W9-BZM-773

SOCIAL THEORY

SOCIAL THEORY:
CONTINUITY AND CONFRONTATION

A READER

edited by Roberta Garner

broadview press

Canadian Cataloguing in Publication Data

Main entry under title:
Social theory: continuity and confrontation: a reader

ISBN 1-55111-235-3

1. Social sciences – Philosophy. I. Garner, Roberta.

H61.S776   1999   300'.1   C99-930737-1

The publisher has made every attempt to locate the authors of the copyrighted material or their heirs and assigns, and would be grateful for information that would allow correction of any errors or omissions in subsequent editions of the work.

Broadview Press, Ltd.
is an independent, international publishing house, incorporated in 1985

North America
Post Office Box 1243, Peterborough, Ontario, Canada K9J 7H5
3576 California Road, Orchard Park, New York, USA 14127
TEL: (705) 743-8990; FAX (705) 743-8353;
E-MAIL: customerservice@broadviewpress.com

United Kingdom and Europe
Turpin Distribution Services, Ltd.,
Blackhorse Rd., Letchworth, Hertfordshire, SO6 EHN
TEL: (1462) 672555; FAX: (1462) 480947; E-MAIL: turpin@rsc.org

Australia
St. Clair Press, Post Office Box 287, Rozelle, NSW 2039
TEL: (612) 818-1942; FAX: (612) 418-1923

www.broadviewpress.com

Broadview Press gratefully acknowledges the support of the Ministry of Canadian Heritage through the Book Publishing Industry Development program.

Printed in Canada

For Larry

CONTENTS

PREFACE

I would like to share with my readers the excitement of reading social theory. My own early efforts to read works of theory were often frustrating—theory at first seemed dry and abstract. It became vital when I saw theoretical concepts used in studies of real life situations and experiences, close to home or in distant cultures; so one goal of this book is to connect classical and early twentieth century theoretical writing to more down-to-earth modern empirical studies. Another is to show how ideas develop both through controversies and continuities. Sociology has never been a field with a single dominant paradigm and a smooth accumulation of knowledge; it is a rush of intellectual whitewater, with many currents, eddies, and unexpected waterfalls. I emphasize the restless, rebellious side of social thought; it appears throughout the book in the body of Marxist theory and the spirit of Nietzsche's influence on Weber, Simmel, and Foucault.

A word about using this reader in teaching social theory courses: it can fit into a frenzied quarter, a fast-moving semester, or two leisurely quarters. It can be paired with any number of theory texts. It can be used as the main or supplementary selection in social and political thought courses, as well as sociology courses.

My colleagues at DePaul create a warm, congenial working environment. Noel Barker is always there to encourage me to think about sociology, as he has so many students, colleagues, and friends. I would like to thank Ted Manley and Heidi Nast for specific suggestions, especially ones that challenge my comfortable assumptions. Bob Rotenberg introduced me to several global perspectives. Melissa Haeffner and Christina Suarez helped to turn plans into pages. My students in the sociological theory core course—which I have taught off and on since the early 1970s—sharpen my ideas and force me to find engaging empirical studies to liven up theoretical concepts.

At Broadview Press, Betsy Struthers brought the book into being: my ideas would not have become a reality without her work in obtaining permissions, organizing the material, and streamlining my writing. Michael Harrison was supportive and encouraging throughout the process, and Barbara Conolly guided the manuscript through key stages.

My family's love makes me feel happy in my work and gives meaning to my projects and endeavors—I am very thankful to all of them.

READING THEORY: A GENERAL INTRODUCTION

In the following pages, we will read the words and ideas of social theorists. We will find continuity: a number of themes appear repeatedly, and certain questions continue to be asked. The answers may change with time and circumstances, but the questions persist. Social theorists also confront and challenge each other's ideas. Theory grows and develops as a result of this controversy. Disagreements force theorists to sharpen their thinking, to look for new empirical evidence, and to discard ideas that don't work.

This reader is organized around continuity and confrontation among ideas. "Continuity" involves the revisiting and rethinking of theories and theoretical questions. "Confrontation" means the growth of theories through disagreement and controversies among theorists.

We will reflect on the relationship between theories and empirical reality, the world of experience and everyday life. Theories are claims that there are patterns in the empirical world; theorists invent concepts that help us to see these patterns. The concepts point to key features of the empirical world. Theorists not only chart the real world, they also try to explain the patterns they see. As social reality changes, theories have to be revised or discarded.

Although theorists challenge each other, it is usually difficult to confirm or disprove a theory. Theories are interpretations of reality; they are not research hypotheses which can be tested with empirical data.

Theorists not only chart and explain social reality; often they also question it. Many theorists take a "negative-critical" view of social institutions. They do not believe that this is the best of all possible worlds: they point to injustices and inequalities among human beings and hope that their ideas can contribute to ending this state of affairs. Controversies among theorists are not only about ways of interpreting reality, but also about prospects for changing it.

Several metaphors are often used to talk about theories. They are said to be constructed or built; theorists make theoretical frameworks, constructions of concepts that are connected to each other. A second commonly used metaphor is visual; theories are perspectives or points of view that focus on some aspect of social reality.

A third metaphor portrays theory as a flowing, changing river, with a mainstream and more controversial countercurrents. The mainstream is formed by ideas that are widely accepted among intellectuals at major universities and publishing houses; the countercurrents are formed by critical and dissenting scholars. Historically, the mainstream has usually been non-Marxist and the major countercurrent, Marxist. There are times when the currents are sharply separated, as in the 1950s, and other times—such as the end of the twentieth century—when they swirl together. Even when they were separate, they were fluid currents, not watertight pipelines. It is a good idea not to think of sociological traditions as completely rigid, distinct systems of ideas; theories have always influenced each other.

Overall, the entire enterprise of theory results in a complex and ever-changing set of overlapping as well as contested ideas. Theorists borrow from each other, recontextualize other theorists' concepts in new frameworks, adapt theory to new empirical and political issues, and challenge each other. A number of questions appear in many theories and form points of connection.

1. What is the nature of modern society, and to what extent is capitalism its key characteristic?
2. How are different types of institutions connected to each other in societies? More specifically, what is the impact of technology, the economy, and culture on each other and on other institutions?
3. How can we best picture the interplay of micro and macro levels of action? By "micro" we mean individual actions and small-scale interactions and by "macro" we mean institutions at the level of societies, nations, and the global system.
4. What is the mix of agency (purposeful human action) and structure (constraining limits) in outcomes? To what extent do human beings "make their own history" individually and collectively, and to what extent is it "made for them" by circumstances inherited from the past?
5. What is the mix of class (economic position) and status (other bases of identity such as racial/ethnic group, gender, and religion) in individual and collective outcomes? How are identities formed? How do identities become the basis of collective action?
6. How do human beings construct social reality?

The works selected here illustrate different ways of thinking about these questions. Some are down-to-earth and address everyday life, while others are very abstract. They come from both the mainstream of academic sociology and the countercurrents. The reader is divided into three parts. Each corresponds to a distinct period in the history of social thought. These differ from each other in terms of the themes and problems addressed by social theory, styles of doing theory, methods of research, and the countries where social theorists worked. The order and placement of the selections allows the reader to see how theories confront each other and how they change historically.

The introductions to each period, type of theory, and individual theorist point out these connections. Biographies of the individual theorists are touched on only briefly; these can be found in many other places (see the Readings at the end of each chapter). In any case, a reading of ideas should never be reduced to the reported facts of an individual's life. Knowing facts (but which facts?) about a person may help us to understand why certain intellectual puzzles appeared in her/his imagination, but ideas take on a life of their own and outlive the individual. Religion, sexual orientation, ethnicity, gender, social class, and psychological states may be factors in the development of these ideas, but they do not explain them. Yet marginality of one kind or another gives a critical edge to a theorist's work, shattering the comfortable taken-for-grantedness in which majorities live their lives; all theorizing is an attack on taken-for-grantedness and in that respect comes easier to minorities.

It is important to keep in mind that individuals change in the course of their lives, and so the writings of a theorist's youth are often different from those of old age. As the maturing and aging process and the historical circumstances change, so do the ideas. Sometimes hope is replaced by pessimism, especially when old age coincides with historical disasters, as World War I brought to several of our theorists. Even in the happiest historical conditions, old age may bring about a sense of limited possibilities, replacing the boundless optimism and freedom of youth, so it may tilt a theorist's work more toward structural determination and away from a focus on autonomy and meaningful action.

Not just writers but readers themselves change, the historical conditions change, and so the texts do not remain the same. To read Marx after the collapse of the Berlin Wall is to encounter a different Marx than the same passages read in the 1960s. When we reread these theorists in the future, we will encounter new perspectives to look at the world in which we live.

Readings

Berger, Peter and Thomas Luckmann. *The Social Construction of Reality.* New York: Doubleday, 1966.

Collins, Randall. *Four Sociological Traditions.* New York: Oxford University Press, 1993.

Collins, Randall and Michael Makowsky. *The Discovery of Society.* New York: McGraw-Hill, 1998.

Farganis, James. *Readings in Social Theory.* New York: McGraw-Hill, 1996.

Ritzer, George. *Sociological Theory.* New York: McGraw-Hill, 1995.

Wallace, Ruth and Alison Wolf. *Contemporary Sociological Theory.* Upper Saddle River, NJ: Prentice-Hall, 1999.

Zeitlin, Irving. *Ideology and the Development of Social Theory.* New York: Prentice-Hall, 1997.

PART I

BEGINNINGS

INTRODUCTION

In Part I we will discover how social theory emerged as a coherent, continuous enterprise in modern Europe. Prior to this period, there had been many astute observers of human societies, such as the Greek historian Herodotus and the North African writer Ibn Khaldun. These writers not only observed cultures and societies, they tried to explain the differences they saw; for example, they tried to relate customs to religious beliefs and culture to political systems, and they made use of explanatory factors such as climate and the history of institutions. These accounts and reflections were not, as yet, part of an ongoing enterprise of social theory in which scholars systematically addressed each other's ideas. Before modern times in Europe, continuity and confrontation were missing from social observation; the observations remained unconnected to each other, and writers about human societies did not yet have the sense of participating in an ongoing tradition. By the nineteenth century, this tradition had taken shape, and social theory had become increasingly an enterprise carried out by a self-conscious community of scholars and theorists.

From the beginning social theory was closely connected to ideology; the analysis of society was always connected to different points of view about the nature of the good society and the causes of social problems. Sociology was born as a modern intellectual enterprise at the same time that ideologies like conservatism, liberalism, socialism, and nationalism emerged, more or less at the end of the eighteenth century and the beginning of the nineteenth; the ideas of sociology as the pursuit of knowledge are often close to the ideas of these contending political forces.

In addition, social theory became increasingly tied to academic disciplines. Social theory became part of the field called "sociology," although political scientists, social revolutionaries, and generic social theorists who did not claim a specific academic discipline also investigated the subject. By the end of the nineteenth century, many social theorists taught at universities, at least part of their lives. Marxist theorists were less likely than others to hold university positions, because they saw themselves as revolutionaries, not pedagogues, and because they were perceived as subversives by academic departments.

During this period, every major theorist was a man and a European. Women did not enter organized scholarly intellectual life till the turn of the century; they published books of travel observations and insightful memoirs, but were simply not included in the more abstract, ongoing conversations about the nature of society that formed the heart of social theory. Equally excluded were all people in colonized societies and in regions outside of the western, Christian world. Most workers and peasants, wherever they lived, were excluded, because they were unlikely to obtain the education needed to enter intellectual and academic life. Elites in the Americas and eastern and southern Europe were marginally included in modern, western intellectual life if they spoke English, French, or German, and appeared like western Europeans in looks and culture; but both distance and western European prejudices kept them at the edge of academic and intellectual life.

The second phase of this period, the later nineteenth century, is called the classical period of social theory. It is dominated by the work of four theorists: Marx, Durkheim, Weber, and Simmel. Durkheim wrote in French, the other three in German. Their work defined the subject matter, central themes, and basic concepts of sociology and the social sciences. All four focused on the nature of modern society; they defined it, each in his own way. They analyzed the effect of social changes such as industrialization, urbanization, the spread of capitalism, revolutions, and the formation of bureaucracies and modern states. These changes are still evident at the beginning of the twenty-first century, and for that reason, the work of the classical theorists remains alive.

CHAPTER ONE

INVENTING THE LENS

INTRODUCTION

In this chapter we will look at the origins of social theory as a systematic pursuit of knowledge about society.

The story begins in Renaissance Italy, when Niccolò Machiavelli wrote about the exercise of power as it really was, not as it should be. The writers of the French Enlightenment continued to look at society as it was, but with a critical eye, in hopes of understanding how human beings could be liberated from cruelty, irrationality, and superstition. Their critical approach brought forth an opposition, a new breed of conservatives prepared to defend existing institutions with the same tools of observation and analysis that the Enlightenment used to attack them. Confrontation was born as a mode of discourse in social theory; the process of debate forced each side to clarify concepts, make its thinking coherent and systematic, and assemble empirical evidence.

The chapter closes with Auguste Comte's early attempt at synthesis, based on the claim that it is possible to preserve social order and hasten progress, both at the same time. He insisted that the structure of society, above and beyond the action of the individual, is a level of reality that requires its own form of inquiry. This idea marks the birth of sociology as a systematic pursuit of knowledge.

1

MACHIAVELLI (1469-1527)

The story of sociology begins with Niccolò Machiavelli and *The Prince*, a book he published in 1513, at the height of the Italian Renaissance. Europe was caught up in a period of dramatic change. In one lifetime—say from 1450 to 1525—a rush of events set the course of modern history for the next 500 years.

> In 1453, the Turks captured Constantinople (now Istanbul) from the Greeks and demonstrated the effective use of cannons and gunpowder; the eastern Mediterranean became part of the Islamic world; and European rulers, merchants, and adventurers felt pressure to expand their sphere westward and southward beyond the Straits of Gibraltar.
>
> In 1458, Johann Gutenberg printed a Bible with movable type; the modern book and the mass dissemination of the printed word were born.
>
> In 1492, the sovereigns of Christian Spain completed their reconquest of the peninsula from Islamic rule and expelled the remaining Moors and Jews. In 1492, Columbus "discovered" the "New" World, the key event of Europe's explosive movement into the rest of the globe. In the years from 1497 to 1502, a Portuguese navigator, Vasco da Gama, led the first European expedition to reach India by sea and established Portuguese power along the coasts of Africa; the African slave trade began to expand.
>
> In 1517 Martin Luther posted his challenge to Roman Catholicism, and the Reformation split the unity of Western Christendom.
>
> In 1519, Ferdinand Magellan's fleet set sail to circumnavigate the globe, returning in 1522. In 1521, Cortez and a handful of men brought down Moctezuma's kingdom, beginning a swift and terrible destruction of the indigenous civilizations of the western hemisphere.

The cultural background of all these momentous and generally violent events was the Renaissance, the glorious rediscovery—more accurately, re-imagining—of the world of the pagan Greeks and Romans: its art, philosophy, and joyous affirmation of human creativity and the human spirit.

In western intellectual history *The Prince* was as explosive as gunpowder. For the first time in centuries someone dared to put in writing a realistic view of human actions. Of course cynical and brutal advice circulated by word of mouth throughout society in the European middle ages (and everywhere else); the practical knowledge of how to rule and control people was shared by kings and queens, knights and sheriffs, slave owners and overseers. However, books were filled with morality and pious platitudes; they dwelled on the exemplary Christian life and the noble character of Christian rulers. (In other literate cultures, the written word fulfilled the same prescriptive function, for example, in the Confucian analects). In short, until the Renaissance, most books were tiresomely normative, not empirical; they prescribed good behaviour rather than observing, describing, and analyzing what human beings really do. *The Prince* broke with the normative tradition of writing; Machiavelli put into his book all the cruel, violent, cunning, coercive, and occasionally even compassionate acts that the ruler must carry out to stay in power. *The Prince* was based on reality, on observations of real people, and not on moral precepts. For this reason, it shocked its readers and was widely censored and banned. Its publication marks the beginning of modern social science—to write about society as it really is, not only as we would like it be: to write about the "is," and not only the "ought to be."

As you will see in the selection, on the surface it appears to be a collection of cynical tips on how to take and hold onto power. Machiavelli used the term "prince" not only for hereditary monarchs but also soldiers of fortune who came to rule territories, elected politicians, and any person who was intent on establishing and maintaining power. Indeed executives today still read and learn from the tips.

Machiavelli's goals in writing *The Prince* went beyond currying favour by offering useful tips to the Medici princes of Florence (to whom it is dedicated). He was writing as an Italian patriot dismayed at Italian rulers' inability to form the large, powerful, centralized states that were beginning to appear in France, England, and Spain. He hoped that his advice to rulers would be taken up by an Italian prince intent on creating a stronger state; he was concerned that a weak, disunited Italy would be invaded and divided by stronger, more cohesive states—and indeed it was.

We can even engage in a leftist reading of *The Prince*, seeing its author as the prototype of a radical democrat revealing the secrets of power to the masses. After all, princes have known the tricks of rule since time immemorial; the lore of power has circulated by word of mouth through royal families and among counsellors and generals since the Bronze Age. To put this lore in writing was a radical leap, a secular parallel to the dissemination of God's word in the form of printed Bibles. Just as people could now freely and directly read God's word, without the intercession of priests, they could now read and understand the workings of earthly powers. The secret oral lore of those in power was made available and transparent to the masses through the medium of writing. Thus *The Prince* is one of the first steps toward the emergence of democratic and revolutionary ideals that characterize modern times. This left or radical reading of *The Prince* is a bit controversial, but intriguing.

As you read this selection note its method as well as its key ideas. Machiavelli often begins by stating his observations as general rules and then supports them with examples from classical antiquity or events in Italy in his own times. This evidence may strike the modern reader as scattershot or anecdotal, but it represents the beginning of a case study method, still popular in our day as a method of educating public administrators, policy planners, lawyers, and executives.

These examples of how to apply general rules in specific contexts allowed Machiavelli to develop his paired concepts of *Fortuna* and *Virtù*. *Fortuna* referred to the external circumstances in which one must act, the situation that Fortune (or fate) doles out to each individual. *Virtù* refers to the qualities of the individual that allow him/her to act effectively within those circumstances. To some extent, *virtù* is inborn in the individual, in boldness, strength of will, courage, and intelligence; but it can be enhanced, and that enhancement is the purpose of *The Prince*.

In this selection, Machiavelli develops another important contrast, the one between the lion who rules through coercion and the fox who rules through cunning.

Keep both of these paired concepts (*Fortuna/virtù*; and lion/fox) in mind, since we will encounter them in other writers in updated forms. *Fortuna/virtù* will reappear in Karl Marx's view that "human beings make history but not in circumstances of their own choosing" and in the contemporary distinction between agency (meaningful action) and structure (external social circumstances). The lion and fox will reappear in theories that address the central question of how power is exercised in different types of societies, whether by coercion or consent.

The Prince
NICCOLÒ MACHIAVELLI

XVII. *Cruelty and compassion; and whether it is better to be loved than feared, or the reverse*

Taking others of the qualities I enumerated above, I say that a prince must want to have a reputation for compassion rather than for cruelty: nonetheless, he must be careful that he does not make bad use of compassion. Cesare Borgia was accounted cruel; nevertheless, this cruelty of his reformed the Romagna, brought it unity, and restored order and obedience. On reflection, it will be seen that there was more compassion in Cesare than in the cruel, Florentine people, who, to escape being called cruel, allowed Pistoia to be devastated.[1] So a prince must not worry if he incurs reproach for his cruelty so long as he keeps his subjects united and loyal. By making an example or two he will prove more compassionate than those who, being too compassionate, allow disorders which lead to murder and rapine. These nearly always harm the whole community, whereas executions ordered by a prince only affect individuals. A new prince, of all rulers, finds it impossible to avoid a reputation for cruelty, because of the abundant dangers inherent in a newly won state. Vergil, through the mouth of Dido, says:

Res dura, et regni novitas me talia cogunt
Moliri, et late fines custode tueri.[2]

Nonetheless, a prince must be slow to take action, and must watch that he does not come to be afraid of his own shadow; his behaviour must be tempered by humanity and prudence so that over-confidence does not make him rash or excessive distrust make him unbearable.

From this arises the following question: whether it is better to be loved than feared, or the reverse. The answer is that one would like to be both the one and the other; but because it is difficult to combine them, it is far better to be feared than loved if you cannot be both. One can make this generalization about men: they are ungrateful, fickle, liars, and deceivers, they shun danger and are greedy for profit; while you treat them well, they are yours. They would shed their blood for you, risk their property, their lives, their children, so long, as I said above, as danger is remote; but when you are in danger they turn against you. Any prince who has come to depend entirely on promises and has taken no other precautions ensures his own ruin; friendship which is bought with money and not with greatness and nobility of mind is paid for, but it does not last and it yields nothing. Men worry less about doing an injury to one who makes himself loved than to one who makes himself feared. The bond of love is one which men, wretched creatures that they are, break when it is to their advantage to do so; but fear is strengthened by a dread of punishment which is always effective.

The prince must nonetheless make himself feared in such a way that, if he is not loved, at least he escapes being hated. For fear is quite compatible with an absence of hatred; and the prince can always avoid hatred if he abstains from the property of his subjects and citizens and from their women. If, even so, it proves necessary to execute someone, this is to be done only when there is proper justification and manifest reason for it. But above all a prince must abstain from the property of others; because men sooner forget the death of their father than the loss of their patrimony. It is always possible to find pretexts for confiscating someone's property; and a prince who starts to live by rapine always finds pretexts for seizing what belongs to others. On the other hand, pretexts for executing someone are harder to find and they are less easily sustained.

However, when a prince is campaigning with his soldiers and is in command of a large army then he need not worry about having a reputation for cruelty because, without such a reputation, no army was ever kept united and disciplined. Among the admirable achievements of Hannibal is included this: that although he led a huge army, made up of countless different races, on foreign campaigns, there was never any dissension, either among the troops themselves or against their leader, whether things were going well or badly. For this, his inhuman cruelty was wholly responsible, It was this, along with his countless other qualities, which made him feared and respected by his soldiers. If it had not been for his cruelty, his other qualities would not have been enough. The historians, having given little thought to this, on the one hand admire what Hannibal achieved, and on the other condemn what made his achievements possible.

That his other qualities would not have been enough by themselves can be proved by looking at Scipio, a man unique in his own time and through all recorded history. His armies mutinied against him in Spain, and the only reason for this was his excessive leniency which allowed his soldiers more licence than was good for military discipline. Fabius Maximus reproached him for this in the Senate and called him a corrupter of the Roman legions. Again, when the Locri were plundered by one of Scipio's officers, he neither gave them satisfaction nor punished his officer's insubordination; and this was all because of his having too lenient a nature. By way of excuse of him some senators argued that many men were better at not making mistakes themselves than at correcting them in others. But in time Scipio's lenient nature would have spoilt his fame and glory had he continued to indulge it during his command; when he lived under orders from the Senate, however, this fatal characteristic of his was not only concealed but even brought him glory.

So, on this question of being loved or feared, I conclude that since some men love as they please but fear when the prince pleases, a wise prince should rely on what he controls, not on what he cannot control. He must only endeavour, as I said, to escape being hated.

XVIII. *How princes should honour their word*
Everyone realizes how praiseworthy it is for a prince to honour his word and to be straightforward rather than crafty in his dealings; nonetheless contemporary experience shows that princes who have achieved great things have been those

who have given their word lightly, who have know how to trick men with their cunning, and who, in the end, have overcome those abiding by honest principles.

You must understand, therefore, that there are two ways of fighting: by law or by force. The first way is natural to men, and the second to beasts. But as the first way often proves inadequate one must need have recourse to the second. So a prince must understand how to make a nice use of the beast and the man. The ancient writers taught princes about this by an allegory, when they described how Achilles and many other princes of the ancient world were sent to be brought up by Chiron, the centaur, so that he might train them his way. All the allegory means, in making the teacher half beast and half man, is that a prince must know how to act according to the nature of both, and that he cannot survive otherwise.

So, as a prince is forced to know how to act like a beast, he must learn from the fox and the lion; because the lion is defenceless against traps and a fox is defenceless against wolves. Therefore one must be a fox in order to recognize traps, and a lion to frighten off wolves. Those who simply act like lions are stupid. So it follows that a prudent ruler cannot, and must not, honour his word when it places him at a disadvantage and when the reasons for which he made his promise no longer exist. If all men were good, this precept would not be good; but because men are wretched creatures who would not keep their word to you, you need not keep your word to them. And no prince ever lacked good excuses to colour his bad faith. One could give innumerable modern instances of this, showing how many pacts and promises have been made null and void by the bad faith of princes: those who have known best how to imitate the fox have come off best. But one must know how to colour one's actions and to be a great liar and deceiver. Men are so simple, and so much creatures of circumstance, that the deceiver will always find someone ready to be deceived.

There is one fresh example I do not want to omit. Alexander VI never did anything, or thought of anything, other than deceiving men; and he always found victims for his deceptions. There never was a man capable of such convincing asseverations, or so ready to swear to the truth of something, who would honour his word less. Nonetheless his deceptions always had the result he intended, because he was a past master in the art.

A prince, therefore, need not necessarily have all the good qualities I mentioned above, but he should certainly appear to have them. I would even go so far as to say that if he has these qualities and always behaves accordingly he will find them harmful; if he only appears to have them they will render him service. He should appear to be compassionate, faithful to his word, kind, guileless, and devout. And indeed he should be so. But his disposition should be such that, if he needs to be the opposite, he knows how. You must realize this: that a prince, and especially a new prince, cannot observe all those things which give men a reputation for virtue, because in order to maintain his state he is often forced to act in defiance of good faith, of charity, of kindness, of religion. And so he should have a flexible disposition, varying as fortune and circumstances dictate. As I said above, he should not deviate from what is good, if that is possible, but he should know how to do evil, if that is necessary.

A prince, then, must be very careful not to say a word which does not seem inspired by the five qualities I mentioned earlier. To those seeing and hearing him, he should appear a man of compassion, a man of good faith, a man of integrity, a kind and a religious man. And there is nothing so important as to seem to have this last quality. Men in general judge by their eyes rather than by their hands; because everyone is in a position to watch, few are in a position to come in close touch with you. Everyone sees what you appear to be, few experience what you really are. And those few dare not gainsay the many who are backed by the majesty of the state. In the actions of all men, and especially of princes, where there is no court of appeal, one judges by the result. So let a prince set about the task of conquering and maintaining his state; his methods will always be judged honourable and will be universally praised. The common people are always impressed by appearances and results. In this context, there are only common people, and there is no room for the few when the many are supported by the state. A certain contemporary ruler, whom it is better not to name, never preaches anything except peace and good faith;[3] and he is an enemy of both one and the other, and if he had ever honoured either of them he would have lost either his standing or his state many times over.

XIX. *The need to avoid contempt and hatred*
Now, having talked about the most important of the qualities enumerated above, I want to discuss the others briefly under this generalization: that the prince should, as I have already suggested, determine to avoid anything which will make him hated and despised. So long as he does so, he will have done what he should and he will run no risk whatsoever if he is reproached for the other vices I mentioned. He will be hated above all if, as I said, he is rapacious and aggressive with regard to the property and the women of his subjects. He must refrain from these. As long as he does not rob the great majority of their property or their honour, they remain content. He then has to contend only with the ambition of a few, and that can be dealt with easily and in a variety of ways. He will be despised if he has a reputation for being fickle, frivolous, effeminate, cowardly, irresolute; a prince should avoid this like the plague and strive to demonstrate in his actions grandeur, courage, sobriety, strength. When settling disputes between his subjects, he should ensure that this judgement is irrevocable; and he should be so regarded that no one ever dreams of trying to deceive or trick him....

Notes

1. Pistoia was a subject-city of Florence, which forcibly restored order there when conflict broke out between two rival factions in 1501-2. Machiavelli was concerned with this business at first hand.
2. "Harsh necessity, and the newness of my kingdom, force me to do such things and to guard my frontiers everywhere." *Aeneid* I, 563.
3. Ferdinand of Aragon.

2

THE ENLIGHTENMENT AND THE CONSERVATIVE REACTION

The Enlightenment emerged in western Europe in the seventeenth and eighteenth centuries. Intellectuals, continuing the work of scientists, attempted to understand the world as a design inherent in nature, possibly set in motion by God as a Prime Mover, but not micro-managed by God's personal intervention. Scientists like Galileo, Newton, and Harvey brought this attitude into studies of the solar system, the behaviour of objects in the earth's gravitational field, and processes in the human body. Observation, experimentation, and analysis replaced the sense that the nature of the world could be defined by ecclesiastical authority or a single sacred text. The Enlightenment, and especially the French *philosophes* as a community of public intellectuals, expanded this perspective into the study of social institutions.

Faith in reason together with observation are at the heart of all social theory. These two linked elements in the pursuit of knowledge do not necessarily lead to a single set of conclusions. They can produce multiple interpretations of reality, based on selection from the enormous range of possible observations and different paths of analysis. Inquiry guided by reason does not produce a single, unquestionable truth, but a discussion among contending views. Disagreement between perspectives is a positive step in the growth of natural and social sciences.

The work of Enlightenment thinkers was not dispassionate inquiry. They were deeply disturbed by the power of the Church and its secular allies in the monarchy to stifle inquiry and punish freedom and diversity of thought. They were also appalled at tortures and gruesome means of execution, like breaking on a wheel and burning heretics, which authorities perpetrated on those who challenged organized religion and the state. These tortures and punishments were not only ways of limiting freedom of thought, they were obviously used to defend existing institutions and the enormous social inequalities and injustices apparent everywhere.

The Enlightenment and the French Revolution created a powerful backlash. Intellectuals who represented the interests of the absolute monarchy and the aristocracy wrote against the new ideas of freedom of thought, civil liberties, religious tolerance, and human rights. They argued for a return to rigid hierarchies, fixed status groups, and established religion. Although leading thinkers of the conservative reaction like Bonald and de Maistre are not widely read today, their challenge to liberal views of society continues to be of interest. They question the atomistic liberal perspective on society that emphasizes individual rights and the individual pursuit of happiness; they argue that society is not merely a collection of individuals, but must be understood as a social order in its own right. These ideas, stripped of their underlying political position, have a role in sociological analysis.

Irving Zeitlin, a professor at the University of Toronto, is a contemporary social theorist who summarizes the thought of the French Enlightenment and the conservative reaction. He "translates" the legacy of the conservative reaction from its archaic original wording into the language of the modern social sciences and summarizes it in ten propositions about society that continue to shape sociology and social thought.

In contrast to the medieval era, the men of the Enlightenment regarded all aspects of human life and works as subject to critical examination—the various sciences, religious beliefs, metaphysics, aesthetics, education, and so on. Self-examination, a scrutiny of their own actions and their own society, was an essential function of thought. By gaining an understanding of the main forces and tendencies of their epoch, human beings could determine their direction and control their consequences. Through reason and science, humanity could attain ever greater degrees of freedom and, hence, ever greater degrees of perfection. Intellectual progress, an idea permeating the thinking of that era, would serve to further humanity's general progress.

The *Philosophes* waged an unceasing war against superstition, bigotry, and intolerance; they fought against censorship and demanded freedom of thought. They attacked the privileges of the feudal classes and their restraints upon the commercial and industrial classes. It was the Enlightenment faith in science and education that provided so powerful an impetus to their work, making them humanitarian, optimistic, and confident. Philosophy was no longer merely a matter of abstract thinking. It acquired the practical function of asking critical questions about existing institutions and demanding that the unreasonable ones, those contrary to human nature, be changed. All obstacles to human perfectibility were to be progressively eliminated. Enlightenment thinking, then, had a *negative-critical* as well as a positive side....

Reason bows neither to the merely factual, the simple data of experience, nor to the "evidence" of revelation, tradition, or authority. Reason together with observation is a facility for the acquisition of truth....[1]

Notes

1. Irving Zeitlin, *Ideology and the Development of Sociological Theory*, 6th ed. (New York: Prentice-Hall, 1997) 2, 4.

The Conservative Reaction
IRVING M. ZEITLIN

Conservative Philosophy and Sociology: A Summary

We have seen how the principles of the Enlightenment, as they became manifest in the Revolution, engendered a conservative philosophical reaction. That reaction, in turn, engendered a new interest in *social order* and various related problems and concepts.

Conservatives, like Burke, Hegel, Bonald, and Maistre, are so called because they desired quite literally to conserve and maintain the prevailing order. Moreover, some of them, as we have seen, sought not so much to conserve the existing order as to regress to a *status quo ante*. The disorder, anarchy, and radical changes those thinkers observed after the Revolution led them to generate concepts that relate to aspects of order and stability: tradition, authority, status, cohesion, adjustment, function, norm, symbol, ritual. As compared with the eighteenth century, the conservative concepts constituted a definite shift of interest from the individual to the group, from criticism of the existing order to its defense, and from social change to social stability.[1]

From the conservative standpoint, the social changes following in the wake of the Revolution had undermined and destroyed fundamental social institutions and had resulted in the loss of political stability. The conservatives traced those results to certain preceding events and processes in European history that had led, they believed, to the progressive weakening of the medieval order and hence to the upheaval of the Revolution. Quite precisely, they singled out Protestantism, capitalism, and science as the major forces. Those processes, furthermore, which were hailed as progressive by their liberal and radical contemporaries, were leading even now to an increasing atomization of peoples. Large "masses" now appeared, presumably unanchored in any stable social groups; widespread insecurity, frustration, and alienation became evident; and, finally, a monolithic secular power had emerged that was dependent for its existence on the mass of rootless individuals.

The conservatives had idealized the medieval order, and from that standpoint the modern era was very wanting indeed. As an antidote to the principles of the *philosophes,* and as a critique of the post-Revolutionary *"disorder,"* the conservatives advanced a number of propositions about society:

1. It is an organic unity with internal laws and development and deep roots in the past, not simply a mechanical aggregate of individual elements. The

conservatives were "social realists" in the sense that they firmly believed in society as a reality greater than the individuals who comprise it. That was in a direct opposition to the social nominalism of the Enlightenment, the view that only individuals exist and that society is simply the name one gives to those individuals in their interrelationships.

2. Society antedates the individual and is ethically superior to him. Man has no existence outside of a social group or context, and he becomes human only by participating in society. Far from individuals constituting society, it is society that creates the individual by means of moral education, to employ Durkheim's term.

3. The individual is an abstraction and not the basic element of a society. Society is composed of relationships and institutions; individuals are simply members of society who fulfill certain statuses and roles—father, son, priest, and so on.

4. The parts of a society are interdependent and interrelated. Customs, beliefs, and institutions are organically intertwined so that changing or remaking one part will undermine the complex relationships maintaining the stability of society as a whole.

5. Man has constant and unalterable needs, which every society and each of its institutions serve to fulfill. Institutions are thus positive agencies by which basic human needs are met. If those agencies are disturbed or disrupted, suffering and disorder will result.

6. The various customs and institutions of a society are positively functional; they either fulfill human needs directly or indirectly by serving other indispensable institutions. Even prejudice is viewed in those terms; it tends to unify certain groups and also increases their sense of security.

7. The existence and maintenance of small groups is essential to society. The family, neighborhood, province, religious groups, occupational groups— those are the basic units of a society, the basic supports of people's lives.

8. The conservatives also conceived of "social organization." The Revolution, as they saw it, had led not to a higher form of organization, but to social and moral disintegration. They wanted to preserve the older religious forms, Catholicism not Protestantism, and sought to restore the religious unity of medieval Europe. Protestantism, in teaching the importance of individual faith, had undermined the spiritual unity of society. And, as we have seen in the case of Bonald, the disorganizing consequences of urbanism, industry, and commerce were recognized.

9. The conservatives insisted, in addition, on the essential importance and positive value of the nonrational aspects of human existence. Man needs ritual, ceremony, and worship. The Philosophes, in their merciless criticism of those activities as irrational vestiges of the past, had weakened the sacred supports of society.

10. Status and hierarchy were also treated as essential to society. The conservatives feared that equality would destroy the "natural" and time-honored

agencies by which values were passed on from one generation to another. Hierarchy was necessary in the family, the Church, and the State, without which social stability was impossible.

Those are some of the major sociological tenets of the conservative legacy—a legacy that greatly influenced such thinkers as Saint-Simon, Comte, and, later, Durkheim. Those thinkers attempted to take conservative ideas and concepts out of their theological-reactionary context and to make them part and parcel of a scientific sociology....

Notes
1. In the present discussion, I have drawn upon a number of points made by Robert A. Nisbet in his article entitled "Conservatism and Sociology," *American Journal of Sociology* (September 1952).

3

EDMUND BURKE (1729-1797)

This selection from *Reflections on the Revolution in France* illustrates the emergence of modern conservative thought. Burke builds on the themes of the conservative reaction outlined in the preceding section, but modifies them to fit the realities of industrial capitalism and liberal democracy. Industrialization expanded, freedom of thought and speech were confirmed as rights of citizens, and more representative political systems emerged; conservatives recognized that it was no longer possible to return to the old ways. It would not be possible to rebuild the absolutist monarchies, to suppress religious freedoms in favour of a single form of Christianity, or to reverse the growth of individual rights and civil liberties. Nor was it possible to retreat from capitalism into the feudal, agrarian way of life that sustained immutable hierarchies, fixed belief systems, and patterns of traditional deference.

Edmund Burke expresses a new form of conservatism, one that accepts change but calls for a slow pace of reform, a pace at which existing institutions such as the monarchy and the established churches are largely preserved and only gradually modified. Burke was a British politician of Irish origin and a member of parliament. He had welcomed the American Revolution, which he believed was fought to preserve existing rights; but he excoriated the French Revolution, which he saw as the wanton destruction of institutions by fanatical intellectuals. His *Reflections on the Revolution* in France is a long essay that denounces the revolution and outlines a conservative view of society.

In the following selection he lays out basic themes of conservative thought, each of which can be illustrated by contemporary conservative positions. Although the selection is only a couple of pages long, it is packed with powerful ideas about the nature of society. Here is a summary of Burke's thought, with contemporary illustrations.

1. One should be careful not to destroy existing institutions, which should be preserved and reformed, not dismantled. They have stood the test of time and generally serve useful functions; to destroy them creates social disorganization and individual unhappiness. Thus for example, conservatives today generally defend and want to preserve the nuclear family and the authoritative position of the father; they believe the weakening of traditional families is a major cause of crime and other kinds of anti-social behaviour. Change has to be a slow process. Any kind of sudden change causes a sense of disorder. In the view of conservatives, the social movements of the 1960s and 1970s created such disorder.

2. The experiences and sensibilities—even the prejudices—of ordinary people are at least as valuable as the ideas of intellectuals. Common sense and widely-shared beliefs are better guides to social action than the sophisticated views of brilliant and well-educated elites. Here Burke expresses a current of anti-intellectualism that persists in conservative thought: intellectuals like to create coherent blueprints and grand visions that they impose on ordinary people. On paper, these blueprints promise a more perfect society; in reality, they are unfeasible and destructive. Implicit in the conservative suspicion of intellectuals is the distrust of centralized policies and plans, especially those articulated and implemented by central governments. Conservatives express trust in local institutions and practices, which they see as being closer to ordinary people and the realities of everyday life. For example, in the United States and Canada, conservatives express distaste for "Washington" and "Ottawa," which are seen as the source of unrealistic and meddlesome policy initiatives.

3. The structure of a society should be formed gradually, through the development of institutions and practices over the course of many generations. The slow growth of institutions and practices assures that they are in harmony with each other. Practices and institutions that don't "work" gradually disappear; the ones that are effective come to function together. Only in this way can institutions form a complex whole. Here Burke again opposes the sudden elimination of institutions and reaffirms the conservative idea that societies are complex systems of which the parts are institutions, not individuals. Change in one institution throws other institutions in disarray. For example, in the view of conservatives, the entry of women into the labour force and the assertion of women's rights by the women's movement may have some merit in the abstract; but in the actual everyday life of many people, these sudden changes in women's roles have also had negative consequences for family unity, childrearing, and social stability.

4. Finally, Burke says, in the language of his day, "Don't micromanage." He is concerned that intellectuals (specifically, the intellectuals spearheading the revolution in France) love to plan out the details of other people's lives. His view is that these details are best left to people to work out for themselves. Once again, we can hear an echo in the position of contemporary conservatives that Big Government has involved itself in too many details of everyday life, telling people how to run their businesses, educate their children, and work out their problems.

Reflections on the Revolution in France
EDMUND BURKE

It is this inability to wrestle with difficulty which has obliged the arbitrary assembly of France to commence their schemes of reform with abolition and total destruction. But is it in destroying and pulling down that skill is displayed? Your mob can do this as well at least as your assemblies. The shallowest understanding, the rudest hand, is more than equal to that task. Rage and phrenzy will pull down more in half an hour, than prudence, deliberation, and foresight can build up in a hundred years. The errors and defects of old establishments are visible and palpable. It calls for little ability to point them out; and where absolute power is given, it requires but a word wholly to abolish the vice and the establishment together. The same lazy but restless disposition, which loves sloth and hates quiet, directs these politicians, when they come to work, for supplying the place of what they have destroyed. To make everything the reverse of what they have seen is quite as easy as to destroy. No difficulties occur in what has never been tried. Criticism is almost baffled in discovering the defects of what has not existed; and eager enthusiasm, and cheating hope, have all the wide field of imagination in which they may expatiate with little or no opposition.

At once to preserve and to reform is quite another thing. When the useful parts of an old establishment are kept, and what is superadded is to be fitted to what is retained, a vigorous mind, steady persevering attention, various powers of comparison and combination, and the resources of an understanding fruitful in expedients are to be exercised; they are to be exercised in a continued conflict with the combined force of opposite vices; with the obstinacy that rejects all improvement, and the levity that is fatigued and disgusted with every thing of which it is in possession. But you may object—"A process of this kind is slow. It is not fit for an assembly, which glories in performing in a few months the work of ages. Such a mode of reforming, possibly might take up many years." Without question it might; and it ought. It is one of the excellencies of a method in which time is amongst the assistants, that its operation is slow, and in some cases almost imperceptible. If circumspection and caution are a part of wisdom, when we work only upon inanimate matter, surely they become a part of duty too, when the subject of our demolition and construction is not brick and timber, but sentient beings, by the sudden alteration of whose state, condition, and habits, multitudes may be rendered miserable. But it seems as if it were the prevalent opinion in Paris, that an unfeeling heart, and an undoubting confidence, are the sole qualifications for a perfect legislator. Far different are my ideas of that high office. The true lawgiver ought to have a heart full of sensibility. He ought to love and respect his kind, and to fear himself. It may be allowed to his temperament to catch his ultimate object with an intuitive glance; but his movements towards it ought to be deliberate. Political arrangement, as it is a work for social ends, is to be only wrought by social means. There mind must conspire with mind. Time is required to produce that union of minds which alone can produce all the good we aim at. Our patience will achieve more than our force. If I might venture to appeal to what is so much out of fashion in Paris, I mean to experience, I should tell you, that in my course I have known, and, according to my measure, have co-operated with great men; and I have never yet seen any plan which has not been mended by the observations of those who were much inferior in understanding to the persons who took the lead in business. By a slow but well-sustained progress the effect of each step is watched; the good or ill success of the first, gives light to us in the second; and so, from light to light, we are conducted with safety through the whole series. We see that the parts of the system do not clash. The evils latent in the most promising contrivances are provided for as they arise. One advantage is as little as possible sacrificed to another. We compensate, we reconcile, we balance. We are enabled to unite into a consistent whole the various anomalies and contending principles that are found in the minds and affairs of men. From hence arises, not an excellence in simplicity, but one far superior, an excellence in composition. Where the great interests of mankind are concerned through a long succession of generations that succession ought to be admitted into some share in the councils which are so deeply to affect them. If justice requires this, the work itself requires the aid of more minds than one age can furnish. It is from this view of things that the best legislators have been often satisfied with the establishment of some sure, solid, and ruling principle in government; a power like that which some of the philosophers have called a plastic nature; and having fixed the principle, they have left it afterwards to its own operation.

4
———

AUGUSTE COMTE (1798-1857)

Auguste Comte was a French social thinker who wrote at the beginning of the nineteenth century, in the aftermath of the French Revolution and the Napoleonic Wars. Comte, like Edmund Burke, hoped that social change could take place without revolution and disorder. He welcomed new developments in science, technology, and the economy, but feared social upheaval and disruption by unruly masses of common folk. He expressed his hopes in the phrase "order and progress." Today we might refer to him as a "technocrat" in that he believed highly trained experts were the best qualified persons to make crucial social and political decisions. He is sometimes credited with having invented the word "sociology"; he believed that sociologists would come to have a leading role in decision-making about society since they had a scientific understanding of it.

Comte believed that the history of every field of knowledge passes through three stages: a theological stage when it is dominated by rigid, traditional, religious ways of thinking; a metaphysical stage when knowledge is expressed in terms of vague, abstract concepts that are formulated without reliable research and data collection; and a scientific stage when knowledge is based on empirical research and a systematic study of reality. Fields of knowledge become scientific at different rates, which he arranged in a "hierarchy of sciences." At the base was mathematics, strictly speaking not a field of empirical research, but an area of knowledge that was foundational to scientific work. At the bottom rung is physics, followed by chemistry, biology, and, at the very top, sociology, which Comte crowned "the queen of the sciences." Each successive rung represents a more complex organization of matter, from atoms (physics) to molecules (chemistry) to cells and tissues formed into organisms (biology) to the grouping and interrelationship of human organisms into society (sociology). (What happened to psychology? Comte left it out because he thought that individual behaviour could be explained either at the sociological level of society and culture or at the biological level.)

Comte pointed out that physics was the first field of knowledge to free itself from the grip of theology and metaphysics; the decisive moment was Galileo's struggle with the Catholic Church, which tried to suppress his findings and teachings in astronomy, especially the Copernican model of the solar system and the discovery of the moons of Jupiter. Though Galileo was silenced and finished his life in virtual house arrest in his villa near Florence, his findings soon were accepted by all educated people in Europe. Chemistry was the next field to liberate itself from theology and metaphysics. The struggle was still underway in biology and sociology, the disciplines closest to human affairs and hence most likely to be a terrain of contention between religion and science.

Comte is also remembered for his use of the term "positivism." This complex concept includes a number of ideas which remain important for understanding social thought. He used it to express his critique of the ideas of Georg Hegel, a major European philosopher at the end of the eighteenth century. Hegel believed that history moves forward dialectically, by a process of negation in which earlier stages of thought and being come to an end and are preserved only in a partial, re-contextualized form within a new totality. Comte found this formulation too metaphysical and perhaps also disturbingly close to revolutionary notions about putting an end to existing institutions and forms of society. He felt that one could not decide *a priori* that historical change always took place through a process of negation; the idea of the dialectic was a prime example of metaphysical rather than scientific thinking. Social change had to be understood empirically, by observing phenomena, not by making claims to know about their inner essences. Comte's concept positivism thus contained both his critique of Hegel's idea of negation and the prescription that science should be empirical and research-oriented.

Positivism is now used to mean the view that science must proceed by the scientific method, by observation, empirical research, and as much as possible, by measurement and experimentation. Scientific work has to meet criteria of validity and reliability. In the view of positivism, the natural sciences are seen as an ideal because they have strict rules of empirical research and widely accepted sets of procedures of experimentation and quantification. In some fields, like cultural studies, humanistic psychology, and qualitative sociology, positivism has come to have a negative connotation, meaning a rigid and unthinking effort to squeeze reflection on human actions into the mold of the natural sciences.

Comte is rarely read nowadays. His writing lacks the flair of Machiavelli's work; unlike Burke and conservative thought, he has little direct influence on any social or political ideologies of the present. Nevertheless, we can still find many traces of his ideas. Managers, administrators, and technocrats share his dream of order and progress, innovation from above without disruption from below. His observations of the history of sciences are perceptive. And while positivism has come to be a negative term, the issues associated with it continue to be debated: to what extent should inquiry into actions of human beings be modeled on empirical methods of the natural sciences?

CHAPTER TWO

CLASSICAL THEORY

INTRODUCTION

In this chapter we will read the theories of four giants in the history of social thought: Karl Marx, Emile Durkheim, Max Weber, and Georg Simmel. These theories are often referred to as classical theory in the social sciences. They were efforts to grasp changes taking place in societies in the nineteenth century: the growth of capitalism, globalization of markets, formation of modern nation-states, industrialization and technological innovation, and urbanization and migration. These changes transformed the world, and many of them are still happening today. The ideas of the four classical theorists are still vital guides to understanding our world. We can see their importance directly by applying them to our own experiences, and we can also trace the impact they had on later theorists. We will read the words of the classical theorists and in the "Legacy" sections look at examples of their impact on contemporary social scientists.

We can summarize classical theory by saying it is like four blindfolded men touching an elephant, trying to figure out what manner of beast it is. The elephant is modern society; the four blindfolded men are Marx, Durkheim, Weber, and Simmel. They touch and name different parts of the elephant, and when they touch the same part, they give it different names. Yet when we read all four descriptions of the elephant, we can see that it is the same creature.

For all four, capitalism is an essential characteristic; for Marx, it is the single defining characteristic, while the others offer a wider and more diffuse analysis of modernity that nevertheless includes capitalism as a central element.

There are many close parallels in their understanding of modern society. For example, Marx's "dead labour" is similar to Simmel's "objective culture": it is human invention and ingenuity embodied in creations that now exist as dead objects independently of the creators. For both, capitalism means an enormous growth of this mass of dead objects that weighs on living people's actions. Weber's "rationalization" and "rational calculation" correspond to Simmel's analysis of quantification in the money economy and Marx's view that all worth comes to be measured by exchange value. For Marx, the commodity form causes this tendency; Weber is more inclined to see the origins of rationalization in religion and disenchantment. Weber's view that status distinctions are slowly being replaced by class inequalities is very close to Marx's discussion of the end of feudal relations, the establishment of juridical equality, and the emergence of class defined in economic terms. Durkheim's "anomie" corresponds to Simmel's analysis of the miser and the spendthrift and Marx's discussion of new wants. All four theorists touch on differentiation, specialization, and a high division of labour. All four see a growth in individualism (or individuation), although Marx especially believes that capitalism quickly reaches the limits of the process of individuation it initially accelerated.

There are considerable differences in the theorists' assessment of the character of the elephant and the direction in which it is headed. Marx sees it in the spirit of revolutionary optimism; it is going to explode into a higher life form. Durkheim looks forward with cautious optimism to a gradual evolution. Weber feels a gloomy pessimism; the behemoth of formal rationality will stamp on the human future. Simmel responds with playful pessimism—enjoy the elephant's antics, but realize it will continue to grow and that it cannot be controlled or tamed.

Readings

Berman, Marshall. *All That Is Solid Melts Into Air*. London: Verso, 1982.

Giddens, Anthony. *Capitalism and Modern Social Theory*. Cambridge, England: Cambridge University Press, 1971.

Hobsbawm, Eric. *The Age of Revolution, 1789-1848*. New York: Mentor Books, 1964.

—. *The Age of Capital, 1848-1875*. New York: Mentor Books, 1975.

—. *The Age of Empire, 1875-1914*. New York: Random House, 1987.

Ritzer, George. *The McDonaldization of Society: An Investigation into the Changing Character of Contemporary Life*. Thousand Oaks, CA: Pine Forge Press/Sage, 1995.

5

KARL MARX (1818-1883)

Karl Marx is one of the few social theorists in this book who enjoys name recognition beyond the ranks of students and scholars. He saw himself as a socialist revolutionary and directed his writing to socialist activists. At the beginning of the twenty-first century, his ideas about a revolution to end capitalism seem far from being fulfilled, yet his analysis of capitalism as a global social, economic, and cultural system remains fresh and incisive. His views of culture, consciousness, and ideas continue to be penetrating and influential.

There are many different ways of reading Marx. Revolutionaries interpret his work differently than scholars. His early writing—the reflections on alienation and ideology—reveals a different man than does his mature analysis of capitalism as a socio-economic system.

In his early writing Marx was still strongly influenced by Hegel and the concept of the dialectic. As I noted in my remarks about Comte, Hegel believed that every process of change—and above all, the unfolding of human history—moves forward through a simultaneous negation and transformation of what existed before. Hegel also postulated that change in history is a process of spiritual and intellectual growth in humanity culminating in a complete consciousness of itself as the subject of history, as an active self-aware force. Marx treated Hegel's philosophy dialectically; he negated or dumped what he believed to Hegel's spiritual mystification of this process as well as Hegel's enthusiasm for the state as an institution. He retained the concept of the logic of historical change, but eliminated spiritual notions and emphasized instead the material and political dimensions of human history. In the course of history, human beings grow in their understanding of nature and society, and in the sophistication of their modes of production; as this understanding expands, they develop a consciousness of, and an ability to create, society as a collective project. Society is no longer seen as a taken-for-granted god-given "natural" force, but as a social construct that we can reshape. We can construct a society in which all human beings can realize their unique potentials, be creative, develop both their individual talents and their sense of community, and experience freedom as well as solidarity.

Later in his life Marx placed more emphasis on the scientific analysis of capitalism as a social and economic system, characterized by private ownership of the means of production, the market mechanism, production of commodities, division of society into classes of owner/employers (the bourgeoisie) and workers (the proletariat), dynamic technology, and high division of labour.

Marx's stand towards capitalism, as we will see in the *Communist Manifesto*, was complex and ambivalent. Capitalism is a society of class inequality, like most societies that preceded it in history; but it is not just "the same old" static type of society as feudalism and slave-based societies, because its mode of production is radically different and new. Capitalism is an economic and social system that fetters—chains—human creativity and locks science, technology, and human labour into the narrow prison cell of private profit. Yet it also contains the promise of scientific understanding, material abundance, and freedom from traditional inequalities, especially those of gender ("patriarchy") and fixed status communities like serfs and nobles. Capitalism promises a society of free, creative, unique individuals; it never delivers on this promise, because of its foundation in differences in the ownership of productive property, but the promise itself is a step forward in human history.

In Marx's most important work, *Capital*, he analyzes the structure of capitalism, beginning with its cell form. The "cell"—the basic unit of the system—is the commodity form. A commodity is something that is bought and sold; in capitalism anything can become a commodity: a manufactured product, land, food, human labour power, care giving and service, scientific knowledge and technological inventions, and ideas and images. In capitalism, all production tends toward commodity production. The only reason to produce anything is in order to be able to sell it in a market. Of course, no one would buy a commodity unless it had use value; but no one who owns the means of production will produce commodities unless they have exchange value, their value in the marketplace where they are sold. Markets have existed for a long time in many societies, but in capitalism, markets and the commodity form have penetrated into every area of life and are the central organizing principle of the whole society, with consequences for culture, ideas, and human relationships.

It is ironic that some of the debates and puzzles that we will trace throughout modern social theory were actually resolved right at the start of this history, in the work of Karl Marx. Marx, unlike many later theorists, immediately recognized both sides of a number of key theoretical confrontations. To think dialectically is to see the bridges between the two sides, to understand that grasping the nature of reality is not a matter of either/or.

Marx thought that human beings take meaningful action, but that we are also in the grip of external, societal forces that shape the way in which we see our choices and limit the effectiveness of our actions. We now often phrase this opposition as the tension between "agency" and "structure." At points in the twentieth century, especially in the ideas of revolutionary movements, it was conceived as the clash of "voluntarism" and "determinism." Marx summed up his position in a succinct and satisfying way: "Human beings make their own history ... but not in circumstances of their own choosing...."[1]

In this context it is important to emphasize that Marx was not an economic or technological determinist. Although he believed that technology and the mode of production (all the activities and relationships through which people create the "human-made" aspects of their world) were crucial in history, he absolutely rejected the idea that technology and the mode of production are external forces. What we call "technology" or "the economy" (or in his words, "the mode of production") are human actions, human acts of creativity, and relationships between people. They are not "things."

Marx saw the interplay of another pair of supposed opposites, culture and social relationships. Social relationships between people, including economic relationships, construct a society. Our consciousness does not arise out of thin air; ideas reflect the experiences of acting and interaction in the context of these relationships. But this does not mean that ideas are unimportant in history or that their form is completely predictable from the structure of social relationships. Although Marx believed that ideas were more a determined than a determining element in society, he was keenly interested in the ideas, culture, and consciousness associated with capitalism (and other class societies).

Marx had a keen insight into the nature of social change. He understood that changes can take place through the accumulation of many small changes that finally add up to a major crisis and social transformation. This concept was derived from a dialectical model of change in which quantitative change in behaviours, institutions, and relationships can suddenly precipitate a qualitative shift, a change that is powerful enough to be termed a revolution. He was also aware that even in a revolution some elements of the old order—habits, beliefs, ways of doing things—may be carried forward into the new; revolutionaries need to be aware of this fact and should strive to hold on to "the rational kernel" of the preceding type of society. A revolution both puts an end to old social practices and preserves them within a new context; the Hegelian concept of *aufhebung* (a German word that means both abrogation and preservation) sums up this recognition of the dual nature of change.

The *Communist Manifesto* begins with Marx and Engels's view of the emergence of capitalism. All historical societies are split by class conflict, which in the long run has always ended either with the destruction of the society or with the emergence of the subordinate class as victors, the new dominant class of a new mode of production and a new social order. The bourgeoisie emerged from feudal society in western Europe, its growth associated with colonization, the growth of manufactures and markets for crafts, new technologies of production and transportation, and the growth of global markets. The bourgeoisie is the capitalist class, the class of owners of capitalist enterprises, seen as a political and cultural as well as an economic force.

The bourgeoisie's political development and consciousness of itself as a class grew in association with its rise as an economic force. Its roots were in the communities of commoners in the middle ages, but as its economic activities grew and flourished, it challenged the ideological and political hold of the landed nobility. By the end of the eighteenth century, its power was such that its most politically active members could spearhead the French Revolution, a decisive moment when most of the privileges, rights, and power of the landed aristocracy were swept away.

The most important section of the *Communist Manifesto* begins with the sentence, "The bourgeoisie has played a most revolutionary role in history." Marx and Engels list all the amazing changes that capitalism has brought about in the world. It has meant unleashing the enormous creative and productive powers of human beings. Global markets and global culture emerge; old prejudices, inequalities, and patriarchal and feudal relationships are swept away. All human relationships, including the structure of professions and the family, are being re-organized along capitalist lines, dominated by the commodity form. All countries are being forced to enter markets and to become like the successful capitalist societies, or risk being humiliated and colonized. Under the competitive pressure inherent in capitalism, technological innovation is a ceaseless process. Culture is in constant flux, as "all that is solid melts into air." This middle section is a great prose poem to capitalism, as a dynamic, revolutionary type of society.

Finally, the authors introduce the metaphor of "fetters," social institutions that limit realization of the potential inherent in capitalism. Capitalism has unleashed the powers of human creativity, but these developments are dangerous for the bourgeoisie. The capitalist class would like to control social change and technological innovation; they fear that the logic of capitalism will lead to a new round of class conflict and their own downfall. The working class, all people whose labour in fact creates the technology and wealth of capitalist society, will begin to organize to end the domination of those few who own the means of production, the bourgeoisie. In Marx and Engels's view, private ownership of the means of production, the appropriation of profit from the exploitation of labour, the market mechanism, and associated socio-political institutions like property law are all forces that now limit rather than expand the possibilities for humankind.

Marx on Ideas and Ideology

In *The German Ideology*, Marx and Engels grapple with the relationship between class structure and ideas. They were writing at a time when many historians and philosophers—especially German ones, hence the book title—were convinced that ideas are the major force for change in society. Most social and historical writing at the time involved tracing the history of ideas expressed by literate elites and gave little attention to social relationships or the lives of ordinary people. Here Marx and Engels reconceptualize the nature of ideas and show how they are produced and disseminated as part of class relationships. Most ideas are best understood as ideology, a system of thought used to justify class inequalities and the social order.

In this passage, the authors present six theses on the nature of ideology.

1. The ideas of the ruling class are the ruling ideas of the age, in other words, these ideas form the dominant ideology. The class that owns the means of material production—mines, factories, plantations—also owns the means of mental production—newspapers, publishing houses, and (in our day) movie production companies and the electronic media. The interests of these two branches of the capitalist class are basically one and the same.

2. Historians of ideas see intellectuals as the active, creative sector of the ruling classes. Marx and Engels question this view: intellectuals create and propagate ideology, but they are not an active force in the mode of production. For example, in capitalism, it is the business owner whose actions have an economic and technological impact, while the university professor merely justifies the market economy.

3. The dominant concepts and values of each age reflect the life conditions of its dominant class: honour, loyalty, faith, and order for the aristocrats of the feudal age; freedom, progress, and equality for the bourgeoisie.

4. These concepts, expressed as values, are a universalized and abstracted form for expressing the interests of the ruling class. Its narrow interests are reformulated by intellectuals into values that can be used to create unity and integration in society, tying subordinate classes into the social order. These universalized concepts have the political purpose of uniting classes into a consensus of values and shared ideals. For example, free enterprise, free markets, and free trade are advantageous to the capitalist class; these interests are then universalized into the concept of "freedom" which has a broader appeal and can serve as a shared value of all classes in capitalism.

5. The political purpose of ideology is often to form a class bloc, to unite intermediate strata and interest groups with the dominant class. For example, the concepts "property rights" and "taxpayers" are used to unite homeowners (who are usually proletarians) with large corporations and the very wealthy. Intellectuals develop and disseminate hegemonic ideas that create support for the ruling class and "naturalize" its right to rule, making its dominance seem logical, commonsensical, and taken-for-granted. To be able to rule with consent, as a fox rather than a lion, a dominant class must present itself as guardian of the whole society, expressing and defending common interests, not merely its own special interests. Hegemony is not a thing, but a process of creating and disseminating ideas, slogans, and notions that sustain a social order. One element of class conflict is contention over ideas; intellectuals

associated with revolutionary classes challenge prevailing hegemony and disseminate new interpretations and visions of the social order.

6. Ideas appear to have a "life of their own." The historian of ideas traces these concepts as though they existed separately from the social conditions in which they were produced and the classes that invented and benefited from them. It is necessary to correct this mistaken approach and analyze culture, ideas, and ideology in their social context.

We must look to *Capital* for Marx's famous section on "commodity fetishism." In the *Communist Manifesto*, Marx and Engels expressed the view that capitalist exploitation is "naked," that the veils of religion and deference present in pre-capitalist systems like feudalism have been torn away. In capitalism, proletarians can see clearly that they are exploited. Here, Marx rethinks this earlier claim about the transparent or unveiled nature of capitalist exploitation. He has come to think that capitalism also has its characteristic mode of mystification, which is no longer framed in religious terms, but in the fetishism of commodities.

To explain the mystification that justifies capitalism, Marx uses the concept of reification: a human action, social process, or concept is erroneously represented as a thing ("res" in Latin), pictured as an external entity that exists outside of ourselves. A process of social construction is mistakenly represented as a fixed thing. The market economy comes to be understood as a "thing" which is external to ourselves, and the "laws of supply and demand" are believed to be natural laws, like the law of gravity. Instead of seeing the market economy as a set of social relations, a process of social construction, we mystify it into a thing that exists independently of human actions and relationships, a thing that compels us to act as we do.

"I can't possibly give you a raise this year; profits are down." "We have to downsize to cut labour costs." "We will cut labour costs (i.e., lay off workers) with a new computer system to keep up with the competition." We read about food crops, milk supplies, or cattle herds being destroyed because there "is a glut on the market," even though we know that there are starving people who need these products. These appeals to the "market" or "the laws of supply and demand" are mystifications that veil the inherent inequality of the social relations between capitalists and workers. The decisions and actions of capitalists are mystified by being represented as unavoidable responses to natural conditions, beyond any human control.

Why does Marx use the phrase "fetishism of commodities" for this reification and mystification? He is comparing it to the creation of idols, fetishes of wood and clay that are believed to embody spirits. The idol is a human creation; but once an idol is made, human beings bow down to it and worship it as a god. In the same way, the market economy is a human creation, a product of social relations, but we mystify it into a fixed, natural, uncontrollable force that is external to our actions. In this mystification, we misinterpret the relationships between people that constitute the economy as relationships between the prices of commodities, the "laws of supply and demand."

Commodities, things made by human beings, take on a life of their own; the economy is believed to be formed by relationships between prices of commodities, not by social relationships between human beings. Especially important in this mystification is the commodity form of human labor power itself. The human ability to create is transformed into a commodity that is bought and sold in the labor market, for wages dictated by "demand and supply."

These passages present in a powerfully succinct form many basic Marxist concepts of the relationship between social conditions (specifically, class relationships) and the values, culture, ideas, and ideologies that arise from and misrepresent these social conditions. A central element of Marxist practice is to expose these misrepresentations and enable us to see the underlying social conditions.

Marx on Machinery and Technology

We now turn from Marx's reflections on ideology to his view of machinery and technology. A passage from *Capital* (see p. 50) describes the use of machinery to increase productivity. Machinery is used to speed up work, reduce labour costs, increase management's control over labour, make workers easily replaceable, and increase profits. Machinery makes it possible to lay off skilled, high-wage workers and replace them with less-skilled employees. In Marx's time this practice often meant replacing adult men by women and children who were paid less because they lacked craft skills. In our time we still see how sophisticated, automated machines can be tended by workers with low skills, low wages, high replaceability, and short training periods; for example, teenagers employed in fast food production.

The potential of technology to emancipate humans from tedious work cannot be realized in capitalism. Instead of being emancipated by technology, human beings are reduced to being appendages of machines. Mechanized work is often broken down into minute, repetitive tasks. The pace of work is fast, too fast to allow day-dreaming and conversation, and too boring to be a source of pleasure and accomplishment. Workers do not experience mechanized work in factories as a satisfying, creative craft, only as a waste of precious years of their lives in a prison-like setting to which they have to submit in order to earn a wage. At the end of the twentieth century, many workers experience similar conditions in computerized office work.

Technology is not a determining force in human society that operates independently of social relationships. It is a complex of "hardware," skills, knowledge, and social relationships connected to other social relationships, especially class relationships. Technology and machinery are created within a set of relationships which shape their use and impact.

Marx and Engels on Communism

Marx and Engels were reluctant to spell out what communism would be like, but in *The German Ideology* (see p. 46) we get a quick, tantalizing glimpse of their wildest fantasies. Usually they distanced themselves from the utopian socialists who liked to plan out all the details of outlandish communal utopias that they believed could be attained in a rather magical way, by a sudden jump from the present into a grand future. Marx and Engels believed that communism was a type of society that could only be achieved through a long, organized, political struggle that had to confront the realities of capitalist society. This struggle would shape the possibilities of the post-capitalist society. Communism still lay far in the future and could be imagined but not planned in any detail.

A stage of socialism, still characterized by a state (a central coercive institution of political power), a division of labour, and a principle of social distribution based on "from and to each according to his/her abilities" would be necessary before communism could emerge. In other words, in socialism societal rewards would be based on talent and hard work, not on ownership of capital. Class fades away, but social roles and specializations still exist in socialist society.

In communism, distribution would be based on unique individual needs and no longer calculated on the basis of individual contributions and abilities. The link between work and livelihood would be completely severed, ending the very notion of work itself. This is a radically individualized vision of the good society, one that clearly requires a high level of technology.

Most people when they hear "communism" think of total equality; but Marx and Engels actually envisioned communism in opposite terms, as a society of total differentiation in which each person is valued in his/her uniqueness and individuality. Social categories, social roles, and specialized labour all cease to exist.

This dream of unique personhood is rooted in Marx and Engels's radical idea that communism means a complete breakdown of the division of labour, the central point of the selection. Communism means that the division between mental and manual labour is completely overcome. Communism means that we can do what we would like to do without ever being labelled in terms of social roles or categories: we can hunt, fish, ranch, and read literature without being a hunter, fisher, rancher, or literary critic. All constraining roles and specializations end.

In communism, each individual enjoys the sensuous pleasure of activities. Once liberated from the need to earn wages and fulfil permanent "role expectations" we would experience our activities as freely chosen and physically pleasurable.

Communism means the overcoming of all practices and actions that were previously represented as natural foundations of the division of labour, most specifically gender. (Incidentally the word "man" in the text is a translation of the more gender-neutral German word "mensch"). The gender division of labour and its apparent naturalness is the original sin of human alienation and exploitation, the initial point of the social construction of unequal roles and relationships, a view that Engels elaborated in *The Origin of the Family, Private Property, and the State*. Marx and Engels contrast a supposedly natural division of labour with the voluntary choice of activities; only the latter is free and unalienated creative activity. We realize our species-being most completely when we free ourselves from the illusion that there is a natural basis to the social order and recognize ourselves as a species that creates our own life conditions.

Marx and Engels's vision is a radical statement about the social construction of gender and "human nature" in general. Human action is always socially constructed; in the past we mystified this social construction by claiming that society reflected a natural order. "Nature" is itself a human construct. In communist society, we finally recognize that we ourselves construct our world, and this recognition frees us to construct it voluntarily and consciously. As Marx phrases it, we then will finally move from prehistory to history.

Most subsequent social thought is a reflection and elaboration of this statement of Marx and Engels, and sometimes a challenge to it. How do we construct our social world? How do we explain and represent these social constructions? How much freedom is possible in social construction and to what extent is human action constrained either by nature or by the weight of the past—what is the dialectic between agency and structure in society? Is a voluntarily and consciously created social order possible?

Notes
1. Karl Marx, *The Eighteenth Brumaire of Louis Bonaparte* (New York: International Publishers) 15.

Readings
Engels, F. *The Origins of the Family, Private Property, and the State*. New York: International Publishers, 1884/1970.

Howard, Dick, and Karl Klare. *The Unknown Dimension: European Marxism since Lenin*. New York: Basic Books, 1972.

Lukacs, Georg. *History and Class Consciousness*. London: Merlin Press, 1968.

Marx, Karl. *Capital*. Vol I. Moscow: Progress Publishers, undated. (based on the 1887 edition).

—. *The Eighteenth Brumaire of Louis Bonaparte*. New York: International Publishers.

Marx, Karl and Friedrich Engels. *The Communist Manifesto*. New York: International Publishers, undated (1885 edition).

—. *The German Ideology*. New York: International Publishers, 1947.

McLellan, David. *The Thought of Karl Marx*. New York: Harper and Row, 1971.

Tucker, Robert C. (ed.). *The Marx-Engels Reader*. New York: W.W. Norton, 1979.

The Communist Manifesto
KARL MARX AND FRIEDRICH ENGELS

[Bourgeois and Proletarians]

The history of all hitherto existing society is the history of class struggles.

Freeman and slave, patrician and plebeian, lord and serf, guild master and journeyman, in a word, oppressor and oppressed, stood in constant opposition to one another, carried on an uninterrupted, now hidden, now open fight, a fight that each time ended, either in a revolutionary reconstitution of society at large, or in the common ruin of the contending classes.

In the earlier epochs of history, we find almost everywhere a complicated arrangement of society into various orders, a manifold gradation of social rank. In ancient Rome we have patricians, knights, plebeians, slaves; in the Middle Ages, feudal lords, vassals, guild-masters, journeymen, apprentices, serfs; in almost all of these classes again, subordinate gradations.

The modern bourgeois society that has sprouted from the ruins of feudal society, has not done away with class antagonism. It has but established new classes, new conditions of oppression, new forms of struggle in place of the old ones.

Our epoch, the epoch of the bourgeoisie, possesses, however, this distinctive feature: It has simplified the class antagonisms. Society as a whole is more and more splitting up into two great hostile camps, into two great classes directly facing each other—bourgeoisie and proletariat.

From the serfs of the Middle Ages sprang the chartered burghers of the earliest towns. From these burgesses the first elements of the bourgeoisie were developed.

The discovery of America, the rounding of the Cape, opened up fresh ground for the rising bourgeoisie. The East Indian and Chinese markets, the colonization of America, trade with the colonies, the increase in the means of exchange and in commodities generally, gave to commerce, to navigation, to industry, an impulse never before known, and thereby, to the revolutionary element in the tottering feudal society, a rapid development.

The feudal system of industry, in which industrial production was monopolized by closed guilds, now no longer sufficed for the growing wants of the new markets. The manufacturing system took its place. The guild-masters were pushed aside by the manufacturing middle class; division of labor between the different corporate guilds vanished in the face of division of labor in each single workshop.

Meantime the markets kept ever growing, the demand ever rising. Even manufacture no longer sufficed. Thereupon, steam and machinery revolutionized industrial production. The place of manufacture was taken by the giant, modern industry, the place of the industrial middle class, by industrial millionaires—the leaders of whole industrial armies, the modern bourgeois.

Modern industry has established the world market, for which the discovery of America paved the way. The market has given an immense development to commerce, to navigation, to communication by land. This development has, in its turn, reacted on the extension of industry; and in proportion as industry, commerce, navigation, railways extended, in the same proportion the bourgeoisie developed, increased its capital, and pushed into the background every class handed down from the Middle Ages.

We see, therefore, how the modern bourgeoisie is itself the product of a long course of development, of a series of revolutions in the modes of production and of exchange.

Each step in the development of the bourgeoisie was accompanied by a corresponding political advance of that class. An oppressed class under the sway of the feudal nobility, it became an armed and self-governing association in the medieval commune; here independent urban republic (as in Italy and Germany), there taxable "third estate" of the monarchy (as in France); afterwards in the period of manufacture proper, serving either the semi-feudal or the absolute monarchy as a counterpoise against the nobility, and in fact cornerstone of the great monarchies in general—the bourgeoisie has at last, since the establishment of modern industry and of the world market, conquered for itself, in the modern representative state, exclusive political sway. The executive of the modern state is but a committee for managing the common affairs of the whole bourgeoisie.

The bourgeoisie has played a most revolutionary role in history.

The bourgeoisie, wherever it has got the upper hand, has put an end to all feudal, patriarchal, idyllic relations. It has pitilessly torn asunder the motley feudal ties that bound man to his "natural superiors," and has left no other bond between man and man than naked self-interest, than callous "cash payment." It has drowned the most heavenly ecstasies of religious fervor, of chivalrous enthusiasm, of Philistine sentimentalism, in the icy water of egotistical calculation. It has resolved personal worth into exchange value, and in place of the numberless indefeasible chartered freedoms, has set up that single, unconscionable freedom—Free Trade. In one word, for exploitation, veiled by religious and political illusions, it has substituted naked, shameless, direct, brutal exploitation.

The bourgeoisie has stripped of its halo every occupation hitherto honored and looked up to with reverent awe. It has converted the physician, the lawyer, the priest, the poet, the man of science, into its paid wage-laborers.

The bourgeoisie has torn away from the family its sentimental veil, and has reduced the family relation to a mere money relation.

The bourgeoisie has disclosed how it came to pass that the brutal display of vigor in the Middle Ages, which reactionaries so much admire, found its fitting complement in the most slothful indolence. It has been the first to show what man's activity can bring about. It has accomplished wonders far surpassing Egyptian pyramids, Roman aqueducts, and Gothic cathedrals; it has conducted expeditions that put in the shade all former migrations of nations and crusades.

The bourgeoisie cannot exist without constantly revolutionizing the instruments of production, and thereby the relations of production, and with them the whole relations of society. Conservation of the old modes of production in unaltered form, was, on the contrary, the first condition of existence for all earlier industrial classes. Constant revolutionizing of production, uninterrupted disturbance of all social conditions, everlasting uncertainty and agitation distinguish the bourgeoisie epoch from all earlier ones. All fixed, fast-frozen relations, with their train of ancient and venerable prejudices and opinions, are swept away, all new-formed ones become antiquated before they can ossify. All that is solid melts into air, all that is holy is profaned, and man is at last compelled to face with sober senses his real conditions of life and his relations with his kind.

The need of a constantly expanding market for its products chases the bourgeoisie over the whole surface of the globe. It must nestle everywhere, settle everywhere, establish connections everywhere.

The bourgeoisie has though its exploitation of the world market given a cosmopolitan character to production and consumption in every country. To the great chagrin of reactionaries, it has drawn from under the feet of industry the national ground on which it stood. All old-established national industries have been destroyed or are daily being destroyed. They are dislodged by new industries, whose introduction becomes a life and death question for all civilized nations, by industries that no longer work up indigenous raw material, but raw material drawn from the remotest zones; industries whose products are consumed, not only at home, but in every quarter of the globe. In place of the old wants, satisfied by the production of the country, we find new wants, requiring for their satisfaction the products of distant lands and climes. In place of the old local and national seclusion and self-sufficiency, we have intercourse in every direction, universal inter-dependence of nations. And as in material, so also in intellectual production. The intellectual creations of individual nations become common property. National one-sidedness and narrow-mindedness become more and more impossible, and from the numerous national and local literatures there arises a world literature.

The bourgeoisie, by the rapid improvement of all instruments of production, by the immensely facilitated means of communication, draws all nations, even the most barbarian, into civilization. The cheap prices of its commodities are the heavy artillery with which it batters down all Chinese walls, with which it forces the barbarians' intensely obstinate hatred of foreigners to capitulate. It compels all nations, on pain of extinction, to adopt the bourgeois mode of production; it compels them to introduce what it calls civilization into their midst, i.e., to become bourgeois themselves. In a word, it creates a world after its own image.

The bourgeoisie has subjected the country to the rule of the towns. It has created enormous cities, has greatly increased the urban population as compared with the rural, and has thus rescued a considerable part of the population from the idiocy of rural life. Just as it has made the country dependent on the towns, so it has made barbarian and semi-barbarian countries dependent on the civilized ones, nations of peasants on nations of bourgeois, the East on the West.

More and more the bourgeoisie keeps doing away with the scattered state of the population, of the means of production, and of property. It has agglomerated population, centralized means of production, and has concentrated property in a few hands. The necessary consequence of this was political centralization. Independent, or but loosely connected provinces, with separate interests, laws, governments, and systems of taxation, became lumped together into one nation, with one government, one code of laws. One national class interest, one frontier, and one customs tariff.

The bourgeoisie, during its rule of scarce one hundred years has created more massive and more colossal productive forces than have all preceding generations together. Subjection of nature's forces to man, machinery, application of chemistry to industry and agriculture, steam-navigation, railways, electric telegraphs, clearing of whole continents for cultivation, canalization of rivers, whole populations conjured out of the ground—what earlier century had even a presentiment that such productive forces slumbered in the lap of social labor?

We see then that the means of production and of exchange, which served as the foundation for the growth of the bourgeoisie, were generated in feudal society. At a certain stage in the development of these means of production and of exchange, the conditions under which feudal society produced and exchanged, the feudal organization of agriculture and manufacturing industry, in a word, the feudal relations of property became no longer compatible with the already developed productive forces; they became so many fetters. They had to be burst asunder; they were burst asunder.

Into their place stepped free competition, accompanied by a social and political constitution adapted to it, and by the economic and political sway of the bourgeois class.

A similar movement is going on before our own eyes. Modern bourgeois society with its relations of production, of exchange and of property, a society that has conjured up such gigantic means of production and of exchange, is like the sorcerer who is no longer able to control the powers of the nether world whom he has called up by his spells. For many a decade past the history of industry and commerce is but the history of the revolt of modern productive forces against modern conditions of production, against the property relations that are the conditions for the existence of the bourgeoisie and of its rule. It is enough to mention the commercial crises that by their periodical return put the existence of the entire bourgeois society on trial, each time more threateningly. In these crises a great part not only of the existing products, but also of the previously created productive forces, are periodically destroyed. In these crises there breaks out an epidemic that, in all earlier epochs, would have seemed an absurdity—the epidemic of over-production. Society suddenly finds itself put back into a state of momentary barbarism; it appears as if a famine, a universal war of devastation had cut off the supply of every means of subsistence; industry and commerce seem to be destroyed. And why? Because there is too much civilization, too much means of subsistence, too much industry, too much commerce. The productive forces at the disposal of society no longer tend to further the development of the conditions of bourgeois property; on the contrary, they have become too powerful for these conditions, by which they are fettered, and no sooner do they overcome these fetters than they bring disorder into the whole of bourgeois society, endanger the existence of bourgeois property. The conditions of bourgeois society are too narrow to comprise the wealth created by them. And how does the bourgeoisie get over these crises? On the one hand, by enforced destruction of a mass of productive forces; the other, by the conquest of new markets, and by the more thorough exploitation of the old ones. That is to say by paving the way for more extensive and more destructive crises, and by diminishing the means whereby crises are prevented.

The weapons with which the bourgeoisie felled feudalism to the ground are now turned against the bourgeoisie itself.

But not only has the bourgeoisie forged the weapons that bring death to itself; it has also called into existence the men who are to wield those weapons—the modern working class—the proletarians.

In proportion as the bourgeoisie, i.e., capital is developed, in the same proportion is the proletariat, the modern working class, developed—a class of laborers, who live only so long as they find work, and who find work only so long as their labor increases capital. These laborers, who must sell themselves piecemeal, are a commodity, like every other article of commerce, and are consequently exposed to all the vicissitudes of competition, to all the fluctuations of the market.

Owing to the extensive use of machinery and to division of labor, the work of the proletarians has lost all individual character, and, consequently, all charm for the workman. He becomes an appendage of the machine, and it is only the most simple, most monotonous, and most easily acquired knack, that is required of him. Hence, the cost of production of a workman is restricted, almost entirely, to the means of subsistence that he requires for his maintenance, and for the propagation of his race. But the price of a commodity, and therefore also of labor, is equal to its cost of production. In proportion, therefore, as the repulsiveness of the work increases, the wage decreases. Nay more, in proportion as the use of machinery and division of labor increases, in the same proportion the burden of toil also increases, whether by prolongation of the working hours, by increased speed of the machinery, etc.

Modern industry has converted the little workshop of the patriarchal master into the great factory of the industrial capitalist. Masses of laborers, crowded into the factory, are organized like soldiers. As privates of the industrial army they are placed under the command of a perfect hierarchy of officers and sergeants. Not only are they slaves of the bourgeois class, and of the bourgeois state; they are daily and hourly enslaved by the machine, by the over-looker, and, above all, by the individual bourgeois manufacturer himself. The more openly this despotism proclaims gain to be its end and aim, the more petty, the more hateful and the more embittering it is.

The less the skill and exertion of strength implied in manual labor, in other words, the more modern industry develops, the more is the labor of men superseded by that of women. Differences of age and sex have no longer any distinctive social validity for the working class. All are instruments of labor, more or less expensive to use according to their age and sex.

No sooner has the laborer received his wages in cash, for the moment escaping exploitation by the manufacturer, than he is set upon by the other portions of the bourgeoisie, the landlord, the shopkeeper, the pawnbroker, etc.

The lower strata of the middle class—the small tradespeople, shopkeepers, and retired tradesmen generally, the handicraftsmen and peasants—all these sink gradually into the proletariat, partly because their diminutive capital does not suffice for the scale on which modern industry is carried on, and is swamped in the competition with the large capitalists, partly because their specialized skill is rendered worthless by new methods of production. Thus the proletariat is recruited from all classes of the population.

The proletariat goes through various stages of development. With its birth begins its struggle with the bourgeoisie. At first the contest is carried on by individual laborers, then by the work people of a factory, then by the operatives of one trade, in one locality, against the individual bourgeois who directly exploits them. They direct their attacks not against the bourgeois conditions of production, but against the instruments of production themselves; they destroy imported wares that compete with their labor, they smash machinery to pieces then set factories ablaze, they seek to restore by force the vanished status of the workman of the Middle Ages.

At this stage the laborers still form an incoherent mass scattered over the whole country, and broken up by their mutual competition. If anywhere they unite to form more compact bodies, this in not yet the consequence of their own active union, but of the union of the bourgeoisie, which class, in order to attain its own political ends, is compelled to set the whole proletariat in motion, and is moreover still able to do so for a time. At this stage, therefore, the proletarians do not fight their enemies, but the enemies of their enemies, the remnants of absolute monarchy, the landowners, the non-industrial bourgeois, the petty bourgeoisie. Thus the whole historical movement is concentrated in the hands of the bourgeoisie.

But with the development of industry the proletariat not only increases in number; it becomes concentrated in greater masses, its strength grows, and it feels that strength more. The various interest and conditions of life within the ranks of the proletariat are more and more equalized, in proportion as machinery obliterates all distinctions of labor and nearly everywhere reduces wages to the same low level. The growing competition among the bourgeois, and the resulting commercial crises, make the wages of the workers ever more fluctuating. The unceasing improvement of machinery, ever more rapidly developing, makes their livelihood more and more precarious; the collisions between individual workmen and individual bourgeois take more and more the character of collisions between two classes. Thereupon the workers begin to form combinations (trade unions) against the bourgeoisie; they club together in order to keep up the rate of wages; they found permanent associations in order to make provision beforehand for these occasional revolts. Here and there the contest breaks out into riots.

Now and then the workers are victorious, but only of a time. The real fruit of their battles lies, not in the immediate result, but in the ever expanding union of the workers. This union is furthered by the improved means of communication which are created by modern industry, and which place the workers of different localities in contact with one another. It was just this contact that was needed to centralize the numerous local struggles, all of the same character, into one national struggle between classes. But every class struggle is a political struggle. And that union, to attain which the burghers of the Middle Ages, with their miserable highways, required centuries, the modern proletarians, thanks to railways, achieved in a few years.

This organization of the proletarians into a class, and consequently into a political party, is continually being upset again by the competition between the workers themselves. But it ever rises up again, stronger, firmer, mightier. It compels legislative recognition of particular interests of the workers, by taking advantage of the divisions among the bourgeoisie itself. Thus the ten-hour bill in England was carried.

Altogether, collisions between the classes of the old society further the course of development of the proletariat in many ways. The bourgeoisie finds itself involved in a constant battle. At first with the aristocracy; later on, with those portions of the bourgeoisie itself whose interests have become antagonistic to the progress of industry; at all times with the bourgeoisie of foreign countries. In all these battles it sees itself compelled to appeal to the proletariat, to ask for its help, and thus, to drag it into the political arena. The bourgeoisie itself, therefore, supplies the proletariat with its own elements of political and general education, in other words, it furnishes the proletariat with weapons for fighting the bourgeoisie.

Further, as we have already seen, entire sections of the ruling classes are, by the advance of industry, precipitated into the proletariat, or are at least threatened in their conditions of existence. These also supply the proletariat with fresh elements of enlightenment and progress.

Finally, in times when the class struggle nears the decisive hour, the process of dissolution going on within the ruling class, in fact within the whole range of old society, assumes such a violent, glaring character, that a small section of the ruling class cuts itself adrift, and joins the revolutionary class, the class that holds the future in its hands. Just as, therefore, at an earlier period a section of the nobility went over to the bourgeoisie, so now a portion of the bourgeoisie goes over to the proletariat, and in particular, a portion of the bourgeois ideologists, who have raised themselves to the level of comprehending theoretically the historical movement as a whole.

Of all the classes that stand face to face with the bourgeoisie today, the proletariat alone is a really revolutionary class. The other classes decay and finally disappear in the face of modern industry; the proletariat is its special and essential product.

The lower middle class, the small manufacturers, the shopkeeper, the artisan, the peasant, all these fight against the bourgeoisie, to save from extinction their existence as fractions of the middle class. They are therefore not revolutionary, but conservative. Nay more, they are reactionary, for they try to roll back the wheel of history. If by chance they are revolutionary, they are so only in view of their impending transfer into the proletariat; they thus defend not their present, but their future interest; they desert their own standpoint to adopt that of the proletariat.

The "dangerous class," the social scum (*Lumpenproletariat*), that passively rotting mass thrown off by the lowest layers of old society, may, here and there, be swept into the movement by a proletarian revolution; its conditions of life, however, prepare it far more for the part of a bribed tool of reactionary intrigue.

The social conditions of the old society no longer exist for the proletariat. The proletarian is without property; his relation to his wife and children has no longer anything in common with bourgeois family relations; modern industrial labor, modern subjection to capital, the same in England as in France, in America as in Germany, has stripped him of every trace of national character. Law, morality, religion, are to him so many bourgeois prejudices, behind which lurk in ambush just as many bourgeois interests.

All the preceding classes that got the upper hand, sought to fortify their already acquired status by subjecting society at large to their conditions of appropriation. The proletarians cannot become masters of the productive forces of society, except by abolishing their own previous mode of appropriation, and thereby also every other previous mode of appropriation. They have nothing of their own to secure and to fortify; their mission is to destroy all previous securities for, and insurances of, individual property.

All previous historical movements were movements of minorities, or in the interest of minorities. The proletarian movement is the self-conscious, independent movement of the immense majority, in the interest of the immense majority. The proletariat, the lowest stratum of our present society, cannot stir, cannot raise itself up, without the whole superincumbent strata of official society being sprung into the air.

Though not in substance, yet in form, the struggle of the proletariat with the bourgeoisie is at first a national struggle. The proletariat of each country must, of course, first of all settle matters with its own bourgeoisie.

In depicting the most general phases of the development of the proletariat, we traced the more or less veiled civil war, raging within existing society, up to the point where that war breaks out into open revolution, and where the violent overthrow of the bourgeoisie lays the foundation for the sway of the proletariat.

Hitherto, every form of society has been based, as we have already seen, on the antagonism of oppressing and oppressed classes. But in order to oppress a class, certain conditions must be assured to it under which it can, at least, continue its slavish existence. The serf, in the periods of serfdom, raised himself to membership in the commune, just as the petty bourgeois, under the yoke of feudal absolutism, managed to develop into a bourgeois. The modern laborer, on the contrary, instead of rising with the progress of industry, sinks deeper and deeper below the conditions of existence of his own class. He becomes a pauper, and pauperism develops more rapidly than population and wealth. And here it becomes evident, that the bourgeoisie is unfit any longer to be the ruling class in society, and to impose its conditions of existence upon society as an overriding law. It is unfit to rule because it is incompetent to assure an existence to its slave within his slavery, because it cannot help letting him sink into such a state, that it has to feed him, instead of being fed by him. Society can no longer live under this bourgeoisie, in other words, its existence is no longer compatible with society.

The essential condition for the existence and sway of the bourgeois class, is the formation and augmentation of capital; the condition for capital is wage-labor. Wage-labor rests exclusively on competition between the laborers. The advance of industry, whose involuntary promoter is the bourgeoisie, replaces the isolation of the laborers, due to competition, by their revolutionary combination, due to association. The development of modern industry, therefore, cuts from under its feet the very foundation on which the bourgeoisie therefore produces and appropriates products. What the bourgeoisie therefore produces, above all, are its own gravediggers. Its fall and the victory of the proletariat are equally inevitable.

The German Ideology
KARL MARX AND FRIEDRICH ENGELS

[On Ideas and Ideology]

The ideas of the ruling class are in every epoch the ruling ideas: i.e. the class, which is the ruling material force of society, is at the same time its ruling intellectual force. The class which has the means of material production at its disposal, has control at the same time over the means of material production so that thereby, generally speaking, the ideas of those who lack the means of mental production are subject to it. The ruling ideas are nothing more than the ideal expression of the dominant material relationships, the dominant material relationships grasped as ideas; hence of the relationships which make the one class the ruling one, therefore the ideas of its dominance. The individuals composing the ruling class possess among other things consciousness, and therefore think. In so far, therefore, as they rule as a class and determine the extent and compass of an epoch, it is self-evident that they do this in their whole range, hence among other things rule also as thinkers, as producers of ideas, and regulate the production and distribution of the ideas of their age: thus their ideas are the ruling ideas of the epoch. For instance, in an age and in a country where royal power, aristocracy and bourgeoisie are contending for mastery and where, therefore, mastery is shared, the doctrine of the separation of powers proves to be the dominant idea and is expressed as an "eternal law." The division of labour, which we saw above as one of the chief forces of history up till now, manifests itself also in the ruling class as the division of mental and material labour, so that inside this class one part appears as the thinkers of the class (its active, conceptive ideologists, who make the perfecting of the illusion of the class about itself their chief source of livelihood), while the others' attitude to these ideas and illusions is more passive and receptive, because they are in reality the active members of this class and have less time to make up illusions and ideas about themselves. Within this class the cleavage can even develop into a certain opposition and hostility between the two parts, which, however, in the case of a practical collision, in which the class itself is endangered, automatically comes to nothing, in which case there also vanishes the semblance that the ruling ideas were not the ideas of the ruling class and had a power distinct from the power of this class. The existence of revolutionary ideas in a particular period presupposes the existence of a revolutionary class; about the premises for the latter sufficient has already been said above.

If now in considering the course of history we detach the ideas of the ruling class from the ruling class itself and attribute to them an independent existence, if we confine ourselves to saying that these or those ideas were dominant, without bothering ourselves about the conditions of production and the producers of these ideas, if we then ignore the individuals and world conditions which are the source of the ideas, we can say, for instance that during the time that the aristocracy was dominant, the concepts honour, loyalty, etc., were dominant, during the dominance of the bourgeoisie the concepts freedom, equality, etc. The ruling class itself on the whole imagines this to be so. This conception of history, which is common to all historians, particularly since the eighteenth century, will necessarily come up against the phenomenon that increasingly abstract ideas hold sway, i.e. ideas which increasingly take on the form of universality. For each new class which puts itself in the place of one ruling before it, is compelled, merely in order to carry through its aim, to represent its interest as the common interest of all the members of society, put in an ideal form; it will give its ideas the form of universality, and represent them as the only rational universally valid ones. The class making a revolution appears from the very start, merely because it is opposed to a class, not as a class but as the representative of the whole of society; it appears as the whole mass of society confronting the one ruling class. It can do this because, to start with, its interest really is more connected with the common interest of all other non-ruling classes, because under the pressure of conditions its interest has not yet been able to develop as the particular interest of a particular class. Its victory, therefore, benefits also many individuals of the other classes which are not winning a dominant position, but only is so far as it now puts these individuals in a position to raise themselves into the ruling class. When the French bourgeoisie overthrew the power of the aristocracy, it thereby made it possible for many proletarians to raise themselves above the proletariat, but only in so far as they became bourgeois. Every new class, therefore, achieves its hegemony only on a broader basis than that of the class ruling previously, in return for which the opposition of the non-ruling class against the new ruling class later develops all the more sharply and profoundly. Both these things determine the fact that the struggle to be waged against this new ruling class, in its turn, aims at a more decided and radical negation of the previous conditions of society than could all previous classes which sought to rule.

This whole semblance, that the rule of a certain class is only the rule of certain ideas, comes to a natural end, of course, as soon as society ceases at last to be organized in the form of class-rule, that is to say as soon as it is no longer necessary to represent a particular interest as general or "the general interest" as ruling....

[On Communism]

And finally, the division of labour offers us the first example of how, as long as man remains in natural society, that is as long as a cleavage exists between the particular and the common interest, as long therefore as activity is not voluntarily, but naturally, divided, man's own deed becomes an alien power opposed to him, which enslaves him instead of being controlled by him. For as soon as labour is distributed, each man has a particular, exclusive sphere of activity, which is forced upon him and from which he cannot escape. He is a hunter, a fisherman, a shepherd, or a critical critic and must remain so if he does not want to lose his means of livelihood; while in communist society, where nobody has one exclusive sphere of activity but each can become accomplished in any branch he wishes society regulates the general production and thus makes it possible for me to do one thing to-day and another to-morrow, to hunt in the morning, fish in the afternoon, rear cattle in the evening, criticize after dinner, just as I have a mind, without ever becoming hunter, fisherman, shepherd or critic.

Capital: Critical Analysis of Capitalist Production
KARL MARX

The Fetishism of Commodities and the Secret Thereof

A commodity appears, at first sight, a very trivial thing, and easily understood. Its analysis shows that it is, in reality, a very queer thing, abounding in metaphysical subtleties and theological niceties. So far as it is a value in use, there is nothing mysterious about it, whether we consider it from the point of view that by its properties it is capable of satisfying human wants, or from the point that those properties are the product of human labour. It is as clear as noon-day, that man, by his industry, changes the forms of the materials furnished by Nature, in such a way as to make them useful to him. The form of wood, for instance, is altered, by making a table out of it. Yet, for all that, the table continues to be that common, every-day thing, wood. But, so soon as it steps forth as a commodity, it is changed into something transcendent. It not only stands with its feet on the ground, but, in relation to all other commodities it stands on its head, and evolves out of its wooden brain grotesque ideas, far more wonderful than "table-turning" ever was.

The mystical character of commodities does not originate, therefore, in their use-value. Just as little does it proceed from the nature of the determining factors of value. For, in the first place, however varied the useful kinds of labour, or productive activities, may be, it is a physiological fact, that they are functions of the human organism, and that each such function, whatever may be its nature or form, is essentially the expenditure of human brain, nerves, muscles, etc. Secondly, with regard to that which forms the ground-work for the quantitative determination of value namely the duration of that expenditure, or the quantity of labour, it is quite clear that there is a palpable difference between its quantity and quality. In all states of society, the labour-time that it costs to produce the means of subsistence, must necessarily be an object of interest to mankind through not of equal interest in different stages of development. And lastly, from the moment that men in any way work for one another, their labour assumes a social form.

Whence, then, arises the enigmatical character of the product of labour so soon as it assumes the form of commodities? Clearly from this form itself. The equality of all sorts of human labour is expressed objectively by their products all being equally values; the measure of the expenditure of labour-power by the duration of that expenditure, takes the form of the quantity of value of the products of labour; and finally, the mutual relations of the producers, within which the social character of their labour affirms itself, take the form of a social relation between the products.

A commodity is therefore a mysterious thing, simply because in it the social character of men's labour appears to them as an objective character stamped upon the product of that labour; because the relation of the producers to the sum total of their own labour is presented to them as a social relation, existing not between themselves, but between the products of their labour. This is the reason why the products of labour become commodities, social things whose qualities are at the same time perceptible and imperceptible by the senses. In the same way the light from an object is perceived by us not as the subjective excitation of our optic nerve, but as the objective form of something outside the eye itself. But, in the act of seeing, there is at all events, an actual passage of light from one thing to another, from the external object to the eye. There is physical relation between physical things. But it is different with commodities. There, the existence of the things quâ commodities, and the value-relation between the products of labour which stamps them as commodities, have absolutely no connexion with their physical properties and with the material relations arising therefrom. There it is definite social relation between men, that assumes, in their eyes, the fantastic form of a relation between things. In order, therefore, to find an analogy, we must have recourse to the mist-enveloped regions of the religious world. In that world the productions of the human brain appear as independent beings endowed with life, and entering into relation both with one another and the human race. So it is in the world of commodities with the products of men's hands. This I call the Fetishism which attaches itself to the products of labour, so soon as they are produced as commodities, and which is therefore inseparable from the production of commodities....

[On Machinery and Technology]

Machinery is put to a wrong use, with the object of transforming the workman, from his very childhood, into a part of a detail-machine. In this way, not only are the expenses of his reproduction considerably lessened, but at the same time his helpless dependence upon the factory as a whole, and therefore upon the capitalist, is rendered complete. Here as everywhere else, we must distinguish between the increased productiveness due to the development of the social process of production, and that due to the capitalist exploitation of that process. In handicrafts and manufacture, the workman makes use of a tool, in the factory, the machine makes use of him. There the movements of the instrument of labour proceed from him, here it is the movements of the machine that he must follow. In manufacture the workmen are parts of a living mechanism. In the factory we have a lifeless mechanism independent of the workman, who becomes its mere living appendage. "The miserable routine of endless drudgery and toil in which the same mechanical process is gone through over and over again, is like the labour of Sisyphus. The burden of labour, like the rock, keeps ever falling back on the worn-out labourer." At the same time that factory work exhausts the nervous system to the uttermost, it does away with the many-sided play of the muscles, and confiscates every atom of freedom, both in bodily and intellectual activity. The lightening of the labour, even, becomes a sort of torture, since the machine does not free the labourer from work, but deprives the work of all interest. Every kind of capitalist production, in so far as it is not only a labour-process, but also a process of creating surplus-value, has this in common, that it is not the workman that employs the instruments of labour, but the instruments of labour that employ the workman. But it is only in the factory system that this inversion for the first time acquires technical and palpable reality. By means of its conversion into an automaton, the instrument of labour confronts the labourer, during the labour-process, in the shape of capital, of dead labour, that dominates, and pumps dry, living labour-power. The separation of the intellectual powers of production from the manual labour, and the conversion of those powers into the might of capital over labour, is, as we have already shown, finally completed by modern industry erected on the foundation of machinery. The special skill of each individual insignificant factory operative vanishes as an infinitesimal quantity before the science, the gigantic physical forces, and the mass of labour that are embodied in the factory mechanism and, together with that mechanism, constitute the power of the "master." This "master" therefore, in whose brain the machinery and his monopoly of it are inseparably united, whenever he falls out with his "hands," contemptuously tells them: "The factory operatives should keep in wholesome remembrance the fact that theirs is really a low species of skilled labour and that there is none which is more easily acquired, or of its quality more amply remunerated, or which by short training of the least expert can be more quickly as well as abundantly, acquired" ... The master's machinery really plays a far more important part in the business of production that the labour and the skill of the operative, which six months' education can teach, and a common labourer can learn. The technical subordination of the workman to the uniform motion of the instruments of labour, and the peculiar composition of the body of workpeople, consisting as it does of individuals of both sexes and of all ages, give rise to a barrack discipline, which is elaborated into a complete system in the factory, and which fully develops the before mentioned labour of overlooking, thereby dividing the workpeople into operatives and overlookers, into private soldiers and sergeants of an industrial army. "The main difficulty [in the automatic factory] ... lay ... above all in training human beings to renounce their desultory habits of work, and to identify themselves with the unvarying regularity of the complex automaton. To devise and administer a successful code of factory discipline, suited to the necessities of factory diligence, was the Herculean enterprise, the noble achievement of Arkwright! Even at the present day, when the system is perfectly organised and its labour lightened to the utmost, it is found nearly impossible to convert persons past the age of puberty, into useful factory hands." The factory code in which capital formulates, like a private legislator, and at his own good will, his autocracy over his workpeople, unaccompanied by that division of responsibility, in other matters so much approved of by the bourgeoisie, and unaccompanied by the still more approved representative system, this code is but the capitalistic caricature of that social regulation of the labour-process which becomes requisite in co-operation on a great scale, and in the employment in common, of instruments of labour and especially of machinery. The place of the slave-driver's lash is taken by the overlooker's book of penalties. All punishments naturally resolve themselves into fines and deductions from wages, and the law-giving talent of the factory Lycurgus so arranges matters, that a violation of his laws is, if possible, more profitable to him than the keeping of them.

We shall here merely allude to the material conditions under which factory labour is carried on. Every organ of sense is injured in an equal degree by artificial elevation of the temperature, by the dust-laden atmosphere, by the deafening noise, not to mention danger to life and limb among the thickly crowded machinery, which, with the regularity of the seasons, issues its list of the killed and wounded in the industrial battle.

Economy of the social means of production, matured and forced as in a hothouse by the factory system, is turned, in the hands of capital, into systematic robbery of what is necessary for the life of the workman while he is at work, robbery of space, light, air, and of protection to his person against the dangerous and unwholesome accompaniments of the productive process, not to mention the robbery of appliances for the comfort of the workman.

6

THE LEGACY OF MARX: STANLEY ARONOWITZ (1933-) AND WILLIAM DIFAZIO (1947-)

In the early twentieth century, the attention of Marxist theorists focused on "Fordism," the capitalist practice of mass production. Management in industrial enterprises introduced machinery to simplify and speed up the labour process, allowing production of large amounts of cheap goods. The term "Fordism" refers to Henry Ford's method of car production; breakdown of production into a sequence of steps and use of an assembly line made possible the hiring of relatively unskilled workers to produce cars for the mass market. Although some crafts workers lost their autonomy and control over the labour process, the working class as a whole enjoyed more access to cheap consumer goods. Ford was proud that his workers could afford the cars they produced.

Fordism is an example of how in the capitalist system technological development is funneled into reorganizing the labour process, not only to make it more productive, but also to bring it more firmly under the control of management. In general, Marxist theorists see science and technology as being subordinated to capital; science and technology are not autonomous institutions but are used to enhance capitalist accumulation.

Stanley Aronowitz and William DiFazio (both professors of sociology) examine the scientific and technical revolution of the late twentieth century. They emphasize that science and technology do not take place in an abstract realm of thought and practice, but in the social context of capitalism, which sets conditions for what scientists and technical workers produce, how they produce it, and how their ideas and inventions are used. The potential of science and technology for enhancing human creativity and reducing drudgery are constantly limited by the "fetters" of capitalism, by the ends and goals for which inventions are used. We can identify a number of these "fetters," evident as problems in the uses of science and technology.

First, technology has the potential of reducing the hours of labour time necessary for meeting our needs and wants, but within the capitalist system such a reduction results in mass unemployment. There is no mechanism for assuring incomes and livelihoods for people who have been "freed" from work by technology; their freedom from work is experienced as a disaster, not an emancipation.

Second is the use of technology to deskill and control workers. For example, computers are used to monitor worker behaviour or to reduce a process to very simple steps. Technology is also used to create "endless" work, to cut into free time, speed up the pace of work, and transform every place into a workplace (homes, hotels, beaches, airplanes, and any other place accessible to laptops and cellphones). All places and moments of time become workplaces and worktime, creating stress and forcing people to become "workaholics" under the spur of competition for sales and jobs.

A third problem is transformation of "knowledge workers" into hired hands of capital. Scientific and technical workers cannot explore and invent according to their own interests and creativity, but find their work is channeled by priorities and funding practices of corporations and governments. Basic science and playful research are discouraged; scientific activity has to be linked to short-term profit or national defense.

Fourth is environmental deterioration and destruction. The benefits of technology are enjoyed in the form of profits and consumer goods for a small proportion of the planet's population, while the costs are borne by society as a whole (both nationally and on a global scale) in terms of health effects, ecosystem damage, extinction of plant and animal species, and clean-up costs. Science and technology are not inherently environmentally damaging; in the capitalist system, however, it is not possible to implement a rational and sustainable type of development.

Three selections from Aronowitz and DiFazio's *The Jobless Future* illustrate their analysis of these issues from a Marxist point of view.

In the first, they sum up the history of subordination of scientific knowledge to capitalist enterprise, with specific examples from several fields of science and technology. In the second, they describe the transformation of people with theoretical knowledge from professionals into salaried workers. Some of their analysis focuses on medicine, in which doctors are decreasingly independent professionals and increasingly employees of corporations that dictate many elements of practice, using criteria of profitability applied by bureaucrats to override doctors' judgements based on scientific claims. (Other theorists, most notably George Ritzer, in a Weberian rather than Marxist tradition, have termed this process the "Macdonaldization" of health care.)[1] Finally, they describe a positive, possible "jobless future," which is not the disaster of mass unemployment that could emerge when computerization and automation are used within the capitalist system to cut labour costs. Instead, it is a world emancipated from work—from drudgery—so that all individuals can develop their creativity, imagination, and participation in a community. Aronowitz and DiFazio disagree with those social thinkers who believe that human beings have an "inherent need to work"; they call this the "dogma" of work, and believe that it has been used as an ideology to lock people into exploited and meaningless kinds of work. Freedom from work means self-managed time. It opens the possibility of people becoming citizens and participating in a community, in civil society. Far from being diametrical opposites, individuality and collectivity are complementary values, and both will be enhanced in a jobless future. This future however can come into being only in a post-capitalist society when capitalist "fetters" are removed from science and technology. In the pages preceding this final vision, the authors outline practical, middle-range steps for moving in this direction, and I strongly urge you to look at their complete set of proposals for getting "beyond the catastrophe."

Note

1. George Ritzer, *The McDonaldization of Society: An Investigation in the Changing Character of Contemporary Life* (Thousand Oaks, CA: Pine Forge Press/Sage, 1995) 4.

Readings

Aronowitz, Stanley. *False Promises*. Durham, NC: Duke University Press, 1991.

Braverman, Harry. *Labor and Monopoly Capitalism*. New York: Monthly Review Press, 1974.

Gorz, Andre. *Paths to Paradise: On the Liberation from Work*. Boston: South End Press, 1985.

Rifkin, Jeremy. *The End of Work: The Decline of the Global Labor Force and the Dawn of the Post-Market Era*. New York: Putnam, 1996.

Ritzer, George. *The McDonaldization of Society: An Investigation into the Changing Character of Contemporary Life*. Thousand Oaks, CA: Pine Forge Press/Sage, 1995.

The Jobless Future
STANLEY ARONOWITZ AND WILLIAM DIFAZIO

The Subordination of Scientific Knowledge

While modern science has always been indebted to some extent to capital, the beginning of the subordination of science to the requirements of capital can be traced to the development of electromagnetism, Babbage's calculating machine experiments, early genetic experiments, and Lyell's development of the science of geology, each of which exhibited characteristics of both the older science and the new technoscience. From Lyell's work in the 1820s and 1830s until the late nineteenth century, geology was constituted by its articulation with the development of the theory of evolution; it was the premier discipline of natural history, of which archaeology and evolutionary biology were, respectively, the study of the history of living things and, specifically, of human evolution. In 1858 Lyell himself presented the papers of Darwin and Wallace on natural selection to the Linneaus Society. With the emergence of coal and oil as crucial fossil fuels in the iron and steel industries, for electricity, and for providing power to the internal combustion engine, however, geology became an industrially linked discipline. Like botany's dual role in evolution and commercial agriculture, Faraday's work on electromagnetism similarly led to new physical discoveries and to broad industrial uses in lighting, the invention of electrical motors and production machinery, Faraday himself stood in both realms: he was the grand old man of British science by the age of forty but also patented his discoveries for commercial uses.[1]

There is no question of the direct subordination of science to industry until later in the nineteenth century when, as we have seen, chemistry was more directly integrated into large corporations. Rather, capital supported the allocation of substantial government funds for research, especially within the universities and independent research institutes. Faraday's employment by the British Royal Institution was an early indication of the end of the era of the so-called gentleman scientist of which Joseph Priestey, Robert Boyle, and Charles Darwin were exemplary figures. Increasingly, physical, chemical, and biological research required elaborate facilities that most larger corporations were unable (or unwilling) to provide because of the uncertain practical results of any basic research. It was not until some U.S. corporations, especially General Electric and American Telephone and Telegraph, became directly involved in transforming Faraday's discoveries into commercial uses that capital entered the research field. Yet despite the extraordinary sophistication of these examples of corporate-sponsored research, few of them were prepared to displace universities as the primary site of basic research.

Babbage's work on the difference engine and on the calculating machine reveals a similar ambiguity between the realism of pure science and practical science. Like his friend Faraday, Babbage was acutely aware of the relevance of his inventions to industry. Himself a prominent, even leading political economist, he made detailed studies of the labour process while working on his computer and saw its development as a potentially important addition to British industry. At the same time, he was interested in the progress of British science and participated actively in the intellectual debates within the Royal Society, the leading forum of the scientific community in Great Britain.

We may observe parallel developments in American science in the latter half of the nineteenth century. By this time, Faraday's discoveries had had an enormous impact on American physicists such as Willard Gibbs and inventors such as Thomas Edison and George Westinghouse. In the United States, the integration of science and technology first took hold in the development of agriculture, which, perhaps in advance of most of Europe, became scientifically based even before the end of the century. This rapid transformation was promoted by the federal government's grants of land to states that agreed to establish colleges devoted in large measure to research and education in agriculture and mechanical technology.

As David Noble has shown, the growth of American industry depended on the emergence of engineering and other technical education programs in these land-grant colleges and private universities.[2] Geological surveys conducted by engineers and scientists were crucially necessary for the discovery of coal and oil resources; experimental physics emerged in the wake of the widespread application of electricity in many sectors of industrial production; and civil engineering expanded with the growth of railroads and roads for wagon, truck, and automobile travel in a sprawling emerging national market. And in addition to these infrastructural aspects of industrial growth, as we have seen, "industrial" engineering became a recognized subdiscipline when, after the Great War, Taylorism and Fordism became crucial technological regimes of production. At the same time, many corporations, especially in the newer industries such as oil, chemicals, steel, communications, and electrical, established research laboratories. Three of the most famous—General Electric's Schenectady laboratory directed by Charles Steinmetz, the Edison labs at Menlo Park, and later the AT&T labs at Kearny and western New Jersey—were responsible for both basic physics research and applications to commercial and industrial uses. Increasingly, however, basic research was centered in universities while the corporations retained significant responsibility for applied science. By 1950 virtually every major corporation whose product was rooted in basic chemical and physical knowledge employed professional scientific and engineering personnel.

Despite much current discussion about the need to privatize basic science, the newest industrially oriented science, molecular biology and its applications to biomedical research, has emerged within universities. The federal government and corporations have funded some of the research on condition that they own the patents to life forms developed in university labs. Given the emerging austerity policies of most state legislatures and the high cost of scientific research, it is not surprising that many scientists have willingly accepted this bargain. The arrangement suggests not only that molecular biology is emerging as a leading technoscience but also that it will remain within universities as long as corporations can benefit directly from discovery and invention.[3]

As continuous-flow technologies came to dominate the workplace, some of the "older" industries such as oil and chemicals that for many years had been based on scientifically wrought knowledge reduced the mass worker and the skilled trades to a minority of the workforce by the 1960s. Similarly, in the telephone industry, computerized processes resulted in a rough parity between professionally and technically trained employees and the manual and clerical workforces. As a result, in both industries, supervisors and nonunion professionals and technicians can operate the facility for considerable periods of time during strikes. In an exemplary instance in the 1960s, during a strike by 3,600 refinery workers against Gulf Oil, six hundred salaried employees successfully operated the plant for a year. Similarly, the communications industry is virtually strikeproof (but not immune to internal industrial action).

These instances suggested, by the mid-1950s, a movement toward a permanent displacement of manual labour, at least within certain types of industries. More important than its relative decline in quantitative terms has been the shift of power over the production process from manual to intellectual labour. With the arrival of the cybernetic revolution (in technological terms) the tendencies already evident in continuous-flow and analog automation technologies are brought to fruition. However much the knowledge entailed in computer programming refers to its origins in crafts and older mechanical-era skills, cybernetics really signals a new era. These skills are now abstracted and converted into self-referential logical symbols. "Computer" languages translated and transmuted these skills so that they no longer appear to have an autonomous existence. Tacit knowledge has been transformed and incorporated into the mathematical system but remains invisible. More striking, intellect no longer appears as a derivation of concrete labour; the abstract symbolic system is now imposed on concrete labour as if from the outside.[4]

So it is not merely that scientifically based technical knowledge has become the dominant productive force; it appears to requalify, even as it continues to subordinate, manual labour. Consequently, for every unit of investment in technological innovations in the cybernetic era, the proportion of intellectual to manual labour increased in two ways: by the elimination of categories of manual labour and by increasing in relative terms the number of qualified intellectual workers while the number of manual workers, whose productive powers are magnified by cybernetic technologies, remains stationary or declines.

This historical reversal, marking the emergence of what various commentators have labeled a new middle class, a new working class, a professional-managerial class, or simply the expansion of a different kind of middle strata, has posed significant issues for the study of professions, for class and stratification analysis, and for the study of work. In 1857 Marx' notebooks for *Capital* published as the *Grundrisse* already asserted that scientific knowledge was rapidly becoming the main productive force: "The entire production process appears as not subsumed under the direct skilfulness of the worker, but rather as the technological application of science. It is hence a tendency of capital to give production a scientific character."[5] Veblen's fundamental insight—arrived at independently of Marx's statement since the *Grundrisse* was not published in German until more than a decade after Veblen's *Engineers and the Price System* (1921)—that technical knowledge had taken hold of the labour process led him to speculate that its bearers were, at least potentially, new historical agents. But Veblen warned that even though engineers were now at the center of the production system they might be subsumed, perhaps permanently, under corporate capital by inducements such as high salaries and easy routes to mobility. Of course, this is precisely what has happened throughout this century. If our thesis that computerization permits a hierarchical bifurcation of scientific and technical labour is right, however, low- and middle-range scientists and engineers may not look forward to occupying a privileged place in the corporate order....

From Professional to Salaried Worker

The technical intellectual is a historically evolved social category whose existence is attributable to the subsumption of science and technology under capital in the late nineteenth century. In contrast to the "traditional" intellectual, who typically was a literary/cultural figure situated either in the universities or in journalism, and the political intellectual, who practiced statecraft or led parties and social movements, the technical intellectual first emerged as a functionary of capital in spheres of instrumental activity, particularly the production and administration of things and signs. Historically, the characteristic technical intellectual was the engineer. Once one of the characteristic sectors of the independent, entrepreneurial middle-class professionals in the late nineteenth century, engineers increasingly became salaried employees. By the time of World War I, engineering, together with law and medicine, had ceased to be a characteristically independent profession.

Half a century later, physicians and attorneys found themselves unable to maintain their independence as the medical and law fields experienced, during the 1960s, their own descent from the independent middle class to the salariat. Today more than half of the graduates of law and medical schools may expect to work for salaries throughout their careers. There is almost no prospect for reversing this trend. A diminishing minority of these professionals, once among the pillars of independent entrepreneurs, can hope to become partners in, or own, their own practices. The fading of this expectation, which was accompanied by the expectation of high income, has caused significant declines in medical school enrollments and a dramatic change in the gender composition of these fields.

Today, more than half of medical and law school students are women, as are a third of all physicians and attorneys, compared to fifteen years ago when only 10 percent of physicians and about 20 percent of attorneys were women. The dramatic alteration of the gender composition of these traditional professions is, of course, not merely the result of their proletarianization; second-wave feminism has contributed to encouraging women to enter these fields, but also to lowering traditional gender barriers.

Becoming salaried employees does not at first signify the loss of traditional markers of professions: they still enjoy a high degree of autonomy in job performance and have credentials that permit both considerable lateral mobility for those who elect to remain practitioners and advancement to management or, an option for attorneys, the judicial bench. In the health field, for example, a small coterie of salaried physicians become top-level managers of the leading institutions. Even staff physicians in most hospitals still make some crucial decisions in their daily practice. Doctors decide on medication, lawyers develop strategies to resolve conflicts within the framework of both laws and the conventions of their profession, and engineers even in CADD-mediated workplaces, must decide among (predetermined) options. In large corporations engineers retain control over a wide range of decisions in the design and processes of industrial production, even if they are subject to constraints imposed by financial and sales managers who may intervene in the design and processes of industrial production to assure cost control and marketability.

Yet there are now two crucial constraints on their autonomy: insofar as they are employed by bureaucratic organizations—public agencies, large law firms and corporations—the range of decision making to which they have access is narrowed; and technological change has recomposed their jobs so that, for most employees, their training exceeds the requirements of job performance. For example, a physician affiliated with a large research hospital in New York City reported to one of the authors that patient care is increasingly governed by computerized information. The computer instructs the nurse when to administer prescribed medicine; the face-to-face ritual of making rounds is virtually eliminated because in many cases doctors simply read the computerized charts hanging from the edge of the patient's bed. And, more broadly, programs have been developed to synthesize information into a diagnosis from which treatment regimens are derived.

In the health industry, computerization is in part a response to chronic shortages of nurses and other trained employees. But the main impetus for the computerization of health services parallels developments in industry and financial services: introducing computers into the workplace is part of a major cost-reduction and productivity-enhancement effort. As a result of computerization, fewer professionals are required on the floor, and the training of and consequently the salaries of paraprofessionals may be reduced; computer-mediated diagnoses and prescriptions standardize patient care, even as they routinize the work of the physician. In addition, most hospitals and other medical centers have introduced management systems that also tend to remove decision making from the health providers.

The routinization of medical work is by no means a universal phenomenon. For even as many staff physicians and professional nurses have been subordinated by the centralization of patient care management and new technologies, a smaller group of administrators, computer-trained physicians, and research scientists have, through the monopolization of new knowledge, enlarged their influence and control over the system. Since the acceleration by molecular biology of medicine as a technoscience over the past decade, knowledge has become more concentrated at the top of hospital and other medical hierarchies. Many staff physicians complain that they are obliged to follow the prescribed regime dictated by the computer program on penalty of discharge or other disciplinary measures. Thus, far from providing new opportunities for staff to interact with the "smart machine" in order to provide better service to patients, the machine is often pitted against the professional as an antagonist. Like skilled craftspersons before them, physicians have suffered not only the loss of opportunities for self-employment but also the loss of autonomy signaled by the decline in their capacity to make independent judgment.

Ending Endless Work

... Like many who have come before us, we believe that among the crucial tools of domination is the practice of "work without end," which chains workers to machines and especially to the authority of those who own and control them—capital and its managerial retainers. To be sure, labour did not enter these relations of domination without thereby gaining some benefit. In the Fordist era, as Hunnicut has brilliantly shown, organized labour exchanged work for consumption and abandoned its historical claim of the right to be lazy, as Paul Lafargue put it.[6] Here, within limits, we affirm that right but confess another: the freedom of people emancipated from labour to become social agents.

Needless to say, we reject the idea that liberal democratic states have already conferred citizenship and that apathy is the crucial barrier preventing many from participating in decision making. Such optimism, unfortunately promulgated by many intellectuals of the left as well as the right, blithely ignores the social conditions that produce "apathy," especially the structural determinants of disempowerment, among them endless work. Nor are we prepared to designate the economic sphere, including the shopfloor "rational-purposive" activity that on the whole has been effectively depoliticized and functions only in terms of the perimeters of instrumental, technical rationality.[7] Management's control over the workplace is an activity of politics. There are winners and losers in the labour process. To render the workplace rational entails a transformation of what we mean by rationality in production, including our conception of skill and its implied "other," unskill, a transformation of what we mean by mental as opposed to physical labour and our judgment of who has the capacity to make decisions under regimes of advanced technologies.

Politics as rational discourse—as opposed to a naked struggle for power — awaits social and economic emancipation. Among the constitutive elements of freedom is self-managed time. Our argument in this book is that there are for the first time in human history the material preconditions for the emergence of the individual and, potentially, for a popular politics. The core material precondition is that labour need no longer occupy a central place in our collective lives nor in our imagination. We do not advocate the emancipation from labour as a purely negative freedom. Its positive content is that, unlike the regime of work without end, it stages the objective possibility of citizenship.

Under these circumstances, we envision civil society as the privileged site for the development of individuals who really are free to participate in a public sphere of their own making. In such a civil society, politics consists not so much in the ritual act of selection, through voting, of one elite over another, but in popular assemblies that could, given sufficient space and time, be both the legislative and the administrative organs. The scope of popular governance would extend from the workplace to the neighbourhood. For as Ernest Mandel has argued, there is no possibility of worker self-management, much less the self-management of society, without ample time for decision making.[8] Thus, in order to realize a program of democratization, we must create a new civil society in which freedom consists in the first place (but only in the first place) in the liberation of time from the external constraints imposed by nature and other persons on the individual.

The development of the individual—not economic growth, cost cutting, or profits—must be the fundamental goal of scientific and technological innovation. The crucial obstacle to the achievement of this democratic objective is the persistence of the dogma of work, which increasingly appears, in its religious-ethical and instrumental-rational modalities, as an obvious instrument of domination.

Notes

1. Joseph Agassi, *Faraday as a Natural Philosopher* (Chicago: University of Chicago Press, 1971).
2. David F. Noble, *America by Design: Science, Technology, and the Rise of Corporate Capitalism* (New York: Knopff, 1977).
3. Martin Kenney, *Bio-Technology: The University-Industrial Complex* (New Haven, Conn.: Yale University Press, 1986).
4. Alfred Sohn-Rethel, *Intellectual and Manual Labour* (London: Macmillan, 1977).
5. Marx, *Grundrisse*, 699.
6. Paul Lafargue, *The Right To Be Lazy* (Chicago: Charles Kerr, 1907).
7. This is a major argument of Jürgen Habermas's theory of communicative action. See especially Habermas's "Toward a Reconstruction of Historical Materialism" in *Communication and the Evolution of Society* (Boston: Beacon, 1979), 131-38.
8. Ernest Mandel, *Late Capitalism* (London: New Left Books, 1979).

7

EMILE DURKHEIM (1858-1917)

Emile Durkheim is the founder of modern sociology. He was radically socio-logical—radical not in a political sense, but in the uncompromising and extreme character of his theory. He insisted that sociology is a science of soci-ety. Explanations of human actions must derive from the level of society, not individual behaviour and motivations. Culture and social structure exist prior and external to individuals.

A simple example may help us understand the external and compelling force of society. All of us are born into at least one language community—Eng-lish, French, Spanish, Tagalog, Urdu, and so on. The grammatical structure, phonetic system, and vocabulary of this language are experienced as absolute-ly fixed, compelling, and beyond our control; at most we may add a word of slang or invent a new technical term, but we will surely not transform this lan-guage in any marked way. The language existed before we were born, it "forces" us to speak and think in certain ways, and it will exist after our death.

Durkheim pictured society and culture in precisely this way—as systems that are external to individuals and compel them to think and act within rigid limits. Language, society, and culture are not subjects, in the sense of entities capable of purposive and conscious action. They have no mind or will of their own. Their power is not intentional, and, though it differs completely from the power of individuals or organizations, it is, indeed, a good deal more com-pelling. We can say things like "Society forces us to..." or "Society con-demns..." as long as we understand that this turn of speech is only a metaphor for a system without an acting, wilful subject.

Durkheim's radical insistence that sociology is about society and culture, not individual action and motivation, underlies the main ideas of his theory. Note the similarity of his view to Comte's placement of sociology at the top of the hierarchy of sciences, as inquiry into the most complex organization of matter. Society and social structures are realities at a level above the individual human organism. Durkheim shares Comte's functionalist, evolutionary, and positive premises.

For Durkheim, functionalism means the idea that society is a system, and that its parts—institutions—contribute to its stability and continued existence. Functionalism does not mean thinking that the system is a good one or that it makes individuals happy. Nor does it suggest that all systems are viable; some function badly and come to an end. Nor does it suggest the divine creation of the system or a purpose for its existence. It only means that the parts of the system are interconnected and that the system persists over time if certain conditions of stability and continuity are met.

Durkheim's sociology was evolutionary in that he was interested in how societies change over time. Societies as systems are not static: changes to them can be either gradual or sudden, qualitative shifts. Durkheim looked at both forms of change. In addition, like Marx, he thought he could discern some progress in the course of history. He was cautiously optimistic about the direction of change in society, believing that it was moving towards "moral individualism," greater opportunities for individuation, personal responsibility, and cultural diversity.

Finally, like Comte, Durkheim was a positivist, in that he rejected the Hegelian notion of a subject in history; history was a process of change in social systems, without a subject, purpose, teleology, or fixed endpoint. As in Comte's case, this position was closely tied to insistence on empirical research. Science, unlike theology and Hegelian philosophy, does not know *a priori* that there is a pattern or an inner logic of things defined by ideal concepts; scientists have to find patterns by studying phenomena. Durkheim was a pioneer in the use of statistics, quantitative data, and data analysis. Statistics show regular patterns of behaviour that reflect the underlying, compelling forces of social structure; statistics based on large numbers of individuals give insight into the supra-individual determination of behaviour. These determinations cannot be discerned in the study of the behaviour of single individuals, and are only seen in the statistical patterning.

Durkheim was especially interested in rates of behaviour, because the rate is an indicator of the condition of society or of a particular social group or community. For example, the fact that the United States has a homicide rate that is considerably higher than Canada's is an indicator of different norms, values, laws (such as those governing gun ownership), and social relationships in the two countries. Rates—especially rates of crime or other "deviant" behaviour— are like measuring body temperature or doing blood tests; the resulting numbers are indicators of the condition of the "body," in this case, society.

Having outlined Durkheim's general orientation towards sociology, we are ready to look at the more specific insights he developed as he studied forms of social cohesion, systems of law, patterns of suicide, and religious beliefs.

One of his first major works was *The Division of Labor in Society* (1893). This title is misleading, promising an economic focus to what is really a study of social cohesion and forms of punishment. Durkheim traces these throughout human history; he uses demographic and economic factors—namely, increasing social density and an increasingly complex division of labour—for a brief and rather perfunctory explanation of the changes he observes. A close reading of the book suggests that his heart is more in the analysis of cohesion and punishment than it is in the demographic and economic explanatory framework.

A central concept in Durkheim's work is the "collective consciousness/conscience." The thesis of *The Division of Labor* is that societies have moved from harsh, punitive, and universally shared collective consciousness/conscience to a more attenuated and individualized form. In French, the two English terms "conscience" and "consciousness" are expressed in the same word, *conscience*; the Anglophone reader needs to imagine these two concepts folded into one. The collective consciousness/conscience is the force of culture, especially the process of normative regulation. It is best to imagine it as a process experienced by individuals, rather than as a "thing," even though it can take a physical form, like a wall plaque of the Ten Commandments, a copy of the Bible or Qur'an, or a law book. We can also picture some elements of the collective consciousness/conscience as the voice of conscience in individual's thoughts, as long as we understand that it does not originate at the individual level, though it is experienced there.

In "primitive" societies, the collective consciousness/conscience is harsh, punitive, intense, rigid, and universally shared. ("Primitive" is not a reflection on individuals' intelligence, but on the forms of cohesion, normative integration, and structural complexity of the society. Unlike most European social scientists of his day, Durkheim was absolutely opposed to any biological, racialist, and essentialist explanations of differences between societies.) We can share the feeling of this type of consciousness/conscience if we dwell on crimes like serial killings, torture-murders, incest, and other heinous crimes. Law associated with the primitive consciousness/conscience is usually repressive; the deviant act creates feelings of loathing that can be balanced only by an action taken against the perpetrator as a person, often execution, corporal punishment, or social segregation. Small towns and small communities (like the Amish) often retain this type of solidarity, with its harsh treatment of deviants.

In modern societies, the collective consciousness/conscience is attenuated. It is less harsh, less punitive, less intensely felt, less rigid, and less shared than in primitive societies. If we think about white collar crimes like tax evasion or embezzlement, we get a sense of this attenuated consciousness/conscience. The acts do not fill us with loathing; we do not feel repulsion about the tax evader as a person; we experience no compulsion to annihilate him or her or to act out a punishment on the body of the evildoer. Law shifts from largely repressive normative regulation to restitution; civil law appears, in which the payment of fines and restitution to victims is the mechanism of punishment and regulation. There is a growing ratio of civil cases to criminal cases (where the older, repressive forms are retained).

Durkheim associates this change in norms and punishments with changes in social solidarity. "Primitive" societies and small communities are characterized by "mechanical solidarity," solidarity based on similarity. It is "mechanical" in the sense of being unreasoning and simple, an identity like that of parts stamped out with a cookie cutter or punch press. Everyone is alike in these societies, sharing the same experiences, views, and feelings. The power of the collective consciousness/conscience is usually associated with religion, especially the codes of prohibitions elaborated by so many religions ("Thou shalt not...").

Modern societies are characterized by "organic solidarity," a cohesion based on differentiation and interdependence. People perform specialized roles in society; there is a greater and more complex division of labour. People are held together by their mutual interdependence, not by their similarity. A society of organic solidarity encourages the formation of a more attenuated but also more complex collective consciousness/conscience.

In *Suicide*, he continued to examine the theme that deviant behaviour is a social fact, a characteristic of societies and not individuals. He analyzed suicide rates of various social groups: Protestants, Catholics, and Jews; men and women; the married and the single; civilians and military personnel; societies in periods of economic booms and societies in periods of recession. He tries to explain differences in the rates in terms of the underlying structure of groups and societies. He identifies two dimensions of difference—social cohesion and normative regulation. Suicide rates are high for the two extreme ends of the dimension of social cohesion. When there is very little cohesion and the individual is isolated, egoistic suicide is common; Durkheim believed that a high degree of individual isolation was the cause of the high Protestant rate, while group cohesion protected Jews from suicide. When there is too much cohesion and individual identity is dissolved in the group, altruistic suicide prevails because the individual is prepared to give up his life for the group. The dimension of normative regulation also has two extreme ends: in conditions of fatalism, there is overregulation, and people kill themselves because of the strict, harsh regime that is imposed on them, as in the case of suicides of slaves and newly married wives. In conditions of anomie, there is an underregulation of wants, and no limits are set on behaviour, a situation that precipitates a sense of confusion and produces a high suicide rate. The concept of anomie explains why the suicide rate often rises during periods of a soaring stock market.

Durkheim was particularly interested in anomie and anomic suicide. He believed that people are unhappy if their wants become unlimited, weakly regulated, and disproportionate to the available means of realizing them. Historically, society has functioned to regulate and limit human desires: people accepted social pressures that defined limited goals and wants. Capitalist society tends to expand these limits and to remove them altogether; far from being discouraged from expressing their wants, people in capitalist society are encouraged to express and pursue them to the utmost. Thus, capitalist society contains powerful pressures toward anomie, to disorientation and confusion that arise out of limitless wants and the inability to satisfy them.

The concept of anomie as a feature of the modern market economy parallels observations of other classical theorists, most notably Marx's comment that capitalism produces new wants, as well as Georg Simmel's analysis of the miser and the spendthrift, both of whom are enthralled by the limitless potential inherent in money. It continues to be a widely-used concept, although it is sometimes applied to any situation of weak or confused norms without Durkheim's focus on limitless wants.

Durkheim's perspective on religion and God was even more innovative. His last major book was *The Elementary Forms of Religious Life*, a daring work in which he argues that religious feeling, the spiritual, the sacred, and God are nothing more than collective representations of the human experience of the power of society. As the basis of his analysis, Durkheim reads and re-interprets ethnographic observations of the Arunta, an aboriginal hunting and gathering tribe of Australia, a place and people he had never seen. This choice of data and method is in keeping with his consistently anti-racist position; social structure and collective consciousness are easier to observe in a "primitive" society, but the fundamental functioning of human society is the same for all races. Using the description of totemic religion from Arunta ethnographies is also disingenuous and ironic, an endrun around the religious sensibilities of his European readers. When Durkheim argues that Arunta religion is nothing more than the collective representation of the overwhelming power of society, he is, of course, saying precisely the same about Judaism and Christianity.

The line of analysis is similar to that of *Suicide* in that it begins with a critique of existing explanations of the phenomenon and moves to Durkheim's own focus on the structure of society. He uses the Arunta ethnographic data to argue against religion being the expression of individual states of mind. He also dismisses the explanation that it is a representation of natural forces, like storms and fertility, an explanation favoured by nineteenth-century rationalists. He argues that religion is always associated with a sense of the sacred, which is, in turn, a representation in supernatural terms of the overwhelming experience of human society. The effervescence of the group massed together for rituals, as well as the terrifying power of social prohibitions, constitute this experience, which human beings then ascribe to a supernatural force. The experience of the force of society is always an experience of power external to the individual and completely beyond his or her control. Thus, it is ascribed to "God," "gods," or "spirits" of nature or ancestors. The specific forms of the collective representation vary with the complexity and structure of society, but the underlying mechanism that produces religious institutions is the same in all societies. "God" is the collective representation of the experience of society as an external and compelling power.

Durkheim uses historical reflection to express two hopes for the future of society. One is implied in the notion of organic solidarity, in which economic interdependence makes it possible to live in societies of cultural diversity. People can live together and feel solidarity, without all having to think and act alike. Durkheim's vision was perhaps based on his experience as a Jew in nineteenth-century France where some ethnic French were very anti-Semitic and believed that Jews could never be "really French"; he hoped to see France become a nation in which the cohesion of the French people could encompass religious and cultural differences among them, so that they could feel solidarity with each other without being identical in their beliefs.

The other hope he expressed was for "moral individualism." He recognized that economic specialization and differentiation undermined the intensity of normative regulation associated with mechanical solidarity and complete alikeness. On the one hand, this attenuation of the collective consciousness/conscience suggested a potential for disorder and *anomie*, that is, weak, conflicting or absent norms and limitless wants. But on the other hand, it also opened the way for more individuation, a greater acceptance and validation of individual differences, a chance for individuals to grow as human beings. The outcome of individuation for society could only be favourable if individuals become more responsible at the same time that they become more differentiated, individuated, and free from rigid regulation of their morality.

These two questions continue to confront most societies. Can societies be truly multicultural, based on multiple diversities, and yet also enjoy solidarity and cohesion? Can individuals be differentiated and freed from rigid regulation of morality, and yet also behave responsibly?

Readings

Alexander, Jeffrey C. *Durkheimian Sociology: Cultural Studies*. New York: Cambridge University Press, 1988.

Durkheim, Emile. *The Division of Labor in Society*. New York: Free Press, 1984.

—. *The Elementary Forms of the Religious Life*. New York: Free Press, 1995.

—. *Suicide*. Glencoe, IL: Free Press, 1966.

Giddens, Anthony. *Emile Durkheim*. New York: Penguin, 1979.

Nisbet, Robert. *Emile Durkheim*. Englewood Cliffs, NJ: Prentice Hall, 1965.

The Rules of Sociological Method
EMILE DURKHEIM

The Normality of Crime

If there is any fact whose pathological character appears incontestable, that fact is crime. All criminologists are agreed on this point. Although they explain this pathology differently, they are unanimous in recognizing it. But let us see if this problem does not demand a more extended consideration.

We shall apply the foregoing rules. Crime is present not only in the majority of societies of one particular species but in all societies of all types. There is no society that is not confronted with the problem of criminality. Its form changes; the acts thus characterized are not the same everywhere; but, everywhere and always, there have been men who have behaved in such a way as to draw upon themselves penal repression. If, in proportion as societies pass from the lower to the higher types, the rate of criminality, i.e., the relation between the yearly number of crimes and the population, tended to decline, it might be believed that crime, while still normal, is tending to lose this character of normality. But we have no reason to believe that such a regression is substantiated. Many facts would seem rather to indicate a movement in the opposite direction. From the beginning of the [nineteenth] century, statistics enable us to follow the course of criminality. It has everywhere increased. In France the increase is nearly 300 per cent. There is, then, no phenomenon that presents more indisputably all the symptoms of normality, since it appears closely connected with the conditions of all collective life. To make of crime a form of social morbidity would be to admit that morbidity is not something accidental, but, on the contrary, that in certain cases it grows out of the fundamental constitution of the living organism; it would result in wiping out all distinction between the physiological and the pathological. No doubt it is possible that crime itself will have abnormal forms, as, for example, when its rate is unusually high. This excess is, indeed, undoubtedly morbid in nature. What is normal, simply, is the existence of criminality, provided that it attains and does not exceed, for each social type, a certain level, which it is perhaps not impossible to fix in conformity with the preceding rules.[1]

Here we are, then, in the presence of a conclusion in appearance quite pathological. Let us make no mistake. To classify crime among the phenomena of normal sociology is not to say merely that it is an inevitable, although regrettable phenomenon due to the incorrigible wickedness of men; it is to affirm that it is a factor in public health, an integral part of all healthy societies.

This result is, at first glance, surprising enough to have puzzled even ourselves for a long time. Once this first surprise has been overcome, however, it is not difficult to find reasons explaining this normality and at the same time confirming it.

In the first place crime is normal because a society exempt from it is utterly impossible. Crime, we have shown elsewhere, consists of an act that offends certain very strong collective sentiments. In a society in which criminal acts are no longer committed, the sentiments they offend would have to be found without exception in all individual consciousness, and they must be found to exist with the same degree as sentiments contrary to them. Assuming that this condition could actually be realized, crime would not thereby disappear; it would only change its form, for the very cause which would thus dry up the sources of criminality would immediately open up new ones....

Imagine a society of saints, a perfect cloister of exemplary individuals. Crimes, properly so called, will there be unknown, but faults which appear venial to the layman will create there the same scandal that the ordinary offense does in ordinary consciousness. If, then, this society has the power to judge and punish, it will define these acts as criminal and will treat them as such. For the same reason, the perfect and upright man judges his smaller failings with a severity that the majority reserve for acts more truly in the nature of an offense. Formerly, acts of violence against persons were more frequent than they are today, because respect for individual dignity was less strong. As this has increased, these crimes have become more rare; and also, many acts violating this sentiment have been introduced into the penal law which were not included there in primitive times.[2]

In order to exhaust all the hypotheses logically possible, it will perhaps be asked why this unanimity does not extend to all collective sentiments without exception. Why should not even the most feeble sentiment gather enough energy to prevent all dissent? The moral consciousness of the society would be present in its entirety in all the individuals, with a vitality sufficient to prevent all acts offending it—the purely conventional faults as well as the crimes. But a uniformity so universal and absolute is utterly impossible; for the immediate physical milieu in which each one of us is placed, the hereditary antecedents, and the social influences vary from one individual to the next, and consequently diversify consciousness. It is impossible for all to be alike, if only because each one has his own organism and that these organisms occupy different areas in space. That is why even among the lower peoples, where individual originality is very little developed, it nevertheless does exist.

Thus, since there cannot be a society in which the individuals do not differ more or less from the collective type, it is also inevitable that, among these divergences, there are some with a criminal character. What confers this character upon them is not the intrinsic quality of a given act but that definition which the collective conscience lends them. If the collective conscience is stronger, if it has enough authority practically to suppress these divergences, it will also be more sensitive, more exacting, and, reacting against the slightest deviations with the energy it otherwise displays only against more considerable infractions, it will attribute to them the same gravity as formerly to crimes. In other words, it will designate them as criminal.

Crime is, then, necessary; it is bound up with the fundamental conditions of all social life and by that very fact it is useful, because these conditions of which it is a part are themselves indispensable to the normal evolution of morality and law....

Nor is this all. Aside from this indirect utility, it happens that crime itself plays a useful role in this evolution. Crime implies not only that the way remains open to necessary changes but that in certain cases it directly prepares these changes. Where crime exists, collective sentiments are sufficiently flexible to take on a new form and crime sometimes helps to determine the form they will take. How many times, indeed, it is only an anticipation of future morality—a step toward what will be! According to Athenian law, Socrates was a criminal, and his condemnation was no more than just. However, his crime, namely, the independence of his thought, rendered a service not only to humanity but to his country. It served to prepare a new morality and faith which the Athenians needed, since the traditions by which they had lived until then were no longer in harmony with the current conditions of life. Nor is the case of Socrates unique; it is reproduced periodically in history. It would never have been possible to establish the freedom of thought we now enjoy if the regulations prohibiting it had not been violated before being solemnly abrogated. At that time, however, the violation was a crime, since it was an offense against sentiments still very keen in the average conscience. And yet this crime was useful as a prelude to reforms which daily became more necessary. Liberal philosophy had as its precursors the heretics of all kinds who were justly punished by secular authorities during the entire course of the Middle Ages and until the eve of modern times.

From this point of view the fundamental facts of criminality present themselves to us in an entirely new light. Contrary to current ideas, the criminal no longer seems a totally unsociable being, a sort of parasitic element, a strange and unassimilable body, introduced into the midst of society.[3] On the contrary, he plays a definite role in social life. Crime, for its part, must no longer be conceived as an evil that cannot be too much suppressed. There is no occasion for self-congratulation when the crime rate drops noticeably below the average level, for we may be certain that this apparent progress is associated with some social disorder. Thus, the number of assault cases never falls so low as in times of want.[4] With the drop in the crime rate, and as a reaction to it, comes a revision, or the need of a revision in the theory of punishment. If indeed, crime is a disease, its punishment is its remedy and cannot be otherwise conceived; thus, all the discussions it arouses bear on the point of determining what the punishment must be in order to fulfil this role of remedy. If crime is not pathological at all, the object of punishment cannot be to cure it, and its true function must be sought elsewhere.

Notes

1. From the fact that crime is a phenomenon of normal sociology, it does not follow that the criminal is an individual normally constituted from the biological and psychological points of view. The two questions are independent of each other. This independence will be better understood when we have shown [...] the difference between psychological and sociological facts.
2. Calumny, insults, slander, fraud, etc.
3. We have ourselves committed the error of speaking thus of the criminal, because of a failure to apply our rule (*Division du travail social*, pp. 395-96).
4. Although crime is a fact of normal sociology, it does not follow that we must not abhor it. Pain itself has nothing desirable about it; the individual dislikes it as society does crime, and yet it is a function of normal physiology. Not only is it necessarily derived from the very constitution of every living organism, but it plays a useful role in life, for which reason it cannot be replaced. It would, then, be a singular distortion of our thought to present it as an apology for crime. We would not even think of protesting against such an interpretation, did we not know to what strange accusations and misunderstandings one exposes oneself when one undertakes to study moral facts objectively and to speak of them in a different language from that of the layman.

8

THE LEGACY OF DURKHEIM: ROBERT MERTON (1910-)

This 1938 article by Robert Merton, a professor of sociology at Columbia University in New York, illustrates the influence of Durkheim on social thought. Merton's discussion of crime, deviance, and social structure continues to have an impact on theories in the fields of criminology and deviant behaviour.

The thesis of the article builds on Durkheim's work in many ways and illustrates continuities in concepts and theoretical reasoning.

First, Merton shares Durkheim's view of society as a structure without a subject. Social structure, culture, and social processes take place without conscious willing or purposive action by individuals, who experience and perceive the structure and make choices about courses of action within structural limits. However, the structure remains external and prior to their actions.

Second, both see crime as an inevitable by-product of this structure. When people's actions fall outside a given cultural and social structure, it is defined as deviant. People who commit deviant acts are not usually pathological individuals. Crime and deviance therefore are "normal" phenomena in two senses: most of the people who commit crimes are psychologically normal, perhaps even above average in intelligence and resolve; the phenomena themselves are "normal" in the sense of being an inevitable feature of society.

Third, Merton explicitly uses the term *anomie*, though his usage is somewhat different from Durkheim's. Durkheim used it to mean a situation of normlessness or weak norms that generate a sense of "limitlessness" or "everything is possible." Merton uses it to refer to a gap between the cultural definition of the good life and the structurally-available means to attain this goal in a legitimate fashion.

Deviant behaviour is bound to appear in a society with a gap between cultural definitions of goals and access to legitimate means to attain the goals. As long as the structural gap remains, we can expect a fairly stable and regular level of deviance. The specific gap that Merton has in mind is that between the culturally defined version of success in capitalist society and the means that are considered legitimate for attaining success. Success is defined as the accumulation of wealth; the legitimate means to achieving it are fairly limited, such as formal education for lucrative professions and investment of inherited capital. Many people are located in class positions in which they cannot hope to follow any of these routes. This gap or disjuncture produces a range of deviant activities which Merton categorizes into a five-part typology.

The more unrestrainedly capitalist a society is, the more we can expect the emergence of deviant behaviour. Societies focused exclusively on wealth as the definition of the good life, with very limited positions near the top and fiercely competitive struggles to get there, are especially likely to experience "innovative" responses—in other words, organized crime, fraud, and corruption. Merton writes about the United States as a particularly clear example of this type of cultural and social structure.

Within capitalist societies, we expect that the lower class would be engaged in more deviant behaviour because they are largely excluded from legitimate means, yet share the culturally defined goal of wealth. Merton was writing primarily about the European-origin lower class, but the theoretical analysis applies just as well to other racial/ethnic groups in so far as they share the cultural definition of success. In the years after this article was published, racially excluded groups like African Americans were able to move more fully into the cultural mainstream of life in the United States and no longer were confined to a separate, limited definition of success. Since they own and inherit far less wealth than whites and often are excluded from the route of first-rate formal education because of restricted and poorly distributed resources for public education at the local and state level, they remain disproportionately excluded from legitimate means. It is thus not surprising that now racial/ethnic minorities, like the European-origin working class, are disproportionately involved in crime.

The reader may be wondering if this article could be interpreted as a Marxist analysis of crime; the thesis is certainly compatible with Marxist theory, but Merton would not have labeled his work that way, perhaps because he did not believe that a revolutionary shift to socialism was likely.

Readings

Adler, Freda and William S. Laufer (eds.). *The Legacy of Anomie Theory*. New Brunswick, NJ: Transaction Press, 1995.

Hagedorn, John. *People and Folks: Gangs, Crime, and the Underclass in a Rustbelt City*. Lakeview Press, 1996.

Merton, Robert. *Social Theory and Social Structure*. New York: Free Press, 1949/1968.

Moore, Joan. *Going Down to the Barrio: Homeboys and Homegirls in Change*. Philadelphia: Temple University Press, 1991.

Padilla, Felix. *The Gang as an American Enterprise*. New Brunswick, NJ: Rutgers University Press, 1992.

Social Structure and Anomie
ROBERT K. MERTON

There persists a notable tendency in sociological theory to attribute the malfunctioning of social structure primarily to those of man's imperious biological drives which are not adequately restrained by social control. In this view, the social order is solely a device of "impulse management" and the "social processing" of tensions. These impulses which break through social control, be it noted, are held to be biologically derived. Nonconformity is assumed to be rooted in original nature.[1] Conformity is by implication the result of an utilitarian calculus or unreasoned conditioning. This point of view, whatever its other deficiencies, clearly begs one question. It provides no basis for determining the nonbiological conditions which induce deviations from prescribed patterns of conduct. In this paper, it will be suggested that certain phases of social structure generate the circumstances in which infringement of social codes constitutes a "normal" response.[2]

The conceptual scheme to be outlined is designed to provide a coherent, systematic approach to the study of socio-cultural sources of deviate behavior. Our primary aim lies in discovering how some social structures exert a definite pressure upon certain persons in the society to engage in nonconformist rather than conformist conduct. The many ramifications of the scheme cannot all be discussed; the problems mentioned outnumber those explicitly treated.

Among the elements of social and cultural structure, two are important for our purposes. These are analytically separable although they merge imperceptibly in concrete situations. The first consists of culturally defined goals, purposes, and interest. It comprises a frame of aspirational reference. These goals are more or less integrated and involve varying degrees of prestige and sentiment. They constitute a basic, but not the exclusive, component of what Linton aptly has called "designs for group living." Some of these cultural aspirations are related to the original drives of man, but they are not determined by them. The second phase of the social structure defines, regulates, and controls the acceptable modes of achieving these goals. Every social group invariably couples its scale of desired ends with moral or institutional regulation of permissible and required procedures for attaining these ends. These regulatory norms and moral imperatives do not necessarily coincide with technical or efficiency norms. Many procedures which from the standpoint of particular individuals would be most efficient in securing desired values, e.g., illicit oil-stock schemes, theft, fraud, are ruled out of the institutional area of permitted conduct. The choice of expedients is limited by the institutional norms.

To say that these two elements, culture goals and institutional norms, operate jointly is not to say that the ranges of alternative behaviors and aims bear some constant relation to one another. The emphasis upon certain goals may vary independently of the degree of emphasis upon institutional means. There may develop a disproportionate, at times, a virtually exclusive, stress upon the value of specific goals, involving relatively slight concern with the institutionally appropriate modes of attaining these goals. The limiting case in this direction is reached when the range of alternative procedures is limited only by technical rather than institutional considerations. Any and all devices which promise attainment of the all important goal would be permitted in this hypothetical polar case.[3] This constitutes one type of cultural malintegration. A second polar type is found in groups where activities originally conceived as instrumental are transmuted into ends in themselves. The original purposes are forgotten and ritualistic adherence to institutionally prescribed conduct becomes virtually obsessive.[4] Stability is largely ensured while change is flouted. The range of alternative behaviors is severely limited. There develops a tradition-bound, sacred society characterized by neophobia. The occupational psychosis of the bureaucrat may be cited as a case in point. Finally, there are the intermediate types of groups where a balance between culture goals and institutional means is maintained. These are the significantly integrated and relatively stable, though changing, groups.

An effective equilibrium between the two phases of the social structure is maintained as long as satisfactions accrue to individuals who conform to both constraints, viz., satisfactions from the achievement of the goals and satisfactions emerging directly from the institutionally canalized modes of striving to attain these ends. Success, in such equilibrated cases, is twofold. Success is reckoned in terms of the product and in terms of the process, in terms of the outcome and in terms of activities. Continuing satisfactions must derive from sheer participation in a competitive order as well as from eclipsing one's competitors if the order itself is to be sustained. The occasional sacrifices involved in institutionalized conduct must be compensated by socialized rewards. The distribution of statuses and roles through competition must be so organized that positive incentives for conformity to roles and adherence to status obligations are provided *for every position* within the distributive order. Aberrant conduct, therefore, may be viewed as a symptom of dissociation between culturally defined aspirations and socially structured means.

Of the types of groups which result from the independent variation of the two phases of the social structure, we shall be primarily concerned with the first, namely, that involving a disproportionate accent on goals. This statement must be recast in a proper perspective. In no group is there an absence of regulatory codes governing conduct, yet groups do vary in the degree to which these folkways, mores, and institutional controls are effectively integrated with the more diffuse goals which are part of the culture matrix. Emotional convictions may cluster about the complex of socially acclaimed ends, meanwhile shifting their support from the culturally defined implementation of these ends. As we shall see, certain aspects of the social structure may generate countermores and antisocial behavior precisely because of differential emphases on goals and regulation. In the extreme case, the latter may be so vitiated by the goal-emphasis that the range of behavior is limited only by considerations of technical expediency. The sole significant question then becomes, which available means is most efficient in netting the socially approved value?[5] The technically most feasible procedure, whether legitimate or not, is preferred to the institutionally prescribed conduct. As this process continues, the integration of the society becomes tenuous and anomie ensues.

Thus, in competitive athletics, when the aim of victory is shorn of its institutional trappings and success in contests becomes construed as "winning the game" rather than "winning through circumscribed modes of activity," a premium is implicitly set upon the use of illegitimate but technically efficient means. The star of the opposing football team is surreptitiously slugged; the wrestler furtively incapacitates his opponent through ingenious but illicit techniques; university alumni covertly subsidize "students" whose talents are largely confined to the athletic field. The emphasis on the goal has so attenuated the satisfactions deriving from sheer participation in the competitive activity that these satisfactions are virtually confined to a successful outcome. Through the same process, tension generated by the desire to win in a poker game is relieved by successfully dealing oneself four aces, or, when the cult of success has become completely dominant, by sagaciously shuffling the cards in a game of solitaire. The faint twinge of uneasiness in the last instance and the surreptious nature of public delicts indicate clearly that the institutional rules of the game are known to those who evade them, but that the emotional supports of these rules are largely vitiated by cultural exaggeration of the success-goal.[6] They are microcosmic images of the social macrocosm.

Of course, this process is not restricted to the realm of sport. The process whereby exaltation of the end generates a literal demoralization, i.e., a deinstitutionalization, of the means is one which characterizes many[7] groups in which the two phases of the social structure are not highly integrated. The extreme emphasis upon the accumulation of wealth as a symbol of success[8] in our own society militates against the completely effective control of institutionally regulated modes of acquiring a fortune.[9] Fraud, corruption, vice, crime, in short, the entire catalogue of proscribed behavior, becomes increasingly common when the emphasis on the culturally induced success-goal becomes divorced from a coordinated institutional emphasis. This observation is of crucial theoretical importance in examining the doctrine that antisocial behavior most frequently derives from biological drives breaking through the restraints imposed by society. The difference is one between a strictly utilitarian interpretation which conceives man's ends as random and an analysis which finds these ends deriving from the basic values of the culture.[10]

Our analysis can scarcely stop at this juncture. We must turn to other aspects of the social structure if we are to deal with the social genesis of the varying rates and types of deviate behavior characteristic of different societies. Thus far, we have sketched three ideal types of social orders constituted by distinctive patterns of relations between culture ends and means. Turning from these types of *culture patterning*, we find five logically possible, alternative modes of adjustment or adaption by *individuals* within the culture-bearing society or group.[11] These are schematically presented in the following table, where (+) signifies "acceptance," (–) signifies "elimination" and (±)signifies "rejection and substitution of new goals and standards."

		Culture goals	*Institutionalized Means*
I.	Conformity	+	+
II.	Innovation	+	–
III.	Ritualism	–	+
IV.	Retreatism	–	–
V.	Rebellion[12]	±	±

Our discussion of the relation between these alternative responses and other phases of the social structure must be prefaced by the observation that persons may shift form one alternative to another as they engage in different social activities. These categories refer to role adjustments in specific situations, not to personality *in toto*. To treat the development of this process in various spheres of conduct would introduce a complexity unmanageable within the confines of this paper. For this reason, we shall be concerned primarily with economic activity in the broad sense, "the production, exchange, distribution and consumption of goods and services" in our competitive society, wherein wealth has taken on a highly symbolic cast. Our task is to search out some of the factors which exert pressure upon individuals to engage in certain of these logically possible alternative responses. This choice, as we shall see, is far from random.

In every society, Adaption I (conformity to both culture goals and means) is the most common and widely diffused. Were this not so, the stability and continuity of the society could not be maintained. The mesh of expectancies which constitutes every social order is sustained by the modal behavior of its members falling within the first category. Conventional role behavior oriented toward the basic values of the group is the rule rather than the exception. It is this fact alone which permits us to speak of a human aggregate as comprising a group or society.

Conversely, Adaptation IV (rejection of goals and means) is the least common. Persons who "adjust" (or maladjust) in this fashion are, strictly speaking, in the society but not of it. Sociologically, these constitute the true "aliens." Not sharing the common frame of orientation, they can be included within the societal population merely in a fictional sense. In this category are *some* of the activities of psychotics, psychoneurotics, chronic autists, pariahs, outcasts, vagrants, vagabonds, tramps, chronic drunkards and drug addicts.[13] These have relinquished, in certain spheres of activity, the culturally defined goals, involving complete aim-inhibition in the polar case, and their adjustments are not in accord with institutional norms. This is not to say that in some cases the source of their behavioral adjustments is not in part the very social structure which they have in effect repudiated nor that their very existence within a social area does not constitute a problem for the socialized population.

This mode of "adjustment" occurs, as far as structural sources are concerned, when both the culture goals and institutionalized procedures have been assimilated throughly by the individual and imbued with affect and high positive value, but where those institutionalized procedures which promise a measure of successful attainment of the goals are not available to the individual. In such instances, there results a twofold mental conflict with the pressure to resort to illegitimate means (which may attain the goal) and inasmuch as the individual is shut off from means which are both legitimate *and* effective. The competitive order is maintained, but the frustrated and handicapped individual who cannot cope with this order drops out. Defeatism, quietism and resignation are manifested in escape mechanisms which ultimately lead the individual to "escape" from the requirements of the society. It is an expedient which arises from continued failure to attain the goal by legitimate measures and from an inability to adopt the illegitimate route because of internalized prohibitions and institutionalized compulsives, *during which process the supreme value of the success-goal has as yet not been renounced*. The conflict is resolved by eliminating *both* precipitating elements, the goals and means. The escape is complete, the conflict is eliminated and the individual is socialized.

Be it noted that where frustration derives from the inaccessibility of effective institutional means for attaining economic or any other type of highly valued "success", that Adaptations II, III and V (innovation, ritualism and rebellion) are also possible. The result will be determined by the particular personality, and thus, the *particular* cultural background, involved. Inadequate socialization will result in the innovation response whereby the conflict and frustration are eliminated by relinquishing the institutional means and retaining the success-aspiration: an extreme assimilation of institutional demands will lead to ritualism wherein the goal is dropped as beyond one's reach but conformity to the mores persists; and rebellion occurs when emancipation from the reigning standards, due to frustration or to marginalist perspectives, leads to the attempt to introduce a "new social order."

Our major concern is with the illegitimacy adjustment. This involves the use of conventionally proscribed but frequently effective means of attaining at least the simulacrum of culturally defined success,—wealth, power, and the like. As we have seen, this adjustment occurs when the individual has assimilated the cultural emphasis on success without equally internalizing the morally prescribed norms governing means for its attainment. The question arises, which phases of our social structure predispose toward this mode of adjustment? We may examine a concrete instance, effectively analyzed by Lohman,[14] which provides a clue to the answer. Lohman has shown that specialized areas of vice in the near north side of Chicago constitute a "normal" response to a situation where the cultural emphasis upon pecuniary success has been absorbed, but where there is little access to conventional and legitimate means for attaining such success. The conventional occupational opportunities of persons in this area are almost completely limited to manual labor. Given our cultural stigmatization of manual labor, and its correlate, the prestige of white collar work, it is clear that the result is a strain toward innovational practices. The limitation of opportunity to unskilled labor and the resultant low income can not compete in terms of conventional standards of achievement with the high income from organized vice.

For our purposes, this situation involves two important features. First such antisocial behavior is in a sense "called forth" by certain conventional values of the culture and by the class structure involving differential access to the approved opportunities for legitimate, prestige-bearing pursuit of the culture goals. The lack of high integration between the means—and—end elements of the cultural pattern and the particular class structure combine to favor a heightened frequency of antisocial conduct in such groups. The second consideration is of equal significance. Recourse to the first of the alternative responses, legitimate effort, is limited by the fact that actual advance toward desired success-symbols through conventional channels is, despite our persisting open-class ideology,[15] relatively rare and difficult for those handicapped by little formal education and few economic resources. The dominant pressure of group standards of success is, therefore, on the gradual attenuation of legitimate, but by and large ineffective, strivings and the increasing use of illegitimate, but more or less effective, expedients of vice and crime. The cultural demands made on persons in this situation are incompatible. On the one hand, they are asked to orient their conduct toward the prospect of accumulating wealth and on the other, they are largely denied effective opportunities to do so institutionally. The consequences of such structural inconsistency are psychopathological personality, and/or antisocial conduct, and/or revolutionary activities. The equilibrium between culturally designated means and ends becomes highly unstable with the progressive emphasis on attaining the prestige-laden ends by any means whatsoever. Within this context, Capone represents the triumph of amoral intelligence over morally prescribed "failure," when the channels of vertical mobility are closed or narrowed[16] in a society which places a high premium on economic affluence and social ascent for all its members.[17]

This last qualification is of primary importance. It suggests that other phases of the social structure besides the extreme emphasis on pecuniary success, must be considered if we are to understand the social sources of antisocial behavior. A high frequency of deviate behavior is not generated simply by "lack of opportunity" or by this exaggerated pecuniary emphasis. A comparatively rigidified class structure, a feudalistic or caste order, may limit such opportunities far beyond the point which obtains in our society today. It is only when a system of cultural values extols, virtually above all else, certain *common* symbols of success *for the population at large* while its social structure rigorously restricts or completely eliminates access to approved modes of acquiring these symbols *for a considerable part of the same population*, that antisocial behavior ensues on a considerable scale. In other words, our egalitarian ideology denies by implication the existence of noncompeting groups and individuals in the pursuit of pecuniary success. The same body of success-symbols is held to be desirable for all. These goals are held to *transcend class lines*, not to be bounded by them, yet the actual social organization is such that there exist class differentials in the accessibility of these *common* success-symbols. Frustration and thwarted aspiration lead to the search for avenues of escape from a culturally induced intolerable situation; or unrelieved ambition may eventuate in illicit attempts to acquire the dominant values.[18] The American stress on pecuniary success and ambitiousness for all thus invites exaggerated anxieties, hostilities, neuroses and antisocial behavior.

This theoretical analysis may go far toward explaining the varying correlations between crime and poverty.[19] Poverty is not an isolated variable. it is one in a complex of interdependent social and cultural variables. When viewed in such a context, it represents quite different states of affairs. Poverty as such, and consequent limitation of opportunity, are not sufficient to induce a conspicuously high rate of criminal behavior. Even the often mentioned "poverty in the midst of plenty" will not necessarily lead to this result. Only insofar as poverty and associated disadvantages in competition for the culture values approved for *all* members of the society is liked with the assimilation of a cultural emphasis on monetary accumulation as a symbol of success is antisocial conduct a "normal" outcome. Thus, poverty is less highly correlated with crime in southeastern Europe than in the United States. The possibilities of vertical mobility in these European areas would seem to be fewer than in this country, so that neither poverty *per se* nor its association with limited opportunity is sufficient to account for the varying correlations. It is only when the full configuration is considered, poverty, limited opportunity and a commonly shared system of success symbols, that we can explain the higher association between poverty and crime in our society than in others where rigidified class structure is coupled with *differential class symbols of achievement.*

In societies such as our own, then, the pressure of prestige bearing success tends to eliminate the effective social constraint over means employed to this end. "The-end-justifies-the-means" doctrine becomes a guiding tenet for action when the cultural structure unduly exalts the end and the social organization unduly limits possible recourse to approved means. Otherwise put, this notion and associated behavior reflect a lack of cultural coordination. In international relations, the effects of this lack of integration are notoriously apparent. An emphasis upon national power is not readily coordinated with an inept organization of legitimate, i.e., internationally defined and accepted, means for attaining this goal. The result is a tendency toward the abrogation of international law, treaties become scraps of paper, "undeclared warfare" serves as a technical evasion, the bombing of civilian populations is rationalized,[20] just as the same societal situation induces the same sway of illegitimacy among individuals.

The social order we have described necessarily produces this "strain toward dissolution." The pressure of such an order is upon outdoing one's competitors. The choice of means within the ambit of institutional control will persist as long as the sentiments supporting a competitive system, i.e., deriving from the possibility of outranking competitors and hence enjoying the favorable response of others, are distributed throughout the entire system of activities and are not confined merely to the final result. A stable social structure demands a balanced distribution of affect among its various segments. When there occurs a shift of emphasis from the satisfactions deriving from competition itself to almost exclusive concern with successful competition, the resultant stress leads to the breakdown of the regulatory structure.[21] With the resulting attenuation of the institutional imperatives, there occurs an approximation of the situation erroneously held by utilitarians to be typical of society generally wherein calculations of advantage and fear of punishment are the sole regulating agencies. In such situations, as Hobbes observed, force and fraud come to constitute the sole virtues in view of their relative efficiency in attaining goals,—which were for him, of course, not culturally derived.

It should be apparent that the foregoing discussion is not pitched on a moralistic plane. Whatever the sentiments of the writer or reader concerning the ethical desirability of coordinating the means-and-goals phases of the social structure, one must agree that lack of such coordination leads to anomie. Insofar as one of the most general functions of social organization is to provide a basis for calculability and regularity of behavior, it is increasingly limited in effectiveness as these elements of the structure become dissociated. At the extreme, predictability virtually disappears and what may be properly termed cultural chaos or anomie intervenes.

This statement, being brief, is also incomplete. It has not included an exhaustive treatment of the various structural elements which predispose toward one rather than another of the alternative responses open to individuals; it has neglected, but not denied the relevance of, the factors determining the specific incidence of these responses; it has not enumerated the various concrete responses which are constituted by combinations of specific values of the analytical variables; it has omitted, or included only by implication, any consideration of the social functions performed by illicit responses; it has not tested the full explanatory power of the analytical scheme by examining a large number of group variations in the frequency of deviate and conformist behavior; it has not adequately dealt with rebellious conduct which seeks to refashion the social framework radically; it has not examined the relevance of cultural conflict for an analysis of culture-goal and institutional-means malintegration. It is suggested that these and related problems may be profitably analyzed by this scheme.

Notes

1. E.g., Ernest Jones, *Social Aspects of Psychoanalysis*, 28, London, 1924. If the Freudian notion is a variety of the "original sin" dogma, then the interpretation advanced in this paper may be called the doctrine of "socially derived sin."

2. "Normal" in the sense of a culturally oriented, if not approved, response. This statement does not deny the relevance of biological and personality differences which may be significantly involved in the *incidence* of deviate conduct. Our focus of interest is the social and cultural matrix; hence we abstract from other factors. It is in this sense, I take it, that James S. Plant speaks of the "normal reactions of normal people to abnormal conditions." See his personality and the reactions of normal people to abnormal conditions." See his *Personality and the Cultural Pattern,* 248, New York, 1937.

3. Contemporary American culture has been said to tend in this direction. See André Siegfried, *America Comes of Age*, 26-37, New York, 1927. The alleged

extreme (?) emphasis on the goals of monetary success and material prosperity leads to dominant concern with technological and social instruments designed to produce the desired result, inasmuch as institutional controls becomes of secondary importance. In such a situation, innovation flourishes as *the range of means* employed is broadened. In a sense, then, there occurs the paradoxical emergence of "materialists" from an "idealistic" orientation. Cf. Durkheim's analysis of the cultural conditions which predispose toward crime and innovation, both of which are aimed toward efficiency, not moral norms. Durkheim was one of the first to see that "contrairement aux idées courantes le criminel n'apparait plus comme un être radicalement insociable, comme une sorte d'element parasitaire, de corps étranger et inassimilable, introduit au sein de la société; c'est un agent régulier de la vie sociale." See *Les Règles de la Méthode Sociologique*, 86-89, Paris, 1927.

4. Such ritualism may be associated with a mythology which rationalizes these actions so that they appear to retain their status as means, but the dominant pressure is in the direction of strict ritualistic conformity, irrespective of such rationalizations. In this sense, ritual has proceeded farthest when such rationalizations are not even called forth.

5. In this connection, one may see the relevance of Elton Mayo's paraphrase of the title of Tawney's well known book. "Actually the problem *is not that of the sickness of an acquisitive society; it is that of the acquisitiveness of a sick society.*" *Human Problems of an Industrial Civilization*, 153, New York, 1933. Mayo deals with the process through which wealth comes to be a symbol of social achievement. He sees this as arising from a state of anomie. We are considering the unintegrated monetary-success goal as an element in producing anomie. A complete analysis would involve both phases of this system of interdependent variables.

6. It is unlikely that interiorized norms are completely eliminated. Whatever residuum persists will induce personality tensions and conflict. The process involves a certain degree of ambivalence. A manifest rejection of the institutional norms is coupled with some latent retention of their emotional correlates. "Guilt feelings," "sense of sin," "pangs of conscience" are obvious manifestations of this unrelieved tension; symbolic adherence to the nominally repudiated values or rationalizations constitute a more subtle variety of tensional release.

7. "Many," and not all, unintegrated groups, for the reason already mentioned. In groups where the primary emphasis shifts to institutional means i.e., when the range of alternatives is very limited, the outcome is a type of ritualism rather than anomie.

8. Money has several peculiarities which render it particularly apt to become a symbol of prestige divorced from institutional controls. As Simmel emphasized, money is highly abstract and impersonal. However acquired, through fraud or institutionally, it can be used to purchase the same goods and services. The anonymity of metropolitan culture, in conjunction with this peculiarity of money, permits wealth, the sources of which may be unknown to the community in which the plutocrat lives, to serve as a symbol of status.

9. The emphasis upon wealth as a success-symbol is possibly reflected in the use of the germ *"fortune"* to refer to a stock of accumulated wealth. This meaning becomes common in the late sixteenth century (Spenser and Shakespeare). A similar usage of the Latin *fortuna* comes into prominence during the first century B.C. Both these periods were marked by the rise to prestige and power of the "bourgeoisie."

10. See Kingsley Davis, "Mental Hygiene and the Class Structure," *Psychiatry*, 1928, I, esp. 62-63; Talcott Parsons, *The Structure of Social Action*, 59-60, New York, 1937.

11. This is a level intermediate between the two planes distinguished by Edward Sapir; namely, culture patterns and personal habit systems. See his "Contribution of Psychiatry to an Understanding of Behavior in Society," *Amer. J. Sociol.*, 1937, 42: 862-70.

12. This fifth alternative is on a plane clearly different from that of the others. It represents a *transitional* response which seeks to *institutionalize* new procedures oriented toward revamped cultural goals shared by the members of the society. It thus involves efforts to *change* the existing structure rather than to perform accommodative actions within this structure, and introduces additional problems with which we are not at the moment concerned.

13. Obviously, this is an elliptical statement. These individuals may maintain some orientation to the values of their particular differentiated groupings within the larger society or, in part, of the conventional society itself. Insofar as they do so, their conduct cannot be classified in the "passive rejection" category (IV). Nels Anderson's description of the behavior and attitudes of the bum, for example, can readily be recast in terms of our analytical scheme. See *The Hobo*, 93-98, et passim, Chicago, 1923.

14. Joseph D. Lohman, "The Participant Observer in Community Studies," *Amer. Sociol. Rev.*, 1937, 2: 890-98.

15. The shifting historical role of this ideology is a profitable subject for exploration. The "office-boy-to-president" stereotype was once in approximate accord with the facts. Such vertical mobility was probably more common then than now, when the class structure is more rigid. (See the following note.) The ideology largely persists, however, possibly because it still performs a useful function for maintaining the *status quo*. For insofar as it is accepted by the "masses," it constitutes a useful sop for those who might rebel against the entire structure, were this consoling hope removed. This ideology now serves to lessen the probability of Adaptation V. In short, the role of this notion has changed from that of an approximately valid empirical theorem to that of an ideology, in Mannheim's sense.

16. There is a growing body of evidence, though none of it is clearly conclusive, to the effect that our class structure is becoming rigidified and that vertical mobility is declining. Taussig and Joslyn found that American business leaders are being *increasingly* recruited from the upper ranks of our society. The Lynds have also found a "diminished chance to get ahead" for the working classes in Middletown. Manifestly, these objective changes are not alone significant; the individual's sub-

jective evaluation of the situation is a major determinant of the response. The extent to which this change inopportunity for social mobility has been recognized by the least advantaged classes is still conjectural, although the Lynds present some suggestive materials. The writer suggests that a case in point is the increasing frequency of cartoons which observe in a tragi-comic vein that "my old man says everybody can't be President. He says if ya can get three days a week study on W.P.A. work ya ain't doin' so bad either," See F.W. Taussig and C.S. Joslyn, *American Business Leaders*, New York, 1932; R.S . And H.M. Lynd, *Middletown in Transition*, 67ff., chap. 12, New York, 1937.

17. The role of the Negro in this respect is of considerable theoretical interest. Certain elements of the Negro population have assimilated the dominant caste's values of pecuniary success and social advancement, but they also recognized that social ascent is at present restricted to their own caste almost exclusively. The pressures upon the Negro which would otherwise derive from the structural inconsistencies we have noticed are hence not identical with those upon lower class whites. See Kingsley Davis, *op.cit.*, 63; John Dollard, *Caste and Class in a Southern Town*, 66 ff., New Haven, 1936; Donald Young, *American Minority Peoples*, 581, New York, 1932.

18. The psychical coordinates of these processes have been partly established by the experimental evidence concerning *Anspruchsniveaus* and levels of performance. See Kurt Lewin, *Versatz, Wille and Bedürfnis*, Berlin, 1926; N.F. Hoppe, "Erfolg und Misserfolg," *Psychol. Forschung*, 1930, 14:1-63; Jerome D. Frank, "Individual Differences in Certain Aspects of the Level of Aspiration," *Amer. J. Psychol.*, 1935, 47: 119-23.

19. Standard criminology texts summarize the data in this field. Our scheme of analysis may serve to resolve some of the theoretical contradictions which P.A. Sorokin indicates. For example, "not everywhere nor always do the poor show a greater proportion of crime ... many poorer countries have had less crime than the richer countries ... The [economic] improvement in the second half of the nineteenth century, and the beginning of the twentieth, has not been followed by a decrease of crime." See his *Contemporary Sociological Theories*, 560-61, New York, 1928. The crucial point is, however, that poverty has varying social significance in different social structures, as we shall see. Hence, one would not expect a linear correlation between crime and poverty.

20. See M.W. Royse, *Aerial Bombardment and the International Regulation of War*, New York, 1928.

21. Since our primary concern is with the socio-cultural aspects of this problem, the psychological correlates have been only implicitly considered. See Karen Horney, *The Neurotic Personality of Our Time*, New York, 1937, for a psychological discussion of this process.

9
———

MAX WEBER (1864-1920)

Max Weber envisioned the study of society as the study of modes of action, by which he meant meaningful, purposive behaviour. This perspective is in sharp contrast to Durkheim's view of society as external structures that function apart from human purpose and will.

The central idea of Weber's work is that action has become increasingly formally rational over the course of history. "Formal rationality" means careful, planned, and calculated matching of means to ends; in formally rational action, human beings identify and use means that they believe are most likely to bring about a desired end. All human beings engage in action, in meaningful behaviour, but such behaviour is not always formally rational. Only in modern societies does the mode of formal rationality pervade all spheres of action.

Another way of thinking about formal rationality is the term "disenchantment." Weber used this word to mean a mode of action stripped of all magical thinking. The human and natural world lose all their magical, mysterious, and miraculous qualities. All action becomes subject to rational calculation.

Weber recognized that formal rationality is only one form of rationality. Unlike substantive rationality, it is dissociated from consideration of the ultimate purpose of action. Formal rationality can come into play in pursuit of inhuman ends, like the murder of millions of people in genocide and modern warfare, and can be applied to the practice of placing profits ahead of human well-being.

Weber wrote about many apparently disparate topics—the history of religion, bureaucratic organization, forms of social inequality, capitalism and Protestantism, collective action and organization that arise from status and class inequality, the relationship between states and societies, and types of power and authority, but all these topics are unified by a sweeping argument that traces increasing domination of human life by rational modes of action over the course of human history.

Weber's work on the history of religion traces the origins of rational action in western and modern culture back to the ideas of the Hebrew prophets. They began the task of dis-enchanting the world, of banishing magical thought. Multitudes of gods and spirits, linked together in inconsistent and mutually-tolerant belief systems, were replaced by a single omnipotent God, who cannot be coaxed or compelled by magic and ritual. God is imagined as a transcendent entity, separate from Creation, rather than immanent like the gods and spirits of nature. Religious thought was codified, made coherent and consistent. A moral breakthrough took place, in which a sacred text called men and women to higher standards of moral action.

This transformation of religious thought set in motion a historical process in which God became increasingly removed from the world of everyday life; the more completely all-powerful God is, the more God is distant from human affairs. The more God is confined to heaven, the more the natural and human environment become a sphere of conscious, rational action. The omnipotence and transcendence of God in human thought leaves open a larger and larger sphere of rational action. Of course, this was not the intention of the Hebrew prophets.

Nor was capitalism the intention of Protestant reformers. The historical linkage of the Protestant Ethic and the spirit of capitalism is an unintentional process in which the tenets of Protestant faith create many of the preconditions for the emergence of capitalism as a coherent and dominant system of thought and action. It is the final stage of the religious transformation sketched above. Protestant thought radically eliminates the role of all miraculous or divinely ordained forces that can intercede or mediate between God and the individual—such as saints, the Blessed Virgin Mary, and the priesthood. Each human being is utterly alone before an omnipotent and distant God. The uncompromisingly puritanical nature of Protestant belief creates an orientation of individual responsibility that underlies the market economy. The idea of a calling creates a new seriousness about the meaning of work. Ascetic attitudes lead to saving and investment, rather than spending wealth on luxury goods.

Weber's analysis of Calvinist predestinarian beliefs is particularly startling. In predestinarian belief, God unilaterally decides who is saved and who is damned. Neither good works nor faith can save the damned, because a truly omnipotent God cannot be compelled by any human actions. Would this belief not lead to a fatalistic, even hedonistic outlook? Weber argues the contrary: desperate to see signs of grace, predestinarian Protestants believed they could discern it in worldly economic success. Success in business and accumulation of wealth could be read as evidence of God's grace, and so religious belief became an incentive for systematic capitalist activities.

Weber traced a parallel historical process in forms of authority and organization. He defined power as the ability to impose one's will. Authority is legitimate power, power exercised with the consent of the ruled. He identified three forms of authority—traditional, charismatic, and rational/legal. Rational/legal authority, lodged in impersonal rules based on a means/ends calculation, has become the predominant type of authority, reflecting the tendency toward rational modes of action. Bureaucracy is the most common modern form of organization based on rational/legal authority.

Our age is dominated by two institutions that embody rational modes of action: the modern state with its bureaucratic organization and impersonal rules, and the capitalist market economy with its profit-seeking firms. We can have little trade-offs between the influence of these two institutions; there can be a slightly "freer" market or a slightly stronger state, but there is no alternative to the logic of formal rationality: the choice is between a socialistic Tweedle Dee or a capitalistic Tweedle Dum. Weber was quite gloomy about the prospects of ever escaping the historical shift towards the dominance of formal rationality; he used the image of an "iron cage" to envision this inevitable and immutable historical trend.

Weber saw these shifts also influencing the nature of stratification systems. He identified three dimensions of inequality: class, economic position, specifically market position; status, identification with communities distinguished by honour or prestige; and political power. Political power is constituted by "party," that is, by purposive formation of political organizations.

Class, status, and party are somewhat independent of each other. For example, in the United States today, a person might enjoy a favourable class position as a successful dentist, but as an African American, his status in a racist society would be relatively low—he might encounter problems in finding housing and be subjected to police harassment and racial profiling. Party, in turn, is not an automatic result of either class or status position; it is based on individual and collective meanings given to these positions and to prospects for collective action. Our dentist might choose to join the American Dental Association to promote professional interests that are related to class position, the NAACP to promote his status interests, or the local Republican organization to promote a broad definition of class interests. Or he might become a socialist, affiliate with the Nation of Islam, or live an entirely privatized life. Class and status positions are translated into specific political action in a process that involves the formation of identity and the efforts of existing organizations to promote those identities and definitions of the situation.

Although the three dimensions are somewhat independent, Weber thought that there was a strong trend toward class becoming relatively more important than status, both in determining individuals' life chances and in defining the overall shape of the stratification system. Status has an archaic character, being based on non-market criteria and ascription rather than individual achievement. Status as the basis for stratification runs counter to the logic of the market in modern societies. The interplay of class and status (and their translation into political organization) is a particularly important issue in culturally diverse societies, in which distinct cultural groups (statuses) persist, along with discrimination, societal efforts to remedy past discrimination, and positive self-identification among status group members. The debate in nations like the United States, Canada, and India over affirmative action and hiring preferences or educational access for indigenous peoples and "scheduled castes" is a symptom of uncertainty about the role that status position should have in determining opportunities in labour markets.

Weber's sociological method was quite distinct from empirical methods used by sociologists today. He was certainly interested in empirical research, but did not frame it in the quantitative or positivist terms favoured by Durkheim. His orientation to method is characterized by three approaches to his subject matter.

He used a "comparative historical method" to reach conclusions. He looked at institutions and modes of action within their historical context and compared different societies. For example, he discussed how the Hebrew prophets had religious ideas that were distinct from those of Hindu Brahmins and Confucian thinkers. Often he compared not only distinct institutions but the linkage between institutions in different types of societies. For example, the linkage between economic activity and Protestant belief is different than that between economic activity and Catholicism.

In making these comparisons he was trying to find a middle ground between two schools of analysis that were popular in his day. The idiographic position held that history must be written entirely as narratives of unique situations; no comparisons can be made across societies or time periods. History can never be a social science, since each event or situation is unique in itself. The nomothetic position was the search for general laws of human behaviour, grand generalizations that are like the "laws of motion" or other laws in the natural sciences. Weber's position was that we want to identify patterns, but these patterns must be carefully contextualized and not pushed to the point where we assert them as "laws" of human behaviour.

A second element of Weber's method is *verstehen*. This German word means understanding. Since Weber, unlike Durkheim, was interested in action and meaning, he thought it was important to understand how people gave meaning to their actions. In our times, this goal might lead to techniques like interviewing, focus groups, or ethnographic observation. This was not at all what Weber did; he achieved an understanding of meaning by reading texts produced by literate elites, which provided insight into the ideas, values, and meaning-giving process in historical societies. We learn what Hebrew prophets thought about God or how Calvinists wrestled with the implications of predestinarian doctrine by reading the words of Isaiah and Calvin. We grasp the spirit of capitalism by reading Benjamin Franklin.

A third element of the method is formulation of "ideal-types." Ideal-types are a definition of an institution or type of society that enumerates key or essential features of the phenomenon. Real life concrete instances of the institution will probably not display all of these defining characteristics. The ideal-type allows us to identify historical conditions under which the institution is likely to emerge and to explore why one or another essential feature may be missing or appears at a different time than the others. Weber identified ideal-types of authority (traditional, charismatic, and rational-legal) and bureaucracy. He used them to discuss how and why these forms appear. An ideal-type is like the concept of "dog": there are no real life instances of a generic dog, only actual specific dogs, but the concept allows us to know when we've spotted one.

Weber remains a giant figure in the social sciences. His emphasis on action rather than structure make him less forbiddingly deterministic than Durkheim. To those who are put off by communism, he offers an analysis of the same issues as Marx without revolutionary conclusions. His basic perspective can be adapted to the analysis of many contemporary phenomena, such as Islamic and Protestant fundamentalism, the McDonaldization of health care in the United States, new forms of corporate structure in an era of global markets, and collective action and social movements. We will see some examples of these new applications and elaborations of Weberian theory in the next selections.

Readings

Gerth, Hans, and C. Wright Mills (eds.). *From Max Weber.* New York: Oxford University Press, 1958.

Giddens, Anthony. *Politics and Sociology in the Thought of Max Weber.* London, 1972.

Riesebrodt, Martin. *Pious Passion: The Emergence of Modern Fundamentalism in the United States and Iran.* Berkeley, CA: University of California Press, 1993.

Ritzer, George. *The McDonaldization of Society: An Investigation into the Changing Character of Contemporary Life.* Thousand Oaks, CA: Pine Forge Press/Sage, 1995.

Essays in Sociology
MAX WEBER

VII. Class, Status, Party

... Now: "classes," "status groups," and "parties" are phenomena of the distribution of power within a community.

2. Determination of Class-Situation by Market-Situation

In our terminology, "classes" are not communities; they merely represent possible, and frequent, bases for communal action. We may speak of a "class" when (1) a number of people have in common a specific causal component of their life chances, in so far as (2) this component is represented exclusively by economic interests in the possession of goods and opportunities for income, and (3) is represented under the conditions of the commodity or labor markets. [These points refer to "class situation," which we may express more briefly as the typical chance for a supply of goods, external living conditions, and personal life experiences, in so far as this chance is determined by the amount and kind of power, or lack of such, to dispose of goods or skills for the sake of income in a given economic order. The term "class" refers to any group of people that is found in the same class situation.]

It is the most elemental economic fact that the way in which the disposition over material property is distributed among a plurality of people, meeting competitively in the market for the purpose of exchange, in itself creates specific life changes. According to the law of marginal utility this mode of distribution excludes the non-owners from competing for highly valued goods; it favors the owners and, in fact, gives to them a monopoly to acquire such goods. Other things being equal, this mode of distribution monopolizes the opportunities for profitable deals for all those who, provided with goods, do not necessarily have to exchange them. It increases, at least generally, their power in price wars with those who, being propertyless, have nothing to offer but their services in native form or goods in a form constituted through their own labor, and who above all are compelled to get rid of these products in order barely to subsist. This mode of distribution gives to the propertied a monopoly on the possibility of transferring property from the sphere of use as a "fortune," to the sphere of "capital goods"; that is, it gives them the entrepreneurial function and all chances to share directly or indirectly in returns on capital. All this holds true within the area in which pure market conditions prevail. "Property" and "lack of property" are, therefore, the basic categories of all class situations. It does not matter whether these two categories become effective in price wars or in competitive struggles.

Within these categories, however, class situations are further differentiated: on the one hand, according to the kind of property that is usable for returns; and, on the other hand, according to the kind of services that can be offered in the market. Ownership of domestic buildings; productive establishments; warehouses; stores; agriculturally usable land, large and small holdings—quantitative differences with possibly qualitative consequences—; ownership of mines; cattle; men (slaves); disposition over mobile instruments of production, or capital goods of all sorts, especially money or objects that can be exchanged for money easily and at any time; disposition over products of one's own labor or of others' labor differing according to their various distances from consumability; disposition over transferable monopolies of any kind—all these distinctions differentiate the class situations of the propertied just as does the "meaning" which they can and do give to the utilization of property, especially to property which has money equivalence. Accordingly, the propertied, for instance, may belong to the class of rentiers or to the class of entrepreneurs.

Those who have no property but who offer services are differentiated just as much according to their kinds of services as according to the way in which they make use of these services, in a continuous or discontinuous relation to a recipient. But always this is the generic connotation of the concept of class: that the kind of chance in the *market* is the decisive moment which presents a common condition for the individual's fate. "Class situation" is, in this sense, ultimately "market situation." The effect of naked possession *per se*, which among cattle breeders gives the non-owning slave or serf into the power of the cattle owner, is only a fore-runner of real "class" formation. However, in the cattle loan and in the naked severity of the law of debts in such communities, for the first time mere "possession" as such emerges as decisive for the fate of the individual. This is very much in contrast to the agricultural communities based on labor. The creditor-debtor relation becomes the bases of "class situations" only in those cities where a "credit market," however primitive, with rates of interest increasing according to the extent of dearth and a factual monopolization of credits, is developed by a plutocracy. Therewith "class struggles" begin.

Those men whose fate is not determined by the chance of using goods or services for themselves on the market, e.g. slaves, are not, however, a "class" in the technical sense of the term. They are, rather, a "status group."

3. Communal Action Flowing from Class Interest

According to our terminology, the factor that creates "class" is unambiguously economic interest, and indeed, only those interests involved in the existence of the "market." Nevertheless, the concept of "class-interest" is an ambiguous one: even as an empirical concept it is ambiguous as soon as one understands by it something other than the factual direction of interests following with a certain probability from the class situation for a certain "average" of those people subjected to the class situation. The class situation and other circumstances remaining the same, the direction in which the individual worker, for instance, is likely to pursue his interests may vary widely, according to whether he is constitutionally qualified for the task at hand to a high, to an average, or to a low degree. In the same way, the direction of interests may vary according to whether or not a *communal* action of a larger or smaller portion of those commonly affected by the "class situation," or even an association among them, e.g. a "trade union," has grown out of the class situation from which the individual may or may not expect promising results. [Communal action refers to that action which is oriented to the feeling of the actors that they belong together.

Societal action, on the other hand, is oriented to a rationally motivated adjustment of interests.] The rise of societal or even of communal action form a common class situation is by no means a universal phenomenon.

The class situation may be restricted in its effects to the generation of essentially *similar* reactions, that is to say, within our terminology, of "mass actions." However, it may not have even this result. Furthermore, often merely an amorphous communal action emerges. For example, the "murmuring" of the workers known in ancient oriental ethics: the moral disapproval of the workmaster's conduct, which in its practical significance was probably equivalent to an increasingly typical phenomenon of precisely the latest industrial development, namely, the "slow down" (the deliberate limiting of work effort) of laborers by virtue of tacit agreement. The degree in which "communal action" and possibly "societal action," emerges from the "mass actions" of the members of a class is linked to general cultural conditions, especially to those of an intellectual sort. It is also linked to the extent of the contrasts that have already evolved, and is especially linked to the *transparency* of the connections between the causes and the consequences of the "class situation." For however different life chances may be, this fact in itself, according to all experience, by no means gives birth to "class action" (communal action by the members of a class). The fact of being conditioned and the results of the class situation must be distinctly recognizable. For only then the contrast of life chances can be felt not as an absolutely given fact to be accepted, but as a resultant from either (1) the given distributions of property, or (2) the structure of the concrete economic order. It is only then that people may react against the class structure not only through acts of an intermittent and irrational protest, but in the form of rational association. There have been "class situations" of the first category (1), of a specifically naked and transparent sort, in the urban centers of Antiquity and during the Middle Ages; especially then, when great fortunes were accumulated by factually monopolized trading in industrial products of these localities or in foodstuffs. Furthermore, under certain circumstances, in the rural economy of the most diverse periods, when agriculture was increasingly exploited in a profit-making manner. The most important historical example of the second category (2) is the class situation of the modern "proletariat."

4. Types of "Class Struggle"
Thus every class may be the carrier of any one of the possibly innumerable forms of "class action," but this is not necessarily so. In any case, a class does not in itself constitute a community. To treat "class" conceptually as having the same value as "community" leads to distortion. That men in the same class situation regularly react in mass actions to such tangible situations as economic ones in the direction of those interests that are most adequate to their average

number is an important and after all simple fact for the understanding of historical events. Above all, this fact must not lead to that kind of pseudo-scientific operation with the concepts of "class" and "class interests" so frequently found these days, and which has found its most classic expression in the statement of a talented author, that the individual may be in error concerning his interests but that the "class" is "infallible" about its interests. Yet, if classes as such are not communities, nevertheless class situations emerge only on the basis of communalization. The communal action that brings forth class situations, however, is not basically action between members of the identical class; it is an action between members of different classes. Communal actions that directly determine the class situation of the worker and the entrepreneur are: the labor market, the commodities market, and the capitalistic enterprise. But, in its turn, the existence of a capitalistic enterprise presupposes that a very specific communal action exists and that it is specifically structured to protect the possession of goods *per se*, and especially the power of individuals to dispose, in principle freely, over the means of production. The existence of a capitalistic enterprise is preconditioned by a specific kind of "legal order." Each kind of class situation, and above all when it rests upon the power of property *per se*, will become most clearly efficacious when all other determinants of reciprocal relations are, as far as possible, eliminated in their significance. It is in this way that the utilization of the power of property in the market obtains its most sovereign importance....

5. Status Honor

In contrast to classes, *status groups* are normally communities. They are, however, often of an amorphous kind. In contrast to the purely economically determined "class situation" we wish to designate as "status situation" every typical component of the life fate of men that is determined by a specific, positive or negative, social estimation of *honor*. This honor may be connected with any quality shared by a plurality, and, of course, it can be knit to a class situation: class distinctions are linked in the most varied ways with status distinctions. Property as such is not always recognized as a status qualification, but in the long run it is, and with extraordinary regularity. In the subsistence economy of the organized neighborhood, very often the richest man is simply the chieftain. However, this often means only an honorific preference. For example, in the so-called pure modern "democracy," that is, one devoid of any expressly ordered status privileges for individuals, it may be that only the families coming under approximately the same tax class dance with one another. This example is reported of certain smaller Swiss cities. But status honor need not necessarily be linked with a "class situation." On the contrary, it normally stands in sharp opposition to the pretensions of sheer property.

Both propertied and propertyless people can belong to the same status group, and frequently they do with very tangible consequences. This "equality" of social esteem may, however, in the long run become quite precarious....

7. "Ethnic" Segregation and "Caste"

Where the consequences have been realized to their full extent, the status group evolves into a closed "caste." Status distinctions are then guaranteed not merely by conventions and laws, but also by *rituals*. This occurs in such a way that every physical contact with a member of any caste that is considered to be "lower" by the members of a "higher" caste is considered as making for a ritualistic impurity and to be a stigma which must be expiated by a religious act. Individual castes develop quite distinct cults and gods.

In general, however, the status structure reaches such extreme consequences only where there are underlying differences which are held to be "ethnic." The "caste" is, indeed, the normal form in which ethnic communities usually live side by side in a "societalized" manner. These ethnic communities believe in blood relationship and exclude exogamous marriage and social intercourse. Such a caste situation is part of the phenomenon of "pariah" peoples and is found all over the world. These people form communities, acquire specific occupational traditions of handicrafts or of other arts, and cultivate a belief in their ethnic community. They live in a "diaspora" strictly segregated from all personal intercourse, except that of an unavoidable sort, and their situation is legally precarious. Yet, by virtue of their economic indispensability, they are tolerated, indeed, frequently privileged, and they live in interspersed political communities. The Jews are the most impressive historical example.

A "status" segregation grown into a "caste" differs in its structure from a mere "ethnic" segregation: the caste structure transforms the horizontal and unconnected coexistences of ethnically segregated groups into a vertical social system of super-and subordination. Correctly formulated: a comprehensive societalization integrates the ethnically divided communities into specific political and communal action. In their consequences they differ precisely in this way: ethnic coexistences condition a mutual repulsion and disdain but allow each ethnic community to consider its own honor as the highest one; the caste structure brings about a social subordination and an acknowledgement of "more honor" in favor of the privileged caste and status groups. This is due to the fact that in the caste structure ethnic distinctions as such have become "functional" distinctions within the political societalization (warriors, priests, artisans that are politically important for war and for building, and so on). But even pariah people who are most despised are usually apt to continue cultivating in some manner that which is equally peculiar to ethnic and to status communities: the belief in their own specific "honor." This is the case with the Jews....

10. Parties

Whereas the genuine place of "classes" is within the economic order, the place of "status groups" is within the social order, that is, within the sphere of the distribution of "honor." From within these spheres, classes and status groups influence one another and they influence the legal order and are in turn influenced by it. But "parties" live in a house of "power."

Their action is oriented toward the acquisition of social "power," that is to say, toward influencing a communal action no matter what its content may be. In principle, parties may exist in a social "club" as well as in a "state." As over against the actions of classes and status groups, for which this is not necessarily the case, the communal actions of "parties" always mean a societalization. For party actions are always directed toward a goal which is striven for in planned manner. This goal may be a "cause" (the party may aim at realizing a program for ideal or material purposes), or the goal may be "personal" (sinecures, power, and from these, honor for the leader and the followers of the party). Usually the party action aims at all these simultaneously. Parties are, therefore, only possible within communities that are societalized, that is, which have some rational order and a staff of persons available who are ready to enforce it. For parties aim precisely at influencing this staff, and if possible, to recruit it from party followers.

In any individual case, parties may represent interests determined through "class situation" or "status situation," and they may recruit their following respectively from one or the other. But they need be neither purely "class" nor purely "status" parties. In most cases they are partly class parties and partly status parties, but sometimes they are neither. They may represent ephemeral or enduring structures. Their means of attaining power may be quite varied, ranging from naked violence of any sort to canvassing for votes with coarse or subtle means: money, social influence, the force of speech suggestion, clumsy hoax, and so on to the rougher or more artful tactics of obstruction in parliamentary bodies.

The sociological structure of parties differs in a basic way according to the kind of communal action which they struggle to influence. Parties also differ according to whether or not the community is stratified by status or by classes. Above all else, they vary according to the structure of domination within the community. For their leaders normally deal with the conquest of a community. They are, in the general concept which is maintained here, not only products of specially modern forms of domination. We shall also designate as parties the ancient and medieval "parties," despite the fact that their structure differs basically from the structure of modern parties. By virtue of these structural differences of domination it is impossible to say anything about the structure of parties without discussing the structural forms of social domination *per se*. Parties, which are always structures struggling of domination, are very frequently organized in a very strict "authoritarian" fashion....

Bureaucracy

1. Characteristics of Bureaucracy

Modern officialdom functions in the following specific manner:

I. There is the principle of fixed and official jurisdictional areas, which are generally ordered by rules, that is, by laws or administrative regulations.

1. The regular activities required for the purposes of the bureaucratically governed structure are distributed in a fixed way as official duties.

2. The authority to give the commands required for the discharge of these duties is distributed in a stable way and is strictly delimited by rules concerning the coercive means, physical, sacerdotal, or otherwise which may be placed at the disposal of officials.

3. Methodical provision is made for the regular and continuous fulfilment of these duties and for the execution of the corresponding rights; only persons who have the generally regulated qualifications to serve are employed.

In public and lawful government these three elements constitute "bureaucratic authority." In private economic domination, they constitute bureaucratic "management." Bureaucracy, thus understood, is fully developed in political and ecclesiastical communities only in the modern state, and, in the private economy, only in the most advanced institutions of capitalism. Permanent and public office authority, with fixed jurisdiction, is not the historical rule but rather the exception. This is so even in large political structures such as those of the ancient Orient, the Germanic and Mongolian empires of conquest, or of many feudal structures of state. In all these cases, the ruler executes the most important measures through personal trustees, table-companions, or court-servants. Their commissions and authority are not precisely delimited and are temporarily called into being for each case.

II. The principles of office hierarchy and of levels of graded authority mean a firmly ordered system of super- and subordination in which there is a supervision of the lower offices by the higher ones. Such a system offers the governed the possibility of appealing the decision of a lower office to its higher authority, in a definitely regulated manner. With the full development of the bureaucratic type, the office hierarchy is monocratically organized. The principle of hierarchical office authority is found in all bureaucratic structures: in state and ecclesiastical structures as well as in large party organizations and private enterprises. It does not matter for the character of bureaucracy whether its authority is called "private" or "public."

When the principle of jurisdictional "competency" is fully carried through, hierarchical subordination—at least in public office—does not mean that the "higher" authority is simply authorized to take over the business of the "lower." Indeed, the opposite is the rule. Once established and having fulfilled its task, an office tends to continue in existence and be held by another incumbent.

III. The management of the modern office is based upon written documents ("the files"), which are preserved in their original or draught form. There is, therefore, a staff of subaltern officials and scribes of all sorts. The body of officials actively engaged in a "public" office, along with the respective apparatus of material implements and the files, make up a "bureau." In private enterprise, "the bureau" is often called "the office."

In principle, the modern organization of the civil service separates the bureau from the private domicile of the official, and, in general, bureaucracy segregates official activity as something distinct from the sphere of private life. Public monies and equipment are divorced from the private property of the official. This condition is everywhere the product of a long development. Nowadays, it is found in public as well as in private enterprises; in the latter, the principle extends even to the leading entrepreneur. In principle, the executive office is separated from the household, business from private correspondence, and business assets from private fortunes. The more consistently the modern type of business management has been carried through the more are these separations in the case. The beginnings of this process are to be found as early as the Middle Ages.

It is the peculiarity of the modern entrepreneur that he conducts himself as the "first official" of his enterprise, in the very same way in which the ruler of a specifically modern bureaucratic state spoke of himself as "the first servant" of the state. The idea that the bureau activities of the state are intrinsically different in character from the management of private economic offices is a continental European notion and, by way of contrast, is totally foreign to the American way.

IV. Office management, at least all specialized office management—and such management is distinctly modern—usually presupposes thorough and expert training. This increasingly holds for the modern executive and employee of private enterprises, in the same manner as it holds for the state official.

V. When the office is fully developed, official activity demands the full working capacity of the official, irrespective of the fact that his obligatory time in the bureau may be firmly delimited. In the normal case, this is only the product of a long development, in the public as well as in the private office. Formerly, in all cases, the normal state of affairs was reversed: official business was discharged as a secondary activity.

VI. The management of the office follows general rules, which are more or less stable, more or less exhaustive, and which can be learned. Knowledge of these rules represents a special technical learning which the officials possess. It involves jurisprudence, or administrative or business management.

The reduction of modern office management to rules is deeply embedded in its very nature. The theory of modern public administration, for instance, assumes that the authority to order certain matters by decree—which has been legally granted to public authorities—does not entitle the bureau to regulate the matter abstractly. This stands in extreme contrast to the regulation of all relationships through individual privileges and bestowals of favor, which is absolutely dominant in patrimonialism, at least in so far as such relationships are not fixed by sacred tradition.

10

THE LEGACY OF WEBER:
JEFF GOODWIN AND THEDA SKOCPOL

In the following selection we see a contemporary application of Weber's concepts and theoretical strategy. The authors not only use Weber's concepts and his way of thinking about a sociological puzzle, they update and extend his perspective as they answer a question about social change in the second half of the twentieth century: how can we explain revolutions in the Third World?

Three terms are key parts of the question. By "revolution" the authors mean a violent, armed struggle that abruptly changes both a political regime and a social order. "Third World" refers to a wide spectrum of places that were neither economically developed, wealthy, industrialized capitalist nations, nor part of the Communist countries in the post-World War II period. Some of these places were independent countries, some were colonies. By "explain" the authors mean "identify all the conditions necessary for the presence of something."

The article begins by questioning and dismissing current explanations and perspectives that the authors find unsatisfactory. They discuss why they think that revolutions cannot be explained solely in terms of class structure, specifically the condition of the peasantry. On this point they are debating contemporary Marxists who argue that the penetration of capitalist economic and social institutions into the countryside inevitably and automatically touches off peasant movements that culminate in successful revolutions. They also dismiss the view that the presence of revolutionary organizations is a sufficient condition for a successful revolution.

When the authors present their own explanation, they reveal Weber's influence: class structure is important in understanding revolutions, but even more important is the form of political action. The variable that allows us to most accurately identify whether or not a successful revolution occurs in a region is the form of political action in that region. The underlying class structure produces revolution only in the presence of certain types of political action. Class structure in and of itself has no agency—it cannot be the source or subject of political action; only people expressing their will and purpose through political organizations have agency, and only they can carry out a revolution.

Political action in this instance has two important and closely related components that are necessary for a revolution to occur: one is the formation of a political coalition larger and more deeply rooted than a vanguard political movement; the other is a regime that fails to include large, key sectors of the population. These two elements are intimately connected to each other: the unwillingness and inability of the regime to gain consent, legitimacy, and the participation of those it rules precipitates the rise of the revolutionary coalition.

The authors proceed to identify two types of regimes that are exclusionary: neo-patrimonial regimes organized by powerful individuals and their families and friends; and direct colonial rule. "Neo-patrimonial" is a concept directly taken from Weber; he used "patrimonial" to describe forms of authority that are not fully modern or rationalized, but are based on customary personal loyalties. A neo-patrimonial regime leaves most people, including the middle class, feeling excluded from political participation; the ruler, his family, and cronies are seen as monopolizing power and economic opportunities.

"Direct colonial rule" (favoured by the French as a strategy of colonial rule) refers to practices of colonial power in which the colonizing country established its own institutions, legal system, and bureaucracies. In "indirect rule" (favoured by the British), the colonial power tried to rule through native chiefs who were co-opted into the service of the colonizers; native legal codes remained in effect, and local native authorities helped the colonial power run the region. Indirect rule gave the colonized a false sense of participation and continuity with pre-colonial institutions; thus, while it was just as one-sided and economically exploitive as direct rule, it provided an illusion of inclusion.

The authors support their analysis with specific examples.

In this article, we can see continuity with Weber's theory and disagreement with Marxist perspectives. The authors provide a good example of applying Weberian concepts to a specific contemporary question. They show the importance of political action and organization as a concept for understanding outcomes. They argue that class structure alone does not help us explain the patterning of outcomes. This position represents a disagreement with many Marxist analyses of revolutions (yet some Marxists might actually agree with this position, seeing the political dimension as not automatically reducible to the effect of class structure). According to Goodwin and Skocpol, we have to focus on the level of politics and purposive action of regimes and organizations to understand why some regions had revolutions and others did not.

Although here the authors challenge a certain type of Marxist approach, Skocpol is actually quite interested in Marxist theory. Marx, as well as Weber, influences her theoretical work on states, revolutions, and social policies.

Readings
Skocpol, Theda. *States and Social Revolutions*. New York: Cambridge University Press, 1979.

—. *Protecting Soldiers and Mothers: The Political Origins of Social Policy in the United States*. Cambridge, MA: Harvard University Press, 1992.

Wolf, Eric. *Peasant Wars of the Twentieth Century*. New York: Harper and Row, 1969.

Explaining Revolutions in the Contemporary Third World
JEFF GOODWIN AND THEDA SKOCPOL

Frontiers of research move with history, although often with a lag. Two decades ago, most comparative research on revolutions remained focused on the classical great revolutions of the West; those of England, France, and Russia. Occasionally, a bold scholar included non-European revolutions (particularly the Chinese and Mexican) in broader comparative studies.[1] It was not until the mid-1970s, however, that comparative scholars began to focus on the features distinctive to Third World social revolutions — the social and political upheavals in smaller, dependent states outside of Europe. At first, perhaps, scholars supposed that such social revolutions would happen only occasionally during decolonization such as those that played themselves out after World War II. Yet modern world history has continued to be punctuated by social revolutions, not only in post-colonial southeast Asia, Algeria, and Portuguese Africa, but also in formally independent states such as Cuba, Ethiopia, Iran, and Nicaragua. As new social revolutions have continued to occur, scholars have been challenged to broaden their scope of comparative studies beyond the classical revolutions of Europe, and they have entertained models of causation applicable across many smaller non-Western nations in the twentieth-century world context.

In this article, we point to what we consider the most promising avenues for comparative analyses of contemporary Third World revolutions. In particular, we shall offer some working hypotheses about the distinctively political conditions that have encouraged revolutionary movements and transfers of power in some, but not all, Third World countries.

Two myths have long coloured popular views about revolutions in the Third World: that destitution, professional revolutionaries, or perhaps both are sufficient to precipitate revolutions; and that local events in Third World countries are easily manipulated by imperialist Great Powers. Thus, in attempting to explain Third World insurgencies, many people point to the incredible poverty found in large parts of Latin America, Africa, and Asia—the sort of sheer misery that capitalist industrialization and redistributive welfare states have largely eliminated, contrary to Karl Marx's expectations, in the advanced capitalist countries. Others have emphasized the role that professional revolutionaries, often backed by foreign powers, have played in "subverting" Third World regimes with the "organizational weapon" of the disciplined revolutionary party. Indeed, many see the hand of Moscow (or Beijing, Havana, or Teheran) behind Third World insurgencies, *exploiting* the social problems of these societies for their own nefarious purposes. Still others see the prime foreign influences on Third World nations as emanating from capitalist powers, especially the United States. When revolutions do not occur in poor nations, it is often suggested, it is because the United States has artificially propped up local agents of capitalist imperialism.

These ideas, however, do not take us very far toward an explanation of just why and where revolutions have occurred in some countries of the contemporary Third World, but not in others. Very many Third World countries are poor, for example, but revolutions have occurred in only a few of them, and not necessarily in the poorest. Why did China and Vietnam have social revolutions, but not India or Indonesia? Why Cuba, one of the more developed Latin American countries when Castro seized power, but not Haiti or the Dominican Republic? Why Nicaragua, but not Honduras? One need merely raise these questions in order to realize that the "misery breeds revolt" hypothesis does not explain very much. Leon Trotsky once wrote that "the mere existence of privations is not enough to cause an insurrection; if it were, the masses would be always in revolt."[2] His point is still relevant for much of today's Third World.

Similarly, although professional revolutionaries have certainly helped to organize and lead many Third World insurgencies, revolutionary groups in many, perhaps most, countries remain small and relatively insignificant sects. The Third World may be the principal theatre of revolutionary conflict in this century, but much of it remains quiescent. And when political passions *have* flared in developing countries, they have more often taken the form of ethnic or subnationalist movements than revolutions. Would-be revolutionaries, Tilly has written, "are almost always with us in the form of millenarian cults, radical cells, or rejects from positions of power. The real question," he emphasizes, "is when such contenders proliferate and/or mobilize."[3] As Goldfrank argues, explanations of revolution that focus on human misery and professional revolutionaries "are not wholly illusory, but as theory they do not take us very far. Both widespread oppression and inflammatory agitation occur with far greater frequency than revolution, or even rebellion."[4]

The great capitalist powers, furthermore, obviously cannot prevent—or reverse—all Third World revolutions, as seen in the difficulties confronted by

France in Vietnam and Algeria and by the United States in Vietnam, Cuba, Nicaragua, and Iran. Imperialist interests certainly exist, but they must operate through local regimes or through *private agents* whose activities are underwritten and strongly shaped by the local regimes. And particular types of regimes in the Third World do not always reliably produce the sort of antirevolutionary stability desired in Paris or Washington, D.C.—any more than local revolutionaries can always produce the changes desired by Moscow, Havana, or Teheran.

Recent academic analyses of Third World insurgencies have helped to dispel myths such as the ones we have just criticized, yet the academic analyses have not replaced the myths with completely adequate arguments. Much of the recent comparative and theoretical literature on Third World revolutions—including the important work of Wolf, Paige, Migdal, Scott, and Popkin—investigates the role of peasants in these upheavals.[5] This body of work examines the specific grievances and motivations for peasant rebellion of peasant support for avowedly revolutionary guerrilla movements, emphasizing that much more than poverty or the activities of professional revolutionaries alone is involved. These writings argue that certain sorts of peasants—not usually the poorest—are more willing or able to rebel than others.

To be sure, the scholars who have recently analyzed Third World revolutions as peasant-based conflicts have their disagreements. At least two important and ongoing debates have come out of this work: the Wolf-Paige debate about just what sort of peasants are revolutionary, and the Scott-Popkin debate on the relative weight of economic, organizational, and cultural determinants of peasant behavior, and on the nature of peasants' psychological motivations for rebelling. We do not propose to rehash these debates here, however, because we believe that they have overemphasized the situation of the peasantry alone. Although the debates about peasants and revolution have enriched our understanding of agrarian socioeconomic relations and peasant political behavior, these debates have focused insufficient analytic attention on two other issues—themselves closely related—which can take us further toward an understanding of revolutionary movements and transfers of power in the contemporary Third World. The first issue is the formation of revolutionary coalitions that invariably extend well beyond peasants alone. The second issue is the relative vulnerability of different sorts of political regimes to the formation of broad revolutionary coalitions and, perhaps, to actual overthrow by revolutionary forces. Drawing from our own recent comparative studies, as well as from political analyses by other scholars, we can explore these matters and suggest a fruitful theoretical approach to explaining why revolutions have happened in some Third World countries but not in others.[6]

From Peasants to Revolutionary Coalitions

Although peasants have undoubtedly been as central to most Third World insurgencies as they were for the classical social revolutions,[7] the characterization of Third World revolutions as *peasant wars* or *agrarian revolutions*—a characterization that sometimes carries an implication of homogeneous peasant communities rebelling spontaneously—has shifted our attention away from the role of other actors in revolutionary dramas. Revolutionary outbreaks and seizures of power are often carried through by coalitions, alliances, or conjunctures of struggles that cut across divides between urban and rural areas and among different social classes and ethnic groupings. (Of course, such revolutionary coalitions tend to break apart or recompose in new ways if and when they actually seize state power, but this is a subject that lies beyond scope of this article.)

With some notable exceptions, the literature that emphasizes the role of peasants in revolutions tends to ignore the role of professional revolutionary organizations, groups that tend to be disproportionately middle class in social composition.[8] This tendency is understandable in part as a reaction against the myth that revolutions are simply the work of small conspiratorial groups of subversives. But even if professional revolutionaries cannot simply *make* revolutions where they will, they have obviously played an important role in organizing, arming, and leading many revolutionary movements. This role, moreover, is often a necessary one. Indeed, except for those peasants who happen to live in relatively autonomous and solitary villages, as did the peasants of France, Russia, and central Mexico, rural cultivators simply do not have the organizational wherewithal to rebel in the absence of outside leaders. Professional revolutionaries, furthermore, have usually been successful precisely to the extent that they have been able to work with *various sorts* of rural folk. This is another point that tends to get lost in debates about just what sorts of peasants are most rebellious. The most successful revolutionary organizations—including those in Vietnam, Zimbabwe, and Nicaragua—have won the support not just of poor or middle peasants, but also of landless and migrant labourers, rural artisans, rich peasants, and even landlords.

What is more, as Gugler and Dix have recently emphasized, urban groups have also played important even crucial roles in a number of Third World revolutions.[9] Indeed, the 1978-1979 overthrow of the Shah of Iran was quintessentially an urban revolution. In Cuba and Nicaragua as well as in Iran, students, professionals, clerics, and even businesspeople, as well as workers and the urban poor, joined or supported broad-based coalitions against dictatorial regimes. Gugler and Dix suggest that the participation of such people may be essential to the success of revolutionaries in all of the more urbanized countries of the contemporary Third World.

How can professional revolutionaries put together broadly based coalitions? Not surprisingly, revolutionary coalitions tend to form around preexisting nationalist, populist, or religious discourses that legitimize resistance to tyranny and, just as important, are capable of aggregating a broad array of social classes and strata. Nationalism, in particular, has proven to be a more inclusive and powerful force for revolutionary mobilization than class struggle alone. Revolutionaries have fared best where they—and not conservative or reformist leaderships—have been able to harness nationalist sentiments. Ironically then, Marxist groups in the Third World have generally been most successful when they have deemphasized class struggle and stressed the goal of national liberation instead—or, at least, when they have attempted to mobilize different types of people through the selective use of both nationalist and class appeals.

Nevertheless, it should be emphasized that revolutionary movements are much more than simply ideological movements. As Popkin and Wickham-Crowley have recently argued, revolutionary movements have won broad popular support when they have been willing and able to deliver state-like collective goods to their constituents.[10] One such collective good is the establishment of "liberated areas" secure from attack by the incumbent regime, whose repressive actions could ensure popular acquiescence with otherwise unappealing armed revolutionaries able to provide little more than a modicum of protection. In addition, the collective goods provided by revolutionaries may also include public education, health services, law and order, and economic reforms such as tax and interest reductions, the elimination of corvée labor, and land reform. Popkin notes that revolutionaries have been particularly effective in winning popular support when they have initially focused on "local goals and goods with immediate payoffs" before attempting to mobilize the population for more difficult tasks—including, ultimately, the overthrow of the incumbent regime. In Vietnam, for example, peasants "in the late 1960s still laughed about the early attempts by young Trotskyites and Communists to organize them for a national revolution, for industrialization, or even for a world revolution! Only later, when peasants (and workers) were organized around smaller and more immediate goals, were larger organizational attempts successful."[11] During the 1960s, a number of Latin American revolutionary groups, which attempted to replicate the Cuban Revolution—including the Sandinistas of Nicaragua—failed to make headway, largely because they were too quick to engage incumbent regimes in armed struggle, well before they had solidified broad popular support through the provision of collective goods.[12]

In addition to collective goods, revolutionary organizations may also offer selective incentives to encourage participation in various sorts of activities, particularly dangerous ones like actual guerilla warfare. Such incentives for actual or potential cadres and fighters, and their families, may include extra tax or rent reductions or an additional increment of land beyond that allocated to supporters in general. In any event, it is the ongoing provisions of such collective and selective goods, not ideological conversion in the abstract, that has played the principal role in solidifying social support for guerrilla armies.

The argument we have just made does not, however, support Tilly's claim that the sudden withdrawal of expected government services drives people to revolt.[13] In many Third World countries, few government services have ever been provided to the bulk of the population. In fact, the evidence suggests that those governments that do not deliver collective goods to people, and then repress reformers who try to do something about the absence of such services, are the governments most likely to generate support for revolutionaries. This analysis, moreover, accords with what we are beginning to learn about ruling revolutionary parties. Walder has recently shown that such parties obtain popular support or compliance not simply through coercion or through impersonal ideological appeals to atomized individuals (as the "totalitarian" image would have it), but through patronage and the development of networks of loyal clients.[14] Revolutionary movements that have to build social support over a long period of time operate in a similar way. In terms of what they are actually doing (and not simply what they are saying), revolutionary movements can usefully be viewed as proto-state organizations, or what Wickham-Crowley calls "guerrilla governments."[15] The presence of revolutionary movements offering collective services in territory claimed by the official state implies a situation of "dual power," in Trotsky's classic phrase.

Revolutionaries are most effective in creating such situations of dual power when they are willing and able to organize precisely those social groupings that the incumbent regime has not incorporated into its own political system. Of course those activists in the Third World who have been schooled in classical Marxist theory have often been content with organizing the urban working class, however small its ranks, and have sometimes eschewed a strategy of armed struggle altogether, even in the face of very repressive regimes. The factors that make revolutionary cadre organizations willing to appeal to broad coalitions, as well as the (undoubtedly somewhat different) factors that prompt them to choose armed struggle, are not sufficiently well understood. Still, even revolutionaries who have attempted to mobilize broad coalitions for armed struggle have been pushed to the margins of politics when and where the regimes they have sought to topple have in some way politically incorporated important social classes and strata that might otherwise have joined revolutionary coalitions. The breadth of revolutionary coalitions is determined, in short, not just by how many groups the cadres try to organize, but also by the political space the incumbent political regime makes *available* to revolutionaries because of the regime's structural characteristics and strategies of rule. Other things being equal, the narrower the regime, and the more repressive, the broader the coalition potentially available to be mobilized by revolutionaries.

This brings us to the second issue largely neglected in recent work on peasants and revolutions, namely, the relative vulnerability of different sorts of political regimes to revolutionary coalitions. Revolutionary movements, needless to say, do not form in a political vacuum. Indeed, political context is absolutely crucial in determining whether such movements will or will not prosper. Recent work on Third World revolutions has not convincingly demonstrated that any one class, class fraction, or class alliance is any more consistently revolutionary than the industrial proletariat was supposed to have been. Exactly who becomes revolutionary, and when, is a preeminently political question. Revolutions are ultimately "made" by revolutionaries, but not of their own free will—not within political contexts they themselves have chosen, to paraphrase Karl Marx, but within very specific sorts of political contexts that are not the same for all who would make revolutions.

Which Regimes are Vulnerable to the Growth of Revolutionary Coalitions?
Revolutionary movements, history suggests, typically coalesce in opposition to closed or exclusionary, as well as organizationally weak (or suddenly weakened), authoritarian regimes. By contrast, multiparty democracies or quasi-democracies, even those in very poor countries like India, Malaysia, the Dominican Republic, and Honduras, have not facilitated the growth of revolutionary coalitions. The ballot box may not always be "the coffin of class consciousness," to use Dawley's evocative phrase, but it has proven to be the coffin of revolutionary movements.[16] Thus far, in fact, avowedly socialist revolutions—which according to classical Marxism were supposed to follow after and build upon the achievements of bourgeois-democratic revolutions—have occurred only in countries that never established liberal-democratic political systems in the first place.

In addition to liberal democracies, so-called "inclusionary" authoritarian regimes—including fascists and state-socialist regimes, as well as the single-party corporatist regimes found in some nations of Africa and Asia—have so far been immune from revolutionary transformations. Although these regimes lack civil rights, they either sponsor mass political mobilization or regulate the official representation of, and bargaining among, various social groups, including working-class and other lower-strata groups. They impose controlled forms of political participation on key social groups, co-opting leaders and handing out certain benefits in the process; this tends to undercut possibilities for political action independent of the existing regime.

Many authoritarian regimes do not, however, bother to mobilize social groups into politics, even in controlled ways; they leave the prerogatives of the state and the benefits of politics entirely in the hands of rulers and narrow cliques. Such exclusionary authoritarian regimes are conducive to the formation of broad revolutionary coalitions for a number of related reasons. First, the economic grievances of groups excluded from the political system tend to be quickly politicized. As Lipset has argued:

> The exclusion of workers from the fundamental political rights of citizenship effectively fuse[s] the struggle for political and economic equality and cast[s] that struggle in a radical mold.... Where the right to combine in the labor market [is] severely restricted, ... the decision to act in politics is forced on trade unions. Whether they [like] it or not, unions [must become] political institutions; they [have] first to change the distribution of political power within the state before they [can] effectively exert power in the market.[17]

Lipset is writing about urban workers, and trade-union organizations in particular, but his analysis also holds for other lower-class groups and their organizational vehicles.

Closed authoritarian regimes also provide a highly visible focus of opposition and a common enemy for groups and classes that may be nursing very different sorts of economic and political grievances (including grievances about one another). Political legitimacy is usually very problematic for authoritarian rulers, especially when religious authorities distance themselves from, or even outright oppose, such regimes, after having previously accepted them. Similarly, the political legitimacy of authoritarian rulers has sometimes been undermined simultaneously in the eyes of many groups when the rulers have orchestrated blatantly fraudulent elections in an effort to justify their continuing power.

Most importantly, perhaps, exclusionary regimes tend to radicalize, or at least neutralize, moderate and reformist politicians, including those that choose to participate in pro forma elections. Such moderates might compete with revolutionaries for popular support, or else initiate a gradual transition to a more open or inclusionary political system, typically through alliances with the armed forces. But exclusionary regimes tend to attack and undermine exactly these moderate elements.

Finally, closed authoritarian regimes, without intending to do so, valorize the potential oppositional role of armed revolutionaries. Because such regimes are so closed, they readily turn to vicious repression when faced with demands for even the most moderate political or economic adjustments. Thus closed authoritarian regimes place a premium on the things armed revolutionaries are best prepared to do—namely, provide opponents of a regime with the means of self-defense, such as guns, clandestine networks, safehouses, and even liberated territory within which to survive and carry on oppositional politics.

Of course, given exclusionary conditions, the growth of revolutionary movements is made even easier when rebels can operate in peripheral areas that the authoritarian regimes they oppose are unable to control. This happens when authoritarian regimes have never fully penetrated certain areas (as in Central America and Lusophone Africa), when they lose control of areas due to war or invasion (as in Southeast Asia), or when they are unable to prevent neighbouring countries from harboring revolutionaries. "[R]evolutionary warfare and its countering," Fairbarn has suggested, "is basically competition in government. The aim of the revolutionary guerrilla is to create a kind of administrative vacuum into which it can insert its own 'parallel hierarchies' or 'alternative government'"[18] If a kind of administrative vacuum already exists on the exclusionary regime's territory, or if it suddenly emerges, then the task of the armed revolutionaries will be the easier.

On the other hand, authoritarian regimes that are militarily and organizationally strong and have secure borders generally do not provide sufficient leeway for armed revolutionaries to mobilize mass support, even though they too tend to radicalize their opponents. Like it or not then some of the most brutal and repugnant authoritarian regimes in the Third World, such as those found in Latin America's southern cone, in various East Asian and Middle Eastern countries, and especially in South Africa, are probably too powerful and ruthless to be toppled by armed struggle.

From the viewpoint of would-be revolutionaries, the ideal situation is to face an exclusionary and repressive authoritarian regime that lacks strong control of its entire territory or borders (or else suddenly loses such control). During World War II, parts of Nazi-occupied Europe fit this formula. More to the point for this analysis of the contemporary Third World, quite a few states in Southeast Asia, Central America, and Africa fall into this category: they are, simultaneously, politically exclusionary, repressive, and not fully in control of their nominal territories. Facing such regimes, revolutionaries can build broad coalitions among many groups fundamentally opposed to the existing political arrangements and authorities, because many groups in society need the coercive means and uncompromising political formulas that the revolutionary cadres have to offer.

Which Regimes are Vulnerable to Actual Overthrow?

Even regimes that confront formidable revolutionary movements, however, do not invariably fall to those forces. Indeed, when speaking of regime vulnerability, a distinction should be made between vulnerability to the *formation* of a mass-based revolutionary movement within the territory a regime claims to rule, and vulnerability to actual *overthrow* by that movement. We need to understand what makes for the second type of vulnerability as well as the first, without analytically collapsing the two.

Unfortunately, the existing theoretical literature on revolutions will not give us the answers we need. Johnson has argued that "flexible" political elites can avert revolutionary takeovers by bringing about "conservative change."[19] This view might seem to account for the failure of a number or revolutionary movements, yet Johnson remains vague, to say the least, about which sorts of political leaderships, operating in which kinds of regimes, can actually accomplish this conservative change. Meanwhile, Huntington is certainly right about the very specific need certain states have to incorporate newly mobilized groups into the political system, if those states are to stave off revolutions.[20] Like Johnson, however, Huntington does not sufficiently explore why some regimes can do this and not others. Huntington argues, for example, that the great revolutions of history have taken place either in highly centralized traditional monarchies (such as Bourbon France, tsarist Russia, and imperial Manchu China) or in narrowly based military dictatorships (such as pre-1911 Mexico, pre-1952 Bolivia, pre-1944 Guatemala, and pre-1959 Cuba),[21] or in colonial regimes (such as Vietnam and Algeria after World War II). Yet, historically, not all centralized monarchies proved susceptible to revolutionary overthrow. More important for our present purposes, not all twentieth-century military dictatorships or colonial regimes have been swept away by revolutions—not even all of those that have faced strong revolutionary movements.

In our view, two specific types of exclusionary and repressive authoritarian regimes are especially vulnerable to actual overthrow by revolutionary movements: neo-patrimonial or Sultanistic dictatorships identified with a foreign power and colonial regimes based on so called direct rule by the colonizing country. These regimes are not only much more narrowly based than other political orders, including other forms of authoritarianism, but they are also more brittle and *unreformable*. They are usually unable to bring about conservative change or the political incorporation of newly mobilized groups that might weaken existing revolutionary movements.

The Susceptibility of Neo-Patrimonial Dictatorships to Revolutionary Takeovers

The vulnerability to revolutionary overthrow of neo-patrimonialism—and, in particular, of the extreme sort of neo-patrimonialism often called Sultanism—has been explored in recent work by Eisenstadt and Goldstone.[22] Sultanistic neo-patrimonial regimes are centered in the personal manipulation of individual dictatorial rulers, who allow no stable group prerogatives in the polity—not even collective prerogatives for military officers or upper social and economic classes. Examples of successful revolutions against such personalist dictatorships include the 1911 Mexican Revolution against the regime of Porfirio Diaz, the 1959 Cuban Revolution against the regime of Fulgencio Batista, the 1979 Nicaraguan Revolution against the regime of Anastazio Somoza, and the 1979 Iranian Revolution against the neo-patrimonial monarchy of the Pahlavi Shahs.

Sultanistic neo-patrimonial regimes are especially vulnerable to actual overthrow by revolutionary movements for several related reasons. First, compared to more impersonal and bureaucratic forms of authoritarian rule, personalist dictators are more likely to generate elite and middle-class opposition. Landlords, businesspeople, clerics, and professionals, for example, often come to resent the blatant corruption of such dictators and their inner circle; their tendency to monopolize significant sectors of economy; their heavy-handed control of the flow of ideas and information in schools and in the press; their use of family connections to monopolize government positions, contracts, and other business and professional opportunities; and their penchant for granting special privileges to foreign capitalists and blindly serving the geopolitical interests of great powers in exchange for foreign aid.

Second, when elites and the middle class join the political opposition, foreign backing for personalist dictators is more likely to be withdrawn, even if those dictators were long supported as the best guarantors of stability. The United States, significantly, was ultimately unwilling to support old allies like Diaz, Batista, Somoza, or the Shah in the face of the broad, multiclass opposition movements to those dictators—even as the United States failed to find or create that elusive, democratic "third force" that could stave off revolution by providing an attractive alternative to both revolution and the status quo.

Finally, the armed forces of Sultanistic neo-patrimonial regimes tend to be especially corrupt and incompetent, in part because the dictator is more concerned with preventing his own personal overthrow by military coup than with establishing an effective fighting force. Coalitions between officers and civilians that might threaten the dictator are discouraged, and reform-minded officers are incessantly purged to prevent such coalitions from coming together through coups. Thus when personalist dictators finally decide to step down after the growth of broad oppositional movements and the withdrawal of foreign sponsorship, their armies, which have been bred and winnowed for sycophantic loyalty to the leader, tend to disintegrate, opening the way for guerrilla armies or irregular forces to seize power.

Despite these special vulnerabilities, however, even long-standing neo-patrimonial dictatorships are not invariably swept away by revolutionaries, and they may not even have to confront significant revolutionary movements.[23] As we suggested earlier, radical groups may simply eschew a strategy of armed struggle, even under very repressive conditions. In addition, the armed forces of neopatrimonial dictatorship—their lack of professionalism notwithstanding—may still manage to control dissidence on their territory and police their borders, leaving little space for revolutionaries to mobilize. Elites and middle classes are not always driven into a coalition with revolutionaries, furthermore, especially if the dictator dispenses patronage according to more or less rational and impersonal criteria and does not repress the moderate opposition in too heavy-handed a fashion. Also, ethnic divisions among the populace may prove too durable and fractious for revolutionaries to bridge, even in the presence of a dictator despised by all. Eisenstadt, in fact, has argued that neo-patrimonial societies make things difficult for revolutionaries, because such societies tend to be characterized by ascriptive, especially ethnic and religious, forms of organization and by the circulation of the elite cliques.[24] Combinations of many of the conditions listed in this paragraph seem to explain why the dictatorship of Mobutu Sese Seko of Zaire has survived for so long, and may account for the recent displacement of Alfredo Stroessner of Paraguay by a rival elite faction.

If neo-patrimonial dictators grant civilian and military moderates some minimal breathing room, furthermore, the threat posed by an emerging (or even potential) revolutionary movement may help forge a civilian-military alliance capable of removing the dictator. This alliance may, in turn, broaden political participation before revolutionaries become sufficiently powerful to bid for power. Ferdinand Marcos of the Phillippines and François Duvalier of Haiti were recently ousted in this manner, although the civilian component of the transition in Haiti has been relatively weak. And in the Philippines, it is too soon to tell whether the democratic opening engineered by Corazon Aquino and her followers will overcome tendencies toward reaction and revolution.

It bears emphasizing, too, that *all* of the counterrevolutionary tasks described above—territorial control, the co-optation or accommodation of elites and the middle class, the removal of an unpopular leader, and the transition to a more open political regime—are more easily accomplished by bureaucratic—(as opposed to neo-patrimonial) authoritarian regimes. Indeed, bureaucratic-authoritarian regimes give power and prerogatives to collectives—such as cohorts of military officers—who can bargain with, or even displace, one another without unraveling the regime. But Sultanistic neo-patrimonial regimes pit personal dictators against elites, and elites against one another, rendering political stability highly dependent on the unrelenting wiliness and vigilance of the individual ruler. Sooner or later however, individual sultans falter or die: and sons, such as the second Iranian Shah or Haiti's "Baby Doc," often prove less strong-willed than their fathers.

The analysis in this section, we might note, raises questions about Tilly's argument that revolutionary movements are more likely to succeed when they can forge alliances with "polity members."[25] Coalitions between polity members and what Tilly calls "challenger groups" are often, if not always, antirevolutionary in their consequences. In fact such coalitions may be formed precisely in order to prevent the further growth of movements led by radical political forces. Contrary to Tilly's hypothesis, social-revolutionary movements seem more likely to seize power when civilian-military coalitions are unable to form and initiate a political *opening* from above.

The Vulnerability of Directly Ruled Colonies

The connection between revolution and particular types of colonial rule has not been explored to the same extent as the connection between revolution and neo-patrimonialism. However, so called direct colonial rule—which occurs when a colony is governed directly by metropolitan officials, and indigenous elites are not allowed to share power nor readied to accept sovereignty after colonialism ends—shares a number of similarities with personalist dictatorships. The resemblances to neo-patrimonialism render direct colonialism especially vulnerable to a revolutionary overthrow. Examples of directly ruled colonies that gave way to broadly based revolutionary coalitions include the former French colonies of Vietnam and Algeria and Portugal's former African colonies, Guinea-Bissau, Angola, and Mozambique. Currently, moreover, direct colonial rule or its equivalent confronts broadly based nationalist movements of a more or less radical complexion in a number of territories: the Israeli-occupied West Bank and Gaza Strip; the Western Sahara, a former Spanish colony now occupied by Morocco; Eritrea, a former Italian colony that was absorbed into Ethiopia; Namibia, a former German colony now occupied by South Africa; East Timor, a former Portuguese colony absorbed into Indonesia; and New Caledonia, a French colony in the South Pacific.

Direct colonial rule cannot easily give way to a stable, nonrevolutionary political system led by either military or civilian elements, for a number of interrelated reasons. Like neo-patrimonialism, direct colonial rule—authoritarian by definition and typically quite repressive—also radicalized its political opponents. Direct colonialism undermines actual or potential moderate and reformist leaderships since, unlike indirect colonialism, it does not attempt to preserve a traditional indigenous elite or to create a new one so that formal political power may one day be "safely" transferred to the colony without jeopardizing the colonizer's economic interests. Direct colonial rule also tends to create more indigenous elite and middle-class opposition than indirect colonial rule. Important business and professional opportunities, as well as upper-level administrative positions, are reserved by and for the colonialists. That exclusion from such positions is based on an explicitly racial criterion, and not on education or ability more generally, can only heighten the alienation of indigenous upper-class and middle-class elements from the colonialists.

The colonial power, like a personalist dictator, also provides a common and highly visible focus of opposition for groups that may have very different reasons for seeking national independence. The armed forces in such colonies, moreover, are not likely to be a force for reform. Direct colonial armies are led by officers whose principal loyalties are to the colonial power and who have few if any connections to indigenous political groups with an interest in decolonization. To be sure, officers and soldiers within direct colonial armies may end up calling for a retreat from colonial wars (as happened in the Portuguese colonial situation at the bitter end). But the sudden withdrawal of colonial armies—like the flight of a dictator—may simply open the way for revolutionaries to seize power.

In addition, directly ruled colonies, like neo-patrimonial dictatorships identified with a foreign power, create contexts in which political symbols of nationalism and cultural self-assertion may be harnessed by revolutionaries in addition to the forces of class struggle. In both types of exclusionary authoritarian regimes, economically rooted grievances come to be directed at political rulers backed by foreign powers, as well as at foreign landlords and businesspeople; as a result, such grievances overlap with and may therefore be subsumed, at least in part within more inclusive demands for *national liberation*. Of course, revolutionaries who confront such regimes typically struggle with balancing class and nationalist issues, but this is a blessed dilemma that their counterparts in indirectly ruled colonies or in independent authoritarian regimes less closely tied to a foreign power do not have the opportunity to confront.

Compared to direct colonialism, indirect colonial rule—as well as more impersonal and bureaucratic forms of authoritarianism in independent countries—tends to be both militarily stronger and more coherent as well as more capable of a transition to an independent and more inclusive political system, including parliamentary democracy. Indirect colonial rule, as noted above, purposely grooms a reliable elite to whom formal political power can be transferred without jeopardizing the economic interests of the colonizer. The armed forces in such colonies, moreover, recruit officers from the indigenous population who tend to have strong loyalties to the local society—as opposed to the colonizing power—or at least strong corporate loyalties, which set them apart from the colonialists. Such officers often become linked to broader forces in the local society that favor political reform and national independence. In contrast, officers in directly ruled colonies and neo-patrimonial regimes are chosen and promoted for their loyalty to the colonizing power or for their purely personal loyalty to the dictator and thus they either cannot or do not form ties to reformist political elites.

Given these considerations, it is not surprising that a number of indirectly ruled colonies *defeated* mass-based revolutionary movements during the 1940s and 1950s, through a combination of military might and transitions to independent or more open political systems. Examples of this phenomenon happened in Malaya, Kenya, and the Philippines. Less formidable rebellions, moreover, were also defeated or contained in India, Indonesia, and Burma. As these lists suggest, the British were particularly adept at avoiding revolutions in their colonies through the use of indirect rule. Significantly, the white settler community in what was then known as Southern Rhodesia unilaterally declared independence from Britain in 1965, precisely in order to avoid a similar process of decolonization. White rule, however, undercut the potential influence of black moderates in Zimbabwe and ensured that armed revolutionaries would dominate the nationalist cause.

More recent political transitions in the formally independent countries of El Salvador, Guatemala, and Peru—all countries where powerful leftist insurgencies are currently underway—have led to the political incorporation of centrist and even some leftist parties and organizations. The political opening in Peru was the most extensive, and its breadth was undoubtedly related to the fact that it was not a calculated response to insurgency, but occurred coincidentally, just as the insurgency began in that country. Whether the political openings in any of these countries will be sufficiently extensive to thwart armed leftist insurgencies remains uncertain, however, particularly in El Salvador, where the armed forces are not especially professional nor the recent political opening especially broad. However, these openings did remove unpopular dictators and are likely to guarantee a continued flow of foreign aid, particularly from the United States. Analogous to the empowerment of indigenous elites in indirectly ruled colonies, these political openings in independent and more bureaucratic authoritarian regimes explain why guerrillas cannot easily come to power. In instances like these, prolonged and even stalemated military struggles can go on and on, while the proponents of reform, revolution, and reaction fight it out.

Conclusion

...[O]ur analysis suggests that revolutionaries in the contemporary Third World are most likely to succeed when civil society as a whole can be politically mobilized to oppose an autonomous and narrowly based direct colonial regime or a Sultanistic neo-patrimonial regime. In her recent comparative study of the Iranian and Nicaraguan revolutions, Farhi suggests that the "most important characteristic of the Iranian and Nicaraguan pre-revolutionary states was their almost total autonomy from internal classes."[26] This has been a characteristic, in fact, of virtually all Third World states that have been toppled by revolutions. In contrast, when radicals confront a state with significant social connections— even if the state is authoritarian and its ties are restricted to the middle and upper classes— then revolutionary coalition building becomes very difficult. Furthermore, if a state traditionally allied with economic elites can politically incorporate at least some popular sectors or organizations, then the prospects for revolutionary success become still more remote.

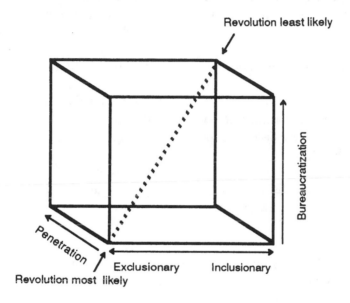

Figure 1. A graphic representation of states according to degrees of (1) *penetration* of national territory, (2) *incorporation* of socially mobilized groups, and (3) *bureaucratization* of the state administration and armed forces

It follows from what we have argued that the Third World has been the principal site of social revolutions in this century, not simply because of the poverty or socioeconomic structures one finds there. The Third World is also where one finds most of the world's exclusionary and repressive political systems, based in administrative organizations and armies that do not fully penetrate civil society or control the territories they claim to rule. By contrast, democratic polities in the First World, and a combination of Communist party patronage and coercive repression in the Second World, have prevented the emergence of strong revolutionary movements (or else, as in Poland, have

Table 1
Some Characteristics of Exclusionary Polities

Patrimonial Dictatorships and Directly Ruled Colonies	*Bureaucratic-Authoritarian Regimes and Indirectly Ruled Colonies*
Relative weak, corrupt, and disorganized civil administration and army	Stronger and more coherent civil administration and army
Political openings difficult: military reformism and civil-military pacts unlikely	Political openings easier: military reformism and civil-military pacts more likely
Basis for popular and elite opposition to ruler	Elite opposition much less likely
External support more likely to be withdrawn, especially as elite opposition develops	External support more likely to persist, especially following a political opening
Probability of state disintegration when dictator or colonial power departs or is removed	State disintegration less likely during political crises and transitions

staved off outright seizures of power by such movements). The unraveling of Communist patronage systems in portions of the Second World may allow the future growth of oppositional movements there. These will often be ethnic separatist, however, rather than revolutionary; and it is hard to imagine that threatened Communist armies will crumble or retreat as patrimonial and colonial armies have done.

Our analysis of the conditions conducive to the formation of revolutionary coalitions and actual transfers of power in the Third World has shifted away from the emphases on the peasantry and the effects of commercial capitalism than characterized earlier comparative approaches. Instead, we have followed in the footsteps of such state—or polity centered analyses of revolutions as Samuel Huntington's *Political Order in Changing Societies*, Charles Tilly's *From Mobilization to Revolution*, and Theda Skocpol's *States and Social Revolutions*—although the hypotheses offered here go beyond what any of these books had to offer.

We have suggested that the structures of states and armies, as well as the political relations between states and various sectors of society, provide the keys to explaining revolutions in the Third World. Revolutionary coalitions have formed and expanded in countries in which one finds not only poverty, imperialism, professional revolutionaries, and peasants of a certain sort, but also political exclusion and severe and indiscriminate (while not overwhelming) repression. In turn, revolutionary movements have actually succeeded in overthrowing those regimes that have been rendered brittle and unreformable by the structural features and strategies of rule characteristic of direct colonialism and Sultanistic neo-patrimonial dictatorship.

Revolutionary movements will undoubtedly continue to emerge in the Third World, where many states are not only exclusionary, but also fiscally, administratively, and militarily weak. And if the past is any guide, such movements will be especially likely to triumph where the political regimes they oppose remain narrow as well as repressive.

Notes

1. For example: Samuel P. Huntington, *Political Order in Changing Societies* (New Haven, Conn.: Yale University Press, 1968); Barrington Moore, Jr., *Social Origins of Dictatorship and Democracy: Lord and Peasant in the Making of the Modern World* (Boston: Beacon Press, 1967); and Eric R. Wolf, *Peasant Wars of the Twentieth Century* (New York: Harper and Row, 1969).

2. Léon Trotsky, *The History of the Russian Revolution*, trans. Max Eastman (New York: Monad Press, 1961; originally 1932), p. 249.

3. Charles Tilly, *From Mobilization to Revolution* (Reading, Mass.: Addison-Wesley, 1978), p. 202.

4. Walter L. Goldfrank, "The Mexican Revolution," in *Revolutions: Theoretical, Comparative, and Historical Studies*, ed. Jack A. Goldstone (San Diego, Calif.: Harcourt Brace Jovanovich, 1986), p. 105. This article originally appeared in *Theory and Society* in 1979.

5. See: Wolf, *Peasant Wars*; Jeffery M. Paige, *Agrarian Revolution: Social Movements and Export Agriculture in the Underdeveloped World* (New York: Free Press, 1975); Joel Migdal, *Peasants, Politics, and Revolution* (Princeton, N.J.: Princeton University Press, 1974); James Scott, *The Moral Economy of the Peasant* (New Haven, Conn.: Yale University Press, 1976); James Scott, "Hegemony and the Peasantry," *Politics & Society* 7 (1977): 267-296; and Samuel L. Popkin, *The Rational Peasant* (Berkeley: University of California Press, 1979).

6. In addition to the works of other scholars cited below, we are drawing upon: Jeff Goodwin, "Revolutionary Movements in Central America: A Comparative Analysis," working paper No. 0007, *Working Paper Series, Center for Research on Politics and Social Organization* (Cambridge, Mass.: Department of Sociology, Harvard University, 1988); Jeff Goodwin, "Revolutionary Movements in Southeast Asia, 1940-1954: A Comparative Analysis," working paper No. 0008, *Working Paper Series, Center for Research on Politics and Social Organization* (Cam

bridge, Mass.: Department of Sociology, Harvard University, 1988); Jeff Goodwin, "States and Revolutions in the Third World: A Comparative Analysis" (Ph.D. diss., Harvard University, November 1988); Theda Skocpol, "What Makes peasants Revolutionary?" Comparative Politics 14, no. 3 (April 1982): 351-375; and Theda Skocpol, "Rentier State and Shi'a Islam in the Iranian Revolution," *Theory and Society* 11, no. 3 (May 1982): 265-283.

7. On peasants in the classic social revolutions, see Theda Skocpol, *States and Social Revolutions: A Comparative Analysis of France, Russia, and China* (Cambridge, Eng.: Cambridge University Press, 1979), chapter 3.

8. Exceptions to this include Migdal, *Peasants, Politics, and Revolution*; and John Dunn, *Modern Revolutions* (Cambridge, Eng.: Cambridge University Press, 1972).

9. Robert H. Dix, "The Varieties of Revolution," *Comparative Politics* 15 (1983): 281-294; Robert H. Dix, "Why Revolutions Succeed and Fail," *Polity* 16 (1984): 423-446; and Josef Gugler, "The Urban Character of Contemporary Revolutions," *Studies in Comparative International Development* 27 (1982): 60-73.

10. Popkin, *Rational Peasant*; and Timothy P. Wickham-Crowley, "The Rise (and Sometimes Fall) of Guerrilla Governments in Latin America," *Sociological Forum* 2 (1987): 473-499.

11. Popkin, *Rational Peasant*, p. 262.

12. Richard Gott, *Guerilla Movements in Latin America* (Garden City, N.Y.: Doubleday, 1971).

13. See Tilly, *From Mobilization to Revolution*, pp. 204-205.

14. See Andrew Walder, *Communist Neo-Traditionalism: Work and Authority in Chinese Industry* (Berkeley: University of California Press, 1986).

15. Wickham-Crowley, "Guerrilla governments in Latin America."

16. Alan Dawley, *Class and Community: The Industrial Revolution in Lynn* (Cambridge, Mass.: Harvard University Press, 1976), p. 70.

17. Seymour Martin Lipset, "Radicalism or Reformism: The Sources of Working-class Politics," *American Political Science Review* 77 (1983): 7.

18. Geoffrey Fairbairn, *Revolutionary Guerrilla Warfare: The Countryside Version* (Harmondsworth, Eng.: Penguin Books, 1974), p. 139.

19. Chalmers Johnson, *Revolutionary Change*, 2d ed., rev. (Palo Alto, Calif.: Stanford University Press, 1982), pp. 95-109.

20. Huntington, *Political Order in Changing Societies*, especially chapter 5.

21. Ibid., p. 275. For Guatemala, Huntington seems to have in mind the short-lived democratic political transition of 1944 away from the dictatorship of General Jorge Ubico. Most analysts, however, ourselves included, do not consider this a social revolution or (in Huntington's terms) a "great revolution."

22. S.N. Eisenstadt, *Revolution and the Transformation of Societies* (New York: Free Press, 1978); and Jack A. Goldstone. "Revolutions and Superpowers," in *Superpowers and Revolutions*, ed. Jonathan P. Adelman (New York: Praeger, 1986). Of course, these scholars are elaborating ideas borrowed from the classic comparative political sociology of Max Weber.

23. In this and the following paragraphs, we have drawn insights especially from

Richard Snyder, "A Comparative Analysis of the vulnerablity of Sultanistic Regimes to Revolution," unpublished Senior Honors Essay, Committee on Degrees in Social Studies, Harvard College, 1989. Snyder examines in depth the cases of Haiti, Paraguay, the Philippines, and Zaire.

24. Eisenstadt, *Revolution and the Transformation of Societies*, especially pp. 282-285.

25. Tilly, *From Mobilization to Revolution*, pp. 213-214.

26. Farideh Farhi, "State Disintegration and Urban-Based Revolutionary Crisis: A Comparative Analysis of Iran and Nicaragua," *Comparative Political Studies* 21 (1988): 231-256.

11

THE LEGACY OF WEBER: ROBERT REICH (1946-)

This selection from Robert Reich's book, *The Work of Nations*, extends and challenges Weber's conclusions about organization and the economy. Robert Reich is an economist, specializing in labour economics and public policy; he was secretary of labour during President Clinton's first administration. Reich builds on the work of Weber as he traces the continued impact of rational calculation on the form and functioning of businesses; however, he believes that rational calculation is now leading away from bureaucratization towards new forms of organization, such as the global web. Rational calculation is a constant in modern society, while bureaucratization was only one historical form for implementing formal rationality.

For a while, managers of capitalist firms and decision-makers in governments both believed that it was rational to increase organizational size and to structure their organizations as big bureaucracies. By the 1950s, sociologists wrote books like *White Collar* by C. Wright Mills and William Whyte's *The Organization Man* to analyze how increasing numbers of people were working in large bureaucracies.

It was widely believed that the most successful business is the vertically integrated firm in which each step of the production process—from extracting raw materials to marketing the finished product—is carried out by the same large organization. In the first part of the century, many companies from auto manufacturers to Hollywood movie studios followed this model. Within each of these companies, corporate structure was rigidly hierarchical, with top-down decision-making. These companies were located in a single country, so that an expansion of the corporation generally meant increased employment opportunities in its "own" country. In the 1950s, the head of General Motors, Charlie Wilson, asserted that "...what was good for our country was good for General Motors, and vice versa."[1]

But a reversal of the trend toward bureaucratization became evident in the 1970s. Giant companies gradually began to change their shape, turning into webs of enterprise. Corporations began to form links with suppliers and distributors, rather than incorporating these functions within their organizational boundaries. Activities were increasingly "out-sourced" to sub-contractors, often located in a different country from corporate headquarters. These practices contributed to lower labour costs and more flexible patterns of production. Information and decision-making no longer flowed exclusively downward. Teams and decentered relationships replaced hierarchical pyramids within the firm; partnerships, brokered relationships, and sub-contracting connected smaller firms to each other and to the large corporations.

The new global webs of enterprise were still governed by considerations of formal rationality, connecting organizational means to the overriding end of profit maximization. What changed was that executives were no longer convinced that bureaucracies were the most rational form in new global markets marked by volatility, big labour cost differentials among nations, the centrality of information as a resource, more sophisticated technologies, and short product cycles. Bureaucracies seemed increasingly unwieldy, ponderous, and unable to respond quickly to changes in market conditions.

Reich identifies these changes and discusses their impact; much of the book is a consideration of the implications of these changes for workers and governments. The new patterns of production reward workers who acquire high skill levels and who can be employed in "high value" enterprises that are replacing "high volume" production. A nation whose workers remain in routine production jobs or low-skill personal service jobs is likely to become a nation of poor people with high unemployment rates. It will inevitably fall into the lower ranks of the global economy. Therefore nations, acting through their governments, have the responsibility to upgrade education and job-training to ensure that workers acquire high skill levels and participate in the function of "symbolic analysis," the managing and use of information, scientific and technical knowledge, and organizational and entrepreneurial know-how.

Reich is concerned that strata of the wealthy and well-educated will increasingly disengage from their poorer and less well-educated fellow citizens. The privileged will live in elegant suburban enclaves and urban luxury complexes, send their children to elite private schools, pursue business ventures on a global scale, and pretend that "ordinary people" don't exist. They will associate only with similar people in other countries, forming an international stratum that is socially, economically, politically, and morally disconnected from production and service workers in its own national hinterlands. Reich does not use the term "bourgeoisie," and in fact pictures the privileged as including top scientists and intellectuals, as well as capitalist entrepreneurs. Nevertheless, his dystopian prospect is not entirely different from Marx's views of class formation in the global capitalist economy.

Notes
1.   Robert Reich, *The Work of Nations* (New York: Vintage, 1992) 48.

Readings

Evans, Peter. *Embedded Autonomy: States and Industrial Transformation*. Princeton, NJ: Princeton University Press, 1995.

Harrison, Bennett. *Lean and Mean: The Changing Landscape of Corporate Power in the Age of Flexibility*. New York: Basic Books, 1995.

Mills, C. Wright. *White Collar*. New York: Oxford University Press, 1951.

Piore, Michael, and Charles Sabel. *The Second Industrial Divide*. New York: Basic Books, 1986.

Whyte, William. *The Organization Man*. New York: Simon and Schuster, 1956.

The Work of Nations
ROBERT B. REICH

> There was ... a mysterious rite of initiation through which, in one way or another, almost every member of the team passed. The term that the old hands used for this rite ... was "signing up." By signing up for the project you agreed to do whatever was necessary for success. You agreed to forsake, if necessary, family, hobbies, and friends—if you had any of these left (and you might not if you had signed up too many times before).... Labor was no longer coerced. Labor volunteered.
> Tracy Kidder, *The Soul of a New Machine* (1981)

The high-value enterprise has no need to control vast resources, discipline armies of production workers, or impose predictable routines. Thus it need not be organized like the old pyramids that characterized standardized production, with strong chief executives presiding over ever-widening layers of managers, atop an even larger group of hourly workers, all following standard operating procedures.

In fact, the high-value enterprise *cannot* be organized this way. The three groups that give the new enterprise most of its value—problem-solvers, problem-identifiers, and strategic brokers—need to be in direct contact with one another to continuously discover new opportunities. Messages must flow quickly and clearly if the right solutions are to be applied to the right problems in a timely way. This is no place for bureaucracy.

Anyone who has ever played the children's game Telephone—in which one person whispers a phrase to the next person in line, who then whispers the phrase to the next, and so on, until the last person announces aloud a phrase that invariably bears no resemblance to the original—knows what can happen when even the simplest messages are passed through intermediaries: "Have a nice day" turns into "Get out of my way." If problem-identifiers had to convey everything they were learning about the needs of their customers upward to top management through layers and layers of middle managers, while problem-solvers had to convey everything *they* were learning about new technologies upward through as many layers, and then both groups had to await top management's decisions about what to do—decisions which then had to travel back down through the same bureaucratic channels—the results would be, to say the least, late and irrelevant, and probably distorted.

Thus one of the strategic broker's tasks is to create settings in which problem-solvers and problem-identifiers can work together without undue interference. The strategic broker is a facilitator and a coach—finding the people in both camps who can learn most from one another, giving them whatever resources they need, letting them go at it long enough to discover new complements between technologies and customer needs, but also providing them with enough guidance so that they don't lose sight of mundane goals like earning a profit.

Creative teams solve and identify problems in much the same way whether they are developing new software, dreaming up a new marketing strategy, seeking a scientific discovery, or contriving a financial ploy. Most coordination is horizontal rather than vertical. Because problems and solutions cannot be defined in advance, formal meetings and agendas won't reveal them. They emerge instead out of frequent and informal communications among team members. Mutual learning occurs within the team, as insights, experiences, puzzles, and solutions are shared—often randomly. One solution is found applicable to a completely different problem; someone else's failure turns into a winning strategy for accomplishing something entirely unrelated. It is as if team members were doing several jigsaw puzzles simultaneously with pieces from the same pile—pieces which could be arranged to form many different pictures. (Such intellectual synergies can be found, on rare occasions, even in university departments.)

Instead of a pyramid, then, the high-value enterprise looks more like a spider's web. Strategic brokers are at the center, but there are all sorts of connections that do not involve them directly, and new connections are being spun all the time. At each point of connection are a relatively small number of people—depending on the task, from a dozen to several hundred. If a group was any larger it could not engage in rapid and informal learning.[1] Here individual skills are combined so that the group's ability to innovate is something more than the simple sum of its parts. Over time, as group members work through various problems and approaches together, they learn about one another's abilities. They learn how they can help one another perform better, who can contribute what to a particular project, how they can best gain more experience together. Each participant is on the look out for ideas that will propel the group forward. Such cumulative experience and understanding cannot be translated into standard operating procedures easily transferable to other workers and other organizations. Each point on the "enterprise web" represents a unique combination of skills.

2

Speed and agility are so important to the high-value enterprise that it cannot be weighed down with large overhead costs like office buildings, plant, equipment, and payroll. It must be able to switch direction quickly, pursue options when they arise, discover new linkages between problems and solutions wherever they may lie.

In the old high-volume enterprise, fixed costs such as factories, equipment, warehouses, and large payrolls were necessary in order to achieve control and predictability. In the high-value enterprise, they are an unnecessary burden. Here, all that really counts is rapid problem-identifying and problem-solving—the marriage of technical insight with marketing know-how, blessed by strategic and financial acumen. Everything else—all of the more standardized pieces—can be obtained as needed. Office space, factories, and warehouses can be rented; standard equipment can be leased; standard components can be bought wholesale from cheap producers (many of them overseas); secretaries, routine data processors, bookkeepers, and routine production workers can be hired temporarily.

In fact, relatively few people actually work for the high-value enterprise in the traditional sense of having steady jobs with fixed salaries. The inhabitants of corporate headquarters, who spend much of their time searching for the right combinations of solutions, problems, strategies and money, are apt to share in the risks and returns of their hunt. When a promising combination is found, participants in the resulting project (some at the center of the web, some at connecting points on the periphery) also may share in any profits rather than take fixed salaries.

With risks and returns broadly shared, and overhead kept to a minimum, the enterprise web can experiment. Experimentation was dangerous in the old high-volume enterprise because failures (like Ford's notorious Edsel) meant that the entire organization had to change direction—retool, retrain, redirect sales and marketing—at a huge cost. But experimentation is the lifeblood of the high-value enterprise, because customization requires continuous trial and error.

Sharing risks and returns has an added advantage. It is a powerful creative stimulus. If they are to spot new opportunities in technologies and markets, problem-solvers, -identifiers, and brokers must be highly motivated. Few incentives are more powerful than membership in a small group engaged in a common task, sharing the risks of defeat and the potential rewards of victory. Rewards are not only pecuniary. The group often shares a vision as well; they want to make their mark on the world.

At the web's outer edges, suppliers of standard inputs (factories, equipment, office space, routine components, bookkeeping, janitorial services, data processing, and so forth) contract to provide or do specific things for a certain time and for a specified price. Such arrangements are often more efficient than directly controlling employees.[2] Suppliers who profit in direct proportion to how hard and carefully they do their jobs have every incentive to find increasingly efficient ways of accomplishing their tasks. Consider the owner of a McDonald's franchise who works fifteen-hour days and keeps the outlet sparkling clean; or the machine operator who, owning the equipment and contracting to do jobs with it (and keep the profits), maintains the machine in perfect condition.[3]

3

Enterprise webs come in several shapes, and the shapes continue to evolve. Among the most common are:

Independent profit centers. This web eliminates middle-level managers and pushes authority for product development and sales down to groups of engineers and marketers (problem-solvers and -identifiers) whose compensation is linked to the unit's profits. Strategic brokers in headquarters provide financial and logistical help, but give the unit discretion over how to spend money up to a certain amount. By 1990, Johnson & Johnson comprised 166 autonomous companies; Hewlett-Packard, some 50 separate business units. General Electric, IBM, AT&T, and Eastman Kodak, among others, were also adopting this approach. For much the same reason, large publishing houses were busily creating "imprints"—small, semiautonomous publishing houses within the structure of the parent firm, each comprising a dozen or so people with considerable responsibility for acquiring and publishing books on their own.

Spin-off partnerships. In this web, strategic brokers in headquarters act as venture capitalists and midwives, nurturing good ideas that bubble up from groups of problem-solvers and -identifiers and then (if the ideas catch on in the market) spinning the groups off as independent businesses in which the strategic brokers at headquarters retain a partial stake. Xerox and 3M have pioneered this form in the United States, but it is nothing new to the Japanese. Hitachi, for example, is actually more than 60 companies, 27 of which are publicly traded. Some venture-capital firms and leveraged-buyout partnerships are coming to resemble the same sort of web, in which risks and returns are shared between headquarters and the managers of the separate businesses.

Spin-in partnerships. In this web, good ideas bubble up outside the firm from independent groups of problem-solvers and -identifiers. Strategic brokers in headquarters purchase the best of them, or form partnerships with the independents, and then produce, distribute, and market the ideas under the firm's own well-known trademark. This sort of arrangement is common to computer software houses. In 1990, for example, over 400 tiny software-developing firms were purchased by big software companies such as Microsoft, Lotus, and Ashton-Tate. The software developers thus received a nice profit on their efforts, while the larger firms maintained a steady supply of new ideas.

Licensing. In this web, headquarters contracts with independent businesses to use its brand name, sell its special formulas, or otherwise market (that is, find applicable problems for) its technologies. Strategic brokers at the center of the web ensure that no licensee harms the reputation of the brand by offering inconsistent or poor quality, and also provide licensees with special bulk services like computerized inventory management or advertising. Most of the ownership and control, however, is left in the hands of licensees. One example is franchises, which are among the fastest-growing businesses in every advanced economy, now selling everything from tax preparation and accounting services to hotel accommodations, cookies, groceries, printing and copying, health care, and bodybuilding. In 1988, American franchisees comprised 509,000 outlets and accounted for $640 billion in sales, amounting to more than 10 percent of the entire national product.[4]

Pure brokering. In the most decentralized kind of web, strategic brokers contract with independent businesses for problem solving and identifying as well as for production. This web is ideal for enterprises that need to shift direction quickly. By 1990, for example, Compaq Computers of Houston (which did not exist in 1982 but eight years later had revenues of $3 billion) was buying many of its most valuable components on the outside (microprocessors from Intel, operating systems from software houses like Microsoft, liquid-crystal screens from Citizen), and then selling the resulting machines through independent dealers to whom Compaq granted exclusive sales territories. The Apple computer costs less than $500 to build, of which $350 was for components purchased on the outside.[5] Meanwhile, the Lewis Galoob Toy company sold more than $50 million worth of tiny gadgets conceived by independent inventors and novelty companies, designed by independent engineers, manufactured and packaged by suppliers in Hong Kong (who contracted out the most labor-intensive work to China and Thailand), and then distributed in America by independent toy companies. Movie studios that once relied on their own facilities, crews, and exclusive stables of actors, directors, and screenwriters were contracting on a project-by-project basis with independent producers, directors, actors, writers, crews, and cinematographers, using rented space and equipment, and relying on independent distributors to get the films into appropriate theaters. Book publishers were contracting not only for authors but also for printing, graphics, artwork, marketing, and all other facets of production. Even automakers were outsourcing more and more of what they produced. (By 1990, Chrysler corporation directly produced only about 30 percent of the value of its cars; Ford, about 50 percent. General Motors bought half its engineering and design services from 800 different companies.)

4

Americans love to debate old categories. Does manufacturing have a future or are we becoming a service economy? Are big businesses destined to expire like prehistoric beasts, to be superseded by small businesses, or are big businesses critical to our economic future? Such questions provide endless opportunities for debate, not unlike the arguments of thirteenth-century Scholastics over how many angels could comfortably fit on a pinhead. Such debates are socially useful in that they create excuses for business seminars, conferences, and magazine articles and thus ensure gainful employment for many. But such debates are less than edifying. Debaters usually can find evidence to support whatever side they choose, depending on how they define their terms. Whether manufacturing is being replaced by a service economy depends on how "manufacturing" and "service" are defined; whether small businesses are replacing large depends equally on what these adjectives are taken to mean. In fact, all manufacturing businesses are coming to entail services, and all large businesses are spinning into webs of smaller businesses.

The federal government's Standard Industrial Classification system is as unhelpful and anachronistic here as before. It defines "establishment" as any business, including one that may be part of a larger company.[6] Thus, not surprisingly, official statistics show that the number of small "establishments" nearly doubled between 1975 and 1990, creating millions of new jobs—just as the high-volume, hierarchical corporation was transforming into a high-value, decentralized enterprise web. But even discounting this statistical sleight of hand, the shift from high-volume hierarchies to high-value webs would create the appearance of a dwindling core simply because core corporations no longer employ many people directly and their webs of indirect employment defy easy measurement.

As stated earlier, by most official measures, America's 500 largest industrial companies failed to create a single net new job between 1975 and 1990, their share of the civilian labor force dropping from 17 percent to less than 10 percent. Meanwhile, after decades of decline, the number of people describing themselves as "self-employed" began to rise.[7] And there has been an explosion in the number of new businesses (in 1950, 93,000 corporations were created in the United States; by the late 1980s, America was adding about 1.3 million new enterprises to the economy each year).[8] Most of the new jobs in the economy appear to come from small businesses,[9] as does most of the growth in research spending.[10] A similar transformation has been occurring in other nations.[11]

But to draw the natural conclusion from these data—that large businesses are being replaced by millions of tiny businesses—is to fall into the same vestigial trap as in the debate over "manufacturing" versus "services": both ignore the weblike relationships that are shaping the new economy. Here, the core corporation is no longer a "big" business, but neither is it merely a collection of smaller ones. Rather, it is an enterprise web. Its center provides strategic insight and binds the threads together. Yet points on the web often have sufficient autonomy to create profitable connections to other webs. There is no "inside" or "outside" the corporation, but only different distances from its strategic center.

The resulting interconnections can be quite complex, stretching over many profit centers, business units, spin-offs, licensees, franchisees, suppliers, and dealers, and then on to other strategic centers, which in turn are linked to still other groups. Throughout the 1980s, for example, IBM (which, as you recall, had jealously guarded its independence even to the point of departing India rather than sharing profits with Indian partners) joined with dozens of companies—Intel, Merrill Lynch, Aetna Life and Casualty, MCI, Comsat, and more than eighty foreign-owned firms—to share problem-solving, problem-identifying, and strategic brokering. Similarly AT&T (which for seventy years had prided itself on having total control over its products and operating systems) found itself in a newly deregulated, unpredictable world of telecommunications, which required hundreds of alliances and joint ventures, and thousands of subcontracts.[12] Core corporations in other mature economies are undergoing a similar transformation. Indeed, as we shall see, their increasingly decentralized enterprise webs are becoming undifferentiated extensions of our own.[13]

The trend should not be overstated. Even by the 1990s there remain large corporations of bureaucratic form and function, which directly employ many thousands of workers and which own substantial physical assets. But these corporations are coming to be the exceptions. That they survive and prosper is despite, rather than because of, their organization. The most profitable firms are transforming into enterprise webs. They may look like the old form of organization from the outside, but inside all is different. Their famous brands adhere to products and services that are cobbled together from many different sources outside the formal boundaries of the firm. Their dignified headquarters, expansive factories, warehouses, laboratories, and fleets of trucks and corporate jets are leased. Their production workers, janitors, and bookkeepers are under temporary contract; their key researchers, design engineers, and marketers are sharing in the profits. And their distinguished executives, rather than possessing great power and authority over this domain, have little direct control over much of anything. Instead of imposing their will over a corporate empire, they guide ideas through the new webs of enterprise.

Notes
1. Information technologies have dramatically reduced the costs of coordinating even relatively large numbers of people without relying on standard operating procedures and other bureaucratic structures. See, for example, T. Malone, J. Yates, and R. Benjamin, "Electronic Markets and Electronic Hierarchies," *Communications of the ACM*, Vol. 30, No. 6 (June 1987).
2. A number of studies have revealed a marked increase in outsourcing and the use of part-time workers during the 1980s. Part of the motive in the United States surely is to avoid paying employee benefits mandated by union contracts or legislation. But interestingly, the same pattern is observable in many other advanced economies where union contracts or legislated benefits are not affected. See I.W. Sengenberger and G. Loveman, *Smaller Units of Employment: A Synthesis of Research on Industrial Organization in Industrial Countries* (Geneva: International Institute for Labor Studies, 1988). Good surveys of the trend toward outsourcing and temporary work can be found in E. Applebaum, "Restructuring Work: Temporary, Part-time, and At-home Employment," In H. Harmann (ed.), *Computer Chips and Paper Clips: Technology and Women's Employment* (Washington, D.C.: National Academy Press, 1987); S. Christopherson, "Flexibility in the U.S. Service Economy and the Emerging Spatial Division of Labour," *Transactions of the British Institute of Geographics*, Vol. 14 (1989).
3. This example is not hypothetical. A Finnish paper company, burdened by tree-harvesting machinery always in need of repair, sold the machines to its operators, and gave them contracts to do their old jobs. Productivity soared, as the operators now kept the machines in better condition and used them with far greater care than before. See *The Economist*, December 24, 1988, p. 16.
4. Figures from *Business Week*, November 13, 1989, p. 83.
5. Apple initially got its microprocessors from Synertek, other chips from Texas Instruments and Motorola, video monitors from Hitachi, power supplies from Astec, and printers from Qume. See James Brian Quinn et al., "Beyond Products: Service-Based Strategy," *Harvard Business Review*, March-April 1990, pp. 58-60.
6. U.S. Office of Management and Budget, SIC Manual (1987), p. 12.

7. In 1975, only 6.9 percent of the U.S. nonfarm work force was "self-employed"; by 1986, it was 7.4 percent. Data from *The State of Small Business: Report of the President* (Washington, D.C.: U.S. Government Printing Office, various issues).

8. David L. Birch, "The Hidden Economy," *The Wall Street Journal*, June 10, 1988, p. 23R.

9. Data from Douglas P. Handler, *Business Demographics* (New York: Dun & Bradstreet, Economic Analysis Department, 1988).

10. According to the national Science Foundation, small firms with fewer than 500 employees doubled their share of America's corporate research and development spending during the 1980s, from 6 percent to 12 percent. National Science Foundation, *Research Report* (Washington, D.C.: National Science Foundation, November 1990), pp. 12-14.

11. See, for example, "München Management," *The Economist*, October 14, 1989, p. 25.

12. My interviews (see "A Note on Additional Sources") confirm the findings of other surveys. See, for example, R. Johnston and Paul Lawrence, "Beyond Vertical Integration: The Rise of the Value-Added Partnership," *Harvard Business Review*, July-August 1988; R. Miles, "Adapting to Technology and Competition: A New Industrial Relations System for the 21st Century," *California Management Review*, Winter 1988; and J. Badaracco, Jr., "Changing Forms of the Corporation," in J. Meyer and J. Gustafson (eds.), *The U.S. Business Corporation* (Cambridge, Mass.:" Ballinger, 1988). See also Jordan D. Lewis, *Partnerships for profit: Structuring and Managing Strategic Alliances* (New York: Free Press, 1990).

13. For a description of the pattern in Europe, see D.J. Sorey and S. Johnson, *Job Generation and Labour Market Changes* (London: Macmillan, 1987).

12

GEORG SIMMEL (1858-1918)

Georg Simmel, who wrote about society at the turn of the century in the years preceding World War I, was a contemporary of Durkheim and Weber. Unlike them he did not have a major university appointment until the last years of his life; excluded from a regular appointment by German anti-semitism and hostile opinions of his work, he lectured at the University of Berlin in a position that we would now describe as part-time. Although his lectures attracted enthusiastic audiences of students, his ideas were not welcomed by senior scholars in Germany who favoured heavy topics and many footnotes; they believed he gave too much attention to superficial and frivolous topics like fashion, sociability, and everyday life in the city. They disliked his writing style, which was witty, ironic, aphoristic, and free of citations.

It was difficult for established scholars in sociology and history to accept a writer who was as much a philosopher as a social scientist, wrote essays rather than research reports, and addressed many of the same themes as the maverick philosopher Friedrich Nietzsche. Weber was also influenced by Nietzsche but, unlike Simmel, he buried this influence deep in scholarly writing; Simmel openly shared Nietzsche's pleasure in contradictions, his aphoristic and unconventional style, and his mixture of lightheartedness and despair about the human condition.

Underlying the playfulness of his topics and writing style was a serious and even pessimistic reflection on the individual and society. Simmel saw a tension between the way individuals experience and create culture ("subjective culture") and culture embodied in material objects and institutions ("objective culture"). He believed that the latter was growing rapidly, overwhelming the former so that individuals were crushed by the weight and force of culture that existed outside of their control and creativity.

A second theme in Simmel's work is the way in which social forms—forms of interaction and culture—are embedded in social structure. To some extent, these forms can be analyzed in their own right apart from historical change in the surrounding structure. For example, he analyzed how interaction is different in dyads and triads, regardless of the cultural and social context in which the dyads and triads appear. He discussed the stranger as a social type who appears in many different kinds of groups and identified secrecy as a widespread phenomenon with its own characteristic forms. These types and forms are virtually independent of the specific cultural context; their characteristics are formal properties of groups and interaction patterns. This element of Simmel's work influenced North American sociology so that he is sometimes remembered most for his formalistic analysis of interaction and his "social geometry."

Yet Simmel was keenly aware that social, economic, and cultural contexts shape forms of interaction. His work on the money economy and the metropolis focuses on the specific forms of interaction, social types, and patterns of mental life that emerge in these contexts. The selection "The metropolis and mental life" spells out these effects of the money economy and the city. The money economy and the city produce an attitude of calculation, dominance of the intellect over the emotions, a blasé and indifferent tone, concern with punctuality, reserve toward others, a desire to "stand out," and enjoyment of anonymity, freedom, and individualism. In the selection from "The miser and the spendthrift" (from *The Philosophy of Money*) Simmel shows how a money economy makes possible certain social types with their own distinct ways of being and acting. The miser, the spendthrift, the prostitute, the poor, and so on appear in the money economy; fashion is a form of action and self-representation associated with it.

Simmel suggests that modern society creates a passion for innovation in form with little regard for content or substance. Playing with forms and formal innovation overwhelm commitment to any specific form and the values it embodies. For example, the arts are subject to wave upon wave of fads and novelties. What is "hot," "trendy," and "fashionable" is valued for its own sake, in clothing, in art, in music, in the media, in technology, and in intellectual currents. The logical extreme of cultural change associated with modern society is the pure play of form. Simmel's insight calls to mind Marx's image that "all that is solid melts into air" in capitalist society.

Simmel delighted in paradox and contradiction, as we see in "The metropolis and mental life." The city both heightens and destroys individuality, as people are treated in impersonal ways and, indeed, come to portray themselves in "shorthand" stereotyped representations conveyed in their stylized dress and speech; yet, at the same time, they are much freer to be individuals than in the small community. The city and the money economy enhance as well as impede autonomy. City life allows people to become anonymous, but it also awakens in them a desire to stand out, to be seen, to enjoy a moment of fame, to draw attention to themselves, to be perceived as unique, and to make an impression, possibly even a violent or outrageous one.

Note the convergence of the thought of Simmel, Marx, and Weber, but the marked divergence in their style and tone. All three emphasize rational calculation, the reduction of values to a quantified bottom line, and rapid social change as characteristics of capitalist society; all three see the ambiguous and paradoxical way in which capitalism both crushes and enhances freedom and individuality. Marx's attitude is one of revolutionary optimism: these characteristics of capitalism are terrible aspects of contemporary society yet also offer a promise of happiness in the future, in a communist society where their positive potential for individual emancipation will be realized. Weber's attitude is one of gloomy pessimism: there is no prospect that the iron cage of formal rationality will open. Simmel's response is playful pessimism: indeed, there is unlikely to be a reversal of these trends and no utopian future is possible—but reality is filled with contradictions and paradoxes so that it is never uniform, fixed, hopeless, or dreary.

Readings

Levine, Donald (ed.). *Georg Simmel on Individuality and Social Forms*. Chicago: University of Chicago Press, 1973.

Sennett, Richard. *The Corrosion of Character: The Personal Consequences of Work in the New Capitalism*. New York: W.W. Norton, 1998.

Simmel, Georg. *The Philosophy of Money*. New York and London: Routledge, 1990.

Weinstein, Deena and Michael Weinstein. *Postmodernized Simmel*. New York: Routledge, 1993.

Wolff, Kurt (ed.). *The Sociology of Georg Simmel*. New York: Free Press, 1985.

The Miser and the Spendthrift
GEORG SIMMEL

The miser [is one who] finds bliss in the sheer possession of money, without proceeding to the acquisition and enjoyment of particular objects. His sense of power is therefore more profound and more precious to him than dominion over specific objects could ever be. As we have seen, the possession of concrete objects is inherently circumscribed; the greedy soul who ceaselessly seeks satisfaction and penetration to the ultimate, innermost absolute nature of objects is painfully rebuffed by them. They are and remain separate, resisting incorporation into the self and thus terminating even the most passionate possession in frustration. The possession of money is free of this contradiction latent in all other kinds of possession. At the cost of not obtaining things and of renouncing all the specific satisfactions that are tied to particulars, money can provide a sense of power far enough removed from actual empirical objects that it is not subject to the limitations imposed by possession of them. Money alone do we own completely and without limitations. It alone can be completely incorporated into the use which we plan for it.

The pleasures of the miser are almost aesthetic. For aesthetic pleasures likewise lie beyond the impermeable reality of the world and depend on its appearance and luster, which are fully accessible to the mind and can be penetrated by it without resistance. The phenomena associated with money are only the clearest and most transparent instances of a series of phenomena in which the same principle is realized in other contexts. I once met a man who, though no longer young and a well-to-do family man, spent all his time learning every skill he could—languages, which he never employed, superb dancing, which he never pursued; accomplishments of every sort, which he never made use of and did not even want to use. This characteristic is precisely that of the miser: satisfaction in the complete possession of a potentiality with no thought whatsoever about its realization. At the same time, it exemplifies an attraction akin to the aesthetic, the mastery of both the pure form and the ideal of objects or of behavior, in respect to which every step toward reality—with its unavoidable obstacles, setbacks, and frustrations—could only be a deterioration, and would necessarily constrain the feeling that objects are potentially absolutely to be mastered.

Aesthetic contemplation, which is possible for any object and only especially easy for the beautiful, most thoroughly closes the gap between the self and the object. It allows an easy, effortless, and harmonious formation of the image of the object as if this image were determined only by the nature of the self. Hence the sense of liberation which accompanies an aesthetic mood; it is characterized by emancipation from the stuffy dull pressure of life, and the expansion of the self with joy and freedom into the objects whose reality would otherwise violate it. Such is the psychological tone of joy in the mere possession of money. The strange coalescing, abstraction, and anticipation of ownership of property which constitutes the meaning of money is like aesthetic pleasure in permitting consciousness a free play, a portentous extension into an unresisting medium, and the incorporation of all possibilities without violation or deterioration by reality. If one defines beauty as *une promesse de bonheur* ["a promise of happiness"], this definition is yet another indicator of the similarity between aesthetic attraction and the attraction of money, because the latter lies in the promise of the joys money makes possible....

It should also be noted that joy in the possession of money also doubtlessly contains an idealistic moment whose importance only appears paradoxical because on the one hand, the means to obtain it are necessarily diminished in the process of obtaining it and on the other hand because this feeling of joy is usually expressed by the individual in a nonidealistic form. This should not obscure the fact that joy in the sheer possession of money is one of the abstract joys, one of the furthest removed from sensuous immediacy, and one of those mediated most exclusively by the process of thinking and fantasy. In this respect it is similar to the joy of victory, which is so strong in some individuals that they simply do not ask what they really gain by winning....

The spendthrift is far more similar to the miser than their apparent polarization would seem to indicate. Let us note that in primitive economies the miserly conservation of valuables is not consistent with the nature of these valuables, that is, with the very limited storage time of agricultural products. Therefore, when their conversion into indefinitely storable money is not practical or is at any rate not a matter of course, one only rarely finds miserly hoarding. Where agricultural products are produced and consumed immediately there usually exists a certain liberality, especially toward guests and the needy. Money is much more inviting to collect and therefore makes such liberality much less likely. Thus Petrus Martyr praises the cocoa-bags which served the ancient Mexicans as money, because they cannot be long hoarded or cached and therefore cannot engender miserliness. Similarly, natural conditions limit the feasibility and attractiveness of prodigality. Prodigal consumption and foolish squandering (except for senseless destruction) are limited by the capacity of household members and outsiders to consume.

But the most important fact is that the waste of money has a different meaning and a new nuance that completely distinguish it from the waste of concrete objects. The latter means that value for any reasonable purposes of the individual is simply destroyed, whereas in the former case it has been purposelessly converted into other values. The wastrel in the money economy (who alone is significant for a philosophy of money) is not someone who senselessly gives his money to the world but one who uses it for senseless purchases, that is, for purchases that are not appropriate to his circumstances. The pleasure of waste must be distinguished from pleasure in the fleeting enjoyment of objects, from ostentation, and from the excitement of the alteration of acquisition and consumption. The pleasure of waste depends simply on the instant of the expenditure of money for no-matter-what objects. For the spendthrift, the attraction of the instant overshadows the rational evaluation either of money or of commodities.

At this point the position of the spendthrift in the instrumental nexus becomes clear. The goal of enjoying the possession of an object is preceded by two steps—first, the possession of money and, second, the expenditure of money for the desired object. For the miser, the first of these grows to be a pleasurable end in itself; for the spendthrift, the second. Money is almost as important to the spendthrift as to the miser, only not in the form of possessing it, but in its expenditure. His appreciation of its worth swells at the instant that money is transformed into other values; the intensity of this feeling is so great that he purchases the enjoyment of this moment at the cost of dissipating all more concrete values.

It is therefore clear to the observer that the indifference about the value of money which constitutes the essence and the charm of prodigality is possible only because money is actually treasured and assumed to be special. For the indifferent man's throwing away of his money would itself be done with indifference. The following case is typical of the enormous waste of the ancien régime: when a lady returned the 4,000—5,000 franc diamond that Prince Conti had sent her, he had it shattered and used the fragments as blotting sand for the note in which he informed her of the incident. Taine adds the following remark about the attitudes of that age: one is the more a man of the world the less one is concerned about money. But precisely herein lies the self-delusion. For as in a dialectic, the conscious and strongly negative stance toward money has the opposite sentiment as its basis, which alone provides it with meaning and attraction.

The same is true of those shops that may be found in the metropolis which, in direct contrast to stores that advertise bargains, smugly boast that they have the *highest* prices. Thus they imply that their customers are the Best People—those who do not ask about prices. But the noteworthy fact is that they do not emphasize what really matters—the quality of their merchandise. Thus they unconsciously do place money above all else, albeit with a reversal of value. Because of its close association with money, a spendthrift's lust easily grows to a monstrous extent and robs its victim of all reasonable sense of proportion. For money lacks the regulation that human capacity imposes on concrete objects. This is exactly the same immoderation that characterizes miserly avarice. The pure potentiality which it seeks instead of the enjoyment of real objects tends toward the infinite. Unlike the latter, it has no inherent or external reasons for restraint. When avarice lacks positive external constraints and limitations, it tends to become completely amorphous and increasingly passionate. This is the reason for the peculiar immoderation and bitterness of inheritance disputes. Since neither effort nor objective apportionment determines one's own claim, no one is inclined a priori to recognize the claims of others. One's own claims therefore, lack all restraint and any encroachment upon them is perceived as a particularly unreasonable injustice....

This is the basis of the nature of miserliness and prodigality: Both reject on principle that calculation of value which alone can stop and limit the instrumental nexus: a calculation based on the consummatory enjoyment of the object. The spendthrift—who is not to be confused with the epicure and the merely frivolous, although all these elements can be blended in a given case— becomes indifferent to the object once he possesses it. For this reason his enjoyment of it is marred by the curse of restlessness and transience. The moment of its beginning is also that of its undoing. The life of the spendthrift is marked by the same demonic formula as that of the miser: every pleasure attained arouses the desire for further pleasure, which can never be satisfied. Satisfaction can never be gained because it is being sought in a form that from the beginning foregoes its ends and is confined to means and to the moment before fulfilment. The miser is the more abstract of the two; *his* goal is reached even earlier than the usual goal. The spend-thrift gets somewhat closer to real objects. He abandons the movement toward a rational goal at a later point [than the miser], at which he stops as though it were the real goal. This formal identity of the two types despite the diametrical opposition of their visible behaviors—and the lack of a regulating substantive aim which suggests a capricious interplay between the two equally senseless tendencies—explain why miserliness and prodigality are often found in the same person, sometimes in different areas of interest and sometimes in connection with different moods. Constricting or expansive moods are expressed in miserliness or prodigality, as though the impulse were the same and merely the valence differed.

The Metropolis and Mental Life
GEORG SIMMEL

The deepest problems of modern life derive from the claim of the individual to preserve the autonomy and individuality of his existence in the face of overwhelming social forces, of historical heritage, of external culture, and of the technique of life. The fight with nature which primitive man has to wage for his *bodily* existence attains in this modern form its latest transformation. The eighteenth century called upon man to free himself of all the historical bonds in the state and in religion, in morals and in economics. Man's nature originally good and common to all, should develop unhampered. In addition to more liberty, the nineteenth century demanded the functional specialization of man and his work; this specialization makes one individual incomparable to another, and each of them indispensable to the highest possible extent. However, this specialization makes each man the more directly dependent upon the supplementary activities of all others. Nietzsche sees the full development of the individual conditioned by the most ruthless struggle of individuals; socialism believes in the suppression of all competition for the same reason. Be that as it may, in all these positions the same basic motive is at work: the person resists to being leveled down and worn out by a social-technological mechanism. An inquiry into the inner meaning of specifically modern life and its products, into the soul of the cultural body, so to speak, must seek to solve the equation which structures like the metropolis set up between the individual and the super-individual contents of life. Such an inquiry must answer the question of how the personality accommodates itself in the adjustments to external forces. This will by my task today.

The psychological basis of the metropolitan type of individuality consists in the *intensification of nervous stimulation* which results from the swift and uninterrupted change of outer and inner stimuli. Man is a differentiating creature. His mind is stimulated by the difference between a momentary impression and the one which preceded it. Lasting impressions, impressions which differ only slightly from one another, impressions which take a regular and habitual course and show regular and habitual contrasts—all these use up, so to speak, less consciousness than does the rapid crowding of changing images, the sharp discontinuity in the grasp of a single glance, and the unexpectedness of onrushing impressions. These are the psychological conditions which the metropolis creates. With each crossing of the street, with the tempo and multiplicity of economic, occupational and social life, the city sets up a deep contrast with small town and rural life with reference to the sensory foundations of psychic life. The metropolis exacts from man as a discriminating creature a different amount of consciousness than does rural life. Here the rhythm of life and sensory mental imagery flows more slowly, more habitually, and more evenly. Precisely in this connection the sophisticated character of metropolitan psychic life becomes understandable—as over against small town life which rests more upon deeply felt and emotional relationships. These latter are rooted in the more unconscious layers of the psyche and grow most readily in the steady rhythm of uninterrupted habituations. The intellect, however, has its locus in the transparent, conscious, higher layers of the psyche; it is the most adaptable of our inner forces. In order to accommodate to change and to the contrast of phenomena, the intellect does not require any shocks and inner upheavals; it is only through such upheavals that the more conservative mind could accommodate to the metropolitan rhythm of events. Thus the metropolitan type of man— which, of course, exists in a thousand individual variants—develops an organ protecting him against the threatening currents and discrepancies of his external environment which would uproot him. He reacts with his head instead of his heart. In this an increased awareness assumes the psychic prerogative. Metropolitan life, thus, underlies a heightened awareness and a predominance of intelligence in metropolitan man. The reaction to metropolitan phenomena is shifted to that organ which is least sensitive and quite remote from the depth of the personality. Intellectuality is thus seen to preserve subjective life against the overwhelming power of metropolitan life, and intellectuality branches out in many directions and is integrated with numerous discrete phenomena.

The metropolis has always been the seat of the money economy. Here the multiplicity and concentration of economic exchange gives an importance to the means of exchange which the scantiness of rural commerce would not have allowed. Money economy and the dominance of the intellect are intrinsically connected. They share a matter-of-fact attitude in dealing with men and with things; and, in this attitude, a formal justice is often coupled with an inconsiderate hardness. The intellectually sophisticated person is indifferent to all genuine individuality, because relationships and reactions result from it which cannot be exhausted with logical operations. In the same manner, the individuality of phenomena is not commensurate with the pecuniary principle. Money is concerned only with what is common to all: it asks for the exchange value, it reduces all quality and individuality to the question: How much? All intimate emotional relations between persons are founded in their individuality, whereas in rational relations man is reckoned with like a number, like an element which is in itself indifferent. Only the objective measurable achievement is of interest. Thus metropolitan man reckons with his merchants and customers, his domestic servants and often even with persons with whom he is obliged to have social intercourse. These features of intellectuality contrast with the nature of the small circle in which the inevitable knowledge of individuality as inevitably produces a warmer tone of behaviour, a behavior which is beyond a mere objective balancing of service and return. In the sphere of the economic psychology of the small group it is of importance that under primitive conditions production serves the customer who orders the good, so that the producer and the consumer are acquainted. The modern metropolis, however, is supplied almost entirely by production for the market, that is, for entirely unknown purchasers who never personally enter the producer's actual field of vision. Through this anonymity the interests of each party acquire an unmerciful matter-of-factness; and the intellectually calculating economic egoisms of both parties need not fear any deflection because of the imponderables of personal relationships. The money economy dominates the metropolis; it has displaced the last survivals of domestic production and the direct barter of goods; it minimizes, from day to day, the amount of work ordered by customers. The matter-of-fact attitude is obviously so intimately interrelated with the money econ-omy, which is dominant in the metropolis, that nobody can say whether the intellectualistic mentality first promoted the money economy or whether the latter determined the former. The metropolitan way of life is certainly the most fertile soil for this reciprocity, a point which I shall document merely by citing the dictum of the most eminent English constitutional historian: throughout the whole course of English history, London has never acted as England's heart but often as England's intellect and always as her moneybag!

In certain seemingly insignificant traits, which lie upon the surface of life, the same psychic currents characteristically unite. Modern mind has become more and more calculating. The calculative exactness of practical life which the money economy has brought about corresponds to the ideal of natural science: to transform the world into an arithmetic problem, to fix every part of the world by mathematical formulas. Only money economy has filled the days of so many people with weighing, calculating, with numerical determinations, with a reduction of qualitative values to quantitative ones. Through the calculative nature of money a new precision, a certainty in the definition of identities and differences, an unambiguousness in agreements and arrangements has been brought about in the relations of life-elements—just as externally this precision has been effected by the universal diffusion of pocket watches. However, the conditions of metropolitan life are at once cause and effect of this trait. The relationships and affairs of the typical metropolitan usually are so varied and complex that without the strictest punctuality in promises and services the whole structure would break down into an inextricable chaos. Above all, this necessity is brought about by the aggregation of so many people with such dif-ferentiated interests, who must integrate their relation and activities into a high-ly complex organism. If all clocks and watches in Berlin would suddenly go wrong in different ways, even if only by one hour, all economic life and com-munication of the city would be disrupted for a long time. In addition an appar-ently mere external factor: long distances, would make all waiting and broken appointments result in an ill afforded waste of time. Thus, the technique of met-ropolitan life is unimaginable without the most punctual integration of all activities and mutual relations into a stable and impersonal time schedule. Here again the general conclusions of this entire task of reflection become obvious, namely, that from each point on the surface of existence—however closely attached to the surface alone—one may drop a sounding into the depth of the psyche so that all the most banal externalities of life finally are connected with the ultimate decisions concerning the meaning and style of life. Punctuality, calculability, exactness are forced upon life by the complexity and extension of metropolitan existence and are not only most intimately connected with its money economy and intellectualistic character. These traits must also color the contents of life and favor the exclusion of those irrational, instinctive, sovereign traits and impulses which aim at determining the mode of life from within, instead of receiving the general and precisely schematized form of life from without. Even though sovereign types of personality, characterized by irrational impulses, are by no means impossible in the city, they are, nevertheless, opposed to typical city life. The passionate hatred of men like Ruskin and Nietzche for the metropolis is understandable in these terms. Their natures discovered the value of life alone in the unschematized existence which cannot be defined with precision for all alike. From the same source of this hatred of the metropolis surged their hatred of money economy and of the intellectualism of modern existence.

The same factors which have thus coalesced into the exactness and minute precision of the form of life have coalesced into a structure of the highest impersonality; on the other hand, they have promoted a highly personal subjectivity. There is perhaps no psychic phenomenon which has been so unconditionally reserved to the metropolis as has the blasé attitude. The blasé attitude results first from the rapidly changing and closely compressed contrasting stimulations of the nerves. From this, the enhancement of metropolitan intellectuality, also, seems originally to stem. Therefore, stupid people who are not intellectually alive in the first place usually are not exactly blasé. A life in boundless pursuit of pleasure makes one blasé because it agitates the nerves to their strongest reactivity for such a long time that they finally cease to react at all. In the same way, through the rapidity and contradictoriness of their changes, more harmless impressions force such violent response, tearing the nerves so brutally hither and thither that their last reserves of strength are spent; and if one remains in the same milieu they have no time to gather new strength. An incapacity thus emerges to react to new sensations with the appropriate energy. This constitutes that blasé attitude which, in fact, every metropolitan child shows when compared with children of quieter and less changeable milieus.

This physiological source of the metropolitan blasé attitude is joined by another source which flows from the money economy. The essence of the blasé attitude consists in the blunting of discrimination. This does not mean that the objects are not perceived, as is the case with the half-wit, but rather than the meaning and differing values of things, and thereby the things themselves, are experienced as insubstantial. They appear to the blasé person in an evenly flat and gray tone; no one object deserves preference to any other. This mood is the faithful subjective reflection of the completely internalized money economy. By being the equivalent to all the manifold things in one and the same way, money becomes the most frightful leveler. For money expresses all qualitative differences of things in terms of "how much?" Money, with all its colorlessness and indifference, becomes the common denominator of all values; irreparably it hollows out the core of things, their individuality, their specific value, and their incomparability. All things float with equal specific gravity in the constantly moving stream of money. All things lie on the same level and differ from one another only in the size of the area which they cover. In the individual case this coloration, or rather discoloration, of things through their money equivalence may be unnoticeably minute. However, through the relations of the rich to the objects to be had for money, perhaps even through the total character which the mentality of the contemporary public everywhere imparts to these objects, the exclusively pecuniary evaluation of objects has become quite considerable. The large cities, the main seats of the money exchange, bring the purchasability of things to the fore much more impressively than do smaller localities. That is why cities are also the genuine locale of the blasé attitude. In the blasé attitude the concentration of men and things stimulate the nervous system of the individual to its highest achievement so that it attains its peak. Through the mere quantitative intensification of the same conditioning factors this achievement is transformed into its opposite and appears in the peculiar adjustment of the blasé attitude. In this phenomenon the nerves find in the refusal to react to their stimulation the last possibility of accommodating to the contents and form of metropolitan life. The self-preservation of certain personalities is bought at the price of devaluating the whole objective world, a devaluation which in the end unavoidably drags one's own personality down into a feeling of the same worthlessness.

Whereas the subject of this form of existence has to come to terms with it entirely for himself, his self-preservation in the face of the large city demands from him a no less negative behavior of a social nature. This mental attitude of metropolitans toward one another we may designate, from a formal point of view, as reserve. If so many inner reactions were responses to the continuous external contacts with innumerable people as are those in the small town, where one knows almost everybody one meets and where one has a positive relation to almost everyone, one would be completely atomized internally and come to an unimaginable psychic state. Partly this psychological fact, partly the right to distrust which men have in the face of the touch-and-go elements of metropolitan life, necessitates our reserve. As a result of this reserve we frequently do not even know by sight those who have been our neighbors for years. And it is this reserve which in the eyes of the small-town people makes us appear to be cold and heartless. Indeed, if I do not deceive myself, the inner aspect of this outer reserve is not only indifference but, more often that we are aware, it is a slight aversion, a mutual strangeness and repulsion, which will break into hatred and fight at the moment of a closer contact, however caused. The whole inner organization of such an extensive communicative life rests upon an extremely varied hierarchy of sympathies, indifference, and aversions of the briefest as well as of the most permanent nature. The sphere of indifference in this hierarchy is not as large as might appear on the surface. Our psychic activity still responds to almost every impression of somebody else with a somewhat distinct feeling. The unconscious, fluid and changing character of this impression seems to result in a state of indifference. Actually this indifference would be just as unnatural as the diffusion of indiscriminate mutual suggestion would be unbearable. From both these typical dangers of the metropolis, indifference and indiscriminate suggestibility, antipathy protects us. A latent antipathy and the preparatory stage of practical antagonism effect the distances and aversions without which this mode of life could not at all be led. The extent and the mixture of this style of life, the rhythm of its emergence and disappearance, the forms in which it is satisfied—all these, with the unifying motives in the narrower sense, form the inseparable whole of the metropolitan style of life. What appears in the metropolitan style of life directly as dissociation is in reality only one of its elemental forms of socialization.

This reserve with its overtone of hidden aversion appears in turn as the form or the cloak of a more general mental phenomenon of the metropolis: it grants to the individual a kind and an amount of personal freedom which has no analogy whatsoever under other conditions. The metropolis goes back to one of the large developmental tendencies of social life as such, to one of the few tendencies for which an approximately universal formula can be discovered. The earliest phase of social formations found in historical as well as in contemporary social structures is this: a relatively small circle firmly closed against neighbouring, strange, or in some way antagonistic circles. However, this circle is closely coherent and allows its individual members only a narrow field for the development of unique qualities and free, self-responsible movements. Political and kinship groups, parties and religious associations begin in this way. The self-preservation of very young associations requires the establishment of strict boundaries and a centripetal unity. Therefore they cannot allow the individual freedom and unique inner and outer development. From this stage social development proceeds at once in two different, yet corresponding, directions. To the extent to which the group grows—numerically, spatially, in significance and in content of life—to the same degree the group's direct, inner unity loosens, and the rigidity of the original demarcation against others is softened through mutual relations and connections. At the same time, the individual gains freedom of movement, far beyond the first jealous delimitation. The individual also gains a specific individuality to which the division of labor in the enlarged group gives both occasion and necessity. The state and Christianity, guilds and political parties, and innumerable other groups have developed according to this formula, however much, of course, the special conditions and forces of the respective groups have modified the general scheme. This scheme seems to me distinctly recognizable also in the evolution of individuality within urban life. The small-town life in Antiquity and in the Middle Ages set barriers against movement and relations of the individual toward the outside, and it set up barriers against individual independence and differentiation within the individual self. These barriers were such that under them modern man could not have breathed. Even today a metropolitan man who is placed in a small town feels a restriction similar, at least, in kind. The smaller the circle which forms our milieu is, and the more restricted those relations to others are which dissolve the boundaries of the individual, the more anxiously the circle guards the achievements, the conduct of life, and the outlook of the individual, and the more readily a quantitative and qualitative specialization would break up the framework of the whole little circle.

The ancient *polis* in this respect seems to have had the very character of a small town. The constant threat to its existence at the hands of enemies from near and afar effected strict coherence in political and military respects, a supervision of the citizen by the citizen, a jealousy of the whole against the individual whose particular life was suppressed to such a degree that he could compensate only by acting as a despot in his own household. The tremendous agitation and excitement, the unique colorfulness of Athenian life, can perhaps be understood in terms of the fact that a people of incomparably individualized personalities struggled against the constant inner and outer pressure of a de-individualizing small town. This produced a tense atmosphere in which the weaker individuals were suppressed and those of stronger natures were incited to prove themselves in the most passionate manner. This is precisely why it was that there blossomed in Athens what must be called, without defining it exactly, "the general human character" in the intellectual development of our species. For we maintain factual as well as historical validity for the following connection: the most extensive and the most general contents and forms of life are most intimately connected with the most individual ones. They have a preparatory stage in common, that is, they find their enemy in narrow formations and groupings the maintenance of which places both of them into a state of defense against expanse and generality lying without and the freely moving individuality within. Just as in the feudal age, the "free" man was the one who stood under the law of the land, that is, under the law of the largest social orbit, and the unfree man was the one who derived his right merely form the narrow circle of a feudal association and was excluded from the larger social orbit— so today metropolitan man is "free" in a spiritualized and refined sense, in contrast to the pettiness and prejudices which hem in the small-town man. For the reciprocal reserve and indifference and the intellectual life conditions of large circles are never felt more strongly by the individual in their impact upon his independence than in the thickest crowd of the big city. This is because the bodily proximity and narrowness of space makes the mental distance only the more visible. It is obviously only the obverse of this freedom if, under certain circumstances, one nowhere feels as lonely and lost as in the metropolitan crowd. For here as elsewhere it is by no means necessary that the freedom of man be reflected in his emotional life as comfort.

It is not only the immediate size of the area and the number of persons which, because of the universal historical correlation between the enlargement of the circle and the personal inner and outer freedom, has made the metropolis the locale of freedom. It is rather in transcending this visible expanse that any given city becomes the seat of cosmopolitanism. The horizon of the city expands in a manner comparable to the way in which wealth develops; a certain amount of property increases in a quasi-automatical way in ever more rapid progression. As soon as a certain limit has been passed, the economic, personal, and intellectual relations of the citizenry, the sphere of intellectual predominance of the city over its hinterland, grow as in geometrical progression. Every gain in dynamic extension becomes a step; not for an equal, but for a new and larger extension. From every thread spinning out of the city, ever new threads grow as if by themselves, just as within the city the unearned increment of ground rent, through the mere increase in communication, brings the owner automatically increasing profits. At this point, the quantitative aspect of life is transformed directly into qualitative traits of character. The sphere of life of the small town is, in the main, self-contained and autarchic. For it is the decisive nature of the metropolis that its inner life overflows by waves into a far-flung national or international area. Weimar is not an example to the contrary, since its significance was hinged upon individual personalities and died with them; whereas the metropolis is indeed characterized by its essential independence even from the most eminent individual personalities. This is the counterpart to the independence, and it is the price the individual pays for the independence, which he enjoys in the metropolis. The most significant characteristic of the metropolis is this functional extension beyond its physical boundaries. And this efficacy reacts in turn and gives weight, importance, and responsibility to metropolitan life. Man does not end with the limits of his body or the area comprising his immediate activity. Rather is the range of the person constituted by the sum of effects emanating from him temporally and spatially. In the same way, a city consists of its total effects which extend beyond its immediate confines. Only this range is the city's actual extent in which its existence is expressed. This fact makes it obvious that individual freedom, the logical and historical complement of such extension, is not to be understood only in the negative sense of mere freedom of mobility and elimination of prejudices and petty philistinism. The essential point is that the particularity and incomparability, which ultimately every human being possesses, be somehow expressed in the working-out of a way of life. That we follow the laws of our own nature—and this after all is freedom—becomes obvious and convincing to ourselves and to others only if the expression of this nature differ from the expressions of others. Only our unmistakableness proves that our way of life has not been superimposed by others.

Cities are, first of all, seats of the highest economic division of labor. They produce thereby such extreme phenomena as in Paris the renumerative occupation of the *quatorzième*. They are persons who identify themselves by signs on their residences and who are ready at the dinner hour in correct attire, so that they can be quickly called upon if a dinner party should consist of thirteen persons. In the measure of its expansion, the city offers more and more the decisive conditions of the division of labor. It offers a circle which through its size can absorb a highly diverse variety of services. At the same time, the concentration of individuals and their struggle for customers compel the individual to specialize in a function from which he cannot be readily displaced by another. It is decisive that city life has transformed the struggle with nature for livelihood into an inter-human struggle for gain, which here is not granted by nature but by other men. For specialization does not flow only from the competition for gain but also from the underlying fact that the seller must always seek to call forth new and differentiated needs of the lured customer. In order to find a source of income which is not yet exhausted, and to find a function which cannot readily be displaced, it is necessary to specialize in one's services. This process promotes differentiation, refinement, and the enrichment of the public's needs, which obviously must lead to growing personal differences within this public.

All this forms the transition to the individualization of mental and psychic traits which the city occasions in proportion to its size. There is a whole series of obvious causes underlying this process. First, one must meet the difficulty of asserting his own personality within the dimensions of metropolitan life. Where the quantitative increase in importance and the expense of energy reach their limits, one seizes upon qualitative differentiation in order somehow to attract the attention of the social circle by playing upon its sensitivity for differences. Finally, man is tempted to adopt the most tendentious peculiarities, that is, the specifically metropolitan extravagances of mannerism, caprice, and preciousness. Now, the meaning of these extravagances does not at all lie in the contents of such behavior, but rather in its form of "being different," of standing out in a striking manner and thereby attracting attention. For many character types, ultimately the only means of saving for themselves some modicum of self-esteem and the sense of filling a position is indirect, through the awareness of others. In the same sense a seemingly insignificant factor is operating, the cumulative effects of which are, however, still noticeable. I refer to the brevity and scarcity of the inter-human contacts granted to the metropolitan man, as compared with social intercourse in the small town. The temptation to appear "to the point," to appear concentrated and strikingly characteristic, lies much closer to the individual in brief metropolitan contacts than in an atmosphere in which frequent and prolonged association assures the personality of an unambiguous image of himself in the eyes of the other.

The most profound reason, however, why the metropolis conduces to the urge for the most individual personal existence—no matter whether justified and successful—appears to me to be the following: the development of modern culture is characterized by the preponderance of what one may call the "objective spirit" over the "subjective spirit." This is to say, in language as well as in law, in the technique of production as well as in art, in science as well as in the objects of the domestic environment, there is embodied a sum of spirit. The individual in his intellectual development follows the growth of this spirit very imperfectly and at an ever increasing distance. If, for instance, we view the immense culture which for the last hundred years has been embodied in things and in knowledge, in institutions and in comforts, and if we compare all this with the cultural progress of the individual during the same period—at least in high status groups—a frightful disproportion in growth between the two become evident. Indeed, at some points we notice a retrogression in the culture of the individual with reference to spirituality, delicacy, and idealism. This discrepancy results essentially from the growing division of labor. For the division of labor demands from the individual an ever more one-sided accomplishment, and the greatest advance in a one-sided pursuit only too frequently means death to the personality of the individual. In any case, he can cope less and less with the overgrowth of objective culture. The individual is reduced to negligible quantity, perhaps less in his consciousness than in his practice and in the totality of his obscure emotional states that are derived from this practice. The individual has become a mere cog in an enormous organization of things and powers which tear from his hands all progress, spirituality, and value in order to transform them from their subjective form into the form of a purely objective life. It needs merely to be pointed out that the metropolis is the genuine arena of this culture which outgrows all personal life. Here in buildings and educational institutions, in the wonders and comforts of space-conquering technology, in the formations of community life, and in the visible institutions of the state, is offered such an overwhelming fullness of crystallized and impersonalized spirit that the personality, so to speak, cannot maintain itself under its impact. On the one hand, life is made infinitely easy for the personality in that stimulation, interests, uses of time and consciousness are offered to it from all sides. They carry the person as if in a stream and one needs hardly to swim for oneself. On the other hand, however, life is composed more and more of these impersonal contents and offerings which tend to displace the genuine personal colorations and incomparabilities. This results in the individual's summoning the utmost in uniqueness and particularization, in order to preserve his most personal core. He has to exaggerate this personal element in order to remain audible even to himself. The atrophy of individual culture through the hypertrophy of objective culture is one reason for the bitter hatred which the preachers of the most extreme individualism, above all Nietzsche, harbor against the metropolis. But it is, indeed, also a reason why these preachers are so passionately loved in the metropolis and why they appear to the metropolitan man as the prophets and saviors of his most unsatisfied yearnings.

If one asks for the historical position of these two forms of individualism which are nourished by the quantitative relation of the metropolis, namely, individual independence and the elaboration of individuality itself, then the metropolis assumes an entirely new rank order in the world history of the spirit. The eighteenth century found the individual in oppressive bonds which had become meaningless—bonds of a political, agrarian, guild, and religious character. They were restraints which, so to speak, forced upon man an unnatural form and outmoded, unjust inequalities. In this situation the cry for liberty and equality arose, the belief in the individual's full freedom or movement in all social and intellectual relationships. Freedom would at once permit the noble substance common to all to come to the fore, a substance which nature had deposited in every man and which society and history had only deformed. Besides this eighteenth-century ideal of liberalism, in the nineteenth century, through Goethe and Romanticism on the one hand and through the economic division of labor, on the other hand, another ideal arose: individuals liberated from historical bonds now wished to distinguish themselves from one another. The carrier of man's values is no longer the "general human being" in every individual, but rather man's qualitative uniqueness and irreplaceability. The external and internal history of our time takes its course within the struggle and in the changing entanglements of these two ways of defining the individual's role in the whole of society. It is the function of the metropolis to provide the arena for this struggle and its reconciliation. For the metropolis presents the peculiar conditions which are revealed to us as the opportunities and the stimuli for the development of both these ways of allocating roles to men. Therewith these conditions gain a unique place, pregnant with inestimable meanings for the development of psychic existence. The metropolis reveals itself as one of those great historical formations in which opposing streams which enclose life unfold, as well as join one another with equal right. However, in this process the currents of life, whether their individual phenomena touch us sympathetically or antipathetically, entirely transcend the sphere for which the judge's attitude is appropriate. Since such forces of life have grown into the roots and into the crown of the whole of the historical life in which we, in our fleeting existence, as a cell, belong only as a part, it is not our task either to accuse or to pardon, but only to understand.[1]

Notes
1. The content of this lecture by its very nature does not derive from a citable literature. Argument and elaboration of its major cultural-historical ideas are contained in my *Philosophie des Geldes* [*The Philosophy of Money*; München und Leipzig: Duncker und Humblot, 1900].

13

THE LEGACY OF SIMMEL: DAVID RIESMAN (1909-)

David Riesman continued Simmel's inquiries into the relationship between social structure and social character. Simmel explored how the metropolis shaped mental life; since the city is the seat of the money economy, his analysis focused not only on the metropolis but also on capitalism as a force that creates a certain type of person—calculating, time-oriented, smart, sophisticated, blasé, individualistic, and liberated from small-town conformity.

Fifty years later, in the late 1940s, Riesman asked what type of person was being formed in the emerging consumer capitalist societies in the developed nations. He identified three periods of history, each with its own character type.

First was the period of tradition-oriented character. It was a period of high birth and death rates, agrarian economies, cohesive communities with shared values, and slow social change. The tradition-oriented character was guided by the strong collective mores and folkways of the community.

The second period was the phase of emerging industrial capitalism, characterized by population growth and a strong emphasis on increasing economic production. Those nations that became developed, industrialized capitalist countries went through this phase. Its characteristic type was inner-directed, guided by internalized norms and values learned from parents; there was an intensity and "drivenness" about the inner-directed, whether they were moralistic or ruthless and greedy (or both). The "self-made man" of nineteenth-century capitalism was the archetype of the inner-directed person, who was more individualistic than the tradition-directed and tended to adhere to internalized values even when separated from community and family.

The third type, the other-directed type, is characteristic of advanced capitalist societies that emphasize services and consumption, rather than industrial production; these societies have stable populations, a result of changing women's roles and effective birth-control methods. The other-directed are guided by peers and the media. They do not have a specific set of internalized values and goals, but only internalized mechanisms that allow them to sense and adapt to changing expectations of others.

Riesman and his research team identified times and places where each of these character types might be found. Most of human history had been spent in tradition-oriented communities, which persisted in agrarian societies. There were still some vestiges of tradition-orientation in the United States among recent immigrants from places like rural Mexico and southern Italy and among African Americans in rural areas of the South. Inner-directed types were located historically in early industrializing nations in western Europe. Although not all inner-directed people were Protestant, there was considerable overlap between their character type and the Protestant Ethic described by Weber. In the postwar United States, inner-directed types could be found in small town America, especially in the Northeast and Midwest, among small business owners, and white Protestants. Riesman pointed out that the other-directed type was as yet mostly an American phenomenon, associated with middle classes in large cities and suburbs of the United States. He believed that this type would eventually become visible in all societies with low birth and death rates and advanced economies.

The research team identified communities and institutions (especially different types of high schools) in the United States where there were likely to be large concentrations of each type and conducted interviews that explored values, norms, patterns of conformity, and the sense of self. These interviews constitute some of the empirical evidence backing up the theory and were published in a volume entitled *Faces in the Crowd*. The theoretical analysis was published in a study called *The Lonely Crowd*. It became popular in the 1950s among educated young people who were producing the Baby Boom and wondering if their children would fit Riesman's predictions.

The following selections from *The Lonely Crowd* illustrate Riesman's ideas about social character, especially his predictions about the other-directed. The selections include a definition of other-direction, a description of how other-direction is formed in the adolescent peer group, and a reflection about how the other-directed experience sex. It concludes with a short quote about "the inside dopester"; Riesman believed that politics was increasingly turning into a spectator sport, rather than an arena for pursuing morality and/or self-interest. The other-directed person is generally cynical about political institutions, but feels compelled to "be in the know." Of course, there are differences by class and education—the readers of the *New York Times* and viewers of the PBS *News Hour* are not identical to readers of *The National Enquirer*; however, the same spirit of inside dopesterism impels them to know a lot about situations they believe they cannot influence themselves.

I hope that you will be as surprised as I always feel when I reread Riesman and see how accurately he predicted the emergence and expansion of other-direction. What he says about teen culture, peer pressure, the media, consumer "choice," sexual practices, and inside-dopesterism seems as fresh today as 50 years ago.

Readings
Lasch, Christopher. *The Culture of Narcissism*. New York: Norton, 1978.

Riesman, David, and Nathan Glazer. *Faces in the Crowd.* New York: Ayer, 1980.

Sennett, Richard. *The Corrosion of Character: The Personal Consequences of Work in the New Capitalism.* New York: W.W. Norton, 1998.

Slater, Philip. *The Pursuit of Loneliness.* Boston: Beacon Press, 1970.

The Lonely Crowd
DAVID RIESMAN

Character and Society

Bearing these qualifications in mind, it seems appropriate to treat contemporary metropolitan America as our illustration of a society—so far, perhaps, the only illustration—in which other direction is the dominant mode of insuring conformity. It would be premature, however, to say that it is already the dominant mode in America as a whole. But since the other-directed types are to be found among the young, in the larger cities, and among the upper income groups, we may assume that, unless present trends are reversed; the hegemony of other-direction lies not far off.

If we wanted to cast our social character types into social class molds, we could say that inner-direction is the typical character of the "old" middle class-the banker, the tradesman, the small entrepreneur, the technically oriented engineer, etc.—while other-direction is becoming the typical character of the "new" middle class—the bureaucrat, the salaried employee in business, etc. Many of the economic factors associated with the recent growth of the "new" middle class are well known. There is a decline in the numbers and in the proportion of the working population engaged in production and extraction—agriculture, heavy industry, heavy transport—and an increase in the numbers and the proportion engaged in white-collar work and the service trades. People who are literate, educated, and provided with the necessities of life by an ever more efficient machine industry and agriculture, turn increasingly to the "tertiary" economic realm. The service industries prosper among the people as a whole and no longer only in court circles.

Education, leisure, services, these go together with an increased consumption of words and images from the new mass media of communications. While societies in the phase of transitional growth step up the process of distributing words from urban centers, the flow becomes a torrent in the societies of incipient population decline. This process, while modulated by profound national and class differences, connected with differences in literacy and loquacity, takes place everywhere in the industrialized lands. Increasingly, relations with the outer world and with oneself are mediated by the flow of mass communication. For the other-directed types political events are likewise experienced through a screen of words by which the events are habitually atomized and personalized—or pseudo-personalized. For the inner-directed person who remain still extant in this period the tendency is rather to systematize and moralize this flow of words.

These developments lead, for large numbers of people, to changes in paths to success and to the requirement of more "socialized" behavior both for success and for marital and personal adaptation. Connected with such changes are changes in the family and in child-rearing practices. In the smaller families of urban life, and with the spread of "permissive" child care to ever wider strata of the population, there is a relaxation of older patterns of discipline. Under these newer patterns the peer-group (the group of one's associates of the same age and class) becomes much more important to the child, while the parents make him feel guilty not so much about violation of inner standards as about failure to be popular or otherwise to manage his relations with these other children. Moreover, the pressures of the school and the peer-group are reinforced and continued—in a manner whose inner paradoxes I shall discuss later—by the mass media: movies, radio, comics, and popular culture media generally. Under these conditions types of character emerge that we shall here term other-directed.... *What is common to all the other-directed people is that their contemporaries are the source of direction for the individual—either those known to him or those with whom he is indirectly acquainted, through friends and through the mass media. This source is of course "internalized" in the sense that dependence on it for guidance in life is implanted early. The goals toward which the other-directed person strives shift with that guidance: it is only the process of striving itself and the process of paying close attention to the signals from others that remain un-altered throughout life.* This mode of keeping in touch with others permits a close behavioral conformity, not through drill in behavior itself, as in the tradition-directed character, but rather through an exceptional sensitivity to the actions and wishes of others....

The three types compared. One way to see the structural differences that mark the three types is to see the differences in the emotional sanction or control in each type.

The tradition-directed person feels the impact of his culture as a unit, but it is nevertheless mediated through the specific, small number of individuals with whom he is in daily contact. These expect of him not so much that he be a certain type of person but that he behave in the approved way. Consequently the sanction for behavior tends to be the fear of being *shamed*.

The inner-directed person has early incorporated a psychic gyroscope which is set going by his parents and can receive signals later on from other authorities who resemble his parents. He goes through life less independent than he seems, obeying this internal piloting. Getting off course, whether in response to inner impulses or to the fluctuating voices of contemporaries, may lead to the feeling of *guilt*.

Since the direction to be taken in life has been learned in the privacy of the home from a small number of guides and since principles, rather than details of behavior, are internalized, the inner-directed person is capable of great stability. Especially so when it turns out that his fellows have gyroscopes too, spinning at the same speed and set in the same direction. But many inner-directed individuals can remain stable even when the reinforcement of social approval is not available—as in the upright life of the stock Englishman isolated in the tropics.

Contrasted with such a type as this, the other-directed person learns to respond to signals from a far wider circle than constituted by his parents. The family is no longer a closely knit unit to which he belongs but merely part of a wider social environment to which he early becomes attentive. In these respects the other directed person resembles the tradition-directed person: both live in a group milieu and lack the inner-directed person's capacity to go it alone. The nature of this group milieu, however, differs radically in the two cases. The other-directed person is cosmopolitan. For him the border between the familiar and the strange—a border clearly marked in the societies depending on tradition-direction—has broken down. As the family continuously absorbs the strange and reshapes itself, so the strange becomes familiar. While the inner-directed person could be "at home abroad" by virtue of his relative insensitivity to others, the other-directed person is, in at sense, at home everywhere and nowhere, capable of a rapid if sometimes superficial intimacy with and response to everyone.

The tradition-directed person takes his signals from others, but they come in a cultural monotone; he needs no complex receiving equipment to pick them up. The other-directed person must be able to receive signals from far and near; the sources are many, the changes rapid. What can be internalized, then, is not a code of behavior but the elaborate equipment needed to attend to such messages and occasionally to participate in their circulation. As against guilt-and-shame controls, though of course these survive, one prime psychological lever of the other-directed person is a diffuse *anxiety*. This control equipment, instead of being like a gyroscope, is like a radar.[1]...

The Peer-group in the Stage of Other-direction
The parents in the era dominated by other-direction lose their once undisputed role; the old man is no longer "the governor"—and the installer of governors. Other adult authorities such as the governess and grandmother either almost disappear or, like the teacher, take on the new role of peer-group facilitator and mediator—a role not too different perhaps from that of many clergy-men who, in the adult congregation, move from morality to morale.

As already indicated, moreover, the city in which the other-directed child grows up is large enough and stratified enough—taking into account its ring of suburbs—to create an age- and class-graded group for him. It will be possible to put him into school and playground, and camp in the summer, with other children of virtually the same age and social position. If the adults are the judge, these peers are the jury. And, as in America the judge is hemmed in by rules which give the jury a power it has in no other common-law land, so the American peer-group, too, cannot be matched for power throughout the middle class-world.

The Trial. While the inner-directed parent frequently forced the pace of the child in its home "duties," as, for example, in cleanliness and toilet-training habits, the other-directed parent, more apt to be permissive in such matters, forces the pace, with like impatience, in the child's social life, though often hardly aware of doing so. Parents today are the stage managers for the meetings of three- and four-year-olds, just as, in earlier eras, the adults managed marriages. Hence, while "self-demand" feeding schedules are gaining ground for infants, self-demand is not observed when it comes to socialization outside the home. The daily schedule is an effort, with mother as chauffeur and booking agent, to cultivate all the currently essential talents, especially the gregarious ones. It is inconceivable to some supervising adults that a child might prefer his own company or that of just one other child.

The child is thus confronted by what we have termed his sociometric peers and is not surrounded by those who are his peers in less visible matters, such as temperament and taste. Yet since there are no *visible* differences he is hard put to it to justify, even to be aware of, these *invisible* differences. On the overt level the situation is highly standardized: any given child faces the culture of the fives or the sixes at a particular moment of the fashion cycle in child-training and child-amusement practices. Indeed it is this very standardization which, as we saw, weakens the power of the parents, whose deviation from the standards is felt by them and by the child to demonstrate their inexperience and inadequacy. In this setting the adults are anxious that the child succeed in the peer-group and therefore are concerned with his "adjustment." They, too, tend to ignore and even suppress invisible differences between their child and the children of others. Such differences might cast doubt on their own adjustment, their own correct tuning to the signals concerning child rearing.

The majority of children learn very fast under these conditions; the same adult authorities who patronize children's intellects (and therefore slow them down) are perhaps not sufficiently impressed with how poised in many social situations modern other-directed children are. These children are not shy, either with adults or with the opposite sex whom they have accompanied to proms and parties and seen daily in and out of school. This adaptability, moreover, prepares the child for a type of social mobility somewhat different from the social-climbing experiences of the parvenue in an inner-directed environment. The latter only rarely acquired the intellectual and social graces of his new associates—or he ridiculously accentuated them. He either kept his rough and lowly manners or painfully tried to learn new ones as he moved up; in either case the standard, limited code of conduct expected of him was unequivocal. In contrast with this the other-directed child is able to move among new associates with an almost automatic adjustment to the subtlest insignia of status.

Bearing in mind these positive achievements of other-directed sociability, let us turn our attention from what the peer-group teaches and evokes to what it represses. Today six-year-olds and up have a phrase—"he [or she] thinks he's *big*" (or "he thinks he's *something*")—which symbolizes the role of the peer-group in the creation of other-directed types. The effort is to cut everyone down to size who stands up or stands out in any direction. Beginning with the very young and going on from there, overt vanity is treated as one of the worst offenses, as perhaps dishonesty would have been in an earlier day. Being high-hat is forbidden.

Temper, manifest jealousy, moodiness—these, too, are offenses in the code of the peer-group. All knobby or idiosyncratic qualities and vices are more or less eliminated or repressed. And judgments of others by peer-group members are so clearly matters of taste that their expression has to resort to the vaguest phrases, constantly changed: cute, lousy, square, darling, good guy, honey, swell, bitch (without precise meaning), etc. Sociometry reflects this situation when it asks children about such things as whom they like to sit next to or not to sit next to, to have for a friend, a leader, and so on. The judgments can be meaningfully scaled because, and only because, they are all based on uncomplicated continua of taste, on which the children are constantly ranking each other.

But to say that judgments of peer-groupers are matters of taste, not of morality or even opportunism, is not to say that any particular child can afford to ignore these judgments. On the contrary he is, as never before, at their mercy. If the peer-group were—and we continue to deal here with the urban middle classes only—a wild, torturing, obviously vicious group, the individual child might still feel moral indignation as a defense against its commands. But like adult authorities in the other-directed socialization process, the peer-group is friendly and tolerant. It stresses fair play. Its conditions for entry seem reasonable and well meaning. But even where this is not so, moral indignation is out of fashion. The child is therefore exposed to trial by jury without any defenses either from the side of its own morality or from the adults. All the morality is the group's. Indeed, even the fact that it is a morality is concealed by the confusing notion that the function of the group is to have fun, to play; the deadly seriousness of the business, which might justify the child in making an issue of it, is therefore hidden.

"The Talk of the Town": The Socialization of Preferences. In the eyes of the jury of peers one may be a good guy one day, a stinker the next. Toleration, let alone leadership, depends on having a highly sensitive response to swings of fashion. This ability is sought in several ways. One way is to surrender any claim to independence of judgment and taste—a kind of plea of nolo contendere. Another is to build a plea for special consideration by acquiring unusual facility in one's duties as a consumer—in performance, that is, of the leisurely arts. With good luck one may even become a taste and opinion leader, with great influence over the jury.

Each particular peer-group has its fandoms and lingoes. Safety consists not in mastering a difficult craft but in mastering a battery of consumer preferences and the mode of their expression. The preferences are for articles or "heroes" of consumption and for members of the group itself. The proper mode of expression requires feeling out with skill and sensitivity the probable tastes of the others and then swapping mutual likes and dislikes to maneuver intimacy.

Now some of this is familiar even in this period depending on inner-direction; it is important, therefore, to realize the degree to which training in consumer taste has replaced training in etiquette. Formal etiquette may be thought of as a means of handling relations with people with whom one does not seek intimacy. It is particularly useful when adults and young, men and women, upper classes and lower classes, are sharply separated and when a code is necessary to mediate exchanges across these lines. Thus etiquette can be at the same time a means of approaching people and of staying clear of them. For some, etiquette may be a matter of little emotional weight—an easy behavioral cloak; for others the ordering of human relations through etiquette can become highly charged emotionally—an evidence of characterological compulsiveness. But in either case etiquette is concerned not with encounters between individuals as such but with encounters between them as representatives of their carefully graded social roles.

In comparison with this, training in consumer taste, which tends to replace etiquette among the other-directed, is useful not so much across age and social class lines as within the jury room of one's age and class peers. As in some groups—children as well as adults—discussion turns to the marginal differentiation between Cadillacs and Lincolns, so in other groups discussion centers on Fords and Chevrolets. What matters in either case is an ability at continual sniffing out of others's tastes, often a far more intrusive process than the exchange of courtesies and pleasantries required by etiquette. Not, of course, that the child always gets close to the others with whom he is exchanging and ratifying preferences—these exchanges are often mere gossip about goods. Yet a certain emotional energy, even excitement, permeates the transaction. For one thing, the other-directed person acquires an intense interest in the ephemeral tastes of the "others"—an interest inconceivable to the tradition-directed or inner-directed child whose tastes have undergone a less differentiated socialization. For another thing, the other-directed child is concerned with learning from these interchanges whether his radar equipment is in proper order.

It has always been true in social classes dominated by fashion that to escape being left behind by a swing of fashion requires the ability to adopt new fashions rapidly; to escape the danger of a conviction for being different from the "others" requires that one can be different—in look and talk and manner— from *oneself* as one was yesterday. Here, also, it is necessary to see precisely what has changed. In general the processes of fashion are expanded in class terms and speeded in time terms. In the leisure economy of incipient population decline the distributive machinery of society improves, in terms of both distribution of income and of commodities. It becomes possible to accelerate swings of fashion as well as to differentiate goods by very minute gradients. For, in its late stages, mass production and mass distribution permit and require a vast increase not only in quantity but in qualitative differences among products—not only as a consequence of monopolistic efforts at marginal differentiation but also because the machinery and organization are present for rapidly designing, producing, and distributing a wide variety of goods.

This means that the consumer trainee has a lot more to learn than in the early days of industrialization. To take one example, the foreigner who visits America is likely to think that salesgirls, society ladies, and movie actresses all dress alike, as compared with the clear status differences of Europe. But the American knows—has to know if he is to get along in life and love—that this is simply an error: that one must look for small qualitative differences that signify style and status, to observe for instance the strained casualness sometimes found in upper-class dress as against the strained formality of working-class dress. In the days of etiquette the differences were far more sharp.

One must listen to quite young children discussing television models, automobile styling, or the merits of various streamliners to see how gifted they are as consumers long before they have a decisive say themselves—though their influence in family councils must not be underestimated. Children join in this exchange of verdicts even if their parents cannot afford the gadgets under discussion; indeed, the economy would slow down if only those were trained as consumers who at any given moment had the wherewithal....

Dating at twelve and thirteen, the child is early made aware of the fact that his taste in emotions as well as in consumer goods must be socialized and available for small talk. Whereas etiquette built barriers between people, socialized exchange of consumer taste requires that privacy either be given up, or be kept, like a liberal theologian's God, in some interstices of one's nature. Before the peer-group jury there is no privilege against self-incrimination....

The other-directed person's tremendous outpouring of energy is channeled into the ever expanding frontiers of consumption, as the inner-directed person's energy was channeled relentlessly into production. Inner-directed patterns often discouraged consumption for adults as well as children. But at other times, and especially in the higher social strata less affected by Puritan asceticism, the inner-directed person consumed—with time out, so to speak, for saving and for good behavior—as relentlessly as he (or his progenitors) produced. Most clearly in the case of upper-class conspicuous consumption, he lusted for possessions and display, once the old tradition-directed restraints had worn away. He pursued with a fierce individualism both the acquisition and consumption of property. To be sure, his goals were socially determined, but less by a contemporary union of consumers than by inherited patterns of desire, hardly less stable than the desire for money itself. Goals such as fine houses, fine horses, fine women, fine objects d'art—these could be investments because their value scarcely changed in the scale of consumer preference.

These relatively stable and individualistic pursuits are today being replaced by the fluctuating tastes which the other-directed person accepts from his peer-group. Moreover, many of the desires that drove men to work and to madness in societies depending on inner-direction are now satisfied relatively easily; they are incorporated into the standard of living taken for granted by millions. But the craving remains. It is a craving for the satisfactions others appear to attain, an objectless craving. The consumer today has most of his potential individuality trained out of him by his membership in the consumers' union. He is kept within his consumption limits not by goal-directed but by other directed guidance, kept from splurging too much by fear of others' envy, and from consuming too little by his own envy of the others.

Today there is no fast line that separates these consumption patterns of the adult world from those of the child, except the objects of consumption themselves. The child may consume comics or toys while the adult consumes editorials and cars; more and more both consume in the same way. In the consumers' union of the peer-group the child's discipline as a consumer begins today very early in life—and lasts late. The inner-directed child was supposed to be job-minded even if the job itself was not clear in his mind. Today the future occupation of all moppets is to be skilled consumers.

This is visible early in children's play-at-consumption, facilitated by a noticeable increase in the range of children's toys. Added to boys' toys, for example production-imitating equipment like trucks and steam shovels or toy soldiers and miniature war materiél, is a whole new range of objects modeled after the service trades: laundry trucks, toy telephones, service stations, and so forth. Added to girls' toys, the doll and her wardrobe, are juvenile make-up outfits and voice recorders.

These props of the child's playtime hours, however, are not so striking as the increasing rationalization of children's preferences in everything they consume. In the period of inner-direction children accepted trade-marked cereals largely because that was what was set for them at table. Today they eat Wheaties, or some other breakfast food, to the tune of some specific reason that all can talk about. "Wheaties makes champions." And comics, children will say if pressed, "relax champions." In this way the other-directed child rapidly learns that there always is and always must be a reason for consuming anything. One "reason" is that the commodity he is consuming is the "best" in its line. As the child develops as a consumer trainee, advertising no longer is given all the credit for answering the question of what is the best in its line. The product approved by most of the others, or by a suitable testimonial from a peer consumer, becomes the "best." The most popular products, by this formula are the products that happen to be used by the most popular. And to be sure, these pace setters themselves have a "reason", often enough picked out from the mass media, if not from the advertising pages; thus the hunt for the reason goes on in an endless regress. Blake wrote: "The child's toys and the old man's reasons/ Are the fruits of the two seasons." In the consumers' union, toys and reasons become amalgamated and, as already stated, the line between childhood and age tends to become an amorphous one.

These patterns place extra burdens on girls, partly because women are the accepted leaders of consumption in our society, partly because women, much more than men, feel pressure to play any role they are accepted in by the men. At every social level boys are permitted a greater amount of aggression then girls; they are also permitted a wider range of preferences and can get by with a good deal of aggressive resistance to the taste-exchanging process.

Finally, the child consumer trainee becomes a tutor in consumption in the home circle, "bringing up" mother as well as father. Teen-agers must initiate adults rather than vice versa; typical is the case, also cited in *Life*, where teachers at a Denver high school imitated the idiomatic greeting style of the "most popular" boy.

The Antagonistic Cooperators of the Peer-Group

It is, possibly, no accident that it was his *greeting style* on which this boy exercised his gifts for opinion leadership and marginal differentiation. For indeed, over and beyond the socialization of consumption preferences and the exchange of consumption shop-talk by this consumers' union, the membership is engaged in *consuming itself*. That is, people and friendships are viewed as the greatest of all consumables; the peer-group is itself a main object of consumption, its own main competition in taste. The "sociometric" exchange of peer-group ratings is ceaseless and is carried on, as a conversation with the self, in "private" also; who is my best friend, my next best, and so on, down to the most dis-liked. The more thoroughly other-directed the individual is, the more unhesitatingly able he is to classify his preferences and to compare them with those of others. In fact, as compared with their inner-directed predecessors, other-directed children are extraordinarily knowledgeable about popularity ratings. Physical prowess probably remains a chief road, though declining, to status among working-class boys. However, popularity among upper middle-class boys and girls seems to hinge on much more vague criteria, frequently impenetrable to the adult observer but, while they last, crystal clear to the peer-group itself.

The tremendous competitive energies which the inner-directed person had available for the sphere of production and, secondarily, for consumption seem now to flow into competition for the much more amorphous security of the peer-group's approval. But just because it is approval for which one is competing one must repress one's overt competitiveness. Here the phrase "antagonistic co-operation," borrowed from other contexts, is apt.

This transformation is so important that we devote several sections to it..., but now we need only note a few reference points. The parents, harking back as they do in their character structures to an earlier era, are themselves competitive—more overtly so than the children. Much of our ideology—free enterprise, individualism, and all the rest—remains competitive and is handed down by parents, teachers, and the mass media. At the same time there has been an enormous ideological shift favoring submission to the group, a shift whose decisiveness is concealed by the persistence of the older ideological patterns. The peer-group becomes the measure of all things; the individual has few defenses the group cannot batter down. In this situation the competitive drives for achievement sponsored in children by the remnants of inner-direction in their parents come into conflict with the cooperative demands sponsored by the peer-group. The child therefore is forced to rechannel the competitive drive for achievement, as demanded by the parents, into his drive for approval from the peers. Neither parent, child, nor the peer-group itself is particularly conscious of this process. As a result all three participants in the process may remain unaware of the degree to which the force of an older individualistic ideology provides the energies for filling out the forms of a newer, group-oriented characterology....

Sex: The Last Frontier

This separation, [of sex from production and reproduction] when it goes beyond the upper class and spreads over almost the whole society, is a sign that a society, through birth control and all that it implies, has entered the population phase of incipient decline by the route of industrialization. In this phase there is not only a growth of leisure, but work itself becomes both less interesting and less demanding for many; increased supervision and subdivision of tasks routinize the industrial process even beyond what was accomplished in the phrase of transitional growth of population. More than before, as job-mindedness declines, sex permeates the daytime as well as the playtime consciousness. It is viewed as a consumption good not only by the old leisure classes but by the modern leisure masses.

The other-directed person, who often suffers from low responsiveness, may pursue what looks like a "cult of effortlessness" in many spheres of life. He may welcome the routinization of his economic roles and of his domestic life; the auto companies may tempt him by self-opening windows and self-shifting gears; he may withdraw all emotion from politics. Yet he cannot handle his sex life in this way. Though there is tremendous insecurity about *how* the game of sex should be played, there is little doubt as to *whether* it should be played or not. Even when we are consciously bored with sex, we must still obey its drive. Sex, therefore, provides a kind of defense against the threat of total apathy. This is one of the reasons why so much excitement is channeled into sex by the other-directed person. He looks to it for reassurance that he is alive. The inner-directed person, driven by his internal gyroscope and oriented toward the more external problems of production, did not need this evidence.

While the inner-directed acquisitive consumer could pursue the ever receding frontiers of material acquisition, these frontiers have lost much of their lure for the other-directed person.... [T]he latter begins as a very young child to know his way around among available consumer goods. He travels widely, to camp or with his family. He knows that the rich man's car is only marginally, if at all, different from his own—a matter at best of a few additional horsepower. He knows anyway that next year's model will be better than this year's. Even if he has not been there, he knows what the night clubs are like; and he has seen television. Whereas the deprived inner-directed person often lusted for possessions as a goal whose glamour a wealthy adulthood could not dim, the other-directed person can scarcely conceive of a consumer good that can maintain for any length of time undisputed dominance over his imagination. Except perhaps sex.

For the consumption of love, despite all the efforts of the mass media, does remain hidden from public view. If someone else has a new Cadillac, the other-directed person knows what that is, and that he can duplicate the experience, more or less. But if someone else has a new lover, he cannot know what that means. Cadillacs have been democratized. So has sexual glamour, to a degree: without the mass production of good-looking, well-groomed youth, the American pattern of sexual competition could not exist. But there is a difference between Cadillacs and sexual partners in the degree of mystery. And with the loss or submergence of moral shame and inhibitions, but not completely of a certain unconscious innocence, the other-directed person has no defenses against his own envy. He is not ambitious to break the quantitative records of the acquisitive consumers of sex like Don Juan, but he does not want to miss, day in day out, the qualities of experiences he tells himself the others are having....

One reason for the change is that women are no longer objects for the acquisitive consumer but are peer-groupers themselves. The relatively unemancipated wife and socially inferior mistresses of the inner-directed man could not seriously challenge the quality of his sexual performance. Today, millions of women, freed by technology from many household tasks, given by technology many "aids to romance," have become pioneers, with men, on the frontier of sex. As they become knowing consumers, the anxiety of men lest they fail to satisfy the women also grows—but at the same time this is another test that attracts men who, in their character, want to be judged by others. The very ability of women to respond in a way that only courtesans were supposed to in an earlier age means, moreover, that qualitative differences of sex experience—the impenetrable mystery—can be sought for night after night, and not only in periodic visits to a mistress or brothel....

The Inside-dopesters

The inside-dopester may be one who has concluded (with good reason) that since he can do nothing to change politics, he can only understand it. Or he may see all political issues in terms of being able to get some insider on the telephone. That is, some inside-dopesters actually crave to *be* on the inside, to join an inner-circle or invent one; others aim no higher than to *know* the inside, for whatever peer-group satisfactions this can bring them.

The inside-dopester of whatever stripe tends to know a great deal about what other people are doing and thinking in the important or "great-issue" spheres of life; he is politically cosmopolitan rather than parochial. If he cannot change the others who dominate his political attention, his characterological drive leads him to manipulate himself in order not to change the others but to resemble them. He will go to great lengths to keep from looking and feeling like the uninformed outsider. Not all other-directed people are inside-dopesters, but perhaps, for the lack of a more mature model, many of them aspire to be.

The inside-dopester is competent in the way that the school system and the mass media of communication have taught him to be competent. Ideology demands that, living in a politically saturated milieu, he knows the political score as he must know the score in other fields of entertainment, such as sports.

Notes
1. The "radar" metaphor was suggested by Karl Wittfogel.

PART II

THE MIDDLE YEARS

INTRODUCTION

In the period running from World War I to the 1960s mainstream social theory continued to be largely an academic enterprise, closely tied to departments of sociology in North America. By the 1920s, many universities in the United States established departments of sociology (as well as political science, anthropology, and social work, other fields that produced social theory), and these departments formed the core of the intellectual enterprise. The institutions that were home to Marxist theorists were often the Communist parties and affiliated publishing houses in western Europe and colonial regions. Marxist intellectuals were divided by their degree of loyalty to the party, with all its implications for the analysis of society.

Europe lagged behind in the development of mainstream social theory in this period, largely because the energy of its intellectual elites was engaged in coping with the devastating aftermath of World War I. European intellectuals lost their sense of progress. This feeling deepened with the Depression and the victories of Fascism in Italy, Germany, Spain, and Japan. World War II left Europe (and many other regions of the world) with millions of casualties and an infrastructure in ruins. Many people spent these years trying to survive under conditions of war, genocide, and economic disaster.

Those regions that had been spared the warfare that devastated Europe and Eastern Asia remained colonies and/or in conditions of great poverty and isolation: Southern Asia, Western Asia, Africa, and Latin America. Intellectuals in these regions were often drawn to struggles against colonialism and dependency, and these immediate political struggles took priority over developing general social theory about global inequalities and uneven development.

The period covered in Part II then, represents the heyday of American social theory ("American" in the sense of United States) in the non-Marxist mainstream. It is strongly marked by characteristics of American culture: pragmatism, a belief that it is possible to solve social problems, individualism, liberalism, and ethnic diversity. It was also a fertile period for developing research methods, the analytical tools of the contemporary social sciences. Quantitative methods, increasingly sophisticated statistical data analysis, and survey research, as well as attention to ethnography and participant-observation—all provided a strong empirical basis for social theory. Outside of the United States and Canada, the most vital and energetic communities of intellectuals involved in social theory were Marxists and anti-colonial writers.

Readings
Hobsbawm, Eric. *The Age of Extremes*. New York: Random House, 1994.

CHAPTER THREE

PRAGMATISM, PROGRESS, ETHNICITY: THE UNITED STATES IN THE SOCIOLOGICAL MIRROR

INTRODUCTION

By the turn of the century, American scholars began to transform sociology into a discipline that matched "new world" values and outlooks. World War I left millions dead, mostly young men who served in the armies of the warring nations. Hundreds of thousands of soldiers died in futile charges across no man's land into artillery fire. The magnitude of the killing, the pointlessness of the war, the sense of betrayal at the hands of governments and military commanders—all created bitter despair and loss of hope in progress. Europe entered "an age of catastrophe" which did not come to an end until after World War II.[1] Mainstream academic sociology, unlike the Marxist current, did not run strong in this setting, and innovative work was done in North America, not Europe.

American values, concerns, issues, and modes of thinking left their mark on sociology as it grew in the first part of the twentieth century. We can identify five American themes.

The first value is pragmatism, a practical, can-do attitude toward the world. Theory, criticism, and contemplation run counter to this spirit of active, down-to-earth mastery of the immediate situation: social problems can be solved. This attitude is more concrete, optimistic, and short-term than the viewpoint of a critical theory that identifies irreparable flaws in the very structure of society and modes of thought.

Pragmatism not only lay at the heart of American values; Pragmatism (with a capital P) was a current of philosophy that became influential among American scholars at the turn of the century. It saw human beings as active and purposeful creatures: biological factors are a component of our selves, but above all we are social beings and develop an active, coping self in society. We are more than a fixed and determined outcome of external forces, social or biological. The sciences, reflecting the character of human beings, develop best when they have an experimental and exploring attitude towards the world. Experience is a crucial component of our understanding of the world; it is important to understand what people experience as well as what they do. We need to listen to the verbalization of experience, not only measure observable behaviour. Pragmatic philosophers such as William James and John Dewey were committed to democracy, which they believed was the political system best suited to supporting the creative, exploring, and active qualities of the human spirit.

A second North American value is a continuing belief in progress. Progress to leading American intellectuals did not mean revolution and a sudden discontinuous leap toward socialism and communism. It meant a slow, steady accumulation of improvements in the human condition: the growth of science and technology applied to increasing physical well-being and efficient production for human needs; the expansion of democracy and the inclusion of previously excluded groups like women and people of colour in political and social life; and the limited, targeted involvement of government in the capitalist economy to ameliorate its negative impact. At the turn of the century, these values guided the Progressive Movement, a social reform movement lodged in the educated white-Anglo middle class that hoped to curb the excesses of robber baron capitalism and bring immigrants into the American way of life; progressive values were also associated with the New Deal, launched by Franklin Delano Roosevelt. They remained an active force in American sociology and in related applied fields like social work and education for most of the twentieth century.

Third is individualism, the ferocious attachment of Americans to the belief that the individual is everything and usually stands in opposition to the collectivity. American sociologists often questioned the insistence of Comte and Durkheim on the "supra-individual" focus of sociology. They were inclined to revert to the viewpoint of Enlightenment liberalism that individuals are the atoms of society, its basic units; society can best be understood as the sum total of individual actions. North American sociologists devoted more time than Europeans to social psychology and micro-sociology, looking at the motivations of individuals, interaction between individuals, and individuals' interpretation of culture.

The fourth theme is cultural diversity. We now use this term to mean a value we cherish, a positive aspect of our society. But in much of North American history it has been a source of pain and a result of conflict: the displacement and extermination of First Nations by white settlers; the enslavement of Africans by Europeans; the war between English and French settlers; the stormy history of immigration from Europe and Asia. Value to be cherished or source of oppression—in either case, contact between people of different cultures was an essential element of life on this continent. European sociology had not been oblivious to the existence of status communities, ethnic castes, and marginalized peoples like the Jews; Weber, for example, had already provided some of the basic concepts for discussing cultural diversity within a society. But in North America, cultural diversity was not merely one topic of many—it had to be at the centre of sociological inquiry.

In the United States sociological analysis of ethnic and cultural diversity first took the form of a focus on "race," on the division and relationship between European and African Americans. Race was a central axis, a major dimension of difference in American society, not just a topic or subfield that was of personal relevance to African American sociologists. Race and ethnicity often were a more important concern than class. Theorizing about race in the United States early in the twentieth century created a framework for the analysis of racial/ethnic relations throughout the world later in the century. Sociologists challenged race as a scientific concept and linked ethnic relations to the study of power.

The fifth value was conservative liberalism. This phrase sounds like an oxymoron, but it is a perfect description of the political ideology of most Americans. They believe in individual rights and the efficacy of the free market and voluntary associations; they distrust government, seeing the state as likely to limit individual rights and interfere with the workings of civil society. They share Burke's conservative views on avoiding top-down, state-directed, and intellectually guided change, but at the same time welcome change that flows out of private decisions in the market.

Although many sociologists leaned toward more positive views of government than other Americans, they shared the general ideology in most respects. Few were socialists, and virtually none were traditional communitarian conservatives; many supported the limited government intervention in the free market represented by the New Deal and postwar administrations of Democrats and moderate Republicans. Conservative liberalism shaped the way they framed solutions to social problems like racism, poverty, gender discrimination, and deviance, which they believed were amenable to public policies. It also shaped their general theoretical understanding of the social order; in their analysis they foregrounded individual action rather than overwhelming collective forces.

Conservative liberalism and individualism influenced North American research methods, leading to a heavy reliance on certain kinds of quantitative data, especially in the postwar period. Collecting and statistically aggregating individual-level data (individual-response data from opinion polls, attitude surveys, and demographic surveys) was believed to be a good way to conceptualize the social order as a whole. Notice how different this methodology is from Weber's method of *verstehen*, with its reliance on texts produced by cultural elites.

These values and concerns formed a foundation for social thought in the United States and influenced choices of theoretical concepts and perspectives as well as research methods. In the following pages we will read selections from theorists who reflect these perspectives.

Notes
1. Eric Hobsbawm, *The Age of Extremes*. New York: Random House, 1994.

14

CHARLES COOLEY (1864-1929) AND GEORGE HERBERT MEAD (1863-1931)

Charles Horton Cooley and George Herbert Mead pioneered the development of a microsociological tradition in theory. Strongly influenced by pragmatic philosophy, both men charted a self that forms in interaction, through language and other types of communication. The self is formed in society; it is flexible and changing; it responds to experience. Society and self are dialectical processes; the self is formed in interaction with others, but at the same time, society is composed of individuals with distinct selves. There is a biological basis to the self, but it becomes a human self only in interaction with others.

Cooley and Mead's position can be distinguished from other social theories. Unlike French theorists in the tradition of Comte and Durkheim, Cooley and Mead did not think of society as external, coercive structures that exist beyond and prior to individual action. Nor did they give much attention to class structure, status inequalities, political action, and large-scale historical change, the focal concerns of Weber and Marx. Their stand toward existing society and culture is relatively accepting and uncritical. They not only parted ways from classical sociology; they also distanced themselves from the schools of psychological theory that were beginning to appear in the early twentieth century. They decisively rejected Freud's idea that there is a huge, irrational unconscious within each of us that has to be retrieved and analyzed before we can understand ourselves. Although Mead is sometimes referred to as a social behaviourist, his position is quite different from that of behavioral psychology, which was becoming a mainstream in that field. The behaviourists in the strict sense of the term were positivists who focused on the analysis of behaviour that could be observed and measured; Mead, on the other hand, was much more interested in internal processes in the mind, processes that could only be inferred rather than directly, empirically observed.

Cooley is most noted for two concepts. One is the distinction between primary groups and secondary groups. Primary groups are relatively small, involve close personal relationships, and have an important part in shaping the self. Secondary groups (or relationships) are more impersonal, often instrumental in nature, and considerably less intense. This definition paralleled Simmel's work on the difference between small-town interpersonal closeness and metropolitan impersonality. It also overlapped a distinction made by a German theorist, Ferdinand Tönnies, who used the term *gemeinschaft* to refer to community, an intense life in common, and *gesellschaft* to refer to association, the looser ties characteristic of modern societies.[1]

Cooley is also remembered for the concept of the looking-glass self, the self formed as one sees the reactions of others to oneself.

> In a large and interesting class of cases, the social reference takes the form of a somewhat definite imagination of how one's self—that is, any idea he appropriates—appears in a particular mind; and the kind of self-feeling one has is determined by the attitude toward this attributed to that other mind. A social self of this sort might be called the reflected or looking-glass self:
>
> > Each to each a looking-glass
> > Reflects the other that doth pass.
>
> As we see our face, figure, and dress in the glass, and are interested in them because they are ours, and pleased or otherwise with them according as they do or do not answer to what we should like them to be, so in imagination we perceive in another's mind some thought of our appearance, manners, aims, deeds, character, friends, and so on, and are variously affected by it.
>
> A self-idea of this sort seems to have three principal elements: the imagination of our appearance to the other person; the imagination of his judgment of that appearance; and some sort of self-feeling, such as pride or mortification. The comparison with a looking glass hardly suggests the second element, the imagined judgment, which is quite essential. The thing that moves us to pride or shame is not the mere mechanical reflection of ourselves, but an imputed sentiment; the imagined effect of this reflection upon another's mind. This is evident from the fact that the character and weight of that other, in whose mind we see ourselves, makes all the difference in our feeling. We are ashamed to seem evasive in the presence of a straight-forward man, cowardly in the presence of brave one, gross in the eyes of a refined one, and so on. We always imagine, and imagining share, the judgments of the other mind.[2]

Mead did not systematically write theory, but expressed his ideas in lectures at the University of Chicago, which were written down, edited, and published by his students in a book entitled *Mind, Self, and Society*.

For Mead, as we see in the following selection, the self is constituted by a dialogue between the "I" and the "me," two distinct processes in the mind. The opinions of others form only part of the self, the "me." The "I" is the acting, spontaneous self, the subject of one's actions; the "me" is the self that is formed as the object of others' actions and views, including one's own reflections on one's self. The complete self is an ongoing conversation between the "I" and the "me."

The "me" is a composite of the social expectations to which one is exposed. For some people the "me" is unitary and coherent; all expectations call for the same behaviour. For others, it may be fragmented and contradictory, formed by multiple competing expectations. In our society, many people have a multiple or fragmented self; for example, peers, parents, and professors may hold contradictory expectations for a college student. Of course, the "me" is not necessarily moral, pro-social, or law-abiding; it can be formed by the expectations of gangs, crime bosses, or death squad commanders. All we can say about the "me" is that it is a social product.

The "I" is spontaneous and not fully predictable. It is the source of truly unconventional and innovative behaviour, and the root cause of change in society. It has a greater capacity for heroic as well as terrible acts than the "me."

The dialogue of the "I" and the "me" was an ingenious way of answering the question "where is society?" As we saw in our reading of Durkheim, society appears to be an external force, yet it is clearly not a tangible thing outside of ourselves. Mead's self-constituting dialogue recognizes both the force of society and the unique individual, placing both within the human mind.

Mead distinguished two processes that form the socially-oriented parts of the self in childhood: play and games. In play, children take on the roles of others; these roles are usually directed towards themselves, often in a serial fashion. A child plays at being a mom, a dad, a teacher, a doctor, and so on, and in each case, uses play to express the expectations of significant others, often adults, towards him/herself. In games a generalized other is formed; when children take part in games, they have to be able to picture the entire configuration of roles and to abide by abstract, fixed rules. Games lead to the internalization of these abstract, fixed rules associated with a group or community as a whole, rather than specific individuals.

Mead speaks as though the behaviour of white middle-class boys of his day is universal; he gives virtually no attention to variation by gender, class, ethnicity, culture, or historical era, apart from a few pejorative remarks about primitive man being like a young child. For example, because it has been observed that, in western culture, boys are more likely to take part in games than are girls, we might ask whether there are gender differences in self-formation, with girls developing selves more closely geared to the expectations of specific individuals (play) and less associated with expectations of a group, team, or larger community (game).

Micro-sociological insight remained largely disconnected from macro-sociological analysis. In its early years, micro-sociology gave little attention to issues of inequality, differences within society, and linkages between self and small groups on the one hand and larger structures and historical change on the other hand. As we will see in Part III and the selection by Patricia and Peter Adler below, these linkages are now a "hot" area of theory.

Notes

1. Ferdinand Tönnies, *Community and Society* (1887; New Brunswick, NJ: Transaction Press, 1988*).*
2. Cooley, Charles. *Human Nature and The Social Order* (New Brunswick, NJ: Transaction Press, 1983) 196-99.

Readings

Cahill, Spencer. *Inside Social Life*. Los Angeles: Roxbury, 1998.

Mead, George Herbert. *Mind, Self, and Society*. Chicago: University of Chicago Press, 1934.

Strauss, Anselm (ed.). *George Herbert Mead on Social Psychology*. Chicago: University of Chicago Press, 1964.

Mind, Self, and Society
GEORGE H. MEAD

The "I" and the "Me"

We have discussed at length the social foundations of the self, and hinted that the self does not consist simply in the bare organization of social attitudes. We may now explicitly raise the question as to the nature of the "I" which is aware of the social "me." I do not mean to raise the metaphysical question of how a person can be both "I" and "me," but to ask for the significance of this distinction from the point of view of conduct itself. Where in conduct does the "I" come in as over against the "me"?...

The "I" is the response of the organism to the attitudes of the others;[1] the "me" is the organized set of attitudes of others which one himself assumes. The attitudes of the others constitute the organized "me," and then one reacts toward that as an "I." I now wish to examine these concepts in greater detail.

There is neither "I" nor "me" in the conversation of gestures; the whole act is not yet carried out, but the preparation takes place in this field of gesture. Now, in so far as the individual arouses in himself the attitudes of the others, there arises an organized group of responses. And it is due to the individual's ability to take the attitudes of these others in so far as they can be organized that he gets self-consciousness. The taking of all of those organized sets of attitudes gives him his "me"; that is the self he is aware of. He can throw the ball to some other member because of the demand made upon him from other members of the team. That is the self that immediately exists for him in his consciousness. He has their attitudes, knows what they want and what the consequence of any act of his will be, and he has assumed responsibility for the situation. Now, it is the presence of those organized sets of attitudes that constitutes that "me" to which he as an "I" is responding. But what that response will be he does not know and nobody else knows. Perhaps he will make a brilliant play or an error. The response to that situation as it appears in his immediate experience is uncertain, and it is that which constitutes the "I."

The "I" is his action over against that social situation within his own conduct, and it gets into his experience only after he has carried out the act. Then he is aware of it. He had to do such a thing and he did it. He fulfils his duty and he may look with pride at the throw which he made. The "me" arises to do that duty—that is the way in which it arises in his experience. He had in him all the attitudes of others, calling for a certain response; that was the "me" of that situation, and his response is the "I."

I want to call attention particularly to the fact that this response of the "I" is something that is more or less uncertain. The attitudes of others which one assumes as affecting his own conduct constitute the "me," and that is something that is there, but the response to it is as yet not given. When one sits down to think anything out, he has certain data that are there. Suppose that it is a social situation which he has to straighten out. He sees himself from the point of view of one individual or another in the group. These individuals, related all together, give him a certain self. Well, what is he going to do? He does not know and nobody else knows. He can get the situation into his experience because he can assume the attitudes of the various individuals involved in it. He knows how they feel about it by the assumption of their attitudes. He says, in effect, "I have done certain things that seems to commit me to a certain course of conduct." Perhaps if he does so act it will place him in a false position with another group. The "I" as a response to this situation, in contrast to the "me" which is involved in the attitudes which he takes, is uncertain. And when the response takes place, then it appears in the field of experience largely as a memory image.

Our specious present as such is very short. We do, however, experience passing events; part of the process of the passage of events is directly there in our experience, including some of the past and some of the future. We see a ball falling as it passes, and as it does pass part of the ball is covered and part is being uncovered. We remember where the ball was a moment ago and we anticipate where it will be beyond what is given in our experience. So of ourselves; we are doing something, but to look back and see what we are doing involves getting memory images. So the "I" really appears experientially as a part of a "me." But on the basis of this experience we distinguish that individual who is doing something from the "me" who puts the problem up to him. The response enters into his experience only when it takes place. If he says he knows what he is going to do, even there he may be mistaken. He starts out to do something and something happens to interfere. The resulting action is always a little different from anything which he could anticipate. This is true even if he is simply carrying out the process of walking. The very taking of his expected steps puts him in a certain situation which has a slightly different aspect from what is expected, which is in a certain sense novel. That movement into the future is the step, so to speak, of the ego, of the "I." It is something that is not given in the "me."

Take the situation of a scientist solving a problem, where he has certain data which call for certain responses. Some of this set of data call for his applying such and such a law, while others call for another law. Data are there with their implications. He knows what such and such coloration means, and when he has these data before him they stand for certain responses on his part; but now they are in conflict with each other. If he makes one response he cannot make another. What he is going to do he does not know, nor does anybody else. The action of the self is in response to these conflicting sets of data in the form of a problem, with conflicting demands upon him as a scientist. He has to look at it in different ways. That action of the "I" is something the nature of which we cannot tell in advance.

The "I," then, in this relation of the "I" and the "me," is something that is, so to speak, responding to a social situation which is within the experience of the individual. It is the answer which the individual makes to the attitude which others take toward him when he assumes an attitude toward them. Now, the attitudes he is taking toward them are present in his own experience, but his response to them will contain a novel element. The "I" gives the sense of freedom, of initiative. The situation is there for us to act in a self-conscious fashion. We are aware of ourselves, and of what the situation is, but exactly how we will act never gets into experience until after the action takes place.

Such is the basis for the fact that the "I" does not appear in the same sense in experience as does the "me." The "me" represents a definite organization of the community there in our own attitudes, and calling for a response, but the response that takes place is something that just happens. There is no certainty in regard to it. There is a moral necessity but no mechanical necessity for the act. When it does take place then we find what has been done. The above account gives us, I think, the relative position of the "I" and "me" in the situation, and the grounds for the separation of the two in behavior. The two are separated in the process but they belong together in the sense of being parts of a whole. They are separated and yet they belong together. The separation of the "I" and the "me" is not fictitious. They are not identical, for, as I have said, the "I" is something that is never entirely calculable. The "me" does call for a certain sort of an "I" in so far as we meet the obligations that are given in conduct itself, but the "I" is always something different from what the situation itself calls for. So there is always that distinction, if you like, between the "I" and the "me." The "I" both calls out the "me" and responds to it. Taken together they constitute a personality as it appears in social experience. The self is essentially a social process going on with these two distinguishable phases. If it did not have these two phases there could not be conscious responsibility, and there would be nothing novel in experience.

Notes
1. For the "I" viewed as the biologic individual, see Supplementary Essays II, III. [George Herbert Mead, *Mind, Self, and Society* (Chicago: University of Chicago Press, 1934).]

15

THE LEGACY OF COOLEY AND MEAD: PATRICIA ADLER (1951-) AND PETER ADLER (1951-)

In this contemporary selection about college athletes, the authors provide an exciting application and update of Cooley and Mead's theories of the self. The top-ranked college team is an ideal milieu for observing the formation of a dazzling and distorted looking-glass self, a "me" based on feelings and expectations of fans and the media. The basic theoretical concepts of Mead and Cooley continue to be useful, while the central importance of spectator sports and the media in contemporary societies adds a new dimension to the construction of the self.

The Adlers extend Mead and Cooley's theoretical work, filling in the gap left in earlier versions of micro-sociological theory. They provide the macro-sociological linkage that had been lacking in early micro-theory by showing us how the self is formed, experienced, and lived in institutions of the larger society. The self is not formed in isolation nor in an unchanging family and small peer group, but in a large, complex, rapidly changing society. At the end of the twentieth century this larger context includes media, institutions of higher education, and intense, commercialized, emotionally charged spectator sports. The Adlers' analysis of the impact of media, schooling, sports, and markets on the self creates a bridge to other types of theory, such as the traditions of Marx and Weber and the analysis of culture.

The Adlers are lively writers and have a knack for selecting thought-provoking topics for field research (an earlier work explored the unpredictable, disorderly, high-rolling lifestyles of cocaine dealers in the southwestern United States). From the Adlers' account we learn that the fabled life of college athletic stars may be stressful, disorienting, and ultimately, disheartening, because the young players lose a realistic sense of self.

Readings

Adler, Patricia. *Wheeling and Dealing: An Ethnography of an Upper Level Drug Dealing and Smuggling Community*. New York: Columbia University Press, 1993.

—. *Peer Power: Preadolescent Culture and Identity*. Rutgers, NJ: Rutgers University Press, 1998.

—, and Peter Adler. *Backboards and Blackboards: College Athletes and Role Engulfment*. New York: Columbia University Press, 1991.

The Gloried Self
PATRICIA ADLER AND PETER ADLER

In this paper we describe and analyze a previously unarticulated form of self-identity: the "gloried" self, which arises when individuals become the focus of intense interpersonal and media attention, leading to their achieving celebrity. The articulation of the gloried self not only adds a new concept to our self-repertoire but also furthers our insight into self-concept formation in two ways: it illustrates one process whereby dynamic contradictions between internal and external pressures become resolved, and it highlights the ascendance of an unintended self-identity in the face of considerable resistance.

The development of the gloried self is an outgrowth of individuals becoming imbued with celebrity.... Development of a gloried self is caused in part by the treatment of individuals' selves as objects by others. A "public person" is created, usually by the media, which differs from individuals' private personas. These public images are rarely as intricate or as complex as individuals [personal] selves; often, they draw on stereotypes or portray individuals in extreme fashion to accentuate their point. Yet the power of these media portrayals, reinforced by face-to-face encounters with people who hold these images, often causes individuals to objectify their selves to themselves. Individuals thus become initially alienated from themselves through the separation of their self-concept from the conception of their selves held by others. Ultimately, they resolve this disparity and reduce their alienation by changing their self-images to bridge the gap created by others perceptions of them, even though they may fight this development as it occurs.

Characteristically, the gloried self is a greedy self, seeking to ascend in importance and to cast aside other self-dimensions as it grows. It is an intoxicating and riveting self, which overpowers other aspects of the individual and seeks increasing reinforcement to fuel its growth. Yet at the same time, its surge and display violate societal mores of modesty in both self-conception and self-presentation. Individuals thus become embroiled in inner conflict between their desire for recognition, flattery, and importance and the inclination to keep feeding this self-affirming element, and the socialization that urges them to fight such feelings and behavioral impulses. That the gloried self succeeds in flourishing, in spite of individuals struggle against it, testifies to its inherent power and its drive to eclipse other self-dimensions.

Drawing on ethnographic data gathered in a college graduate athletics setting, we discuss the creation and the character of the gloried self, showing its effects on the individuals in whom it develops.... Over a five-year period (1980-1985), we conducted a participant-observation study of a major college basketball program.... The research was conducted at a medium-sized (6,000 students) private university (hereafter referred to as "the University") in the mid-south central portion of the United States, with a predominantly white, suburban, middle-class student body. The basketball program was ranked in the top 40 of Division I NCAA schools throughout our research, and in the top 20 for most of two seasons. The team played in post-season tournaments every year, and in four complete seasons won approximately four times as many games as it lost. Players generally were recruited from the surrounding area; they were predominantly black (70 percent) and ranged from lower to middle class.... We analyze [these] athletes, the athletes' experiences and discuss the aggrandizing effects of celebrity in fostering the gloried self's ascent to prominence. Then we look at the consequent changes and diminishments in the self that occur as the price of this self-aggrandizement....

The Experience of Glory

Experiencing glory was exciting, intoxicating, and riveting. Two self-dimensions were either created or expanded in the athletes we studied: the reflected self and the media self....

The Reflected Self

As a result of the face-to-face interactions between team members and people they encountered through their role as college athletes' impressions of themselves were modified and changed. As Cooley (1902) and Mead (1934) were the first to propose, individuals engage in role-taking; their self-conceptions are products of social interaction, affected by the reflected impressions of others. According to Cooley (1902), these "looking-glass" selves are formed through a combination of cognitive and affective forces; although individuals react intellectually to the impressions they perceive others are forming about them, they also develop emotional reactions about these judgements. Together, these reactions are instrumental in shaping their self-images.

The forging and modification of reflected selves began as team members perceived how people *treated* them; subsequently, they formed *reactions* to that treatment. One of the first things they all noticed was that they were sought intensely by strangers Large numbers of people, individually and in groups, wanted to be near them, to get their autographs, to touch them, and to talk to them. People treated them with awe and respect. One day, for example, the head coach walked out of his office and found a woman waiting for him. As he turned towards her, she threw herself in front of him and began to kiss his feet, all the while telling him what a great man he was. More commonly, fans who were curious about team matters approached players, trying to engage them in conversation. These conversations sometimes made the players feel awkward, because, although they wanted to be polite to their fans, they had little to say to them. Carrying on an interaction was often difficult. As one player said:

> People come walking up to you, and whether they're timid or pushy, they still want to talk. It's like, here's their hero talking face-to-face with them, and they want to say anything just so they can have a conversation with them. It's *hero-worshipping*. But what do actually say to your hero when you see him?

These interactions, then, often took the form of ritualized pseudo-conversations, in which players and their fans offered each other stylized but empty words.

Many fans [identified with players] socially and expect[ed] them to respond in kind. Players found themselves thrust into a "pseudo-intimacy" (Bensman and Lilienfeld 1979) with these fans, who had seen them so often at games and on television. Yet their relationship with players was one sided; fans often expected players to reciprocate their feelings of intimacy. As a result of their celebrity, team members ... were open to engagement in personal interaction with individuals whom they did not know at all.

Players also found themselves highly prized in interacting with boosters (financial supporters of the team). Boosters showered all players with invitations to their houses for team meetings or dinner. They fought jealously to have players seen with them or gossiped about as having been in their houses. It soon became apparent to players that boosters derived social status from associating with them.... This situation caused players to recognize that they were "glory bearers," so filled with glory that they could confer it on anyone by their mere presence. They experienced a sense of the "Midas touch": they had an attribute (fame) that everybody wanted and which could be transmitted. Their ability to cast glory onto others and their desirability to others because of this ability became an important dimension of their new, reflected self-identity.

The Media Self

A second dimension of the self created from the glory experience was influenced largely by media portrayals.... Most of the athletes who came to the University had received some media publicity in high school (68 percent); but the national level of the print and video coverage they received after arriving, coupled with the intensity of the constant focus, caused them to develop more compelling and more salient media selves than they had possessed previously.

Radio, television, and newspaper reporters covering the team often sought out athletes for "human interest" stories. These features presented media-framed angles that cast athletes into particular roles and tended to create new dimensions of their selves. Images were created from a combination of individuals' actual behaviour and reporters' ideas of what made good copy. Thus, through media coverage, athletes were cast into molds that frequently were distorted or exaggerated reflections of their behaviour and self conceptions.

Team members, for whom the media had created roles, felt as if they had to live up to these portrayals. For instance, two players were depicted as "good students"—shy, quiet, religious, and diligent. Special news features emphasized their outstanding traits, illustrating how they went regularly to class, were humanitarian, and cared about graduating. Yet one of them lamented:

> Other kids our age, they go to the fair and they walk around with a beer in their hand, or a cigarette; but if me or Dan were to do that, then people would talk about that. We can't go over to the clubs, or hang around, without it relaying back to Coach. We can't even do things around our teammates, because they expect us to be a certain way. The media has created this image of us as the "good boys," and now we have to live up to it.

Other players (about 20 percent) were embraced for their charismatic qualities; they had naturally outgoing personalities and the ability to excite a crowd. These players capitalized on the media coverage, exaggerating their antics to gain attention and fame. Yet the more they followed the media portrayal, the more likely it was to turn into a caricature of their selves. One player described how he felt when trapped by his braggart media self:

> I used to like getting in the paper. When reporters came around, I would make those Mohammed Ali type outbursts—I'm gonna do this, I'm gonna do that. And they come around again, stick a microphone in your face, 'cause they figure somewhere Washington will have another outburst. But playing that role died out in me. I think sometimes the paper pulled out a little too much from me that wasn't me. But people seen me as what the paper said, and I had to play that role.

Particular roles notwithstanding, all the players shared the media-conferred sense of self as celebrity. Raised to the status of stars, larger than life, they regularly read their names and statements in the newspaper; saw their faces on television, or heard themselves whispered about on campus. One team member described the consequences of this celebrity:

> We didn't always necessarily agree with the way they wrote about us in the paper; but people who saw us expected us to be like what they read there. A lot of times it made us feel uncomfortable, acting like that, but we had to act

like they expected us to, for the teams sake. We had to act like this was what we was really like.

Ironically, however, the more they interacted with people through their dramaturgically induced media selves, the more many of the team members felt familiar and comfortable with those selves. ("We know what to do, we don't have to think about it no more.") The media presented the selves and the public believed in them, so the athletes continued to portray them. Even though they attempted to moderate these selves, part of them pressed for their legitimacy and acceptance. Over time, the athletes believed these portrayals increasingly and transformed their behaviour into more than mere "impression management" (Goffman 1959).... [They] went through a gradual process of ... becoming more engrossed or more deeply involved in their media selves. The recurrent social situations of their everyday lives served as the foil against which both their public and their private selves developed. The net effect of having these selves placed upon them and of interacting through them with others was that athletes eventually integrated them into their core self.

Self-Aggrandizement

Athletes were affected profoundly by encounters with the self-images reflected onto them by others, both in person and through the media. It was exciting and gratifying to be cast as heroes. Being presented with these images and feeling obligated to interact with people through them, athletes added a new self to their repertoire: a glorified self. This self had a greater degree of aggrandizement than their previous identities. The athletes may have dreamed of glory, but until now they had never formed a structured set of relationships with people who accorded it to them. Yet although they wanted to accept and enjoy this glory, to allow themselves to incorporate it into a full-blown self-identity, they felt hesitant and guilty. They wrestled with the competing forces of their desires for extravagant pleasure and pride and the normative guidelines of society, which inhibited these desires. The athletes' struggle with factors inhibiting and enhancing their self-aggrandizement shows how and why they ultimately developed gloried selves.

Inhibiting Factors

Players knew they had to be careful both about feeling important and about showing these feelings. The norms of our society dictate a more modest, more self-effacing stance. Consequently the players worked hard to suppress their growing feelings of self-aggrandizement in several ways. First, they drew on their own feelings of *fear* and *insecurity*. Although it violated the norms of their peer culture to reveal these feelings, most of the athletes we interviewed (92 percent) had doubts or worries about their playing abilities or futures.

Second they tried to *discount* the flattery of others as exaggerated or false.... Athletes ... tended to evaluate their behaviour less globally than did their audience and to interpret their successes as based less on their own outstanding characteristics than on some complex interaction of circumstances.

Third, the athletes' feelings of importance and superiority were constrained by the actions of the coach and by the norms of their peer subculture. For his part, the coach tried to keep players' self-aggrandizement in check by *puncturing* them whenever he thought they were becoming too "puffed" (conceited). He "dragged" (criticized, mocked) them both in team meetings and in individual sessions, trying to achieve the right balance of confidence and humility.

In addition, players punctured their teammates by ridiculing each other publicly in their informal sessions in the dorms. Each one claimed to be the best player on the team, and had little praise for others. The athletes did not actually think their teammates had no talent; rather, the peer subculture allowed little room for "glory passing."As a result, except for the braggarts (about 20 percent of the group), none of the players expressed in public how good they felt and how much they enjoyed being treated as stars. Instead, they tried largely to suppress the feelings of excitement, intoxication, and aggrandizement, not to let themselves be influenced by the reflected sense of glory. As one player remarked:

> You feel it coming up on you and you know you got to fight it. You can't be letting your head get all out of control.

Fourth, the coach helped to *normalize* the athletes' experiences and reactions by placing them in the occupational perspective. Being adulated was part of the job, he believed, and this job was no more special than any other.... He conveyed this sense of occupational duty to his players and assistants. Like him, they had to "get with the program," to play to the public and help support people's sense of involvement with the team. In public, then, players feigned intimacy with total strangers and allowed themselves to be worshiped, meanwhile being told that this was merely a job.

Enhancing Factors

Yet as tired as they were, as repetitive as this behaviour became, the athletes knew that this job was unlike any other. The excitement, the centrality, and the secrecy, which did not exist in the everyday world made this arena different. As one assistant coach explained:

The times were exciting. There was always something going on, something happening, some new event occurring each day. We felt like we were newsmakers, we were important. We touched so many more lives, were responsible for so many more people, and so many more people cared, wanted to know something from us. It was very intoxicating. Everyone even close felt the excitement, just from elbow-rubbing.

Athletes also were influenced in their developing feelings of self-importance by the concrete results of their behaviour.... [T]hey were able to observe the outcomes of their behaviour and use them to form and modify assessments of their selves. Thus, when the team was winning, their feelings of importance, grandeur, talent, and invincibility soared; when they lost, they felt comparatively incompetent, powerless, and small. Because the team's record throughout our research period was overwhelmingly successful, team members reviewed the outcomes of their contests and the season records, and concluded that they were fine athletes and local heroes....

One result of receiving such intense personal interest and media attention was that players developed "big heads." They were admired openly by so many people and their exploits were regarded as so important that they began to feel more notable. Although they tried to remain modest, all of the players found that their celebrity caused them to lose control over their sense of self-importance. As one player observed:

You try not to let it get away from you. You feel it coming all around you. People building you up. You say to yourself that you're the same guy you always were and that nothing has changed. But what's happening to you is so unbelievable. Even when you were sitting at home in high school imagining what college ball would be like, you could not imagine this. All the media, all the fans, all the pressure. And all so suddenly, with no time to prepare or ease into it. Doc, it got to go to your head. You try to fight it, and you think you do, but you got to be affected by it, you got to get a big head.

Although the players fought to normalize and diminish their feelings of self-aggrandizement, they were swept away in spite of themselves by the allure of glory, to varying degrees. Their sense of glory fed their egos, exciting them beyond their ability to manage or control it. They had never before been such glory-generating figures, had never felt the power that was now invested in them by the crowds or worshipful fans. They developed deep, powerful feelings affirming how good it felt.

All the members of the University's basketball program developed gloried selves, although the degree varied according to several factors. To some extent, their aggrandizement and glorification were affected by the level of attention they received. Individuals with more talent, who held central roles as team stars, were the focus of much media and fan attention. Others, who possessed the social and interpersonal attributes that made them good subjects for reporters, fruitful topics of conversation for boosters, and charismatic crowd pleasers, also received considerable notice. In addition, those who were more deeply invested in the athletic role were more likely to develop stronger gloried selves. They looked to this arena for their greatest rewards and were the most susceptible to its aggrandizing influence. Finally, individuals resisted or yielded to the gloried self depending on personal attributes. Those who were ... more modest and more self-effacing tried harder to neutralize the effects and had more difficulty in forging grandiose self-conceptions than those who were boastful or pretentious.

The Price of Glory

Athletes' self-aggrandizement, as we have seen, was a clear consequence of the glory experience. Self-diminishment was a corresponding and concomitant effect. Athletes paid a price for becoming gloried in the form of self-narrowing or self-erosion. They sacrificed both the multi-dimensionality of their current selves and the potential breadth of their future selves; various dimensions of their identities were either diminished, detached, or somehow changed as a result of their increasing investment in their gloried selves.

Self-Immediacy

One of the first consequences of the ascent of the gloried self was a loss of future orientation. In all their lives, from the most celebrated player to the least, these individuals had never experienced such a level of excitement, adulation, intensity, and importance. These sensations were immediate and real, flooding all team members' daily lives and overwhelming them. As a result, their focus turned toward their present situation and became fixed on it.

This reaction was caused largely by the absorbing quality of the moment. During the intensity of the season (and to a lesser extent during the off season), their basketball obligations and involvements were prominent. When they were lying exhausted in their hotel rooms, hundreds of miles from campus, or on their beds after a grueling practice, the responsibilities of school seemed remote and distant. One player described his state of preoccupation:

> I've got two finals tomorrow and one the next day. I should be up in the room studying right now. But how can I get my mind on that when I know I've got to guard Michael Jordan tomorrow night?

Their basketball affairs were so much more pressing, not only in the abstract but also because other people made specific demands on them, that it was easy to relegate all other activities to a position of lesser importance.

Many players who had entered college expecting to prepare themselves for professional or business careers were distracted from those plans and relinquished them (71 percent). The demands of the basketball schedule became the central focus of their lives; the associated physical, social, and professional dimensions took precedence over all other concerns. Despite their knowledge that only two percent of major-college players eventually play in the NBA (Coakley 1986; Leonard and Reyman 1988), they all clung to the hope that they would be the ones to succeed. One of the less outstanding athletes on the team expressed the players' commonly held attitude toward their present and their future:

> You have to have two goals, a realistic and an unrealistic. Not really an unrealistic, but a dream. We all have that dream. I know the odds are against it, but I feel realistically that I can make the NBA. I have to be in the gym every day, lift weights, more or less sacrifice my life to basketball. A lot.

To varying degrees, all players ceased to think about their futures other than as a direct continuation of the present. They were distracted from long-term planning and deferment of gratification in favor of the enormous immediate gratification they received from their fans and from celebrity. What emerged was a self that primarily thought about only one source of gratification—athletic fame—and that imagined and planned for little else.

The players imagined vaguely that if they did not succeed as professional athletes, a rich booster would provide them with a job. Although they could observe older players leaving the program without any clear job opportunities, they were too deeply absorbed in the present to recognize the situation. Ironically, they came to college believing that it would expand their range of opportunities ... yet they sacrificed the potential breadth of their future selves by narrowing their range of vision to encompass only that which fed their immediate hunger for glory.

Diminished Awareness

Locked into a focus on the present and stuck with a vision of themselves that grew from their celebrity status, all team members, to varying degrees, became desensitized to the concerns of their old selves. They experienced a heightened sensitivity and reflectivity toward the gloried self and a loss of awareness of the self-dimensions unrelated to glory. Nearly everyone they encountered interacted with them, at least in part, through their gloried selves. As this self-identity was fed and expanded, their other selves they tended to atrophy. At times the athletes seemed to be so blinded by their glory that they would not look beyond it....

This diminished awareness had several consequences. First, in becoming so deeply absorbed in their gloried selves, athletes relegated non-athletic concerns to secondary, tertiary, or even lesser status. These concerns included commitments to friends, relatives, and school. For example, many athletes (54 percent) began each semester vowing that it would be different this time, but each semester they "forgot" to go to class. Reflecting on this occurrence, one player mused:

> You don't think, it's not like you goin' to be a bad boy today, or you goin' to pull the wool over someone's eyes. You just plain ol' forget. You sleep through it.

For a while the athletes could ignore the facts and the consequences of their behaviour, but this denial wore thin as the semester progressed, and they fell behind more noticeably Then they moved into a stage of neutralization, blaming boring professors, stupid courses, exhaustion, coaches' demands, or injury.

Second, their new personas were expanded, even in their interactions with friends. Players referred to this situation as being "puffed," and each accused the others of it:

> Sometimes I can't even talk to Rich no more. He's so puffed on the head you can't get him to talk sense, he's lost touch with reality. It's like it's full of jello in there and he's talking a bunch of hot air.

What the athletes sensed as filling the heads of these puffed players was the self-image created by the glory experience.

Third, some athletes plunged into various acts because these acts fed their gloried selves (60 percent). They distanced themselves from their old values and took potentially career-ending risks. For example, when a player who filled a substitute role was "red-shirted" (excused from play without losing his scholarship or expending a year of eligibility) for the year because of injury, he was willing to give up this desirable and protective status when asked to do so by the coach. He was convinced easily, despite his secondary position, that the team could not function without him; like others, he blocked off the warnings and the caution that stemmed from an awareness of other needs and interests. The same lack of reflectiveness and self-awareness prevented players with chronic injuries, those who were hobbling and could no longer jump, from admitting to themselves that their playing days were over, that their gloried selves had to retire.

Self-Detachment

For some team members and at times for all, the distinction between their gloried selves and their other selves became more than a separation; the distance and the lack of reflectiveness grew into detachment. In the most extreme cases (18 percent), some athletes developed a barrier between this new, exciting, glamorous self and their old, formerly core selves. They found it increasingly difficult to break through that barrier. They experienced a dualism between these selves, as if occasionally they represented discrete individuals and not multiple facets of the same person; at times, they shifted back and forth between them. Ultimately, the different images became so disparate that they could not be fused, or else individuals became so deeply involved in their gloried selves that they lost control over their efforts to constrain and integrate them. The more these individuals interacted with others through this self, the more it developed a life and a destiny of its own.

For instance, one of the most popular players on the team developed a gloried self that was tied to his self-proclaimed nickname "Apollo." Charismatic and enthusiastic whenever he was in public, he generated enormous amounts of attention and adulation through his outgoing personality. On the court he would work the crowd, raising their emotions, exhorting them to cheer, and talking brashly to opposing players. Reporters thronged to him, because he was colorful, lively, and quotable. In public settings, he was always referred to by his nickname.

Yet, although this player deliberately had created the Apollo identity, eventually it began to control him. It led him to associate at times with people who valued him only for that self; it surfaced in interactions with friends when he had not called it forth. It led him to detach himself from responsibility for things he did while in that persona. As he reported:

> I had a summer job working for some booster at a gas station. I figured he wanted to show off that he had Apollo pumping his gas. I'd go into my act for the customers and the other employees, how fine I was, lotta times show up late or not at all. I figured he wouldn't fire me. But he did. Looking back, I can't see how I just up and blew that job. That ain't like me. That was Apollo done that, not me.

Other team members, who did not go so far as to create separate identities for their gloried selves, still experienced feelings of bifurcation. Their former selves were mundane and commonplace compared to their new, vibrant selves. These contrasting selves called forth different kinds of character and behavior. At times, the team members found it difficult to think of themselves as integrated persons, incorporating these divergent identities into one overall self. Feelings of fragmentation haunted them.

Discussion

As we have shown, high school graduates entered the world of college athletics and underwent a fundamental transformation. Thrust into a whirlwind of adulation and celebrity, they reacted to the situation through a process of simultaneous self-aggrandizement and self-diminishment. The gloried self expanded, overpowering all ... other ... self dimensions; it became the aspect of self in which they lived and invested. They immersed themselves single-mindedly in this portion of their selves, and the feedback and gratification they derived from this identity dwarfed their other identities. They had not anticipated this situation, but gradually, as they were drawn into the arena of glory, they were swept away by stardom and fame. Their commitment to the athletic self grew beyond anything they had ever imagined or intended. Once they had experienced the associated power and centrality, they were reluctant to give them up. They discarded their other aspirations, lost touch with other dimensions of their selves (even to the point of detachment), and plunged themselves onto the gloried self.

Athletes' gloried selves arose originally as dramaturgical constructions. Other people, through the media or face to face, conferred these identities on athletes through their expectations of them. Athletes responded by playing the corresponding roles because of organizational loyalty, interactional obligations, and enjoyment. Yet in contrast to other roles, which can be played casually and without consequence, athletes' actions in these roles increased their commitment and their self-involvement in them and made the athletes "more or less unavailable for alternative lines of action" (Kornhauser 1962:321). The gloried self not only influenced athletes' future behaviour but also transformed their self-conceptions and identities.... [This] entire process ... illustrates the relationship between dramaturgical roles and real selves, showing how the former comes to impinge upon and influence the latter.

References

Bensman, Joseph and Robert Lilienfeld. 1979. *Between Public and Private.* New York: Free Press.

Coakley, Jay J. 1986. *Sport in Society.* 3d. ed. St. Louis: Mosby.

Cooley, Charles H. 1902. *Human Nature and Social Order.* New York: Scribners.

Goffman, Erving. 1959. *The Presentation of Self in Everyday Life.* New York: Doubleday.

Kornhauser, William. 1962. "Social Bases of Political Commitment: A Study of Liberals and Radicals." pp 321-339 in *Human Behaviour and Social Processes,* ed. A.M. Rose. Boston: Houghton Mifflin.

Leonard, Wilbert and Jonathon Reyman. 1988. "The Odds of Attaining Professional Athlete Status: Refining the Computations." *Sociology of Sports Journal 5:* 162-169.

Mead, George Herbert. 1934. *Mind, Self, and Society.* Chicago: University of Chicago Press.

16

W.E.B. DuBois (1868-1963)

DuBois was a leading figure of twentieth-century social thought; his writing encompassed several distinct perspectives, moving from an influence of Weber and Pragmatism in his early work to Marxist and Pan-Africanist positions later. The selections reflect the Pragmatist and Weberian influences, but show how DuBois transformed these theoretical positions in his analysis of the United States as a racially divided society as he pioneered ways of studying power and culture.

The Weberian influence is most notable in DuBois's discussion of class, status, and political organization in African American history. African Americans form a status group in Weber's sense, a community with a sense of identity, assigned a rank in a system of prestige and honour held in the society at large. As members of a status group, African Americans are seen as having a relatively fixed position. But African Americans also occupy class positions in United States society. These class positions are more varied, flexible, and mutable than their status positions. Yet the majority of African Americans at the time of DuBois's writing were poor sharecroppers, landless labourers, domestic servants, or owners of tiny farms from which they could barely eke out a subsistence living. Status and class were not entirely independent dimensions, but neither were they reducible to each other. Racial status had its own logic of subordination, associated with but distinct from economic class.

Status and class in turn could be translated into collective action, into power and party, as Weber used the terms. The objective character of class and the subjective, but largely non-political, feelings associated with status identity, can both be transformed into meaningful, organized collective action under certain circumstances. As DuBois outlines in the essay (and elaborates in the rest of the book), African Americans exemplify the interplay of status and class, on the one hand, with collective action on the other hand. This discussion is an excellent example of a Weberian analysis of these three dimensions applied to a specific situation.

From Pragmatic philosophy DuBois drew an interest in how individuals see and respond to their situation, in understanding and characterizing the nature of experience at the individual level.

He went beyond these influences to develop a series of new concepts about representation and power, largely organized as visual metaphors expressed in poetic, lyrical language. Notice how his work closely parallels Cooley's idea of the looking-glass self, but with considerably more nuance and a firmer sense of the social and historical context.

One of these new concepts is the notion of double-consciousness. People see themselves as others see them, and this reflective, looking-glass self is particularly disturbing in any society characterized by cultural diversity and inequality. The looking-glass self is likely to appear as a distorted image of the self for both dominant and subordinate social groups.

A second visual metaphor to describe the experience of multicultural, ethnically stratified societies is "second sight." DuBois displays considerable ambivalence about the double-consciousness of African Americans. He suggests it is painful and that people strive to develop a unified consciousness. And yet he states very clearly that the African American is a "seventh son..." In folk belief in many cultures, a seventh child is especially lucky. The African American is born with a veil, that is, like a child born with a caul (part of the amniotic sac, which sometimes clings to the baby); this too is a lucky sign, and a child born with a caul is believed to have special, magical powers. The African American is born with second sight, a folk expression meaning a magical insight into the nature and flow of things. DuBois quickly, and somewhat inexplicably, reverses himself to identify the painful aspects of double-consciousness. The reader should, however, linger on the positive, almost magical side of the image. Double-consciousness, like the perspective of Simmel's stranger, confers a clearer image of society.

DuBois confronts the issues of representation in a culturally divided and stratified society. Some groups are defined as problems by the dominant group: the "Negro problem" in the United States or the "Jewish problem" in Europe, with its ominous foreshadowing of a final solution.

The subordinate or excluded group is not only presented as a problem in itself, all of its characteristics and behaviours are problematized. Representations focus on its shortcomings as essential features of the group as a whole. Its crimes, illegitimate children, and failings are counted by social scientists and presented to the public. The representation of the group to the larger society is increasingly dominated by these images. The reader will certainly recognize this type of representation in contemporary social science and media reports; for example, in the United States, African Americans and Latinos appear in TV images of crime and drugs in numbers disproportionate to their actual involvement. Without using the term "stereotype," DuBois pioneers the concept.

A third representational issue he raised is the representation of history. The history of African Americans and of Africa itself remains shadowy and de-valued, even to African Americans. They are not connected in a representational form to the great African civilizations, especially ancient Egypt, in the same way that European Americans feel and display a connectedness with ancient Greece, Rome, and medieval Europe. African and African American history are thus lost in the present, both to African Americans and to others. New texts about history have to come into being in order for African Americans to develop self-awareness and for other ethnic groups to recognize them as descendants of coherent cultures and great civilizations. This re-representing involves several processes: a recognition of the African character of ancient Egyptian culture; a validation of more recent African cultures, typically dismissed in nineteenth-century European and American historiography as "savage"; a reconnection of African Americans to the cultures from which they were cut off by the Middle Passage and slavery; and a recovery of African American history, despite its painfulness.

Finally, DuBois presents one of the first portraits of what a multicultural society might look like (a theme you may remember also appeared in Durkheim's work on organic solidarity, at about the same time). He outlines the idea that individuals might have a bi- or multi- cultural identity. Cultures are neither segregated nor assimilated; at both the individual and societal level, an ongoing duality is possible, so that we can live "at the hyphen" and are not forced into an either/or choice. At the societal level, different cultures can be seen as making distinct contributions. The whole is a composite of multiple contributions. Many ethnic traditions are integral parts of the multicultural society. All Americans are African Americans, culturally, regardless of where their ancestors came from.

Recently, Orlando Patterson has called this position an interactive view of American ethnic and race relations. Patterson goes beyond both sides in the debate on African American assimilation—one being that the African legacy was obliterated in a process of forced assimilation, and the other being that people of African ancestry have retained elements of African cultures. No, says Patterson, reality in the United States (and more obviously so in Caribbean and South American cultures) is also formed by "white" people incorporating elements of "black" culture into their own lives. The process is two-way.

DuBois points to the unequivocal example of musical forms; a hundred years after the publication of this essay, it is even clearer that all twentieth-century music in the United States, and increasingly globally, is in part African. Language is probably another area of African influence, with the rhythms of American speech and its rich vocabulary of popular culture shaped by African-based pronunciation patterns and African American vernaculars (local variants of a language). Both DuBois (and later Patterson) point to the way in which African American experience shaped United States political culture, namely ideas of freedom and democracy. The definition of freedom and the images of freedom were shaped in the interaction of the founding fathers (many of them slaveowners) and their slaves.

A final noteworthy feature of the essay is the way DuBois begins with an episode from his own life. This is uncharacteristic of the theorists of the period, who liked to write in an abstract way; scholarly writing in most of the twentieth century suppressed the "I." It is only in postmodern writing that authors become less timid about positioning themselves at the centre of their work, allowing us to see it as their creation, constructed by their choices, rather than pretending that it reflects an entirely objective truth that came into being without their intervention. DuBois lets us know that he is not disconnected from the people about whom he writes.

In short, we see in this essay many of the themes to which postmodern social thought will return a hundred years later: individual identity in a multicultural society; the complex "interactive" culture of such a society, even though it may be masked by accounts that leave out some groups' contributions; the issues of cultural representation and misrepresentation, including the re-imagining of a historical past; the interplay among economic position (class), communitarian, fixed, and traditional status, and collective political action; the work of social theory as a form of literature and self-narrative; and the painful, yet magical second sight bestowed on children of the diaspora.

While *The Souls of Black Folk* is the more famous and often quoted work, Du Bois's "The Souls of White Folk" (from *Darkwater*) is of equal importance, because it states explicitly what is already implied in the earlier work: a system of racial/ethnic inequality cannot be understood without analyzing the ideology and behaviour of the oppressing group. Race relations in the United States and the colonial world system of the nineteenth and twentieth centuries cannot be explained in terms of the characteristics of people of colour; analysis must center on the formation of a "white race" and the articulation of an ideology of white supremacy. As Du Bois points out, whiteness is a relatively recent social construction associated with the expansion of slavery and colonialism. In "The Souls of White Folk," he outlined a theory of the social construction of identity linked to the analysis of power and structural inequality.

Du Bois's pioneering insights into ideology, representation, and inequality became central elements of theories of social construction and critical race theory. Gender theorists focus on the construction of masculinity as the key to understanding gender inequality, and theories of ethnic relations highlight the historical construction of whiteness and the emergence of white supremacist ideology and practices.

Readings

DuBois, W.E.B. *The Philadelphia Negro: A Social Study*. 1899; Philadelphia: University of Pennsylvania Press, 1996.

Lewis, David Levering. *W.E.B. Dubois: Biography of a Race, 1868-1919*. New York: Henry Holt, 1994.

Patterson, Orlando. *Freedom in the Making of Western Culture*. New York: Basic Books, 1991.

—. *The Ordeal of Integration: Progress and Resentment in America's "Racial" Crisis*. Washington, DC: Counterpoint, 1998.

West, Cornel. *Race Matters*. Boston: Beacon Press, 1993.

The Souls of Black Folk
W.E.B. DuBois

Between me and the other world there is ever an unasked question: unasked by some through feelings of delicacy; by others through the difficulty of rightly framing it. All, nevertheless, flutter round it. They approach me in a half-hesitant way, eye me curiously or compassionately, and then, instead of saying directly, How does it feel to be a problem? they say, I know an excellent colored man in my town; or, I fought at Mechanicsville; or, Do not these Southern outrages make your blood boil? At these I smile, or am interested, or reduce the boiling to a simmer, as the occasion may require. To the real question, How does it feel to be a problem? I answer seldom a word.

And yet, being a problem is a strange experience,—peculiar even for one who has never been anything else, save perhaps in babyhood and in Europe. It is in the early days of rollicking boyhood that the revelation first bursts upon one, all in a day, as it were. I remember well when the shadow swept across me. I was a little thing, away up in the hills of New England, where the dark Housatonic winds between Hoosac and Taghkanic to the sea. In a wee wooden schoolhouse, something put it into the boys' and girls' heads to buy gorgeous visiting cards—ten cents a package—and exchange. The exchange was merry, till one girl, a tall newcomer, refused my card,—refused it peremptorily with a glance. Then it dawned upon me with a certain suddenness that I was different from the others; or like, mayhap, in heart and life and longing, but shut out from their world by a vast veil. I had thereafter no desire to tear down that veil, to creep through; I held all beyond it in common contempt, and lived above it in a region of blue sky and great wandering shadows. That sky was bluest when I could beat my mates at examination-time, or beat them at a foot-race, or even beat their stringy heads. Alas, with the years all this fine contempt began to fade; for the words I longed for, and all their dazzling opportunities, were theirs, not mine. But they should not keep these prizes, I said; some, all, I would wrest from them. Just how I would do it I could never decide: by reading law, by healing the sick, by telling the wonderful tales that swam in my head,—some way. With other black boys the strife was not so fiercely sunny: their youth shrunk into tasteless sycophancy, or into silent hatred of the pale world about them and mocking distrust of everything white; or wasted itself in a bitter cry, Why did God make me an outcast and a stranger in mine own house? The shades of the prisonhouse closed round about us all: walls strait and stubborn to the whitest, but relentlessly narrow, tall, and unscalable to sons of night who must plod darkly on in resignation, or beat unavailing palms against the stone, or steadily, half hopelessly, watch the streak of blue above.

After the Egyptian and Indian, the Greek and Roman, the Teuton and Mongolian, the Negro is a sort of seventh son, born with a veil, and gifted with second-sight in this American world,—a world which yields him no true self-consciousness, but only lets him see himself through the eyes of others, of measuring one's soul by the tape of a world that looks on in amused contempt and pity. One ever feels his twoness,—an American, a Negro; two souls, two thoughts, two unreconciled strivings; two warring ideals in one dark body, whose strength alone keeps it from being torn asunder.

The history of the American Negro is the history of this strife,—this longing to attain self-conscious manhood, to merge his double self into a better and truer self. In this merging he wishes neither of the older selves to be lost. He would not Africanize America, for America has too much to teach the world and Africa. He would not bleach his Negro soul in a flood of white Americanism, for he knows that Negro blood has a message for the world. He simply wishes to make it possible for a man to be both a Negro and an American, without being cursed and spit upon by his fellows, without having the doors of Opportunity closed roughly in his face.

This, then, is the end of his striving: to be a coworker in the kingdom of culture, to escape both death and isolation, to husband and use his best powers and his latent genius. These powers of body and mind have in the past been strangely wasted, dispersed, or forgotten. The shadow of a mighty Negro past flits through the tales of Ethiopia the Shadowy and of Egypt the Sphinx. Through history, the powers of single black men flash here and there like falling stars, and die sometimes before the world has rightly gauged their brightness. Here in America, in the few days since Emancipation, the black man's turning hither and thither in hesitant and doubtful striving has often made his very strength to lose effectiveness, to seem like absence of power, like weakness. And yet it is not weakness,—it is the contradiction of double aims.

The double-aimed struggle of the black artisan—on the one hand to escape white contempt for a nation of mere hewers of wood and drawers of water, and on the other hand to plough and nail and dig for a poverty-stricken horde— could only result in making him a poor craftsman, for he had but half a heart in either cause. By the poverty and ignorance of his people, the Negro minister or doctor was tempted toward quackery and demagogy; and by the criticism of the other world, toward ideals that made him ashamed of his lowly tasks. The would-be black *savant* was confronted by the paradox that the knowledge his people needed was a twice-told tale to his white neighbors, while the knowl- edge which would teach the white world was Greek to his own flesh and blood. The innate love of harmony and beauty that set the ruder souls of his people a- dancing and a-singing raised but confusion and doubt in the soul of the black artists; for the beauty revealed to him was the soul-beauty of a race which his larger audience despised, and he could not articulate the message of another people. This waste of double aims, this seeking to satisfy two unreconciled ideals, has wrought sad havoc with the courage and faith and deeds of ten thou- sand thousand people,—has sent them often wooing false gods and invoking false means of salvation, and at times has even seemed about to make them ashamed of themselves.

Away back in the days of bondage they thought to see in one divine event the end of all doubt and disappointment; few men ever worshipped Freedom with half such unquestioning faith as did the American Negro for two centuries. To him, so far as he thought and dreamed, slavery was indeed the sum of all villainies, the cause of all sorrow, the root of all prejudice; Emancipation was the key to a promised land of sweeter beauty than ever stretched before the eyes of wearied Israelites. In song and exhortation swelled one refrain—Liberty; in his tears and curses the God he implored had Freedom in his right hand. At last it came,—suddenly, fearfully, like a dream. With one wild carnival of blood and passion came the message in his own plaintive cadences:—

> "Shout, O children!
> Shout, you're free!
> For God has bought your liberty!"

Years have passed away since then,—ten, twenty, forty; forty years of national life, forty years of renewal and development, and yet the swarthy spec- tre sits in its accustomed seat at the Nation's feast. In vain do we cry to this our vastest social problem:—

> "Take any shape but that, and my firm nerves
> Shall never tremble."

The Nation has not yet found peace from its sins; the freedman has not yet found in freedom his promised land. Whatever of good may have come in these years of change, the shadow of a deep disappointment rests upon the Negro people,—a disappointment all the more bitter because the unattained ideal was unbounded save by the simple ignorance of a lowly people.

The first decade was merely a prolongation of the vain search for freedom, the boon that seemed ever barely to elude their grasp,—like a tantalizing will-o'-the-wisp, maddening and misleading the headlesss host. The holocaust of war, the terrors of the Ku-Klux-Klan, the lies of carpet-baggers, the disorganization of industry, and the contradictory advice of friends and foes, left the bewildered serf with no new watchword beyond the old cry for freedom. As the time flew, however, he began to grasp a new idea. The ideal of liberty demanded for its attainment powerful means, and these the Fifteeenth Amendment gave him. The ballot, which before he had looked upon as a visible sign of freedom, he now regarded as the chief means of gaining and perfecting the liberty with which war had partially endowed him. And why not? Had not votes made war and emancipated millions? Had not votes enfranchised the freedmen? Was anything impossible to a power that had done all this? A million black men started with renewed zeal to vote themselves into the kingdom. So the decade flew away, the revolution of 1876 came, and left the half-free serf weary, wondering, but still inspired. Slowly but steadily, in the following years, a new vision began gradually to replace the dream of political power,—a powerful movement, the rise of another ideal to guide the unguided, another pillar of fire by night after a clouded day. It was the ideal of "book-learning"; the curiosity, born of compulsory ignorance, to know and test the power of the cabalistic letters of the white man, the longing to know. Here at least seemed to have been discovered the mountain path to Canaan; longer than the highway of Emancipation and law, steep and rugged, but straight, leading to heights high enough to overlook life.

Up the new path the advance guard toiled, slowly, heavily, doggedly; only those who have watched and guided the faltering feet, the misty minds, the dull understandings of the dark pupils of these schools know how faithfully, how piteously, this people strove to learn. It was weary work. The cold statistician wrote down the inches of progress here and there, noted also where here and there a foot had slipped or some one had fallen. To the tired climbers, the horizon was ever dark, the mists were often cold, the Canaan was always dim and far away. If, however, the vistas disclosed as yet no goal, no resting-place, little but flattery and criticism, the journey at least gave leisure for reflection and self-examination; it changed the child of Emancipation to the youth with dawning self-consciousness, self-realization, self-respect. In those sombre forests of his striving his own soul rose before him, and he saw himself,—darkly as through a veil; and yet he saw in himself some faint revelation of his power, of his mission. He began to have a dim feeling that, to attain his place in the world, he must be himself, and not another. For the first time he sought to analyze the burden he bore upon his back, that dead-weight of social degradation partially masked behind a half-named Negro problem. He felt his poverty: without a cent, without a home, without land, tools, or savings, he had entered into competition with rich, landed, skilled neighbors. To be a poor man is hard, but to be a poor race in a land of dollars is the very bottom of hardships. He felt the weight of his ignorance,—not simply of letters, but of life, of business, of the humanities; the accumulated sloth and shirking and awkwardness of decades and centuries shackled his hands and feet. Nor was his burden all poverty and ignorance. The red stain of bastardy, which two centuries of systematic legal defilement of Negro women had stamped upon his race, meant not only the loss of ancient African chastity, but also the hereditary weight of a mass of corruption from white adulterers, threatening almost the obliteration of the Negro home.

A people thus handicapped ought not to be asked to race with the world, but rather allowed to give all its time and thought to its own social problems. But alas! while sociologists gleefully count his bastards and his prostitutes, the very soul of the toiling, sweating black man is darkened by the shadow of a vast despair. Men call the shadow prejudice, and learnedly explain it as the natural defence of culture against barbarism, learning against ignorance, purity against crime, the "higher" against the "lower" races. To which the Negro cries Amen! and swears that to so much of this strange prejudice as is founded on just homage to civilization, culture, righteousness, and progress, he humbly bows and meekly does obeisance. But before that nameless prejudice that leaps beyond all this he stands helpless, dismayed, and well-nigh speechless; before that personal disrespect and mockery, the ridicule and systematic humiliation, the distortion of fact and wanton license of fancy, the cynical ignoring of the better and the boisterous welcoming of the worse, the all-pervading desire to inculcate disdain for everything black, from Toussaint to the devil,—before this there rises a sickening despair that would disarm and discourage any nation save that black host to whom "discouragement" is an unwritten word.

But the facing of so vast a prejudice could not but bring the inevitable self-questioning, self-disparagement, and lowering of ideals which ever accompany repression and breed in an atmosphere of contempt and hate. Whisperings and portents came borne upon the four winds: Lo! we are diseased and dying, cried the dark hosts; we cannot write, our voting is vain; what need of education, since we must always cook and serve? And the Nation echoed and enforced this self-criticism, saying: Be content to be servants, and nothing more; what need of higher culture for half-men? Away with the black man's ballot, by force or fraud,—and behold the suicide of a race! Nevertheless, out of the evil came something of good,—the more careful adjustment of education to real life, the clearer perception of the Negroes' social responsibilities, and the sobering realization of the meaning of progress.

So dawned the time of *Sturm und Drang*: storm and stress to-day rocks our little boat on the mad waters of the world-sea; there is within and without the sound of conflict, the burning of body and rending of soul; inspiration strives with doubt, and faith with vain questionings. The bright ideals of the past,— physical freedom, political power, the training of brains and the training of hands,—all these in turn have waxed and waned, until even the last grows dim and overcast. Are they all wrong,—all false? No, not that, but each alone was over-simple and incomplete,—the dreams of a credulous race-childhood, or the fond imaginings of the other world which does not know and does not want to know our power. To be really true, all these ideals must be melted and welded into one. The training of the schools we need today more than ever,—the training of deft hands, quick eyes and ears, and above all the broader, deeper, higher culture of gifted minds and pure hearts. The power of the ballot we need in sheer self-defence,—else what shall save us from a second slavery? Freedom, too, the long-sought, we still seek,—the freedom of life and limb, the freedom to work and think, the freedom to love and aspire. Work, culture, liberty,—all those we need, not singly but together, not successively but together, each growing and aiding each, and all striving toward that vaster ideal that swims before the Negro people, the ideal of human brotherhood, gained through the unifying ideal of Race; the ideal of fostering and developing the traits and talents of the Negro, not in opposition to or contempt for other races, but rather in large conformity to the greater ideals of the American Republic, in order that some day on American soil two world-races may give each to each those characteristics both so sadly lack. We the darker ones come even now not altogether empty-handed: there are today no truer exponents of the pure human spirit of the Declaration of Independence than the American Negroes; there is no true American music but the wild sweet melodies of the Negro slave; the American fairy tales and folklore are Indian and African' and all in all, we black men seem the sole oasis of simple faith and reverence in a dusty desert of dollars and smartness. Will America be poorer if she replace her brutal dyspeptic blundering with light-hearted but determined Negro humility? or her coarse and cruel wit with loving jovial good-humor? or her vulgar music with the soul of the Sorrow Songs?

Merely a concrete test of the underlying principles of the great republic is the Negro Problem, and the spiritual striving of the freedmen's sons is the travail of souls whose burden is almost beyond the measure of their strength, but who beat it in the name of an historic race, in the name of this the land of their fathers' fathers, and in the name of human opportunity....

The Souls of White Folk
W.E.B. DuBois

... I know many souls that toss and whirl and pass, but none there are that intrigue me more than the Souls of White Folk.

Of them I am singularly clairvoyant. I see in and through them. I view them from unusual points of vantage. Not as a foreigner do I come, for I am native, not foreign, bone of their thought and flesh of their language. Mine is not the knowledge of the traveler or the colonial composite of dear memories, words, and wonder. Nor yet is my knowledge that which servants have of masters, or mass of class, or capitalist of artisan. Rather I see these souls undressed and from the back and side. I see the working of their entrails. I know their thoughts and they know that I know. This knowledge makes them now embarassed, now furious! They deny my right to live and be and call me misbirth! My word is to them mere bitterness and my soul, pessimism. And yet as they preach and strut and shout and threaten, crouching as they clutch at rags of facts and fancies to hide their nakedness, they go twisting, flying by my tired eyes and I see them ever stripped—ugly, human.

The discovery of personal whiteness among the world's peoples is a very modern thing—a nineteenth and twentieth century matter, indeed. The ancient world would have laughed at such a distinction. The Middle Age regarded skin color with mild curiousity; and even up into the eighteenth century we were hammering our national manikins into one, great, Universal Man, with fine frenzy which ignored color and race even more than birth. Today we have changed all that, and the world in a sudden, emotional conversion has discovered that it is white and by that token, wonderful!

This assumption that of all the hues of God whiteness alone is inherently and obviously better than brownness or tan leads to curious acts; even the sweeter souls of the dominant world as they discourse with me on weather, weal, and woe are continually playing above their actual words an obligato of tune and tone, saying:

"My poor, un-white thing! Weep not nor rage. I know, too well, that the curse of God lies heavy on you. Why? That is not for me to say, but be brave! Do your work in your lowly sphere, praying the good Lord that into heaven above, where all is love, you may, one day, be born—white!"

I do not laugh. I am quite straight-faced as I ask soberly:

"But what on earth is whiteness that one should so desire it?" Then always, somehow, some way, silently but clearly, I am given to understand that whiteness is the ownership of the earth forever and ever, Amen!...

17

___

THE CHICAGO SCHOOL

The Chicago School refers to urban sociologists at the University of Chicago in the 1920s and 1930s; this type of sociological work continued into the post-war period, and eventually the term came to be used for a style of sociology that is still practised today. Its basic premises include:

1. embedding theory in research, so that theorizing is not the formulation of abstract concepts but ideas closely connected to empirical findings;
2. doing fieldwork, especially using ethnographic methods, such as participant-observation and analysis of life narratives, with data collected in a specific place;
3. emphasizing a specific place or environment, so that the research is always grounded in a community, neighbourhood, city, or organization (such as a bar or hospital) and does not lead to the formulation of abstract concepts distant from empirical observation;
4. recording details of the lives and speech of specific individuals, so that the fieldwork is always about human lives and activities: dance hall girls, muggers, physicians, residents of the slum or the Gold Coast, street gangs, etc.;
5. focusing on topics like ethnicity, cultural diversity in the modern metropolis, deviance and disorganization, and the ways of life of different social classes—often topics central to the North American experience in the first decades of the twentieth century as well as now;
6. keeping a relatively short time frame, suitable for observing processes like immigration, assimilation, ethnic conflict, and urban growth, and avoiding the long historical dimension of classical theory; and
7. writing in a lively way about real people—actual individuals whose actions, interactions, and voices are recorded in fieldnotes, interviews, and life narratives.

Chicago School sociology offers an implicit social theory: society is constantly formed by the actions of people in specific settings, cultural milieus and actual places. The field research *is* the theory. This grounded style of theorizing later became one of the elements of a theory called "symbolic interactionism."

The perspective of the Chicago School is lively and gut-level, not abstract and cerebral. It is an excellent starting point for the student who is eager to do sociology, to start observing and writing, to talk to real people, to be out on the street, in the bars, parks, cafes, squad cars, housing projects, clubs, and markets of the great metropolis. After a term or two of sociology courses, everyone can begin Chicago School fieldwork, and that is part of its continuing appeal.

Chicago School sociology shares Weber's concept of social action, but is radically different in its research methods, time frame, and level of abstraction from Weber's historically-contextualized *verstehen*. Weber's concepts of class, status, and party appear in Chicago School work (as we will see in our selection), but these categories are much closer than his concepts to people's everyday life experiences and ways of talking about their reality. The Chicago School shares little of Marx's transcendent and negative-critical stance; Chicago School sociologists hoped to resolve social problems but in more down-to-earth and immediate ways than Marx. They were strongly influenced by Simmel, and shared his interest in interaction and the modern metropolis, but were less involved in his philosophical concerns.

Here, in a selection from the opening chapter of St. Clair Drake and Horace Cayton's *Black Metropolis*, published in 1945, we see many Chicago School characteristics. The work is about an actual place—the south side of Chicago; the writing is concrete and vivid; attention is devoted to ethnicity, class, and the dialectic of American identity and ethnic culture; spatial patterns are a central topic of the research; class, racial status, and party ("advancing the race") are described in a down-to-earth way.

Of course, race relations in the United States changed in the two decades after the publication of *Black Metropolis*, yet the authors' conclusions about the mix of class (realized in free competition) and fixed racial status in the lives of African Americans are still relevant today, even if the mix has shifted toward free competition.

Readings

Addams, Jane. *Twenty Years at Hull House*. Urbana, IL: University of Illinois Press, 1990.

Deegan, Mary Jo. *Jane Addams and the Men of the Chicago School, 1892-1918*. New Brunswick, NJ: Transaction Press, 1988.

Henslin, James. *Down to Earth Sociology*. New York: Free Press, 1999.

Stebner, Eleanor. *The Women of Hull House*. Albany, NY: SUNY Press, 1997.

Thomas, W.I. and Florian Znaniecki. *The Polish Peasant in Europe and America*. Urbana, IL: University of Illinois Press, 1995.

Zorbaugh, Harvey. *The Gold Coast and the Slum*. Chicago: University of Chicago Press, 1954.

Black Metropolis
ST. CLAIR DRAKE (1911-1990) AND HORACE CAYTON (1903-1970)

Ezekiel saw a wheel—
Wheel in the middle of a wheel—
The big wheel run by faith,
An' the little wheel run by the grace of God—
Ezekiel saw a wheel.
—Negro spiritual

Stand in the center of the black belt—at Chicago's 47th st. and South Parkway. Around you swirls a continuous eddy of faces—black, brown, olive, yellow, and white. Soon you will realize that this is not "just another neighborhood" of Midwest Metropolis. Glance at the newsstand on the corner. You will see the Chicago dailies—the *Tribune*, the *Times,* the *Herald-American*, the *News*, the *Sun*. But you will also find a number of weeklies headlining the activities of Negroes—Chicago's *Defender*, *Bee*, *News-Ledger*, and *Metropolitan News*, the Pittsburgh *Courier*, and a number of others. In the nearby drugstore colored clerks are bustling about. (They are seldom seen in other neighborhoods.) In most of the other stores, too, there are colored salespeople, although a white proprietor or manager usually looms in the offing. In the offices around you, colored doctors, dentists, and lawyers go about their duties. And a brown-skinned policeman saunters along swinging his club and glaring sternly at the urchins who dodge in and out among the shoppers.

Two large theaters will catch your eye with their billboards featuring Negro orchestras and vaudeville troupes, and the Negro great and near-great of Hollywood—Lena Horne, Rochester, Hattie McDaniels.

On a spring or summer day this spot, "47th and South Park," is the urban equivalent of a village square. In fact, Black Metropolis has a saying, "if you're trying to find a certain Negro in Chicago, stand on the corner of 47th and South Park long enough and you're bound to see him." There is continuous and colorful movement here—shoppers streaming in and out of stores; insurance agents turning in their collections at a funeral parlor; club reporters rushing into a newspaper office with their social notes; irate tenants filing complaints with the Office of Price Administration; job-seekers moving in and out of the United States Employment Office. Today a picket line may be calling attention to the "unfair labor practices" of a merchant. Tomorrow a girl may be selling tags on the corner for a hospital or community house. The next day you will find a group of boys soliciting signatures to place a Negro on the All-Star football team. And always a beggar or two will be in the background—a blind man, cup in hand, tapping his way along, or a legless veteran propped up against the side of a building. This is Bronzeville's central shopping district, where rents are highest and Negro merchants compete fiercely with whites for the choicest commercial spots. A few steps away from the intersection is the "largest Negro-owned department store in America," attempting to challenge the older and more experienced white retail establishments across the street. At an exclusive "Eat Shoppe" just off the boulevard, you may find a Negro Congressman or ex-Congressman dining at your elbow, or former heavyweight champion Jack Johnson, beret pushed back on his head, chuckling at the next table; in the private dining-room there may be a party of civic leaders, black and white, planning reforms. A few doors away, behind the Venetian blinds of a well-appointed tavern, the "big shots" of the sporting world crowd the bar on one side of the house, while the respectable "élite" takes its beers and "sizzling steaks" in the booths on the other side.

Within a half-mile radius of "47th and South Park" are clustered the major community institutions: the Negro-staffed Provident Hospital; the George Cleveland Hall Library (named for a colored physician); the YWCA; the "largest colored Catholic church in the country"; the "largest Protestant congregation in America"; the Black Belt's Hotel Grand; Parkway Community House; and the imposing Michigan Boulevard Garden Apartments for middle-income families.

As important as any of these is the large four-square-mile green, Washington Park—playground of the South Side. Here in the summer thousands of Negroes of all ages congregate to play softball and tennis, to swim, or just lounge around. Here during the Depression, stormy crowds met to listen to leaders of the unemployed.

Within Black Metropolis, there are neighborhood centers of activity having their own drugstores, grocery stores, theaters, poolrooms, taverns, and churches, but "47th and South Park" overshadows all other business areas in size and importance.

If you wander about a bit in Black Metropolis you will note that one of the most striking features of the area is the prevalence of churches, numbering some 500. Many of these edifices still bear the marks of previous ownership—six-pointed Stars of David, Hebrew and Swedish inscriptions, or names chiseled on old cornerstones which do not tally with those on new bulletin boards. On many of the business streets in the more run-down areas there are scores of "storefront"churches. To the uninitiated, this plethora of churches is no less baffling than the bewildering variety and the colorful extravagance of the names. Nowhere else in Midwest Metropolis could one find, within a stone's throw of one another, a Hebrew Baptist Church, a Baptized Believers' Holiness Church, a Universal Union Independent, a Church of Love and Faith, Spiritual, a Holy Mt. Zion Methodist Episcopal Independent, and a United Pentecostal Holiness Church. Or a cluster such as St. John's Christian Spiritual, Park Mission African Methodist Episcopal, Philadelphia Baptists, Little Rock Baptist, and the Aryan Full Gospel Mission, Spiritualist.

Churches are conspicuous, but to those who have eyes to see they are rivaled in number by another community institution, the policy station, which is to the Negro community what the race-horse bookie is to white neighborhoods. In these mysterious little shops, tucked away in basements or behind stores, one may place a dime bet and hope to win $20 if the numbers "fall right." Definitely illegal, but tolerated by the law, the policy station is a ubiquitous institution, absent only from the more exclusive residential neighborhoods.

In addition to these more or less legitimate institutions, "tea pads" and "reefer dens," "buffet flats" and "call houses" also flourish, known only to the habitués of the underworld and to those respectable patrons, white and colored, without whose faithful support they could not exist. (Since 1912, when Chicago's Red-light District was abolished, prostitution has become a clandestine affair, though open "street-walking" does occur in isolated areas.) An occasional feature story or news article in the daily press or in a Negro weekly throws a sudden light on one of these spots—a police raid or some unexpected tragedy; and then, as in all communities, it is forgotten.

In its thinking, Black Metropolis draws a clear line between the "shady" and the "respectable," the "sporting world" and the world of churches, clubs, and polite society. In practice, however, as we shall see, the line is a continuously shifting one and is hard to maintain, in the Black Metropolis as in other parts of Midwest Metropolis.

This is a community of stark contrasts, the facets of its life as varied as the colors of its people's skins. The tiny churches in deserted and dilapidated stores, with illiterately scrawled announcements on their painted windows, are marked off sharply from the fine edifices on the boulevards with stained-glass windows and electric bulletin boards. The rickety frame dwellings, sprawled along the railroad tracks, bespeak a way of life at an opposite pole from that of the quiet and well-groomed orderliness of middle-class neighborhoods. And many of the still stately-appearing old mansions, long since abandoned by Chicago's wealthy whites, conceal interiors that are foul and decayed.

The Anatomy of a Black Ghetto

... [T]he Black Belt has higher rates of sickness and death than the rest of the city, and the lowest average incomes. But misery is not spread evenly over the

Black Ghetto, for Black Metropolis, as a part of Midwest Metropolis, has followed the same general pattern of city growth. Those Negroes who through the years have become prosperous tend to gravitate to stable neighborhoods far from the center of the city.[1] They have slowly filtered southward within the Black Belt. Always, however, they hit the invisible barbed-wire fence of restrictive covenants. The fence may be moved back a little here and there, but never fast enough nor far enough.

Out of this moving about, this twenty-five-year-old search for a "better neighborhood," has arisen a spatial pattern *within* the Black Belt similar to that found in the city as a whole. E. Franklin Frazier, a Negro sociologist, was the first to demonstrate clearly this progressive differentiation statistically. His *Negro Family in Chicago* graphically portrayed the existence of "zones" based on socio-economic status within Black Metropolis. The Cayton-Warner Research, some years later, revealed what happens in ghetto when the successful and ambitious can't get out and when the city does not provide the poor and the vicious with enough living space, or enough incentive and opportunity to modify their style of life. The "worst" areas begin to encroach upon the "more desirable areas," and large "mixed" areas result. These, in turn, become gradually "worst," and the "more desirable" areas begin to suffer from "blight" and become "mixed."

A few people from time to time do manage to escape from the Black Ghetto into the city's residential and commuters' zones. They are immediately encysted by restrictive covenants and "sealed off." Such settlements—"satellite areas"—are unable to expand freely, although there is a tendency, in time, for the white people in immediate proximity to move away.

The Spirit of Bronzeville

"Ghetto" is a harsh term, carrying overtones of poverty and suffering, of exclusion and subordination. In Midwest Metropolis it is used by civic leaders when they want to shock complacency into action. Most of the ordinary people in the Black Belt refer to their community as "the South Side," but everybody is also familiar with another name for the area—Bronzeville. This name seems to have been used originally by an editor of the Chicago *Bee*, who, in 1930, sponsored a contest to elect a "Mayor of Bronzeville." A year or two later, when this newspaperman joined the *Defender* staff, he took his brain-child with him. The annual election of the "Mayor of Bronzeville" grew into a community event with a significance far beyond that of a circulation stunt. Each year a Board of Directors composed of outstanding citizens of the Black Belt takes charge of the mock-election. Ballots are cast at corner stores and in barbershops and poolrooms. The "Mayor," usually a businessman, is inaugurated with a colorful ceremony and a ball. Throughout his tenure he is expected to serve as a symbol of the community's aspirations. He visits churches, files protests with the Mayor of the city, and acts as official greeter of visitors to Bronzeville. Tens of thousands of people participate in the annual election of the "Mayor." In 1944-45, a physician was elected mayor.

...Throughout the remainder of this book we shall use the term "Bronzeville" for Black Metropolis because it seems to express the feeling that the people have about their own community.[2] They *live* in the Black Belt and to them it is more than the "ghetto" revealed by statistical analysis.

The Axes of Life: What are the dominating interests, the "centers of orientation," the lines of attention, which claim the time and money of Bronzeville— the "axes of life"[3] around which individual and community life revolves? The most important of these are: (1) Staying Alive; (2) Having a Good time; (3) Praising God; (4) Getting Ahead; (5) Advancing the Race.

The majority of Bronzeville's people will insist that they came to Midwest Metropolis to "better their condition." Usually they mean that they were seeking an opportunity to sell their labor for a steady supply of money to expend on food, clothing, housing, recreation, and plans for the future. They were also searching for adequate leisure time in which to enjoy themselves. Such goals are a part of the general American Dream. (But when a Negro talks about "bettering his condition" he means something more: he refers also to finding an environment where exclusion and subordination by white men are not rubbed in his face—as they are in the South.)

Staying Alive

Before people can enjoy liberty or pursue happiness, they must maintain life. During the Fat Years the problem of earning a living was not an acute one for Negroes in Chicago. More than three-fourths of the Negro men and almost half of the women were gainfully employed, though their work tended to be heavy or menial. Wages were generally lower than for the bulk of the white working people, but they permitted a plane of living considerably higher than anything most parts of the South had to offer. Though the first few years of the Depression resulted in much actual suffering in Bronzeville, the WPA eventually provided a bedrock of subsistence which guaranteed food and clothing. The ministrations of social workers and wide education in the use of public health facilities seem to have actually raised the level of health in the Black Ghetto during the Depression years.[4] The Second World War once more incorporated Negroes into the productive economic life of Midwest Metropolis, and most of them had plenty of money to spend for the first time in a decade.

The high infant mortality and general death rates, the high incidence of disease, and the overcrowding and hazardous work, have all operated to keep the rate of natural increase for Negroes below that for whites. The man in the street is not aware of these statistical indices, but he does experience life in the Black Belt as a struggle for existence, a struggle which he consciously interprets as a fight against white people who deny Negroes the opportunity to compete for—and hold—"good jobs." Civic leaders, who see the whole picture, are also acutely aware of the role played by inadequate health and recreational facilities and poor housing. They also recognize the need for widespread adult education which will teach recent migrants how to make use of public health facilities and to protect themselves against disease. (The struggle for survival proceeds on an unconscious level, except when it is highlighted by a depression, a race riot, or an economic conflict between Negroes and whites.)

Enjoying Life

Bronzeville's people have never let poverty, disease, and discrimination "get them down." The vigor with which they enjoy life seems to belie the gloomy observations of the statisticians and civic leaders who know the facts about the Black Ghetto. In the Lean Years as well as the Fat, Bronzeville has shared the general American interest in "having a good time." Its people like the movies and shows, athletic events, dancing, card-playing, and all the other recreational activities--commercial and noncommercial—which Midwest Metropolis offers. The recreations of an industrial society reflect the need for an escape from the monotony of machine-tending and the discipline of office and factory. For the people of Bronzeville, "having a good time" also serves another function—escape from the tensions of contact with white people. Absorption in "pleasure" is, in part at least, a kind of adjustment to their separate, subordinate status in American life.

If working as servants, Negroes must be properly deferential to the white people upon whom they depend for meager wages and tips. In fact, they often have to overdo their act in order to earn a living; as they phrase it, they have to "Uncle Tom" to "Mr. Charley" a bit to survive. If working in a factory, they must take orders from a white managerial personnel and associate with white workers who, they know, do not accept them as social equals. If self-employed, they are continually frustrated by the indirect restrictions imposed upon Negro business and professional men. If civil servants, they are in continuous contact with situations that emphasize their ghetto existence and subordinate status. But, when work is over, the pressure of the white world is lifted. Within Bronzeville Negroes are at home. They find rest from white folks as well as from labor, and they make the most of it. In their homes, in lodge rooms and clubhouses, pool parlors and taverns, cabarets and movies, they can temporarily shake off the incubus of the white world. Their recreational activities parallel those of white people, but with distinctive nuances and shadings of behavior. What Bronzeville considers a good time—the pattern for enjoying life—is intimately connected with economic status, education, and social standing. A detailed discussion of recreational habits is therefore reserved for those chapters dealing with social class. Suffice it here to say that Bronzeville's people treasure their inalienable right to pursue happiness.

Praising the Lord
It is a matter for continuous surprise that churches in America's large urban communities are able to compete with secular interests and to emerge even stronger than the church in rural areas.[5] Despite the fact that only about half of the adults in America claim church membership, the strong Protestant and Catholic tradition in the culture retains its hold upon the minds of the American people. The church and religion have been displaced from the center of the average man's life, but remain an important side-interest for many people. The general trend toward secularization of interests has affected men more strongly than women, but probably the majority of Americans pay some lip-service to religion and participate occasionally in the rites and ceremonies—at least upon occasions of birth, marriage, and death.

It has become customary in America to refer to Negroes as a "religious people." The movies and the radio, by their selection of incident and dialogue, tend to reinforce this prevalent conception. A walk through Bronzeville also seems to lend confirmation to this belief, for the evidences of an interest in "praising the Lord" are everywhere—churches are omnipresent. Negroes have slightly more than their expected share of churches and twice their share of preachers; a large proportion of the people seem to enjoy "praising the Lord." The spirit of Bronzeville is tinctured with religion, but like "having a good time" the real importance of the church can be understood only by relating it to the economic and social status of the various groups in Bronzeville.

Getting Ahead
The dominating individual drive in American life is not "staying alive," nor "enjoying life," nor "praising the Lord"—it is "getting ahead." In its simplest terms this means progressively moving from low-paid to higher-paid jobs, acquiring a more comfortable home, laying up something for sickness and old age, and trying to make sure that the children will start out at a higher economic and cultural level than the parents. Individuals symbolize their progress by the way they spend their money—for clothes, real estate, automobiles, donations, entertaining; and the individual's choice is dictated largely in terms of the circle of society in which he moves or which he wishes to impress. These circles

or groupings are myriad and complex, for not all people set their goals at the same distance. Out of the differential estimates of the meaning of success arise various social classes and "centers of orientation."

There are, of course, some small groups in Midwest Metropolis, as elsewhere, who interpret success in noneconomic terms, who prize "morality," or "culture," or talent and technical competence. In general, however, Americans believe that if a man is *really* "getting ahead," if he is *really* successful, his accomplishments will become translated into an effective increase in income. People are expected to "cash in" on brains or talent or political power.

For thousands of Negro migrants from the South, merely arriving in Bronzeville represented "getting ahead." Yet Negroes, like other Americans, share the general interest in getting ahead in more conventional terms. The Job Ceiling and the Black Ghetto limit free competition for the money and for residential symbols of success. Partly because of these limitations (which are not peculiar to Chicago) it has become customary among the masses of Negroes in America to center their interest upon living in the immediate present or upon going to heaven—upon "having a good time" or "praising the Lord." Though some derive their prestige from the respect accorded them by the white world, or by the professional and business segments of the Negro world, most Negroes seem to adopt a pattern of conspicuous behavior and conspicuous consumption. Maintaining a "front" and "showing off" become very important substitutes for getting ahead in the economic sense. Leadership in various organizations often constitutes the evidence that a man has "arrived."

Leaders in Bronzeville, like Negro leaders everywhere since the Civil War, are constantly urging the community to raise its sights above "survival," "enjoying life," and "praising the Lord". They present "getting ahead" as a *racial* duty as well as a personal gain. When a Negro saves money, buys bonds, invests in a business or in property, he is automatically "advancing The Race."[6] When Negroes "waste their substance," they are "setting The Race back." This appraisal of their activity is widely accepted by the rank and file, but leaders sometimes press their shots too hard. When they do so, they often get a response like that of the domestic servant who resented the attempts of a civic leader to discourage elaborate social club dances during the Depression: "We [the social club] give to the Federated Home and about ten or fifteen other institutions. If we want to give a dance, I think that's our business. We poor colored people don't have much as it is, and if we sat around and thought about our sufferings we'd go crazy."

Advancing the Race
White people in Midwest Metropolis become aware of Negroes only occasionally and sporadically. Negroes, however, live in a state of intense and perpetu-

al awareness that they are a black minority in a white man's world. The Job Ceiling and the Black ghetto are an ever present experience. Petty discriminations (or actions that might be interpreted as such) occur daily. Unpleasant memories of the racial and individual past are a part of every Negro's personality structure. News and rumors of injustice and terror in the south and elsewhere circulate freely through Negro communities at all times. "Race consciousness" is not the work of "agitators" or "subversive influences"—it is forced upon Negroes by the very fact of their separate-subordinate status in American life. And it is tremendously reinforced by life in a compact community such as Black Metropolis, set within the framework of a large white community.

Negroes are ill at ease in the land of their birth. They are bombarded with the slogans of democracy, liberty, freedom, equality, but they are not allowed to participate freely in American life. They develop a tormenting ambivalence toward themselves and the larger society of which they are a part. America rejects them; so they tend to hate. But it is the only land they know; so they are sentimentally attached to it. Their skin color and social origins subject them to discrimination and contumely; so they often (consciously or unconsciously) despise The Race. The people they know most intimately, however, are colored, and men cannot totally hate themselves and their friends. Thus their moods fluctuate between shame and defiance. Their conversation becomes a bewildering mixture of expressions of "racial depreciation" and "race pride."

The Cult of Race: Negroes feel impelled to prove to themselves continually that they are not the inferior creatures which their minority status implies. Thus, ever since emancipation, Negro leaders have preached the necessity for cultivating "race pride." They have assiduously repeated the half truth that "no other race has ever made the progress that Negroes have made in an equivalent length of time." They have patiently attempted to popularize an expanding roster of Race Heroes—individuals who have attained success or prominence, "Catching up with the white folks" has been developed as the dominating theme of inspirational and exhortations, and the Negro "firsts" and "onlies" are set up as Race Heroes.[7] "Beating the white man at his own game" becomes a powerful motivation for achievement and explains the popularity of such personalities as Joe Louis or Jesses Owens, George Washington Carver or outstanding soldier-heroes. A myth of "special gifts" has also emerged, with Negroes (and whites also) believing that American Negroes have some inborn, unusual talent as dancers, musicians, artists and athletes.

In the period between the First and the Second World Wars, this emphasis upon race pride became a mass phenomenon among the Negroes in large urban communities. Race consciousness was transformed into a positive and aggressive defensive racialism. Negroes in Black Metropolis, as in other communities, feeling the strength of their economic and political power, have become increasingly aware of the achievements of individual Negroes, and have developed an absorbing interest in every scrap of evidence that "The Race is advancing," or is "catching up with white folks," or is "beating the white man at his own game." Unable to compete freely *as individuals,* the Negro masses take intense vicarious pleasure in watching Race heroes vindicate them in the eyes of the white world.

Race pride is a defensive reaction that can become a mere verbal escape mechanism. Negro leaders are therefore perpetually involved in an effort to make race pride more than an end in itself: to utilize it as a morale builder, as the raw material of "racial solidarity." They seek to use it for "advancing The Race." They foster race pride in order to elicit support for collective action—the support of Negro business enterprises, the organization of petition and protest, the focusing of economical and political power. The most persistent theme of speeches and editorials in Bronzeville is: "Negroes must learn to stick together." The leaders use it also to encourage individual achievement, by interpreting the success of one Negro as the success of all. Out of this interplay between race consciousness, race pride, and race solidarity arise certain definite social types: the Race Hero, the Race Leader, the Race Man, the Race Woman.

The average person in Bronzeville is primarily interested in "staying alive," "getting ahead," "having a good time" and "praising the Lord." Conscious preoccupation with "racial advancement" is fitful and sporadic, though always latent. The masses leave "the burden of The Race" to those individuals who are oriented around "service"—the Race Leaders. Some of these are people who devote much of their leisure time to charitable organizations or associations for racial advancement. For others solving the race problem is a full-time job. For instance, a score or so of individuals in Bronzeville are elected and appointed politicians who "represent The Race." There are also a few civic leaders who earn their living by administering social agencies such as the Urban League, the YMCA, the YWCA, settlement houses, and similar organizations. In Bronzeville, too, there are numerous "self-appointed leaders"—men and women, often illiterate and poverty stricken, who feel the call to "lead The Race out of bondage." They harangue their small groups of followers on the streets, in store-fronts, or in the public parks with a fanaticism that alienates them from the masses as well as from the affluent and educated.

Most of the people in Bronzeville do not hold membership in any of the organizations for "racial advancement," such as the National Association for the Advancement of Colored People (NAACP), the national Negro Congress, the Urban League, or the Council of Negro Organizations. They follow the activities of Race leaders in the Negro press, they cheer and applaud an occasionally highly publicized victory over those who maintain the Job Ceiling and the Black Ghetto. They grumble persistently about "lack of leadership." They contribute an occasional nickel or dime to drives for funds. But when some inciting incident stirs them deeply, they close ranks and put up a scrap—for a community housing project, to remove a prejudiced policeman, to force a recalcitrant merchant to employ Negroes. And they periodically vote for Negroes to represent them in state, local, and national bodies. In general, "solving the race problem" is left in the hands of Race Leaders—the "racial watchdogs," as one Bronzeville preacher called them.

Race Leadership: Race Leaders are expected to put up some sort of aggressive fight against the exclusion and subordination of Negroes. They must also stress "catching up with white folks," and this involves the less dramatic activity of appeals for discipline within the Black Belt, and pleas for Negroes to take advantage of opportunities to "advance." A Race Leader has to fight the Job Ceiling and Black Ghetto and at the same time needle, cajole, and denounce Negroes themselves for inertia, diffidence, and lack of race pride; and the functions sometimes conflict.

There is rather widespread agreement in Bronzeville on what an ideal Race Leader should be. When the people are asked to describe a "real Race Leader" they always stress "sincerity" as a cardinal virtue: A Race Leader, they say

... knows the difficulties of the race and fights without a selfish reason;
... is a sincere person with some moral principle;
... is sincere and has a plan;
... has a constant, sincere interest in the race;
... is sincere and people know he is not after some hidden personal interest;
... has the interest and well-being of the Negro race uppermost in his life.

"Everybody will tell you," a young stenographer observed, "that a real Race Leader is 'square'!"

Sincerity is prized, but, as one of the persons quoted above stated, a leader must have a plan. Theories about solving the race problem range all the way from amalgamation to emigration to Africa, from sympathy with Communism to the demand for a "49th Negro state." The "accepted leaders," however, tend to be people who stress the use of political and economic pressure (without violence) and gradual advancement by slowly raising the economic and educational level of the entire group.

"An ardent racialist without ability is not a race leader," comments a clerical worker; "he must have something to contribute." A leader must be able to formulate and present the Negroes' demands and aspirations to white people. Many people insist that a real leader must be "calm, well poised, well trained." Some think he should be "an educated person who has a great deal of influence with whites and prestige with Negroes." The more conservative people feel that he should also be a person who "believes strongly in caution and patience" and who is "adept in the arts of personal and political compromise."

Bronzeville knows that the powers of its leaders are limited, that in the final analysis the white majority can break any leader who is too aggressive. It is well aware that white America makes concessions to Negroes primarily from the imperatives of economic necessity and political expediency rather than from devotion to democratic ideals. Out of this knowledge arises a kind of cynical realism which does not expect too much from leaders.

Bronzeville knows, too, that "leaders are human," that they are motivated by the desire for power and prestige as well as by the "service" ideal. The whole business of "advancing The Race" offers wide opportunities for fraud, graft, and chicanery. There are opportunities for "selling out to the white folks," diverting funds from "the cause," or making a racket out of race. People try to draw a line between "sincere Race Leaders" and those Race Men who "are always clamoring everything for The Race, just for the glory of being known." They will characterize some leaders as being "like the William Randolf Hearst variety of patriot whose Americanism means a chance to make more money." They are skeptical of those who, "when you see them, are always talking about The Race." Sincerity is hard to test, however, and Bronzeville seems to expect that its leaders will "cash in" on their positions, in terms of personal influence if not in terms of money.

The Race Man: Frustrated in their isolation from the main streams of American life, and in their impotence to control their fate decisively, Negroes tend to admire an aggressive Race Man even when his motives are suspect.[8] They will applaud him, because, in the face of the white world, he remains "proud of his race and always tries to uphold it whether it is good or bad, right or wrong," because he sees "only the good points of the race." One high school girl explained that "the Race Man is interested in the welfare of the people. Everybody says that they admire a Race Man, but behind the scenes they may not regard him as being sincere. The Race Man is usually a politician or a business man. He sponsors movements for the benefit of the people. It is a way of securing honor and admiration form the people. Personally, I admire a Race Man even if he seeks his own advancement." A well-known minister interpreted the admiration for the Race Man as follows: "The people are emotionally enthusiastic about a Race Man. They know that a Race Man may not be quite as sincere as some of the more quiet leaders. Still, the very fact of his working for the race gives him prestige in their eyes." A Race Man is one type of Race Hero.

The Race Hero: If a man "fights for The Race," if he seems to be "all for The Race," if he is "fearless in his approach to white people," he becomes a Race Hero. Similarly any Negro becomes a hero if he beats the white man at his own game or forces the white world to recognize his talent or service or achievement. Racketeer or preacher, reactionary or Communist, ignoramus or savant—if a man is an aggressive, vocal, uncompromising Race Man he is everybody's hero. Even conservative Negroes admire colored radicals who buck the white world. Preachers may oppose sin, but they will also express a seeking admiration for a Negro criminal who decisively outwits white people. Even the quiet, well-disciplined family man may get a thrill when a "bad Negro" blows his top and goes down with both guns blazing at the White Law. Such identification is usually covert and unconscious, and may even be feared and regretted by the very persons who experience it. Race pride sometimes verges upon the vindictive, but it is a direct result of the position to which white America has consigned the Negro group.

World Within a World

The people of Bronzeville have, through the years, crystallized certain distinctive patterns of thought and behavior. Their tenacious clinging to life, their struggle for liberty, their quest for happiness, have resulted in the proliferation of institutions. The customs and habits of Bronzeville's people are essentially American but carry overtones of subtle difference. Bronzeville has all the major institutions found in any other Chicago neighborhood—schools and churches, a wide range of stores and shops, varied commercial amusements, segments of the city political machine, and numerous voluntary associations. And besides, as a low-income community it has had more than its share of relief stations and never enough playgrounds, clinics, and similar social services.

While Bronzeville's institutions differ little in form from those in other Midwest Metropolis communities, they differ considerably in content. The dissimilarity springs primarily from two facts: Because the community is spiritually isolated from the larger world, the development of its families, churches, schools, and voluntary associations has proceeded quite differently from the course taken by analogous white institutions; and, second, Bronzeville's "culture" is but a part of a larger, national Negro culture, its people being tied to thirteen million other Negroes by innumerable bonds of kinship, associational and church membership, and a common minority status. The customs inherited by Bronzeville have been slowly growing up among American Negroes in the eighty years since slavery.

But Bronzeville is also a part of Midwest Metropolis, and Negro life is organically bound up with American life. Negroes attend the same movies, read the same daily papers, study the same textbooks, and participate in the same political and industrial activity as other Americans. They know white America far better than white America knows them. Negroes live in two worlds and they must adjust to both. Their institutions reflect the standards of both. In so far as Midwest Metropolis is a "wide-open town," in so far as it has a "sporting tradition," to the extent that it is young and rapidly changing, Bronzeville reflects these characteristics.

Notes

1. Faris and Dunham describe Black Metropolis as " ... in general, similar in character to the foreign-born slum area," but add: "In the parts farther to the south live the Negroes who have resided longer in the city and who have been more successful economically. These communities have much the same character as the nearby apartment house areas inhabited by native-born whites." (Robert E.L. Faris, and H. Warren Dunham, *Mental Disorders in Urban Areas*, University of Chicago, 1939, p. 20.)

2. The expression "Bronze" when counterposed to "Black" reveals a tendency on the part of Negroes to avoid referring to themselves as "black." And, of course, as a descriptive term, the former is even more accurate than the latter, for most Negroes *are* brown.

3. The term "axes of life" has been used by Samuel M. Strong, of the Cayton-Warner Research, to describe the dominant interests of Bronzeville. It is used here with some modifications of the original list that Strong compiled. (Cf. Samuel M. Strong, "The Social Type Method: Social Types in the Negro Community of Chicago," unpublished Ph.D. Thesis, University of Chicago, 1940.

4. Data concerning pre-Depression incomes assembled for this study indicate that in a significant number of cases even the bare subsistence level permitted by relief allowances and WPA wages constituted a definitely higher material standard of living for the lowest income group than did the wages earned in private industry during the Fat Years.

5. "City churches, collectively speaking, are succeeding better than rural ones." (H. Paul Douglass and Edmund deS. Brunner, *The Protestant Church as a Social Institution,* Harper, New York, 1935, p. 44.)

6. "Service" is a key word in American life, cherished alike by Rotarian and labor leader, politician and priest. All forms of intense individual competition are sanctified under the name of "service," and individual success is represented as "service" to the community. The struggle for prestige, too, is dressed up as "service." Bronzeville, like the rest of Midwest metropolis, has its frequent money-raising drives for charitable institutions and its corps of enthusiastic volunteers who, under the auspices of churches, lodges, clubs, and social agencies, function as part-time

civic leaders. "Service" in Bronzeville is usually interpreted as "Advancing the Race."

7. Among Bronzeville's "firsts" are: Dr. Daniel Williams, "First man to suture a human heart"; Dr. Julian Lewis, "first Negro to serve on the faculty of the University of Chicago's medical school"; and Robert R. Taylor, "first Negro to serve as the head of this Chicago Housing Authority." Among the "onlies" are the only Negro on the schoolboard of the city, and the only Negro on the library board.

8. The term Race Man is used in a dual sense in Bronzeville. It refers to any person who has a reputation as an uncompromising fighter against attempts to subordinate Negroes. It is also used in a derogatory sense to refer to people who pay loud lip-service to "race pride." It is interesting to note that Bronzeville is somewhat suspicious, generally, of its Race Men, but tends to be more trustful of the Race Woman. "A Race Woman is sincere," commented a prominent businessman; "she can't capitalize on her activities like a Race Man." The Race woman is sometimes described as "forceful, outspoken, and fearless, a great advocate of race pride" ... "devoted to the race" ... "studies the conditions of the people" ... "the Race is uppermost in her activities" ... "you know her by the speeches she makes" ... "she champions the rights of Negroes"... "active in civic affairs." The Race woman is idealized as a "fighter," but her associated role of "uplifter" seems to be accepted with less antagonism than in the case of the Race Man. She is sometimes described as "continually showing the Negro people why they should better their condition economically and educationally." cynics are apt to add: "intelligent and forceful but has little influence with whites." Certain women were repeatedly named as "good Race Women"—one or two local Bronzeville women who were active in civic organizations, and such nationally known figures as Mrs. Mary Mcleod Bethune.

18

THE LEGACY OF AMERICAN SOCIOLOGY: WILLIAM JULIUS WILSON (1935-)

William Julius Wilson, formerly a professor of sociology at the University of Chicago and currently at Harvard, exemplifies the public intellectual. He works within the tradition of North American progressive and pragmatic political thought, giving new energy to the ideals of thinkers like John Dewey and W.E.B. DuBois. Social research is not a value-free enterprise of pure inquiry, but a pursuit of knowledge that can make society more just and equitable. Sociological knowledge can give us insight into social problems and help us understand which solutions cut deeply enough to end the problems, rather than put a band-aid on them. This approach requires both the negative-critical sociological imagination of the Enlightenment, Karl Marx, and C. Wright Mills, and a faith in the possibility of social change without revolution.

Wilson is influenced by the classical theoretical tradition of Marx and Weber. Like Marx, he sees that problems of crime, social disorganization, and disintegrating family life have their origin in upheavals in the capitalist mode of production. As the selection makes clear, the transformation of the United States economy has left many city people stranded in jobless neighbourhoods. Wilson shares Weber's attention to both class and status; in this case, race as a form of status distinction. The problems of the urban poor are not only problems of economic displacement but also the result of white racism practiced in one form or another over nearly 400 years. For Wilson, as for Weber, class and race are two distinct dimensions of inequality, not reducible into one or the other.

But Wilson does not share Weber's pessimism nor Marx's optimistic belief that the end of capitalism is the next item on history's agenda. He is a public intellectual within the framework of contemporary North American society and politics; he recognizes the persistence of capitalism and strives to solve problems in the near future, within the structure of capitalism. His focus is short-term and long-term change in public policy, with faith that government can be an effective lever for social change when it is pressured by progressive coalitions. In the last chapter of *When Work Disappears*, Wilson lays out the long-term policies he believes will be most effective in reducing urban poverty. His primary focus is substantial transformations in the United States educational system such as: improving performance standards; private-public partnerships for advanced technical, scientific, and math training in high school; early child-welfare support services; and consistent planning of the school-to-work transition. Better relations between cities and suburbs are also part of his long-term policy package. His short-term policies include a variety of measures to boost employment and sustain incomes in poor urban areas.

As you read Wilson's analysis of the experience and impact of joblessness, notice how many threads of theory and research he pulls together, in addition to classical theory and progressive-pragmatic perspectives. He uses both quantitative and qualitative data, allowing them to complement each other, rather than stand in acrimonious opposition. Like sociologists of the Chicago School, he uses empirical research at the neighbourhood level as an essential element of theory building. It is necessary to see how large economic and social trends play themselves out at the local and neighbourhood level, to understand these trends as spatial processes, and to hear voices of real people telling their stories in their own words.

We can also see here reflections of pragmatic social psychology (as well as pragmatic-progressive political thought). Economic dislocation, racism, joblessness, and neighbourhood deterioration form a cruel looking-glass for the urban poor. Making ends meet is a daily struggle, and setbacks—a sick child, a burglary, a layoff, a cancelled bus route to a suburban job—can undo years of struggle to save money and establish job stability. Feelings of self-efficacy are lowered by the impact of extreme economic marginality. Wilson's looking-glass is larger than Cooley's; it shows us the mirrored self within the big historical and global framework of racism and capitalism.

Readings

Massey, Douglas and Nancy Denton. *American Apartheid: Segregation and the Making of the Underclass.* Cambridge, MA: Harvard University Press, 1993.

Wilson, William J. (ed.) *The Ghetto Underclass: Social Science Perspectives.* Newbury Park, CA: Sage, 1993.

—. *Poverty, Inequality, and the Future of Social Policy.* New York: Russell Sage Foundation, 1995.

—. (ed.). *Sociology and the Public Agenda.* Newbury Park, CA: Sage, 1993.

—. *The Truly Disadvantaged: The Inner City, The Underclass, and Public Policy.* Chicago, IL: University of Chicago Press, 1987/1990.

When Work Disappears
WILLIAM JULIUS WILSON

Societal Change and Vulnerable Neighbourhoods

The disappearance of work in many inner-city neighborhoods is partly related to the nationwide decline in the fortunes of low-skilled workers. Although the growing wage inequality has hurt both low-skilled men and women, the problem of declining employment has been concentrated among low-skilled men. In 1987-89, a low-skilled male worker was jobless eight and a half weeks longer than he would have been in 1967-69 (Topel, 1993; Juhn, Murphy, and Topel, 1991). Moreover, the proportion of men who "permanently" dropped out of the labor force was more than twice as high in the late 1980s than it had been in the late 1960s Juhn, Murphy, and Pierce, 1991, 1993; Topel, 1993). A precipitous drop in real wages—that is, wages adjusted for inflation—has accompanied the increases in joblessness among low income workers. If you arrange all wages into five groups according to wage percentile (from highest to lowest), you see that men in the bottom fifth of this income distribution experienced more than a 30 percent drop in real wages between 1970 and 1989 (Juhn, Murphy, and Topel, 1991).

Even the low-skilled workers who are consistently employed face problems of economic advancement. Job ladders—opportunities of promotion within firms—have eroded, and many less-skilled workers stagnate in dead-end, low-paying positions. This suggests that the chances of improving one's earnings by changing jobs have declined: if jobs inside a firm have become less available to the experienced workers in that firm, they are probably even more difficult for outsiders to obtain (Blank, 1994).

But there is a paradox here. Despite the increasing economic marginality of low-wage workers, unemployment dipped below 6 percent in 1994 and early 1995, many workers are holding more than one job, and overtime work has reached a record high. Yet while tens of millions of new jobs have been created in the past two decades, men who are well below retirement age are working less than they did two decades ago (Rose, 1994; Nasar, 1994)—and a growing percentage are neither working nor looking for work. The proportion of male workers in the prime of their life (between the ages of 22 and 58) who worked in a given decade fulltime, year-round, in at least eight out of ten years declined from 79 percent during the 1970s to 71 percent in the 1980s (Rose, 1994). While the American economy saw a rapid expansion in high technology and services, especially advanced services, growth in blue-collar factory, transportation, and construction jobs, traditionally held by men, has not kept pace with the rise in the working age population (Nasar, 1994). These men are working less as a result.

The growth of a nonworking class of prime-age males along with a larger number of those who are often unemployed, who work part-time, or who work in temporary jobs is concentrated among the poorly educated, the school dropouts, and minorities (Rose, 1994; Nasar, 1994). In the 1970s, two-thirds of prime age male workers with less than a high school education worked full time, year round, in eight out of ten years. During the 1980s, only half did so. Prime-age black men experienced a similar sharp decline. Seven out of ten of all black men worked full-time, year-round, in eight out of ten years in the 1970s, but only half did so in the 1980s. The figures for those who reside in the inner city are obviously even lower (Rose, 1994).

One study estimates that since 1967 the number of prime-age men who are not in school, not working, and not looking for work for even a single week in a given year has more than doubled for both whites and nonwhites (respectively, from 3.3. to 7.7 percent and 5.8 percent to 13.2 percent) (Buron, Haveman, and O'Donnell, 1994). Data from this study also revealed that one-quarter of all male high school dropouts had no official employment at all in 1992. And of those with high school diplomas, one out of ten did not hold a job in 1993, up sharply from 1967 when only one out of fifty reported that he had had no job throughout the year. Among prime age nonwhite males, the share of those who had no jobs at all in a given year increased from 3 percent to 17 percent during the last quarter century.

These changes are related to the decline of the mass production system in the United States. The traditional American economy featured rapid growth in productivity and living standards (Marshall, 1994; Rifkin, 1995). The mass production system benefited from large quantities of cheap natural resources, economies of scale, and processes that generated higher uses of productivity through shifts in market forces from agriculture to manufacturing and that caused improvements in one industry (for example, reduced steel costs) to lead to advancements in others (for example, higher sales and greater economies of scale in the automobile industry). In this system plenty of blue-collar jobs were available to workers with little formal education. Today, most of the new jobs for workers with limited education and experience are in the service sector, which hires relatively more women (Nasar, 1994; Freeman, 1994; Holzer, 1995). One study found that the U.S. created 27 clerical, sales, and service jobs per thousand of working-age population in the 1980s (McKinsey & Co., 1994). During the same period, the country lost 125 production, transportation, and laborer jobs per thousand of working-age population. In another study the social scientists Robert Lerman and Martin Rein revealed that from 1989 to

1993, the period covering the economic downturn, social service industries (health, education, and welfare) added almost 3 million jobs, while 1.4 million jobs were lost in all other industries. The expanding job market in social services offset the recession-linked job loss in other industries (Lerman and Rein, forthcoming).[1]

The movement of lower-educated men into the growth sectors of the economy has been slow. For example, "the fraction of men who have moved into so-called pink-collar jobs like practical nursing or clerical work remains negligible" (Nasar, 1994). The large concentration of women in the expanding social service sector partly accounts for the striking gender differences in job growth. Unlike lower-educated men, lower-educated women are working more, not less, than in previous years. The employment patterns among lower-educated women, like those with higher education and training, reflect the dramatic expansion of social service industries, between 1989 and 1993, jobs held by women increased by 1.3 million, while those held by men barely rose at all (by roughly 100,000) (Lerman and Rein, forthcoming).

Although the wages of low-skilled women (those with less than twelve years of education) rose slightly in the 1970s, they flattened out in the 1980s, and continued to remain below those of low-skilled men. The wage gap between low-skilled men and women shrank not because of gains made by female workers but mainly because of the decline in real wages for men. The unemployment rates among low-skilled women are slightly lower than those among their male counterparts (Blank, 1994). However, over the past decade their rates of participation in the labor force have stagnated and have fallen further behind the labor-force-participation rates among more highly educated women, which continue to rise. The unemployment rates among both low-skilled men and women are five times that among their college-educated counterparts.

Among the factors that have contributed to the growing gap in employment and wages between low-skilled and college-educated workers is the increased internationalization of the U.S. Economy. As the economists Richard B. Freeman and Lawrence F. Katz point out:

> In the 1980s, trade imbalances implicitly acted to augment the nations' supply of less educated workers, particularly those with less than a high school education. Many production and routine clerical tasks could be more easily transferred abroad than in the past. The increased supply of less educated workers arising from trade deficits accounted for as much as 15 percent of the increase in college-high school wage differential from the 1970s to the mid1980s. In contrast, a balanced expansion of international trade, in which growth in exports matches the growth of imports, appears to have fairly neutral effects

on relative labor demand. Indeed, balanced growth of trade leads to an upgrading in jobs for workers without college degrees, since export-sector jobs tend to pay higher wages for "comparable" workers than do import-competing jobs. (Freeman and Katz, 1994, p. 46)

The lowering of unionization rates, which accompanied the decline in the mass production system, has also contributed to shrinking wages and nonwage compensation for less skilled workers. As the economist Rebecca Blank has pointed out, "unionized workers typically receive not only higher wages, but also more non-wage benefits. As the availability of union jobs has declined for unskilled workers, non-wage benefits have also declined" (Blank, 1994, p. 17).

Finally, the wage and employment gap between skilled and unskilled workers is growing partly because education and training are considered more important than ever in the new global economy. At the same time that changes in technology are producing new jobs, they are making many others obsolete. The workplace has been revolutionized by technological changes that range from the development of robotics to information highways (Marshall, 1994). While educated workers are benefitting from the pace of technological change, involving the increased use of computer-based technologies and microcomputers, more routine workers face the growing threat of job displacement in certain industries. For example, highly skilled designers, engineers, and operators are needed for the jobs associated with the creation of a new set of computer-operated machine tools; but these same exciting new opportunities eliminate jobs for those trained only for manual, assembly-line work. Also, in certain businesses, advances in word processing have increased the demand for those who not only know how to type but can operate specialized software as well; at the same time, these advances reduce the need for routine typists and secretaries. In the new global economy, highly educated and thoroughly trained men and women are in demand. This may be seen most dramatically in the sharp differences in employment experiences among men. Unlike men with lower education, college-educated men are working more, not less.[2]

The shift in demand has been especially devastating for those low-skilled workers whose incorporation into the mainstream economy has been marginal or recent. Even before the economic restructuring of the nation's economy, low-skilled African-Americans were at the end of the employment queue (Lieberson, 1980). Their economic situation has been further weakened because they tend to reside in communities that not only have higher jobless rates and lower employment growth but lack access to areas of higher employment and employment growth as well. Moreover,... they are far more likely than other ethnic and racial groups to face negative employer attitudes.

Of the changes in the economy that have adversely affected low-skilled African-American workers, perhaps the most significant have been those in the manufacturing sector. One study revealed that in the 1970s "up to half of the huge employment declines for less-educated blacks might be explained by industrial shifts away from manufacturing toward other sectors."[3] Another study reported that since the 1960s "deindustrialization" and the "erosion in job opportunities especially in the Midwest and Northeast ... bear responsibility for the growth of the ranks of the 'truly disadvantaged'" (Bluestone, Stevenson, and Tilly, 1991, p. 25). The manufacturing losses in some northern cities have been staggering. In the twenty-year period from 1967 to 1987, Philadelphia lost 64 percent of its manufacturing jobs; Chicago lost 60 percent; New York City, 58 percent; Detroit, 51 percent. In absolute numbers, these percentages represent the loss of 160,000 jobs in Philadelphia, 326,000 in Chicago, 520,000— over half a million—in New York, and 108,000 in Detroit (Kasarda, 1995).

Another study examined the effects of economic restructuring in the 1980s by highlighting the changes in both the variety and the quality of blue-collar employment in general (Gittleman and Howell, 1993). Jobs were grouped into a small number of relatively homogeneous clusters on the basis of job quality (which was measured in terms of earning, benefits, union protection, and involuntary part-time employment). The authors found that both the relative earnings and employment rates among unskilled black workers were lower for two reasons: traditional jobs that provide a living wage (high-wage blue-collar, of which roughly 50 percent were manufacturing jobs) declined, as did the quality of secondary jobs on which they increasingly had to rely, leading to lower relative earnings for the remaining workers in the labor market. As employment prospects worsened, rising proportions of low-skilled black workers dropped out of the legitimate labor market.

Data from the Chicago Urban Poverty and Family Life Survey show that efforts by out-of-school inner-city black men to obtain blue-collar jobs in the industries in which their fathers had been employed have been hampered by industrial restructuring. "The most common occupation reported by respondents at ages 19 to 28 changed from operative and assembler jobs among the oldest cohorts to service jobs (waiters and janitors) among the youngest cohort" (Testa and Krogh, 1989, p. 77). Fifty-seven percent of Chicago's employed inner-city black fathers (aged 15 and over and without undergraduate degrees) who were born between 1950 and 1955 worked in manufacturing and construction industries in 1974. By 1987, industrial employment in this group had fallen to 31 percent. Of those born between 1956 and 1960, 52 percent worked in these industries as late as 1978. But again, by 1987 industrial employment in this group fell to 28 percent.[4] No other male ethnic group in the inner city experienced such an overall precipitous drop in manufacturing employment.... These employment changes have accompanied the loss of traditional manufacturing and other blue-collar jobs in Chicago. As a result, young black males have turned increasingly to the low-wage service sector and unskilled laboring jobs for employment, or have gone jobless. The strongly held U.S. cultural and economic belief that the son will do at least as well as the father in the labor market does not apply to many young inner-city males.

If industrial restructuring has hurt inner-city black workers in Chicago, it has had serious consequences for African-Americans across the nation. "As late as the 1968-70 period," states John Kasarda, "more than 70 percent of all blacks working in metropolitan areas held blue-collar jobs at the same time that more than 50 percent of all metropolitan workers held white-collar jobs. Moreover, of the large numbers of urban blacks classified as blue-collar workers during the late 1960s, more than half were employed in goods-producing industries" (Kasarda, 1995, p. 239).

The number of employed black males ages 20 to 29 working in manufacturing industries fell dramatically between 1973 and 1987 (from three of every eight to one in five). Meanwhile, the share of employed young black men in the retail trade and service jobs rose sharply during that period (from 17 to almost 27 percent and from 10 to nearly 21 percent, respectively). And this shift in opportunities was not without economic consequences: in 1987, the average annual earnings of 20-to 29-year-old males who held jobs in the retail trade and service sectors were 25 to 30 percent less than those of males employed in manufacturing sectors (Sum and Fogg, 1990). This dramatic loss in earnings potential affects every male employed in the service sector regardless of color.

The structural shifts in the distribution of industrial job opportunities are not the only reason for the increasing joblessness and declining earnings among young black male workers. There have also been important changes in the patterns of occupational staffing within firms and industries, including those in manufacturing. These changes have primarily benefited those with more formal education. Substantial numbers of new professional, technical, and managerial positions have been created. However, such jobs require at least some years of post-secondary education. Young high school dropouts and even high school graduates "have faced a dwindling supply of career jobs offering the real earnings opportunities available to them in the 1960s and early 1970s" (Sum and Fogg, 1990, p. 51).

In certain urban areas the prospects for employment among workers with little education have fallen sharply. John Kasarda examined employment changes in selected urban centers and found that major northern cities had consistent employment losses in industries with low mean levels of employee education and employment gains in industries in which the workers had higher levels of education (Kasarda, 1995). For example, during the 1980s New York

City lost 135,000 jobs in industries in which the workers averaged less than twelve years of education, and gained almost 300,000 jobs in industries in which workers had thirteen or more years of education. Philadelphia lost 55,000 jobs in the lower-education industries and gained 40,000 jobs for workers with high school plus at least some college. Baltimore and Boston also experienced substantial losses in industries employing low-education workers and major gains in industries employing more educated workers.

Kasarda's study also documents the growing importance of education in nine "economically transforming" northern cities and in Los Angeles. The jobs traditionally held by high school dropouts declined in all nine northern cities between 1980 and 1990, while those held by college graduates increased.[5] "Los Angeles, which experienced a 50 percent increase in city [urban] jobs held by college graduates; also experienced a 15 percent growth in jobs held by those who have not completed high school. The latter no doubt reflects the large immigration of Hispanic workers and other minorities" who have little education (Kasarda, 1995, pp. 247, 250).

To some degree, these changes reflect overall improvements in educational attainment within the urban labor force. However, they "were not nearly as great as the concurrent upward shifts in the education of city jobholders" (Kasarda, 1995, p. 250). Moreover, much of the increase in the "college-educated" jobs in each city reflected the educational status of suburban commuters, while much of the decrease in the "less than high school" category reflected the job losses of city residents, few of whom could aspire to a four-year postsecondary degree.

As pointed out earlier, most of the new jobs for workers with limited training and education are in the service sector and are disproportionately held by women. This is even more true for those who work in social services, which include the industries of health, education, and welfare. As we have seen, within central cities the number of jobs for less educated workers has declined precipitously. However, many workers stayed afloat thanks to jobs in the expanding social service sector, especially black women with less than a high school degree. Robert Lerman and Martin Rein (forthcoming) report that among all women workers, the proportion employed in social services climbed between 1979 and 1993 (from 28 to 33 percent). The health and education industries absorbed nearly all of this increase. Of the 54 million female workers in 1993, almost one-third were employed in social service industries. Social services tend to feature a more highly educated workforce. Only 20 percent of all female workers with less than a high school degree were employed in social services in 1993. (The figure for comparable males is even less. Only 4 percent of employed less educated men held social service jobs in 1993.) Nonetheless, the proportion of less educated female workers in social services is up notably from 1989.

Indeed, despite the relatively higher educational level of social service workers, the research of Lerman and Rein reveals that 37 percent of employed less educated black women in central cities worked in social services in 1993, largely in jobs in hospitals, elementary schools, nursing care, and child care. In central cities in the largest metropolitan areas, the fraction of low-educated African-American female workers in social services sharply increased form 30.5 percent in 1979 to 40.5 percent in 1993.[6] Given the overall decline of jobs for less educated central city workers, the opportunity for employment in the social service industries prevented many inner-city workers from joining the growing ranks of the jobless. Less educated black female workers depend heavily on social service employment. Even a small number of less educated black males were able to find jobs in social services. Although only 4 percent of less educated employed males worked in social services in 1993, 12 percent of less educated employed black men in the central cities of large metropolitan areas held social service jobs (Lerman and Rein, forthcoming). Without the growth of social service employment, the rates of inner-city joblessness would have risen beyond their already unprecedented high levels.

The demand in the labor market has shifted toward higher-educated workers in various industries and occupations. The changing occupational and industrial mix is associated with increases in the rates of joblessness (unemployment and "dropping out" of, or nonparticipation in, the labor force) and decreases in the relative wages of disadvantaged urban workers.[7]

The factors contributing to the relative decline in the economic status of disadvantaged workers are not solely due to those on the demand side, such as economic restructuring. The growing wage differential in the 1980s is also a function of two supply-side factors—the decline in the relative supply of college graduates and the influx of poor immigrants. "In the 1970s the relative supply of college graduates grew rapidly, the result of the baby boomers who enrolled in college in the late 1960s and early 1970s in response to the high rewards for college degrees and the fear of being drafted for the Vietnam War," state Freeman and Katz. "The growth in supply overwhelmed the increase in demand for more educated workers, and the returns to college diminished" (1994, p. 47). In the 1980s, the returns for college increased because of declining growth in the relative supply of college graduates.

Also in the 1980s, a large number of immigrants with little formal education arrived in the United States from developing countries, and affected the wages of poorly educated native workers, especially those who had dropped out of high school. According to one estimate, nearly one-third of the decline in earnings for male high school dropouts compared with other workers in the 1980s may be linked to immigration (Freeman and Katz, 1994; Borjas, Freeman, and Katz, 1992). However, although the increase in immigration contributed to the growing inequality, it is only one of several factors depressing the wages of low-skilled workers. As Sheldon Danziger and Peter Gottschalk point out in this connection, "Immigrants are heavily concentrated in a few states, such as California and Florida ... inequality did rise in these states, but it rose in most areas, even those with very few immigrants" (1995, p. 133; also Topel, 1994).

Joblessness and declining wages are also related to the recent growth in ghetto poverty. The most dramatic increases in ghetto poverty occurred between 1970 and 1980, and they were mostly confined to the large industrial metropolises of the Northeast and Midwest, regions that experienced massive industrial restructuring and loss of blue-collar jobs during that decade (Jargowsky and Bane, 1991). But the rise in ghetto poverty was not the only problem. Industrial restructuring had devastating effects on the social organization of many inner-city neighborhoods in these regions. The fate of the West Side black community of North Lawndale vividly exemplifies the cumulative process of economic and social dislocation that has swept through Chicago's inner city.

After more than a quarter century of continuous deterioration, North Lawndale resembles a war zone. Since 1960, nearly half of its housing stock has disappeared; the remaining units are mostly rundown or dilapidated. Two large factories anchored the economy of this West Side neighborhood in its good days—the Hawthorne plant of Western Electric, which employed over 43,000 workers; and an International Harvester plant with 14,000 workers. The world headquarters for Sears, Roebuck and Company was located there, providing another 10,000 jobs. The neighborhood also had a Copenhagen snuff plant, a Sunbeam factory, and a Zenith factory, a Dell Farm food market, and Alden's catalog store, and a U.S. Post Office bulk station. But conditions rapidly changed. Harvester closed its doors in the late 1960s. Sears moved most of its offices to the Loop in downtown Chicago in 1973; a catalog distribution center with a workforce of 3,000 initially remained in the neighborhood but was relocated outside of the state of Illinois in 1987. The Hawthorne plant gradually phased out its operations and finally shut down in 1984.

The departure of the big plants triggered the demise or exodus of the smaller stores, the banks, and other businesses that relied on the wages paid by the large employers. "To make matters worse, scores of stores were forced out of business or pushed out of the neighborhoods by insurance companies in the wake of the 1968 riots that swept through Chicago's West Side after the assassination of Dr. Martin Luther King, Jr. Others were simply burned or abandoned. It has been estimated that the community lost 75 percent of its business establishments from 1960 to 1970 alone" (Wacquant and Wilson, 1989, pp. 91-92). In 1986, North Lawndale, with a population of over 66,000 had only one bank and one supermarket; but it was also home to forty-eight state lottery agents, fifty currency exchanges, and ninety-nine licensed liquor stores and bars (Chicago *Tribune*, 1986).

The impact of industrial restructuring on inner-city employment is clearly apparent to urban blacks. The UPFLS survey posed the following question: "Over the past five or ten years, how many friends of yours have lost their jobs because the place where they worked shut down—would you say none, a few, some, or most?" Only 26 percent of the black residents in our sample reported that none of their friends had lost jobs because their workplace shut down. Indeed, both black men and black women were more likely to report that their friends had lost jobs because of plant closings than were the Mexicans and the other ethnic groups in our study. Moreover, nearly half of the employed black fathers and mothers in the UPFLS survey stated that they considered themselves to be at high risk of losing their jobs because of plant shutdowns. Significantly fewer Hispanic and white parents felt this way.[8]

Some of the inner-city neighborhoods have experienced more visible job losses than others. But residents of the inner city are keenly aware of the rapid depletion of job opportunities. A 33-year-old unmarried black male of North Lawndale who is employed as a clerical worker stated: "Because of the way the economy is structured, we're losing more jobs. Chicago is losing jobs by the thousands. There just aren't any starting companies here and it's harder to find a job compared to what it was years ago."

A similar view was expressed by a 41-year-old black female, also from North Lawndale, who works as a nurse's aide:

> Chicago is really full of peoples. Everybody can't get a good job. They don't have enough good jobs to provide for everybody. I don't think they have enough jobs period.... and all the factories and the places, they closed up and moved out of the city and stuff like that, you know. I guess it's one of the reasons they haven't got too many jobs now, 'cause a lot of the jobs now, factories and business, they're done moved out. So that way it's less jobs for lot of peoples.

Respondents from other neighborhoods also reported on the impact of industrial restructuring. According to a 33-year-old South Side janitor:

> The machines are putting a lot of people out of jobs. I worked for *Time* magazine for seven years on a videograph printer and they come along with the Abedic printer, it cost them half a million dollars: they did what we did in half the time, eliminated two shifts.

"Jobs were plentiful in the past," stated a 29-year-old unemployed black male who lives in one of the poorest neighborhoods on the South Side.

You could walk out of the house and get a job. Maybe not what you want but you could get a job. Now, you can't find anything. A lot of people in this neighborhood, they want to work but they can't get work. A few, but a very few, they just don't want to work. The majority they want to work but they can't find work.

Finally, a 41-year-old hospital worker from another impoverished South Side neighborhood associated declining employment opportunities with decreasing skill levels:

Well, most of the jobs have moved out of Chicago. Factory jobs have moved out. There are no jobs here. Not like it was 20, 30 years ago, and people aren't skilled enough for the jobs that are here. You don't have enough skilled and educated people to fill them.

The increasing suburbanization of employment has accompanied industrial restructuring and has further exacerbated the problems of inner-city joblessness and restricted access to jobs. "Metropolitan areas captured nearly 90 percent of the nation's employment growth; much of this growth occurred in booming 'edge cities' at the metropolitan periphery. By 1990, many of these 'edge cities' had more office space and retail sales than the metropolitan downtowns" (Kasarda, 1995, pp. 215-16). Over the last two decades, 60 percent of the new jobs created in the Chicago metropolitan area have been located in the northwest suburbs of Cook and Du Page counties (Reardon, 1991). African-Americans constitute less than 2 percent of the population in these areas.

In *The Truly Disadvantaged,* I maintained that one result of these changes for many urban blacks has been a growing mismatch between the suburban location of employment and minorities' residence in the inner city.[9] Although studies based on data collected before 1970 showed no consistent or convincing effects on black employment as a consequence of this spatial mismatch, the employment of inner-city blacks relative to suburban blacks has clearly deteriorated since then (Holzer, 1991; Ellwood, 1986). Recent research, conducted mainly by urban and labor economists, strongly shows that the decentralization of employment is continuing and that employment in manufacturing, most of which is already suburbanized, has decreased in central cities, particularly in the Northeast and Midwest.[10] As Farrell Bloch, an economic and statistical consultant, points out, "Not only has the number of manufacturing jobs been decreasing, but new plants now tend to locate in the suburbs to take advantage of cheap land, access to highways, and low crime rates; in addition, businesses shun urban locations to avoid buying land from several different owners, paying high demolition costs for old buildings and arranging parking for employees and customers" (Bloch, 1994, p. 124).

Blacks living in central cities have less access to employment, as measured by the ratio of jobs to people and the average travel time to and from work, than do central-city whites. Moreover, unlike most other groups of workers across the urban/suburban divide, less educated central-city blacks receive lower wages than suburban blacks who have similar levels of education. And the decline in earnings of central-city blacks is related to the decentralization of employment—that is, the movement of jobs from the cities to the suburbs—in metropolitan areas.

But are the differences in employment between city and suburban blacks mainly the result of changes in the location of jobs? (Holzer, 1991; Jencks and Mayer, 1989; Frey, 1985; Grier and Grier, 1988). It is possible that in recent years the migration of blacks to the suburbs has become much more selective than in earlier years, so much so that the changes attributed to job location are actually caused by this selective migration. The pattern of black migration to the suburbs in the 1970s was similar to that of whites during the 1950s and 1960s in the sense that it was concentrated among the better-educated and younger city residents. However, in the 1970s this was even more true for blacks, creating a situation in which the education and income gaps between city and suburban blacks seemed to expand at the same time that the differences between city and suburban whites seemed to contract. Accordingly, if one were to take into account differences in education, family background, and so on, how much of the employment gap between city and suburbs would remain?

This question was addressed in a study of the Gautreaux program in Chicago (Rosenbaum and Popkin, 1991). The Gautreaux program was created under a 1976 court order resulting from a judicial finding of widespread discrimination in the public housing projects of Chicago. The program has relocated more than 4,000 residents from public housing into subsidized housing in neighborhoods throughout the Greater Chicago area. The design of the program permitted the researchers, James E. Rosenbaum and Susan J. Popkin, to contrast systematically the employment experiences of a group of low-income blacks who had been assigned private apartments in the suburbs with the experiences of a control group with similar characteristics and histories who had been assigned private apartments in the city. Their findings support the spatial mismatch hypothesis. After taking into account the personal characteristics of the respondents (including family background, family circumstances, levels of human capital, motivation, length of time since the respondent first enrolled in the Gautreaux program), Rosenbaum and Popkin found that those who moved to apartments in the suburbs were significantly more likely to have a job after the move than those placed in the city. When asked what makes it easier to obtain employment in the suburbs, nearly all the suburban respondents mentioned the high availability of jobs.

The African-Americans surveyed in the UPFLS clearly recognized a spatial mismatch of jobs. Both black men and black women saw greater job prospects outside the city. For example, only one-third of black fathers from areas with poverty rates of at least 30 percent reported that their best opportunities for employment were to be found in the city. Nearly two-thirds of whites and Puerto Ricans and over half of Mexicans living in similar neighborhoods felt this way. Getting to suburban jobs is especially problematic for the jobless individuals in the UPFLS because only 28 percent have access to an automobile. This rate falls even further to 18 percent for those living in the ghetto areas.

Among two-car middle-class and affluent families, commuting is accepted as a fact of life; but it occurs in a context of safe school environments for children, more available and accessible day care, and higher incomes to support mobile, away-from-home lifestyles. In a multitiered job market that requires substantial resources for participation, most inner-city minorities must rely on public transportation systems that rarely provide easy and quick access to suburban locations. A 32-year-old unemployed South Side welfare mother described the problem this way:

> There's not enough jobs. I thinks Chicago's the only city that does not have a lot of opportunities opening in it. There's not enough factories, there's not enough work. Most all the good jobs are in the suburbs. Sometimes it's hard for the people in the city to get to the suburbs, because everybody don't own a car. Everybody don't drive.

After commenting on the lack of jobs in his area, a 29-year-old unemployed South Side black male continued:

> You gotta go out in the suburbs, but I can't get out there. The bus go out there but you don't want to catch the bus out there, going two hours each ways. If you have to be at work at eight that mean you have to leave for work at six, that mean you have to get up at five to be at work at eight. Then when wintertime come you be in trouble.

Another unemployed South Side black male had this to say": "Most of the time ... the places be too far and you need transportation and I don't have none right now. If I had some I'd probably be able to get one [a job]. If I had a car and went way into the suburbs, 'cause there ain't none in the city." This perception was echoed by an 18-year-old unemployed West Side black male:

> They are most likely hiring in the suburbs. Recently, I think about two years ago, I had a job but they say that I need some transportation and they say that

the bus out in the suburbs run at a certain time. So I had to pass that job up because I did not have no transport.

An unemployed unmarried welfare mother of two from the West Side likewise stated:

Well, I'm goin' to tell you: most jobs, more jobs are in the suburbs. It's where the good jobs and stuff is but you gotta have transportation to get there and it's hard to be gettin' out there in the suburbs. Some people don't know where the suburbs is, some people get lost out there. It is really hard, but some make a way.

One employed factory worker from the West Side who works a night shift described the situation this way:

From what I, I see, you know, it's hard to find a good job in the inner city 'cause so many people moving, you know, west to the suburbs and out of state.... Some people turn jobs down because they don't have no way of getting out there.... I just see some people just going to work—and they seem like they the type who just used to—they coming all the way from the city and go on all the way to the suburbs and, you know, you can see'em all bundled and—catching one bus and the next bus. They just used to doing that.

But the problem is not simply one of transportation and the length of commuting time. There is also the problem of the travel expense and of whether the long trek to the suburbs is actually worth it in terms of the income earned—after all, owning a car creates expenses far beyond the purchase price, including insurance, which is much more costly for city dwellers than it is for suburban motorists. "If you work in the suburbs you gotta have a car," stated an unmarried welfare mother of three children who lives on Chicago's West Side, "then you gotta buy gas. You spending more getting to the suburbs to work, than you is getting paid, so you still ain't getting nowhere."

Indeed, one unemployed 36-year-old black man from the West Side of Chicago actually quit his suburban job because of the transportation problem. "It was more expensive going to work in Naperville, transportation and all, and it wasn't worth it.... I was spending more money getting to work than I earned working."

If transportation poses a problem for those who have to commute to work from the inner city to the suburbs, it can also hinder poor ghetto residents' ability to travel to the suburbs just to seek employment. For example, one unemployed man who lives on the South Side had just gone to O'Hare Airport looking for work with no luck. His complaint: "The money I spent yesterday, I coulda kept that in my pocket—I coulda kept that. 'Cause you know I musta spent about $7 or somethin'. I coulda kept that."

Finally, in addition to enduring the search-and-travel costs, inner-city black workers often confront racial harassment when they enter suburban communities. A 38-year-old South Side divorced mother of two children who works as hotel cashier described the problems experience by her son and his coworker in one of Chicago's suburbs:

> My son, who works in Carol Stream, an all-white community, they've been stopped by a policeman two or three times asking them why they're in the community. And they're trying to go to work. They want everyone to stay in their own place. That's what society wants. And they followed them all the way to work to make sure. 'Cause it's an all-white neighborhood. But there're no jobs in the black neighborhoods. They got to go way out there to get a job.

These informal observations on the difficulties and cost of travel to suburban employment are consistent with the results of a recent study by the labor economist Harry J. Holzer, Keith R. Ihlanfeldt, and David L. Sjoquist. In addition to finding that the lack of automobile ownership among inner-city blacks contributed significantly to their lower wages and lower rate of employment, these authors also reported that African-American "spend more time traveling to work than whites," that "the time cost per mile traveled is ... significantly higher for blacks," and that the resulting gains are relatively small. Overall, their results suggest that the amount of time and money spent in commuting, when compared with the actual income that accrues to inner-city blacks in low-skill jobs in the suburbs, acts to discourage poor people from seeking employment far from their own neighborhoods. Holzer and his colleagues concluded that it was quite rational for blacks to reject these search-and-travel choices when assessing their position in the job market (Holzer, Ihlanfeldt, and Sjoquist, 1994, pp. 323, 324).

Changes in the industrial and occupational mix, including the removal of jobs from urban centers to suburban corridors, represent external factors that have helped to elevate joblessness among inner-city blacks. But important social and demographic changes within the inner city are also associated with the escalating rates of neighborhood joblessness....

Notes

1. Social services increased from 17 percent of total employment in 1979 to 21 percent in 1993. Lerman and Rein (forthcoming).
2. In the decade of the 1980s, 79 percent worked at least eight out of ten months, up from 77 percent during the 1970s. Rose (1994) and Nasar (1994).

3. Bound and Holzer (1993), p. 395. Also see Bound and Freeman (1992); Acs and Danziger (1993); and Johnson and Oliver (1992). Studies measuring the effects of declining manufacturing on black male *income*, as opposed to employment, reach different conclusions. On the basis of these studies, declining manufacturing does not appear to have the same adverse effects on black income as it does on black employment. See Bartik (forthcoming) and Danziger and Gottschalk (1993).

4. For a discussion of these findings, see Krogh (1993).

5. The nine northern cities were Baltimore, Boston, Chicago, Cleveland, Detroit, New York, Philadelphia, St. Louis, and Washington, D.C. Twenty-five percent of the jobs held by high school graduates disappeared in these nine northern cities between 1980 and 1990, including a decrease of more than 50 percent in Detroit and St. Louis and nearly 50 percent in Cleveland and Baltimore. On the other hand, those held by college graduates rose by at least 40 percent, except in Detroit and Cleveland, which experienced more modest increases of 12 and 33 percent, respectively. Kasarda (1995).

6. Only 17 percent of less educated female workers held jobs in social services in 1989. See Lerman and Rein (forthcoming).

7. The decline in wages has also been notable among rural workers, although some groups suffered greater income loss than others. As William O'Hare and Anne Pauti point out: "Men, blacks, and part-time workers experienced a bigger decline in wages than did women, whites, or full-time workers. Wages of young rural workers in every sector declined, but those in extractive industries, manufacturing and trade experienced the biggest decrease in earnings. Deterioration of wages of young rural workers was found in every region of the country except New England" (1990, p. 5).

8. Only one-third of the employed Hispanic parents, one-quarter of white fathers, and one-fifth of white mothers felt that they might lose their jobs because of plant shutdowns.

9. This was a thesis first put forth by John Kain in his classic 1968 article. Kain (1968).

10. Holzer (1991). Also see Holzer, Ihlanfeldt, and Sjoquist (1994); Ihlanfeldt and Sjoquist (1990); Ihlanfeldt, and Sjoquist, (1991); Fernandez (1991); and Zax and Kain (1992).

References

Acs, Gregory and Sheldon Danziger. 1993. "Educational Attainment, Industrial Structure, and Earnings: 1973-87." *Journal of Human Resources* 28: 618-48.

Bartik, Timothy J. Forthcoming. "The Distributional Effects of Local Labor Market Demand and Industrial Mix." *Journal of Labor Economics.*

Blank, Rebecca. 1994. "Outlook for the U.S. Labor Market and Prospects for Low-Wage Entry Jobs." Working paper, Center for Urban Affairs, Northwestern University.

Bluestone, Barry, Mary Stevenson, and Christ Tilly. 1991. "The Deterioration in Labor

Market Prospects for Young Men with Limited Schooling: Assessing the Impact of 'Demand Side' Factors." Paper presented at the annual meeting of the Eastern Economic Association, March 14-15, Pittsburgh.

Borjas, George, Richard Freeman, and Lawrence Katz. 1992. "On the Labor Market Effects of Immigration and Trade." In *Immigration and the Work Force,* edited by George Borjas and Richard Freeman, pp. 213-44. Chicago: University of Chicago Press (for NBER).

Bound, John, and Richard J. Freeman. 1992. "What Went Wrong? The Erosion of the Relative Earnings of Young Black Men in the 1980s." *Quarterly Journal of Economics* 107 (February) 201-33.

Bound, John, and Harry Holzer. 1993. "Industrial Shifts, Skills Levels, and the Labor Market for White and Black Men." *Review of Economics and Statistics* 75 (August): 387-96.

Buron, Lawrence, Robert Haveman, and Owen O'Donnell. 1994. "Recent Trends in U.S. Male Work and Wage Patterns: An Overview." Unpublished manuscript, University of Wisconsin, December.

Chicago *Tribune.* 1986. *The American Millstone.* Chicago: Contemporary Books.

Danziger, Sheldon H., and Peter Gottschalk. 1995. *America Unequal.* Cambridge: Harvard University Press.

Danziger, Sheldon H., and Peter Gottschalk, eds. 1993. *Uneven Tides: Rising Inequality in America.* New York: Russell Sage Foundation.

Ellwood, David T. 1986. "The Spatial Mismatch Hypothesis: Are There Teenage Jobs Missing in the Ghetto?" In *The Black Youth Employment Crisis*, edited by Richard B. Freeman and Harry J. Holzer, pp. 147-48. Chicago: University of Chicago Press.

Fernandez, Roberto M. 1991. "Race, Space and Job Accessibility: Evidence from a Plant Relocation." Unpublished manuscript, Northwestern University.

Freeman, Richard B., ed. 1994. *Working Under Different Rules.* New York: Russell Sage Foundation.

Freeman, Richard B. and Lawrence F. Katz. 1994. "Rising Wage Inequality: The United States vs. Other Advanced Countries." In *Working Under Different Rules*, edited by Richard B. Freeman, pp. 29-62. New York: Russell Sage Foundation.

Gittleman, Maury B., and David R. Howell. 1993. "Job Quality and Labor Market Segmentation in the 1980s: A New Perspective on the Effects of Employment Restructuring by Race and Gender." Working paper no. 82, Jerome Levy Economics Institute, Bard College, March.

Grier, Eunice S., and George Grier. 1988. "Minorities in Suburbia: A Mid-1980s Update." Report to the Urban Institute Project on Housing Mobility, March. Washington, DC: Urban Institute Press.

Holzer, Harry J. 1991. "The Spatial Mismatch Hypothesis: What Has the Evidence Shown?" *Urban Studies* 28: 105-22.

Holzer, Harry J. 1995. *What Employers Want: Job Prospects for Less-Educated Workers.* New York: Russell Sage.

Holzer, Harry J., Keith R. Ihlanfeldt, and David L. Sjoquist. 1994. "Work, Search and Travel Among White and Black Youth." *Journal of Urban Economics* 35: 320-45.

Ihlanfeldt, Keith R., and David L. Sjoquist. 1990. "Job Accessibility and Racial Differences in Youth Employment Rates." *American Economic Review* 80: 67-76.

—. "The Effect of Job Access on Black Youth Employment: A Cross Sectional Analysis." *Urban Studies* 28: 255-65.

Jargowsky, Paul A. and Mary Jo Bane. 1991. "Ghetto Poverty in the United States, 1970-1980." In *The Urban Underclass,* edited by Christopher Jencks and Paul E. Peterson, pp. 235-73. Washington, DC: Brookings Institution.

Johnson, James and Melvin Oliver. 1992. "Structural Changes in the U.S. Economy and Black Male Joblessness: A Reassessment." In *Urban Labor Markets and Job Opportunity,* edited by G. Peterson and W. Vromaneds, pp. 113-47. Washington, DC: Urban Institute Press.

Juhn, Chinhui, Kevin M. Murphy, and Brooks Pierce. 1991. "Accounting for the Slowdown in Black-White Wage Convergence." In *Workers and Their Wages: Changing Patterns in the United States,* edited by Marvin H. Kosters, pp. 107-43. Washington, DC: American Enterprise Press.

—. 1993. "Wage Inequality and the Rise in Returns to Skill." *Journal of Political Economy* 101: 410-42.

Juhn, Chinhui, Kevin M. Murphy, and Robert H. Topel. 1991. "Why Has the Natural Rate of Unemployment Increased Over Time?" *Brookings Papers on Economic Activity* 2: 75-126.

Kain, John. 1968. "Housing Segregation, Negro Employment and Metropolitan Decentralization." *Quarterly Journal of Economics* 26: 110-30.

Kasarda, John D. 1995. "Industrial Restructuring and the Changing Location of Jobs." In *State of the Union: America in the 1990s*, vol. 1, edited by Reynolds Farley. New York: Russell Sage Foundation.

Krogh, Marilyn. 1993. "A Description of the Work Histories of Fathers Living in the Inner City of Chicago." Working paper, Center for the Study of Urban Inequality, University of Chicago.

Lerman, Robert I. and Martin Rein. Forthcoming. *Social Service Employment: An International Perspective.* New York: Russell Sage Foundation.

Lieberson, Stanley. 1980. *A Piece of the Pie: Black and White Immigrants Since 1880.* Berkeley: University of California Press.

Marshall, Ray. 1994. "School-to-Work Processes in the United States." Paper presented at the Carnegie Corporation/Johann Jacobs Foundation, November 3-5, Marbach Castle, Germany.

McKinsey & Co. 1994. *Employment Performance.* Washington, DC: McKinsey Global Institute, November.

Nasar, Sylvia. 1994. "The Men in Prime of Life Spend Less Time Working." *New York Times*, December 1.

O'Hare, William, and Anne Pauti. 1990. *Declining Wages of Young Workers in Rural America*. Staff Working Papers, Population Reference Bureau, Washington, DC.

Reardon, Patrick. 1991. "Study Links City Jobless, Suburban Housing." *Chicago Tribune*, May 1.

Rifkin, Jeremy. 1995. *The End of Work: The Decline of the Global Labor Force and the Dawn of the Post-Market Era.* New York: Putnam's.

Rose, Stephen J. 1994. "On Shaky Ground: Rising fears About Incomes and Earnings." Research report no. 94-02, National Commission for Employment Policy, Washington, DC, October.

Rosenbaum, James E. and Susan J. Popkin. 1991. "Employment and Earnings of Low-Income Blacks Who Move to Middle-Class Suburbs." In *The Urban Underclass.* edited by Christopher Jencks and Paul E. Peterson, pp. 342-56. Washington, DC: Brookings Institution.

Sum, Andrew and Neal Fogg. 1990. "The Changing Economic Fortunes of Young Black Men in America." *Black Scholar* 21 (January, February and March): 47-55.

Testa, Mark, and Marilyn Krogh. 1995. "The Effect of Employment on Marriage Among Black Males in Inner-City Chicago." In *The Decline in Marriage Among African Americans: Causes, Consequences and Policy Implications*, edited by M. Belinda Tucker and Claudia Mitchell-Kernan, pp. 59-95. New York: Russell Sage Foundation.

Topel, Robert. 1993. "What Have We Learned from Empirical Studies of Unemployment and Turnover?" *AEA Papers and Proceedings* 83: 110-15.

Wacquant, Loïc J.D., and William Julius Wilson. 1989. "Poverty, Joblessness and the Social Transformation of the Inner City." In *Reforming Welfare Policy*, edited by D. Ellwood and P. Cottingham, pp. 70-102. Cambridge: Harvard University Press.

Zax, Jeffrey, and John Kain. 1992. "Moving to the Suburbs: Do Relocating Companies Leave Their Black Employees Behind?" Unpublished manuscript, Harvard University.

CHAPTER FOUR

MARXISM IN THE INTERWAR PERIOD

INTRODUCTION

By the mid-1920s and 1930s, Marxist theorists had to contend with the fact that socialist revolutions did not succeed beyond the borders of Russia. Western and Central Europe, as well as China, had seen large communist and socialist movements and even attempted revolutions, but none of them came to power. In the countries where these movements were strongest—Germany, Italy, Spain, and China—they were suppressed by fascist and right-wing counter movements and regimes—the Nazis, the Italian Fascists, Franco's Falange, and nationalist Kuomintang forces. These right-wing forces were also large movements that captured mass bases of support in the middle strata. In liberal democracies such as Great Britain and the United States, the left-wing movements remained relatively small and were channelled into activities like electoral politics and union organizing.

The revolutionary organization of the proletariat and its ability to capture the state were clearly not automatic outcomes of the growth of capitalism; even the economic crises of the 1920s and 1930s did not automatically expand socialism as an ideology or as an organized movement. In the interwar period, fascist movements and ideologies extended their hold on millions of people. Marxist theory needed to focus on why bourgeois rule was so tenacious; it had to explain the rise of right-wing ideologies, movements, and regimes. In short, it had to elaborate stronger theories of culture and politics.

At least two of these theoretical developments in Marxism remain of great value to sociologists and students of culture.

One set of theories was formulated by the Frankfurt Institute, a group of social scientists in Germany during this period. The theorists of the Frankfurt Institute were influenced by psychoanalysis as well as Marxism and by other currents of Central European intellectual life. Their focus was culture and ideology, the media and other culture industries, the transformation of culture into a commodity in capitalist societies, and the slogans and images that relentlessly pour into people's minds. They were fascinated by the way that commercialized forms of culture penetrated not only the conscious but even the unconscious mental processes of people in capitalist societies. They saw as their primary task the critical analysis of culture.

When the Nazis came to power, the Institute had to disband, and its members went into exile; many of them were Jews, some were close to communist or socialist organizations, and all were critical intellectuals with a left orientation—exactly the sort of people the Nazis planned to destroy. Several came to the United States and had a formative influence on North American sociology as well as postwar developments in European social theory.

The legacy of the Frankfurt Institute was rich, but complex and ambiguous. Former Frankfurt Institute theorists in the United States were central in development of modern social science research methods and data analysis, in areas such as multivariate statistical analysis and empirical research on authoritarian, fascist, and ethnocentric personality structure.[1] They also expanded the project of critical theory; this theory is anti-positivist, grounds social theory in philosophy and history, and questions prevailing ideology and consciousness, including the social sciences themselves.[2]

Walter Benjamin's "The work of art in an age of mechanical reproduction" exemplifies the analysis of culture and media in capitalist society. Unlike some theorists associated with the Frankfurt Institute, Benjamin was not hostile to new media technologies; he emphasized their liberating potential, inherent in their destruction of the artwork's "aura" and their disrespect for bourgeois cultural treasures. His analysis of art and culture in an age of mechanical reproduction is just as applicable to video and computer-mediated communication as it was to photography and film.

A second important force in the development of a Marxist theory of culture and politics was the work of Antonio Gramsci, an intellectual associated with the Italian Communist Party. His elaboration of the Marxist concept of hegemony remains of outstanding importance in contemporary sociology; as we shall see in Gitlin's article, this concept is part of a larger framework for analyzing politics and culture.

Notes

1. Theodor Adorno, E. Frenkel-Brunswick, D. Levinson, and R. Sanford, *The Authoritarian Personality* (New York: Norton, 1950/93).
2. Herbert Marcuse, *Eros and Civilization* (New York: Random House, 1962) and *Negations* (Boston: Beacon Press, 1968); Max Horkheimer and Theodor Adorno, *The Dialectic of Enlightenment* (New York: Herder and Herder, 1972).

19

WALTER BENJAMIN (1892-1940)

In this selection we encounter one of the most imaginative and unusual of the Marxist theorists, Walter Benjamin. His focus was primarily culture—literature, books, theatre, the media, and consumer goods. He treasured the paradoxical and the magical. He brought to Marxist analysis a visionary, utopian outlook; he wedded Marxist concepts like class struggle to surrealism and Dada, to the mystical and Messianic side of the Jewish tradition, and to writers like Baudelaire and Kafka. He believed that no matter how revolutionary one's thoughts, if they were expressed in a conventional, academic writing style they would inevitably be swallowed up in the routines of bourgeois culture. So he experimented with fragmentary and provocative ways of organizing his ideas, parallel to the playful, disruptive innovations that surrealists, Dada, and the Soviet Constructivists were bringing to the visual arts.

One set of themes in Benjamin's work revolved around urban experience in capitalist society. There are many similarities between Benjamin and Simmel's writing, perhaps because they shared origins in an intellectual, upper-middle-class Jewish milieu in Berlin. Like Simmel, Benjamin was fascinated by the street scene, the character of the *flaneur* (the person who "hangs out" and strolls through the city, enjoying all that it has to offer), and the enticement of commodities and fashions. Both saw these social types and urban diversions as results of the money economy, and both expressed a deep ambivalence about their observations—a playful enjoyment, mingled with a concern that capitalism is highly destructive of communities and individuals. Benjamin, living in more sombre times than Simmel, chose to frame these concerns in Marxist terms.

Just as Simmel wrote about shopping, fashion, and the metropolitan scene, Benjamin envisioned a writing project about the Paris Arcades. The Arcades were splendid glass and iron structures of nineteenth-century Paris where new consumer goods were beautifully displayed in shop windows; they were the forerunners of great shopping boulevards like Fifth Avenue in New York. Benjamin saw how important the magic of consumer goods was to capitalism, even in its early phase when it appeared to be still guided by an orientation to production rather than mass consumption. He hoped to combine the topic of the Arcades with innovations in his style of writing, expressing his reflections entirely in the form of de-contextualized quotes from literary works. We can see in this a forerunner of deconstructionism, hoping to jar conventional views of the world by ripping ideas out of their comfortable, taken-for-granted intellectual settings.

An even more unconventional and imaginative theme in Benjamin's work is the idea that revolutions are about the reorganization of time. This fascination with the nature of time derived not only from Marx's reflections on history, but also from the Jewish Messianic tradition. The present is responsible for the past, and class struggle is about the past as much as it is about the present and future. Only class struggle and revolution allow us to redeem the past, to redeem the lives of "enslaved ancestors." On the other hand, the victory of fascism and reaction would mean that not even the dead will be spared; the forces of reaction try to rewrite the past, obliterating and defiling our collective memories of struggle and survival.

Like Marx, Benjamin was reluctant to describe the future after the revolution. Unlike Marx, he specifically cites the Jewish prohibition against soothsaying and fortune telling; it is not for us to try to foretell the future, it is enough to believe that "every second of time was the strait gate through which the Messiah might enter."[1] The revolution is best envisioned as an explosive moment, a break from the normal flow of time. Our moments of joy and pleasure—often pleasure that is sensuous, transgressive, and beyond social control—are tiny bursts of this utopian future into the present. The promise of happiness contained in these moments allows us to picture human emancipation. We can see the similarity of this idea to Marx's description of communism as the free development of each individual in an idyllic life of hunting, fishing, ranching, and literary criticism. The appeal of this vision lies in its outlandishness, sensuality, and playfulness—its complete break with Marx's usually angry analysis of the real state of things under capitalism. For Benjamin as well, the class struggle must include a utopian leap of the imagination.

Benjamin writes in a relatively conventional style here, but his conclusion is a surprising one. We are accustomed to reading a Marxist critique of the modern media; we expect a Marxist to say that the media are simply ways of disseminating bourgeois ideology and escapist pap to exhausted workers. Far from seeing the modern media as tightening the hold of bourgeois ideology, Benjamin sees them as potentially breaking it. In the past, the work of culture had a special aura, a sacred quality that functioned ideologically, to hold the masses in awe. Painting, music, and theatre served the ruling classes. Once art was entirely part of religion and served ritual purposes intimately connected to organized religion's ideological function. In the nineteenth century, in capitalist society, art lost these religious functions, but works of art retained their aura. They were believed to be unique and were associated with cliches such as genius and authenticity. Catchphrases about the work of genius and the solitary genius mystify reality.

In the age of mechanical reproduction, works of culture are stripped of their aura. They lose their sacred qualities and their uniqueness. Photographs and movies (and in our own day, videos, computer texts and images, and "virtual realities") knock cultural treasures off their pedestal. We realize that movies, for example, are produced in a factory-like process; they are really fragments edited into a semblance of a whole by technicians. The dis-assembly of the actor's work and its re-assembly into a movie undermine the notion of genius. Slow-motion, time lapse photography, voice-overs, montage (and in our day, instant replays) shatter the apparent unity, reality, and cohesiveness of the representation. It is revealed to be a construct that is collectively produced and patched together. This in turn leads us to question reality itself. Authority is undermined, as anyone knows who has seen a referee or umpire's judgment put into question by an instant replay.

The mechanical reproduction of a work of art democraticizes cultural production. After Gutenberg, anyone could become a reader because books became so easily available; almost anyone could become a writer. With the camera, everyone could create visual representations of the real world. Video and computers continue this process. Anyone can make a video, anyone can be a critic. This theme is now being elaborated by postmodern theorists who claim that the line between high and low culture is completely blurred.

Benjamin was delighted, not dismayed, by the artwork's loss of its aura. The pretensions of bourgeois culture had been thoroughly punctured. Mechanical reproduction created a breach in bourgeois ideology. Benjamin was suspicious of cultural treasures, which the bourgeoisie carried along like spoils in a triumphal procession; at best, these treasures were only possible due to the labour of many exploited ordinary people, and often they must be seen primarily as a record of horrors and barbarism.[2] Mechanical reproduction challenged bourgeois ideology.

Fascism brought about Benjamin's death, as it did Gramsci's. When the Nazis came to power in Germany, he went to France; when France came under the rule of the Nazis and the collaborationist Vichy government, he tried to flee to the United States by way of Spain. Although he obtained a US emergency visa and a Spanish transit visa, he was refused permission to cross the border between France and Spain after an exhausting trek through the mountains. He took his own life; the following day, the rest of the group of refugees was allowed to enter Spain.[3]

Notes
1. Walter Benjamin, "Theses on the Philosophy of History," *Illuminations* (New York: Schocken, 1969) 253-64.

2. Benjamin 256.
3. Hannah Arendt, "Introduction," *Illuminations* (New York: Schocken, 1969) 18.

Readings

Alter, Robert. *Necessary Angels: Tradition and Modernity in Kafka, Benjamin, and Scholem*. Cambridge, MA: Harvard University Press, 1991.

Broderson, Momme. *Walter Benjamin: A Biography*. London: Verso, 1996.

Jay, Martin. *The Dialectical Imagination*. Boston: Little, Brown, 1973.

Wolin, Richard. *Walter Benjamin: An Aesthetic of Redemption*. Berkeley, CA: University of California Press, 1994.

The Work of Art in an Age of Mechanical Reproduction
WALTER BENJAMIN

Preface

When Marx undertook his critique of the capitalistic mode of production, this mode was in its infancy. Marx directed his efforts in such a way as to give them prognostic value. He went back to the basic conditions underlying capitalistic production and through his presentation showed what could be expected of capitalism in the future. The result was that one could expect it not only to exploit the proletariat with increasing intensity, but ultimately to create conditions which would make it possible to abolish capitalism itself.

The transformation of the superstructure, which takes place far more slowly than that of the substructure, has taken more than half a century to manifest in all areas of culture the change in the conditions of production. Only today can it be indicated what form this has taken. Certain prognostic requirements should be met by these statements. However, theses about the art of the proletariat after its assumption of power or about the art of a classless society would have less bearing on these demands that theses about the developmental tendencies of art under present conditions of production. Their dialectic is no less noticeable in the superstructure than in the economy. It would therefore be wrong to underestimate the value of such theses as a weapon. They brush aside a number of outmoded concepts, such as creativity and genius, eternal value and mystery—concepts whose uncontrolled (and at present almost uncontrollable) application would lead to a processing of data in the Fascist sense. The concepts which are introduced into the theory of art in what follows differ from the more familiar terms in that they are completely useless for the purposes of Fascism. They are, on the other hand, useful for the formulation of revolutionary demands in the politics of art.

I

In principle a work of art has always been reproducible. Manmade artifacts could always be imitated by men. Replicas were made by pupils in practice of their craft, by masters for diffusing their works, and, finally, by third parties in the pursuit of gain. Mechanical reproduction of a work of art, however, represents something new. Historically, it advanced intermittently and in leaps at long intervals, but with accelerated intensity. The Greeks knew only two procedures of technically reproducing works of art: founding and stamping. Bronzes, terra cottas, and coins were the only art works which they could produce in quantity. All others were unique and could not be mechanically reproduced. With the woodcut graphic art became mechanically reproducible for the first time, long before script became reproducible by print. The enormous changes which printing, the mechanical reproduction of writing, has brought about in literature are a familiar story. However, within the phenomenon which we are here examining from the perspective of world history, print is merely a special, though particularly important, case. During the Middle Ages engraving and etching were added to the woodcut; at the beginning of the nineteenth century lithography made its appearance.

With lithography the technique of reproduction reached an essentially new stage. This much more direct process was distinguished by the tracing of the design on a stone rather than its incision on a block of wood or its etching on a copperplate and permitted graphic art for the first time to put its products on the market, not only in large numbers as hitherto, but also in daily changing forms. Lithography enabled graphic art to illustrate everyday life, and it began to keep pace with printing. But only a few decades after its invention, lithography was surpassed by photography. For the first time in the process of pictorial reproduction, photography freed the hand of the most important artistic functions which henceforth devolved only upon the eye looking into a lens. Since the eye perceives more swiftly than the hand can draw, the process of pictorial reproduction was accelerated so enormously that it could keep pace with speech. A film operator shooting a scene in the studio captures the images at the speed of an actor's speech. Just as lithography virtually implied the illustrated newspaper, so did photography foreshadow the sound film. The technical reproduction of sound was tackled at the end of the last century. These convergent endeavors made predictable a situation which Paul Valéry pointed up in this sentence: "Just as water, gas, and electricity are brought into our houses from far off to satisfy our needs in response to a minimal effort, so we shall be supplied with visual or auditory images, which will appear and disappear at a simple movement of the hand, hardly more than a sign" (*op. cit,* p. 226). Around 1900 technical reproduction had reached a standard that not only permitted it to reproduce all transmitted works of art and thus to cause the most profound change in their impact upon the public; it also had captured a place of its own among the artistic processes. For the study of this standard nothing is more revealing than the nature of the repercussions that these two different manifestations—the reproduction of works of art and the art of the film—have had on art in its traditional form.

II

Even the most perfect reproduction of a work of art is lacking in one element: its presence in time and space, its unique existence at the place where it happens to be. This unique existence of the work of art determined the history to which it was subject throughout the time of its existence. This includes the changes which it may have suffered in physical condition over the years as well as the various changes in its ownership.[1] The traces of the first can be revealed only by chemical or physical analyses which it is impossible to perform on a reproduction; changes of ownership are subject to a tradition which must be traced from the situation of the original.

The presence of the original is the prerequisite to the concept of authenticity. Chemical analyses of the patina of a bronze can help to establish this, as does the proof that a given manuscript of the Middle Ages stems from an archive of the fifteenth century. The whole sphere of authenticity is outside technical—and, of course, not only technical—reproducibility.[2] Confronted with its manual reproduction, which was usually branded as a forgery, the original preserved all its authority; not so *vis à vis* technical reproduction. The reason is twofold. First, process reproduction is more independent of the original than manual reproduction. For example, in photography, process reproduction can bring out those aspects of the original that are unattainable to the naked eye yet accessible to the lens, which is adjustable and chooses its angle at will. And photographic reproduction, with the aid of certain processes, such as enlargement or slow motion, can capture images which escape natural vision. Secondly, technical reproduction can put the copy of the original into situations which would be out of reach for the original itself. Above all, it enables the original to meet the beholder halfway, be it in the form of a photograph or a phonograph record. The cathedral leaves its locale to be received in the studio of a lover of art; the choral production, performed in an auditorium or in the open air, resounds in the drawing room.

The situations into which the product of mechanical reproduction can be brought may not touch the actual work of art, yet the quality of its presence is always depreciated. This holds not only for the art work but also, for instance, for a landscape which passes in review before the spectator in a movie. In the case of the art object, a most sensitive nucleus—namely, its authenticity—is interfered with whereas no natural object is vulnerable on that score. The authenticity of a thing is the essence of all that is transmissible from its beginning, ranging from its substantive duration to its testimony to the history which it has experienced. Since the historical testimony rests on the authenticity, the former, too, is jeopardized by reproduction when substantive duration ceases to matter. And what is really jeopardized when the historical testimony is affected is the authority of the object.[3]

One might subsume the eliminated element in the term "aura" and go on to say: that which withers in the age of mechanical reproduction is the aura of the work of art. This is a symptomatic process whose significance points beyond the realm of art. One might generalize by saying: the technique of reproduction detaches the reproduced object from the domain of tradition. By making many reproductions it substitutes a plurality of copies for a unique existence. And in permitting the reproduction to meet the beholder or listener in his own particular situation, it reactivates the object reproduced. These two processes lead to a tremendous shattering of tradition which is the obverse of the contemporary crisis and renewal of mankind. Both processes are intimately connected with the contemporary mass movements. Their most powerful agent is the film. Its social significance, particularly in its most positive form, is inconceivable without its destructive, cathartic aspect, that is, the liquidation of the traditional value of the cultural heritage. This phenomenon is most palpable in the great historical films. It extends to ever new positions. In 1927 Abel Gance exclaimed enthusiastically: "Shakespeare, Rembrandt, Beethoven will make films ... all legends, all mythologies and all myths, all founders of religion, and the very religions ... await their exposed resurrection, and the heroes crowd each other at the gate."[4] Presumably without intending it, he issued an invitation to a far-reaching liquidation.

III

During long periods of history, the mode of human sense perception changes with humanity's entire mode of existence. The manner in which human sense perception is organized, the medium in which it is accomplished, is determined not only by nature but by historical circumstances as well. The fifth century, with its great shifts of population, saw the birth of the late Roman art industry and the Vienna Genesis, and there developed not only an art different from that of antiquity but also a new kind of perception. The scholars of the Viennese school, Riegl and Wickhoff, who resisted the weight of classical tradition under which these later art forms had been buried, were the first to draw conclusions from them concerning the organization of perception at the time. However far-reaching their insight, these scholars limited themselves to showing the significant, formal hallmark which characterized perception in late Roman times. They did not attempt—and, perhaps, saw no way—to show the social transformations expressed by these changes of perception. The conditions for an analogous insight are more favorable in the present. And if changes in the medium of contemporary perception can be comprehended as decay of the aura, it is possible to show its social causes.

The concept of aura which was proposed above with reference to historical objects may usefully be illustrated with reference to the aura of natural ones. We define the aura of the latter as the unique phenomenon of distance, however close it may be. If, while resting on a summer afternoon, you follow with your eyes a mountain range on the horizon or a branch which casts its shadow over you, you experience the aura of those mountains, of that branch. This image makes it easy to comprehend the social bases of the contemporary decay of the aura. It rests on two circumstances, both of which are related to the increasing significance of the masses in contemporary life. Namely, the desire of contemporary masses to bring things "closer" spatially and humanly, which is just as ardent as their bent toward overcoming the uniqueness of every reality by accepting its reproduction.[5] Every day the urge grows stronger to get hold of an object at very close range by way of its likeness, its reproduction. Unmistakably, reproduction as offered by picture magazines and newsreels differs from the image seen by the unarmed eye. Uniqueness and permanence are as closely linked in the latter as are transitoriness and reproducibility in the former. To pry an object from its shell, to destroy its aura, is the mark of a perception whose "sense of the universal equality of things" has increased to such a degree that it extracts it even from a unique object by means of reproduction. Thus is manifested in the field of perception what in the theoretical sphere is noticeable in the increasing importance of statistics. The adjustment of reality to the masses and of the masses to reality is a process of unlimited scope, as much for thinking as for perception.

IV

The uniqueness of a work of art is inseparable from its being imbedded in the fabric of tradition. This tradition itself is thoroughly alive and extremely changeable. An ancient statue of Venus, for example, stood in a different traditional context with the Greeks, who made it an object of veneration, than with the clerics of the Middle Ages, who viewed it as an ominous idol. Both of them, however, were equally confronted with its uniqueness, that is, its aura. Originally the contextual integration of art in tradition found its expression in the cult. We know that the earliest art works originated in the service of a ritual— first the magical, then the religious kind. It is significant that the existence of the work of art with reference to its aura is never entirely separated from its ritual function.[6] In other words, the unique value of the "authentic" work of art has its basis in ritual, the location of its original use value. This ritualistic basis, however remote, is still recognizable as secularized ritual even in the most profane forms of the cult of beauty.[7] The secular cult of beauty, developed during the Renaissance and prevailing for three centuries, clearly showed that ritualistic basis in its decline and the first deep crisis which befell it. With the advent of the first truly revolutionary means of reproduction, photography, simultaneously with the rise of socialism, art sensed the approaching crisis which has become evident a century later. At the time, art reacted with the doctrine of *l'art pour l'art*, that is, with a theology of art. This gave rise to what might be called a negative theology in the form of the idea of "pure" art, which not only denied any social function of art but also any categorizing by subject matter. (In poetry, Mallarmé was the first to take this position.)

An analysis of art in the age of mechanical reproduction must do justice to these relationships, for they lead us to an all-important insight: for the first time in world history, mechanical reproduction emancipates the work of art from its parasitical dependence on ritual. To an ever greater degree the work of art reproduced becomes the work of art designed for reproducibility.[8] From a photographic negative, for example, one can make any number of prints; to ask for the "authentic" print makes no sense. But the instant the criterion of authenticity ceases to be applicable to artistic production, the total function of art is reversed. Instead of being based on ritual, it begins to be based on another practice—politics.

V

Works of art are received and valued on different planes. Two polar types stand out: with one, the accent is on the cult value; with the other, on the exhibition value of the work.[9] Artistic production begins with ceremonial objects destined to serve in a cult. One may assume that what mattered was their existence, not their being on view. The elk portrayed by the man of the Stone Age on the walls of his cave was an instrument of magic. He did expose it to his fellow men, but in the main it was meant for the spirits. Today the cult value would seem to demand that the work of art remain hidden. Certain statues of gods are accessible only to the priest in the cella; certain Madonnas remain covered nearly all year round; certain sculptures on medieval cathedrals are invisible to

the spectator on ground level. With the emancipation of the various art practices from ritual go increasing opportunities for the exhibition of their products.
It is easier to exhibit a portrait bust that can be sent here and there than to exhibit the statue of a divinity that has its fixed place in the interior of a temple. The
same holds for the painting as against the mosaic or fresco that preceded it. And
even though the public presentability of a mass originally may have been just
as great as that of a symphony, the latter originated at the moment when its
public presentability promised to surpass that of the mass.

With the different methods of technical reproduction of a work of art, its
fitness for exhibition increased to such an extent that the quantitative shift
between its two poles turned into a qualitative transformation of its nature. This
is comparable to the situation of the work of art in prehistoric times when, by
the absolute emphasis on its cult value, it was, first and foremost, an instrument
of magic. Only later did it come to be recognized as a work of art. In the same
way today, by the absolute emphasis on its exhibition value the work of art
becomes a creation with entirely new functions, among which the one we are
conscious of, the artistic function, later may be recognized as incidental.[10] This
much is certain: today photography and the film are the most serviceable exem-
plifications of this new function.

VI

In photography, exhibition value begins to displace cult value all along the line.
But cult value does not give way without resistance. It retires into an ultimate
retrenchment: the human countenance. It is no accident that the portrait was the
focal point of early photography. The cult of remembrance of loved ones,
absent or dead, offers a last refuge for the cult value of the picture. For the last
time the aura emanates from the early photographs in the fleeting expression of
a human face. This is what constitutes their melancholy, incomparable beauty.
But as man withdraws from the photographic image, the exhibition value for
the first time shows its superiority to the ritual value. To have pinpointed this
new stage constitutes the incomparable significance of Atget, who, around
1900, took photographs of deserted Paris streets. It has quite justly been said of
him that he photographed them like scenes of crime. The scene of a crime, too,
is deserted; it is photographed for the purpose of establishing evidence. With
Atget, photographs become standard evidence for historical occurrences, and
acquire a hidden political significance. They demand a specific kind of
approach; free-floating contemplation is not appropriate to them. They stir the
viewer; he feels challenged by them in a new way. At the same time picture
magazines begin to put up signposts for him, right ones or wrong ones, no matter. For the first time, captions have become obligatory. And it is clear that they
have an altogether different character than the title of a painting. The directives

which the captions give to those looking at pictures in illustrated magazines soon become even more explicit and more imperative in the film where the meaning of each single picture appears to be prescribed by the sequence of all preceding ones....

VIII

The artistic performance of a stage actor is definitely presented to the public by the actor in person; that of the screen actor, however, is presented by a camera, with a twofold consequence. The camera that presents the performance of the film actor to the public need not respect the performance as an integral whole. Guided by the cameraman, the camera continually changes its position with respect to the performance. The sequence of positional views which the editor composes from the material supplied him constitutes the completed film. It comprises certain factors of movement which are in reality those of the camera, not to mention special camera angles, close-ups, etc. Hence, the performance of the actor is subjected to a series of optical tests. This is the first consequence of the fact that the actor's performance is presented by means of a camera. Also, the film actor lacks the opportunity of the stage actor to adjust to the audience during his performance, since he does not present his performance to the audience in person. This permits the audience to take the position of a critic, without experiencing any personal contact with the actor. The audience's identification with the actor is really an identification with the camera. Consequently the audience takes the position of the camera; its approach is that of testing.[11] This is not the approach to which cult values may be exposed.

IX

For the film, what matters primarily is that the actor represents himself to the public before the camera, rather than representing someone else. One of the first to sense the actor's metamorphosis by this form of testing was Pirandello. Though his remarks on the subject in his novel *Si Gira* were limited to the negative aspects of the question and to the silent film only, this hardly impairs their validity. For in this respect, the sound film did not change anything essential. What matters is that the part is acted not for an audience but for a mechanical contrivance—in the case of the sound film, for two of them. "The film actor," wrote Pirandello, "feels as if in exile—exiled not only from the stage but also from himself. With a vague sense of discomfort he feels inexplicable emptiness: his body loses its corporeality, it evaporates, it is deprived of reality, life, voice, and the noises caused by his moving about, in order to be changed into a mute image, flickering an instant on the screen, then vanishing into silence.... The projector will play with his shadow before the public, and he himself must be content to play before the camera."[12] This situation might also be characterized as follows: for the first time—and this is the effect of the film—man has to operate with his whole living person, yet forgoing its aura. For aura is tied to his presence; there can be no replica of it. The aura which, on the stage, emanates from Macbeth, cannot be separated for the spectators from that of the actor. However, the singularity of the shot in the studio is that the camera is substituted for the public. Consequently, the aura that envelops the actor vanishes, and with it the aura of the figure he portrays.

It is not surprising that it should be a dramatist such as Pirandello who, in characterizing the film, inadvertently touches on the very crisis in which we see the theater. Any thorough study proves that there is indeed no greater contrast than that of the stage play to a work of art that is completely subject to or, like the film, founded in, mechanical reproduction. Experts have long recognized that in the film "the greatest effects are almost always obtained by "acting" as little as possible...." In 1932 Rudolf Arnheim saw "the latest trend ... in treating the actor as a stage prop chosen for its characteristics and ... inserted at the proper place."[13] With this idea something else is closely connected. The stage actor identifies himself with the character of his role. The film actor very often is denied this opportunity. His creation is by no means all of a piece; it is composed of many separate performances. Besides certain fortuitous considerations, such as cost of studio, availability of fellow players, décor, etc., there are elementary necessities of equipment that split the actor's work into a series of mountable episodes. In particular, lighting and its installation require the presentation of an event that, on the screen, unfolds as a rapid and unified scene, in a sequence of separate shootings which may take hours at the studio; not to mention more obvious montage. Thus a jump from the window can be shot in the studio as a jump from a scaffold and the ensuing flight, if need be, can be shot weeks later when outdoor scenes are taken. Far more paradoxical cases can easily be construed. Let us assume that an actor is supposed to be startled by a knock at the door. If his reaction is not satisfactory, the director can resort to an expedient: when the actor happens to be at the studio again he has a shot fired behind him without his being forewarned of it. The frightened reaction can be shot now and be cut into the screen version. Nothing more strikingly shows that art has left the realm of the "beautiful semblance" which, so far, had been taken to be the only sphere where art could thrive.

X

The feeling of strangeness that overcomes the actor before the camera, as Pirandello describes it, is basically of the same kind as the estrangement felt before one's own image in the mirror. But now the reflected image has become separable, transportable. And where is it transported? Before the public.[14] Never for a moment does the screen actor cease to be conscious of this fact.

While facing the camera he knows that ultimately he will face the public, the consumers who constitute the market. This market, where he offers not only his labor but also his whole self, his heart and soul, is beyond his reach. During the shooting he has as little contact with it as any article made in a factory. This may contribute to that oppression, that new anxiety which, according to Pirandello, grips the actor before the camera. The film responds to the shriveling of the aura with an artificial build-up of "personality" outside the studio. The cult of the movie star, fostered by the money of the film industry, preserves not the unique aura of the person but the "spell of the personality," the phony spell of a commodity. So long as the movie-makers' capital sets the fashion, as a rule no other revolutionary merit can be accredited to today's film than the promotion of a revolutionary criticism of traditional concepts of art. We do not deny that in some cases today's films can also promote revolutionary criticism of social conditions, even of the distribution of property. However, our present study is no more specifically concerned with this than is the film production of Western Europe.

It is inherent in the technique of the film as well as that of sports that everybody who witnesses its accomplishments is somewhat of an expert. This is obvious to anyone listening to a group of newspaper boys leaning on their bicycles and discussing the outcome of a bicycle race. It is not for nothing that newspaper publishers arrange races for their delivery boys. These arouse great interest among the participants, for the victor has a opportunity to rise from delivery boy to professional racer. Similarly, the newsreel offers everyone the opportunity to rise from passer-by to movie extra. In this way any man might even find himself part of a work of art, as witness Vertoff's *Three Songs About Lenin* or Ivens's *Borinage*. Any man today can lay claim to being filmed. This claim can best be elucidated by a comparative look at the historical situation of contemporary literature.

For centuries a small number of writers were confronted by many thousands of readers. This changed toward the end of the last century. With the increasing extension of the press, which kept placing new political, religious, scientific, professional, and local organs before the readers, an increasing number of readers became writers—at first, occasional ones. It began with the daily press opening to its readers space for "letters to the editor." And today there is hardly a gainfully employed European who could not, in principle, find an opportunity to publish somewhere or other comments on his work, grievances, documentary reports, or that sort of thing. Thus, the distinction between author and public is about to lose its basic character. The difference becomes merely functional; it may vary from case to case. At any moment the reader is ready to turn into a writer. As expert, which he had to become willy-nilly in an extremely specialized work process, even if only in some minor respect, the reader gains access to authorship. In the Soviet Union work itself is given a voice. To present it verbally is part of a man's ability to perform the work. Literary license is now founded on polytechnic rather than specialized training and thus becomes common property.[15]

All this can easily be applied to the film, where transitions that in literature took centuries have come about in a decade. In cinematic practice, particularly in Russia, this change-over has partially become established reality. Some of the players whom we meet in Russian films are not actors in our sense but people who portray *themselves*—and primarily in their own work process. In Western Europe the capitalistic exploitation of the film denies consideration to modern man's legitimate claim to being reproduced. Under these circumstances the film industry is trying hard to spur the interest of the masses through illusion-promoting spectacles and dubious speculations.

XI

The shooting of a film, especially of a sound film, affords a spectacle unimaginable anywhere at any time before this. It presents a process in which it is impossible to assign to a spectator a viewpoint which would exclude from the actual scene such extraneous accessories as camera equipment, lighting machinery, staff assistants, etc.—unless his eye were on a line parallel with the lens. This circumstance, more than any other, renders superficial and insignificant any possible similarity between a scene in the studio and one on the stage. In the theater one is well aware of the place from which the play cannot immediately be detected as illusionary. There is no such place for the movie scene that is being shot. Its illusionary nature is that of the second degree, the result of cutting. That is to say, in the studio the mechanical equipment has penetrated so deeply into reality that its pure aspect freed from the foreign substance of equipment is the result of a special procedure, namely, the shooting by the specially adjusted camera and the mounting of the shot together with other similar ones. The equipment-aspect of reality here has become the height of artifice; the sight of immediate reality has become an orchid in the land of technology.

Even more revealing is the comparison of these circumstances, which differ so much from those of the theater, with the situation in painting. Here the question is: How does the cameraman compare with the painter? To answer this we take recourse to an analogy with a surgical operation. The surgeon represents the polar opposite of the magician. The magician heals a sick person by the laying on of hands; the surgeon cuts into the patient's body. The magician maintains the natural distance between the patient and himself; though he reduces it very slightly by the laying on of hands, he greatly increases it by virtue of his authority. The surgeon does exactly the reverse; he greatly diminishes the distance between himself and the patient by penetrating into the patients's body, and increases it but little by the caution with which his hand moves among the organs. In short, in contrast to the magician—who is still hidden in the medical practitioner—the surgeon at the decisive moment abstains from facing the patient man to man; rather, it is through the operation that he penetrates into him.

Magician and surgeon compare to painter and cameraman. The painter maintains in his work a natural distance from reality, the cameraman penetrates deeply into its web.[16] There is a tremendous difference between the pictures they obtain. That of the painter is a total one, that of the cameraman consists of multiple fragments which are assembled under a new law. Thus, for contemporary man the representation of reality by the film is incomparably more significant than that of the painter, since it offers, precisely because of the thoroughgoing permeation of realty with mechanical equipment, an aspect of reality which is free of all equipment. And that is what one is entitled to ask from a work of art.

XIII

... By close-ups of the things around us, by focusing on hidden details of familiar objects, by exploring commonplace milieus under the ingenious guidance of the camera, the film, on the one hand, extends our comprehension of the necessities which rule our lives; on the other hand, it manages to assure us of an immense and unexpected field of action. Our taverns and our metropolitan streets, our offices and furnished rooms, our railroad stations and our factories appeared to have us locked up hopelessly. Then came the film and burst this prison-world asunder by the dynamite of the tenth of a second, so that now, in the midst of its far-flung ruins and debris, we calmly and adventurously go traveling. With the close-up, space expands; with slow motion, movement is extended. The enlargement of a snap-shot does not simply render more precise what in any case was visible, though unclear: it reveals entirely new structural formations of the subject. So, too, slow motion not only presents familiar qualities of movement but reveals in them entirely unknown ones "which, far from looking like retarded rapid movements, give the effect of singularly gliding, floating, supernatural motions."[17] Evidently a different nature opens itself to the camera than opens to the naked eye—if only because an unconsciously penetrated space is substituted for a space consciously explored by man. Even if one has a general knowledge of the way people walk, one knows nothing of a person's posture during the fractional second of a stride. The act of reaching for a lighter or a spoon is familiar routine, yet we hardly know what really goes on between hand and metal, not to mention how this fluctuates with our moods. Here the camera intervenes with the resources of its lowerings and liftings, its interruptions and isolations, its extensions and accelerations, its enlargements and reductions. The camera introduces us to unconscious optics as does psychoanalysis to unconscious impulses....

Notes

1. Of course, the history of a work of art encompasses more than this. The history of the "Mona Lisa," for instance, encompasses the kind and number of its copies made in the 17th, 18th, and 19th centuries.

2. Precisely because authenticity is not reproducible, the intensive penetration of certain (mechanical) processes of reproduction was instrumental in differentiating and grading authenticity. To develop such differentiations was an important function of the trade in works of art. The invention of the woodcut may be said to have struck at the root of the quality of authenticity even before its late flowering. To be sure, at the time of its origin a medieval picture of the Madonna could not yet be said to be "authentic." It became "authentic" only during the succeeding centuries and perhaps most strikingly so during the last one.

3. The poorest provincial staging of *Faust* is superior to a Faust film in that, ideally, it competes with the first performance at Weinmar. Before the screen it is unprofitable to remember traditional contents which might come to mind before the stage—for instance, that Goethe's friend Johann Heinrich Merck is hidden in Mephisto, and the like.

4. Abel Gance, "Le Temps de l'image est venu," *L'Art cinématographique*, Vol., 2, pp. 94 f, Paris, 1927.

5. To satisfy the human interest of the masses may mean to have one's social function removed from the field of vision. Nothing guarantees that a portraitist of today, when painting a famous surgeon at the breakfast table in the midst of his family, depicts his social function more precisely than a painter of the 17th century who portrayed his medical doctors as representing this profession, like Rembrandt in his "Anatomy Lesson."

6. The definition of the aura as a "unique phenomenon of a distance however close it may be" represents nothing but the formulation of the cult value of the work of art in categories of space and time perception. Distance is the opposite of closeness. The essentially distant object is the unapproachable one. Unapproachability is indeed a major quality of the cult image. True to its nature, it remains "distant, however close it may be." The closeness which one may gain from its subject matter does not impair the distance which it retains in its appearance.

7. To the extent to which the cult value of the painting is secularized the ideas of its fundamental uniqueness lose distinctness. In the imagination of the beholder the uniqueness of the phenomena which hold sway in the cult image is more and more displaced by the empirical uniqueness of the creator or of his creative achievement. To be sure, never completely so; the concept of authenticity always transcends mere genuineness. (This is particularly apparent in the collector who always retains some traces of the fetishist and who, by owning the work of art,

shares in its ritual power.) Nevertheless, the function of the concept of authenticity remains determinate in the evaluation of art; with the secularization of art, authenticity displaces the cult value of the work.

8. In the case of films, mechanical reproduction is not, as with literature and painting, an external condition for mass distribution. Mechanical reproduction is inherent in the very technique of film production. This technique not only permits in the most direct way but virtuality causes mass distribution. It enforces distribution because the production of a film is so expensive that an individual who, for instance, might afford to buy a painting no longer can afford to buy a film. In 1927 it was calculated that a major film, in order to pay its way, had to reach an audience of nine million. With the sound film, to be sure, a setback in its international distribution occurred at first: audiences became limited by language barriers. This coincided with the Fascist emphasis on national interests. It is more important to focus on this connection with Facism than on this setback, which was soon minimized by synchronisation. The simultaneity of both phenomena is attributable to the depression. The same disturbances which , on a larger scale, led to an attempt to maintain the existing property structure by sheer force led the endangered film capital to speed up the development of the sound film. The introduction of the sound film brought about a temporary relief, not only because it again brought the masses into the theaters but also because it merged new capital from the electrical industry with that of the film industry. Thus, viewed from the outside, the sound film promoted national interests, but seen from the inside it helped to internationalize film production even more than previously.

9. This polarity cannot come into its own in the aesthetics of Idealism. Its idea of beauty comprises these polar opposites without differentiating between them and consequently excludes their polarity. Yet in Hegel this polarity announces itself as clearly as possible within the limits of Idealism. We quote from his *Philosophy of History*:

> "Images were known of old. Piety at an early time required them for worship, but it could do without *beautiful* images. These might even be disturbing. In every beautiful painting there is also something nonspiritual, merely external, but its spirit speaks to man through its beauty. Worshipping, conversely, is concerned with the work as an object, for it is but a spiritless stupor of the soul.... Fine art has arisen ... in the church ... , although it has already gone beyond its principle as art."

Likewise, the following passage from *The Philosophy of Fine Art* indicates that Hegel sensed a problem here.

> "We are beyond the stage of reverence for works of art as divine and objects deserving our worship. The impression they produce is one of a more reflective kind, and the emotions they arouse require a higher test...."—G. W. F. Hegel, *The Philosophy of Fine Art*, trans., with notes, by F. P. B. Osmaston, Vol. 1, p. 12, London, 1920.

The transition form the first kind of artistic reception to the second characterizes the history of artistic reception in general. Apart from that, a certain oscillation between these two polar modes of reception can be demonstrated for each work of art. Take the Sistine Madonna. Since Hubert Grimme's research it has been known that the Madonna originally was painted for the purpose of exhibition. Grimme's research was inspired by the question: What is the purpose of the molding in the foreground of the painting which the two cupids lean upon? How, Grimme asked further, did Raphael come to furnish the sky with two draperies? Research proved that the Madonna had been commissioned for the public lying-in-state of Pope Sixtus. The Popes lay in state in a certain side chapel of St. Peter's. On that occasion Raphael's picture had been fastened in a nichelike background of the chapel, supported by the coffin. In this picture Raphael portrays the Madonna approaching the papal coffin in clouds from the background of the niche, which was demarcated by green drapes. At the obsequies of Sixtus a pre-eminent exhibition value of Raphael's picture was taken advantage of. Some time later it was placed on the high altar in the church of the Black Friars at Piacenza. The reason for this exile is to be found in the Roman rites which forbid the use of paintings exhibited at obsequies as cult objects on the high altar. This regulation devalued Raphael's picture to some degree. In order to obtain an adequate price nevertheless, the Papal See resolved to add to the bargain the tacit toleration of the picture above the high altar. To avoid attention the picture was given to the monks of the far-off provincial town.

10. Bertolt Brecht, on a different level, engaged in analogous reflections: "If the concept of 'work of art' can no longer be applied to the thing that emerges once the work is transformed into a commodity, we have to eliminate this concept with cautious care but without fear, lest we liquidated the function of the very thing as well. For it has to go thorough this phase without mental reservation, and not as noncommittal deviation form the straight path; rather, what happens here with the work of art will change it fundamentally and erase its past to such an extent that should the old concept be taken up again—and it will, why not?—it will no longer stir any memeroy of the thing it once designated."

11. "The film ... provides—or could provide—useful insight into the details of human actions.... Character is never used as a source of motivation; the inner life of the persons never supplies the principal cause of the plot and seldom is its main result." (Bertolt Brecht, *Versuche*, "Der Dreigroschenprozess," p. 268.) The expansion of the field of the testable which mechanical equipment brings about for the actor corresponds to the extraordinary expansion of the field of the testable brought about for the individual through economic conditions. Thus, vocational aptitude tests become constantly more important. What matters in these tests are segmental performances of the individual. The film shot and the vocational aptitude test are taken before a committee of experts. The camera director in the studio occupies a place identical with that of the examiner during aptitude tests.

12. Luigi Pirandello, *Si Gira*, quoted by Léon Pierre-Quint, "Signification du cinéma," *L'Art cinématographique, op. cit.*, pp. 14-15.

13. Rudolf Arnheim, *Film als Kunst*, Berlin, 1932, pp. 176 f. In this context certain seemingly unimportant details in which the film director deviates from stage prac-

tices gain in interest. Such is the attempt to let the actor play without make-up, as made among others by Dreyer in his *Jeanne d'Arc*. Dreyer spent months seeking the forty actors who constitute the Inquisitors' tribunal. The search for these actors resembled that for stage properties that are hard to come by. Dreyer made every effort to avoid resemblances of age, build, and physiognomy. If the actor thus becomes a stage property, this latter, on the other hand, frequently functions as actor. At least it is not unusual for the film to assign a role to the stage property. Instead of choosing at random from a great wealth of examples, let us concentrate on a particularly convincing one. A clock that is working will always be a disturbance on the stage. There it cannot be permitted its function of measuring time. Even in a naturalistic play, astronomical time would clash with theatrical time. Under these circumstances it is highly revealing that the film can, whenever appropriate, use time as measured by a clock. From this more than from many other touches it may clearly be recognized that under certain circumstances each and every prop in a film may assume important functions. From here it is but one step to Pudovkin's statement that "the playing of an actor which is connected with an object and is built around it ... is always one of the strongest methods of cinematic construction." (W. Pudovkin, *Filmregie und Filmmanuskript,* Berlin, 1928, p. 126) The film is the first art form capable of demonstrating how matter plays tricks on man. Hence, films can be an excellent means of materialistic representation.

14. The change noted here in the method of exhibition caused by mechanical reproduction applies to politics as well. The present crisis of the bourgeois democracies comprises a crisis of the conditions which determine the public presentations of the rulers. Democracies exhibit a member of government direct and personally before the nations' representatives. Parliament is his public. Since the innovations of camera and recording equipment make it possible for the orator to become audible and visible to an unlimited number of persons, the presentation of the man of politics before camera and recording equipment becomes paramount. Parliaments, as much as theaters, are deserted. Radio and film not only affect the function of the professional actor but likewise the function of those who also exhibit themselves before this mechanical equipment, those who govern. Though their tasks may be different, the change affects equally the actor and the ruler. The trend is toward establishing controllable and transferrable skills under certain social conditions. This results in a new selection, a selection before the equipment from which the star and the dictator emerge victorious.

15. The privileged character of the respective techniques is lost. Aldous Huxley writes:

"Advances in technology have led ... to vulgarity.... Process reproduction and the rotary press have made possible the indefinite multiplication of writing and pictures. Universal education and relatively high wages have created an enormous public who know how to read and can afford to buy reading and pictorial matter. A great industry has been called into existence in order to supply these commodities. Now, artistic talent is a very rare phenomenon; whence it follows ... that, at every epoch and in all countries, most art has been bad. But the proportion of trash in the total artistic output is greater now than at any other period. That it must be so is a matter of simple arithmetic. The population of Western Europe has a little more than doubled during the last century. But the amount of reading—and seeing—matter has increased, I should imagine, at least twenty and possibly fifty or even a hundred times. If there were n men of talent in a population of x millions, there will presumably be 2n men of talent among 2x millions. The situation may be summed up thus. For every page of print and pictures published a century ago, twenty or perhaps even a hundred pages are published today. But for every man of talent then living, there are now only two men of talent. It may be of course that, thanks to universal education, many potential talents which in the past would have been stillborn are now enabled to realize themselves. Let us assume, then, that there are now three or even four men of talent to every one of earlier times. It still remains true to say that the consumption of reading—and seeing—matter has far outstripped the natural production of gifted writers and draughtsmen. It is the same with hearing-matter. Prosperity, the gramophone and the radio have created an audience of hearers who consume an amount of hearing-matter that has increased out of all proportion to the increase of population and the consequent natural increase of talented musicians. It follows from all this that in all the arts the output of trash is both absolutely and relatively greater than it was in the past; and that it must remain greater for just so long as the world continues to consume the present inordinate quantities of reading-matter, seeing-matter, and hearing-matter."—Aldous Huxley, *Beyond the Mexique Bay. A Travellers's Journal,* London, 1949, pp. 274 ff. First published in 1934.

This mode of observation is obviously not progressive.

16. The boldness of the cameraman is indeed comparable to that of the surgeon. Luc Durtain lists among specific technical sleights of hand those "which are required in surgery in the case of certain difficult operations. I choose as an example a case from oto-rhino-laryngology; ... the so-called endonasal perspective procedure; or I refer to the acrobatic tricks of larynx surgery which have to be performed following the reversed picture in the laryngoscope. I might also speak of ear surgery which suggest the precision work of watchmakers. What range of the most subtle muscular acrobatics is required from the man who wants to repair or save the human body! We have only to think of the couching of a cataract where there is virtually a debate of steel with early fluid tissue, or of the major abdominal operations (laparotomy)." Luc Durtain, *op. Cit.*

17. Rudolf Arnheim, *loc.cit.*, p. 138.

20

ANTONIO GRAMSCI (1891-1937)

Antonio Gramsci's work offers a rich legacy of engagement with Machiavelli's ideas about political power and with non-Marxist theories of culture and ideology. He remains a leading influence not only within Marxism but also in political sociology and cultural analysis.

As an intellectual in the Italian Communist Party, Gramsci was imprisoned by the Fascist regime and held for eleven years; he died shortly after his release. Most of his writing was accomplished in the difficult circumstances of a Fascist prison; he lacked books and paper, and his words were subject to scrutiny of prison censors. Furthermore, as a political activist he wanted to address the reality of Italy in the 1920s and 1930s, rather than weave academic theories, so there are many references to modern Italian history. For these reasons, his work is not an easy read for the contemporary student, especially outside of Italy.

The central concept in Gramsci's work is hegemony, a form of rule in which the ruled consent to the exercise of power. It is similar to Machiavelli's notion of the power of the fox who rules by cunning rather than coercion and to Weber's concepts of authority and legitimacy. Gramsci observed that in many bourgeois societies, the proletariat and other subordinate classes seem to consent to the power of capitalists. Subordinate classes are generally not in a state of constant rebellion or revolution; most of the time they go along with the existing state of affairs, with capitalist control of the economy and the workplace. They accord the bourgeoisie a right to rule, accepting the legitimacy of bourgeois domination of society.

How and in what circumstances can an economically dominant class translate its economic dominance into cultural and political power? An economically dominant class (for example, employers and owners of capital in capitalist society or landholders in feudal society) must have a way of establishing its rule throughout the institutions of society, otherwise its hold over resources and labour is likely to be constantly challenged. How does it translate its dominance in the relations of production into a more general hold on society? Are there mechanisms to establish and maintain power apart from coercion, which is an unstable and thoroughly unpopular form of domination?

Gramsci was particularly interested in the role of intellectuals in this translation of economic power into political and cultural power. In most societies the economically dominant classes produce a stratum of organic intellectuals that function to create consent. Gramsci used the term "organic" to mean that the intellectuals are thoroughly intertwined with the class structure, that they grow with it and fulfil a specific function within it. In all class societies the function of organic intellectuals is to create the cultural conditions for consent to inequality. For example, in the European Middle Ages, priests created the images of salvation, the good Christian life, the divine right of kings, and many other ideas that justified feudal relations of production. In capitalist society, journalists, the media in general, and professors create the sense that capitalism is efficient, egalitarian, natural, etc. You may remember that Marx was quite interested in this division of ruling classes into an active, economically-involved fraction and an intellectual, theorizing fraction, which justifies class inequality by the ideas it produces and disseminates.

The best kind of hegemony is the most effortless kind, in which people are induced to think about the world in only one way, so that no alternative thoughts are possible. Hegemony is a process that shapes common sense itself. When people can no longer think outside of the framework of hegemonic culture, their allegiance to class rule is complete. For example, in capitalist societies most people believe that the superiority of capitalism over socialism is "just common sense." Socialism seems silly, utopian, laughable, or sinister; it is associated with goofy professors, Stalinist secret police, the gulag of labour camps, meddlesome government bureaucrats, dangerous Reds, etc. It is impossible to think of an alternative to capitalism; when we try to do it, these disagreeable images well up, despite our efforts to think beyond them. A huge reservoir of notions, prejudices, images, and feelings seems to have been built up within us, largely unconsciously, through the gradual accumulation of stereotypes, slogans, and visual images. At an even more fundamental level, common sense talks to us in the voice of fatalism and acceptance: "This is the way the world works, this is human nature, it cannot be any other way." Hegemony at its most effective keeps us from thinking subversive thoughts or dreaming of rebellion.

Gramsci, as a communist revolutionary, was particularly committed to developing revolutionary intellectuals. Just as the bourgeoisie had its own organic intellectuals, the proletariat as a revolutionary force had to produce a cadre of intellectuals. Without organic intellectuals, proletarians might be able to organize to defend or enlarge their own immediate interests, but it was unlikely that they would be able to capture the state, take political power, and redirect society in a new, socialist, direction.

There are several tasks in which revolutionary organic intellectuals must be involved. One is the articulation of a vision of a socialist society that is a genuine alternative to capitalism. The second is to bring the subordinate classes and strata of capitalist society into a revolutionary movement. Gramsci referred to this task as the "formation of a historic bloc." The two polarized classes of capitalist society, bourgeoisie and proletariat, contend for the loyalty and support of the wide array of intermediate strata. For example, the bourgeoisie appeals to white collar workers as part of the middle class and to small business owners in terms of property rights. These ideological ploys bring intermediate strata into the bloc of the bourgeoisie, aligning them with capitalists against the working class. Revolutionary intellectuals have to voice alternative views of society that reveal shared interests between the proletariat and other subordinate groups.

Gramsci thought that it was not enough merely to put forth an ideology of a revolutionary bloc; once in power the proletariat might have to sacrifice some of its immediate interests to establish its political power and moral authority as a new ruling class. For example, in a socialist society, factory workers' interest in low food prices might have to be weighed against the interests of its allied class, the peasantry, who hope to be paid well enough for its produce to raise its own living standard.

Gramsci used the term "corporatist" as the opposite of hegemonic. A hegemonic class establishes its right to rule, using words and deeds to implant its moral authority on the ruled. It becomes hegemonic by defining itself as the representative of society as a whole, of the public interest and not only its own class interests. "What is good for capitalism is good for everybody; capitalism creates jobs, the market is the best way of distributing goods and services, and so on." On the other hand, a corporatist group acts only in terms of its immediate self-interest, usually defined in narrowly economic terms. It defends its short-term interests against other groups with little or no regard for the common good and the public interest. As long as the proletariat acts as a corporatist group, other strata will see it only as a special interest. Gramsci believed that intellectuals had an essential role in transforming the proletariat from a corporatist group defending its own rights into a hegemonic class that addresses the needs of a large bloc; only then can the proletariat lead a revolution and establish a socialist society.

To develop his ideas about how the proletariat can become a new ruling force in society, Gramsci turned once again to Machiavelli's analysis of power. Like Lenin, Gramsci saw the need for a vanguard party that articulates a socialist vision of society and organizes local class struggles into a revolutionary movement. Ultimately it is the vanguard party that implements the capture and transformation of the state; the state apparatus is used to change society from a capitalist to a socialist structure. There is nothing conspiratorial or underhanded about the vanguard party *vis à vis* its proletarian constituency; a revolution cannot be carried out by a class as an unorganized category of people— some type of structure is necessary. Gramsci understood that the revolutionary transformation of society from capitalism to socialism posed enormous problems of consolidating power and establishing hegemony. These problems were similar to those faced by Renaissance rulers attempting to wield power in the turbulent atmosphere of Italian city-states, in situations where old traditions counted for nothing. Thus, Gramsci called the revolutionary communist party "the modern prince." It was a collective rather than an individual prince, but it faced the same challenges of creating viable states, and of using its own resources of courage, boldness, and intelligence to mold new societies.

Gramsci developed his theory of hegemony by comparing different societies, focusing on the relationship between the state ("government" in contemporary North American parlance), civil society, and class power. He saw three distinct patterns in Western societies: the Russian case, which produced a successful socialist revolution; the stable bourgeois democracies like Great Britain and the United States; and the fascist and Nazi regimes.

In the case of Tsarist Russia the state had appeared to be extremely powerful, but it did not rest on a solid foundation of consent. It defended the interests of the rich—capitalists and landowners—in a heavy-handed, repressive way. Ordinary people—workers and peasants—accorded little consent to this power. They were not involved in civic associations and institutions that tied them to the ruling classes. Class rule was based on coercion: police forces, the Cossack troops, attacks on peaceful strikes and demonstrations, brutal punishments, and exile in Siberia. When the Tsarist state weakened in World War I, it was easy for the Russian revolutionaries to topple it.

In contrast, in the bourgeois democracies class rule was hegemonic. Not only did the capitalist class enjoy consent, it was also firmly tied to the subordinate strata in institutions and voluntary associations. Its rule through the state was backed up by cross-class associations of civil society. Churches, political parties, local community organizations, and interest groups tied bourgeoisie and proletariat to each other and integrated the proletariat into the capitalist social order. The state was not an isolated guardpost defending capitalist dominance by itself; in Gramsci's metaphor, the state was backed up by "the trenches of civil society," organizations and associations in which the proletariat came to feel part of the system and saw its interests aligned with those of capital.

He summarized this difference: "In Russia the State was everything, civil society was primordial and gelatinous; in the West, there was a proper relation between State and civil society, and when the State trembled a sturdy structure of civil society was at once revealed. The State was only an outer ditch, behind which there stood a powerful system of fortresses and earthworks...."[1]

Fascist and Nazi regimes, such as the ones that came to power in Italy and Germany, represented a third configuration of class, state, and civil society. Here the bourgeoisie had also been unable to establish themselves as a fully hegemonic ruling class. The tremendous shock of World War I set in motion powerful socialist and communist movements that the bourgeoisie was unable to contain. A majority of the working class no longer accorded the bourgeoisie the right to rule and began to organize to overthrow capitalism. The bourgeoisie had to turn to a mass movement based in the middle strata—fascism—to repress the working class movements. In these societies, the balance of forces was such that a stand-off developed between the bourgeoisie and proletariat. It could only be resolved in favour of the bourgeoisie by the abandonment of bourgeois democracy and the establishment of a fascist state that repressed the proletarian movements.

Gramsci traced the weak hegemony of the bourgeoisie through an historical analysis to show how it grew out of the unresolved relationship between the bourgeoisie and the agrarian ruling strata of pre-industrial times and backward regions, powerful landed interests such as owners of *latifundia* (estates worked by landless labourers) in southern Italy. Extending his analysis to Germany, historians have pointed to a similar position occupied by the Junkers, owners of estates in the eastern part of the country. Being unable to displace these quasi-feudal ruling classes completely, the bourgeoisie was in a weak position to establish itself as a hegemonic force in capitalist society.

To sum up: in the work of Gramsci we see first and foremost the development of a Marxist theory of culture and politics. Gramsci builds on and elaborates Marx's observations of hegemony and the ruling ideas of class formations. We can also trace the influence of Machiavelli's thought on Gramsci's views of how power is established and how a ruler consolidates a hold on society. Like Machiavelli, Gramsci believes that the lion—the ruler who relies on coercive power alone—is usually in a weaker position than the fox. He uses Machiavelli's analysis of the prince to identify the tasks faced by the modern prince, the revolutionary party intent on establishing and consolidating a new state and society. Finally, note how Gramsci provides a Marxist analysis of many issues that intrigued Weber: authority, legitimacy, and the role of ideas in the exercise of power; the relationship between social categories (class and status) and political organizations that claim to express their interests ("party"); and the relationship between states and societies.

Notes

1. Antonio Gramsci, *Selections from the Prison Notebooks* (New York: International Publishers, 1971) 238.

Readings

Cammett, John. *Antonio Gramsci and the Origins of Italian Communism*. Stanford, CA: Stanford, 1967.

Clark, Martin. *Antonio Gramsci and the Revolution that Failed*. New Haven, CT: Yale University Press, 1977.

Fernia, Joseph. *Gramsci's Political Thought: Hegemony, Consciousness, and the Revolutionary Process*. New York: Oxford University Press, 1987.

Fontana, Benedetto. *Hegemony and Power: On the Relation between Gramsci and Machiavelli*. Minneapolis, MN: University of Minnesota Press, 1993.

Gramsci, Antonio. *Further Selections from the Prison Notebooks*. Ed. and trans. Derek Boothman. Minneapolis, MN: University of Minnesota Press, 1995.

Harris, David. *From Class Struggle to the Politics of Pleasure: The Effects of Gramscianism on Cultural Studies*. London and New York: Routledge, 1992.

Mouffe, Chantal. *Gramsci and Marxist Theory*. London and Boston: Routledge and Kegan Paul, 1979.

The Prison Notebooks
ANTONIO GRAMSCI

The Formation Of The Intellectuals

Are intellectuals an autonomous and independent social group, or does every social group have its own particular specialised category of intellectuals? The problem is a complex one, because of the variety of forms assumed to date by the real historical process of formation of the different categories of intellectuals.

The most important of these forms are two:

1. Every social group, coming into existence on the original terrain of an essential function in the world of economic production, creates together with itself, organically, one or more strata[1] of intellectuals which give it homogeneity and an awareness of its own function not only in the economic but also in the social and political fields. The capitalist entrepreneur creates alongside himself the industrial technician, the specialist in political economy, the organisers of a new culture, of a new legal system, etc. It should be noted that the entrepreneur himself represents a higher level of social elaboration, already characterised by a certain directive [*dirigente*][2] and technical (i.e. intellectual) capacity: he must have a certain technical capacity, not only in the limited

sphere as well, at least in those which are closest to economic production. He must be an organiser of masses of men; he must be an organiser of the "confidence" of investors in his business, of the customers for his product, etc.

If not all entrepreneurs, at least an *élite* amongst them must have the capacity to be an organiser of society in general, including all its complex organism of services, right up to the state organism, because of the need to create the conditions most favourable to the expansion of their own class; or at the least they must possess the capacity to choose the deputies (specialised employees) to whom to entrust this activity of organising the general system of relationships external to the business itself. It can be observed that the "organic" intellectuals which every new class creates alongside itself and elaborates in the course of its development, are for the most part "specialisations" of partial aspects of the primitive activity of the new social type which the new class has brought into prominence.[3]

Even feudal lords were possessors of a particular technical capacity, military capacity, and it is precisely from the moment at which the aristocracy loses its monopoly of technico-military capacity that the crisis of feudalism begins. But the formation of intellectuals in the feudal world and in the preceding classical world is a question to be examined separately: this formation and elaboration follows ways and means which must be studied concretely. Thus it is to be noted that the mass of the peasantry, although it performs an essential function in the world of production, does not elaborate its own "organic" intellectuals, nor does it "assimilate" any stratum of "traditional" intellectuals, although it is from the peasantry that other social groups draw many of their intellectuals and a high proportion of traditional intellectuals are of peasant origin.[4]

2. However, every "essential" social group which emerges into history out of the preceding economic structure, and as an expression of a development of this structure, has found (at least in all of history up to the present) categories of intellectuals already in existence and which seemed indeed to represent an historical continuity uninterrupted even by the most complicated and radical changes in political and social forms.

The most typical of these categories of intellectuals is that of the ecclesiastics, who for a long time (for a whole phase of history, which is partly characterised by this very monopoly) held a monopoly of a number of important services: religious ideology, that is the philosophy and science of the age, together with schools, education, morality, justice, charity, good works, etc. The category of ecclesiastics can be considered the category of intellectuals organically bound to the landed aristocracy. It had equal status juridically with the aristocracy, with which it shared the exercise of feudal ownership of land and the use of state privileges connected with property.[5] But the monopoly held by the ecclesiastics in the superstructural field[6] was not exercised without a struggle or without limitations, and hence there took place the birth, in various forms (to be gone into and studied concretely), of other categories, favoured and enabled to expand by the growing strength of the central power of the monarch, right up to absolutism. Thus we find the formation of the *noblesse de robe*, with its own privileges, a stratum of administrators, etc., scholars and scientists, theorists, non-ecclesiastical philosophers, etc.

Since these various categories of traditional intellectuals experience through an *"esprit de corps"* their uninterrupted historical continuity and their special qualification, they thus put themselves forward as autonomous and independent of the dominant social group. This self-assessment is not without consequences in the ideological and political field, consequences of wide-ranging import. The whole of idealist philosophy can easily be connected with this position assumed by the social complex of intellectuals and can be defined as the expression of that social utopia by which the intellectuals think of themselves as "independent," autonomous, endowed with a character of their own, etc.

One should note however that if the Pope and the leading hierarchy of the Church consider themselves more linked to Christ and to the apostles than they are to senators Agnelli and Benni,[7] the same does not hold for Gentile and Croce, for example: Croce in particular feels himself closely linked to Aristotle and Plato, but he does not conceal, on the other hand, his links with senators Agnelli and Benni, and it is precisely here that one can discern the most significant character of Croce's philosophy.

What are the "maximum" limits of acceptance of the term "intellectual"? Can one find a unitary criterion to characterise equally all the diverse and disparate activities of intellectuals and to distinguish these at the same time and in an essential way from the activities of other social groupings? The most widespread error of method seems to me that of having looked for this criterion of distinction in the intrinsic nature of intellectual activities, rather than in the ensemble of the system of relations in which these activities (and therefore the intellectual groups who personify them) have their place within the general complex of social relations. Indeed the worker or proletarian, for example, is not specifically characterised by his manual or instrumental work, but by performing this work in specific conditions and in specific social relations (apart from the consideration that purely physical labour does not exist and that even Taylor's phrase of "trained gorilla"[8] is a metaphor to indicate a limit in a certain direction: in any physical work, even the most degraded and mechanical, there exists a minimum of technical qualification, that is, a minimum of creative intellectual activity.) And we have already observed that the entrepreneur, by virtue of his very function, must have to some degree a certain number of qualifications of an intellectual nature although his part in society is determined not by these, but by the general social relations which specifically characterise the position of the entrepreneur within industry.

All men are intellectuals, one could therefore say: but not all men have in society the function of intellectuals.[9]

When one distinguishes between intellectuals and non-intellectuals, one is referring in reality only to the immediate social function of the professional category of the intellectuals, that is, one has in mind the direction in which their specific professional activity is weighted, whether towards intellectual elaboration or towards muscular-nervous effort. This means that, although one can speak of intellectuals, one cannot speak of non-intellectuals, because non-intellectuals do not exist. But even the relationship between efforts of intellectual-cerebral elaboration and muscular-nervous effort is not always the same, so that there are varying degrees of specific intellectual activity. There is no human activity from which every form of intellectual participation can be excluded: *homo faber* cannot be separated from *homo sapiens.*[10] Each man, finally, outside his professional activity, carries on some form of intellectual activity, that is, he is a "philosopher," an artist, a man of taste, he participates in a particular conception of the world, has a conscious line of moral conduct, and therefore contributes to sustain a conception of the world or to modify it, that is, to bring into being new modes of thought.

The problem of creating a new stratum of intellectuals consists therefore in the critical elaboration of the intellectual activity that exists in everyone at a certain degree of development, modifying its relationship with the muscular-nervous effort towards a new equilibrium, and ensuring that the muscular-nervous effort itself, in so far as it is an element of a general practical activity, which is perpetually innovating the physical and social world, becomes the foundation of a new and integral conception of the world. The traditional and vulgarised type of the intellectual is given by the man of letters, the philosopher, the artist. Therefore journalists, who claim to be men of letters, philosophers, artists, also regard themselves as the "true" intellectuals. In the modern world, technical education, closely bound to industrial labour even at the most primitive and unqualified level, must form the basis of the new type of intellectual.

On this basis the weekly *Ordine Nuovo*[11] worked to develop certain forms of new intellectualism and to determine its new concepts, and this was not the least of the reasons for its success, since such a conception corresponded to latent aspirations and conformed to the development of the real forms of life. The mode of being of the new intellectual can no longer consist in eloquence, which is an exterior and momentary mover of feelings and passions, but in active participation in practical life, as constructor, organiser, "permanent persuader" and not just a simple orator (but superior at the same time to the abstract mathematical spirit); from technique-as-work one proceeds to technique-as-science and to the humanistic conception of history, without which one remains "specialised" and does not become "directive"[12] (specialised and political).

Thus there are historically formed specialised categories for the exercise of the intellectual function. They are formed in connection with all social groups, but especially in connection with the more important, and they undergo more extensive and complex elaboration in connection with the dominant social group. One of the most important characteristics of any group that is developing towards dominance is its struggle to assimilate and to conquer "ideologically" the traditional intellectuals, but this assimilation and conquest is made quicker and more efficacious the more the group in question succeeds in simultaneously elaborating its own organic intellectuals.

The enormous development of activity and organisation of education in the broad sense in the societies that emerged from the medieval world is an index of the importance assumed in the modern world by intellectual functions and categories. Parallel with the attempt to deepen and to broaden the "intellectuality" of each individual, there has also been an attempt to multiply and narrow the various specialisations. This can be seen from educational institutions at all levels, up to and including the organisms that exist to promote so-called "high culture" in all fields of science and technology.

School is the instrument through which intellectuals of various levels are elaborated. The complexity of the intellectual function in different states can be measured objectively by the number and gradation of specialised schools: the more extensive the "area" covered by education and the more numerous the "vertical" "levels" of schooling, the more complex is the cultural world, the civilisation, of a particular state. A point of comparison can be found in the sphere of industrial technology: the industrialisation of a country can be measured by how well equipped it is in the production of machines with which to produce machines, and in the manufacture of ever more accurate instruments for making both machines and further instruments for making machines, etc. The country which is best equipped in the construction of instruments for experimental scientific laboratories and in the construction of instruments with which to test the first instruments, can be regarded as the most complex in the technical-industrial field, with the highest level of civilisation, etc. The same applies to the preparation of intellectuals and to the schools dedicated to this preparation; schools and institutes of high culture can be assimilated to each other. In this field also, quantity cannot be separated from quality. To the most refined technical-cultural specialisation there cannot but correspond the maximum possible diffusion of primary education and the maximum care taken to expand the middle grades numerically as much as possible. Naturally this need to provide the widest base possible for the selection and elaboration of the top intellectual qualifications—i.e. to give a democratic structure to high culture and top-level technology—is not without its disadvantages: it creates the possibility of vast crises of unemployment for the middle intellectual strata, and in all modern societies this actually takes place.

It is worth noting that the elaboration of intellectual strata in concrete reality does not take place on the terrain of abstract democracy but in accordance with very concrete traditional historical processes. Strata have grown up which traditionally "produce" intellectuals and these strata coincide with those which have specialised in "saving," i.e., the petty and middle landed bourgeoisie and certain strata of the petty and middle urban bourgeoisie. The varying distribution of different types of school (classical and professional)[13] over the "economic" territory and the varying aspirations of different categories within these strata determine, or give form to, the production of various branches of intellectual specialisation. Thus in Italy the rural bourgeoisie produces in particular state functionaries and professional people, whereas the urban bourgeoisie produces technicians for industry. Consequently it is largely northern Italy which produces technicians and the South which produces functionaries and professional men.

The relationship between the intellectuals and the world of production is not as direct as it is with the fundamental social groups but is, in varying degrees, "mediated" by the whole fabric of society and by the complex of superstructures, of which the intellectuals are, precisely, the "functionaries." It should be possible both to measure the "organic quality" [organicità] of the various intellectual strata and their degree of connection with a fundamental social group, and to establish a gradation of their functions and of the superstructures from the bottom to the top (from the structural base upwards). What we can do, for the moment, is to fix two major superstructural "levels": the one that can be called "civil society," that is the ensemble of organisms commonly called "private," and that of "political society" or "the State." These two levels correspond on the one hand to the function of "hegemony" which the dominant group exercises throughout society and on the other hand to that of "direct domination" or command exercised through the State and "juridical" government. The functions in question are precisely organisational and connective. The intellectuals are the dominant group's "deputies" exercising the subaltern functions of social hegemony and political government. These comprise:

1. The "spontaneous" consent given by the great masses of the population to the general direction imposed on social life by the dominant fundamental group; this consent is "historically" caused by the prestige (and consequent

confidence) which the dominant group enjoys because of its position and function in the world of production.

2. The apparatus of state coercive power which "legally" enforces discipline on those groups who do not "consent"either actively or passively. This apparatus is, however, constituted for the whole of society in anticipation of moments of crisis of command and direction when spontaneous consent has failed.

This way of posing the problem has as a result a considerable extension of the concept of intellectual, but it is the only way which enables one to reach a concrete approximation of reality. It also clashes with preconceptions of caste. The function of organising social hegemony and state domination certainly gives rise to a particular division of labour and therefore to a whole hierarchy of qualifications in some of which there is no apparent attribution of directive or organisational functions. For example, in the apparatus of social and state direction there exists a whole series of jobs of a manual and instrumental character (non-executive work, agents rather than officials or functionaries).[14] It is obvious that such a distinction has to made just as it is obvious that other distinctions have to be made as well. Indeed, intellectual activity must also be distinguished in terms of its intrinsic characteristics, according to levels which in moments of extreme opposition represent a real qualitative difference—at the highest level would be the creators of the various sciences, philosophy, art, etc., at the lowest the most humble "administrators" and divulgators of pre-existing, traditional, accumulated intellectual wealth.[15]

In the modern world the category of intellectuals, understood in this sense, has undergone an unprecedented expansion. The democratic-bureaucratic system has given rise to a great mass of functions which are not all justified by the social necessities of production, though they are justified by the political necessities of the dominant fundamental group. Hence Loria's[16] conception of the unproductive "worker" (but unproductive in relation to whom and to what mode of production?), a conception which could in part be justified if one takes account of the fact that these masses exploit their position to take for themselves a large cut out of the national income. Mass formation has standardised individuals both psychologically and in terms of individual qualification and has produced the same phenomena as with other standardised masses: competition which makes necessary organisations for the defence of professions, unemployment, over-production in the schools, emigration, etc.

Notes
(Notes by Quentin Hoare and Geoffrey Nowell Smith, editors and translators,

Selections from the Prison Notebooks of Antonio Gramsci [New York: International Publishers, 1971])

1. The Italian word here is *"ceti"* which does not carry quite the same connotations as "strata," but which we have been forced to translate in that way for lack of alternatives. It should be noted that Gramsci tends, for reasons of censorship, to avoid using the word class in contexts where its Marxist overtones would be apparent, preferring (as for example in this sentence) the more neutral "social group." The word "group," however, is not always a euphemism for "class," and to avoid ambiguity Gramsci uses the phrase "fundamental social group" when he wishes to emphasise the fact that he is referring to one or other of the major social classes (bourgeoisie, proletariat) defined on strict Marxist terms by its position in the fundamental relations of production. Class groupings which do not have this fundamental role are often described as "castes" (aristocracy, etc.). The word "category," on the other hand, which also occurs on this page, Gramsci tends to use in the standard Italian sense of members of a trade or profession, though also more generally. Throughout this edition we have rendered Gramsci's usage as literally as possible (see note on Gramsci's Terminology, p.xiii).

2. See note on Gramsci's Terminology.

3. Mosca's *Elementi di Scienza Politica* (new expanded edition, 1923) are worth looking at in this connection. Mosca's so-called "political class"* is nothing other than the intellectual category of the dominant social group. Mosca's concept of "political class" can be connected with Pareto's concept of the *elite*, which is another attempt to interpret the historical phenomenon of the intellectuals and their function in the life of the state and of society, Mosca's book is an enormous hotchpotch, of a sociological and positive character, plus the tendentiousness of immediate politics which makes it less indigestible and livelier from literary point of view.

    * Usually translated in English as "ruling class," which is also the title of the English version of Mosca's *Elementi* (G. Mosca, *The Ruling Class,* New York 1939). Gaetano Mosca (1858-1941)was, together with Pareto and Michels, one of the major early Italian exponents of the theory of political *élites*. Although sympathetic to fascism, Mosca was basically a conservative, who saw the *élite* in rather more static terms than did some of his fellows.

4. Notably in Southern Italy, See, "The Different Position of Urban and Rural-type Intellectuals," [*Selections from the Notebooks of Antonio Gramsci*] pp. 14-23. Gramsci's general argument, here as elsewhere in the *Quaderni,* is that the person of peasant origin who becomes an "intellectual" (priest, lawyer, etc.) generally thereby ceases to be organically linked to his class of origin. One of the essential differences between, say, the Catholic Church and the revolutionary party of the working class lies in the fact that, ideally, the proletariat should be able to generate its own "organic" intellectuals within the class and who remain intellectuals *of* their class.

5. For one category of these intellectuals, possibly the most important after the eccle-

siastical for its prestige and the social function it performed in primitive societies, the category of *medical men* in the wide sense, that is all those who "struggle" or seem to struggle against death and disease, compare the *Storia della medicina* of Arturo Castiglioni. Note that there has been a connection between religion and medicine, and in certain areas there still is: hospitals in the hands of religious orders for certain organisational functions, apart from the fact that wherever the doctor appears, so does the priest (exorcism, various forms of assistance, etc.). Many great religious figures were and are conceived of as great "healers": the idea of miracles, up to the resurrection of the dead. Even in the case of kings the belief long survived that they could heal with the laying on of hands, etc.

6. From this has come the general sense of "intellectual" or "specialist" of the word *"chierico"* (clerk, cleric) in many languages of romance origin or heavily influenced, through church Latin, by the romance languages, together with its correlative *"laico"* (lay, layman) in the sense of profane, non-specialist.

7. Heads of FIAT and Montecatini (Chemicals) respectively. For Agnelli, of whom Gramsci had direct experience during the *Ordine Nuovo* period, see note II on p. 286 [*Selections from the Prison Notebooks of Antonio Gramsci*].

8. For Frederick Taylor and his notion of the manual worker as a "trained gorilla," see Gramsci's essay *Americanism and Fordism,* pp. 277-318 [*Selections from the Prison Notebooks of Antonio Gramsci*].

9. Thus, because it can happen that everyone at some time fries a couple of eggs or sews up a tear in a jacket, we do not necessarily say that everyone is a cook or a tailor.

10. i.e. Man the maker (or tool-bearer) and Man the thinker.

11. The *Ordine Nuovo,* the magazine edited by Gramsci during his days as a militant in Turin, ran as a "weekly review of Socialist culture" in 1919 and 1920. See Introduction [*Selections from the Prison Notebooks of Antonio Gramsci*] pp.xxxvff.

12. *"Dirigente."* This extremely condensed and elliptical sentence contains a number of key Gramscian ideas: on the possibility of proletarian cultural hegemony through domination of the work process, on the distinction between organic intellectuals of the working class and traditional intellectuals from outside, on the unity of theory and practice as a basic Marxist postulate, etc.

13. The Italian school system above compulsory level is based on a division between academic ("classical" and "scientific") education and vocational training for professional purposes. Technical and, at the academic level, "scientific" colleges tend to be concentrated in the Northern industrial areas.

14. *"funzionari"*; in Italian usage the word is applied to the middle and higher echelons of the bureaucracy. Conversely "administrators." (*"amministratori"*) is used here (end of paragraph) to mean people who merely "administer" the decisions of others. The phrase "non-executive work" is a translation of "[*impiego*] di ordine e non di concetto" which refers to distinctions within clerical work.

15. Here again military organisation offers a model of complex gradations between subaltern officers, senior officers and general staff, not to mention the NCO's, whose importance is greater than is generally admitted. It is worth observing that

all these parts feel a solidarity and indeed that it is the lower strata that display the most blatant *esprit de corps,* from which they derive a certain "conceit"* which is apt to lay them open to jokes and witticisms.

    * *"boria."* This is a reference to an idea of Vico.

16. The notion of the "unproductive labourer" is not in fact an invention of Loria's but has its origins in Marx's definitions of production and unproductive labour in *Capital*, which Loria, in his characteristic way, both vulgarised and claimed as his own discovery.

21

THE LEGACY OF CULTURAL MARXISM: TODD GITLIN (1943–)

Todd Gitlin, a professor of sociology and a media critic, explicitly turns to Antonio Gramsci and the concept of hegemony to analyze television programming. He rejects several alternative forms of media criticism—the tendency to focus on specific single programs; the effort to explain media characteristics as a simple, direct result of ownership patterns; and the view that all media content is straightforward ideological indoctrination. Gitlin looks at television and sees a more complicated picture than these types of critiques can encompass. Television programming now includes a wide range of shows and characters, more sensitivity about divisive social issues, and more tolerance of ambiguity. Gitlin's point is that these changes represent a more complex and powerful form of hegemony.

Gitlin wants to show that hegemony is a complicated process. It is not embedded in any one show, by itself, nor can it simply be seen in the contents of shows. Hegemony is constructed through the entire spectrum of media production, is built into the structure of TV programming, and is solidified by incorporating elements of resistance and opposition; "alternative and oppositional values are brought into the cultural system, and domesticated into hegemonic forms at times, by the routine workings of the market."[1]

Gitlin outlines five key terms for the analysis, in addition to framing, the way a narrative or problem is presented.

1. *Format and formula*. Time is standardized (a characteristic of capitalism we already found in Simmel's discussion) and divisions are domesticated into a repetitive and predictable pattern.
2. *Genre*. Both within and across genres, there is response to changes in popular moods or climates. For example, westerns gave way to Cold War spy dramas and science fiction; within the perennial genre favourites of police and courtroom dramas, there were changes in style, taste, and framing of details. What does not change is a framing that affirms dominant values such as individualism and technical know-how.
3. *Setting and character type*. The range has widened in these areas, but it is still narrow. Some stereotypes have disappeared or softened, but there is still a large range of people and settings that are considered taboo or unappealing to viewers.
4. *Slant*. Over several decades there has been a shift from simply excluding divisive social issues (racism, domestic violence, diversity in sexual orientation, political differences, etc.) to domesticating them, that is, bringing

them into a standardized format and conventional resolutions of the problems. Generally there is growing tolerance in television programming for diversity in private matters—for example for cultural diversity among ethnic groups or acceptance of homosexuality—but the limits are narrower for public, organized, and political challenges to the status quo.

5. *Solution.* There is now a greater leeway for ambiguous endings. Ambiguity itself can be a hegemonic discourse; it can be used to suggest that action to change a status quo is likely not to produce a positive or intended effect. For example, when a union drive or other collective action is shown as having an ambiguous or unanticipated outcome, the framing indicates that such action should probably not be undertaken.

Although Gitlin's examples are dated, the overall patterns and trends he identifies have continued. The importance of this article is in showing how hegemony has to be studied in terms of large, long-term patterns of media framing that can include the incorporation of diversity and even oppositional elements within a larger structure of affirming dominant values and domesticating difference.

Notes
1. Todd Gitlin, *The Whole World Is Watching* (Berkely, CA: University of California Press, 1980) 431.

Readings
Chomsky, Noam. *Manufacturing Consent: The Political Economy of the Mass Media.* New York: Pantheon, 1988.

Hertsgaard, Mark. *On Bended Knee: The Press and the Reagan Presidency.* New York: Schocken Books, 1989.

Schudson, Michael. *Discovering the News.* New York: Basic Books, 1981.

Prime Time Ideology:
The Hegemonic Process in Television Entertainment
TODD GITLIN

Every society works to reproduce itself—and its internal conflicts—within its cultural order, the structure of practices and meanings around which the society takes shape. So much is tautology. In this paper I look at contemporary mass media in the United States as one cultural system promoting that reproduction. I try to show how ideology is relayed through various features of American television, and how television programs register larger ideological structures and changes. The question here is not, What is the impact of these programs? but rather a prior one, What do these programs mean? For only after thinking through their possible meanings as cultural objects and as signs of cultural interactions among producers and audiences may we begin intelligibly to ask about their "effects."

The attempt to understand the sources and transformations of ideology in American society has been leading social theorists not only to social-psychological investigations, but to a long overdue interest in Antonio Gramsci's (1971) notion of ideological hegemony. It was Gramsci who, in the late twenties and thirties, with the rise of Fascism and the failure of the Western European working-class movements, began to consider why the working class was not necessarily revolutionary; why it could, in fact, yield to Fascism. Condemned to a Fascist prison precisely because the insurrectionary workers' movement in Northern Italy just after World War I failed, Gramsci spent years trying to account for the defeat, resorting in large measure to the concept of hegemony: bourgeois domination of the thought, the common sense, the lifeways and everyday assumptions of the working class. Gramsci counterposed "hegemony" to "coercion"; these were two analytically distinct processes through which ruling classes secure the consent of the dominated. Gramsci did not always make plain where to draw the line between hegemony and coercion; or rather, as Perry Anderson shows convincingly (1976),[1] he drew the line differently at different times. Nonetheless, ambiguities aside, Gramsci's distinction was a great advance for radical thought, for it called attention to the routine structures of everyday thought—down to "commonsense" itself—which worked to sustain class domination and tyranny. That is to say, paradoxically, it took the working class seriously enough as a potential agent of revolution to hold it accountable for its failures.

Because Leninism failed abysmally throughout the West, Western Marxists and non-Marxist radicals have both been drawn back to Gramsci, hoping to address the evident fact that the Western working classes are not predestined toward socialist revolution.[2] In Europe this fact could be taken as strategic rather than normative wisdom on the part of the working class; but in America the working class is not only hostile to revolutionary *strategy,* it seems to disdain the socialist *goal* as well. At the very least, although a recent Peter Hart opinion poll showed that Americans abstractly "favor" workers' control, Americans do not seem to care enough about it to organize very widely in its behalf. While there are abundant "contradictions" throughout American society, they are played out substantially in the realm of "culture" or "ideology," which orthodox Marxism had consigned to the secondary category of "superstructure." Meanwhile, critical theory—especially in the work of T.W. Adorno and Max Horkheimer—had argued with great force that the dominant forms of commercial ("mass") culture were crystallizations of authoritarian ideology; yet despite the ingenuity and brilliance of particular feats of critical exegesis (Adorno, 1954, 1974; Adorno and Horkheimer, 1972), they seemed to be arguing that the "culture industry" was not only meretricious but wholly and statically complete. In the seventies, some of their approaches along with Gramsci's have been elaborated and furthered by Alvin W. Gouldner (1976; see also Kellner, 1978) and Raymond Williams (1973), in distinctly provocative ways.

In this paper I wish to contribute to the process of bringing the discussion of cultural hegemony down to earth. For much of the discussion so far remains abstract, almost as if cultural hegemony were a substance with a life of its own, a sort of immutable fog that has settled over the whole public life of capitalist societies to confound the truth of the proletarian telos. Thus to the questions, "Why are radical ideas suppressed in the schools?", "Why do workers oppose socialism?" and so on, comes the single Delphic answer: hegemony. "Hegemony" becomes the magical explanation of last resort. And as such it is useful neither as explanation nor as guide to action. If "hegemony" explains everything in the sphere of culture, it explains nothing.

Concurrent with the theoretical discussion, but on a different plane, looms an entire sub-industry criticizing and explicating specific mass-cultural products and straining to find "emancipatory" if not "revolutionary" meanings in them. Thus in 1977 there was cacophony about the TV version of *Roots;* this year the trend-setter seems to be TV's handling of violence. Mass media criticism becomes mass-mediated, an auxiliary sideshow serving cultural producers as well as the wider public of the cultural spectacle. Piece by piece we see fast and furious analysis of this movie, that TV show, that book, that spectator sport. Many of these pieces have merit one by one, but as a whole they do not accumulate toward a more general theory of how the cultural forms are managed and reproduced—and how they change. Without analytic point, item-by-item analyses of the standard fare of mass culture run the risk of degenerating into high-toned gossip, even a kind of critical groupie-ism. Unaware of the ambiguity of their own motives and strategies, the partial critics may be yielding to a displaced envy, where criticism covertly asks to be taken into the spotlight along with the celebrity culture ostensibly under criticism. Yet another trouble is that partial critiques in the mass-culture tradition don't help us understand the *hold* and the *limits* of cultural products, the degree to which people do and do not incorporate mass-cultural forms, sing the jingles, wear the corporate T-shirts, and most important, permit their life-worlds to be demarcated by them.

My task in what follows is to propose some features of a lexicon for discussing the forms of hegemony in the concrete. Elsewhere I have described some of the operations of cultural hegemony in the sphere of television news, especially in the news's framing procedures for opposition movements (Gitlin, 1977 a, b).[3] Here I wish to speak of the realm of entertainment: about television entertainment in particular—as the most pervasive and (in the living room sense) *familiar* of our cultural sites—and about movies secondarily. How do the *formal* devices of TV prime-time programs encourage viewers to experience themselves as anti-political, privately accumulating individuals (also see Gitlin, 1977c)? And how do these forms express social conflict, containing and diverting the images of contrary social possibilities? I want to isolate a few of the routine devices, though of course in reality they do not operate in isolation; rather, they work in combination, where their force is often enough magnified (though they can also work in contradictory ways). And, crucially, it must be borne in mind throughout this discussion that the forms of mass-cultural production do not either spring up or operate independently of the rest of social life. Commercial culture does not *manufacture* ideology; it *relays* and *reproduces* and *processes* and *packages* and *focuses* ideology that is constantly arising both from social elites and from active social groups and movements throughout the society (as well as within media organizations and practices).

A more complete analysis of ideological process in a commercial society would look both above and below, to elites and to audiences. Above, it would take a long look at the economics and politics of broadcasting, at its relation to the FCC, the Congress, the President, the courts; in case studies and with a developing theory of ideology it would study media's peculiar combination and refraction of corporate, political, bureaucratic and professional interests, giving the media a sort of limited independence—or what Marxists are calling "relative autonomy"—in the upper reaches of the political-economic system. Below, as Raymond Williams has insisted, cultural hegemony operates within a whole social life-pattern; the people who consume mass-mediated products are also the people who work, reside, compete, go to school, live in families. And there are good many traditional and material interests at stake for audiences: the political inertia of the American population now, for example, certainly has something to do with the continuing productivity of the goods producing and distributing industries, not simply with the force of mass culture. Let me try to avoid misunderstanding at the outset by insisting that *I will not be arguing that the forms of hegemonic entertainment superimpose themselves automatically and finally onto the consciousness or behavior of all audiences at all times:* it remains for sociologists to generate what Dave Morley (1974)[4] has called "an ethnography of audiences," and to study what Ronald Abramson (1978) calls "the phenomenology of audiences" if we are to have anything like a satisfactory account of how audiences consciously and unconsciously process, transform, and are transformed by the contents of television. For many years the subject of media effects was severely narrowed by a behaviorist definition of the problem (see Gitlin, 1978a); more recently, the "agenda-setting function" of mass media has been usefully studied in news media, but not in entertainment. (On the other hand, the very pervasiveness of TV entertainment makes laboratory study of its "effects" almost inconceivable.) It remains to incorporate occasional sociological insights into the actual behavior of TV audiences[5] into a more general theory of the interaction—a theory which avoids both the mechanical assumptions of behaviorism and the trivialities of the "uses and gratifications" approach.

But alas, that more general theory of the interaction is not on the horizon. My more modest attempt in this extremely preliminary essay is to sketch an approach to the hegemonic thrust of some TV forms, not to address the deflection, resistance, and reinterpretation achieved by audiences. I will show that hegemonic ideology is systematically preferred by certain features of TV programs, and that at the same time alternative and oppositional values are brought into the cultural system, and domesticated into hegemonic forms at times, by the routine workings of the market. Hegemony is reasserted in different ways at different times, even by different logics; if this variety is analytically messy, the messiness corresponds to a disordered ideological order, a contradictory society. This said, I proceed to some of the forms in which ideological hegemony is embedded: *format* and *formula; genre; setting* and *character type; slant;* and *solution.* Then these particulars will suggest a somewhat more fully developed theory of hegemony.

Format and Formula
Until recently at least, the TV schedule has been dominated by standard lengths and cadences, standardized packages of TV entertainment appearing, as the announcers used to say, "same time, same station." This week-to-weekness— or, in the case of soap operas, day-to-dayness—obstructed the development of

characters; at least the primary characters had to be preserved intact for next week's show. Perry Mason was Perry Mason, once and for all; if you watched the reruns, you couldn't know from character or set whether you were watching the first or the last in the series. For commercial and production reasons which are in practice inseparable—and this is why ideological hegemony is not reducible to the economic interests of elites—the regular schedule prefers the repeatable formula: it is far easier for production companies to hire writers to write for standardized, static characters than for characters who develop. Assembly-line production works through regularity of time slot, of duration, and of character to convey images of social steadiness: come what may, *Gunsmoke* or *Kojak* will check in to your mind at a certain time on a certain evening. Should they lose ratings (at least at the "upscale" reaches of the "demographics," where ratings translate into disposable dollars),[6] their replacements would be—for a time, at least!—equally reliable. Moreover, the standard curve of narrative action—stock characters encounter new version of stock situation; the plot thickens, allowing stock characters to show their standard stuff; the plot resolves—over twenty-two or fifty minutes is itself a source of rigidity and forced regularity.

In these ways, the usual programs are performances that rehearse social fixity: they express and cement the obduracy of a social world impervious to substantial change. Yet at the same time there are signs of routine obsolescence, as hunks of last year's regular schedule drop from sight only to be supplanted by this season's attractions. Standardization and the threat of evanescence are curiously linked: they match the intertwined processes of commodity production, predictability and obsolescence, in a high-consumption society. I speculate that they help instruct audiences in the rightness and naturalness of a world that, in only apparent paradox, regularly requires an irregularity, an unreliability which it calls progress. In this way, the regular changes in TV programs, like the regular elections of public officials, seem to affirm the sovereignty of the audience while keeping deep alternatives off the agenda. Elite authority and consumer choice are affirmed at once—this is one of the central operations of the hegemonic liberal capitalist ideology.

Then too, by organizing the "free time" of persons into end-to-end interchangeable units, broadcasting extends, and harmonizes with, the industrialization of time. Media time and school time, with their equivalent units and curves of action, mirror the time of clocked labor and reinforce the seeming naturalness of clock time. Anyone who reads Harry Braverman's *Labor and Monopoly Capital* can trace the steady degradation of the work process, both white and blue collar, through the twentieth century, even if Braverman has exaggerated the extent of the process by focusing on managerial *strategies* more than on actual work *processes*. Something similar has happened in other life-sectors.[7] Leisure is industrialized, duration is homogenized, even excitement is routinized, and the standard repeated TV format is an important component of the process. And typically, too, capitalism provides relief from these confines for its more favored citizens, those who can afford to buy their way out of the standardized social reality which capitalism produces. Thus Sony and RCA now sell home video recorders, enabling consumers to tape programs they'd otherwise miss. The widely felt need to overcome assembly-line "leisure" time becomes the source of a new market—to sell the means for private, commoditized solutions to the time-jam.

Commercials, of course, are also major features of the regular TV format. There can be no question but that commercials have a good deal to do with shaping and maintaining markets—no advertiser dreams of cutting advertising costs as long as the competition is still on the air. But commercials also have important *indirect* consequences on the contours of consciousness overall: they get us accustomed to thinking of ourselves and behaving as a *market* rather than a *public*, as consumers rather than citizens. Public problems (like air pollution) are propounded as susceptible to private commodity solutions (like eyedrops). In the process, commercials acculturate us to interruption through the rest of our lives. Time and attention are not one's own; the established social powers have the capacity to colonize consciousness, and unconsciousness, as they see fit. By watching, the audience one by one consents. Regardless of the commercial's "effect" on our behavior, we are consenting to its domination of the public space. Yet we should note that this colonizing process does not actually require commercials, as long as it can form discrete packages of ideological content that call forth discontinuous responses in the audience. Even public broadcasting's children's shows take over the commercial forms to their own educational ends—and supplant narrative forms by herky-jerky bustle. The producers of *Sesame Street*, in likening knowledge to commercial products ("and now a message from the letter B"), may well be legitimizing the commercial form in its discontinuity and in its invasiveness. Again, regularity and discontinuity, superficially discrepant, may be linked at a deep level of meaning. And perhaps the deepest privatizing function of television, its most powerful impact on public life, may lie in the most obvious thing about it: we receive the images in the privacy of our living rooms, making public discourse and response difficult. At the same time, the paradox is that at any given time many viewers are receiving images discrepant with many of their beliefs, challenging their received opinions....

Genre[8]

The networks try to finance and choose programs that will likely attract the largest conceivable audiences of spenders; this imperative requires that the broadcasting elites have in mind some notion of popular taste from moment to moment. Genre, in other words, is necessarily somewhat sensitive; in its rough outlines, if not in detail, it tells us something about popular moods. Indeed, since there are only three networks, there is something of an oversensitivity to a given success; the pendulum tends to swing hard to replicate a winner. Thus *Charlies's Angels* engenders *Flying High* and *American Girls,* about stewardesses and female reporters respectively, each on a long leash under male authority.

Here I suggest only a few signs of this sensitivity to shifting moods and group identities in the audience. The adult western of the middle and late fifties, with its drama of solitary righteousness and suppressed libidinousness, for example, can be seen in retrospect to have played on the quiet malaise under the surface of the complacency of the Eisenhower years, even in contradictory ways. Some lone heroes were identified with traditionally frontier-American informal and individualistic relations to authority (Paladin in *Have Gun, Will Travel*, Bart Maverick in *Maverick*), standing for sturdy individualism struggling for hedonistic values and taking law-and-order wryly. Meanwhile, other heroes were decent officials like *Gunsmoke*'s Matt Dillon, affirming the decency of paternalistic law and order against the temptations of worldly pleasure. With the rise of the Camelot mystique, and the vigorous "long twilight struggle" that John F. Kennedy personified, spy stories like *Mission: Impossible* and *The Man From Uncle* were well suited to capitalize on the macho CIA aura. More recently, police stories, with cops surmounting humanist illusions to draw thin blue lines against anarcho-criminal barbarism, afford a variety of official ways of coping with "the social issue," ranging from *Starsky and Hutch's* muted homoeroticism to *Barney Miller*'s team pluralism. The single-women shows following from *Mary Tyler Moore* acknowledge in their privatized ways that some sort of feminism is here to stay, and work to contain it with hilarious versions of "new life styles" for single career women. Such shows probably appeal to the market of "upscale" singles with relatively large disposable incomes, women who are disaffected from the traditional imagery of housewife and helpmeet. In the current wave of "jiggle" or "T&A" shows patterned on *Charlie's Angels* (the terms are widely used in the industry), the attempt is to appeal to the prurience of the male audience by keeping the "girls" free of romance, thus catering to male (and female?) backlash against feminism. The black sitcoms probably reflect the rise of a black middle class with the purchasing power to bring forth advertisers while also appealing *as comedies*—for conflicting reasons, perhaps—to important parts of the white audience. (Serious black drama would be far more threatening to the majority audience.)

Whenever possible it is illuminating to trace the transformations in a genre over a longer period of time. For example, the shows of technological prowess have metamorphosed over four decades as hegemonic ideology has been contested by alternative cultural forms. In work not yet published, Tom Andrae of the Political Science Department at the University of California, Berkeley, shows how the Superman archetype began in 1933 as a menace to society; then became something of a New Dealing, anti-Establishmentarian individualist casting his lot with the oppressed and, at times, against the State; and only in the forties metamorphosed into the current incarnation who prosecutes criminals in the name of "the American way." Then the straight-arrow Superman of the forties and fifties was supplemented by the whimsical, self-satirical Batman and the Marvel Comics series of the sixties and seventies, symbols of power gone silly, no longer prepossessing. In playing against the conventions, their producers seem to have been exhibiting the self-consciousness of genre so popular among "high arts" too, as with Pop and minimal art. Thus shifts in genre presuppose the changing mentality of critical masses of writers and cultural producers; yet these changes would not take root commercially without corresponding changes in dispositions (even the self-consciousness) of large audiences. In other words, changes in cultural ideals and in audience sensibilities must be harmonized to make for shifts in genre or formula.

Finally, the latest form of technological hero corresponds to an authoritarian turn in hegemonic ideology, as well as to a shift in popular (at least children's) mentality. The seventies generation of physically augmented, obedient, patriotic super-heroes (*The Six Million Dollar Man* and *The Bionic Woman*) differ from the earlier waves in being organizational products through and through; these team players have no private lives from which they are recruited task by task, as in *Mission: Impossible*, but they are actually *invented* by the State, to whom they owe their lives.

Televised sports too is best understood as an entertainment genre, one of the most powerful.[9] What we know as professional sports today is inseparably intertwined with the networks' development of the sports market. TV sports is rather consistently framed to reproduce dominant American values. First, although TV is ostensibly a medium for the eyes, the sound is often decisive in taking the action off the field. The audience is not trusted to come to its own conclusions. The announcers are not simply describing events ("Reggie Jackson hits a ground ball to shortstop"), but interpreting them ("World Series 1978! It's great to be here"). One may see here a process equivalent to advertising's project of taking human qualities out of the consumer and removing them to the product: sexy perfume, zesty beer.

In televised sports, the hegemonic impositions have, if anything, probably become more intense over the last twenty years. One technique for interpreting the event is to regale the audience with bits of information in the form of "stats." "A lot of people forget they won eleven out of their last twelve games...." "There was an extraordinary game in last year's World Series...." "Rick Barry hasn't missed two free throws in a row for 72 games...." "The last time the Warriors were in Milwaukee Clifford Ray *also* blocked two shots in the second quarter." How *about* that? The announcers can't shut up; they're constantly chattering. And the stat flashed on the screen further removes the action from the field. What is one to make of all this? Why would anyone want to know a player's free throw percentage not only during the regular season but during the playoffs?

But the trivialities have their reason: they amount to an interpretation that flatters and disdains the audience at the same time. It flatters in small ways, giving you the chance to be the one person on the block who already possessed this tidbit of fact. At the same time, symbolically, it treats you as someone who really knows what's going on in the world. Out of control of social reality, you may flatter yourself that the substitute world of sports is a corner of the world you can really grasp. Indeed, throughout modern society, the availability of statistics is often mistaken for the availability or knowledge and deep meaning. To know the number of megatons in the nuclear arsenal is not to grasp its horror; but we are tempted to bury our fear in the possession of comforting fact. To have made "body counts" in Vietnam was not to be in control of the countryside, but the U.S. Army flattered itself that the stats looked good. TV sports shows, encouraging the audience to value stats, harmonize with a stat-happy society. Not that TV operates independently of the sports event itself; in fact, the event is increasingly organized to fit the structure of the broadcast. There are extra time-outs to permit the network to sell more commercial time. Michael Real of San Diego State University used a stopwatch to calculate that during the 1974 Super Bowl, the football was actually moving for—seven minutes (Real, 1977). Meanwhile, electronic billboards transplant the stats into the stadium itself.

Another framing practice is the reduction of the sports experience to a sequence of individual achievements. In a fusion of populist and capitalist dogma, everyone is somehow the best. This one has "great hands," this one has "a great slam dunk," that one's "great on defense." This indiscriminate commendation raises the premium on personal competition, and at the same time undermines the meaning of personal achievement: everyone is excellent at something, as at a child's birthday party. I was most struck by the force of this sort of framing during the NBA basketball playoffs of 1975, when, after a season of hearing Bill King announce the game over local KTVU, I found myself watching and hearing the network version. King's Warriors were not CBS's. A fine irony: King with his weird mustache and San Francisco panache was talking about team relations and team strategy; CBS, with its organization-man team of announcers, could talk of little besides the personal records of the players. Again, at one point during the 1977 basketball playoffs, CBS's Brent Musburger gushed: "I've got one of the greatest players of all time [Rick Barry] and one of the greatest referees of all time [Mendy Rudolph] sitting next to me! ... I'm surrounded by experts!" All in all, the network exalts statistics, personal competition, expertise. The message is: The way to understand things is by storing up statistics and tracing their trajectories. This is training in observation without comprehension.

Everything is technique and know-how; nothing is purpose. Likewise, the instant replay generates the thrill of recreating the play, even second-guessing the referee. The appeal is to the American tradition of exalting means over ends: this is the same spirit that animates popular science magazines and do-it-yourself. It's a complicated and contradictory spirit, one that lends itself to the preservation of craft values in a time of assembly-line production, and at the same time distracts interest from any desire to control the goals of the central work process.

The significance of this fetishism of means is hard to decipher. Though the network version appeals to technical thinking, the announcers are not only small-minded but incompetent to boot. No sooner have they dutifully complimented a new acquisition as "a fine addition to the club" than often enough he flubs a play. But still they function as cheerleaders, revving up the razzle-dazzle rhetoric and reminding us how uniquely favored we are by the spectacle. By staying tuned in, somehow we're "participating" in sports history indeed, by proxy, in history itself. The pulsing theme music and electronic logo reinforce this sense of hot-shot glamor. The breathlessness never lets up, and it has its pecuniary motives: if we can be convinced that the game really is fascinating (even if it's a dog), we're more likely to stay tuned for the commercials for which Miller Lite and Goodyear have paid $100,000 a minute to rent our attention.

On the other hand, the network version does not inevitably succeed in forcing itself upon our consciousness and defining our reception of the event. TV audiences don't necessarily succumb to the announcers' hype. In semi-public situations like barrooms, audiences are more likely to see through the trivialization and ignorance and—in "para-social interaction"—to tell the announcers off. But in the privacy of living rooms, the announcers' framing probably penetrates farther into the collective definition of the event. It should not be surprising that one fairly common counter-hegemonic practice is to watch the broadcast picture without the network sound, listening to the local announcer on the radio.

Setting and Character Type
Closely related to genre and its changes are setting and character type. And here again we see shifting market tolerances making for certain changes in content, while the core of hegemonic values remains virtually impervious.

In the fifties, when the TV forms were first devised, the standard TV series presented—in Herbert Gold's phrase—happy people with happy problems. In the seventies it is more complicated: there are unhappy people with happy ways of coping. But the set itself propounds a vision of consumer happiness. Living rooms and kitchens usually display the standard package of consumer goods. Even where the set is ratty, as in *Sanford and Son,* or working-class, as in *All in the Family,* the bright color of the TV tube almost always glamorizes the surroundings so that there will be no sharp break between the glorious color of the program and the glorious color of the commercial. In the more primitive fifties, by contrast, it was still possible for a series like *The Honeymooners* or *The Phil Silvers Show* (Sergeant Bilko) to get by with one or two simple sets per show: the life of a good skit was in its accomplished *acting*. But that series, in its sympathetic treatment of working-class mores, was exceptional. Color broadcasting accomplishes the glamorous ideal willy-nilly.

Permissible character types have evolved, partly because of changes in the structure of broadcasting power. In the fifties, before the quiz show scandal, advertising agencies contracted directly with production companies to produce TV series (Barnouw, 1970). They ordered up exactly what they wanted, as if by the yard; and with some important but occasional exceptions—I'll mention some in a moment—what they wanted was glamor and fun, a showcase for commercials. In 1954, for example, one agency wrote to the playwright Elmer Rice explaining why his *Street Scene,* with its "lower class social level," would be unsuitable for telecasting:

> We know of no advertiser or advertising agency of any importance in this country who would knowingly allow the products which he is trying to advertise to the public to become associated with the squalor ... and general "down" character ... of *Street Scene*....

On the contrary it is the general policy of advertisers to glamorize their products, the people who buy them, and the whole American social and economic scene.... The American consuming public as presented by the advertising industry today is middle class, not lower class; happy in general, not miserable and frustrated.... (Barnouw, 1970:33).

Later in the fifties, comedies were able to represent discrepant settings, permitting viewers both to identify and to indulge their sense of superiority through comic distance: *The Honeymooners* and *Bilko*, which capitalized on Jackie Gleason's and Phil Silvers' enormous personal popularity (a personality cult can always perform wonders and break rules), were able to extend dignity to working-class characters in anti-glamourous situations (see Czitrom, 1977).

Beginning in 1960, the networks took direct control of production away from advertisers. And since the networks are less provincial than particular advertisers, since they are more closely attuned to general tolerances in the population, and since they are firmly in charge of a buyers' market for advertising (as long as they produce shows that *some* corporation will sponsor), it now became possible—if by no means easy—for independent production companies to get somewhat distinct cultural forms, like Norman Lear's comedies, on the air. The near-universality of televisions set ownership, at the same time, creates the possibility of a wider range of audiences, including minority-group, working-class and age-segmented audiences, than existed in the fifties, and thus makes possible a wider range of fictional characters,. Thus changes in the organization of TV production, as well as new market pressures, have helped to change the prevalent settings and character types on television.

But the power of corporate ideology over character types remains very strong, and sets limits on the permissible; the changes from the fifties through the sixties and seventies should be understood in the context of essential cultural features that have *not* changed. To show the quality of deliberate choice that is often operating, consider a book called *The Youth Market*, by two admen, published in 1970, counselling companies on ways to pick "the right character for your product":

> But in our opinion, if you want to create your own hard-hitting spokesman to children, the most effective route is the superhero-miracle worker. He certainly can demonstrate food products, drug items, many kinds of toys, and innumerable household items.... The character should be adventurous. And he should be on the right side of the law. A child must be able to mimic his hero, whether he is James Bond, Superman or Dick Tracy; to be able to fight and shoot to kill without punishment or guilt feeling (Helitzer and Heyel, 1970).

If this sort of thinking is resisted within the industry itself, it's not so much because of commitments to artistry in television as such, but more because there are other markets that are not "penetrated" by these hard-hitting heroes. The industry is noticing, for example, that *Roots* brought to the tube an audience who don't normally watch TV. The house-using-television levels during the week of *Roots* were up between six and twelve percent over the programs of the previous year (*Broadcasting*, Jan. 31, 1977). Untapped markets—often composed of people who have, or wish to have, somewhat alternative views of the world—can only be brought in by unusual sorts of programming. There is room in the schedule for rebellious human slaves just as there is room for hard-hitting patriotic-technological heroes. In other words—and contrary to a simplistic argument against television manipulation by network elites—the receptivity of enormous parts of the population is an important limiting factor affecting what gets on television. On the other hand, network elites do not risk investing in *regular* heroes who will challenge the core values of corporate capitalist society: who are, say, explicit socialists, or union organizers, or for that matter born-again evangelists. But like the dramatic series *Playhouse 90* in the fifties, TV movies permit a somewhat wider range of choice than weekly series. It is apparently easier for producers to sell exceptional material for one-shot showings—whether sympathetic to lesbian mothers, critical of the 1950s blacklist or of Senator Joseph McCarthy. Most likely these important exceptions have prestige value for the networks.

Slant

Within the formula of a program, a specific slant often pushes through, registering a certain position on a particular public issue. When issues are politically charged, when there is overt social conflict, programs capitalize on the currency. ("Capitalize" is an interesting word, referring both to use and to profit.) In the program's brief compass, only the most stereotyped characters are deemed to "register" on the audience, and therefore slant, embedded in character, is almost always simplistic and thin. The specific slant is sometimes mistaken for the whole of ideological tilt or "bias," as if the bias dissolves when no position is taken on a topical issue. But the week-after-week angle of the show is more basic, a hardened definition of a routine situation *within which* the specific topical slant emerges. The occasional topical slant then seems to anchor the program's general meanings. For instance, a 1977 show of *The Six Million Dollar Man* told the story of a Russian-East German plot to stop the testing of the new B-1 bomber; by implication, it linked the domestic movement against the B-1 to the foreign Red menace. Likewise, in the late sixties and seventies, police and spy dramas have commonly clucked over violent terrorists and heavily armed "anarchist" maniacs, labeled as "radicals" or "revolutionaries," giving the cops a chance to justify their heavy armament and crude machismo. But the other common variety of slant is sympathetic to forms of deviance which are either private (the lesbian mother shown to be a good mother to her children) or quietly reformist (the brief vogue for *Storefront Lawyers* and the like in the early seventies). The usual slants, then, fall into two categories: either (a) a legitimation of depoliticized forms of deviance, usually ethnic or sexual; or (b) a delegitimation of the dangerous, the violent, the out-of-bounds.

The slants that find their way into network programs, in short, are not uniform. Can we say anything systematic about them? Whereas in the fifties family dramas and sit-coms usually ignored—or indirectly sublimated—the existence of deep social problems in the world outside the set, programs of the seventies much more often domesticate them. From *Ozzie and Harriet* or *Father Knows Best* to *All in the Family* or *The Jeffersons* marks a distinct shift for formula, character, and slant: a shift, among other things, in the image of how a family copes with the world outside. Again, changes in content have in large part to be referred back to changes in social values and sensibilities, particularly the values of writers, actors, and other practitioners: there is a large audience now that prefers acknowledging and domesticating social problems directly rather than ignoring them or treating them only indirectly and in a sublimated way; there are also media practitioners who have some roots in the rebellions of the sixties. Whether hegemonic style will operate more by exclusion (fifties) than by domestication (seventies) will depend on the level of public dissensus as well as on internal factors of media organization (the fifties blacklist of TV writers probably exercised a chilling effect on subject matter and slant; so did the fact that sponsors directly developed their own shows).

Solution

Finally, cultural hegemony operates through the solutions proposed to difficult problems. However grave the problems posed, however rich the imbroglio, the episodes regularly end with the click of a solution: an arrest, a defiant smile, an I-told-you-so explanation. The characters we have been asked to care about are alive and well, ready for next week. Such a world is not so much fictional as fake. However deeply the problem is located within society, it will be solved among a few persons: the heroes must attain a solution that leaves the rest of the society untouched. The self-enclosed world of the TV drama justifies itself, and its exclusions, by "wrapping it all up." Occasional exceptions are either short-lived, like *East Side, West Side,* or independently syndicated outside the networks, like Lear's *Mary Hartman, Mary Hartman.* On the networks, *All in the Family* has been unusual in sometimes ending obliquely, softly or ironically, refusing to pretend to solve a social problem that cannot, in fact, be solved by the actions of the Bunkers alone. The Lou Grant show is also partial to downbeat, alienating endings.

Likewise, in mid-seventies mass-market films like *Chinatown, Rollerball, Network* and *King Kong*, we see an interesting form of closure: as befits the common cynicism and helplessness, society owns the victory. Reluctant heroes go up against vast impersonal forces, often multinational corporations like the same Gulf & Western (sent up as "Engulf & Devour" in Mel Brooks's *Silent Movie*) that, through its Paramount subsidiary, produces some of these films. Driven to anger or bitterness by the evident corruption, the rebels break loose—only to bring the whole structure crashing down on them. (In the case of King Kong, the great ape falls of his own weight—from the World Trade Center roof, no less—after the helicopter gunships "zap" him.) These popular films appeal to a kind of populism and rebellious-ness, usually of a routine and vapid sort, but then close off the possibilities of effective opposition. The rich and the incoherent rebels get bought or killed.

Often the sense of frustration funnelled through these films is diffuse and ambiguous enough to encourage a variety of political responses. While many left-wing cultural critics raved about *Network*, for example, right-wing politicians in southern California campaigned for proposition 13 using the film's slogan, "I'm mad as hell and I'm not going to take it any more." Indeed, *the fact that the same film is subject to a variety of conflicting yet plausible interpretations may suggest a crisis in hegemonic ideology.* The economic system is demonstrably troubled, but the traditional liberal recourse, the State, is no longer widely enough trusted to provide reassurance. Articulate social groups do not know whom to blame; public opinion is fluid and volatile, and people at all levels in the society withdraw from public participation.[10] In this situation, commercial culture succeeds with diverse interest groups, as well as with the baffled and ambivalent, precisely by propounding ambiguous or even self-contradictory situations and solutions.

The Hegemonic Process in Liberal Capitalism

Again it bears emphasizing that, for all these tricks of the entertainment trade, the mass-cultural system is not one-dimensional. High-consumption corporate capitalism implies a certain sensitivity to audience taste, taste which is never wholly manufactured. Shows are made by guessing at audience desires and tolerances, and finding ways to speak to them that perpetuate the going system.[11] (Addressing one set of needs entails scanting and distorting others, ordinarily the less mean, less invidious, less aggressive, less reducible to commodity forms.) The cultural hegemony system that results is not a closed system. It leaks. Its very structure leaks, at the least because it remains to some extent competitive. Networks sell the audience's attention to advertisers who want what they think will be a suitably big, suitably rich audience for their products; since the show is bait, advertisers will put up with—or rather buy into—a great many possible baits, as long as they seem likely to attract a buying audience. In the news, there are also traditions of real though limited journalistic independence, traditions whose modern extension causes businessmen, indeed, to loathe the press. In their 1976 book *Ethics and Profits,* Leonard Silk and David Vogel quote a number of big businessmen complaining about the raw deal they get from the press. A typical comment: "Even though the press is a business, it doesn't reflect business values." That is, it has a certain real interest in truth—partial, superficial, occasion—and celebrity-centered truth, but truth nevertheless.

Outside the news, the networks have no particular interest in truth as such, but they remain sensitive to currents of interest in the population, including the yank and haul and insistence of popular movements. With few ethical or strategic reasons not to absorb trends, they are adept at perpetrating them with new formats, new styles, tie-in commodities (dolls, posters, T-shirts, fan magazines) that fans love. In any case, it is in no small measure because of the economic drives themselves that *the hegemonic system itself amplifies legitimated forms of opposition.* In liberal capitalism, hegemonic ideology develops by domesticating opposition, absorbing it into forms compatible with the core ideological structure. Consent is managed by absorption as well as by exclusion. The hegemonic ideology changes in order to remain hegemonic; that is the peculiar nature of the dominant ideology of liberal capitalism.

Raymond Williams (1977) has insisted rightly on the difference between two types of non-hegemonic ideology: *alternative* forms, presenting a distinct by supplementary and containable view of the world and *oppositional* forms, rarer and more tenuous within commercial culture, intimating an authentically different social order. Williams makes the useful distinction between *residual* forms, descending from declining social formations, and *emergent* forms, reflecting formations on the rise. Although it is easier to speak of these possibilities in the abstract than in the concrete, and although it is not clear what the emergent formations are (this is one of the major questions for social analysis now), these concepts may help organize an agenda for thought and research on popular culture. I would add to Williams own carefully modulated remarks on the subject only that there is no reason *a priori* to expect that emergent forms will be expressed as the ideologies of rising *classes,* or as " proletarian ideology" in particular; currently in the United States the emergent forms have to do with racial minorities and other ethnic groups, with women, with singles, with homosexuals, with old-age subcultures, as well as with technocrats and with political interest groups (loosely but not inflexibly linked to corporate interests) with particular strategic goals (like the new militarists of the Committee on the Present Danger). Analysis of the hegemonic ideology and its rivals should not be allowed to lapse into some form of what C. Wright Mills (1948) called the "labor metaphysic."

One point should be clear: the hegemonic system is not cut-and-dried, not definitive. It has continually to be reproduced, continually superimposed, continually to be negotiated and managed, in order to override the alternative and, occasionally, the oppositional forms. To put it another way: major social conflicts are transported *into* the cultural system, where the hegemonic process frames them, form and content both, into compatibility with dominant systems of meaning. Alternative material is routinely *incorporated*: brought into the body of cultural production. Occasionally oppositional material may succeed in being indigestible; that material is excluded from the media discourse and returned to the cultural margins from which it came, while *elements* of it are incorporated into the dominant forms.

In these terms, *Roots* was an alternative form, representing slaves as unblinkable facts of American history, blacks as victimized humans and humans nonetheless. In the end, perhaps the story is dominated by the chance for upward mobility; the upshot of travail is freedom. Where Alex Haley's book is subtitled "The Saga of an American Family," ABC's version carries the label—and the self-congratulation—"The *Triumph* of an American Family." It is hard to say categorically which story prevails; in any case there is a tension, a struggle, between the collective agony and the triumph of a single family. That struggle is the friction in the works of the hegemonic system.

And all the evident friction within television entertainment—as well as within the schools, the family, religion, sexuality, and the State—points back to a deeper truth about bourgeois culture. In the United States, at least, hegemonic ideology is extremely complex and absorptive; it is only by absorbing and domesticating conflicting definitions of reality and demands on it, in fact, that it remains hegemonic. In this way, the hegemonic ideology of liberal capitalism is dramatically different from the ideologies of pre-capitalist societies, and from the dominant ideology of authoritarian socialist or fascist regimes. What permits it to absorb and domesticate critique is not something accidental to capitalist ideology but rather its core. *The hegemonic ideology of liberal capitalist society is deeply and essentially conflicted in a number of ways.* As Daniel Bell (1976) has argued, it urges people to work hard, but proposes that real satisfaction is to be found in leisure, which ostensibly embodies values opposed to work.[12] More profoundly, at the center of liberal capitalist ideology there is a tension between the affirmation of patriarchal authority—currently enshrined in the national security state—and the affirmation of individual worth and self-determination. Bourgeois ideology in all its incarnations has been from the first a contradiction in terms, affirming "life, liberty and the pursuit of happiness," or "liberty, equality, fraternity," as if these ideals are compatible, even mutually dependent, at all times in all places, as they were for one revolutionary group at one time in one place. But all anti-bourgeois movements wage their battles precisely in terms of liberty, equality or fraternity (or, recently, sorority); they press on liberal capitalist ideology *in its own name.*

Thus we can understand something of the vulnerability of bourgeois ideology, as well as its persistence. In the twentieth century, the dominant ideology has shifted toward sanctifying consumer satisfaction as the premium definition of "the pursuit of happiness," in this way justifying corporate domination of the economy. What is hegemonic in consumer capitalist ideology is precisely the notion that happiness, or liberty, or equality, or fraternity can be affirmed through the existing private commodity forms, under the benign, protective eye of the national security state. This ideological core is what remains essentially unchanged and unchallenged in television entertainment, at the same time the inner tensions persist and are even magnified.

Author's Note

An earlier version of this paper was delivered to the 73rd Annual Meeting of the American Sociological Association, San Francisco, Sept, 1978. Thanks to Victoria Bonnell, Bruce Dancis, Wally Goldfrank, Karen Shapiro, and several anonymous reviewers for stimulating comments on earlier drafts.

Notes

1. Anderson has read Gramsci closely to tease out this and other ambiguities in Gramsci's diffuse and at times Aesopian texts. (Gramsci was writing in a Fascist prison, he was concerned about passing censorship, and he was at times gravely ill.)
2. In my reading, the most thoughtful specific approach to this question since Gramsci, using comparative structural categories to explain the emergence or absence of socialist class consciousness, is Mann (1973). Mann's analysis takes us to structural features of American society that detract from revolutionary consciousness and organization. Although my paper does not discuss social structural and historical features, I do not wish their absence to be interpreted as a belief that culture is all-determining. This paper discusses aspects of the hegemonic culture, and makes no claims to a more sweeping theory of American society.
3. In Part III of the latter, I discuss the theory of hegemony more extensively Published in *The Whole World is Watching: Mass Media and the New Left, 1965-70*, Berkeley: University of California Press, 1980.
4. See also, Willis (n.d.) for an excellent discussion of the limits of both ideological analysis of cultural artifacts and the social meaning system of audiences, when each is taken by itself and isolated from the other.
5. Most strikingly, see Blum's (1964) findings on black viewers putting down TV shows while watching them. See also Willis' (n.d.) program for studying the substantive meanings of particular pop music records for distinct youth subcultures; but note that it is easier to study the active uses of music than TV, since music is more often heard publicly and because, there being so many choices, the preference for a particular set of songs or singers or beats expresses more about the mentality of the audience than is true for TV.
6. A few years ago, *Gunsmoke* was cancelled although it was still among the top ten shows in Nielsen ratings. The audience was primarily older and disproportionately rural, thus an audience less well sold to advertisers. So much for the networks' democratic rationale.

7. Borrowing "on time," over commensurable, arithmetically calculated lengths of time, is part of the same process: production, consumption and acculturation made compatible.

8. I use the term *loosely* to refer to general categories of TV entertainment, like "adult wester," "cops and robber," "black shows." Genre is not an objective feature of the cultural universe, but a conventional name for a convention, and should not be reified—as both cultural analysis and practice often do—into a cultural essence.

9. This discussion of televised sports was published in similar form (Gitlin, 1978b).

10. In another essay I will be arguing that forms of pseudo-participation (including cult movies like *Rocky Horror Picture Show* and *Animal House,* along with religious sects) are developing simultaneously to fill the vacuum left by the declining of credible radical politics, and to provide ritual forms of expression that alienated groups cannot find within the political culture.

11. See the careful, important and unfairly neglected discussion of the tricky need issue in Leiss, 1976. Leiss cuts through the Frankfurt premise that commodity culture addresses false needs by arguing that audience needs for happiness, diversion, self-assertion and so on are ontologically real; what commercial culture does is not to invent needs (how could it do that?) but to insist upon the possibility of meeting them through the purchase of commodities. For Leiss, all specifically human needs are social; they develop within one social form or another. From this argument—and, less rigorously but more daringly from Ewen (1976)—flow powerful political implications I cannot develop here. On the early popularity of entertainment forms which cannot possibly be laid at the door of a modern "culture industry" and media-produced needs, see Altick (1978).

12. There is considerable truth in Bell's thesis. Then why do I say "ostensibly"? Bell exaggerates his case against "adversary culture" by emphasizing changes in avant-garde culture above all (Pop Art, happenings, John Cage, etc.); if he looked at *popular* culture, he would more likely find ways in which aspects of the culture of consumption *support* key aspects of the culture of production. I offer my discussion of sports as one instance. Morris Dickstein's (1977) affirmation of the critical culture of the sixties commits the counterpart error of overemphasizing the importance of *other* selected domains of literary and avant-garde culture.

References

Abramson, Ronald (1978) Unpublished manuscript, notes on critical theory distributed at the West Coast Critical Communications Conference, Standord University.

Adorno, Theodor W. (1954) "How to look at television." *Hollywood Querterly of Film, Radio and Television.* Spring. Reprinted 1975: 474-488 in Beranrd Rosenberg and David Manning White (eds.), *Mass culture.* New York: The Free Press.

—. (1974) "The stars down to earth. The Los Angeles Times Astrology column." *Telos* 19. Spring 1974: (1957) 13-90.

Adorno, Theodor W. and Max Horkheimer (1972) "The culture industry: Enlightenment as mass deception." pp. 120-167 in Adorno and Horkheimer, *Dialectic of Enlightenment* (1944). New York: Seabury.

Altick, Richard (1978) *The Shows of London.* Cambridge: Harvard University Press.

Anderson, Perry (1976) "The antinomies of Antonio Gramsci." *New Left Review* 100 (November 1976-January 1977): 5-78.

Barnouw, Erik (1970) *The Image Empire.* New York: Oxford University Press.

Bell, Daniel (1976) *The Cultural Contradictions of Capitalism.* New York: Basic Books.

Blum, Alan F. (1964) "Lower-class Negro television spectators: The concept of pseudo-Jovial scepticism." P.p. 429-435 in Arthur B. Shostak and William Gomberg (eds.), *Blue Collar World.* Englewood Cliffs, N.J.: Prentice-Hall.

Braverman, Harry (1974) *Labor and Monopoly Capital: The Degradation of Work in the Twentieth Century.* New York: Monthly Review Press.

Czitrom, Danny (1977) "Bilko: A sitcom for all seasons." *Cultural Correspondence* 4:16-19.

Dickstein, Morris (1977) *Gates of Eden.* New York: Basic Books.

Ewen, Stuart (1976) *Captains of Consciousness.* New York: McGraw-Hill.

Gitlin, Todd (1977a) "Spotlights and shadows: Television and the culture of politics." *College English* April: 789-801.

—. (1977b) "'The whole world is watching': Mass media and the new left, 1965-70." Doctoral dissertation, University of California, Berkeley.

—. (1977c) "The televised professional." *Social Policy* (November/December): 94-99.

—. (1978a) "Media sociology: the dominant paradigm." *Theory and Society* 6: 205-253.

—. (1978b) "Life as instant replay." *East Bay Voice* (November-December): 14.

Gouldner, Alvin W. (1976) *The Dialectic of Ideology (and Technology).* New York: Seabury.

Gramsci, Antonio (1971) *Selections From the Prison Notebooks.* Quintin Hoare and Geoffrey Nowell Smith (eds.), New York: International Publishers.

Helitzer, Melvin and Carl Heyel (1970) The Youth Market: Its Dimensions, Influence and Opportunities for You: Quoted pp. 62-63 in William Melody, *Children's Television* (1973). New Haven: Yale University Press.

Kellner, Douglas (1978) "Ideology, Marxism, and advanced capitalism." *Socialist Review* 42 (November-December): 37-66.

Leiss, William (1976) *The Limits to Satisfaction.* Toronto: University of Toronto Press.

Mann, Michael (1973) *Consciousness and Action Among the Western Working Class.* London: Macmillan.

Mills, C. Wright (1948) *The New Men of Power.* New York: Harcourt, Brace.

Morley, Dave (1974) "Reconceptualising the media audience: Towards an ethnography of audiences." Mimeograph, Centre for Contemporary Cultural Studies, University of Birmingham.

Real, Michael R. (1977) *Mass-Mediated Culture.* Englewood Cliffs, N.J.: Prentice-Hall.

Silk, Leonard and David Vogel (1976) *Ethics and Profits.* New York: Simon and Schuster.

Williams, Raymond (1973) "Base and superstructure in Marxist cultural theory." *New Left Review* 82.

—. (1977) *Marxism and Literature.* New York: Oxford University Press.

Willis, Paul (n.d.) "Symbolism and practice: A theory for the social meaning of pop music." Mimeograph, Centre for Contemporary Cultural Studies, University of Birmingham.

CHAPTER FIVE

POSTWAR PERSPECTIVES

INTRODUCTION

In the period after World War II, three perspectives—structural-functionalism, conflict theories, and symbolic interactionism—were the leading types of sociological theory. The most active centres of sociological theory were still in North America, particularly in the United States, and their development reflected national cultural and political trends.

The first perspective to emerge was "structural functionalism." Structural-functional theorists tried to take American sociology beyond the Chicago School's fieldwork-based empirical study of communities, urban form, ethnic relations, and deviance. They returned to the work of Durkheim and Weber, but interpreted it in a conservative light, with an emphasis on social cohesion and shared values. Their reading of Durkheim connected their work with the French structuralist tradition and its roots in the conservative reaction. In the Cold War climate of hostility to anything even faintly associated with Soviet Communism, they explicitly avoided re-reading Marx.

Structural functional theory was based on four major premises:

1. Society can be understood as a system; sociology is the study of social systems, which are coherent and relatively stable over time. Sociology is not the study of individual actions and dispositions.
2. Culture and values are generally shared within a society and form part of the glue that holds societies together.
3. Institutions—as regular, recurrent patterns of social roles—contribute to social stability, and in that sense can be said to have functions.
4. Sociologists must understand stability; the social order is in a state of dynamic equilibrium most of the time in most societies. Most change is slow and involves the gradual shedding of dysfunctional institutions and the ongoing adjustment of institutions to each other. In the course of human history, societies have generally become more complex, with more differentiated kinds of institutions.

"Conflict theory" emerged as a challenge to structural functionalism. Its leading theorists, most notably C. Wright Mills, rejected the notion that society is a relatively harmonious system, a coherent whole. Although not prepared to call themselves Marxists, conflict theorists read Marx. They also read Weber in a very different light than structural functionalists; their Weber was a conflict theorist who studied power, struggles within states and organizations, and collective action by classes and status groups. The first works in conflict theory also drew on North American political thought, especially ideals of radical democracy and left-wing populism.

Conflict theory included these basic premises:

1. Society is not a system; it is formed by groups with objectively and subjectively opposed interests, in competition and contention with one another.
2. These groups usually have unequal power in society and unequal life chances. Wealth, power, status, and opportunities are not equally distributed; these inequalities are a central feature of societies.
3. The conflicting groups do not share values. In so far as they appear to have a common culture, it is really an ideology that favours a dominant group; this ideology is imposed on subordinate groups through institutions like the media, schooling, and religion.
4. Conflicting groups are not just categories in a social structure; sooner or later, people in these categories develop awareness or consciousness of inequalities and organize to change society. Therefore an important task of sociology is to study the conditions under which people develop this awareness and begin to take purposive, collective, and politicized action.
5. The most important kinds of changes are discontinuous and arise out of collective action, purposive political struggles initiated by subordinate groups. Armed uprising and revolutions are important forms of social change.
6. Institutions do not just function in a neutral way, to sustain a social order; they function on behalf of the groups that hold power.

For example, structural functionalists would say that schools function to socialize the next generation, teaching skills, knowledge, and shared values; schools prepare young people for labour markets. Conflict theorists would say that schools inculcate ideology and impose habits of mind that support authority and inequality; schools sort and select young people, generally along lines of existing inequalities, and use grading and tracking to perpetuate social privilege. In the conflict perspective, schools do not simply have functions of social reproduction; they reproduce inequalities.

Structural functionalists would say that the criminal justice system protects society from criminals. Conflict theorists see courts and prisons as part of the coercive arm of the state, holding subordinate groups down and suppressing any type of rebellious activity. Police are not the citizen's friends, defending law and order, but an occupying force imposing an unjust social order on the community.

The third perspective is "symbolic interactionism" (and other micro-theories). It is less politically radical than conflict theory, but challenges structural functionalism in terms of the basic subject matter of sociology. Its roots are in the liberal social thought of the Enlightenment, with its emphasis on the individual as the basis of society. Pragmatic philosophy and the work of Cooley and Mead are among its more recent ancestors in the United States. Symbolic interactionists also re-read Simmel, focusing on his work on interaction, sociability, and social forms while giving less attention to his examination of capitalism. The basic premises include:

1. There is no such thing as society. Society is a reified concept; symbolic interactionists deny that society exists as a thing. Look around! There is no such thing as society; there are only interacting individuals (and the material objects we have made).
2. The fundamental element of human life is language, communication, and the use of symbols; we interact with each other and think for ourselves using language. Language (and related symbolic gestures) has to be the focus of sociological study.
3. Society is really an open-ended process of interaction. It may not have any discernable historical patterns. Change goes on all the time, and we can observe it, but we should not rush into any conclusions about its large-scale direction or patterning.
4. Most individuals act in a relatively rational way, not always in economically rational terms, but in terms of their own understanding of their situation. Human action and interaction is best understood as pragmatic coping with situations.

If we look carefully at these three perspectives we can see that there is some overlap between them. Structural functionalists and conflict theories actually share functional analysis; the difference is not in the concept "function" but in the analysis of what or whom the function serves. Symbolic interactionists cleared away all the structural and systemic concepts shared by conflict theorists and structural functionalists, but they shared conflict theorists' interest in social action, in the meaning and purpose of human activities, and in the resistance of the marginalized and oppressed. Symbolic interactionist theory was even politically radical at times, but at a micro-level; symbolic interactionists engaged with definitions of reality and the process by which these definitions are imposed on individuals. For example, they analyzed how mental patients are stigmatized and labelled. They liked to study deviant behaviour, showing how deviance is socially constructed.

In the 1950s, structural functionalism reigned supreme and was the type of theory taught from sociology textbooks and in most departments in North

America; conflict theory and symbolic interactionism were subterranean traditions among sociology graduate students and maverick young faculty. By the later 1960s, all three traditions had become part of the sociological canon in North America; they were included in most introductory sociology textbooks and were assumed to be in the repertoire of the graduating senior and the new recruit to graduate school.

No sooner were these three perspectives canonized, than they began to disintegrate and come under challenge. Each perspective followed a distinct trajectory of disintegration.

The first casualty was probably conflict theory. By the later 1960s it was increasingly replaced by new variants of Marxism; young sociologists were no longer reluctant to use that label, and it was becoming trendy to be a Marxist again, in western Europe, North America, and many of the emerging new nations. Conflict theory begin to mutate into Marxism and neo-Marxism.

But at the very moment that Marxism was on the verge of replacing conflict theory, new kinds of conflict theory appeared—especially feminist theory and conflict-multiculturalism (theories that put an emphasis on contending cultural/ethnic groups and traditions in a society). All these theories of societal disunity, inequality, and struggle continued to be lumped together as conflict theories, but they became increasingly strange bedfellows. Some concepts continued to appear across the variants of conflict theory (inequality, hegemony and ideology, domination, collective action and conflict, resistance and opposition, etc.), but in many other ways, Marxism, feminism, and conflict-multiculturalism were incompatible. In the real world of political action in the 1970s, Marxists, feminists, and movements of ethnic/cultural nationalism were having difficulties forming viable coalitions. In the realm of theory, conflict theory as a unified tradition no longer held together. This reflection of reality into theory is not surprising; many young radicals were also students, especially in the social sciences, and they brought their movement experiences into their theoretical work.

Structural functionalism also lost its cohesion and popularity. By the 1970s, under the onslaught of conflict theories and interactionism, hardly anyone wanted to admit to being a structural functionalist, so that the conventional centre of sociology began to fragment into many smaller sub-fields of increasingly specialized knowledge and middle range theory (of health, law and society, the sociology of gender, deviance and criminology, and literally scores of areas). Most of these, in fact, loosely held to some basic premises of structural functionalism, but often mixed in with conflict perspectives and interactionist analysis. Concepts like role, structure, and institution continued to be in common use. Mainstream sociologists did not share conflict theorists' belief that society was irrevocably divided into groups with incompatible interests.

Symbolic-interactionist theory also split and proliferated, giving rise to a bewildering multiplicity of overlapping micro approaches. Most of them still centred on individual action, interaction, and meaning, but used different terminology and expressed subtle differences of focus and method. They included ethnomethodology, rational choice theory, and frame analysis. Micro theories such as rational choice theory emphasized pragmatic decision-making; others such as ethnomethodology emphasized the invisible rules of communication.

Meanwhile, by the later 1970s, a new hybrid appeared in theories of social construction, which united some elements of conflict theory with symbolic interactionist premises. Social constructionists argued that the categories of social inequality—especially race and gender—are socially constructed. They are not natural, nor are they fixed. They emerge in a process of social definition. Social constructionists believe a key step towards greater social equality is the deconstruction of those categories of thought and language that define and create difference. For example, if we can show how "men and women" are created in language and interaction that creates difference, we are taking a radical and necessary step towards reducing the very real, everyday consequences of that difference. Social constructionists showed how "white" and "black" people were created in racist ideology through a number of processes that included the transformation of European ethnic and cultural groups into "whites."

The bell tolled for the canon, but its trinitarian structure remained enshrined in introductory textbooks well into the 1990s. Indeed, the conceptual differences outlined here still make quite a lot of sense for distinguishing different ways of doing sociology and looking at social processes. However, sociologists now see them as no longer a satisfactory statement about innovative directions at the frontier of social theory.

22

STRUCTURAL FUNCTIONALISM: TALCOTT PARSONS (1902-1979)

A long economic boom took place after World War II in most economically developed regions. In North America, high employment and low inflation created a sense of prosperity within a few years of the end of the war in 1945. The boom came later in war-ravaged western Europe and Japan. The socialist economies of the Soviet bloc also enjoyed high growth rates.

Government played an active role in this boom. The specifics of government activism varied a bit from country to country. In the United States, for example, the federal government guaranteed home mortgages and provided college scholarships for veterans; it also engaged in huge road-building efforts, ostensibly as part of national defense, that subsidized suburban development. The defense industries of the "garrison state" and the "military industrial complex" had a multiplier effect, putting money in the pockets of working people as well as defense contractors. In western Europe, governments with a leftwing or labour orientation went further, developing health care systems and physical infrastructure. These forms of government activism amplified the effects of the long economic boom and spread them to a large proportion of the population; the result was a general sense of prosperity. In the words of scholars and journalists of the period, poverty was now confined to pockets of the unfortunate, mainly African Americans in the United States, the elderly poor, and a few disadvantaged rural areas and backward regions. The patterns varied from country to country, but the same sense of prosperity and the ideal of life in the nuclear family appeared in most industrialized capitalist nations.

Prosperity and family formation in the postwar years created a sense that industrial capitalist societies were finally settling into a long-term phase of stability, not only in their economies, but also in their family structure and social institutions. The shape of the 1950s appeared to be the shape of the future: the growth of a middle class that included both production workers and white collar employees; stable nuclear families; a strong gender division of labour with dads as breadwinners and moms as homemakers; limited and manageable social problems like crime and poverty that could be handled within existing institutions; and stable political institutions in which individuals' political choices were predictably influenced by institutions such as unions and professional associations.

Structural-functional sociology mirrored these real-life developments. It emphasized societal stability and the match between institutions like the economy, the family, the political system, and the value system. Functional analysis had been present in social theory from its inception at the end of the eighteenth century. After all, most societies do last a fairly long time, there is stability in the social order, and institutions do mesh with each other. Revolutions and other forms of social collapse are rare events. This stability had been celebrated by conservative thinkers, as we read in the opening chapter; but even radical intellectuals with a commitment to social transformation had to acknowledge and explain stability as a reality.

Structural-functional theory not only drew on concepts pioneered by conservative reactionaries, Burke, and Comte. It also offered a conservative reading of Durkheim and Weber. Structural-functional theorists interpreted these two classical theorists in a way that supported structural-functional analysis. For example, the evolutionary side of Durkheim—his hope for a future society that transcended the existing state of affairs—was downplayed. Weber was presented as diametrically opposed to Marx, emphasizing ideas and values in contrast to material conditions as the engine of social change. Weber's interest in social conflict and his insistence on historical analysis were not highlighted; neither was the gloomy feeling tone of his ideas about the future of modern society, the iron cages of bureaucracies, and the chilling formal rationality of the state and the market.

The 1950s was the period in which structural-functional theory enjoyed its heyday. Theory focused on how social systems achieve a dynamic stability, how institutions function together and how roles held by individuals mesh with institutional tasks. Even though structural-functional theory sometimes had a celebratory ring—endorsing as well as explaining social order—it nevertheless offered a powerful set of concepts for understanding the relative stability of most societies.

The concept of system is central to the theory. The roots of this concept lie in the organic metaphor of eighteenth-century social thought, but by the 1950s the system concept had become far more sophisticated and was increasingly based on contemporary biological and engineering models. How do we know that a society or a configuration of roles and actions constitutes a system? Because it has a degree of continuity and stability—and it is this continuity and stability that we want to understand in more detail.

Systems have parts—subsystems or elements that are necessary to the continuity of the whole. In societies, these parts are not individuals but institutions. As long as they function—carry out tasks that are necessary for system stability—the larger system can continue. When many institutions break down, or when a few key institutions fall apart, the system as a whole becomes weak.

The institutions (or other system components) not only have to function as separate components, they have to be articulated with one another in a coherent way. This articulation is not usually planned by people; it develops over time by trial and error. For example, family structure and the economy have to correspond to each other. If the economy is a market system in which it is assumed that people will change jobs and investments, shifting rather rapidly and flexibly from one region or industry to another, families have to be small, geographically mobile, and geared to producing individuals who are prepared to enter and flourish in the rapidly changing world of the market. Large extended families, local loyalties, and devotion to tradition may get in the way of the market; to put it differently, the experience of the market encourages families to shrink, move around, and raise their children to be flexible and innovative. (As you remember from reading the *Communist Manifesto*, Marx observed this process too and felt ambivalent about it.) There are conscious choices at the individual level in this process, but from a systemic view, much of it develops over time, as dysfunctional institutions, roles, and behaviours are gradually extinguished. In some societies, the articulation of structures may fail to work itself out, leading to weaker systems. Structural-functionalist theory does not guarantee functional systems!

The "atoms" of social systems in structural-functional theory are social roles. Individuals fill these roles, but the individual is not the basic unit of the system. Institutions have manifest functions that correspond to group and individual purposes, but also latent functions that are not intended or understood by social actors.

Social systems differ in complexity. While all human beings are equal, the social systems in which they participate are not structured identically. We cannot speak of "primitive people," but we can assert that a modern industrial society has a more complex organization than a small hunting and gathering society. Modern industrial societies are complex in terms of the number and differentiation of institutions, the number and differentiation of roles, and the articulation of multiple institutions with each other. In a hunting and gathering band-level society, most roles are kinship roles; functions are embedded in the institution of kinship. Modern, complex societies have differentiated institutions (family, economy, religion, media, political system, military, civic associations, and so on). These differentiated institutions are articulated with each other in complicated ways.

Structural functionalists are sometimes caricatured as celebrating a completely static social order. This portrayal is unfair; they were keenly interested in how societies remain in dynamic equilibrium. They realized that not all institutions or roles are functional, so they wanted to understand how dysfunctional ones disappear or change and how institutions that may be out of sync with each other change in such a way that the system returns to a new level of stability. Yet many critics of structural-functional theory believe that the perspective carries with it a subtle endorsement of existing institutional arrangements, especially family structures, gender roles, and social inequalities. If an institution or form of behaviour exists—especially if it exists over a long period—it is probably serving a function, according to structural functionalists. Thus the theory flirts with the notion that "what is real is rational" and that it could not be otherwise.

Some inequalities may be functional; others may be dysfunctional or irrelevant to system functioning. Structural-functional theory does not provide enough analysis of which is which; it gives little insight into either the historical causes of inequalities or their long-term effects.

Yet, despite these criticisms, structural-functional theory is a powerful way of understanding social reality. It forces us to think about stability and to recognize that most societies and institutions change only slowly. Like the work of Comte, it makes us think about a social system that operates apart from the motivations (and happiness) of individuals. It emphasizes overall, systemic, structural characteristics, especially the interconnection of institutions.

Talcott Parsons was a leading structural functionalist. His work exemplifies many of the strengths and weaknesses of the theory. Its strengths lie in the effort to create a general conceptualization of the social system, a framework of concepts that could be used in the analysis of many different kinds of societies and institutions. The problems are the flip side of the strengths: the terminology and analysis are often so abstract as to be disconnected from any observations of actual societies, social actions or behaviours, specific cultures, and historical transformations. The abstraction of the language makes Parsons's work difficult to read.

In the following reading, Parsons identifies the functional imperatives of the social system and the subsystems with which each imperative is associated. In other words, these are the tasks that must be fulfilled if a society or subsystem is to survive. His functional imperatives are often referred to by the letters *AGIL*. *A* stands for adaptation, the extraction and organization of the resources needed for survival, at whatever is deemed an appropriate level. *G* stands for goal attainment; it is the system function of decision-making, guiding or managing the system and assigning priorities to activities and purposes. *I* is the function of integration, of holding the subsystems together, of articulating the various subsystems with each other. Finally, *L* is latency, here referred to as pattern maintenance, which means reproducing the system over time. In addition, systems are characterized by distinct boundaries and by "boundary maintaining devices." The systems could be whole societies, institutions within societies, organizations (with their divisions or departments forming subsystems), or even individual human beings.

Brought down from the high level of abstraction at which Parsons wrote, these four functions can be loosely identified with distinct institutions in modern societies. Adaptation is the function of the economy, goal attainment is the function of government, and integration is carried out primarily by the legal system. Latency/pattern maintenance is the function of the family, above all; it motivates individuals—i.e., molds personality systems—to assume roles and prepares a new generation to fulfil social roles. Latency and integration are also functions of the media and religious institutions that generate and diffuse ideologies and take care of the cultural system. Notice that the functions do not correspond perfectly or in a simple one-to-one way to the institutions that we usually talk about in everyday discourse—government, the media, the family, religious institutions, the economy. A single institution may be involved in carrying out more than one of the imperatives, and each imperative may be sustained by more than one institution.

The advantage of the extremely high level of abstraction is that functions can be discussed separately from actual institutions in any given society. This allows us to compare societies that have completely different structures and institutional forms.

In simple or primitive social systems, these functions are carried out largely within and by the kinship system. In modern, complex societies they are carried out by differentiated and specialized institutions. The task of articulating and integrating the institutions is very complex. Motivating individuals is also a more difficult task in modern, large, and diverse societies than in small, community-like, band-level societies.

Readings
Alexander, Jeffrey. *Neofunctionalism*. Beverly Hills: Sage, 1985.

Functional Imperatives
TALCOTT PARSONS

The most strategic starting point for explaining this basic set of classifications is the category of functions, the link between the structural and the dynamic aspects of the system. I have suggested that it is possible to reduce the essential functional imperatives of any system of action, and hence of any social system, to four, which I have called pattern-maintenance, integration, goal-attainment, and adaptation. These are listed in order of significance from the point of view of cybernetic control of action processes in the system type under consideration

The Function of Pattern Maintenance. The function of pattern-maintenance refers to the imperative of maintaining the stability of the patterns of institutionalized culture defining the structure of the system. There are two distinct aspects of this functional imperative. The first concerns the character of the normative pattern itself; the second concerns its state of "institutionalization." From the point of view of the individual participant in a social system, this may be called his motivational *commitment* to act in accordance with certain normative patterns; this, as we shall see, involves their "internalization" in the structure of his personality.

Accordingly, the focus of pattern-maintenance lies in the structural category of *values*, which will be discussed presently. In this connection, the essential function is maintenance, at the cultural level, of the stability of institutionalized values through the processes which articulate values with the belief system, namely, religious beliefs, ideology, and the like. Values, of course, are subject to change, but whether the empirical tendency be toward stability or not, the potentialities of disruption from this source are very great, and it is essential to look for mechanisms that tend to protect such order—even if it is orderliness in the process of change.

The second aspect of this control function concerns the motivational commitment of the individual—elsewhere called "tension-management." A very central problem is that of the mechanisms of socialization of the individual, i.e., of the processes by which the values of the society are internalized in his personality. But even when values have become internalized, the commitments involved are subject to different kinds of strain. Much insight has recently been gained about the ways in which such mechanisms as ritual, various types of expressive symbolism, the arts, and indeed recreation, operate in this connection. Durkheim's analysis of the functions of religious ritual may be said to constitute the main point of departure here.

Pattern-maintenance in this sense plays a part in the theory of social systems, as of other systems of action, comparable to that of the concept of inertia in mechanics. It serves as the most fundamental reference point to which the analysis of other, more variable factors can be related. Properly conceived and used, it does not imply the empirical predominance of stability over change. However, when we say that, because of this set of functional exigencies, social systems show a *tendency* to maintain their structural patterns, we say essentially two things. First, we provide a reference point for the orderly analysis of a whole range of problems of variation which can be treated as arising from sources *other* than processes of structural change in the system, including, in the latter concept, its dissolution. Second, we make it clear that when we do analyze structural change we are dealing with a different kind of theoretical problem than that involved in equilibration. Hence, there is a direct relation between the function of pattern-maintenance—as distinguished from the other three functional imperatives—and the distinction between problems of equilibrium analysis, on the one hand, and the analysis of structural change on the other. The distinction between these two types of problems comes to focus at this point in the paradigm.

The Function of Goal-Attainment. For purposes of exposition it seems best to abandon the order of control set forth above and to concentrate next upon the function of goal-attainment and its relation to adaptation. In contrast to the constancy of institutionalized cultural patterns, we have emphasized the variability of a system's relation to its situation. The functions of goal-attainment and adaptation concern the structures, mechanisms, and processes involved in this relation.

We have compared pattern-maintenance with inertia as used in the theory of mechanics. Goal-attainment then becomes a "problem" in so far as there arises some discrepancy between the inertial tendencies of the system and its "needs" resulting from interchange with the situation. Such needs necessarily arise because the internal system and the environing ones cannot be expected to follow immediately the changing patterns of process.[1] A goal is therefore defined in terms of equilibrium. It is a directional change that tends to reduce the discrepancy between the needs of the system, with respect to input-output interchange, and the conditions in the environing systems that bear upon the "fulfilment" of such needs. Goal-attainment or goal-orientation is thus, by contrast with pattern-maintenance, essentially tied to a specific situation.

A social system with only one goal, defined in relation to a generically crucial situational problem, is conceivable. Most often, however, the situation is complex, with many goals and problems. In such a case two further considerations must be taken into account. First, to protect the integrity of the system, the several goals must be arranged in some scale of relative urgency, a scale sufficiently flexible to allow for variations in the situation. For any complex system, therefore, it is necessary to speak of a system of goals rather than of a single unitary goal, a system, however, which must have some balance between integration as a system and flexile adjustment to changing pressures.

For the social system as such, the focus of its goal-orientation lies in its relation as a system to the personalities of the participating individuals. It concerns, therefore, not commitment to the values of the society, but motivation to contribute what is necessary for the functioning of the system; these "contributions" vary according to particular exigencies. For example, considering

American society, one may suggest that, given the main system of values, there has been in the cold-war period a major problem of motivating large sectors of the population to the level of national effort required to sustain a position of world leadership in a very unstable and rapidly changing situation. I would interpret much of the sense of frustration expressed in isolationism and McCarthyism as manifestations of the strains resulting from this problem.[2]

The Function of Adaptation. The second consequence of plurality of goals, however, concerns the difference between the functions of goal-attainment and adaptation. When there is only one goal, the problem of evaluating the usefulness of facilities is narrowed down to their relevance to attaining this particular goal. With plurality of goals, however, the problem of "cost" arises. That is, the same scarce facilities will have *alternative* uses within the system of goals, and hence their use for one purchase means sacrificing the gains that would have been derived from their use for another. It is on this basis that an analytical distinction must be made between the function of effective goal-attainment and that of providing disposable facilities independent of their relevance to any particular goal. The adaptive function is defined as the provision of such facilities.

Just as there is a pluralism of lower-order, more concrete goals, there is also a pluralism of relatively concrete facilities. Hence there is a parallel problem of the organization of such facilities in a system. The primary criterion is the provision of flexibility, so far as this is compatible with effectiveness; for the system, this means a maximum of generalized disposability in the processes of allocation between alternative uses. Within the complex type of social system, this disposability of facilities crystallizes about the institutionalization of money and markets. More generally, at the macroscopic social-system level, the function of goal-attainment is the focus of the political organization of societies, while that of adaptation is the focus of economic organization.[3]

The most important kinds of facilities involve control of physical objects, access to the services of human agents and certain cultural elements. For their mechanisms of control to be at all highly generalized, particular units of such resources must be "alienable," i.e., not bound to specific uses through ascription. The market system is thus a primary focus of the society's organization for adaptation. Comparable features operate in less differentiated societies, and in more differentiated subsystems where markets do not penetrate, such as the family.[4]

Within a given system, goal-attainment is a more important control than adaptation. Facilities subserve the attainment of goals, not vice versa—though of course the provision or "production" of facilities may itself be a goal, with a place within the more general system of goals. There are, however, complications in the implication of this statement.

The Function of Integration. The last of the four functional imperatives of a system of action—in our case, a social system—is that of integration. In the control hierarchy, this stands between the functions of pattern-maintenance and goal-attainment. Our recognition of the significance of integration implies that all systems, except for a limiting case, are differentiated and segmented into relatively independent units, i.e., must be treated as boundary maintaining systems within an environment of other systems, which in this case are other subsystems of the same, more inclusive system. The functional problem of integration concerns the mutual adjustments of these "units" or subsystems from the point of view of their "contributions," to the effective functioning of the system as a whole. This, in turn, concerns their relation to the pattern-maintenance problem, as well as to the external situation through processes of goal-attainment and adaptation.

In a highly differentiated society, the primary focus of the integrative function is found in its system of legal norms and the agencies associated with its management, notably the courts and the legal profession. Legal norms at this level, rather than that of a supreme constitution, govern the *allocation* of rights and obligations, of facilities and rewards, between different units of the complex system; such norms facilitate internal adjustments compatible with the stability of the value system or its orderly change, as well as with adaptation to the shifting demands of the external situation. The institutionalization of money and power are primarily integrative phenomena, like other mechanisms of social control in the narrower sense. These problems will be further discussed in later sections of this essay.

For any given type of system—here, the social—the integrative function is the focus of its most distinctive properties and processes. We contend, therefore, that the problems focusing about the integrative functions of social systems constitute the central core of the concerns of sociological theory. This point of view will guide our analyses in subsequent introductory discussions and will receive strong emphasis in selections presented at various points in the Reader. Until a broad structural outline of the social system has been presented, it seems best to defer further discussion of the ways in which the integrative function meshes more specifically with the others.

Notes

1. When we speak of the *pattern* of the system tending to remain constant, we mean this in an analytical sense. The outputs to environing systems need not remain constant in the same sense, and their variations may disturb the relationship to the environing system. Thus scientific investigation may be stably institutionalized in a structural sense but result in a continuing output of new knowledge, which is a dynamic factor in the system's interchanges with its situation.

2. Cf. The paper, Parsons, "McCarthyism and American Social Tension," *Yale Review,* Winter 1955. Reprinted as Chap. 7, "Structure and Process" in *Modern Societies.*

3. It should be noted that the above formulation of the function of adaptation carefully avoids any implication that "passive" adjustment is the keynote of adaptation. Adaptation is relative to the values and goals of the system. "Good adaptation" may consist either in passive acceptance of conditions with a minimization of risk or in active mastery of conditions. The inclusion of active mastery in the concept of adaptation is one of the most important tendencies of recent developments in biological theory. An important relation between the two functional categories of goal-attainment and adaptation and the old categories of ends and means should be noted. The basic discrimination of ends and means may be said to be the special case, for the personality system, of the more general discrimination of the functions of goal-attainment and adaptation. In attempting to squeeze analysis of social behavior into this framework, utilitarian theory was guilty both of narrowing it to the personality case (above all, denying the independent analytical significance of social systems) and of overlooking the independent significance of the functions of pattern-maintenance and of integration of social systems themselves.

4. The importance of adaptive flexibility for the functioning of families as systems is well illustrated in the study of Robert Angell, *The Family Encounters the Depression* (New York: Chas. Scribner's Sons, 1936).

23

CONFLICT THEORY: C. WRIGHT MILLS (1916-1962)

The work of C. Wright Mills represents the emergence of conflict theories in postwar North American sociology. Of Texan origin, which contributed to his image as a maverick and radical from the heartland, he was a professor of sociology at Columbia University during the most intense period of the Cold War. The 1950s was a period of political timidity and enforced conformity when many intellectuals avoided expressing ideas and opinions for which they could have been labeled as reds or subversives. Mills courageously opposed this political timidity in his writing and teaching.

He took a critical view of trends in sociology and in society. Within the field of sociology he questioned "grand theory" and "abstracted empiricism." By using these terms he attacked the tendency of sociologists—especially structural functionalists—to develop concepts that were drained of political meaning. Concepts like "functional imperatives" and "system integration" were so broad and abstract as to be completely detached from public issues, political concerns, historical change, and people's everyday lives; Mills thought that these concepts and theories expressed tautologies and platitudes.

Mills was also critical of the direction in which sociologists were taking empirical research in the 1950s—the trend toward quantification, statistical analysis, survey research, and a positivist outlook. He believed that increasingly sophisticated statistical analysis and survey methodologies obscured rather than clarified the issues of the times; fragmented data based on isolated individual questionnaire responses were displacing a broad historical and political understanding of society.

In his own writing Mills offered a vigorous alternative to abstracted empiricism. He analyzed political and social institutions in the United States. In *The Power Elite* he identified the three-fold elite that he believed ruled the United States: the executives of the largest corporations, the upper-level leadership of the executive branch of the federal government, and the decision-makers in the military-industrial complex (the department of defense, top military officers, and major defense contractors). The presidency and the executive branch of the federal government represented these interests; they were gaining power, while Congress was increasingly relegated to the role of offering more local and limited special interests a sphere of action. The main loser in this process was the public at large, composed of ordinary citizens who had no political contacts and no forum in which to voice concerns.

In *White Collar*, Mills described the transformation of the old entrepreneurial middle class into a new stratum of employees of large organizations, mostly corporations and government agencies. The new middle class was composed of a huge sales force, technical intellectuals with narrowly defined areas of expertise, clerical workers, and low-level managers and supervisors. It had lost the independent spirit and autonomous political organization of the middle classes of the past.

Mills was concerned that the media were transforming the United States from a society of political discussion and public debate into a mass society in which the media disseminated opinions and the masses could no longer talk back. More and more people were becoming receivers of opinions via the new channels of communication. The town meeting and even the small town newspaper had permitted an exchange of political ideas; the new corporate media allowed only a one-way flow of opinions and images. Universities were also becoming part of a corporate system, producing knowledge for specific ends defined by elites and abandoning the critical spirit of the liberal arts and sciences.

Mills and other conflict theorists were deeply influenced by Marx and Marxist thought; Mills edited *The Marxists*, an anthology aimed at bringing back this intellectual legacy to the United States after McCarthyism. Mills however did not label himself a Marxist, and indeed there are major differences between his theories of society and Marxism. Mills did not see all inequality as emerging from the mode of production; like Weber, he identified several distinct dimensions of inequality and treated power as a variable that can be independent from economic class. The concept of power elite, rather than ruling class, signals this difference between Mills and Marxists. He did not insist on the bourgeoisie and the proletariat as the antagonistic classes of a polarized structure, nor did he share Marxist ideas about the unfolding of a historical process. In many ways, his version of conflict theory was much closer to Weber than to Marx, and his concerns about the direction of society overlapped and updated Weber's critique of bureaucracy and formal rationality.

Mills also differed from many Marxists in his commitment to North American traditions of social criticism and radical democracy. His solution to the economic inequalities and power differences in corporate America was not a vanguard party and a proletarian revolution, but a re-opening of political debate, public discussion, and citizen participation in politics.

Mills had an enormous influence on a younger generation of sociologists, the graduate students of the 1960s. They continued his inquiries, probing the social organization of the media, the universities, the corporations, and the state. His work was read not only by sociologists but by student radicals in the protest movements of the 1960s, especially during the civil rights movement and the formation of Students for a Democratic Society. Later in the decade some activists fell in love with unrealistic dreams of Third World revolution and Marxist-Leninist models; they lost sight of Mills's vision of radical democracy rooted in North American values and informed by North American traditions of pragmatism, progressive politics, and critical social thought.

The selection is from the opening pages of *The Sociological Imagination*. Mills is calling for a practice of sociology that connects it to public issues. The sociologist must be a public intellectual; critical skills must be linked to political engagement. The sociologist is first and foremost a citizen of a society.

Readings

Horowitz, Irving Louis. *C. Wright Mills: An American Utopian*. New York: Free Press, 1983.

Mills, C. Wright. *The Marxists*. New York: Dell, 1962.

—. *The Power Elite*. New York: Oxford University Press, 1956.

—. *The Sociological Imagination*. New York: Grove Press, 1959.

—. *White Collar*. New York: Oxford University Press, 1951.

The Sociological Imagination
C. WRIGHT MILLS

Nowadays men often feel that their private lives are a series of traps. They sense that within their everyday worlds, they cannot overcome their troubles, and in this feeling, they are often quite correct: What ordinary men are directly aware of and what they try to do are bounded by the private orbits in which they live; their visions and their powers are limited to the close-up scenes of job, family, neighborhood; in other milieux, they move vicariously and remain spectators. And the more aware they become, however vaguely, of ambitions and of threats which transcend their immediate locales, the more trapped they seem to feel.

Underlying this sense of being trapped are seemingly impersonal changes in the very structure of continent-wide societies. The facts of contemporary history are also facts about the success and the failure of individual men and women. When a society is industrialized, a peasant becomes a worker; a feudal lord is liquidated or becomes a businessman. When classes rise or fall, a man is employed or unemployed; when the rate of investment goes up or down, a man takes new heart or goes broke. When wars happen, an insurance salesman becomes a rocket launcher; a store clerk, a radar man; a wife lives alone; a child grows up without a father. Neither the life of an individual nor the history of a society can be understood without understanding both.

Yet men do not usually define the troubles they endure in terms of historical change and institutional contradiction. The well-being they enjoy, they do not usually impute to the big ups and downs of the societies in which they live. Seldom aware of the intricate connection between the patterns of their own lives and the course of world history, ordinary men do not usually know what this connection means for the kinds of men they are becoming and for the kinds of history-making in which they might take part. They do not possess the quality of mind essential to grasp the interplay of man and society, of biography and history, of self and world. They cannot cope with their personal troubles in such ways as to control the structural transformations that usually lie behind them.

Surely it is no wonder. In what period have so many men been so totally exposed at so fast a pace to such earthquakes of change? That Americans have not known such catastrophic changes as have the men and women of other societies is due to historical facts that are now quickly becoming "merely history." The history that now affects every man is world history. Within this scene and this period, in the course of a single generation, one sixth of mankind is transformed from all that is feudal and backward into all that is modern, advanced, and fearful. Political colonies are freed; new and less visible forms of imperialism installed. Revolutions occur; men feel the intimate grip of new kinds of authority. Totalitarian societies rise, and are smashed to bits—or succeed fabulously. After two centuries of ascendancy, capitalism is shown up as only one way to make society into an industrial apparatus. After two centuries of hope, even formal democracy is restricted to a quite small portion of mankind. Everywhere in the underdeveloped world, ancient ways of life are broken up and vague expectations become urgent demands. Everywhere in the overdeveloped world, the means of authority and of violence become total in scope and bureaucratic in form. Humanity itself now lies before us, the supernation at either pole concentrating its most co-ordinated and massive efforts upon the preparation of World War Three.

The very shaping of history now outpaces the ability of men to orient themselves in accordance with cherished values. And which values? Even when they do not panic, men often sense that older ways of feeling and thinking have collapsed and that newer beginnings are ambiguous to the point of moral stasis. Is it any wonder that ordinary men feel they cannot cope with the larger worlds with which they are so suddenly confronted? That they cannot understand the meaning of their epoch for their own lives? That—in defense of selfhood—they become morally insensible, trying to remain altogether private men? Is it any wonder that they come to be possessed by a sense of the trap?

It is not only information that they need—in this Age of Fact, information often dominates their attention and overwhelms their capacities to assimilate it. It is not only the skills of reason that they need—although their struggles to acquire these often exhaust their limited moral energy.

What they need, and what they feel they need, is a quality of mind that will help them to use information and to develop reason in order to achieve lucid summations of what is going on in the world and of what may be happening within themselves. It is this quality, I am going to contend, that journalists and scholars artists and publics, scientists and editors are coming to expect of what may be called the sociological imagination.

1

The sociological imagination enables its possessor to understand the larger historical scene in terms of its meaning for the inner life and the external career of a variety of individuals. It enables him to take into account how individuals, in the welter of their daily experience, often become falsely conscious of their social positions. Within that welter, the framework of modern society is sought, and within that framework the psychologies of a variety of men and women are formulated. By such means the personal uneasiness of individuals is focused upon explicit troubles and the indifference of publics is transformed into involvement with public issues.

The first fruit of this imagination—and the first lesson of the social science that embodies it—is the idea that the individual can understand his own experience and gauge his own fate only by locating himself within his period, that he can know his own chances in life only by becoming aware of those of all individuals in his circumstances. In many ways it is a terrible lesson; in many ways a magnificent one. We do not know the limits of man's capacities for supreme effort or willing degradation, for agony or glee, for pleasurable brutality or the sweetness of reason. But in our time we have come to know that the limits of "human nature" are frighteningly broad. We have come to know that every individual lives, from one generation to the next, in some society; that he lives out a biography, and that he lives it out within some historical sequence. By the fact of his living he contributes, however minutely, to the shaping of this society and to the course of its history, even as he is made by society and by its historical push and shove.

The sociological imagination enables us to grasp history and biography and the relations between the two within society. That is its task and its promise. To recognize this task and this promise is the mark of the classic social analyst. It is characteristic of Herbert Spencer—turgid, polysyllabic, comprehensive; of E.A. Ross—grateful, muckraking, upright; of Auguste Comte and Emile Durkheim; of the intricate and subtle Karl Mannheim. It is the quality of all that is intellectually excellent in Karl Marx; it is the clue to Thorsten Veblen's brilliant and ironic insight, to Joseph Schumpeter's many-sided constructions of reality; it is the basis of the psychological sweep of W. E. H. Lecky no less than of the profundity and clarity of Max Weber. And it is the signal of what is best in contemporary studies of man and society.

No social study that does not come back to the problems of biography, of history and of their intersections within a society has completed its intellectual journey. Whatever the specific problems of the classic social analysis, however limited or however broad the features of social reality they have examined, those who have been imaginatively aware of the promise of their work have consistently asked three sorts of questions:

(1) What is the structure of this particular society as a whole? What are its essential components and how are they related to one another? How does it differ from other varieties of social order? Within it, what is the meaning of any particular feature for its continuance and for its change?

(2) Where does this society stand in human history? What are the mechanics by which it is changing? What is its place within and its meaning for the development of humanity as a whole? How does any particular feature we are examining affect, and how is it affected by, the historical period in which it moves? And this period—what are its essential features? How does it differ from other periods? What are its characteristic ways of history-making?

(3) What varieties of men and women now prevail in this society and in this period? And what varieties are coming to prevail? In what ways are they selected and formed, liberated and repressed, made sensitive and blunted? What kinds of "human nature" are revealed in the conduct and character we observe in this society in this period? And what is the meaning for "human nature" of each and every feature of the society we are examining?

Whether the point of interest is a great power state or a minor literary mood, a family, a prison, a creed—these are the kinds of questions the best social analysts have asked. They are the intellectual pivots of classic studies of man in society—and they are the questions inevitably raised by any mind possessing the sociological imagination. For that imagination is the capacity to shift from one perspective to another—from the political to the psychological; from examination of a single family to comparative assessment of the national budgets of the world; from the theological school to the military establishment;

from considerations of an oil industry to studies of contemporary poetry. It is the capacity to range from the most impersonal and remote transformations to the most intimate features of the human self—and to see the relations between the two. Back of its use there is always the urge to know the social and historical meaning of the individual in the society and in the period in which he has his quality and his being.

That, in brief, is why it is by means of the sociological imagination that men now hope to grasp what is going on in the world, and to understand what is happening in themselves as minute points of the intersections of biography and history within society. In large part, contemporary man's self-conscious view of himself as at least an outsider, if not a permanent stranger, rests upon an absorbed realization of social relativity and of the transformative power of history. The sociological imagination is the most fruitful form of this self-consciousness. By its use men whose mentalities have swept only a series of limited orbits often come to feel as if suddenly awakened in a house with which they had only supposed themselves to be familiar. Correctly or incorrectly, they often come to feel that they can now provide themselves with adequate summations, cohesive assessments, comprehensive orientations. Older decisions that once appeared sound now seem to them products of a mind unaccountably dense. Their capacity for astonishment is made lively again. They acquire a new way of thinking, they experience a transvaluation of values; in a word, by their reflection and by their sensibility, they realize the cultural meaning of the social sciences.

2

Perhaps the most fruitful distinction with which the sociological imagination works is between "the personal troubles of milieu" and the "public issues of social structure." This distinction is an essential tool of the sociological imagination and a feature of all classic work in social science.

Troubles occur within the character of the individual and within the range of his immediate relations with others; they have to do with his self and with those limited areas of social life of which he is directly and personally aware. Accordingly, the statement and the resolution of troubles properly lie within the individual as a biographical entity and within the scope of his immediate milieu—the social setting that is directly open to his personal experience and to some extent his willful activity. A trouble is a private matter: values cherished by an individual are felt by him to be threatened.

Issues have to do with matters that transcend these local environments of the individual and the range of his inner life. They have to do with the organization of many such milieux into the institutions of a historical society as a whole, with the ways in which various milieux overlap and interpenetrate to form the larger structure of social and historical life. An issue is a public matter: some value cherished by publics is felt to be threatened. Often there is a debate about what that value really is and about what it is that really threatens it. This debate is often without focus if only because it is the very nature of an issue, unlike even widespread trouble, that it cannot very well be defined in terms of the immediate and everyday environments of ordinary men. An issue, in fact, often involves a crisis in institutional arrangements, and often too it involves what Marxists call "contradictions" or "antagonisms."

In these terms, consider unemployment. When, in a city of 100,000, only one man is unemployed, that is his personal trouble, and for its relief we properly look to the character of the man, his skills, and his immediate opportunities. But when in a nation of 50 million employees, 15 million men are unemployed, that is an issue, and we may not hope to find its solution within the range of opportunities open to any one individual. The very structure of opportunities has collapsed. Both the correct statement of the problem and the range of possible solutions require us to consider the economic and political institutions of the society, and not merely the personal situation and character of a scatter of individuals.

Consider war. The personal problem of war, when it occurs, may be how to survive it or how to die in it with honor; how to make money out of it; how to climb into the higher safety of the military apparatus; or how to contribute to the war's termination. In short, according to one's values, to find a set of milieux and within it to survive the war or make one's death in it meaningful. But the structural issues of war have to do with its cause; with what types of men it throws up into command; with its effects upon economic and political, family and religious institutions, with the unorganized irresponsibility of a world of nation-states.

Consider marriage. Inside a marriage a man and a woman may experience personal trouble, but when the divorce rate during the first four years of marriage is 250 out of every 1,000 attempts, this is an indication of a structural issue having to do with the institutions of marriage and the family and other institutions that bear upon them.

Or consider the metropolis—the horrible, beautiful, ugly, magnificent sprawl of the great city. For many upper-class people, the personal solution to "the problem of the city" is to have an apartment with private garage under it in the heart of the city, and forty miles out, a house by Henry Hill, garden by Garrett Eckbo, on a hundred acres of private land. In these two controlled environments—with a small staff at each end and a private helicopter connection—most people could solve many of the problems of personal milieux caused by the facts of the city. But all this, however splendid, does not solve the public issues that the structural fact of the city poses. What should be done with this wonderful monstrosity? Break it all up into scattered units, combining residence and work? Refurbish it as it stands? Or, after evacuation, dynamite it and build new cities according to new plans in new places? What should those plans be? And who is to decide and to accomplish whatever choice is made? These are structural issues; to confront them and to solve them requires us to consider political and economic issues that affect innumerable milieux.

In so far as an economy is so arranged that slumps occur, the problem of unemployment becomes incapable of personal solution. In so far as war is inherent in the nation-state system and in the uneven industrialization of the world, the ordinary individual in his restricted milieu will be powerless—with or without psychiatric aid—to solve the troubles this system or lack of system imposes upon him. In so far as the family as an institution turns women into darling little slaves and men into their chief providers and unweaned dependents, the problem of a satisfactory marriage remains incapable of purely private solution. In so far as the overdeveloped megalopolis and the overdeveloped automobile are built-in features of the overdeveloped society, the issues of urban living will not be solved by personal ingenuity and private wealth.

What we experience in various and specific milieux, I have noted, is often caused by structural changes. Accordingly, to understand the changes of many personal milieux we are required to look beyond them. And the number and variety of such structural changes increase as the institutions within which we live become more embracing and more intricately connected with one another. To be aware of the idea of social structure and to use it with sensibility is to be capable of tracing such linkages among a great variety of milieux. To be able to do that is to possess the sociological imagination.

24

SYMBOLIC INTERACTION AND OTHER MICRO-PERSPECTIVES: HOWARD BECKER (1928-) AND ERVING GOFFMAN (1922-1982)

Symbolic-interactionist theory had multiple roots. One was the work of Cooley and Mead, the Pragmatic theorists who charted the formation of the self in interaction and role taking; they identified the reciprocal formation of self and society. Second was the Chicago School with its emphasis on observation of the flow of everyday life. And third was rebellion against structural functionalism with its large impersonal systems, absence of human agency, and abstract detachment from actual situations. Symbolic interactionists called for "grounded theory," theory that emerged from observation.

Symbolic interactionists also challenged theories in psychology that gave no attention to what people said and quantified conclusions about behaviour using experimental designs. For symbolic interactionists, society and self were not fixed, measurable, external quantities but a constant flow of action, interaction, and self-reflection in countless situations of human life. The essence of sociology was observing and documenting these situations and writing about them in a perceptive, engaging way. There are no laws of behaviour or system imperatives, only an ongoing flux of human interaction.

Symbolic interactionists were often drawn to extreme situations in which these processes of interaction, negotiation of identities, and self-reflection were most visible. Among these situations were drug states and addictions. Symbolic interactionists did not believe that these were simply caused by the chemical properties of a drug; a "high" and an "addiction" were socially constructed conditions in which individuals came to experience themselves on the basis of the expectations and responses of others. Highs and addictions reflected the definitions of drug states that prevailed in communities of users. New users in these social contexts learned from others what to expect and how to behave; their identity as a drug user (and in the case of heroin, an addict) was learned.

In the late 1950s and 1960s Howard Becker compiled his observations of jazz musicians and marijuana users in *Outsiders*. He showed how deviance is a socially constructed category, a view we already saw in Durkheim's work; the jazz musicians and marijuana users were not inherently deviant, only deviant in the context of then-current norms about race, drugs, and lifestyles. Even more radical was his finding that a high is not a fixed product of the chemical properties of marijuana, but a condition that is verbally defined, recognized, and learned only in interaction with more experienced users.

A number of other perspectives with a focus on interaction and symbolic processes emerged in the later 1950s, 1960s, and 1970s; one of the most influential was the work of Erving Goffman. Goffman developed a dramaturgical model to analyze interaction and self-presentation; this model suggests that interaction is much like a theatrical performance. Individuals and teams perform roles and act out scenes, sometimes tightly scripted and sometimes loosely improvised. The self is a performed self, constantly presented in an effort to manage impressions. Space is organized into backstage areas for relaxation and rehearsal and frontstage areas in which the performance is presented to the public; the teachers' lounge and the classroom are corresponding examples.

Goffman's work, like Becker's, contained a critical edge, exposing many of the pretensions of institutions and social life. This critical edge is most evident in his work on mental hospitals and other total institutions. Based on his observation in a large mental hospital, Goffman revealed the ways in which staff labeled patients, constantly discredited their self-identity, and imposed one or another medical view of mental illness on them. The patient is processed through the stages of a moral career which finally produces an apathetic and manipulative self that can play the games necessary for survival in the asylum and, perhaps, obtain eventual release. Mental hospitals are only one of many types of total institutions—prisons, schools, boot camps, sects and cults, and the military are other examples. All operate to break down a self by batch processing; labeling; isolation from external support; and regimes of physical, mental, and emotional restrictions. Goffman's critical analysis of these institutions and their use of medical, psychological, and social science jargon paralleled the work of Michel Foucault who was developing his own theories of knowledge, power, and micro-politics as he engaged in the prisoners' rights movement (see below, selection 33).

Goffman developed the concept of framing, the pattern or form in which an idea or position is stated, especially in the media. As the term implies, frames limit understandings and perceptions. They are words and images that emerge from and sustain certain types of ideological assumptions through which we comprehend reality, negotiate it, and believe we understand it. Frames involve selection of some experiences, neglect or discounting of other experiences, choices of words and symbols for expressing experiences, and systems of classifying and categorizing them. Framing occurs not only in interpersonal communication, but also in the media and social movement ideologies. Although Goffman made no direct references to Marxist theory, frame analysis is a contemporary way of addressing issues that intrigued Gramsci and other Marxists. How is thought—common sense itself—forced into certain channels that limit and constrain our understanding of social reality? How is a hegemonic consciousness perpetuated by education and media in order to preclude critical thinking?

Symbolic interactionism and Goffman's work form a body of conflict theory at the micro-level. These theorists took a negative-critical stand toward the status quo, but without mention of structural inequalities, oppressive institutions, societal elites, class domination, or any of the usual terms of conflict theories. For the micro-theorists, power is a game played at the level of interaction and communication, and inequality is an interactive and symbolic strategy. Most of the micro-theorists of the postwar period consistently took the side of the outcast, outsider, and underdog in the game of power–the deviant, the incarcerated, the mental patient, the addict. In Part III we will see how the analysis of power and inequality at the level of interaction and culture has now become a mainstream of social theory. The pioneering role of North American microsociologists in the period between 1955 and 1975 is unfortunately sometimes forgotten in tracing this history.

Readings

Becker, Howard, Blanche Geer, Everett Hughes, and Anselm Strauss. *Boys in White: Student Culture in Medical School.* New Brunswick, NJ: Transaction: 1991.

Blumer, Herbert. *Symbolic Interaction: Perspective and Method.* Englewood Cliffs, NJ: Prentice-Hall, 1969.

Charon, Joel. *Symbolic Interaction.* Englewood Cliffs, NJ: Prentice-Hall, 1997.

Denzin, Norman. *The Alcoholic Society: Addiction and Recovery of the Self.* New Brunswick, NJ: Transaction, 1993.

Goffman, Erving. *Asylums: Essays on the Social Situation of Mental Patients and Other Inmates.* New York: Doubleday, 1961.

—. *Frame Analysis: An Essay on the Organization of Experience.* New York: Harper and Row, 1974.

—. *The Presentation of Self in Everyday Life.* New York: Doubleday, 1959.

—. *Stigma: Notes on the Management of a Spoiled Identity.* New York: Simon and Schuster, 1986.

Strauss, Anselm. *Basics of Qualitative Research: Grounded Theory Procedures and Techniques.* Thousand Oaks, CA: Sage.

—. *Mirrors and Masks: The Search for Identity.* New Brunswick, NJ: Transaction, 1997.

Outsiders
HOWARD S. BECKER

Becoming a Marihuana User

An unknown, but probably quite large, number of people in the United States use marihuana. They do this in spite of the fact that it is both illegal and disapproved.

The phenomenon of marihuana use has received much attention, particularly from psychiatrists and law enforcement officials. The research that has been done, as is often the case with research on behavior that is viewed as deviant, is mainly concerned with the question: why do they do it? Attempts to account for the use of marihuana lean heavily on the premise that the presence of any particular kind of behavior in an individual can best be explained as the result of some trait which predisposes or motivates him to engage in that behavior. In the case of marihuana use, this trait is usually identified as psychological, as a need for fantasy and escape from psychological problems the individual cannot face.[1]

I do not think such theories can adequately account for marihuana use. In fact, marihuana use is an interesting case for theories of deviance, because it illustrates the way deviant motives actually develop in the course of experience with the deviant activity. To put a complex argument in a few words: instead of the deviant motives leading to the deviant behavior, it is the other way around; the deviant behavior in time produces the deviant motivation. Vague impulses and desires—in this case, probably most frequently a curiosity about the kind of experience the drug will produce—are transformed into definite patterns of action through the social interpretation of a physical experience which is in itself ambiguous. Marihuana use is a function of the individual's conception of marihuana and of the uses to which it can be put, and this conception develops as the individual's experience with the drug increases.[2]

The research reported in this and the next chapter deals with the career of the marihuana user. In this chapter, we look at the development of the individual's immediate physical experience with marihuana. In the next, we consider the way he reacts to the various social controls that have grown up around use of the drug. What we are trying to understand here is the sequence of changes in attitude and experience which lead to *the use of marihuana for pleasure.* This way of phrasing the problem requires a little explanation. Marihuana does not produce addiction, at least in the sense that alcohol and the opiate drugs do. The user experiences no withdrawal sickness and exhibits no ineradicable craving for the drug.[3] The most frequent pattern of use might be termed "recreational." The drug is used occasionally for the pleasure the user finds in it, a relatively casual kind of behavior in comparison with that connected with the use of addicting drugs. The report of the New York City Mayor's Committee on Marihuana emphasizes this point:

> A person may be a confirmed smoker for a prolonged period, and give up the drug voluntarily without experiencing any craving for it or exhibiting withdrawal symptoms. He may, at some time later on, go back to its use. Others may remain infrequent users of the cigarette, taking one or two a week, or only when the "social setting" calls for participation. From time to time we had one of our investigators associate with a marihuana user. The investigator would bring up the subject of smoking. This would invariably lead to the suggestion that they obtain some marihuana cigarettes. They would seek a "tea-pad," and if it was closed the smoker and our investigator would calmly resume their previous activity, such as the discussion of life in general or the playing of pool. There were apparently no signs indicative of frustration in the smoker at not being able to gratify the desire for the drug. We consider this point highly significant since it is so contrary to the experience of users of other narcotics. A similar situation occurring in one addicted to the use of morphine, cocaine or heroin would result in a compulsive attitude on the part of the addict to obtain the drug. If unable to secure it, there would be obvious physical and mental manifestations of frustration. This may be considered presumptive evidence that there is no true addiction in the medical sense associated with the use of marihuana.[4]

In using the phrase "use for pleasure," I mean to emphasize the noncompulsive and casual character of the behavior. (I also mean to eliminate from consideration here those few cases in which marihuana is used for its prestige value only, as a symbol that one is a certain kind of person, with no pleasure at all being derived from its use.)

The research I am about to report was not so designed that it could constitute a crucial test of the theories that relate marihuana use to some psychological trait of the user. However, it does show that psychological explanations are not in themselves sufficient to account for marihuana use and that they are, perhaps, not even necessary. Researchers attempting to prove such psychological theories have run into two great difficulties, never satisfactorily resolved, which the theory presented here avoids. In the first place, theories based on the existence of some predisposing psychological trait have difficulty in accounting for that group of users, who turn up in sizable numbers in every study,[5] who do not exhibit the trait of traits which are considered to cause the behavior. Second, psychological theories have difficulty in accounting for the great variability over time of a given individual's behavior with reference to the drug. The same person will at one time be unable to use the drug for pleasure, at a later stage be able and willing to do so, and still later again be unable to use it in this way. These changes, difficult to explain from a theory based on the user's needs for "escape" are readily understandable as consequences of changes in his conception of the drug. Similarly, if we think of the marihuana user as someone who has learned to view marihuana as something that can give him pleasure, we have no difficulty in understanding the existence of psychologically "normal" users.

In doing the study, I used the method of analytic induction. I tried to arrive at a general statement of the sequence of changes in individual attitude and experience which always occurred when the individual became willing and able to use marihuana for pleasure, and never occurred or had not been permanently maintained when the person was unwilling to use marihuana for pleasure. The method requires that *every* case collected in the research substantiate the hypothesis. If one case is encountered which does not substantiate it, the researcher is required to change the hypothesis to fit the case which has proven his original idea wrong.[6]

To develop and test my hypothesis about the genesis of marihuana use for pleasure, I conducted fifty interviews with marihuana users. I had been a professional dance musician for some years when I conducted this study and my first interviews were with people I had met in the music business. I asked them to put me in contact with other users who would be willing to discuss their experiences with me. Colleagues working on a study of users of opiate drugs made a few interviews available to me which contained, in addition to material on opiate drugs, sufficient material on the use of marihuana to furnish a test of my hypothesis.[7] Although in the end half of the fifty interviews were conducted with musicians, the other half covered a wide range of people, including laborers, machinists, and people in the professions. The sample is, of course, in no sense "random"; it would not be possible to draw a random sample, since no one knows the nature of the universe from which it would have to be drawn.

In interviewing users, I focused on the history of the person's experience with marihuana, seeking major changes in his attitude toward it and in his actual use of it, and the reasons for these changes. Where it was possible and appropriate, I used the jargon of the user himself.

The theory starts with the person who has arrived at the point of willingness to try marihuana. (I discuss how he got there in the next chapter.) He knows others use marihuana to "get high," but he does not know what this means in any concrete way. He is curious about the experience, ignorant of what it may turn out to be, and afraid it may be more than he has bargained for.

The steps outlined below, if he undergoes them all and maintains the attitudes developed in them, leave him willing and able to use the drug for pleasure when the opportunity presents itself.

Learning the Technique
The novice does not ordinarily get high the first time he smokes marihuana, and several attempts are usually necessary to induce this state. One explanation of this may be that the drug is not smoked "properly," that is, in a way that insures sufficient dosage to produce real symptoms of intoxication. Most users agree that it cannot be smoked like tobacco if one is to get high:

> Take in a lot of air, you know, and ... I don't know how to describe it, you don't smoke it like a cigarette, you draw in a lot of air and get it deep down in your system and then keep it there. Keep it there as long as you can.

Without the use of some such technique[8] the drug will produce no effects, and the user will be unable to get high:

> The trouble with people like that [who are not able to get high] is that they're just not smoking it right, that's all there is to it. Either they're not holding it down long enough, or they're getting too much air and not enough smoke, or the other way around or something like that. A lot of people just don't smoke it right, so naturally nothing's gonna happen.

If nothing happens, it is manifestly impossible for the user to develop a conception of the drug as an object which can be used for pleasure, and use will therefore not continue. The first step in the sequence of events that must occur if the person is to become a user is that he must learn to use the proper smoking technique so that his use of the drug will produce effects in terms of which his conception of it can change.

Such a change is, as might be expected, a result of the individual's participation in groups in which marihuana is used. In them the individual learns the proper way to smoke the drug. This may occur through direct teaching:

> I was smoking like I did an ordinary cigarette. He said, "No, don't do it like that." He said, "suck it, you know, draw in and hold it in your lungs till you ... for a period of time."
> I said, "Is there any limit of time to hold it?"
> He said, "No, just till you feel that you want to let it out, let it out." So I did that three of four times.

Many new users are ashamed to admit ignorance and, pretending to know already, must learn through the more indirect means of observation and imitation:

> I came on like I had turned on [smoked marihuana] many times before, you know. I didn't want to seem like a punk to this cat. See, like I didn't know the first thing about it—how to smoke it, or what was going to happen, or what. I just watched him like a hawk—I didn't take my eyes off him for a second, because I wanted to do everything just as he did it. I watched how he held it, how he smoked it, and everything. Then when he gave it to me I just came on cool, as though I knew exactly what the score was. I held it like he did and took a poke just the way he did.

No one I interviewed continued marihuana use for pleasure without learning a technique that supplied sufficient dosage for the effects of the drug to appear. Only when this was learned was it possible for a conception of the drug as an object which could be used for pleasure to emerge. Without such a conception marihuana use was considered meaningless and did not continue.

Learning to Perceive the Effects

Even after he learns the proper smoking technique, the new user may not get high and thus not form a conception of the drug as something which can be used for pleasure. A remark made by a user suggested the reason for this difficulty in getting high and pointed to the next necessary step on the road to being a user:

> As a matter of fact, I've seen a guy who was high out of his mind and didn't know it.
> [How can that be, man?]
> Well, it's pretty strange, I'll grant you that, but I've seen it. This guy got on with me, claiming that he'd never got high, one of those guys, and he got completely stoned. And he kept insisting that he wasn't high. So I had to prove to him that he was.

What does this mean? It suggests that being high consists of two elements: the presence of symptoms caused by marihuana use and the recognition of these symptoms and their connection by the user with his use of the drug. It is not enough, that is, that the effects be present; alone, they do not automatically provide the experience of being high. The user must be able to point them out to himself and consciously connect them with having smoked marihuana before he can have this experience. Otherwise, no matter what actual effects are produced, he considers that the drug has had no effect on him: "I figured it either had no effect on me or other people were exaggerating its effect on them, you know. I thought it was probably psychological, see." Such persons believe the whole thing is an illusion and that the wish to be high leads the user to deceive himself into believing that something is happening when, in fact, nothing is. They do not continue marihuana use, feeling that "it does nothing" for them.

Typically, however, the novice has faith (developed from his observation of users who do get high) that the drug actually will produce some new experience and continues to experiment with it until it does. His failure to get high worries him, and he is likely to ask more experienced users or provoke comments from them about it. In such conversations he is made aware of specific details of his experience which he may not have noticed or may have noticed by failed to identify as symptoms of being high:

> I didn't get high the first time.... I don't think I held it in long enough. I probably let it out, you know, you know, you're a little afraid. The second time I wasn't sure, and he [smoking companion] told me, like I asked him for some of the symptoms or something, how would I know, you know ... so he told me to sit on a stool. I sat on—I think I sat on a bar stool—and he said, "let your feet hang," and then when I got down my feet were real cold, you know.
>
> And I started feeling it, you know. That was the first time. And then about a week after that, sometime pretty close to it, I really got on. That was the first time I got on a big laughing kick, you know. Then I really knew I was on.

One symptom of being high is an intense hunger. In the next case the novice becomes aware of this and gets high for the first time:

> They were just laughing the hell out of me because like I was eating so much. I just scoffed [ate] so much food, and they were just laughing at me, you know. Sometimes I'd be looking at them, you know, wondering why they're laughing, you know, not knowing what I was doing. [Well, did they tell you why they were laughing eventually?] Yeah, yeah, I come back, "Hey, man, what's happening?" Like, you know, like I'd ask, "What's happening?" and all of a sudden I feel weird, you know. "Man, you're on, you know. You're on pot [high on marihuana]." I said, "No, am I?" Like I don't know what's happening.

The learning may occur in more indirect ways:

> I heard little remarks that were made by other people. Somebody said, "My legs are rubbery," and I can't remember all the remarks that were made because I was very attentively listening for all these clues for what I was supposed to feel like.

The novice, then, eager to have this feeling, picks up from other users some concrete referents of the term "high" and applies these notions to his own experience. The new concepts make it possible for him to locate these symptoms among his own sensations and to point out to himself a "something different" in his experience that he connects with drug use. It is only when he can do this that he is high. In the next case, the contrast between two successive experiences of a user makes clear the crucial importance of the awareness of the symptoms in being high and re-emphasizes the important role of interaction with other users in acquiring the concepts that make this awareness possible:

[Did you get high the first time you turned on?] Yeah, sure. Although, come to think of it, I guess I really didn't. I mean, like that first time it was more or less of a mild drunk. I was happy, I guess, you know what I mean. But I didn't really know I was high, you know what I mean. It was only after the second time I got high that I realized I was high the first time. Then I knew that something different was happening.

[How did you know that?] How did I know? If what happened to me that night would of happened to you, you would've known, believe me. We played the first tune for almost two hours—one tune! Imagine, man! We got on the stand and played this one tune, we started at nine o'clock. When we got finished I looked at my watch, it's a quarter to eleven. Almost two hours on one tune. And it didn't seem like anything.

I mean, you know, it does that to you. It's like you have much more time or something. Anyway, when I saw that, man, it was too much. I knew I must really be high or something if anything like that could happen. See, and then they explained to me that that's what it did to you, you had a different sense of time and everything. So I realized that that's what it was. I knew then. Like the first time, I probably felt that way, you know, but I didn't know what's happening.

It is only when the novice becomes able to get high in this sense that he will continue to use marijuana for pleasure. In every case in which use continued, the user had acquired the necessary concepts with which to express to himself the fact that he was experiencing new sensations caused by the drug. That is, for use to continue, it is necessary not only to use the drug so as to produce effects but also to learn to perceive these effects when they occur. In this way marihuana acquires meaning for the user as an object which can be used for pleasure.

With increasing experience the user develops a greater appreciation of the drug's effects: he continues to learn to get high. He examines succeeding experiences closely, looking for new effects, making sure the old ones are still there.

Out of this there grows a stable set of categories for experiencing the drug's effects whose presence enables the user to get high with ease.

Users, as they acquire this set of categories, become connoisseurs. Like experts in wines, they can specify where a particular plant was grown and what time of year it was harvested. Although it is usually not possible to know whether these attributions are correct, it is true that they distinguish between batches of marihuana, not only according to strength, but also with respect to the different kinds of symptoms produced.

The ability to perceive the drug's effects must be maintained if use is to continue; if it is lost, marihuana use ceases. Two kinds of evidence support this statement. First, people who become heavy users of alcohol, barbiturates, or opiates do not continue to smoke marihuana, largely because they lose the ability to distinguish between its effects and those of the other drugs.[9] They no longer know whether the marihuana gets them high. Second, in those few cases in which an individual uses marihuana in such quantities that he is always high, he is apt to feel the drug has no effect on him, since the essential element of a noticeable difference between feeling high and feeling normal is missing. In such a situation, use is likely to be given up completely, but temporarily, in order that the user may once again be able to perceive the difference.

Learning to Enjoy the Effects

One more step is necessary if the user who has now learned to get high is to continue use. He must learn to enjoy the effects he has just learned to experience. Marihuana-produced sensations are not automatically or necessarily pleasurable. The taste for such experience is a socially acquired one, not different in kind from acquired tastes for oysters or dry martinis. The user feels dizzy, thirsty; his scalp tingles; he misjudges time and distances. Are these things pleasurable? He isn't sure. If he is to continue marihuana use, he must decide that they are. Otherwise, getting high, while a real enough experience, will be an unpleasant one he would rather avoid.

The effects of the drug, when first perceived, may be physically unpleasant or at least ambiguous:

> It started taking effect, and I didn't know what was happening, you know, what it was, and I was very sick. I walked around the room, walking around the room trying to get off, you know; it just scared me at first, you know. I wasn't used to that kind of feeling.

In addition, the novice's naïve interpretation of what is happening to him may further confuse and frighten him, particularly if he decides, as many do, that he is going insane:

> I felt I was insane, you know. Everything people done to me just wigged me. I couldn't hold a conversation, and my mind would be wandering, and I was always thinking, oh, I don't know, weird things, like hearing music different.... I get the feeling that I can't talk to anyone. I'll goof completely.

Given these typically frightening and unpleasant first experiences, the beginner will not continue use unless he learns to redefine the sensations as pleasurable:

> It was offered to me, and I tried it. I'll tell you one thing. I never did enjoy it at all. I mean it was just nothing that I could enjoy. [Well, did you get high when you turned on?] Oh, yeah, I got definite feelings from it. But I didn't enjoy them. I mean I got plenty of reactions, but they were mostly reactions of fear. [You were frightened?] Yes. I didn't enjoy it. I couldn't seem to relax with it, you know. If you can't relax with a thing, you can't enjoy it, I don't think.

In other cases the first experiences were also definitely unpleasant, but the person did become a marihuana user. This occurred, however, only after a later experience enabled him to redefine the sensations as pleasurable:

> [This man's first experience was extremely unpleasant, involving distortion of spatial relationships and sounds, violent thirst, and panic produced by these symptoms.] After the first time I didn't turn on for about, I'd say, ten months to a year.... It wasn't a moral thing; it was because I'd gotten so frightened, bein' so high. An' I didn't want to go through that again, I mean, my reaction was, "Well, if this is what they call bein' high, I don't dig [like] it.".... So I didn't turn on for a year almost, accounta that....
>
> Well, my friends started, an' consequently I started again. But I didn't have any more, I didn't have that same initial reaction, after I started turning on again.
>
> [In interaction with his friends he became able to find pleasure in the effects of the drug and eventually became a regular user.]

In no case will use continue without a redefinition of the effects as enjoyable.

This redefinition occurs, typically, in interaction with more experienced users who, in a number of ways, teach the novice to find pleasure in this experience which is at first so frightening.[10] They may reassure him as to the temporary character of the unpleasant sensations and minimize their seriousness, at the same time calling attention to the more enjoyable aspects. An experienced user describes how he handles new comers to marihuana use:

> Well, they get pretty high sometimes. The average person isn't ready for that,

and it is a little frightening to them sometimes. I mean, they've been high on lush [alcohol], and they get higher that way than they've ever been before, and they don't know what's happening to them. Because they think they're going to keep going up, up, up till they lose their minds or begin doing weird things or something. You have to like reassure them, explain to them that they're not really flipping or anything, that they're gonna be all right. You have to just talk them out of being afraid. Keep talking to them, reassuring, telling them it's all right. And come on with your own story, you know: "The same thing happened to me. You'll get to like that after awhile." Keep coming on like that; pretty soon you talk them out of being scared. And besides they see you doing it and nothing horrible is happening to you, so that gives them more confidence.

The more experienced user may also teach the novice to regulate the amount he smokes more carefully, so as to avoid any severely uncomfortable symptoms while retaining the pleasant ones. Finally, he teaches the new user that he can "get to like it after awhile." He teaches him to regard those ambiguous experiences formerly defined as unpleasant as enjoyable. The older user in the following incident is a person whose tastes have shifted in this way, and his remarks have the effect of helping others to make a similar redefinition:

A new user had her first experience of the effects of marihuana and became frightened and hysterical. She "felt like she was half in and half out of the room" and experienced a number of alarming physical symptoms. One of the more experienced users present said, "She's dragged because she's high like that. I'd give anything to get that high myself. I haven't been that high in years."

In short, what was once frightening and distasteful becomes, after a taste for it is built up, pleasant, desired, and sought after. Enjoyment is introduced by the favorable definition of the experience that one acquires from others. Without this, use will not continue, for marihuana will not be for the user an object he can use for pleasure.

In addition to being a necessary step in becoming a user, this represents an important condition for continued use. It is quite common for experienced users suddenly to have an unpleasant or frightening experience, which they cannot define as pleasurable, either because they have used a larger amount of marihuana than usual or because the marihuana they have used turns out to be of a higher quality than they expected. The user has sensations which go beyond any conception he has of what being high is and is in much the same situation as the novice, uncomfortable and frightened. He may blame it on an overdose and simply be more careful in the future. But he may make this the occasion for a rethinking of his attitude toward the drug and decide that it no longer can give him pleasure. When this occurs and is not followed by a redefinition of the drug as capable of producing pleasure, use will cease.

The likelihood of such a redefinition occurring depends on the degree of the individual's participation with other users. Where this participation is intensive, the individual is quickly talked out of his feeling against marihuana use. In the next case, on the other hand, the experience was very disturbing, and the aftermath of the incident cut the person's participation with other users to almost zero. Use stopped for three years and began again only when a combination of circumstances, important among which was a resumption of ties with users, made possible a redefinition of the nature of the drug:

> It was too much, like I only made about four pokes, and I couldn't even get it out of my mouth, I was so high, and I got real flipped. In the basement, you know, I just couldn't stay in there anymore. My heart was pounding real hard, you know, and I was going out of my mind; I thought I was losing my mind completely. So I cut out of this basement, and this other guy, he's out of his mind, told me, "Don't leave me, man. Stay here." And I couldn't.
>
> I walked outside, and it was five below zero, and I thought I was dying, and I had my coat open; I was sweating, I was perspiring. My whole insides were all ... , and I walked about two blocks away, and I fainted behind a bush. I don't know how long I laid there. I woke up, and I was feeling the worst, I can't describe it at all, so I made it to a bowling alley, man, and I was trying to act normal, I was trying to shoot pool, you know, trying to act real normal, and I couldn't lay and I couldn't stand up and I couldn't sit down, and I went up and laid down where some guys that spot pins lay down, and that didn't help me, and I went down to a doctor's office. I was going to go in there and tell the doctor to put me out of my misery ... because my heart was pounding so hard, you know.... So then all week end I started flipping, seeing things there and going through hell, you know, all kinds of abnormal things.... I just quit for a long time then.
>
> [He went to a doctor who defined the symptoms for him as those of a nervous breakdown caused by "nerves" and "worries." Although he was no longer using marihuana, he had some recurrences of the symptoms which led him to suspect that "it was all his nerves."] So I just stopped worrying, you know; so it was about thirty-six months later I started making it again. I'd just take a few pokes, you know. [He first resumed use in the company of the same user-friend with whom he had been involved in the original incident.]

A person, then, cannot begin to use marihuana for pleasure, or continue its use for pleasure, unless he learns to define its effects as enjoyable, unless it becomes and remains an object he conceives of as capable of producing pleasure.

In summary, an individual will be able to use marihuana for pleasure only when he goes through a process of learning to conceive of it as an object which can be used in this way. No one becomes a user without (1) learning to smoke the drug in a way which will produce real effects; (2) learning to recognize the effects and connect them with drug use (learning, in other words, to get high); and (3) learning to enjoy the sensations he perceives. In the course of this process he develops a disposition or motivation to use marihuana which was not and could not have been present when he began use, for it involves and depends on conceptions of the drug which could only grow out of the kind of actual experience detailed above. On completion of this process he is willing and able to use marihuana for pleasure.

He has learned, in short, to answer "Yes" to the question: "Is it fun?" The direction his further use of the drug takes depends on his being able to continue to answer "Yes" to this question and, in addition, on his being able to answer "Yes" to other questions which arise as he becomes aware of the implications of the fact that society disapproves of the practice: "Is it expedient?" "Is it moral?" Once he has acquired the ability to get enjoyment by using the drug, use will continue to be possible for him. Considerations of morality and expediency, occasioned by the reactions of society, may interfere and inhibit use, but use continues to be a possibility in terms of his conception of the drug. The act becomes impossible only when the ability to enjoy the experience of being high is lost, through a change in the user's conception of the drug occasioned by certain kinds of experience with it.

Notes

1. See, as examples of this approach, the following: Eli Marcovitz and Henry J. Meyers, "The Marihuana Addict in the Army," *War Medicine*, VI (December, 1944), 382-391; Herbert S. Gaskill, "Marihuana, an Intoxicant," *American Journal of Psychiatry,* CII (September, 1945), 202-204; Sol Charen and Luis Perelman, "Personality Studies of Marihuana Addicts," *American Journal of Psychiatry*, CII (March, 1946), 674-682.
2. This theoretical point of view stems from George Herbert Mead's discussion of objects in *Mind, Self and Society* (Chicago: University of Chicago Press, 1934), pp. 277-280.
3. Cf. Rogers Adams, "Marihuana," *Bulletin of the New York Academy of Medicine*, XVIII (November, 1942), 705-730.
4. The New York City Mayor's Committee on Marihuana, *The Marihuana Problem in the City of New York* (Lancaster, Pennsylvania: Jacques Cattell Press, 1944), pp. 12-13.
5. Cf. Lawrence Kolb, "Marihuana," *Federal Probation,* II (July, 1938), 22-25; and Walter Bromberg, "Marihuana: A Psychiatric Study," *Journal of the American Medical Association*, CXIII (July 1, 1939), 11.

6. The method is described in Alfred R. Lindesmith, *Opiate Addiction* (Bloomington, Indiana: Principia Press, 1947), chap. 1. There has been considerable discussion of this method in the literature. See, particularly, Ralph H. Turner, "The Quest for Universals in Sociological Research," *American Sociological Review,* 18 (December, 1953), 604-611, and the literature cited there.

7. I wish to thank Solomon Kobrin and Harold Finestone for making these interviews available to me.

8. A pharmacologist notes that this ritual is in fact an extremely efficient way of letting the drug into the blood stream. See R.P. Walton, *Marihuana: America's New Drug Problem* (Philadelphia: J.B. Lippincott, 1938). P. 48.

9. "Smokers have repeatedly stated that the consumption of whiskey while smoking negates the potency of the drug. They find it very difficult to get 'high' while drinking whiskey and because of that smokers will not drink while using the 'weed.'" (New York city Mayor's committee on Marihuana, *The Marihuana Problem in the City of New York*, op. cit., p. 13.)

10. Charen and Perlman, *op. cit.*, p. 679.

25

STRUCTURAL MARXIST THEORY: LOUIS ALTHUSSER (1918-1990)

The work of Louis Althusser exemplifies structural Marxist theory, one of the major currents of Marxist thought in the postwar period.

Althusser was born in Algeria of French parents. According to his own account, his parents' loveless marriage and his mother's overprotectiveness led to years of constricted, immature sexual and emotional life. In his youth he was influenced by radical social ideas of the Catholic Church. His brilliant academic career was interrupted by a long period of imprisonment in a German prisoner-of-war camp at the beginning of World War II; he resumed it successfully after the war, eventually holding the prestigious post of a professor at the *Ecole Normale Supérieure*, an elite institution of higher education in Paris. He was a member of the French Communist Party, but had a troubled relationship with it, criticizing many of its positions. He suffered from severe, recurrent episodes of depression that often led to hospitalization; during a particularly devastating attack in 1980, he killed his wife, a homicide for which he did not stand trial, but instead was held for a long time in mental hospitals.

In Althusser's work we see that Marxists can make use of structural-functional logic. Marxism is quite comfortable with functional explanations—but always with a special spin. For Marxists, "structure" and "function" are not class-neutral terms: the function of structures is to perpetuate class rule. Marxism takes structural-functional theory and puts the concept of class at its heart.

Marx had already used functional explanations to analyze institutions of capitalist society. For example, in the *Communist Manifesto* he had described the executive of the modern state as a committee for managing the common affairs of the whole bourgeoisie. In other words, in a system that is characterized by multiple markets and competing interests within the dominant class itself, system stability requires an institution that defines and pursues the common goals of the class, apart from their special, competing business objectives. Stock and bond markets, domestic retailers, high-tech industries, low-wage manufacturers—all these sectors of capital often have opposed short-term interests; within each of these sectors, there is also competition between firms. The executive branch of government articulates and serves the interests of the bourgeoisie as a whole, above and beyond these competing interests. Marx also used functional logic when he described the emergence of intellectuals who create and disseminate "the ruling ideas of the age." Althusser highlighted and extended the functional logic in Marx's analysis.

Class societies face the functional imperative of reproducing class relations, the relations of production. For Althusser, as for the structural functionalists, "face" here means a system need, not necessarily recognized by actual human beings in their actions; if the system imperative is not fulfilled, the society will not continue to exist.

The structures that fulfil the function of reproduction include the repressive state apparatuses (police, courts, prisons and "corrections," the military, and all other institutions that use coercion); even more important are the ideological state apparatuses, structures that purvey ideology. For Marxists, ideology means false ideas about society that sustain class rule—ideas and values that obscure, mystify, misinform, and mislead about class domination. These false ideas are one of the forces that impede the proletariat (the majority of people who must work for a living and do not own the means of production) from collective action to put an end to capitalism. False ideas include individualistic hopes ("Go for the gold!"), limited understanding of how the world works ("Business creates jobs"), and fatalism or cynicism ("It's a dog-eat-dog world—always was, always will be" and "same old, same old.")

In Althusser's work we can see continuities not only with Marx, but also with Gramsci; the repressive and ideological apparatuses represent our old friends the lion and the fox. But Althusser avoids the language of action, intentionality, agency, and a purposive subject which pervade Machiavelli and Gramsci. He pictures history as a process without a subject, a process of structural change that must be analyzed scientifically without reference to the meanings people impute to their actions. The object of scientific analysis is the social formation, the type of society whose structure is determined by the mode of production (like capitalism or feudalism). In this respect, Althusser is in the Comte/Durkheim tradition of French structuralism, but with Marxist emphasis on the mode of production as the determining element of the structure as a whole.

Notice the similarity of Althusser and Parson's analysis. Althusser's "reproduction of class relations" is the analog of "pattern maintenance." Like Parsons, Althusser points out that there is no simple one-to-one match of functions and institutions; several institutions may contribute to the same function (for instance, churches and schools to ideological functions) and most functions are distributed across several institutions. In capitalist society, the repressive apparatus tends to be relatively unitary, lodged in the state, but ideological apparatuses are multiple and relatively autonomous from class structure, from the state, and from each other. This is a Marxist formulation of Parsons's observation that modern societies are characterized by a high degree of institutional differentiation and complex forms of articulation.

In Althusser's analysis, ideology not only functions to reproduce class relations, it also has a function of holding the system together, of articulation or system integration. Once again, we see a parallel to the structural-functional view that "values" are the glue that holds complex societies together. As Althusser puts it, it is ruling ideology that assures harmony between the various apparatuses.

Althusser ends his discussion by arguing that in capitalism the education system has taken the place of the church as the dominant ideological apparatus. It may be useful to keep in mind that he was writing in France, a country which has a powerful, centralized, and well-organized public school system. Readers in other countries, especially the United States, might assign the role of ideological dominance to the privately owned media; in this case, the absence of central, state co-ordination implies an even more complex structure of ideological integration.

Of course, in structural Marxism—in absolute contrast to structural-functionalism—each apparatus or institution is the site of class struggle. Ideological and economic dominance are always contested.

Readings

Benton, Ted. *The Rise and Fall of Structural Marxism: Althusser and His Influence.* London: Macmillan, 1994.

Elliot, Gregory. *Althusser: A Critical Reader.* Cambridge, MA: Blackwell, 1994.

Resch, Robert Paul. *Althusser and the Renewal of Marxist Social Theory.* Berkeley, CA: University of California Press, 1992.

*Ideology and Ideological State Apparatuses
(Notes Towards an Investigation)*
LOUIS ALTHUSSER

... How is this reproduction of the (diversified) skills of labour power provided for in a capitalist regime? Here, unlike social formations characterized by slavery or serfdom, the reproduction of the skills of labour power tends (this is a tendential law) decreasingly to be provided for "on the spot" (apprenticeship within production itself), but is achieved more and more outside production: by the capitalist education system, and by other instances and institutions.

What do children learn at school? They go varying distances in their studies, but at any rate they learn to read, to write and to add—i.e. a number of techniques, and a number of other things as well, including elements (which may be rudimentary or on the contrary thoroughgoing) of "scientific" or "literary culture," which are directly useful in the different jobs in production (one instruction for manual workers, another for technicians, a third for engineers, a final one for higher management, etc.). Thus they learn "know-how."

But besides these techniques and knowledges, and in learning them, children at school also learn the "rules" of good behaviour, i.e. the attitude that should be observed by every agent in the division of labour, according to the job he is "destined" for: rules of morality, civic and professional conscience, which actually means rules of respect for the socio-technical division of labour and ultimately the rules of the order established by class domination. They also learn to "speak proper French," to "handle" the workers correctly, i.e. actually (for the future capitalists and their servants) to "order them about" properly, i.e. (ideally) to "speak to them" in the right way, etc.

To put this more scientifically, I shall say that the reproduction of labour power requires not only a reproduction of its skills, but also, at the same time, a reproduction of its submission to the rules of the established order, i.e. a reproduction of submission to the ruling ideology for the workers, and a reproduction of the ability to manipulate the ruling ideology correctly for the agents of exploitation and repression, so that they, too, will provide for the domination of the ruling class "in words."

In other words, the school (but also other State institutions like the Church, or other apparatuses like the Army) teaches "know-how," but in forms which ensure *subjection to the ruling ideology* or the mastery of its "practice." All the agents of production, exploitation and repression, not to speak of the "professionals of ideology" (Marx), must in one way or another be "steeped" in this ideology in order to perform their tasks "conscientiously"—the tasks of the exploited (the proletarians), of the exploiters (the capitalists), of the exploiters' auxiliaries (the managers), or of the high priests of the ruling ideology (its "functionaries"), etc.

The reproduction of labour power thus reveals as its *sine qua non* not only the reproduction of its "skills" but also the reproduction of its subjection to the ruling ideology or of the "practice" of that ideology, with the proviso that it is not enough to say "not only but also" for it is clear that *it is in the forms and under the forms of ideological subjection that provision is made for the reproduction of the skills of labour power.*

But this is to recognize the effective presence of a new reality: *ideology....*

...What are the ideological State apparatuses (ISAs)?

They must not be confused with the (repressive) State apparatus. Remember that in Marxist theory, the State Apparatus (SA) contains: the Government, the Administration, the Army, the Police, the Courts, the Prisons, etc., which constitute what I shall in future call the Repressive State Apparatus. Repressive suggests that the State Apparatus in question "functions by violence"—at least ultimately (since repression, e.g. administrative repression, may take non-physical forms).

I shall call Ideological State Apparatuses a certain number of realities which present themselves to the immediate observer in the form of distinct and specialized institutions. I propose an empirical list of these which will obviously have to be examined in detail, tested, corrected and reorganized. With all the reservations implied by this requirement, we can for the moment regard the following institutions as Ideological State Apparatuses (the order in which I have listed them has no particular significance):

- the religious ISA (the system of the different Churches),
- the educational ISA (the system of the different public and private "Schools"),
- the family ISA,[1]
- the legal ISA,[2]
- the political ISA (The political system, including the different Parties),
- the trade-union ISA,
- the communications ISA (press, radio and television etc.),
- the cultural ISA (Literature, the Arts, sports, etc.).

I have said that the ISAs must not be confused with the (Repressive) State Apparatus. What constitutes the difference?

As a first moment, it is clear that while there is *one* (Repressive) State Apparatus, there is a *plurality* of Ideological State Apparatuses. Even presupposing that it exists, the unity that constitutes this plurality of ISAs as a body is not immediately visible.

As a second moment, it is clear that whereas the—unified—(Repressive) State Apparatus belongs entirely to the *public* domain, much the larger part of the Ideological State Apparatuses (in their apparent dispersion) are part, on the contrary, of the *private* domain. Churches, Parties, Trade Unions, families, some schools, most newspapers, cultural ventures, etc., etc., are private.

We can ignore the first observation for the moment. But someone is bound to question the second, asking me by what right I regard as Ideological *State* Apparatuses, institutions which for the most part do not possess public status, but are quite simply *private* institutions. As a conscious Marxist, Gramsci already forestalled this objection in one sentence. The distinction between the public and the private is a distinction internal to bourgeois law, and valid in the (subordinate) domains in which bourgeois law exercises its "authority." The domain of the State escapes it because the latter is "above the law": the State, which is the State *of* the ruling class, is neither public nor private; on the contrary, it is the precondition for any distinction between public and private. The same thing can be said from the starting-point of our State Ideological Apparatuses. It is unimportant whether the institutions in which they are realized are "public" or "private." What matters is how they function. Private institutions can perfectly well "function" as Ideological State Apparatuses. A reasonably thorough analysis of any one of the ISAs proves it.

But now for what is essential. What distinguishes the ISAs from the (Repressive) State Apparatus is the following basic difference: the Repressive State Apparatus functions "by violence," whereas the Ideological State Apparatuses *function "by ideology."*

I can clarify matters by correcting this distinction. I shall say rather that every State Apparatus, whether Repressive or Ideological "functions" both by violence and by ideology, but with one very important distinction which makes it imperative not to confuse the Ideological State Apparatuses with the (Repressive) State Apparatus.

This is the fact that the (Repressive) State Apparatus functions massively and predominantly *by repression* (including physical repression), while functioning secondarily by ideology. (There is no such thing as a purely repressive apparatus.) For example, the Army and the Police also function by ideology both to ensure their own cohesion and reproduction, and in the "values" they propound externally.

In the same way, but inversely, it is essential to say that for their part the Ideological State Apparatuses function massively and predominantly *by ideology*, but they also function secondarily by repression, even if ultimately, but only ultimately, this is very attentuated and concealed, even symbolic. (There is no such thing as a purely ideological apparatus.) Thus Schools and churches use suitable methods of punishment, expulsion, selection, etc., to "discipline" not only their shepherds, but also their flocks. The same is true of the Family.... The same is true of the cultural IS Apparatus (censorship, among other things), etc.

Is it necessary to add that this determination of the double "functioning" (predominantly, secondarily) by repression and by ideology, according to whether it is a matter of the (Repressive) State Apparatus or the Ideological State Apparatuses, makes it clear that very subtle explicit or tacit combinations may be woven from the interplay of the (Repressive) State Apparatus and the Ideological State Apparatuses? Everyday life provides us with innumerable examples of this, but they must be studied in detail if we are to go further than this mere observation.

Nevertheless, this remark leads us towards an understanding of what constitutes the unity of the apparently disparate body of the ISA. If the ISAs "function" massively and predominantly by ideology, what unifies their diversity is precisely this functioning, insofar as the ideology by which they function is always in fact unified, despite its diversity and its contradictions, *beneath the ruling ideology,* which is the ideology of "the ruling class." Given the fact that the "ruling class" in principle holds State power (openly or more often by means of alliances between classes or class fractions), and therefore has at its disposal the (Repressive) State Apparatus, we can accept the fact that this same ruling class is active in the Ideological State Apparatuses insofar as it is ultimately the ruling ideology which is realized in the Ideological State Apparatuses, precisely in its contradictions. Of course, it is a quite different thing to act by laws and decrees in the (Repressive) State Apparatus and to "act" through the intermediary of the ruling ideology in the Ideological State Apparatuses. We must go into the details of this difference—but it cannot mask the reality of a profound identity. To my knowledge, *no class can hold State power over a long period without at the same time exercising its hegemony over and in the State Ideological Apparatuses.* I only need one example and proof of this: Lenin's anguished concern to revolutionize the educational Ideological State Apparatus (among others), simply to make it possible for the Soviet proletariat, who had seized State power, to secure the future of the dictatorship of the proletariat and the transition to socialism.[3]

This last comment puts us in a position to understand that the Ideological State Apparatuses may be not only the *stake*, but also the *site* of class struggle, and often of bitter forms of class struggle. The class (or class alliance) in power cannot lay down the law in the ISAs as easily as it can in the (repressive) State apparatus, not only because the former ruling classes are able to retain strong positions there for a long time, but also because the resistance of the exploited classes is able to find means and occasions to express itself there, either by the utilization of their contradictions, or by conquering combat positions in them in struggle.[4]

Let me run through my comments.

If the thesis I have proposed is well-founded, it leads me back to the classical Marxist theory of the State, while making it more precise in one point. I argue that it is necessary to distinguish between State power (and its possession by ...) on the one hand, and the State Apparatus on the other. But I add that the State Apparatus contains two bodies: the body of institutions which represent the Repressive State Apparatus on the one hand, and the body of institutions which represent the body of Ideological State Apparatuses on the other.

But if this is the case, the following question is bound to be asked, even in the very summary state of my suggestions: what exactly is the extent of the role of the Ideological State Apparatuses? What is their importance based on? In other words: to what does the "function" of these Ideological State Apparatuses, which do not function by repression but by ideology, correspond?

On the Reproduction of the Relations of Production
I can now answer the central question which I have left in suspense for many long pages: *how is the reproduction of the relations of production secured?*

In the topographical language (Infrastructure, Superstructure), I can say: for the most part,[5] it is secured by the legal-political and ideological superstructure.

But as I have argued that it is essential to go beyond this still descriptive language, I shall say: for the most part,[6] it is secured by the exercise of State power in the State Apparatuses, on the one hand the (Repressive) State Apparatus, on the other the Ideological State Apparatuses.

What I have just said must also be taken into account, and it can be assembled in the form of the following three features:

1. All the State Apparatuses function both by repression and by ideology, with the difference that the (Repressive) State Apparatus functions massively and predominantly by repression, whereas the Ideological State Apparatuses function massively and predominantly by ideology.
2. Whereas the (Repressive) State Apparatus constitutes an organized whole whose different parts are centralized beneath a commanding unity, that of the politics of class struggle applied by the political representatives of the ruling classes in possession of State power, the Ideological State Apparatuses are multiple, distinct, "relatively autonomous" and capable of providing an objective field to contradictions which express, in forms which may be limited or extreme, the effects of the clashes between the capitalist class struggle and the proletarian class struggle, as well as their subordinate forms.
3. Whereas the unity of the (Repressive) State Apparatus is secured by its unified and centralized organization under the leadership of the representatives of the classes in power executing the politics of the class struggle of the classes in power, the unity of the different Ideological State Apparatuses is secured, usually in contradictory forms, by the ruling ideology, the ideology of the ruling class.

Taking these features into account, it is possible to represent the reproduction of the relations of production[7] in the following way, according to a kind of "division of labour."

The role of the repressive State apparatus, insofar as it is a repressive apparatus, consists essentially in securing by force (physical or otherwise) the political conditions of the reproduction of relations of production which are in the last resort *relations of exploitation.* Not only does the State apparatus contribute generously to its own reproduction (the capitalist State contains political dynasties, military dynasties, etc.), but also and above all, the State apparatus secures by repression (from the most brutal physical force, via mere administrative commands and interdictions, to open and tacit censorship) the political conditions for the action of the Ideological State Apparatuses.

In fact, it is the latter which largely secure the reproduction specifically of the relations of production, behind a "shield" provided by the repressive State apparatus. It is here that the role of the ruling ideology is heavily concentrated, the ideology of the ruling class, which holds State power. It is the intermediation of the ruling ideology that ensures a (sometimes teeth-gritting) "harmony" between the repressive State apparatus and the Ideological State Apparatuses, and between the different State Ideological Apparatuses.

We are thus led to envisage the following hypothesis, as a function precisely of the diversity of ideological State Apparatuses in their single, because shared, role of the reproduction of the relations of production.

Indeed we have listed a relatively large number of ideological State apparatuses in contemporary capitalist social formations: the educational apparatus, the religious apparatus, the family apparatus, the political apparatus, the trade-union apparatus, the communications apparatus, the "cultural" apparatus, etc.

But in the social formations of that mode of production characterized by "serfdom" (usually called the feudal mode of production), we observe that although there is a single repressive State apparatus which, since the earliest known Ancient States, let alone the Absolute Monarchies, has been formally very similar to the one we know today, the number of Ideological State Apparatuses is smaller and their individual types are different. For example, we observe that during the Middle Ages, the Church (the religious ideological State apparatus) accumulated a number of functions which have today devolved on to several distinct ideological State apparatuses, new ones in relation to the past I am invoking, in particular educational and cultural functions. Alongside the Church there was the family Ideological State Apparatus, which played a considerable part, incommensurable with its role in capitalist social formations. Despite appearances, the Church and the Family were not the only Ideological State Apparatuses. There was also a political Ideological State Apparatus (the Estates General, the *Parlement,* the different political factions and Leagues, the ancestors of the modern political parties, and the whole political system of the free Communes and then of the *Villes*). There was also a powerful "proto-trade-union" Ideological State Apparatus, if I may venture such an anachronistic term (the powerful merchants and bankers' guilds and the journeymen's associations, etc). Publishing and Communications, even, saw an indisputable development, as did the theatre; initially both were integral parts of the Church, then they became more and more independent of it.

In the pre-capitalist historical period which I have examined extremely broadly, it is absolutely clear that *there was one dominant Ideological State Apparatus, the Church,* which concentrated within it not only religious functions, but also educational ones, and a large proportion of the functions of communications and "culture." It is no accident that all ideological struggle, from the sixteenth to the eighteenth century, starting with the first shocks of the Reformation, was *concentrated* in an anti-clerical and anti-religious struggle; rather this is a function precisely of the dominant position of the religious ideological State apparatus.

The foremost objective and achievement of the French Revolution was not just to transfer State power from the feudal aristocracy to the merchant-capitalist bourgeoisie, to break part of the former repressive State apparatus and replace it with a new one (e.g., the national popular Army)—but also to attack the number-one Ideological State Apparatus: the Church. Hence the civil constitution of the clergy, the confiscation of ecclesiastical wealth, and the creation of new ideological State apparatuses to replace the religious ideological State apparatus in its dominant role.

Naturally, these things did not happen automatically: witness the Concordat, the Restoration and the long class struggle between the landed aristocracy and the industrial bourgeoisie throughout the nineteenth century for the establishment of bourgeois hegemony over the functions formerly fulfilled by the Church: above all by the Schools. It can be said that the bourgeoisie relied on the new political, parliamentary-democratic, ideological State apparatus, installed in the earliest years of the Revolution, then restored after long and violent struggles, for a few months in 1848 and for decades after the fall of the Second Empire, in order to conduct its struggle against the Church and wrest its ideological functions away from it, in other words, to ensure not only its own political hegemony, but also the ideological hegemony indispensable to the reproduction of capitalist relations of production.

That is why I believe that I am justified in advancing the following Thesis, however precarious it is. I believe that the ideological State apparatus which has been installed in the *dominant* position in mature capitalist social formations as a result of a violent political and ideological class struggle against the old dominant ideological State apparatus, is the *educational ideological apparatus.*

This thesis may seem paradoxical, given that for everyone, i.e. in the ideological representation that the bourgeoisie has tried to give itself and the classes it exploits, it really seems that the dominant ideological State apparatus in capitalist social formations is not the Schools, but the political ideological State apparatus, i.e. the regime of parliamentary democracy combining universal suffrage and party struggle.

However, history, even recent history, shows that the bourgeoisie has been and still is able to accommodate itself to political ideological State apparatuses other than parliamentary democracy: the First and Second Empires, Constitutional Monarchy (Louis XVIII and Charles X), Parliamentary Monarchy (Louis-Philippe), Presidential Democracy (de Gaulle), to mention only France. In England this is even clearer. The Revolution was particularly "successful" there from the bourgeois point of view, since unlike France, where the bourgeoisie, partly because of the stupidity of the petty aristocracy, had to agree to being carried to power by peasant and plebeian *"journées révolutionnaries,"* something for which it had to pay a high price, the English bourgeoisie was able to "compromise" with the aristocracy and "share" State power and the use of the State apparatus with it for a long time (peace among all men of good will in the ruling classes!). In Germany it is even more striking, since it was behind a political ideological State apparatus in which the imperial Junkers (epitomized by Bismarck), their army and their police provided it with a shield and leading personnel, that the imperialist bourgeoisie made its shattering entry into history, before "traversing" the Weimar Republic and entrusting itself to Nazism.

Hence I believe I have good reasons for thinking that behind the scenes of its political ideological State Apparatus, which occupies the front of the stage, what the bourgeoisie has installed as its number-one, i.e. as its dominant ideological State apparatus, is the educational apparatus, which has in fact replaced in its functions the previously dominant ideological State apparatus, the church. One might even add: the School-Family couple has replaced the Church-Family couple.

Why is the educational apparatus in fact the dominant ideological State apparatus in capitalist social formations, and how does it function?

For the moment it must suffice to say:

1. All ideological State apparatuses, whatever they are, contribute to the same result: the reproduction of the relations of production, i.e. of capitalist relations of exploitation.
2. Each of them contributes towards this single result in the way proper to it. The political apparatus by subjecting individuals to the political State ideology, the "indirect" (parliamentary) or "direct" (plebiscitary or fascist) "democratic" ideology. The communications apparatus by cramming every "citizen" with daily doses of nationalism, chauvinism, liberalism, moralism, etc, by means of the press, the radio and television. The same goes for the cultural apparatus (the role of sport in chauvinism is of the first importance), etc. The religious apparatus by recalling in sermons and the other

great ceremonies of Birth, Marriage and Death, that man is only ashes, unless he loves his neighbour to the extent of turning the other cheek to whoever strikes first. The family apparatus ... but there is no need to go on.

3. This concert is dominated by a single score, occasionally disturbed by contradictions (those of the remnants of former ruling classes, those of the proletarians and their organizations): the score of the Ideology of the current ruling class which integrates into its music the great themes of the Humanism of the Great Forefathers, who produced the Greek Miracle even before Christianity, and afterwards the Glory of Rome, the Eternal City, and the themes of Interest, particular and general, etc. nationalism, moralism and economism.

4. Nevertheless, in this concert, one ideological State apparatus certainly has the dominant role, although hardly anyone lends an ear to its music: it is so silent! This is the School.

It takes children from every class at infant-school age, and then for years, the years in which the child is most "vulnerable," squeezed between the family-State apparatus and the educational State apparatus, it drums into them, whether it uses new or old methods, a certain amount of "know-how" wrapped in the ruling ideology (French, arithmetic, natural history, the sciences, literature) or simply the ruling ideology in its pure state (ethics, civic instruction, philosophy). Somewhere around the age of sixteen, a huge mass of children are ejected "into production": these are the workers or small peasants. Another portion of scholastically adapted youth carries on: and, for better or worse, it goes somewhat further, until if falls by the wayside and fills the posts of small and middle technicians, white-collar workers, small and middle executives, petty bourgeois of all kinds. A last portion reaches the summit, either to fall into intellectual semi-employment, or to provide, as well as the "intellectuals of the collective labourer," the agents of exploitation (capitalists, managers), the agents of repression (soldiers, policemen, politicians, administrators, etc.) and the professional ideologists (priests of all sorts, most of whom are convinced "laymen").

Each mass ejected *en route* is practically provided with the ideology which suits the role it has to fulfil in class society: the role of the exploited (with a "highly-developed" "professional," "ethical," "civic," "national" and a-political consciousness); the role of the agent of exploitation (ability to give the workers orders and speak to them: "human relations"), of the agent of repression (ability to give orders and enforce obedience "without discussion", or ability to manipulate the demagogy of a political leader's rhetoric), or of the professional ideologist (ability to treat consciousnesses with the respect, i.e. with the contempt, blackmail, and demagogy they deserve, adapted to the accents of Morality, of Virtue, of "Transcendence," of the Nation, of France's World Role, etc.).

Of course, many of these contrasting Virtues (modesty, resignation, submissiveness on the one hand, cynicism, contempt, arrogance, confidence, self-importance, even smooth talk and cunning on the other) are also taught in the Family, in the Church, in the Army, in Good Books, in films and even in the football stadium. But no other ideological State apparatus has the obligatory (and not least, free) audience of the totality of the children in the capitalist social formation, eight hours a day for five or six days out of seven.

But it is by an apprenticeship in a variety of know-how wrapped up in the massive inculcation of the ideology of the ruling class that the *relations of production* in a capitalist social formation, i.e. the relations of exploited to exploiters and exploiters to exploited, are largely reproduced. The mechanisms which produce this vital result for the capitalist regime are naturally covered up and concealed by a universally reigning ideology of the School, universally reigning because it is one of the essential forms of the ruling bourgeois ideology: an ideology which represents the School as a neutral environment purged of ideology (because it is ... lay), where teachers respectful of the "conscience" and "freedom" of the children who are entrusted to them (in complete confidence) by their "parents" (who are free, too, i.e. the owners of their children) open up for them the path to the freedom, morality and responsibility of adults by their own example, by knowledge, literature and their "liberating" virtues.

I ask the pardon of those teachers who, in dreadful conditions, attempt to turn the few weapons they can find in the history and learning they "teach" against the ideology, the system and the practices in which they are trapped. They are a kind of hero. But they are rare and how many (the majority) do not even begin to suspect the "work" the system (which is bigger than they are and crushes them) forces them to do, or worse, put all their heart and ingenuity into performing it with the most advanced awareness (the famous new methods!). So little do they suspect it that their own devotion contributes to the maintenance and nourishment of this ideological representation of the School, which makes the School today as "natural," indispensable-useful and even beneficial for our contemporaries as the Church was "natural", indispensable and generous for our ancestors a few centuries ago.

In fact, the Church has been replaced today *in its role as the dominant Ideological State Apparatus* by the School. It is coupled with the Family just as the Church was once coupled with the Family. We can now claim that the unprecedentedly deep crisis which is now shaking the education system of so many States across the globe, often in conjunction with a crisis (already proclaimed in the *Communist Manifesto*) shaking the family system, takes on a political meaning, given that the School (and the School-Family couple) constitutes the dominant Ideological State Apparatus, the Apparatus playing a determinant part in the reproduction of the relations *of* production of a mode of production threatened in its existence by the world class struggle.

Notes

1. The family obviously has other "functions" than that of an ISA. It intervenes in the reproduction of labour power. In different modes of production it is the unit of production and/or the unit of consumption.

2. The "Law" belongs both to the (Repressive) State Apparatus and to the system of the ISAs.

3. In a pathetic text written in 1937, Krupskaya relates the history of Lenin's desperate efforts and what she regards as his failure.

4. What I have said in these few brief words about the class struggle, in the ISAs is obviously far from exhausting the question of the class struggle.

   To approach this question, two principles must be borne in mind:

   The first principle was formulated by Marx in the Preface to *A Contribution to the Critique of Political Economy*: "In considering such transformations [a social revolution] a distinction should always be made between the material transformation of the economic conditions of production, which can be determined with the precision of natural science, and the legal, political, religious, aesthetic or philosophic—in short, ideological forms in which men become conscious of this conflict and fight it out." The class struggle is thus expressed and exercised in ideological forms, thus also in the ideological forms of the ISAs. But the class struggle *extends far beyond* these forms, and it is because it extends beyond them that the struggle of the exploited classes may also be exercised in the forms of the ISAs, and thus turn the weapon of ideology against the classes in power.

   This by virtue of the *second principle*: the class struggle extends beyond the ISAs because it is rooted elsewhere than in ideology, in the infrastructure, in the relations of production, which are relations of exploitation and constitute the base for class relations.

5. For the most part. For the relations of production are first reproduced by the materiality of the processes of production and circulation. But it should not be forgotten that ideological relations are immediately present in these same processes.

6. See note above.

7. *For that part* of reproduction to which the Repressive State Apparatus and the Ideological State Apparatus *contribute.*

PART III

RADIANT TOMORROWS

INTRODUCTION

Part III begins in the later 1960s and 1970s, when changes in social thought reflected changes in society during the last decades of the twentieth century. The long post-World War II economic boom in the capitalist nations wound down in the 1970s and was followed by new areas of growth, particularly associated with new computer technologies. In the communist bloc, economic, technological, and political stagnation became irreversible and precipitated a collapse of the party and the system as a whole. New social movements emerged and shifted collective action from class-based organization to more fluid bases of identity and solidarity. The formation of large trade zones, like the European Union, as well as policies of international organizations like the International Monetary Fund and the World Trade Organization, buoyed market mechanisms, while government guidance of economies and societies weakened; markets globalized and transnational migration grew. The Third World ceased to be a area of post-colonial underdevelopment, and fragmented into many different zones, some with booming economies, others plunged into absolute poverty. A postmodern intellectual and cultural climate set in. Social theory tried to explain these changes, but was also transformed by them.

It was not only the theories themselves that were affected. Concepts and categories, especially those used to classify people, also melted into thin air. The hitherto fixed, "ascribed," demographic categories like sex, age, race, religion, and national origin turned out to be highly unstable socially constructed identities, lodged in discourses and practices, not in some essential and immutable quality of individuals. "Sex" became "gender"; "Nations" turned into "imagined communities." Old racial and ethnic categories disappeared, replaced by highly fluid identities that proliferated or became lumped together (for instance, when immigrants to the United States from mnay countries became grouped together as "Asians"). "Classes" could no longer be seen as fixed groups defined by clear, objective characteristics such as ownership and employment status; the notion that it was only a matter of time for consciousness to automatically catch up to objective location in the class structure was discredited. "Class" was now an emergent process of self-definition. Suddenly everything was in quotation marks; identities were formed by categories of discourse, words that had to be set in quotes.

The body became central to social theory. Most previous social theory was disembodied; it focused on interaction, social structures, and dialogues within the "mind"—all involving disembodied social selves. Apart from some remarks by Marx about the impact of machinery on human beings, most theory was written as though people were not physical bodies. The influence of Foucault and feminism put embodiment at the centre of social theory and tied issues of embodiment to power relations and social construction of selves and identities.

New types of people engaged in social theory. The doors of the theoretical community are more open than they ever have been before. In a hundred years, the enterprise of social theory changed from a club entered only by European men of bourgeois social origin into a community in which a much broader range of people participate. The dominance of the United States has come to an end; western Europe is once again a major player, but not only people of western European origin write theory now. The former colonial world is an active area of theoretical development. Women are still at the margins of theory, often confining themselves to feminist theory, but they are entering the conversation in increasing numbers. As universities open their doors to a broader, less affluent spectrum of students, people of working-class origin enter an intellectual enterprise that was once exclusively bourgeois.

All these changes in culture and global life have contributed to a postmodern mood. The word "postmodern" means many different things. At the most grandiose level, some intellectuals use it to mean a rolling back of the Enlightenment, and maybe even loss of a Platonic faith in transcendent ideals at work in history and society. We are less inclined to believe in historical redemption, whether Messianic or in the form of secular progress. What we have in society now is about "as good as it gets." The mood is one of enjoyment of appearance, of the surface of life, instead of a search for a better social order that can be brought forth from the present unjust and oppressive one. This view suggests a fading of the negative-critical perspective in social theory.

Other observers use "postmodern" in a more modest, limited, and down-to-earth way to mean societies and cultures that are based on advanced electronic technologies, globalized in markets and communication systems, and highly media oriented. This more limited use of postmodern allows ample room for new types of social theory, and these are explored here.

Readings
Alexander, Jeffrey C., and Piotr Sztompka. *Rethinking Progress: Movements, Forces, and Ideas at the End of the Twentieth Century*. Boston: Unwin Hyman, 1990.

CHAPTER SIX

MELTING RAYS

INTRODUCTION

The three-fold categories—structural functionalism, conflict theory, and symbolic interactionism—began to to lose their boundaries, to melt into each other and into new types of theory. Partly for this reason, the first chapter of Part III is called "Melting Rays": new theories were like powerful beams that caused this distintegration and combination of previous theories.

The agency/structure dualism that was so marked in the difference between structural functionalism and symbolic interactionism was overcome; a more dialectical view of duality, rather than dualism, emerged from new theoretical work, especially that of three European theorists—Jürgen Habermas, Anthony Giddens, and Pierre Bourdieu.

The increasing emphasis on culture as a master concept pulls together many theoretical themes into a single, complex position that emphasizes social construction. There are many different kinds of social constructionism, but their unifying theme is the way in which identities and unequal social relations are culturally constructed in discourse and practice. ("Discourse" is a concept that is fairly close to the old concept of "symbolic interaction"—people saying things to each other and themselves.) This type of theory was influenced by the work of Michel Foucault, a French post-structuralist theorist.

The collapse of communism and the end of the Cold War posed serious problems for Marxist social theory. Born into a peripheral area of the global economy, bearing the brunt of fascist attack in World War II, and drawn into a spiralling postwar arms race, the Soviet version of socialism could not catch up to capitalism. With the failure of the Soviet model came the failure of the vanguard party as a revolutionary organization and the means of managing the transition to socialism. In the final analysis, it was objective conditions of initial backwardness, war, and technological lag that sunk the Soviet Union, but the Communist Party had certainly not provided an attractive model of political participation.

In some ways, the collapse of communism liberated Marxist theory from the need to explain and justify really existing socialism in the Soviet bloc and China. It was freer now to concentrate on its negative-critical role, its analysis of capitalism. Indeed, most of the observations of capitalism that Marx and

Engels offer in the *Communist Manifesto* are truer now than ever before: globalization in markets and investments; the emergence of worldwide communications and culture; the increasing concentration of capital in huge firms formed by mega mergers; the total collapse of all systems that fail to become capitalist or try to resist doing so; the accelerated pace of technological change; and the commodification of all relationships and activities. Marx's analysis of capitalism remains first rate, although he and other Marxists had underestimated the resilience of the system in key respects: formally democratic political systems are able to absorb great amounts of discontent and defuse class conflict; national and ethnic diversity in the global labour force continues to fragment the proletariat; and technological advances have led to qualitative leaps in living standards in many global regions, reducing the impetus for finding an alternative to capitalism.

26

CONTEMPORARY EUROPEAN THEORISTS

In the last third of the twentieth century, the centres of social thought shifted back to Europe after a long exile in North America. A wealthy and powerful western European community rose from the ashes of World War II and with it came the leisure and intellectual energy for theorizing. Tumultuous student-worker movements in the 1960s, a subsequent conservative consolidation, and the irreversible stagnation and collapse of Soviet socialism raised questions about the emerging structure of developed societies, the nature of modernity, and the role of theory in social change.

Three names are often associated with this resurgence of European social thought: Jürgen Habermas in Germany, Pierre Bourdieu in France, and Anthony Giddens in Britain, and each responds to concepts and questions raised by the classical theorists. Each offers an extensive, comprehensive set of concepts for thinking about society. Like the work of Talcott Parsons and the structural functionalists, these conceptual frameworks sometimes veer off into grand abstractions; unlike them, they retain a critical edge and are influenced by Marx.

All three of the contemporary-classical theorists concern themselves with four questions, answering them in similar ways, although they introduce distinct terms.

1. How can we best conceptualize the mix of agency (purposive action) and structure (compelling "external" circumstances) that produces society? Readers may remember that Durkheim leaned toward the structural side, Weber toward agency, and Marx insisted on a dialectic between these two forces.
2. How can we conceptualize the integration of micro and macro levels? At the micro level we find interaction, local meanings, communication, and individual actions; at the macro level we speak of structures, institutions, the larger society, and national and global processes. This question pushes us toward a synthesis of Marxist and structural-functionalist theory on the one hand, with symbolic-interactionist theories on the other hand.
3. Can we retain a negative-critical thrust to theorizing, yet accurately think about society as it is? If our starting point is a future utopia, an emancipatory vision as it appears to be for Marxists, will this goal inevitably distort our understanding of empirical reality? How can we best conceptualize modern society, and what potentials for change does it have within itself?
4. What concepts of the classical theorists are still essential? Which can be brought forward to our times? Which need to be revised, renamed, or reshuffled? Which are to be discarded?

All three of these theorists work at a high level of abstraction. They melt most of the structure/agency dualism left as a legacy of the postwar period with its distinct division between structural functionalists and interactionists.They also soften the line between conflict and other types of theory; they retain a critical edge but do not commit themselves to organized, identifiable, conflicting groups in contemporary society. They melt together themes in Marx, Weber, Durkheim, and Simmel.

There are a number of features that these theories have in common, ways in which they retain and revise elements of classical social thought.

1. They attempt to overcome the agency/structure dualism that entered postwar social theory, returning to the more dialectical view proposed by Marx.
2. They try to de-reify structure and to avoid writing of structure as an external thing as Durkheim and structural functionalists sometimes appeared to do. Structure is located in rules and resources that shape practice (Giddens), in a shared and internalized habitus as well as capital and position in fields (Bourdieu), and in system processes that affect lifeworlds (Habermas). While rejecting reified concepts of structure, they also distinguish themselves from the classical symbolic interactionists; they do not write as though interaction and communication are consciously and freely directed by individuals.
3. They define modern society in similar ways, emphasizing disjunction between the local (lifeworlds; communities that are spatially and temporally unified) and the national-global (system; processes disembedded in time and space).
4. They retain an emphasis on capitalism as a central element of modernity, but make fewer claims than Marxists about its laws of motion, class formation, linear evolution, revolutionary end, etc.
5. They retain the concern of Weber and the critical theorists that rationality is being replaced by formal rationalization, or instrumental reason.
6. They retain Weber and Marx's interest in class, but experiment with new ways of thinking about class formation, class structure, and class consciousness; this focus is most evident in the work of Bourdieu.
7. They retain Weber and Marx's interest in how a class-in-itself (or people in other types of specific positions and statuses) becomes a group of social actors, with identity, purpose, and organization. They emphasize that this is not a determined outcome.

Short selections from the three theorists illustrate their attention to definitions of concepts; their effort to define new concepts or revisit and redefine existing concepts is itself a response to new social conditions and not only a reaction to issues within the field of theory. In the half century after World War II, most economically developed societies became more open; rigid types of class barriers softened, especially as educational opportunities expanded; the sharp lines between working-class and middle-class communities blurred; in many parts of the world, formal democracy prevailed over authoritarian and totalitarian political systems; capitalism became more flexible; white collar jobs increased as a proportion of the labour force; and through pension plans and other investment opportunities, many working people believed they entered the ranks of the propertied classes. All of these real life developments forced European theorists to move away from concepts that emphasized social determination of life chances and lifeways towards North American methodological individualism. However, they were not prepared to move to a purely individual-centred analysis, nor did they abandon class and power as fundamental categories.

For example, Habermas struggles with the definition of democracy (as well as reason and communication) because, while formal democracy has expanded in the postwar period, it was not accompanied by real public participation. Bourdieu develops concepts like "habitus" and "field" and Giddens posits his "structuration theory" explicitly in order to capture the fluidity and flexibility of contemporary society and social inequalities. The determinism and rigidity implicit in the concept of structure fails to capture the character of postwar societies which allow individuals considerable opportunities and choices. Yet the North American individualism and voluntarism that pervade symbolic-interactionist theory need to be tempered by greater recognition of structural constraint and power differences between actors. Both Bourdieu and Giddens are especially intrigued by the ambiguities and paradoxes of an educational system that offers equal opportunities yet consistently reproduces inequalities—a system in which working-class young people appear to choose their own failure.

For Bourdieu and Giddens, society is not formed by individual will or purely subjective impulses, yet neither is it a determined structure. Bourdieu's habitus and field and Giddens's structuration theory, in which action is constrained but not determined by rules and resources, are attempts to theorize the dialectic between individual actions and constraining forces. These in turn are sometimes external to the actor—for example, differences in coercive power or economic resources—and sometimes internalized, as in the disposition toward modes of action implied by habitus.

The selections illustrate how these three theorists grapple with concepts; the reader is referred to Bourdieu and Giddens' writing on education to see more down-to-earth analysis, in which the concepts are applied rather than only defined. It is also important to note that all three theorists write extensively on their debts to and differences from leading theorists of the past: Marx, for all three; Durkheim for Bourdieu and Giddens; Weber for Giddens and Habermas; and the symbolic interactionists and Goffman for Giddens.

The Bourdieu selections are reflections on habitus and field. In the first one he discusses habitus, and in the second one he focuses on social fields, associating them with activities that intellectuals often deem frivolous (the gatherings of high society and beautiful people covered by gossip columns and the French equivalents of *People*). Here he also addresses the complicated question of how capital in one field can be used to acquire advantages in another. Bourdieu distinguishes field from apparatus, as he differentiates his broader and more flexible concept from the more rigid one used by Althusser and many Marxists. Finally, Bourdieu addresses the question whether sociology is deterministic; like Freud and Marx, he asserts that the possibility of freedom is enlarged, not narrowed, by our understanding of determining forces. Furthermore, these apparent laws are not really physical laws, but only prevailing historical constraints; by showing the historical limits of such laws, the sociologist sides with the dominated and points the way toward a future that is different than the present.

The selection by Giddens differentiates structuration from structure and discusses rules and resources. Giddens maintains that while individual actors are the "atoms" of interactions and social systems, the rules and resources that shape their actions are properties of collectivities and communities. Note how Giddens begins with a salute to Marx as a forerunner of structuration theory and then proceeds to add a stronger element of collectivity and constraint to interactionist theory. It is most helpful to keep in mind the nature of language (in fact, Giddens uses that as a starting point), in which speakers are both infinitely creative yet rigidly bound by the grammar, sounds, and meanings of their speech communities. Language perfectly illustrates structuration in which individual action is constrained by rules and resources and yet remains unpredictable and free.

Readings

Layder, Derek. *Modern Social Theory*. London: University College London Press, 1997.

Ritzer, George. *Modern Sociological Theory*. New York: McGraw-Hill, 1992.

27

JÜRGEN HABERMAS (1929-)

Jürgen Habermas is most directly influenced by Marx and Weber, as well as the critical theory developed by the Frankfurt School. Critical theory must be turned on the processes of communication to expose distortion and to enable us to attain undistorted communication. With this central theoretical project, Habermas connects Marxist theories of consciousness with the analysis of language and communication.

The public sphere, potentially an area of undistorted communication, has become increasingly restricted in capitalist society; everyday interaction is de-politicized and privatized, and technocratic jargon and media patterns of communication are the dominant modes of discourse. Local lifeworlds, small cultural spheres of everyday interaction and construction of meaning, are increasingly colonized by system processes associated with the state and the capitalist economy. Power and money, rather than shared communication, dictate the terms of everyday life.

This domination cannot be reversed by a backwards-looking defense of simple, homogenous, undifferentiated lifeworlds, such as small towns, ethnic enclaves, and tight-knit religious faiths. Emancipation becomes possible if interaction within the lifeworld engages with the system processes, challenging them through rational communication. Rationality must be freed from its subordination to formal rationalization, instrumental reason (or means-rationality) associated with power and money.

The system lays claim to rationality, but its rationality is only a means-rationality used to expand the forces of power and money. Small besieged lifeworlds have responded by rejecting rationality in all its forms, throwing out the baby of rationality with the bathwater of formal rationalization.

We can see here how Habermas develops Marxist ideas of consciousness, critical theory's critique of instrumental reason, and Weber's critique of rationalization. He attempts to rescue rationality from Weber's pessimistic tendency to couple it with formal rationalization. He also transforms Marxist theory by adding increased emphasis on communication and interaction; this new emphasis, based on twentieth phenomenology, interactionist theory, and modern theories of communication and cognitive development, clarifies the process by which subjective consciousness can be transformed.

Habermas also expands Marxist notions of crisis from economic crisis to crises in political, cultural, and intra-personal spheres—crises of legitimation, rationality, and motivation.

A close reading of Marx and Weber shows that these concepts are already present in the original texts: Weber was careful to distinguish means- and end-rationality; Marx gave attention to factories and modern work organization as providing sites for communication among proletarians, and he certainly saw the connections between economic, political, cultural processes. But Habermas's re-reading of these texts, and their elaboration in light of later communication theories, amounts to a new theoretical synthesis.

Three central values that guide Habermas's work are democracy, communication, and rationality. A problem of all three concepts is that we usually encounter them in their debased, manipulated, narrowed, and false forms. The words are in constant danger of losing their meaning when they are captured and used by corporations, the media, and power elites; their new false meanings are virtually the opposite of their true meanings—"democracy" means a process of compromise among ruling elites, "rationality" means instrumental reason that treats people as things, and "communication" means manipulation and distortion in speech in the private interest of corporations and ruling elites. Therefore the first step for theory is a negative-critical one, attacking and exposing these false uses of concepts. Here Habermas differentiates the broader, true meaning of democracy from the narrow meaning that political scientists, as well as the public, have come to accept.

Readings

Habermas, Jürgen. *The Theory of Communicative Action.* Vol 2: *Lifeworld and System: A Critique of Functionalist Reason.* Boston: Beacon Press, 1989.

—. *The Philosophical Discourse of Modernity.* Cambridge, MA: MIT Press, 1987.

Formal Democracy
JÜRGEN HABERMAS

Democracy, in this view, is no longer determined by the content of a form of life that takes into account the generalizable interests of all individuals. It counts now as only a method for selecting leaders and the accoutrements of leadership. Under "democracy," the conditions under which all legitimate interests can be fulfilled by way of realizing the fundamental interests in self-determination and participation are no longer understood. It is now only a key for the distribution of rewards conforming to the system, that is, a regulator for the satisfaction of private interests. This democracy makes possible *prosperity without freedom.* It is no longer tied to political equality in the sense of an equal distribution of political power, that is, of the chances to exercise power. Political equality now means only the formal right to equal opportunity of access to power, that is, "equal eligibility for election to positions of power." Democracy no longer has the goal of rationalizing authority through the participation of citizens in discursive processes of will-formation. It is intended, instead, to make possible *compromises* between ruling elites. Thus, the substance of classical democratic theory is finally surrendered. No longer *all* politically consequential decisions, but only those decisions of the government still *defined as political*, are to be subject to the precepts of democratic will-formation. In this way, a pluralism of elites, replacing the self-determination of the people, makes privately exercised social power independent of the pressures of legitimation and immunizes it against the principle of rational formation of will....

28

PIERRE BOURDIEU (1930-)

Bourdieu is in a dialogue with Durkheim and Marx. From Durkheim he derives an emphasis on structure which he extends to culture as well as social relations. From Marx he brings the centrality of social class to the analysis of society. Social classes are among the most compelling "social facts," the most powerful type of external constraint. Classes are distinguished by four kinds of capital: economic (productive property); social (positions in influential networks and groupings); cultural (skills, habits, knowledge, tastes, and educational credentials); and symbolic (manipulation of symbols to express and legitimate the other three types of capital). The field of power relationships in turn structures the fields in which these types of capital are deployed.

Factions within the major classes are further distinguished by their control of various types as well as various amounts of capital. For example, the haute bourgeoisie is dominant in economic capital, which it uses to acquire social and cultural capital. In contrast, intellectuals are placed by Bourdieu in a dominated position at the bottom of the upper class; they have cultural capital but little economic or political power.

Bourdieu introduces the concept of "habitus." Habitus is the shared mode of perception, judgment, and behavioural dispositions of a category of people, particularly a class. This concept combines elements of Marx's consciousness (including false consciousness) with Durkheim's collective conscience/consciousness. Like the collective conscience/consciousness, the habitus is often unconscious as well as conscious. Most individuals are not aware of this sum total of their shared dispositions, the internalized structures which propel them to act in the social world, "externalizing their internality."

Individuals as carriers of a class culture express their tastes, not only in big political issues, but also in the details of food preferences, clothing, arts and popular culture, and habits of thought and language. Habitus is a process that mediates between class and individual dispositions, tastes, and habits.

Actions are constrained, but not determined by these cultural structures. Bourdieu emphasizes that habitus is not a determining force; not all individuals in the same class have an identical habitus, and exactly what actions result from the habitus cannot be predicted. The influence of Jean-Paul Sartre and French existentialism is visible in this area of Bourdieu's thought; habitus and field are internalized and external structures of possibilities, not forces that lead to fixed, determined outcomes. Over a large number of individuals, however, habitus tends to reproduce social class.

For example, a lower-class child may fail school courses, be chronically truant, and drop out in the early years of secondary school, not only because of peer pressure or uncaring teachers, but because the entire force of the habitus militates against sitting still, reading textbooks, using bookish language, competing for grades, expressing oneself in writing, carrying books home, being quietly studious, doing homework, and scores of other matters of taste, style, self-concept, and behaviour. The lower-class child may have a cultural fund of sports skills and lore, vivid slang and folk expressions, fashion and musical styles, and street sense, but this capital is worthless currency in formal education.

Bourdieu is influential in the sociology of education, where the concepts of cultural capital and habitus help explain why a public school system with formal equality and well-intentioned teachers (and in Europe, if not in the United States, relatively uniform per pupil expenditures and national performance standards) can nevertheless reproduce so much social inequality.

Bourdieu also responds to Weber and Marx's interest in explaining how classes as objective locations in a structure ("class in itself") are transformed into social actors ("class for itself"). Class formation as a process of cultural and social construction, as well as any ensuing class conflict, involve the mobilization of symbols. These are not predictable processes because different types of capital, multiple factions within classes, and individual differences in class origins and destinations produce extremely complicated patterns in the transformation of classes into organizational actors.

Readings

Bourdieu, Pierre. *On Television*. New York: New Press, 1999.

Bourdieu, Pierre, Edward Lipuma, Moishe Postone, and Craig Calhoun (eds.). *Bourdieu: Critical Perspectives*. Chicago: University of Chicago Press, 1993.

Bourdieu, Pierre, and Passeron, Jean-Claude. *Reproduction in Education, Society and Culture*. London: Sage, 1970/1990.

Swartz, David. *Culture and Power: The Sociology of Pierre Bourdieu*. Chicago: University of Chicago, 1997.

Sociology in Question
PIERRE BOURDIEU

[Bourdieu on habitus and field]

The idea of *habitus* has a long tradition behind it. The Scholastics used it to translate Aristotles's *hexis*. You find it in Durkheim, who, in *L'Évolution pédagogique en France,* notes that Christian education had to solve the problems raised by the need to mould a Christian *habitus* with a pagan culture. It's also in Marcel Mauss, in his famous text on the techniques of the body. But neither of those authors gives it a decisive role to play.

Why did I revive that old word? Because with the notion of *habitus* you can refer to something that is close to what is suggested by the idea of habit, while differing from it in one important respect. The *habitus*, as the word implies, is that which one has acquired, but which has become durably incorporated in the body in the form of permanent dispositions. So the term constantly reminds us that it refers to something historical, linked to individual history, and that it belongs to a genetic mode of thought, as opposed to essentialist modes of thought (like the notion of competence which is part of the Chomskian lexis).[1] Moreover, by *habitus* the Scholastics also meant something like a property, a *capital*. And indeed, the *habitus* is a capital, but one which, because it is embodied appears as innate.

But then why not say "habit"? Habit is spontaneously regarded as repetitive, mechanical, automatic, reproductive rather than productive. I wanted to insist on the idea that the *habitus* is something powerfully generative. To put it briefly, the *habitus* is a product of conditionings which tends to reproduce the objective logic of those conditionings while transforming it. It's a kind of transforming machine that leads us to "reproduce" the social conditions of our own production, but in a relatively unpredictable way, in such a way that one cannot move simply and mechanically from knowledge of the conditions of production to knowledge of the products. Although this capacity for generating practices or utterances or works is in no way innate and is historically constituted, it is not completely reducible to its conditions of production not least because it functions in a *systematic* way. One can only speak of a linguistic *habitus*, for example, so long as it is not forgotten that it is only one dimension of the *habitus* understood as a system of schemes for generating and perceiving practices, and so long as one does not autonomize the production of speech *vis-à-vis* production of aesthetic choices, or gestures, or any other possible practice. The *habitus* is a principle of invention produced by history but relatively detached from history: its dispositions are *durable*, which leads to all sorts of effects of hysteresis (of time lag, of which the example *par excellence* is Don Quixote). It can be understood by analogy with a computer program (though it's a mechanistic and therefore dangerous analogy)—but a self-correcting program. It is constituted from a systematic set of simple and partially interchangeable principles, from which an infinity of solutions can be invented, solutions which cannot be directly deduced from its conditions of production.

So the *habitus* is the principle of a real autonomy with respect to the immediate determinations of the "situation." But that does not mean that it is some kind of a-historical essence of which the existence is merely the development, in short, a destiny defined once and for all. The adjustments that are constantly required by the necessities of adaptation to new and unforseen situations may bring about durable transformations of the *habitus*, but these will remain within certain limits, not least because the *habitus* defines the perception of the situation that determines it.

The "situation" is, in a sense, the permissive condition of the fulfilment of the *habitus*. When the objective conditions of fulfilment are not present, the *habitus*, continuously thwarted by the situation, may be the site of explosive forces (resentment) which may await (and even look for) the opportunity to break out and which express themselves as soon as the objective conditions for this (e.g. the power of an authoritarian foreman) are offered. (The social world is an immense reservoir of accumulated violence, which is revealed when it encounters the conditions for its expression.) In short, in reaction against instantaneist mechanism, one is led to insist on the "assimilatory" capacities of the *habitus*; but the *habitus* is also a power of adaptation, it constantly performs an adaptation to the external world which only exceptionally takes the form of a radical conversion....

Q. *What distinction do you make between a field and an apparatus?*
A. A fundamental one, I think. The idea of the "apparatus" reintroduces pessimistic functionalism: it's an "infernal engine," programmed to bring about certain ends. The educational system, the State, the Church, the parties, are not apparatuses, but fields. However, in certain conditions, they may start functioning as apparatuses. Those conditions need to examined.

In a field, agents and institutions are engaged in struggle, with unequal strengths, and in accordance with the rules constituting that field of play, to appropriate the specific profits at stake in that game. Those who dominate the field have the means to make it function to their advantage; but they have to reckon with the resistance of the dominated agents. A field becomes an apparatus when the dominant agents have the means to nullify the resistance and the reactions of the dominated, in other words, when the lower clergy, or the grass-roots activists, or the working classes, etc., can only *suffer* domination; when all movement runs downwards and the effects of domination are such that the struggle and dialectic that are constitutive of the field come to an end. There is history so long as there are people who revolt, who make trouble. The "total" or totalitarian institution, the asylum, prison or concentration camp as described by Goffman, or the totalitarian state, attempts to institute the end of history.

The difference between fields and apparatuses is seen clearly in revolutions. Revolutionaries behave as if it were sufficient to seize control of the "state apparatus" and to reprogramme the machine, in order to have a radically different social order. In fact, the political will has to reckon with the logic of the social fields, extremely complex universes in which political intentions may be hijacked, turned upside down (this is as true of the action of the dominant groups as of subversive action, as is shown by everything that is described in the inadequate language of "recuperation," which is still naïvely teleological). All political action can only be sure of achieving the desired effects so long as it is dealing with apparatuses, that is, organizations in which the dominated agents are reduced to execution, to carrying out orders "to the death" (activists, soldiers, etc.). Thus apparatuses are just one state, one which can be regarded as pathological, of fields.

[Bourdieu on different kinds of capital]

To return to the question of the kinds of capital, I think it's a very difficult question and I realize, when I tackle it, that I am moving outside the charted area of established truths, where one is sure of immediately attracting approval, esteem, and so on. (At the same time, I think that the scientifically most fruitful positions are often the most risky ones, and therefore the socially most improbable.) As regards economic capital, I leave that to others; it's not my area. What concerns me is what is abandoned by others. Because they lack the interest or the theoretical tools for these things, cultural capital and social capital. Very recently I've tried to set out in simple terms for didactic purposes what I mean by these notions. I try to construct rigorous definitions that are not only descriptive concepts, but means of *construction,* which make it possible to produce things that one could not see previously. Take social capital, for example: one can give an intuitive idea of it by saying that it is what ordinary language calls "connections." (It often happens that ordinary language designates very important social facts; but it masks them at the same time, by the effect of familiarity, which leads one to imagine that one already knows, that one has understood everything, and which stops research in its tracts. Part of the work of social science consists in dis-covering what is both unveiled and veiled by ordinary language. This means running the risk of being accused of stating the self-evident, or, worse, of labouriously translating, into a heavily conceptual language, the basic verities of common sense or the more subtle and more agreeable intuitions of moralists and novelists. When, that is, people do not accuse the sociologist of saying things that are simultaneously banal and untrue, which just goes to show the extraordinary resistances that sociological analysis arouses.)

To return to social capital: by constructing this concept, one acquires the means of analysing the logic whereby this particular kind of capital is accumulated, transmitted and reproduced, the means of understanding how it turns into economic capital and, conversely, what work is required to convert economic capital into social capital, the means of grasping the function of institutions such as clubs or, quite simply, the *family*, the main site of the accumulation and transmission of that kind of capital, and so on. We are a long way, it seems to me, from common-sense "connections," which are only one manifestation among others of social capital. The "social round" and all that is related in the high-society gossip columns of *Le Figaro, Vogue* or *Jours de France* cease to be, as is generally thought, exemplary manifestations of the idle life of the "leisure class" or the "conspicuous consumption" of the wealthy, and can be seen instead as a particular form of social labour, which presupposes expenditure of money, time and a specific competence and which tends to ensure the (simple or expanded) reproduction of social capital. (It can be seen, incidentally, that some ostensibly very critical discourses miss what is essential, because intellectuals are not very "sensitive" to the form of social capital that accumulates and circulates in "society" gatherings and tend to sneer, with a mixture of fascination and resentment, rather than analyse.)

So it was necessary to construct the object that I call social capital which immediately brings to light that publishers' cocktail parties or reciprocal reviewing are the equivalent, in the intellectual field, of the "social work" of the aristocracy—to see that high-society socializing is, for certain people, whose power and authority are based on social capital, their principal occupation. An enterprise based on social capital has to ensure its own reproduction through a specific form of labour (inaugurating monuments, chairing charities, etc.) That presupposes professional skills, and therefore an apprenticeship, and an expenditure of time and energy. As soon as this object is constructed, one can carry out genuine comparative studies, talk to historians about the nobility in the Middle Ages, reread Saint-Simeon and Proust, or, of course, the work of the ethnologists.

At the same time, you are quite right to ask the question. Since what I do is not at all theoretical work, but scientific work that mobilizes all the theoretical resources for the purposes of empirical analysis, my concepts are not always what they ought to be. For example, I constantly raise the problem of the conversion of one kind of capital into another, in terms that do not completely satisfy even me. It's an example of a problem that could not be posed explicitly—it posed itself before one knew it—until the notion of kinds of capital had been constructed. Practice is familiar with this problem. In certain games (in the intellectual field, for example, in order to win a literary prize or the esteem of one's peers), economic capital is inoperative. To become operational it has to undergo a transmutation. That's the function, for example, of the "social work" that made it possible to transmute economic capital—always at the root in the last analysis—into nobility. But that's not all. What are the laws governing that conversion? What defines the exchange rate at which one kind of capital is converted into another? In every epoch there is a constant struggle over the rate of exchange between the different kinds of capital, a struggle among the different fractions of the dominant class, whose overall capital is composed in differing proportions of the various kinds of capital. Those who in nineteenth-century France were called the "capacities" have a constant interest in the revaluing of cultural capital with respect to economic capital. It can be seen—and this is what makes sociological analysis so difficult, that these things that we take as our object, cultural capital, economic capital, etc., are themselves at stake in struggles within the reality that we are studying and what we say about them will itself become a stake in struggles.

Analysis of these laws of conversion is not complete, far from it, and if there is one person for whom it's a problem, it's myself. Which is fine. There's a host of questions, very fertile ones I think, that I ask myself or that are put to me, objections that are raised and that were only made possible because these distinctions had been made. Research is perhaps the art of creating fruitful problems for oneself—and creating them for other people. Where things were simple, you bring out problems. And then you find yourself facing a much more sticky reality. Of course, I could have produced one of the courses of Marxism-without-tears on the social classes that have sold so well in the last few years, under the name of theory, or even science. Or even sociology—you find yourself dealing with things that are both suggestive, and worrying (I know the effect that what I do has on the guardians of orthodoxy and I think I also have some idea why it has that effect and I'm delighted that it does). The idea of being both suggestive and worrying is one that suits me fine.

Q. *But isn't there something static about the theory of the social classes that you put forward? You describe a state of the structure without saying how it changes.*

A. What statistical analysis can grasp is a moment, a state of a game with two, three, four or six players, or whatever. It gives a photograph of the piles of tokens of various colours that they have won in the previous rounds and which they will play in the rounds to come. Capital apprehended instantaneously is a product of history that will produce more history. I'll simply say that the strategies of the different players will depend on their resources in tokens, and more specifically on the overall volume of their capital (the number of tokens) and the structure of this capital, that's to say the composition of the piles (those who have lots of red tokens and a few yellow ones, that is, a lot of economic capital and little cultural capital, will not play in the same way as those who have many yellow tokens and few red ones). The bigger their pile, the more audacious they can be (bluff), and the more yellow tokens (cultural capital) they have, the more they will stake on the yellow squares (the educational system). Each player sees the play of the others, that is, their way of playing, their style, and he derives clues from this regarding their hand, tacitly hypothesizing that the former, is a manifestation of the latter. He may even have direct knowledge of part or all of the capital of the others (educational qualifications play the role of calls in bridge). In any case, he uses his knowledge of the properties of the other players, that is, their strategy, to guide his own play. But the principle of his anticipations is nothing other than the sense of the game, that is, the practical mastery of the relationship between tokens and play (what we express when we say of a property, a garment or a piece of furniture, for example—that it's "petit-bourgeois"). This sense of the game is the product of the progressive internalization of the immanent laws of the game. It's what Thibaut and Riecken grasp, for example, when their respondents, questioned about two people who give blood, spontaneously assume that the person of higher class is free, the person of lower class forced (although we do not know, and it would be very interesting to know how the proportion of those who make this assumption varies between upper- and lower-class respondents).

Obviously the image I have just used is only valid as a didactic device. But I think it gives an idea of the real logic of social change and gives a sense of how artificial it is to oppose the static to the dynamic.

[Bourdieu on determinism]

Q. *Doesn't your sociology imply a deterministic view of man? What role, if any, is left for human freedom?*

A. Like every science, sociology accepts the principle of determinism understood as a form of the principle of sufficient reason. The science which must give the reasons for that which it thereby postulates that nothing is without a reason for being. The sociologist adds: "social reason"—nothing is without a specifically social reason for being. Faced with a statistical table, he postulates that there is a social factor that explains that distribution, and if, having found it, there is a residue, then he postulates the existence of another social factor, and so on. (That's what makes people sometimes imagine a sociological imperialism: but it's fair enough—every science has to use its own means to account for the greatest number of things possible, including things that are apparently or really explained by other sciences. It's on that condition that it can put real questions to the other sciences—and to itself and destroy apparent reasons or raise clearly the problem of overdetermination).

Having said that, people are often referring to two quite different things under the term "determinism"—objective necessity, implied in reality itself, and "experiential," apparent, subjective necessity, the *sense* of necessity or freedom. The degree to which the social world *seems* to us to be determined depends on the knowledge we have of it. On the other hand, the degree to which the world is *really* determined is not a question of opinion; as a sociologist, it's not for me to be "for determinism" or "for freedom," but to discover necessity, if it exists, in the places where it is. Because all progress in the knowledge of the laws of the social world increases the degree of perceived necessity, it is natural that social science is increasingly accused of "determinism" the further it advances.

But, contrary to appearances, it's by raising the degree of perceived necessity and giving a better knowledge of the laws of the social world that social science gives more freedom. All progress in knowledge of necessity is a progress in *possible* freedom. Whereas misrecognition of necessity contains a form of recognition of necessity, and probably the most absolute, the most total form, since it is unaware of itself as such, knowledge of necessity does not at all imply the necessity of that recognition. On the contrary, it brings to light the possibility of choice that is implied in every relationship of the type *"if X, then Y."* The freedom that consists in choosing to accept or refuse the "if" has no meaning so long as one is unaware of the relationship that links it to a "then...." By bringing to light the laws that presuppose non-intervention of (that's to say, unconscious acceptance of the conditions of realization of the expected effects), one extends the scope of freedom. A law that is unknown is a nature, a destiny (that's true, for example, of the relationship between inherited cultural capital and educational achievement); a law that is known appears as a possibility of freedom.

Q. *Isn't it dangerous to speak of laws?*
A. Yes, undoubtedly. And, as far as possible, I avoid doing so. Those who have an interest in things taking their course (that's to say in the "if" remaining unchanged) see the "law" (when they see it at all) as a destiny, an inevitability inscribed in social nature (which gives the iron laws of the oligarchies of the neo-Machiavellians, such as Michels or Mosca). In fact, a social law is a historical law, which perpetuates itself so long as it is allowed to operate, that's to

say as long as those whose interests it serves (sometimes unknown to them) are able to perpetuate the conditions of its efficacy.

What we have to ask is what we are doing when we state a social law that was previously unknown (such as the law of the transmission of cultural capital). One may claim to be fixing an eternal law, as the conservative sociologists do with the tendency towards the concentration of power. In reality, science needs to know that it merely records, in the form of tendential laws, the logic that is characteristic of a *particular game, at a particular moment,* and which plays to the advantage of those who dominate the game and are able, *de facto* or *de jure*, to define the rules of the game.

Having said that, as soon as the law has been stated, it may become a stake in struggles, the struggle to conserve, by conserving the conditions of the functioning of the law, the struggle to transform, by changing these conditions. Bringing the tendential laws to light is a precondition for the success of actions aimed at frustrating them. The dominant groups have an interest in the law, and therefore in a physicalist interpretation of the law, which pushes it back to the state of an infra-conscious mechanism. By contrast, the dominated groups have an interest in the discovery of the law as such, that is, as a historical law, which could be abolished if the conditions of its functioning were removed. Knowledge of the law gives them a chance, a possibility of countering the effects of the law, a possibility that does not exist so long as the law is unknown and operates unbeknown to those who undergo it. In short just as it de-naturalizes, so sociology de-fatalizes.

Notes
1. [By "genetic" Bourdieu means an analysis of origins, not biological inheritance. –Editor]

29

ANTHONY GIDDENS (1938-)

Anthony Giddens calls his central concept "structuration." He is probably the least concerned of the three with producing a negative-critical perspective and the most distant from structural and Marxist theories. Structuration theory is in many ways a revision of symbolic interactionism, continuing to emphasize interaction and agency. Giddens however recognizes more constraints on actors than classic interactionists who often wrote as though the conscious, even rational, motivations of actors were enough to explain the flow of an interaction. For Giddens, structure impinges on actors through rules that guide their practice and interactions—sometimes unconsciously—and through resources that they are able to bring to and derive from these practices and interactions. Structure exists as rules and resources, which both constrain and enable actors. Actors do not fully control resources nor do they make rules; in many cases they are not consciously aware of the rules. They act, but not always meaningfully, let alone rationally.

For example, the rules and resources that a group of white Los Angeles Police Department officers bring to an encounter with an African American motorist suspected of driving under the influence of alcohol or drugs are quite different from the rules and resources the motorist brings to the situation. The rules and resources are not the result of the wishes and will of the actors, nor are they equal. These two sets of actors are in distinct positions and have distinct identities.

Rules and resources tend to come bundled together in what Giddens calls "structural sets." The patterning of social relationships governed by these structural sets persist over time and exist in a spatial territory. This patterning is similar to the concept of institution in structural-functional sociology. Notice however that Giddens's terms like "practice" and "position" assume much less about stability, legitimacy, and institutionalization than the structural-functional term "role."

While Giddens specifically rejects evolutionary theorizing, he is keenly interested in the nature of modern society. One of his early works concerns Durkheim, Weber, and Marx's views of capitalism, and he continues to include capitalism, along with industrialization, surveillance, the industrialization of war, and the power of the nation-state, as elements of modernity. At a more fundamental level than these institutions, modernity involves a re-organization of time and space. Time was standardized as capitalism developed (a concept we have also seen in Marx, Simmel, and Gitlin). Social processes are now increasingly disconnected from physical places; for example, a corporation is not headquartered where its factories stand; a student can register for courses at a remote terminal; money flows and stock market transactions are globalized. Giddens uses the term "disembedding" for this disconnection of practices, social relations, and interactions from distinct places and times. Money and professional expertise are two types of practices that are associated with this disembedding, the increased abstraction of actions from real, closely connected points in time and space.

All societies are concerned with risk and with interpersonal trust, but the meaning of these terms is transformed in societies characterized by disembedding of activities from local contexts of interaction. Evaluating the integrity of a stockbroker half way around the world is quite different from evaluating produce at the local grocery. Here we can see a convergence of Giddens's ideas with Habermas's discussion of system and lifeworld, as well as an expansion of themes we saw in Simmel, Marx, and Weber.

Readings

Giddens, Anthony. *The Class Structure of Advanced Societies*. London: Hutchinson, 1973.

—. *Introduction to Sociology*. New York: W.W. Norton, 1996.

Giddens, Anthony, and Christopher Pierson. *Conversations with Anthony Giddens*. Palo Alto, CA: Stanford University Press, 1999.

Studies in Social and Political Theory
ANTHONY GIDDENS

Notes on the theory of structuration

Everything that has a fixed form, such as the product, etc., appears as merely a moment, a vanishing moment in ... [the] movement ... [of society]. The direct production process itself appears only as a moment. The conditions and objectifications of the process are themselves equally moments of it, and its only subjects are the individuals, but individuals in mutual relationships, which they equally reproduce and produce anew ... in which they renew themselves even as they renew the world of wealth they create. Marx, *Grundisse*

Linguists commonly recognize three sorts of activities in which the speaker of a language engages: he is able to produce "acceptable" sentences, to "understand" sentences, and make judgements about "potentially acceptable" sentences.[1] This is a useful classification when applied to the activities of a social actor more generally: the study of speech and language provides us with important insights into the conduct of social life, not because the latter is like a language or can be represented as an "information system," "sign system," etc., but because language is such a central feature of social life that it exemplifies certain characteristics of all social activity. The three types of linguistic activity mentioned above are what a person "knows" when he knows how to speak a particular language. Similarly, what an actor "knows" when he knows how to sustain social encounters with others within a specific community is how to produce "acceptable" modes of action, to "understand" both what he himself says and does and what others say and do, and to make judgements about "potentially acceptable" forms of activity. "Acceptability" here has to be taken to involve two elements (which are not always empirically discrete): the identification or typification of "meaningful acts," and the normative evaluation of such acts. The capability of judging potentially acceptable activities within the context of interaction with others is basic to the reflexive monitoring of conduct, and is characteristically applied as part of the rationalization of action; but it is also crucial to social research itself, as a means of acquiring the mutual knowledge[2] necessary to generate "adequate" characterizations of social conduct.

The production of interaction can in this way be treated as an active, contingent accomplishment of social actors, grounded in the reflexive rationalization of action, and located contextually. A crucial move in social theory, however, concerns the conceptual transition between production and reproduction. Most leading schools of social theory divide between those which opt for a voluntaristic approach (often connected to subjectivism), and those which adopt some version of social determinism. Neither is able satisfactorily to reconcile a theory of action with an acknowledgement of the fundamental importance of institutional analysis in the explanation of human social conduct. Both voluntaristic and deterministic schools of social theory actually tend to culminate in a similar viewpoint in this respect: one which identifies "structure" with "constraint" and thereby opposes "structure" to "action." Placing the notion of what I have called the duality of structure as central conceptually, connects social production and social reproduction by rejecting these oppositions. Structure enters into the explanation of action in a dual way: as the medium of its production and at the same time as its outcome in the reproduction of social forms. Thus the study of social reproduction cannot be conceived as the aggregation of numerous "productive acts," which tends to be the conclusion that voluntaristic forms of social theory lead to; nor, on the other hand, can the production of action, as a rationalized accomplishment, be treated as merely "structurally determined." Marx has some apt comments on the first of these position, discussing the conditions involved in the reproduction of capital. Such conditions, he says, can only be grasped if we concern ourselves with "the ensemble of social production." We must consider, "not the single capitalist, and the single labourer, but the capitalist class and the labouring class, *not isolated acts of production*, but capitalist production in its full continuous renewal, and on is social scale."[3] As Balibar points out, Marx here characterizes the isolated act of production "twice negatively": "as something which is not repeated and as something done by an individual."[4] However, Balibar, following Althusser, treats this as a basis for proclaiming a particularly direct form of structural determinism, in which actors appear merely as the "bearers of a mode of production."

Clarification of the implications of the above paragraph demands two things: a formal consideration of how the term "structure" is to be applied, and an amplification of the content of a theory of structuration. If "structure" is to be used not to refer to "patterns of social relationships," but rather to refer to rules and resources, we obviously then have to specify how the latter terms are to be used—and how they connect to the notion of "system." What are rules, and what are resources, in this terminology? I shall subsequently distinguish two types (which in actual social life may only represent two aspects) of "rules," but for the moment I shall confine my attention to general remarks. A preliminary approach to explicating a notion of "rule" that will be appropriate here can be derived from Wittgenstein's analysis of "knowing a rule."[5] A player in a game knows a particular rule of the game, when he knows "how to play according to that rule," when he knows "how to go on."[6] The rules involved in a social activity are not like those of most games in one crucial respect: that they are more frequently the subject of disputation over their central character or legitimacy; but this is not relevant at this stage of the discussion. To know a rule is to know, then, what one is supposed to do, and others are supposed to do, in all situations to which that rule applies, or potentially applies. A person may grasp a rule through observing regularity in what people do; but a rule as such is not a generalization of what people do. A rule can be formally stated as an abstract precept of the form, "when in situation $a, b, c \ldots$, activity $n, m, u \ldots$ is appropriate or called for." To apply a rule is to generate a form of ("meaningful") activity. This does not imply, however, that "meaningful" action can be simply equated with "rule-following" conduct, as Winch holds.[7] One reason for this is that "what happens" in any given situation of the application of rules to generate social interaction depends on the resources that those who are party to that interaction are able to mobilize in the encounter. "What happens" here has to include not just the "outcome" of interaction, in respect of motivations that participants bring to it, but in principle may concern the very nature of that interaction itself. For if knowledge (mutual knowledge) of rules is the condition of the production of interaction, it is not in and of itself a condition of how those rules are "interpreted" or are made to "count." These latter depend upon the relative influence that those who participate in the interaction bring to bear upon its course. The resources thus mobilized may be of many different kinds; all that needs to be said at this juncture is that a "resource" is any kind of advantage or capability which actors may draw upon to affect the character or the outcome of a process of interaction.

It may still sound odd to claim that the notion of "structure" can be most usefully applied in social analysis to refer to generative rules and resources. But it is not a particularly idiosyncratic usage, for the following reasons. First, it should be emphasized that social rules are not to be treated as properties of specific actors, but only of collectivities. It may indeed be true, if Wittgenstein's arguments about the impossibility of a private language are correct, that the very notion of a rule as an "individual property" is logically contradictory.[8] Second, application of the concept of "structure" in the sense I wish to suggest, can only be carried through in conjunction with that of "system," and more specifically with that of "systems of social interaction." Rules and resources are not distributed in a random form in society, but are co-ordinated with one another, in and through the coordination of the systems of interaction in whose production and reproduction they are implicated. Third, this usage does not imply that structure is inert. Rules and resources are the media of the accomplishment of social interaction, and as such are constantly embroiled in the flux of social life....

The application of semantic rules as interpretative schemes in actual contexts of interaction normally draws heavily upon tacit knowledge. The fact that such knowledge has been "taken for granted" by social researchers, just as it is by lay actors in their day-to-day life, undoubtedly has hindered this being made available as a phenomenon for study.[9] Moreover, since semantic rules are often in a way "familiar," because they are tacitly employed by members of a community, their formal elucidation as precepts may appear trivial or banal. Under the heading of "semantic rules" I include all types of rules that are drawn upon as interpretative schemes to make sense of what actors say and do, and of the cultural objects they produce. Some important aspects of the application of interpretative schemes (typifications) in everyday life have been well analysed by Schutz.[10] But the tacitly known rules involved in "meaningful" interaction also overlap with those involved in the encoding of information in symbolism and in myth, which are presumably transformational in character.[11] Under the heading of "moral rules" I classify all types of rules that are drawn upon as norms in the evaluation of conduct. Which has argued that an indication of whether behaviour is "rule-following" is given by whether or not it makes sense to ask of that behaviour, "Is there a right and wrong way of doing it?[12] I want to say, however, that there are two senses in which one may distinguish "right" (acceptable) and "wrong" (unacceptable) ways of doing things, corresponding to the differentiation of semantic and moral rules. One is that an act may be appropriately described or identified; the other is that it may be evaluatively the "right" or "wrong" way to behave in a particular set of circumstances. It is obviously important to recognize that interpretative schemes and norms interlace in actual conditions of social life. For how an act is evaluated depends upon how it is characterized, both in terms of what an actor "did" and what he "intended to do."

The latter comment connects directly with the significance of the use of power in social interaction. I shall make no attempt to classify substantive forms of power relation here: the facilities that may be brought to a situation of interaction range from command of verbal skills to the application of means of physical violence. The capabilities that an actor has to influence the events involved in a sequence of interaction depends upon the resources he is able to mobilize. "Resources" I treat as properties of structure; actors "possess" resources in a parallel sense to that in which they "know" rules. This is clear enough in the case, for instance, of the mobilization of authority rights in the context of interaction, where such rights "belong" to the individual actor only in the sense that he can—in principle—demand and obtain certain responses from others. Authority is a structured resource that can be potentially drawn upon by actors to influence the conduct of others. But the same holds true of many (not all) capabilities that are seemingly wholly "individualized." Thus command of verbal or dialectical skill as a facility uses as a resource knowledge of (acceptable) language structures. In its aspect as resources, power may be defined as "transformative capacity."[13]

While social systems only exist in so far as they are continually produced and reproduced via the duality of structure, the conditions influencing such processes of structuration can be analysed as "impersonal" connections. But generalizations which establish such connections are inherently unstable in respect of the shifting compass of the rationalization of action. The conceptions of structure, and structural causation, involved here cross-cut the traditional lines of the debate over the status of methodological individualism. Social systems only exist as transactions between actors; but their structural features cannot be explicated except as properties of communities or collectivities. The debate has not led to much in the way of any definite outcome in some degree because its participants have followed conventional assumptions in not recognizing a distinction between system and structure.

Notes

1. Cf. T.G. Bever and D.T. Langendoen, "The interaction of speech perception and grammatical structure in the evolution of language," in Robert R. Stockwell and Ronald K.S. Macauley, *Linguistic Change and Generative Theory*, Blommington, 1972.
2. My *New Rules of Sociological Method*, pp. 88 ff.
3. Karl Marx, *Capital*, London, 1970, vol. I, p. 572.
4. Etienne Balibar, "On reproduction," in Louis Althusser and Etienne Balibar, *Reading Capital*, London, 1970, pp. 263-4.
5. Ludwig Wittgenstein, *Philosophical Investigations*, Oxford, 1972 [New York, 1973], S217 ff. and *passim*.
6. Many philosophers have suggested that it is useful to distinguish between "constitutive" and "regulative" rules. But it can be shown that all social rules have "constitutive" and "regulative" aspects, as is suggested indeed by the common root which "rule" and "regulate" share. cf. Max Black, "The analysis of rules," in *Models and Metaphors*, Ithaca, 1962.
7. Peter Winch, *The Idea of a Social Science*, London (new edition)[New York], 1970, cf. my *New Rules of Sociological Method*, pp. 44 ff.
8. Cf. O.R. Jones, *The Private Language Argument*, London, 1971.
9. Harold Garfinkel, *Studies in Ethnomethodology*, Englewood Cliffs, 1967.
10. Alfred Schutz, *Collected Papers*, The Hague, 1967, 2 vols.; Alfred Schutz and Thomas Luckmann, *The Structures of the Life-World* [Evanston, 1973], London, 1974.
11. For a recent critique of semiology, see Dan Sperber, *Rethinking Symbolism*, Cambridge (UK), 1975.
12. Winch, op.cit., pp. 58-62.
13. Cf. "Remarks on the theory of power," pp. 129-34.

30
———

UNDERSTANDING THE THIRD TECHNOLOGICAL REVOLUTION: BELL (1919-), MANDEL (1923-1995), TOFFLER (1928-), AND CASTELLS

In this section we will see the value and limitations of social theories as aids to understanding the enormous technological, economic, and social changes that took place in the last third of the twentieth century. By 1970, data showed changes taking place in the economy. What were the best concepts and theories for making sense of these statistics? What kind of political and social future was likely to come about as a result of the technological and economic changes signalled by these data?

Daniel Bell was a leading sociologist of the postwar period. He was deeply influenced by Marx and Weber; his work responds to questions raised by these two classical theorists and does not fall easily into the tripartite categories of the period—structural functionalism, conflict theory, and symbolic interactionism. He uses Marxist concepts like capitalism and contradiction, but without Marxist faith in class conflict, proletarian consciousness, and revolution. In some of his work, like the selection here, he shares Weber's views about the expansion of rationalization.

The Coming of Post-Industrial Society: A Venture in Social Forecasting was published in 1973 in a climate of stagflation in capitalist economies, the onset of Brezhnev-era stagnation in the Soviet bloc, and the end of the long postwar economic boom. The percentage of the labour force in manufacturing was declining in the developed economies. Bell does not focus on the short-term slowdowns, but on the meaning of long-term trends; he interprets the situation as a symptom of a turning point, the cusp between industrial and post-industrial society. The trends toward post-industrial society latent in advanced industrial capitalism were now clearly visible. He identifies five key features of post-industrial society; of these five, the essential one is the application of theoretical knowledge to innovation and planning. Compare Bell's views to Robert Reich's analysis of economic change, as well as Stanley Aronowitz and William DiFazio's discussion of technology.

At almost the same moment, Ernst Mandel published *Late Capitalism*, a Marxist analysis of the same phenomena. Mandel looked at essentially the same economic data as Bell, but came to strikingly different conclusions. First of all, he rejected the term post-industrial, pointing out that the process is actually total industrialization, with advanced technology penetrating previously low-tech areas like agriculture, the production of raw materials (which have become manufactured synthetics), and the superstructure of information and ideology. This complete penetration of technology, which Mandel called the "Third Technological Revolution," corresponds to the application of theoretical knowledge in Bell's paradigm. (The First Technological Revolution was the invention of the steam engine and its use in factory production of manufactured goods—the industrial revolution; the Second Technological Revolution centred on electricity and the internal combustion engine.) Mandel wrote: "Late capitalism, far from representing a 'post-industrial society,' thus appears as the period in which all branches of the economy are fully industrialized for the first time."[1]

The reduction in turnover time of fixed capital becomes a major issue for advanced capitalism, according to Mandel. Anyone who experiences pressure to replace a perfectly good computer or to install new software after using a system for only a couple of years has a gut feeling for this problem. Systems become obsolete before they are fully developed and problem-free. The result is a paradoxical situation in which shorter and shorter product cycles require longer and longer periods of financial and technical planning. This structure of accelerated innovation and the need for long-term planning take place in the market economy with its inherent tendencies toward instability. The result is a squeeze on profits that generates pressure on firms to protect themselves from accelerated turnover in fixed capital by creating and manipulating sheltered markets. Much of the squeeze is displaced onto labour, as firms seek to lower wages in order to compensate for technology costs. Pollution, an international arms race in both nuclear and conventional weapons, and a shift of private costs into the public sector are additional fallout from firms' efforts to cope with the problem of accelerated turnover.

Bell and Mandel, looking at similar data and the same underlying economic and technological changes, came to different conclusions about society. Bell, as we see in the selection, envisioned the application of science and technology leading to increasing rationalization and centralization of power, especially at the level of national governments. Mandel believed it would lead to global social and political instability and a spiralling crisis in the capitalist system.

Twenty-five years later, neither socio-political forecast seems particularly accurate, although the Third Technological Revolution continues. The anti-statist policies of the Reagan and Thatcher period, the push toward more market and less government, the formation of supra-national free trade areas like the North American Free Trade Agreement and the European Union all seem to have prevented—or at least postponed—both Bell's and Mandel's scenarios. Governments undertook measures to reduce their role in guiding the economy. These anti-government government policies undercut the state-level planning envisioned by Bell. There is no unified social actor, like national government or an international agency, to actually order a mass society. On the contrary, international agencies like the World Trade Organization and the International Monetary Fund take action to maintain and expand markets rather than replace them with centralized planning structures.

Nor did the perennial Marxist prediction of unmanageable global crisis come true. On the contrary, like a forest fire, a series of crises cleared out the economic deadwood (often at terrible cost to people who lost their jobs and businesses) and prepared the system for new growth at the end of the century. East Asian countries moved from agrarian poverty into industrial and post-industrial development, although it was often spotty and uneven. Latin American countries experienced a return to democracy from military dictatorships in the southern cone and Central America; in many, the middle class expanded. Computers and telecommunication systems drew more of the world into a net-worked society, as sociologist Manuel Castells terms it. Poverty, pollution, and population pressures remained enormous, interlinked problems, but the market persisted as the major mechanism for innovation.

It is sobering for the fan of theory to admit that the most accurate social scenario for the Third Technological Revolution was probably Alvin Toffler's *Future Shock*. It is the least explicitly theorized of the three books, the least connected to a negative-critical tradition of social thought. Written for a mass readership, Toffler's book predicts neither centralized and rationalized planning nor growing systemic crisis, although it gently urges efforts to regulate change and cushion its impact. Toffler accepts continuity in society at the same time that he focuses on change and innovation. He implicitly assumes that most of the new technology will be absorbed through the market and that it will lead to social change by a process of diffusion and gradual adaptation. The "Third Wave" as Toffler calls the Third Technological Revolution, will produce enormous change, but in an incremental fashion, in an organic process embedded in the market and in the organizations and movements of civil society. Impermanence, novelty, and diversity will characterize culture.

A recent addition to the analysis of post-industrial technology and society is Manuel Castells's trilogy, *The Information Age*, especially its first volume, *The Rise of the Network Society*. Castells argues that in the 1970s capitalism entered a new phase of informationalism, characterized by new technologies of computerization, communication networks, biotechnology, and multimedia systems. Using concepts derived from both Karl Marx and Daniel Bell, Castells makes clear that he considers informationalism a new mode of development while capitalism remains the prevailing mode of production. Capitalist relations of production shape the form and use of technological innovations, but informationalism has a logic of its own that produces changes in social relations and institutions.

The informational mode of development and network society are globalizing and disruptive of local and traditional cultures; thus, they generate a backlash in the form of movements and the development of anti-network identities and communities, such as Christian and Islamic fundamentalisms, the Zapatistas, and the militia/patriot movement in the United States. Yet these movements themselves use new network technologies of communication. Like earlier forms of capitalism, informational capitalism develops unevenly; some global regions (North America, Western Europe, the Pacific Basin) move ahead while others (Africa south of the Sahara, Russia) are pushed to the margins. Unlike Bell, Castells observes a weakening of centralized poltiical systems, especially the nation-state. Informationalism develops through market mechanisms, corporate decision-making, and communication networks rather than by state-level planning. Like Giddens, Castells examines the way informational capitalism disembeds social processes and relationships from time and space through lightning-fast, computer-mediated communication across the globe. Informational capitalism is also characterized by a pervasive, corporate-produced multimedia environment that makes the expression of self-identity and historically rooted cultures increasingly difficult. Castells comments:

> ... global networks of instrumental exchanges selectively switch on and off individuals, groups, regions, and even countries, according to their relevance in fulfilling the goals processed in the network, in a relentless flow of strategic decisions. It follows a fundamental split between abstract, universal instrumentalism, and historically rooted, particularistic identities. Our societies are increasingly structured around a bipolar opposition between the Net and the Self.[2]

Notes
1. Ernst Mandel, *Late Capitalism* (London: New Left Books, 1975) 191.
2. Manuel Castells. *The Network Society* (Malden, MA and Oxford, UK: Blackwell, 1996) 3.

Readings
Bell, Daniel. *The Cultural Contradictions of Capitalism.* New York: Basic Books, 1996.

Castells, Manuel. *The Information Age.* Malden, MA, and Oxford, UK: Blackwell, 1996.

Mandel, Ernst. *Late Capitalism.* London: Verso, 1975.

Toffler, Alvin. *Future Shock.* New York: Random House, 1970.

The Coming of Post-Industrial Society: A Venture in Social Forecasting
DANIEL BELL

Introduction

The concept of the post-industrial society is a large generalization. Its meaning can be more easily understood if one specifies five dimensions, or components, of the term:

1. Economic sector: the change from a goods-producing to a service economy;
2. Occupational distribution: the pre-eminence of the professional and technical class;
3. Axial principle: the centrality of theoretical knowledge as the source of innovation and of policy formulation for the society.
4. Future orientation: the control of technology and technological assessment;
5. Decision-making: the creation of a new "intellectual technology."

Creation of a service economy. About thirty years ago, Colin Clark, in his *Conditions of Economic Progress,* analytically divided the economy into three sectors—primary, secondary, and tertiary—the primary being principally agriculture; the secondary, manufacturing or industrial; and the tertiary, services. Any economy is a mixture in different proportions of each. But Clark argues that, as nations became industrialized, there was an inevitable trajectory whereby, because of sectoral differences in productivity, a larger proportion of the labor force would pass into manufacturing, and as national incomes rose, there would be a greater demand for services and a corresponding shift in that slope.

By this criterion, the first and simplest characteristic of a post-industrial society is that the majority of the labor force is no longer engaged in agriculture or manufacturing but in services, which are defined, residually, as trade, finance, transport, health, recreation, research, education, and government.

Today, the overwhelming number of countries in the world are still dependent on the primary sector: agriculture, mining, fishing, forestry. These economies are based entirely on natural resources. Their productivity is low, and they are subject to wide swings of income because of the fluctuations of raw material and primary-product prices. In Africa and Asia, agrarian economies account for more than 70 percent of the labor force. In western and northern Europe, Japan, and the Soviet Union, the major portion of the labor force is engaged in industry or the manufacture of goods. The United States today is the only nation in the world in which the service sector accounts for more than half the total employment and more than half the Gross National Product. It is the first service economy, the first nation, in which the major portion of the population is engaged in neither agrarian nor industrial pursuits. Today about 60 percent of the United States labor force is engaged in services; by 1980, the figure will have risen to 70 percent.

The term "services," if used generically, risks being deceptive about the actual trends in the society. Many agrarian societies such as India have a high proportion of persons engaged in services, but of a personal sort (e.g. household servants) because labor is cheap and usually underemployed. In an industrial society different services tend to increase because of the need for auxiliary help for production, e.g. transportation and distribution. But in a post-industrial society the emphasis is on a different kind of service. If we group services as personal (retail stores, laundries, garages, beauty shops); business (banking and finance, real estate, insurance); transportation, communication and utilities, and health, education, research, and government; then it is the growth of the last category which is decisive for post-industrial society. And this is the category that represents the expansion of new intelligentsia—in the universities, research organizations, professions, and government.

The pre-eminence of the professional and technical class. The second way of defining a post-industrial society is through the change in occupational distributions; i.e. not only *where* people work, but the *kind* of work they do. In large measure, occupation is the most important determinant of class and stratification in the society.

The onset of industrialization created a new phenomenon, the semi-skilled worker who could be trained within a few weeks to do the simple routine operations required in machine work. Within industrial societies, the semi-skilled worker has been the single largest category in the labor force. The expansion of the service economy, with its emphasis on office work, education, and government, has naturally brought about a shift to white-collar occupations. In the United States, by 1956, the number of white-collar workers, for the first time in the history of industrial civilization, outnumbered the blue collar workers in the occupational structure. Since then the ratio has been widening steadily; by 1970 the white-collar workers outnumbered the blue-collar by more than five to four.

But the most startling change has been the growth of professional and technical employment—jobs that usually require some college education—at a rate twice that of the average.

The primacy of theoretical knowledge. In identifying a new and emerging social system it is not only in the extrapolated social trends, such as the creation of a service economy or the expansion of the professional and technical class, that one seeks to understand fundamental social change. Rather, it is through some specifically defining characteristic of a social system, which becomes the axial principle, that one establishes a conceptual schema. Industrial society is the coordination of machines and men for the production of goods. Post-industrial society is organized around knowledge, for the purpose of social control and the directing of innovation and change; and this in turn gives rise to new social relationships and new structures which have to be managed politically.

Now, knowledge has of course been necessary in the functioning of any society. What is distinctive about the post-industrial society is the change in the character of knowledge itself. What has become decisive for the organization of decisions and the direction of change is the certainty of *theoretical* knowledge—the primacy of theory over empiricism and the codification of knowledge into abstract systems of symbols that, as in any axiomatic system, can be used to illuminate many different and varied areas of experience.

Every modern society now lives by innovation and the social control of change, and tries to anticipate the future in order to plan ahead. This commitment to social control introduces the need for planning and forecasting into society. It is the altered awareness of the nature of innovation that makes theoretical knowledge so crucial.

One can see this, first, in the changed relationship between science and technology. Almost all the major industries we still have—steel, electric power, telegraph, telephone, automobiles, aviation—were nineteenth-century industries (although steel begins in the eighteenth century and aviation in the twentieth), in that they were mainly the creation of inventors, inspired and talented tinkerers who were indifferent to science and the fundamental laws underlying their investigations. Kelly and Bessemer, who (independently) created the oxidation process that makes possible the steel converter and the mass production of steel, were unaware of their contemporary, Henry Clifton Sorby, whose work in metallurgy disclosed the true microstructure of steel. Alexander Graham Bell, inventor of the telephone, was in Clerk Maxwell's opinion a mere elocutionist who "to gain his private ends [money] has become an electrician." Edison's work on "etheric sparks," which led to the development of the electric light and generated a vast new revolution in technology, was undertaken outside the theoretical research in electromagnetism and even in hostility to it. But the further development of electrodynamics, particularly in the replacement of steam engines, could only come from engineers with formal training in mathematical physics. Edison as one biographer has written, lacked "the power of abstraction."[1]

What might be called the first "modern" industry, because of its intricate linking of science and technology, is chemistry, since one must have a theoretical knowledge of the macromolecules one is manipulating in order to do chemical synthesis—the recombination and transformation of compounds.[2] In 1909 Walter Nerst and Fritz Haber converted nitrogen and hydrogen to produce synthetic ammonia. Working from theoretical principles first predicated by the Frenchman Henri Le Chatelier in 1888, the two German chemists provided a spectacular confirmation of Kant's dictum that there is nothing so practical as a good theory.[3] The irony, however, lies in the use of the result.

War is a technological forcing house, but modern war has yoked science to technology in a radically new way. Before World War I, every General Staff calculated that Germany would either win a quick, smashing victory or, if France could hold, the war would end quickly in a German defeat (either in the field or at the negotiating table). The reasoning was based on the simple fact that Chile was Germany's (and the world's) major source of the natural nitrates needed for fertilizer and for explosives and, in wartime, Germany's access to Chile would be cut off by the British Navy. In 1913 Germany used about 225,000 tons of nitrogen, half of which was imported. Stocks began to fall, but the Haber-Bosch process for the manufacture of synthetic ammonia developed so rapidly that by 1917 it accounted for 45 percent of Germany's production of nitrogen compounds. By the armistice Germany was almost self-sufficient in nitrogen,[4] and because she was able to hold out, the war became a protracted struggle of static trench warfare and slaughter.

In the latter sense, World War I was the very last of the "old" wars of human civilization. But with the new role of science it was also the first of the "new" wars. The eventual symbolic fusion of science and war was, of course, in World War II the atom bomb. It was a demonstration, as Gerald Holton has written, "that a chain of operations, starting in a scientific laboratory, can result in an event of the scale and suddenness of a mythological occurrence." Since the end of World War II the extraordinary development of scientific technology has led to hydrogen bombs, distant-early-warning networks coordinated in real time through computer systems, intercontinental ballistics missiles, and, in Vietnam, the beginning of an "automated" battlefield through the use of large-scale electronic sensing devices and computer-controlled retaliatory strikes. War, too, has now come under the "terrible" dominion of science, and the shape of war, like all other human activity, has been drastically changed.

In a less direct but equally important way, the changing relation between theory and empiricism is reflected in the formulation of government policy, particularly in the management of the economy....

The development of modern economics, in this respect, has been possible because of the computer. Computers have provided the bridge between the body of formal theory and the large data bases of recent years; out of this has come modern econometrics and the policy orientation of economics.[5] One major area has been the models of interdependencies among industries such as the input-output matrices developed by Wassily Leontieff, which simplify the general equilibrium system of Walras and show, empirically, the transactions between industries, or sectors, or regions. The input-output matrix of the American economy is a grid of 81 industries, from Footwear and other Leather Products (1) to Scrap, Used, and Secondhand Goods (81) grouped into the productive, distributive, and service sectors of the economy. A dollar-flow table shows the distribution of the output of any one industry to each (or any) of the other 80 sectors. The input-output matrix shows the mix and proportions of inputs (from each or several industries) which go into a specific unit of output (in dollar value or physical production terms). An inverse matrix shows the indirect demand generated by a product as well as the direct demand. Thus, one can trace the effect of the final consumer demand say for automobiles on the amount (or value) of iron ore, even though the automobile industry buys no iron ore directly. Or one can see what proportion of iron ore, as a raw material, goes into such final products as autos, ships, buildings, and the like. In this way, one can chart the changes in the nature of final demands in terms of the differential effects on each sector of the economy.[6] Input-output tables are now the basic tools for national economic planning and they have been applied in regional planning, through computerized models, to test the effect on trade of changes in population distributions.

The large econometric models of the economy, such as the Brookings model discussed earlier, allow one to do economic forecasting, while the existence of such computer models now enables economists to do policy "experiments," such as the work of Fromm and Taubman in simulating eight different combinations of fiscal and monetary policy for the period 1960-1962, in order to see which policy might have been the most effective.[7] With these tools one can test different theories to see whether it is now possible to do "fine tuning" of the economy.

It would be technocratic to assume that the managing of an economy is only a technical offshoot of a theoretical model. The overriding considerations are political, and set the frames of decision. Yet the economic models indicate the boundaries of constraint within which one can operate, and they can specify the consequences of alternative political choices.[8] The crucial point is that economic policy formulations, though not an exact art, now derive from theory, and often must find justification in theory. The fact that a Nixon administration in 1972 could casually accept the concept of a "full employment budget," which sets a level of government expenditures *as if* there were full utilization of resources (thus automatically accepting deficit financing) is itself a measure of the degree of economic sophistication that government has acquired in the past thirty years.

The joining of science, technology, and economics in recent years is symbolized by the phrase "research and development" (R & D). Out of this have come the science-based industries (computers, electronics, optics, polymers) which increasingly dominate the manufacturing sector of the society and which provide the lead, in product cycles, for the advanced industrial societies. But these science-based industries, unlike industries which arose in the nineteenth century, are primarily dependent on theoretical work prior to production. The computer would not exist without the work in solid-state physics initiated forty years ago by Felix Bloch. The laser came directly out of I.I. Rabi's research thirty years ago on molecular optical beams. (One can say, without being overly facile, that U.S. Steel is the paradigmatic corporation of the first third of the twentieth century, General Motors of the second third of the century, and IBM of the final third. The contrasting attitudes of the corporations toward research and development are a measure of these changes.)

What is true of technology and economics is true, albeit differentially, of all modes of knowledge: the advances in a field become increasingly dependent on the primacy of theoretical work, which codifies what is known and points the way to empirical confirmation. In effect, theoretical knowledge increasingly becomes the strategic resource, the axial principle, of a society. And the university, research organizations and intellectual institutions, where theoretical knowledge is codified and enriched, become the axial structures of the emergent society.

The planning of technology. With the new modes of technological forecasting, my fourth criterion, the post-industrial societies may be able to reach a new dimension of societal change, the planning and control of technological growth.

Modern industrial economies became possible when societies were able to create new institutional mechanisms to build up savings (through banks, insurance companies, equity capital through the stock market, and government levies, i.e. loans or taxes) and to use this money for investment. The ability consistently to re-invest annually at least 10 percent of GNP became the basis of what W.W. Rostow has called the "take-off" point for economic growth. But a modern society, in order to avoid stagnation or "maturity" (however that vague word is defined), has had to open up new technological frontiers in order to maintain productivity and higher standards of living. If societies become more dependent on technology and new innovation, then a hazardous "indeterminacy" is introduced into the system. (Marx argues that a capitalist economy had to expand or die. Later Marxists, such as Lenin or Rosa Luxemburg, assumed that such expansion necessarily had to be geographical; hence the theory of imperialism. But the greater measure of expansion has been capital-intensive or technological.) Without new technology, how can growth be maintained? The development of new forecasting and "mapping techniques" makes possible a novel phase in economic history—the conscious, planned advance of technological change, and therefore the reduction of indeterminacy about the economic future (Whether this can actually be done is a pregnant question....)

But technological advance, as we have learned, has deleterious side effects, with second-order and third-order consequences that are often overlooked and certainly unintended. The increasing use of cheap fertilizers was one of the elements that created the revolution in agricultural productivity, but the run-off of nitrates into the rivers has been one of the worst sources of pollution. The introduction of DDT as a pesticide saved many crops, but also destroyed wildlife and birds. In automobiles, the gasoline engine was more effective than steam, but it has smogged the air. The point is that the introduction of technology was uncontrolled, and its initiators were interested only in single-order effects.

Yet none of this has to be. The mechanisms of control are available as well. As a number of studies by a panel of the National Academy of Science has shown, if these technologies had been "assessed" before they were introduced, alternative technologies or arrangements could have been considered. As the study group reported:

> The panel believes that in some cases an injection of the broadened criteria urged here might have led, or might in the future lead, to the selection or encouragement of different technologies or at least modified ones—functional alternatives with lower "social costs" (though not necessarily lower total costs). For example, bioenvironmental rather than primarily chemical devices might have been used to control agricultural pests, or there might have been design alternatives to the purely chemical means of enhancing engine efficiency, or mass transit alternatives to further reliance upon the private automobile.[9]

Technology assessment is feasible. What it requires is a political mechanism that will allow such studies to be made and set up criteria for the regulation of new technologies.[10]...

The rise of a new intellectual technology. "The greatest invention of the nineteenth century," Alfred North Whitehead wrote, "was the invention of the method of invention. A new method entered into life. In order to understand our epoch, we can neglect all the details of change, such as railways, telegraphs, radios, spinning machines, synthetic dyes. We must concentrate on the method itself; that is the real novelty, which has broken up the foundations of the old civilization."[11]

In the same spirit, one can say that the methodological promise of the second half of the twentieth century is the management of organized complexity (the complexity of large organizations and systems, the complexity of theory with a large number of variables), the identification and implementation of strategies for rational choice in games against nature and games between persons, and the development of a new intellectual technology which, by the end of the century, may be as salient in human affairs as machine technology has been for the past century and a half....

I have called the applications of these new developments "intellectual technology" for two reasons. Technology, as Harvey Brooks defines it, "is the use of scientific knowledge to specify ways of doing things in a *reproducible* manner."[12] In this sense, the organization of a hospital or an international trade system is a *social* technology, as the automobile or a numerically controlled tool is a *machine* technology. An *intellectual* technology is the substitution of algorithms (problem-solving rules) for intuitive judgments. These algorithms may be embodied in an automatic machine or a computer program or a set of instructions based on some statistical or mathematical formula; the statistical and logical techniques that are used in dealing with "organized complexity" are efforts to formalize a set of decision rules. The second reason is that without the computer, the new mathematical tools would have been primarily of intellectual interest, or used, in Anatol Rappoport's phrase, with "very low resolving power." The chain of multiple calculations that can be readily made, the multivariate analyses that keep track of the detailed interactions of many variables, the simultaneous solution of several hundred equations—these feats which are the foundation of comprehensive numeracy—are possible only with a tool of intellectual *technology,* the computer.

What is distinctive about the new intellectual technology is its effort to define rational action and to identify the means of achieving it. All situations involve constraints (costs, for example) and contrasting alternatives. And all action takes place under conditions of certainty, risk, or uncertainty. Certainty exists when the constraints are fixed and known. Risk means that a set of possible outcomes is known and the probabilities for each outcome can be stated. Uncertainty is the case when the set of possible outcomes can be stipulated, but the probabilities are completely unknown. Further, situations can be defined as "games against nature," in which the constraints are environmental, or "games between persons," in which each person's course of action is necessarily shaped by the reciprocal judgments of the others' intentions.[13] In all these situations, the desirable action is a strategy that leads to the optimal or "best" solution; i.e. one which either maximizes the outcome or, depending upon the assessment of the risks and uncertainties, tries to minimize the losses. Rationality can be defined as judging, between two alternatives, which one is capable of yielding that preferred outcome.[14]

Intellectual technology makes its most ambitious claims in systems analysis. A system, in this sense, is any set of reciprocal relationships in which a variation in the character (or numerical value) of one of the elements will have determinate—and possibly measurable—consequences for all the others in the system. A human organism is a determinate system; a work-group whose members are engaged in specialized tasks for a common objective is a goal-setting system; a pattern of bombers and bases forms a variable system; the economy as a whole is a loose system.

The problem of the number of variables has been a crucial factor in the burgeoning fields of systems analysis for military or business decisions. In the design of an airplane, say, a single performance parameter (speed, or distance, or capacity) cannot be the measure of the intrinsic worth of a design, since these are all interrelated....

The goal of the new intellectual technology is, neither more nor less, to realize a social alchemist's dream: the dream of "ordering" the mass society. In this society today, millions of persons daily make billions of decisions about what to buy, how many children to have, whom to vote for, what job to take, and the like. Any single choice may be as unpredictable as the quantum atom responding erratically to the measuring instrument, yet the aggregate patterns could be charted as neatly as the geometer triangulates the height and the horizon. If the computer is the tool, then decision theory is its master. Just as Pascal sought to play dice with God, and the physiocrats attempted to draw an economic grid that would array all exchanges among men, so the decision theorists seek their own *tableau entier*—the compass of rationality, the "best" solution to the choices perplexing men.

That this dream—as utopian, in its way, as the dreams of a perfect commonwealth—has faltered is laid, on the part of its believers, to the human resistance to rationality. But it may also be due to the very idea of rationality which guides the enterprise—the definition of function without a justification of reason. This, too, is a theme I explore in these essays.

Notes
1. Matthew Josephson, *Edison* (New York, 1959), p. 361.
2. Aviation is an interesting transition. The first inventors were tinkerers, but the field could develop only through the use of scientific principles. Langley (1891) and Zahm (1902-1903) started the new science of aerodynamics by studying the behavior of air currents over different types of airfoils. At the same time, in 1900,

the Wright brothers began tinkering with gliders, and in 1903 put a gasoline-powered engine into an airplane. But further work was possible only through the development, after 1908, of experiments (such as models in wind tunnels) and mathematical calculations (such as airflows over different angles of wings) based on physical laws.

3. See Eduard Farber, "Man Makes His Materials," in Kransberg and Pursell, eds. *Technology and Western Civilization,* vol. 2 (New York, 1967).

4. See L.F. Haber, *The Chemical Industry, 1900-1930* (Oxford, 1971), chap. 7, pp. 198-203. As Haber writes:

> "The Haber process ... was still largely an unknown factor when the Great War broke out. The synthesis of ammonia ... represents one of the most important advances in industrial chemistry.... The process, discovered by Fritz Haber and developed industrially by Carl Bosch, was the first application of high-pressure synthesis; the technology of ammonia production, appropriately modified, was used later in the synthesis of methanol and the hydrogenation of coal to petroleum. Its influence extends to present-day techniques of oil refining and use of cracker gases from refining operations for further synthesis." Ibid., p. 90.

5. Charles Wolf, Jr., and John H. Enns have provided a comprehensive review of these developments in their paper "Computers and Economics," Rand Paper P. 4724. I am indebted to them for a number of illustrations.

6. Mathematically speaking, an input-output matrix represents a set of simultaneous linear equations—in this case 81 equations with 81 variables which are solved by matrix algebra. See Wassilly Leontieff, *The Structure of the American Economy: Theoretical and Empirical Explorations in Input-Output Analysis* (New York, 1953). Ironically, when the Bureau of Labor Statistics tried to set up an input-output grid for the American economy in 1949, it was opposed by business on the ground that it was a tool for socialism, and the money was initially denied.

7. Their conclusions: that the largest impact on real GNP came from increases in government nondurable and construction expenditures. Income-tax cuts were less of a stimulant than increase in expenditures. Gary Fromm and Paul Taubman, *Policy Simulations with an Econometric Model* (Brookings Institution, Washington, D.C., 1968), cited in Wolf and Enns, op. cit.

8. With modern economic tools, Robert M. Solow argues, an administration can, within limits, get the measure of economic activity it wants, for the level of government spending can redress the deficits of private spending and step up economic activity. But in so doing, an administration has to choose between inflation or full employment; this dilemma seems to be built into the market structure of capitalist economies. An administration has to make a trade-off—and this is a political choice. Democrats have preferred full employment and inflation, Republicans price stability and slow economic growth.

In the last few years, however, there has been the new phenomenon—simultaneous high unemployment and high inflation. For reasons that are not clear, unemployment no longer "disciplines" an economy into bringing prices down, either because of substantial welfare cushions (e.g. unemployment insurance), wage-push pressure in organized industries, or the persistent expectation of price rises that discounts inflation.

The two turning points in modern economic policy were President Kennedy's tax cut in 1964, which canonized Keynesian principles in economic policy, and President Nixon's imposition of wage and price controls in 1971. Though mandatory controls were relaxed in 1973, the option to use them now remains.

9. *Technology: Processes of Assessment and Choice,* Report of the National Academy of Sciences, U.S. House of Representatives, committee on Science and Astronautics, July 1969.

10. To further the idea of technology assessment, the National Academy of Engineering undertook three studies in developing fields, that of computer-assisted instruction and instructional television; subsonic aircraft noise; and multiphasic screening in health diagnosis. The study concluded that technology assessment was feasible, and outlined the costs and scope of the necessary studies. In the case of technological teaching aids, the study considered eighteen different impacts they might have. In the case of noise, they examined the costs and consequences of five alternative strategies, from relocating airports or soundproofing nearby homes to modifying the airplanes or their flight patterns. See *A Study of Technology Assessment,* Report of the Committee on Public Engineering Policy, national Academy of Engineering, July 1969.

The idea of "technology assessment" grew largely out of studies made by the House Science and Astronautics Committee, and in 1967 a bill was introduced in the House by Congressman Daddario for a Technology Assessment Board. The bill was passed in 1972 and the Congress, not the Executive, is charged with setting up a Technology Assessment Office.

11. *Science and the Modern World*, p. 141.

12. Harvey Brooks, "Technology and the Ecological Crisis," lecture given at Amherst, May 9, 1971, p. 13 from unpublished text, emphasis added. For an application of these views, see the reports of two committees chaired by Professor Brooks, Technology, Processes of Assessment and *Choice, Report of the National Academy of Science,* published by the Committee on Science and Astronauticism, U.S. House of Representatives, July 1969; and, *Science Growth and Society*, OECD (Paris, 1971).

13. Most of the day-to-day problems in economics and management involve decision-making under conditions of certainty; i.e. the constraints are known. These are such problems as proportions of product mixes under know assumptions of cost and price, production scheduling by size, network paths, and the like. Since the objectives are clear (the most efficient routing, or the best profit yield from a product mix), the problems are largely mathematical and can be solved by such techniques as linear programming. The theory of linear programming derives from a 1937 paper by John von Neumann the general equilibrium of a uniformly expanding closed economy. Many of the computational procedures were developed by the Soviet economist L.V. Kantorovich, whose work was ignored by the regime until Stalin's death. Similar techniques were devised in the late 1940s by the Rand

mathematician G.B. Dantzig, in his simplex method. The practical application of linear programming had to await the development of the electronic computer and its ability (in some transportation problems, for example) to handle 3200 equations and 600,000 variables in sequence. Robert Dorfman has applied linear programming to the theory of the firm, and Dorfman, Samuelson and Solow used it in 1958 in an inter-industry model of the economy to allow for substitutability of supply and a criterion function that allows a choice of solutions for different objectives within a specified sector of final demand.

Criteria for decision-making under conditions of uncertainty were introduced by the Columbia mathematical statistician Abraham Wald in 1939. It specifies a "maximin" criterion in which one is guided by an expectation of the worst outcome. Leonid Hurwicz and L.J. Savage have developed other strategies, such as Savage's charmingly named "criteria of regret," whose subjective probabilities may cause one to increase or decrease a risk.

Game theory has a long history but the decisive turn occurred in a 1928 paper of John von Neumann which provided a mathematical proof of a general minimax strategy for a two-person game. The 1944 book by von Neumann and Morgenstern, *Theory of games and Economic Behavior* (Princeton), extended the theory of games with more than two persons and applied the theorem to economic behavior. The strategy proposed by von Neumann and Morgenstern—that of minimax, or the minimization of maximum loss- is defined as the rational course under conditions of uncertainty.

Games-and-decision theory was given an enormous boost during World War II, when its use was called "operations research." There was, for example, the "duel" between the airplane and the submarine. The former had to figure out the "best" search pattern for air patrol of a given area; the other had to find the best escape pattern when under surveillance. Mathematicians in the Anti-Submarine Warfare Operations Research Group, using a 1928 paper of von Neumann, figured out a tactical answer.

The game-theory idea has been widely applied—sometimes as metaphor, sometimes to specify numerical values for possible outcomes—in bargaining and conflict situations. See Thomas C. Schelling, *The Strategy of Conflict* (Cambridge, Mass., 1960).

14. R. Duncan Luce and Howard Raiffa, *Games and Decisions* (New York, 1957). My discussion of rationality is adapted from the definition on p. 50; that of risk, certainty, and uncertainty from p. 13.

31

MARSHALL MCLUHAN (1911-1980)

Marshall McLuhan was a theorist of literature whose ideas about media and global culture stimulated discussion among social theorists. He was a quirky writer, given to aphorisms, puns, hyperbole, and provocative fragments, rather than a systematic and consistent style of exposition. He invented several phrases that captured the popular imagination and continue to be useful pointers to key features of contemporary culture: "The medium is the message" and "the global village."

McLuhan periodized human history into three phases, each characterized by a patterning of human relationships, activities, and technologies through which culture is formed: Oral, written/print, and television. Each pattern is associated with a distinct form of consciousness, a distinct mentality. McLuhan was no more a technological determinist than Marx; for both, technology (or *techne* for McLuhan, who liked the Greek concept) is a complex of human practices, not simply machinery or other physical objects by themselves.

Oral societies are characterized by intensely felt personal relationships; communication is always a direct interpersonal act. The person as speaker and the group as listener and responder are closely connected to each other. The person is important, but always embedded in the life of the group. Variation and multiplicity are possible. For example, myths and legends may have multiple versions, each one as good as the other. Tradition appears to dominate the society, yet the oral medium permits a constant flux of small changes, as tradition is effortlessly reworded and reinterpreted to fit new circumstances. Many oral societies have polytheistic or animist conceptions of the sacred, corresponding to hearing of many voices. The world teems with spiritual beings.

The way people think and feel in societies in which oral communication is the only (or predominant) medium is different from the thoughts and feelings of people in societies dominated by writing. Although writing had been around for several thousand years, the written word became the leading mass medium with the invention of movable type. McLuhan invented the term "Gutenberg Galaxy" to refer to the constellation of mentalities, thought patterns, and cultural forms characteristic of societies organized around the written and printed word as the medium of communication.

Writing and print shape a different mentality or form of consciousness. The individual, rather than the person embedded in group life, stands out. Beginning with the sacred books of the monotheistic faiths (Judaism, Christianity, and Islam), and greatly accelerated by the printed word and the Protestant

Reformation, the realm of the sacred narrows to a single transcendent and omnipotent God, known through his indisputable Word. Thought becomes highly linear, sequential, and analytical. For McLuhan, writing is a "hot" medium, a medium that forces a specific interpretation on the receiver of the message.

In a reversal of oral societies' effortless transformation of tradition through retelling, writing preserves the past in the perfected form of the book, and yet—or therefore—has a strong sense of abandoning the past. This sense may be one of progress and scientific development, or it may be an outraged fundamentalism that demands to return to tradition; in either case, there is a sense of historical change. In both oral and written cultures, the past is both preserved and annihilated, but in diametrically opposite ways. In oral cultures, people are attached to traditions but constantly, continuously, and unconsciously transform them in the retelling. In written cultures, the past is put into a physical container, the book, which establishes a fixed point in time and produces consciousness of the movement of history.

Radio extended some of the characteristics of writing. For McLuhan, radio is a particularly "hot" medium, that rapidly brought into existence a generation of political orators who created intense feelings in the listeners—Hitler, Father Coughlin, and others on the fascist right; Franklin Roosevelt and his fireside chats; and orators of the anti-imperialist movements, especially in the Arab world. Radio forces the imagination into a narrow channel of words and feelings.

Television marks the beginning of a new era. The medium of television diffuses the message, not just because television is blurry (a problem that can be solved by high-definition transmissions), but for several other reasons as well, such as multiple channels and the disjuncture between word and image. Television is a "cool" medium that allows the viewer a wide range of possibilities in interpreting images. Indeed, television has wiped out the intensity of the political orator who now seems ridiculous ranting and raving in a cool medium. Irony (itself a form of message based on the existence of multiple levels), detachment, playfulness, and multiple interpretations characterize television consciousness.

The culture of television recreates some features of oral culture, especially ambiguity, greater tolerance of multiple interpretations, and receiver involvement in decoding messages. It therefore reawakens some characteristics of oral culture. But McLuhan was not offering a cyclical theory of history; the reawakened characteristics of oral culture are contextualized in completely new circumstances, and television creates its own forms of consciousness.

As a Canadian, McLuhan was keenly interested in how media shift identities. He saw that Canadian national identity was challenged both by ethnic/cultural loyalties within Canada (especially among Francophones and First

Nations) and by the economic and cultural dominance of the United States. He suggested that one of the ways in which television impacts modern identity is a "retribalization." This retribalization does not mean only the re-awakening of ethnic/cultural solidarities that challenge modern nation states from within, it also means a global rebuilding of village life, an intense, communal, and concrete type of consciousness that repeats some features of oral cultures. Television creates "the global village," transnational identities, worldwide information flows, global gossip, and a sense of interconnectedness.

In selections from *Understanding Media*, McLuhan offers some of the defining characteristics of hot and cool media. He comments on the role of ads in modern consciousness, introducing the notion of icon as a compressed image and mosaic as a text or image of fragments glued together.

Readings

Ang, Ien. *Living Room Wars: Rethinking Media Audiences for a Postmodern World*. New York and London: Routledge, 1995.

McLuhan, Marshall. *Gutenberg Galaxy: The Making of Typographic Man*. Toronto: University of Toronto Press, 1962.

—. *Understanding Media*. Cambridge, MA: MIT Press, 1994.

McLuhan, Marshall, and Bruce Powers. *The Global Village: Transformations in World Life and Media in the 21st Century*. New York: Oxford University Press, 1992.

Understanding Media
MARSHALL MCLUHAN

Media Hot and Cold

"The rise of the waltz," explained Curt Sachs in the *World History of the Dance*, "was a result of that longing for truth, simplicity, closeness to nature, and primitivism, which the last two-thirds of the eighteenth century fulfilled." In the century of jazz we are likely to overlook the emergence of the waltz as a hot and explosive human expression that broke through the formal feudal barriers of courtly and choral dance styles.

There is a basic principle that distinguishes a hot medium like radio from a cool one like the telephone, or a hot medium like the movie from a cool one like TV. A hot medium is one that extends one single sense in "high definition." High definition is the state of being well filled with data. A photograph is, visually, "high definition." A cartoon is "low definition," simply because very little visual information is provided. Telephone is a cool medium, or one of low definition, because the ear is given a meager amount of information. And speech is a cool medium of low definition, because so little is given and so much has to be filled in by the listener. On the other hand, hot media do not leave so much to be filled in or completed by the audience. Hot media are, therefore, low in participation, and cool media are high in participation or completion by the audience. Naturally, therefore, a hot medium like radio has very different effects on the user from a cool medium like the telephone.

A cool medium like hieroglyphic or ideogrammic written characters has very different effects from the hot and explosive medium of the phonetic alphabet. The alphabet, when pushed to a high degree of abstract visual intensity, became typography. The printed word with its specialist intensity, burst the bonds of medieval corporate guilds and monasteries, creating extreme individualist patterns of enterprise and monopoly. But the typical reversal occurred when extremes of monopoly brought back the corporation, with its impersonal empire over many lives. The hotting-up of the medium of writing to repeatable print intensity led to nationalism and the religious wars of the sixteenth century. The heavy and unwieldy media, such as stone, are time binders. Used for writing, they are very cool indeed, and serve to unify the ages; whereas paper is a hot medium that serves to unify spaces horizontally, both in political and entertainment empires.

Any hot medium allows of less participation than a cool one, as a lecture makes for less participation than a seminar, and a book for less than dialogue. With print many earlier forms were excluded from life and art, and many were given strange new intensity. But our own time is crowded with examples of the principle that the hot form excludes, and the cool one includes. When ballerinas began to dance on their toes a century ago, it was felt that the art of the ballet had acquired anew "spirituality." With this new intensity, male figures were excluded from ballet. The role of women had also become fragmented with the advent of industrial specialism and the explosion of home functions into laundries, bakeries, and hospitals on the periphery of the community. Intensity or high definition engenders specialism and fragmentation in living as in entertainment, which explains why any intense experience must be "forgotten," "censored," and reduced to a very cool state before it can be "learned" or assimilated. The Freudian "censor" is less of a moral function than an indispensable condition of learning. Were we to accept fully and directly every shock to our various structures of awareness, we would soon be nervous wrecks, doing double-takes and pressing panic buttons every minute. The "censor" protects our central system of values, as it does our physical nervous system by simply cooling off the onset of experience a great deal. For many people, this cooling system brings on a lifelong state of psychic *rigor mortis*, or of somnambulism, particularly observable in periods of new technology.

An example of the disruptive impact of a hot technology succeeding a cool one is given by Robert Theobald in *The Rich and the Poor.* When Australian natives were given steel axes by the missionaries, their culture, based on the stone axe, collapsed. The stone axe had not only been scarce but had always been a basic status symbol of male importance. The missionaries provided quantities of sharp steel axes and gave them to women and children. The men had even to borrow these from the women, causing a collapse of male dignity. A tribal and feudal hierarchy of traditional kind collapses quickly when it meets any hot medium of the mechanical, uniform, and repetitive kind. The medium of money or wheel or writing, or any other form of specialist speed-up of exchange and information, will serve to fragment a tribal structure....

Ads

Keeping Upset with the Joneses

The continuous pressure is to create ads more and more in the image of audience motives and desires. The product matters less as the audience participation increases. An extreme example is the corset series that protests that "it is not the corset that you feel." The need is to make the ad include the audience experience. The product and the public response become a single complex pattern. The art of advertising has wondrously come to fulfill the early definition of anthropology as "the science of man embracing woman." The steady trend in advertising is to manifest the product as an integral part of large social purposes and processes. With very large budgets the commercial artists have tended to develop the ad into an icon, and icons are not specialist fragments or aspects but unified and compressed images of complex kind. They focus a large region of experience in tiny compass. The trend in ads, then, is away from the consumer picture of product to the producer image of process. The corporate image of process includes the consumer in the producer role as well.

This powerful new trend in ads toward the iconic image has greatly weakened the position of the magazine industry in general and the picture magazines in particular. Magazine features have long employed the pictorial treatment of themes and news. Side by side with these magazines features that present shots and fragmentary points of view, there are the new massive iconic ads with their compressed images that include producer and consumer, seller and society in a single image. The ads make the features seem pale, weak, and anemic. The features belong to the old pictorial world that preceded TV mosaic imagery.

It is the powerful mosaic and iconic thrust in our experience since TV that explains the paradox of the upsurge of *Time* and *Newsweek* and similar magazines. These magazines present the news in a compressed mosaic form that is a real parallel to the ad world. Mosaic news is neither narrative, nor point of view, nor explanation, nor comment. It is a corporate image in depth of the community in action and invites maximal participation in the social process.

Ads seem to work on the very advanced principle that a small pellet or pattern in a noisy, redundant barrage of repetition will gradually assert itself. Ads push the principle of noise all the way to the plateau of persuasion. They are quite in accord with the procedures of brain-washing. This depth principle of onslaught on the unconscious may be the reason why.

Many people have expressed uneasiness about the advertising enterprise in our time. To put the matter abruptly, the advertising industry is a crude attempt to extend the principles of automation to every aspect of society. Ideally, advertising aims at the goal of a programmed harmony among all human impulses and aspirations and endeavors. Using handicraft methods, it stretches out toward the ultimate electronic goal of a collective consciousness. When all production and all consumption are brought into a preestablished harmony with all desire and all effort, then advertising will have liquidated itself by its own success.

Since the advent of TV, the exploitation of the unconscious by the advertiser has hit a snag. TV experience favors much more consciousness concerning the unconscious than do the hard-sell forms of presentation in the press, the magazine, movie, or radio. The sensory tolerance of the audience has changed, and so have the methods of appeal by the advertisers. In the new cool TV world, the old hot world of hard-selling, earnest-talking salesmen has all the antique charm of the songs and togs of the 1920s. Mort Sahl and Shelley Berman are merely following, not setting, a trend in spoofing the ad world. They discovered that they have only to reel off an ad or news item to have the audience in fits. Will Rogers discovered years ago that any newspaper read aloud from a theater stage is hilarious. The same is true today of ads. Any ad put into a new setting is funny. This is a way of saying that any ad consciously attended to is comical. Ads are not meant for conscious consumption. They are intended as subliminal pills for the subconscious in order to exercise an hypnotic spell, especially on sociologists. That is one of the most edifying aspects of the huge educational enterprise that we call advertising, whose twelve-billion-dollar annual budget approximates the national school budget. Any expensive ad represents the toil, attention, testing, wit, art, and skill of many people. Far more thought and care go into the composition of any prominent ad in a newspaper or magazine than go into the writing of their features and editorials. Any expensive ad is as carefully built on the tested foundations of public stereotypes or "sets" of established attitudes, as any skyscraper is built on bedrock. Since highly skilled and perceptive teams of talent cooperate in the making of an ad for any established line of goods whatever, it is obvious that any acceptable ad is a vigorous dramatization of communal experience. No group of sociologists can approximate the ad teams in the gathering and processing of exploitable social data. The ad teams have billions to spend annually on research and testing of reactions, and their products are magnificent accumulations of material about the shared experience and feelings of the entire community. Of course, if ads were to depart from the center of this shared experience, they would collapse at once, by losing all hold on our feelings.

It is true, of course, that ads use the most basic and tested human experience of a community in grotesque ways. They are as incongruous, if looked at consciously, as the playing of "Silver Threads among the Gold" as music for a strip-tease act. But ads are carefully designed by the Madison Avenue frogmen-of-the-mind for semiconscious exposure. Their mere existence is a testimony, as well as a contribution, to the somnambulistic state of a tired metropolis.

After the Second War, an ad-conscious American army officer in Italy noted with misgiving that Italians could tell you the names of cabinet ministers, but not the names of commodities preferred by Italian celebrities. Furthermore, he said, the wall space of Italian cities was given over to political, rather than commercial, slogans. He predicted that there was small hope that Italians would ever achieve any sort of domestic prosperity or calm until they began to worry about the rival claims of cornflakes and cigarettes, rather than the capacities of public men. In fact, he went so far as to say that democratic freedom very largely consists in ignoring politics and worrying, instead, about the threat of scaly scalp, hairy legs, sluggish bowels, saggy breasts, receding gums, excess weight, and tired blood.

The army officer was probably right. Any community that wants to expedite and maximize the exchange of goods and services has simply got to homogenize its social life. The decision to homogenize comes easily to the highly literate population of the English-speaking world. Yet it is hard for oral cultures to agree on this program of homogenization, for they are only too prone to translate the message of radio into tribal politics, rather than into a new means of pushing Cadillacs. This is one reason that it was easy for the retribalized Nazi to feel superior to the American consumer. The tribal man can spot the gaps in the literate mentality very easily. On the other hand, it is the special illusion of literate societies that they are highly aware and individualistic. Centuries of typographic conditioning in patterns of lineal uniformity and fragmented repeatability have, in the electric age, been given increasing critical attention by the artistic world. The lineal process has been pushed out of industry, not only in management and production, but in entertainment, as well. It is the new mosaic form of the TV image that has replaced the Gutenberg structural assumptions. Reviewers of William Burroughs' *The Naked Lunch* have alluded to the prominent use of the "mosaic" term and method in his novel. The TV image renders the world of standard brands and consumer goods merely amusing. Basically, the reason is that the mosaic mesh of the TV image compels so much active participation on the part of the viewer that he develops a nostalgia for pre-consumer ways and days. Lewis Mumford gets serious attention when he praises the cohesive form of medieval towns as relevant to our time and needs.

Advertising got into high gear only at the end of the last century, with the invention of photoengraving. Ads and pictures then became interchangeable and have continued so. More important, pictures made possible great increases in newspaper and magazine circulation that also increased the quantity and profitability of ads. Today it is inconceivable that any publication, daily or periodical, could hold more than a few thousand readers without pictures. For both the pictorial ad or the picture story provide large quantities of instant information and instant humans, such as are necessary for keeping abreast in our kind of culture. Would it not seem natural and necessary that the young be provided with at least as much training of perception in this graphic and photographic world as they get in the typographic? In fact, they need more training in graphics, because the art of casting and arranging actors in ads is both complex and forcefully insidious.

Some writers have argued that the Graphic Revolution has shifted our culture away from private ideals to corporate images. That is really to say that the photo and TV seduce us from the *literate* and private "point of view" to the complex and inclusive world of the group icon. That is certainly what advertising does. Instead of presenting a private argument or vista, it offers a way of life that is for everybody or nobody. It offers this prospect with arguments that concern only irrelevant and trivial matters. For example, a lush car ad features a baby's rattle on the rich rug of the back floor and says that it has removed unwanted car rattles as easily as the user could remove the baby's rattle. This kind of copy has really nothing to do with rattles. The copy is merely a punning gag to distract the critical faculties while the image of the car goes to work on the hypnotized viewer. Those who have spent their lives protesting about "false and misleading ad copy" are godsends to advertisers, as teetotalers are to brewers, and moral censors are to books and films. The protesters are the best acclaimers and accelerators. Since the advent of pictures, the job of the ad copy is as incidental and latent, as the "meaning" of a poem is to a poem, or the words of a song are to a song. Highly literate people cannot cope with the nonverbal art of the pictorial, so they dance impatiently up and down to express a pointless disapproval that renders them futile and gives new power and authority to the ads. The unconscious depth-messages of ads are never attacked by the literate, because of their incapacity to notice or discuss nonverbal forms of arrangement and meaning. They have not the art to argue with pictures. When early in TV broadcasting hidden ads were tried out, the literate were in a great panic until they were dropped. The fact that typography is itself mainly subliminal in effect and that pictures are, as well, is a secret that is safe from the book-oriented community.

When the movies came, the entire pattern of American life went on the screen as a nonstop ad. Whatever any actor or actress wore or used or ate was such an ad as had never been dreamed of. The American bathroom, kitchen, and car, like everything else, got the *Arabian Nights* treatment. The result was that all ads in magazines and the press had to look like scenes from a movie. They still do. But the focus has had to become softer since TV.

With radio, ads openly went over to the incantation of the singing commercial. Noise and nausea as a technique of achieving unforgettability became universal. Ad and image making became, and have remained, the one really dynamic and growing part of the economy. Both movie and radio are hot media, whose arrival pepped up everybody to a great degree, giving us the Roaring Twenties. The effect was to provide a massive platform and a mandate for sales promotion as a way of life that ended only with *The Death of a Salesman* and the advent of TV. These two events did not coincide by accident. TV introduced that "experience in depth" and the "do-it-yourself" pattern of living that has shattered the image of the individualist hard-sell salesman and the docile consumer, just as it has blurred the formerly clear figures of the movie stars. This is not to suggest that Arthur Miller was trying to explain TV to America on the eve of its arrival, though he could as appropriately have titled his play "The Birth of the PR Man." Those who saw Harold Lloyd's *Work of Comedy* film will remember their surprise at how much of the 1920s they had forgotten. Also, they were surprised to find evidence of how naive and simple the Twenties really were. That age of the vamps, the sheiks, and the cavemen was a raucous nursery compared to our world, in which children read *MAD* magazine for chuckles. It was a world still innocently engaged in expanding and exploding, in separating and teasing and tearing. Today, with TV, we are experiencing the opposite process of integrating and interrelating that is anything but innocent. The simple faith of the salesman in the irresistibility of his line (both talk and goods) now yields to the complex togetherness of the corporate posture, the process and the organization.

Ads have proved to be a self-liquidating form of community entertainment. They came along just after the Victorian gospel of work, and they promised a

Beulah land of perfectibility, where it would be possible to "iron shirts without hating your husband." And now they are deserting the individual consumer-product in favor of the all-inclusive and never-ending process that is the Image of any great corporate enterprise. The Container Corporation of America does not feature paper bags and paper cups in its ads, but the container *function*, by means of great art. The historians and archeologists will one day discover that the ads of our time are the richest and most faithful daily reflections that any society ever made of its entire range of activities. The Egyptian hieroglyph lags far behind in this respect. With TV, the smarter advertisers have made free with fur and fuzz, and blur and buzz. They have, in a word, taken a skin-dive. For that is what the TV viewer is. He is a skin-diver, and he no longer likes garish daylight on hard, shiny surfaces, though he must continue to put up with a noisy radio sound track that is painful.

32
———

THE LEGACY OF MCLUHAN: IEN ANG

Ien Ang addresses questions raised by Marshall McLuhan. She points to local appropriation and reworking of global media products to fit local identities and cultures. Her work exemplifies many of the characteristics of theory at the turn of the century. Capitalism remains a central concept but it is no longer associated with Marxist hopes for revolution and transcendence. Culture is also a central concept, replacing earlier interest in structure, social relationships, institutions, roles, and so on. The unit of analysis is the whole world, a unified field that is both global and local. Television is a prime example of Giddens' contention that our times are characterized by the disembedding of processes from local, fixed, unified space and time. Ang uses the term postmodern to mean a recognition of the limits of the universalizing and rationalizing force of western, capitalist culture that had expanded in the high modern period; it turns out that people within local cultures resist and redefine these large systemic processes associated with capitalism and westernization. The global village is not so much one community, as a number of networked, linked local villages.

The reader can immediately note an ongoing dialogue between Ang and many of the other theorists in this volume: with Marx about capitalist globalization; with Jameson about the nature of postmodern culture; with DuBois about multiple consciousness and cultural complexity; with Mead and Becker about the construction of meaning by audiences that always actively and collectively interpret experiences; with Giddens and Habermas about disembedding of social and cultural processes in space and time; with Gramsci, Gitlin, Foucault, and Willis about the ambiguous borders between hegemony and resistance; with Benjamin about television as ultimate destroyer of the aura of works of art, with enormous possibilities for both domination and emancipation; with McLuhan, Hall, and Appadurai about global culture and the global village.

The postmodern is the open-ended nature of this dialogue, the inability to come to closure, the "yes, but" of its twists and turns: total commodification of culture under capitalism, but the persistence of resistance everywhere; globalization of communication, but the continued vitality and diversity of local cultures; the juggernaut of instrumental reason, but its consistent overturning by rational and irrational actions.

Living Room Wars
IEN ANG

Global Media/Local Meaning

Marshall McLuhan's idea of the global village, of the whole world united through long-distance communication technologies, has recently gained renewed popularity as a result of a number of heavily televised historic events such as the fall of the Berlin Wall, the Tiananmen Square Massacre, the Gulf War, the civil wars in Bosnia and Somalia. It is largely through the representational practices of Ted Turner's Cable News Network (CNN) that the Gulf War could be dubbed the "Third World War"—a war in which the whole world presumably participated through the electronic collapsing of time and space induced by satellite television technology. Indeed, CNN's unprecedented triumph in catapulting the "War in the Gulf" (as CNN's caption went) as a "simultaneous happening" into billions of dispersed living rooms worldwide seems to confirm Turner's self-proclaimed ambition, in the name of world peace and harmony, to turn the world instantly into one big global audience. As Australian cultural critic McKenzie Wark has observed:

> The whole thing about the media vector is that its tendency is toward *implicating* the entire globe. Its historic tendency is toward making any and every point a possible connection—everyone and everything is a potential object and/or subject of a mediated relation, realized instantly. In the Gulf War, to see it [on CNN] was to be implicated in it. [...] We are all, always, already—there. (Wark 1994: 15)

However, this perception can be sustained only from a productivist view of the process of mass communications, which needs to be complemented with the specific productivities of the receiving end of the process. In other words, the idea of a unified and united global village imagines the global audience as an anonymous "taxonomic collective" (Ang 1991: chapter 3), gathered together as one large diasporic community participating in "the live broadcasting of history" (Dayan and Katz 1992). Indeed, as Wark says, "we are all, always, already—there." But at the same time we are also *not* there. As audiences of the Gulf War on CNN, we were present and absent at the same time. To put it differently, at one level CNN is indeed a spectacular embodiment of the "annihilation of space by time" brought about by what Harold Innis (1951) has called space-binding communication media. The emphasis on speed of delivery and immediacy of transmission does indeed produce a structure of temporal synchronicity which makes space irrelevant: a wide variety of dispersed locales are, at this structural level, and assuming that they are so "fortunate" to be able to receive CNN directly, symbolically bound together by the simultaneous appearance of the same images on the TV screen. At another level, however, the spatial dimension cannot be discounted when it comes to what happens to those images once they arrive in specific locations. At this cultural level, at once more mundane and more fluid local realities can themselves present an unpredictable interpretive screen through which the intruding electronic screen images are filtered. At the level of the day-to-day, space cannot be annihilated because the social specificity of any locality is inevitably marked by its characteristics as a place. In other words, global media do affect, but cannot control local meanings.

Two weeks after the launch of Operation Desert Storm on 15 January 1991, I asked my students at the University of Amsterdam to write down how they experienced the event that seemed to preoccupy and usurp all public discourse in those cold winter days (winter, that is, in the Northern hemisphere only). It should be noted that CNN is available as a regular 24-hour-a-day cable channel to Dutch television audiences and that about 90 per cent of Dutch homes are cabled, making the American news network into a virtually omnipresent, ready service in that country, which is by no means the case in many other parts of the world—a reminder that the presumably "global" is by no means "universal." From my students' responses, a rather consistent pattern emerged. During the first few days after the war broke out, there was an obsessive fascination with its minute-to-minute goings-on which CNN purported to inform us about. Any spare time was spent in front of the TV set, motivated by a haunting sense of involvement which was soon superseded by a desire to detach: after less than a week or so, fascination was replaced by indifference and, to some, resentment about the excessive nature of the media's coverage of the war. The initial interest gave way to a more routine form of (dis)engagement. In other words, what gradually but inevitably occurred was a kind of "resistance" against the imposed complicity created by the news media, a quiet revolt against the position of well-informed powerlessness induced by the media's insistence on keeping us continuously posted. As one student exclaimed: "It's as if nothing else happened anymore!" What these students articulated, then, was a clear determination to defy the global media's orchestrated colonization of their attention and interest. For most of them, the war remained a limited media reality which did not succeed in totally encroaching on the intimate texture of their local, everyday concerns.

I invoke this small case-study here in order to raise some questions about a particularly pressing cultural and political problematic on the verge of the twenty-first century: the consequences of the increasing scale and rapidity of global flows of media products and technologies as a result of the growing economic power of the transnational communications corporations, and the construction of global media markets that go with their activities. The case-study suggests that by considering the perspective of media audiences in our analysis, we can avoid mistaking "world politics" as constructed by CNN and other news media for "the whole story." Media reality has not completely erased social reality, as is often claimed by radical postmodernists, counter posed as it is by the centrifugal forces of the local micro-circumstances in which people live out their everyday lives, where different concerns take on priority. At the same time, Wark (1994) is right to stress that even if we get bored with the CNN coverage, we are still, willy-nilly, implicated in it. We can switch off the TV set, but as its images pervade the texture of our everyday worlds, the distinction between media reality and social reality becomes blurred. What needs to be addressed, then, is the complicated relationship between global media and local meanings, their intricate interconnections as well as disjunctions (Appadurai 1990; Morley1992: chapter 13).

It is often said that emerging from the ever more comprehensive expansion of the capitalist culture industries is a "global culture." How should we conceptualize and analyse this monstrous beast? No doubt, the liberal discourse in which CNN's Ted Turner appropriated McLuhan's global village idea falls short here, incapable and unprepared as it is to see beyond the optimistic, happy pluralist rhetoric of "free flow of information" and "democratic participation." This rhetoric was already criticized and discarded in the 1970s and 1980s by critical theorists who, mostly speaking in the name of Third World perspectives and interests, forcefully emphasized the deep imbalance of those flows and the "cultural imperialism" that is implicated in that process (for a critical overview, see Tomlinson 1991). But the cultural imperialism thesis, on its part, provides an equally flawed account of "global culture," evoking an unrelenting and all-absorbing, linear process of cultural homogenization seen as the result of unambiguous domination of subordinated peoples and cultures by a clearly demarcated powerful culture, usually designated as American or European, or, more generally, as "Western" culture. It is not only the residual elements of hypodermic needle theories of "media effects" that make such a view problematic. A more fundamental problem is its implicit assumption of "culture" as organic, self-contained entity with fixed boundaries, whose traditional wholesomeness is presumed to be crushed by the superimposition of another, equally self-contained, "dominant culture." As a result, talk about cultural imperialism often tends to collude with a defence of conservative positions of cultural puritanism and protectionism. To put it differently, this perspective too easily equates the "global" as the site of cultural erosion and destruction, and the "local" as the site of pristine cultural "authenticity." It is such a dichotomized, binary counterposing of the "global" and the "local" that I wish to challenge here. As I have already suggested in chapter 8, the global and the local should not be conceived as two distinct, separate and opposing realities, but as complexly articulated, mutually constitutive. Global forces only display their effectivity in particular localities; local realities today can no longer be thought outside of the global sphere of influence, for better or for worse.

The transnational dissemination of mass-mediated culture is, given the hegemonic strength of global capitalism in today's world economy, an irreversible process that cannot be structurally transcended, at least not in the foreseeable future. But this does not mean that it is not actively and differentially responded to and negotiated with in concrete local contexts and conditions. These local responses and negotiations, culturally diverse and geographically dispersed, need to be taken into account if we are to understand the complex and contradictory dynamics of today's "global culture." In this respect, as Mike Featherstone (1990) has remarked, it is preferable to speak about globalization, to think in terms of complex *processes* of global integration rather than in terms of static and given polarities of "global" and "local." Globalization—defined by Roland Robertson as "the concrete structuration of the world as a whole" (1990:20), the series of developments by which the world becomes a "single place"—should not be thought of in simple, linear terms. It is not a sweeping, all-absorbing process; and, above all, it is an always unfinished, and necessarily unfinishable, process precisely because this single global place we live in is also a deeply fractured one.

The construction of a "global culture," then, should not be conceived as a process of straightforward homogenization, in which all cultural difference and diversity is gradually eradicated and assimilated. Rather, globalization involves a checkered process of systemic desegregation in which local cultures lose their autonomous and separate existence and become thoroughly interdependent and interconnected. Nowadays, as I will indicate later, local cultures everywhere tend to reproduce themselves precisely, to a large extent, through the appropriation of global flows of mass-mediated forms and technologies.

In this sense, the integrative effects of globalization should be conceived in a conditional rather than a substantive sense. What becomes increasingly "globalized" is not so much concrete cultural contents (although global distribution does bring, say, the same movies to many dispersed locals), but, more importantly and more structurally, the parameters and infrastructure which determine the conditions of existence for local cultures. It can be understood, for example, as the dissemination of a limited set of economic, political, ideological and pragmatic conventions and principles which govern and mould the accepted ways in which media production, circulation and consumption are organized throughout the modern world. This is one sense in which the claim that "the media are American" (Tunstall 1977) has a quintessential validity. After all, it is in the United States that many of these principles and conventions, now often taken for granted and fully routinized, were first explored and perfected. As the commercial principle of production of culture for profit becomes ever more dominant, for example, it brings with it a spread of concomitant practices such as marketing, advertising and audience research, all heavily institutionalized, specialized practices which were first developed in the United States in the early twentieth century. Furthermore, the commodification of media culture is an increasingly global phenomenon which brings with it the adoption of peculiarly modernist cultural arrangements such as the fashion system with its principle of planned obsolescence, framed within risk-reducing strategies of innovation through repetition. In television, for example, this takes the form of a continuous rehashing of relatively constant formats and genres (e.g. the cop show, the sitcom, the soap opera) and a standardization of scheduling routines. Again, it is in American commercial television that such profit-maximizing strategies have been most perfected, from where they have been increasingly globalized, that is, taken as the commonsense way of doing things.

However, it is the particular appropriation and adaptation of such standardized rules and conventions within local contexts and according to local traditions, resources and preferences that the non-linear, fractured nature of cultural globalization displays itself. The evolution of the film and television industries in Hong Kong is a point in case. In the 1950s, Cantonese movies dominated the Hong Kong market, drawing on traditional Cantonese cultural forms such as opera, musicals and contemporary melodrama. Their popularity declined in the 1960s and early 1970s, when Hollywood films consistently out grossed locally produced Chinese films. By the 1980s, however, the most popular film genres in Hong Kong were once again locally produced, in the Cantonese language, but evincing definite elements of "indigenization" of the Western action adventure movie format. The contemporary genre of Cantonese Kung Fu movies, for example, appropriated and refracted James Bond-style film narratives by using fists and martial arts as weapons, as well as drawing on traditional Cantonese values such as vengeance for friends and kin, loyalty to close acquaintances and punishment to traitors (Lee 1991).

Culturally speaking, it is hard to distinguish here between the "foreign" and the "indigenous," the "imperialist" and the "authentic": what has emerged is a highly distinctive and economically viable hybrid cultural form in which the global and the local are inextricably intertwined, in turn leading to the modernized reinvigoration of a culture that continues to be labelled and widely experienced as "Cantonese." In other words, what counts as "local" and therefore "authentic" is not a fixed content, but subject to change and modification as a result of the domestification of imported cultural goods. As Joseph Tobin observes in the context of Japanese consumer culture, "[w]hat was marked as foreign and exotic yesterday can become foreign but familiar today and traditionally Japanese tomorrow" (1992: 26). Tobin mentions the example of sukiyaki, now considered a "traditional" Japanese food but actually a dish borrowed from the Europeans. The same is happening in Japan with the hamburger, where McDonald's Biggu Makku is becoming increasingly Japanized and where hybrids such as a "riceburger" have been invented.

A similar, well-known story has been told about the telenovela, a genre which had its origins in the American daytime soap opera but soon evolved into a distinctively Latin American genre. Telenovelas became so popular in that part of the world that they gradually displaced American imports from the TV schedules and become an intrinsic part of local popular culture (Vink 1988; Mattelart and Mattelart 1990). A similar erosion of the hegemony of American imports has taken place wherever there is competition from local productions, which almost everywhere tend to be more popular than American programmes (McNeely and Soysal 1989).

Of course, all too euphoric evaluations of such developments as evidence of "global pluralism" and "local autonomy" should be countered and confronted with the remark that they still remain framed within the concerns of capitalist culture, now at the national level rather than the transnational one. Nevertheless, what such examples do indicate is that the apparent increasing global integration does not simply result in the elimination of cultural diversity, but, rather, provides the context for the production of new cultural forms which are marked by local specificity. If, in other words, the global is the site of the homogeneous (or the common) and the local the site of the diverse and the distinctive, then the latter can—in today's integrated world-system—only constitute and reconstitute itself in and through concrete reworkings and appropriations of the former. Diversity then, is to be seen not in terms of local autonomy but in terms of local reworkings and appropriations. The diverse is not made up of fixed, originary differences, but is an ever-fluctuating, ever-evolving proliferation of "expressions of possibilities active in any situation, some accommodating, others resistant to dominant cultural trends or interpretations" (Marcus and Fischer 1986: 116). Two things follow from this. First, we have to recognize the hybrid, syncretic and creolized, always-already "contaminated" nature of diversity in today's global cultural order, a fluid diversity emanating from constant cultural traffic and interaction rather than from the persistence of original, rooted and traditional "identities." Second, we can agree with Ulf Hannerz (1992) that contemporary global culture, what he calls "the global ecumene," is bounded not through a replication of uniformity but through an organization or orchestration of diversity; a diversity that never adds up to a perfectly coherent, unitary whole.

At a more fundamental level, this discussion leads me to explore the relationship of the globalization of culture and the predicament of modernity. After all, modernity has been presented as one of the most sweeping globalizing forces in history—if anything, as dominant ideology would have it, the whole ought to "modernize" itself, become "modern." But what does this mean in cultural terms? One of the most eloquent descriptions of the modern experience comes from Marshall Berman:

> There is a mode of vital experience—experience of space and time, of self and others, of life's possibilities and perils—that is shared by men and women all over the world today. I will call this body of experience "modernity." To be modern is to find ourselves in an environment that promises us adventure, power, joy, growth, transformation of ourselves and the world—and at the same time, that threatens to destroy everything we have, everything we know, everything we are. Modern environments and experiences cut across all boundaries of geography and ethnicity, of class and nationality, of religion and ideology: in this sense, modernity can be said to unite all mankind [sic]. But [and here comes an important qualification, I.A.] it is a paradoxical unity, a unity of disunity: it pours us all into a maelstrom of perpetual disintegration and renewal, of struggle and contradiction, of ambiguity and anguish. To be modern is to be part of a universe in which, as Marx said, "all that is solid melts into air." (Berman 1982: 1)

In this sweeping, totalizing generalization, Berman articulates the very central feature of modernist discourse—seeing modernity as a relentlessly universalizing force, imposing a singular type of hyper-individualized experience, destroying traditional connections and meanings on which old certainties were based. But he is only half right. When we look at what is actually happening in global culture today, we can see that not all that was solid has melted into air: on the contrary, the globalizing force of capitalist modernity has not dissolved the categorial solidities of geography, gender, ethnicity, class, nationality, religion, ideology, and so on, which still have crucial impacts on the ways in which people experience and interpret the world and create and recreate their cultural environments, although the way they do so has been reframed by and within the structuring moulds of the modern itself.

Moreover, at the mundane level of daily life people build new solidities on the ruins of the old ones. When old ties and bonds and systems of meaning were eroded by the dissemination of the modern, they were replaced by new ones: people form new senses of identity and belonging, new symbolic commodities. But these new solidities are of a different nature than the old, traditional ones: they are less permanent, less total, less based on fixed territories, more dynamic, more provisional, and above all they are often based on the resources offered by global modern culture itself. To put it differently, it is not enough to define the modern as a singular, universal and abstract experience formally characterized by a constant revolutionizing impulse; instead, we should emphasize that there are many, historically particular and localized ways of being modern, shaped by and within particular conditions and power relations.

At issue here, of course, is the question, not of postmodernism, but of postmodernity. I would like to oppose the tendency of the discourse of postmodernism to speak about contemporary culture in purely or primarily aesthetic terms, emphasizing elements such as pastiche, collage, allegory and spectacle. Lash and Urry see this kind of postmodernist cultural form as a more or less direct effect of what they call the "disorganised capitalism" of today (1987: 286), while Fredric Jameson (1991) has, in a famous essay, dubbed postmodernism "the cultural logic of late capitalism." The importance here is not to reduce the postmodern to "mere" style, but to see it much more broadly as describing some fundamental aspects of social formation and meaning production in life dominated by the forces of global capitalism. To be sure, the reduction of the postmodern to an artistic attitude, an -ism, a superstructural phenomenon, might be particularly biased to the situation in the developed West, where the epithets of modernity and modernism can arguably be attached to a "real" and protracted historical period (say, 1789-1968) and where the *post*-modern is often experienced as either a demystification or a betrayal of "the project of modernity" and its modernist ideals (Habermas 1983). In the context of this discussion, however, I find it more useful to approach postmodernity not just as that which comes *after* the modern in a chronological sense, but more profoundly as those modes of social experience and practice which respond, synchronically as well as diachronically, to the cultural contradictions brought about by, and inherent in, modernity itself.

In this sense, it is worth asserting that the peripheries of the world, those at the receiving end of the forces of globalization, where capitalist modernization has been an imposed state of affairs rather than an internal development as was the case in Europe, have always been more truly postmodern than Europe itself, because in those contexts the eclectic juxtaposition and amalgamation of "global" and "local" cultural influences have always been a social necessity and therefore an integrated mode of survival rather than a question of aesthetics. Becoming modern, in these cases has always been ridden with power and violence; it could never have been a matter of simply embracing the new, as Berman would have it—but then, he described a peculiarly romanticized way of becoming modern—but has been one of being *forced* to "let all that is solid melt into air" by Western powers, and of becoming experienced in the improvised and makeshift forms of new solidities in order to negotiate the consequences of an imposed entry into the "modern world-system." As a result, being "modern" here has always-already been a fractured experience, always a matter of negotiating with an Other which presents itself as both the site of power and object of desire. As Hannerz, a Swedish anthropologist, has astutely remarked:

> [T]he First World has been present in the consciousness of many Third World people a great deal longer than the Third World has been on the minds of most First World People. The notion of the sudden engagement between the cultures of center and periphery may thus in large part be an imaginative byproduct of the late awakening to global realities of many of us inhabitants of the center. (Hannerz 1991: 110)

This is not to ignore the unequal power relations that continue to characterize the relentlessly globalizing tendencies of modern capitalism, which have only become more overwhelming in scale and scope in the late twentieth century. It is, however, to point to the unpredictable, often incongruous and highly creative (though not necessarily desired or desirable) cultural consequences of these power relations as they intervene in shaping particular local contexts, particularly those positioned at the relatively powerless receiving end of transnational cultural and media flows. It is here, in these peripheries, where the intricate intertwinings of global media and local meaning—not their binary counterposing—are most likely to be a taken-for granted aspect of everyday experience, where postmodernity—in the sense of an always-already "disintegrated" modernity, a modernity whose completion has failed from the start (see Ang and Stratton 1996)—is most manifestly palpable as a "condition" of daily life.

Therefore, let me finish with three stories in order to illuminate the profound incoherence of the current global cultural (dis)order, that of the "modern world-system," three stories located in three very differently positioned global peripheries (for not all peripheries are the same). What they do have in common is the fact that they all have to grapple with the unsolicited "invasion" of global media from a centre which is undeniably American. But, as Hannerz observes: "Anglo culture, the culture of the WASPs, may have provided the metropolis, the Standard, the mainstream, but as it reaches out toward every corner of society, it becomes creolized itself" (1992: 226).

This is certainly what happened when Hollywood videos first entered the lived reality of the Warlpiri people, an isolated Aboriginal community in the

Australian Central Desert, in the early 1980s. There is a lot of concern about the ability of traditional cultures to survive this new electronic invasion but, as the late anthropologist Eric Michaels, who spent three years among the Warlpiri, notes this concern is all too often cast within the long tradition of a Western racist paternalism intent on "protecting" these "primitive," "preliterate," "prehistorical" people from the ravages of "modernity." Ironically, such a stance only serves to monopolize the "modern" to the West, forever relegating indigenous Australians at the realm of an ahistorical "non-modern." Such a stance also disavows the very historical fact that the current plight of Aboriginal people—dispossessed from their own land, living forever in a colonized state—was precipitated precisely by the globalizing force of European modernity. That many of these communities still survive after two hundred years of forced contact is an indication of their cultural strength, not their helplessness, in managing and accommodating the brute and powerful impositions from outside. Michaels noticed that electronic media were remarkably attractive and accessible to the Warlpiri, in contrast with print and literacy. This, according to Michaels, is not because audiovisual images do not need active interpretation and "reading" to be made sense of; on the contrary:

> It could prove promising that the most popular genres appear to be action/adventure, soaps, musicals, and slapstick.[...] As the least character-motivated, most formulaic fictions, they may encourage active interpretation and cross-culturally varied readings [where] culture-specific references are either minimal or unnecessary for the viewer's enjoyment. From this perspective, it would seem difficult to see in the introduction of imported video and television programs the destruction of Aboriginal culture. Such a claim can only be made in ignorance of the strong traditions and preferences in graphics, the selectivity of media and contents, and the strength of interpretation of the Warlpiri. (Michaels 1994 [1987]: 96)

This is not to indiscriminately celebrate or congratulate the Warlpiri on their ingenious resilience, for what Michaels is interested in is not so much such a "romanticism of the oppressed," but rather the more complicated idea that video might be relatively compatible with traditional Warlpiri culture (which Michaels contrasts with the great resistance against reading and literature within the community) only because it enables an evocative mode of interpretation which is congruous with the Warlpiri graphic system, the way writing does not (and which might thus be much more destructive to Aboriginal culture, as Michaels more or less suggests). In this sense, what might be called "Aboriginal modernity" is an extremely precarious and fragile, perhaps transitory cultural formation.

Cut now to Trinidad, a place which is peripheral in the global scenario in a very different way than Aboriginal Australia. It is an independent nation-state with its own, formally "sovereign" cultural apparatus and national media industry, but contrary to, for example, Hong Kong or India or even Nigeria, Trinidad cannot be, and will arguably never be, the primary producer of the images and goods from which it constructs its own cultural modernity (Miller 1992). As such small postcolonial nations will generally depend heavily on Western products, it is, again, the transformative properties of local consumption which are crucial for an appreciation of their cultural distinctiveness.

When British anthropologist Daniel Miller went to Trinidad to document contemporary life on this South Caribbean island, he was soon confronted with the centrality of the American soap opera *The Young and the Restless* in the population's everyday cultural experience. Why? Miller interprets this popularity by associating it with the uniquely Trinidadian concept of bacchanal. If one asks Trinidadians to describe their country in one word, by far the commonest response is "bacchanal," "said with a smile which seemed to indicate affectionate pride triumphing over potential shame" (Miller 1992: 176). Bacchanal designates a way of experiencing the everyday world in terms of gossip, scandal, exposure, confusion and disorder, representing a local sense of truth for many Trinidadians, who are acutely aware of the fluidity and dynamism of their national reality precisely because of its location on the periphery, subject to uncontrollable external forces, past and present. *The Young and the Restless,* says Miller, could become central to the Trinidadian imaginary because it "reinforces bacchanal as the lesson of recession which insists that [...] the façade of stability is a flimsy construction which will be blown over in the first storm created by true nature" (ibid.: 179). The fact that it is an imported product of mass-mediated culture that could acquire this centrality, muses Miller, stems precisely from the fact that local TV productions cannot incorporate clear expressions of bacchanal, concerned as they are with the "serious," official concerns of the nation-state. Instead, what the popular consumption of *The Young and the Restless* in Trinidad accomplishes is not only the indigenization of the soap opera as Trinidadian, but also "the refinement of the concept of Trinidad as the culture of bacchanal" (ibid.). Miller provides a useful historical context for this apparently paradoxical state of affairs:

> It is hard to talk of a loss of tradition here, since Trinidad was born into modernity in its first breath, a slave colony constructed as producer of raw materials for the industrialising world. The result is an extremely fluid society which makes itself up as it goes along. (Miller 1992: 179)

The fact that, in the late 1980s, an American soap opera became a key instrument for forging a highly specific sense of Trinidadian culture reveals the way in which the local can construct its syncretic, postmodern brand of cultural identity through consumption of the global. As Miller usefully concludes, "authenticity," if we still want to retain that word, "has increasingly to be judged a posteriori not a priori, according to local consequences not local origins" (1992: 181).

As with the case of the popularity of Hollywood videos among the Warlpiri, however, this isn't to suggest that the power of the transnational media industry is in any sense diminished. It is, however, to at least entertain the possibility that at the level of culture, meaning and identity, "the interplay of center and periphery could go on and on, never settling into a fixed form precisely because of the openness of the global whole" (Hannerz 1992: 266).

In the end, however, we do need to return to the persistent asymmetry between centre and periphery, and to the very substantial Americanness of much of "global" media, not only in terms of corporate ownership and working principles, but also, more flagrantly, in terms of symbolic content: images, sounds, stories, names. No amount of transformative interpretation will change this. And even though CNN implicated all of us into vicarious participation in the supposedly global Gulf War, the experiential disjuncture between "here" and "there" remains, as McKenzie Wark narrates:

> It was difficult, as an Australian, not to experience the war as something that happened in America, performed, acted, and sponsored by Americans, for Americans. On television, most voices were American. All the images looked American. Even Saddam seemed to be an American. As American as Lon Chaney or Bela Lugosi. Iraq seemed to be a place in America. A place like Wounded Knee or Kent State or the Big Muddy. (Wark 1994: 13)

Australia—Wark's Australia, not that of the Warlpiri—can hardly be called a periphery in the same way as Trinidad; like the Netherlands or Sweden, it is better described as part of the "semi-periphery," a part of "the West" but relatively marginal within it. Nevertheless, as Wark astutely observes, every (white) Australian who grew up after the Second World War knows "the feeling of growing up in a simulated America," resulting in "perverse intimacy with the language and cultural reference points which nevertheless takes place elsewhere" (1994: 14). And not only in Australia. Although this experience of decenteredness in an imaginary geography—a paradox which might quite appropriately be called "postmodern"—has become a rather common one throughout the globe, its cultural consequences in particular localities have hardly begun to be understood.

Perhaps it is precisely because of this paradox, this dominant Americanness which presents itself as global and universal, that my Dutch students quickly lost interest in CNN's representation of the "War in the Gulf," and why this first truly "living room war" did not become "authenticized" in the local experience of those who, from a "global" perspective, would be reduced to the status of "silent majority" (Baudrillard 1983).

References

Ang, Ien. *Desperately Seeking the Audience*. London/New York: Routledge, 1991.

Appadurai, A. "Disjuncture and difference in the global cultural economy." *Public Culture*, 2 (2), 1990: 1-24.

Baudrillard. J. *In the Shadow of the Silent Majorities*. New York: Semiotext(e), 1983.

Berman, Marshall. *All That Is Solid Melts Into Air*. New York: Simon and Schuster: 1982.

Featherstone, Mike. (ed.). *Global Culture*. London: Sage, 1990.

Habermas, Jurgen. "Modernity—an incomplete product." In H. Foster (ed.), *The Anti-Aesthetic*. Port Townsend, WA: Bay Press, 1983.

Hannerz, Ulf. *Cultural Complexity*. New York: Columbia University Press, 1992.

Innis, H. *The Bias of Communication*. Toronto: University of Toronto Press, 1951.

Jameson, Fredric. *Postmodernism or the Cultural Logic of Late Capitalism*. London: Verso, 1991.

Lash, S., and J. Urry. *The End of Organized Capitalism*. Cambridge: Polity Press, 1987.

Lee, P.S.N. "The absorption and indigenisation of foreign media culture: A study on a cultural meeting point of the east and west: Hong Kong." *Asian Journal of Communication*, 1 (2),: 52-72, 1991.

Mattelart, M., and A. Mattelart. *The Carnival of Images*. New York: Bergin and Garvey, 1990.

Marcus, G.E., and Fischer, M.M. *Anthropology a Cultural Critique*. Chicago/London: University of Chicago Press, 1986.

Michaels, E. "Hollywood iconography: A Warlpiri reading." In his *Bad Aboriginal Art*. Minneapolis: University of Minnesota Press, 1994.

Miller, D. *"The Young and the Restless* in Trinidad: A case of the local and the global in mass consumption." In R. Silverstone and E. Hirsch (eds.), *Consuming Technologies*. London: Routledge, 1992.

Morley, D. *Television, Audiences, and Cultural Studies*. London: Routledge, 1992.

Robertson, Roland. "Mapping the global condition: Globalization as the central concept." In M. Featherstone (ed.), *Global Culture*. London: Sage, 1990.

Tobin, J.J. "Introduction: Domesticating the west." In J.J. Tobin (ed.), *Remade in Japan: Everyday Life and Consumer Taste in a Changing Society*. New Haven/London: Yale University Press, 1992.

Tomlinson, J. *Cultural Imperialism.* London: Pinter Publishers, 1991.

Tunstall, J. *The Media are American.* London: Constable, 1977.

Vink, N. *The Telenovela and Emancipation.* Amsterdam: Royal Tropical Institute, 1988.

Wark, M. *Virtual Geographies: Living with Global Media Events.* Bloomington/Indianapolis: Indiana University Press, 1994.

33

MICHEL FOUCAULT (1926-1984)

The work of Michel Foucault has transformed modern social theory. All the categories of Marxist, conflict, and mainstream thinking have been melted in air by the radical innovations of the French theorist, a professor at several major universities. Yet his work also shows strong continuity with ideas of the conservative reaction, Comte and Durkheim, a French tradition that de-emphasizes the individual and highlights the compelling and external character of culture.

Foucault's ideas evolved through a series of books, including *Madness and Civilization*, *Discipline and Punish*, *The Archaeology of Knowledge*, and *The History of Sexuality*. The titles recall Durkheim's *Suicide* and his work on crime and punishment: like Durkheim, Foucault focused on deviance and on acts and conditions that appear to be highly personal and individually unique—sex and insanity—and was intent on showing that these apparently individual behaviours can only be understood by examining prevailing cultural frameworks, "discursive formations."

A discursive formation is a way of representing the nature of society and human beings. It is a framework of words and images through which we see ourselves at any point in time. These words and images are shared by the entire society (and by groups of societies like the "West"). In some societies they are said to be religious, while in others they claim to be scientific. In all cases, the discursive formations are systems of knowledge, claims to understand the nature of human beings and the world in which we live. Historical change involves change in discursive formations, major shifts from one to another form.

A discursive formation is a set of round holes into which the unpredictable, multishaped pegs of human experience are crammed. The round holes define what is "normal" and "deviant," "sane" and "insane," "natural" and "unnatural." These terms have to be put in quotation marks because they have no intrinsic meaning. The cramming of human acts and experiences into the categories of the discursive formation always involves exercise of power and enactment of punishments. It is always met by some degree of resistance.

For example, human sexuality is nothing more than bodies and pleasures. It has no intrinsic organization. The discursive formations of successive epochs impose categories like "good" and "evil," "natural" and "unnatural," "virtuous" and "sinful" on these experiences. They are claims to knowing and classifying the true nature of sexuality. In classical antiquity, sexuality was believed to be an expression of dominance; penetration was seen as an act of dominance, engaged in by adult men with women, slaves, and/or adolescent boys of the men's own social class. There was some ambivalence about the boys, because they were going to mature into a category of social equals, unlike women and slaves. Christian teachings radically rearranged the categories and the meaning of the acts, defining all same-sex relations as "sinful."

Foucault's analysis of madness is similar. In all ages, some people's behaviour fails to fit a norm. The mad may be allowed to roam around freely or, as in modern times until the 1970s, they may be placed in prison-like insane asylums. They may be defined in religious terms or, in modern times, subjected to medical analysis and treatment.

The definition of crime and the punishments it receives also vary. In the period of European history before the French Revolution, criminals were punished by corporal and capital punishment, subjected to gruesome tortures, and exhibited in public spectacles. The Enlightenment and French Revolution marked the start of new ways of thinking about crime and punishment. After this turning point, criminals were incarcerated, separated, and isolated from society. Emerging human sciences like medicine, psychology, and sociology claimed to understand the causes of crime and to be able to effect rehabilitation, the transformation of the character and behaviour of criminals. The emphasis now is on corrections and the imposition of order and self-control on the imprisoned criminal.

Foucault saw these changes in the treatment of the mad and the criminal as a central feature of the modern discursive formation, characterized by the dominance of the sciences—biology, psychology, sociology—and by the translation of these disciplines' claims into fields of practice such as medicine, psychotherapy, and social work. All these fields constitute disciplines of power; that is, they are focused on the imposition of order, regulation of behaviour, and social control. Technologies of all kinds—medication, electroshock, lobotomies, behaviour modification, management practices, and computerized surveillance and record-keeping—are put to the service of control. Like all systems of power, these disciplines employ a "gaze," a form of scrutiny exercised by those with power upon those without power. Doctors examine patients, psychotherapists look at the mad and the troubled, educators monitor children: these are all examples of surveillance.

Modern formations are characterized by increasing emphasis on self-monitoring and self control. The ideal modern person suppresses impulses of all kinds, especially sexual, violent, and unruly ones. The gaze of surveillance is turned upon oneself, and this self-scrutiny is the most pervasive and effective form of social control. If people cannot monitor and curb impulses on their own, they turn to physicians and helping professions for treatment.

In short, knowledge in modern times is organized in terms of scientific claims, rather than religious judgements, and power is exercised in the context of expertise and scientific knowledge. The "gaze" is always a detached, affectively neutral, scientific gaze—the gaze of the researcher and the dispassionate diagnostician.

These ideas of Foucault are closely connected to theories we read earlier in the volume. They are in line with Durkheim's analysis of the shift away from repressive laws. But where Durkheim was at least moderately optimistic about evolution toward a more humane and less rigid system of social control, Foucault sees the new forms as no less oppressive than the old ones.

Foucault sees society in ways that are similar to the ideas of the conservative reaction, Comte and Durkheim, but turns each of their values upside-down. The conservative reaction celebrated social compulsion; Foucault loathes it in both its traditional and modern forms. Comte hailed the emergence of the human sciences, the exercise of expertise, and the prospect of order and progress; Foucault attacks them. Durkheim believed modern structures of normative regulation are more humane than old ones; Foucault sees them as new forms of control. He agrees with the French tradition of analyzing the external and compelling character of culture. He also shares its perspective on crime and social deviance, in which these phenomena are not seen as social problems, but as fundamental expressions of society.

Foucault's ideas are close to Weber's concerns about the iron cage of formal rationality and instrumental reason. Like Weber, he foresees a society in which rationality becomes a repressive and inhumane force. Science's claim to the complete understanding of nature gives its practioners a hold on human action that is hard to break. Both Weber and Foucault were influenced by the work of Friedrich Nietzsche, a nineteenth-century critic of liberal rationalism.

Foucault confronts two other social theorists, Sigmund Freud and Karl Marx. His work on sexuality is a direct challenge to Freud's view that each individual's self is formed around repressed and unconscious infantile sexual impulses. Freud's view implies that there is a "true self," and that psychoanalysis can uncover it, restoring a person to health in the process. The person can never, of course, return to the world of infantile sexuality, but he or she can, at least, understand how they were forced out of Paradise. Foucault does not believe there is such a thing as the true self, nor is there a consistent, universally human process of repressing infantile sexual impulses. Sexuality is a cultural product, varying among cultures. It has no true form, repressed, infantile, or whatever. The subject—each individual's sense of self—is constituted by processes of power and knowledge within a discursive formation. The concept of a true self, formed by repression of sexual impulses but accessible with the help of a psychoanalyst, is the target of Foucault's attack in *The History of Sexuality*.

Foucault challenges Marx in several ways. First, Foucault believes power is exercised at many sites; the mode of production is certainly one of them, but not necessarily the determining or most important one. Power is not lodged only or primarily in a distinct social group, the ruling class, or even in a definable category like the economically dominant class. Second, resistance is omnipresent, not focused in a movement, let alone one led by the proletariat. Like power, resistance appears always and everywhere. Power is always met by resistance, and the two processes appear throughout the formation. Resistance is as strong in the university lecture hall, in school, at the office water cooler, in bed, in prison, in the mental hospital day room, and at the rock concert as it is on the factory floor or the socialist party headquarters. It is an on-going micro-process, with no particular endpoint. Third, Foucault shared the view of many other French intellectuals in the 1960s and 1970s: the effort to channel resistance into an oppositional movement of proletarians against capitalism had disastrous consequences—The Party and the State. Foucault was writing at a time of growing disillusionment among leftwing intellectuals with real socialism in the Soviet bloc and China and growing disengagement from the western European Communist Parties. He was politically active in the prisoners' rights movement in France, supporting the civil rights of the incarcerated. Sharing Marx's vision of human emancipation, he did not pursue it in contemporary Marxist theory and practice, but in a more individual and anarchic perspective of the outsider and deviant.

Foucault's work revolutionized social theory. Its radical social constructionism, the paired concepts "power and knowledge," the critique of the human sciences, and the idea that resistance is a pervasive phenomenon—these elements of Foucault's thought became incorporated into feminist theory, revisions in Marxist theory, and mainstream cultural studies.

Both Foucault readings are from *Discipline and Punish* (actually *Surveiller et Punir*, in the French title). They reveal his method, which is extremely unconventional. He proceeds by investigating unusual and bizarre historical materials, reconstructing the histories of deviance and punishment with fragmentary, quasi-anecdotal evidence that highlights those phenomena he believes are most important; for example, accounts of a particularly bizarre murder, gruesome details of an execution, records of a reform school, personal memoirs of a hermaphrodite. These strange, unsystematically accumulated details are like the intense light of a search beam, thrown back into the darkness of history, illuminating key elements of landscapes of deviance, crime, madness, and punishment.

In the first reading, Foucault shows us images of the Before and After, the shift from pre-modern to modern punishment. In a pre-modern situation, the attempted regicide, Robert Damien, is torn apart in a horrifying public spectacle of torture and execution. After the French Revolution, punishment is replaced by "corrections"; the timetable of a reformatory exemplifies the new order. The deviant is hidden away, incarcerated in a prison or insane asylum. Order is imposed on an unruly body, every motion is prescribed and monitored. Control over the deviant's time is essential to the imposition of order; every minute of the day is accounted for. The deviant is subjected to constant surveillance.

In the second reading, Foucault uses the metaphor of the "Panopticon," an imaginary institution of total and constant surveillance, as an image of modern society. The gaze of the monitors can be turned upon all inmates at all times, eventually inducing them to monitor themselves.

Readings

Foucault, Michel. *The Archaeology of Knowledge*. New York: Pantheon, 1982.

—. *Discipline and Punish: The Birth of the Prison*. New York: Vintage, 1979.

—. *The History of Sexuality*. New York: Vintage, 1990.

—. *Madness and Civilization*. New York: Vintage, 1965.

Macey, David. *The Lives of Michel Foucault: A Biography*. New York: Random House, 1993.

Sawicki, Jana. *Disciplining Foucault: Feminism, Power, and the Body*. New York: Routledge, 1991.

Smart, Barry. *Michel Foucault*. Chichester, England: Ellis Horwood, 1985.

The Body of the Condemned
MICHEL FOUCAULT

On 2 March 1757 Damiens the regicide was condemned "to make the *amende honorable* before the main door of the Church of Paris," where he was to be "taken and conveyed in a cart, wearing nothing but a shirt, holding a torch of burning wax weighing two pounds"; then, "in the said cart, to the Place de Grève, where, on a scaffold that will be erected there, the flesh will be torn from his breasts, arms, thighs and calves with red-hot pincers, his right hand, holding the knife with which he committed the said parricide, burnt with sulphur, and, on those places where the flesh will be torn away, poured molten lead, boiling oil, burning resin, wax and sulphur melted together and then his body drawn and quartered by four horses and his limbs and body consumed by fire, reduced to ashes and his ashes thrown to the winds" (*Pièces originale ...*, 372-4).

"Finally, he was quartered," recounts the *Gazette d'Amsterdam* of 1 April 1757. "This last operation was very long, because the horses used were not accustomed to drawing: consequently, instead of four, six were needed; and when that did not suffice, they were forced, in order to cut off the wretch's thighs, to sever the sinews and hack at the joints....

"It is said that, though he was always a great swearer, no blasphemy escaped his lips; but the excessive pain made him utter horrible cries, and he often repeated: 'My God, have pity on me! Jesus, help me!' the spectators were all edified by the solicitude of the parish priest of St Paul's who despite his great age did not spare himself in offering consolation to the patient."

Bouton, an officer of the watch, left us his account:

The sulphur was lit, but the flame was so poor that only the top skin of the hand was burnt, and that only slightly. Then the executioner, his sleeves rolled up, took the steel pincers, which had been especially made for the occasion, and which were about a foot and a half long, and pulled first at the calf of the right leg, then at the thigh, and from there at the two fleshy parts of the right arm; then at the breasts. Though a strong, sturdy fellow, this executioner found it so difficult to tear away the pieces of flesh that he set about the same spot two or three times, twisting the pincers as he did so, and what he took away formed at each part a wound about the size of a six-pound crown piece.

After these tearings with the pincers, Damiens, who cried out profusely, though without swearing, raised his head and looked at himself; the same executioner dipped an iron spoon in the pot containing the boiling potion, which he poured liberally over each wound. Then the ropes that were to be harnessed to the horses were attached with cords to the patient's body; the horses where then harnessed and placed alongside the arms and legs, one at each limb.

Monsieur Le Breton, the clerk of the court, went up to the patient several times and asked him if he had anything to say. He said he had not; at each torment, he cried out, as the damned in hell are supposed to cry out, "Pardon, my God! Pardon, Lord." Despite all this pain, he raised his head from time to time and looked at himself boldly. The cords had been tied so tightly by the men who pulled the ends that they caused him indescribable pain. Monsieur Le Breton went up to him again and asked him if he had anything to say; he said no. Several confessors went up to him and spoke to him at length; he willingly kissed the crucifix that was held out to him; he opened his lips and repeated: "Pardon, Lord."

The horses tugged hard, each pulling straight on a limb, each horse held by an executioner. After a quarter of an hour, the same ceremony was repeated and finally, after several attempts, the direction of the horses had to be changed, thus: those at the arms were made to pull towards the head, those at the thighs towards the arms, which broke the arms at the joints. This was repeated several times without success. He raised his head and looked at himself. Two more horses had to be added to those harnessed to the thighs, which made six horses in all. Without success.

Finally, the executioner, Samson, said to Monsieur Le Breton that there was no way or hope of succeeding, and told him to ask their Lordships if they wished him to have the prisoner cut into pieces. Monsieur Le Breton, who had come down from the town, ordered that renewed efforts be made, and this was done; but the horses gave up and one of those harnessed to the thighs fell to the ground. The confessors returned and spoke to him again. He said to them (I heard him): "Kiss me, gentlemen." The parish priest of St Paul's did not dare to, so Monsieur de Marsilly slipped under the rope holding the left arm and kissed him on the forehead. The executioners gathered round and Damiens told them not to swear, to carry out their task and that he did not think ill of them; he begged them to pray to God for him, and asked the parish priest of St Paul's to pray for him at the first mass.

After two or three attempts, the executioner Samson and he who had used the pincers each drew out a knife from his pocket and cut the body at the thighs instead of severing the legs at the joints; the four horses gave a tug and carried of the two thighs after them, namely, that of the right side first, the other following; then the same was done to the arms, the shoulders, the arm-pits and the four limbs, the flesh had to be cut almost to the bone, the horses pulling hard carried off the right arm first and the other afterwards.

When the four limbs had been pulled away, the confessors came to speak to him; but his executioner told them that he was dead, though the truth was that I saw the man move, his lower jaw moving from side to side as if he were talking. One of the executioners even said shortly afterwards that when they had lifted the trunk to throw it on the stake, he was still alive. The four limbs were untied from the ropes and thrown on the stake set up in the enclosure in line with the scaffold, then the trunk and the rest were covered with logs and faggots, and fire was put to the straw mixed with this wood.

... In accordance with the decree, the whole was reduced to ashes. The last piece to be found in the embers was still burning at half-past ten in the evening. The pieces of flesh and the trunk had taken about four hours to burn. The officers of whom I was one, as also was my son, and a detachment of archers remained in the square until nearly eleven o'clock.

There were those who made something of the fact that a dog had lain the day before on the grass where the fire had been, had been chased away several times, and had always returned. But it is not difficult to understand that an animal found this place warmer than elsewhere" (quoted in Zevaes, 201-14).

Eighty years later, Léon Faucher drew up his rules "for the House of young prisoners in Paris":

Art. 17. The prisoners' day will begin at six in the morning in winter and at five in summer. They will work for nine hours a day throughout the year. Two hours a day will be devoted to instruction. Work and the day will end at nine o'clock in winter and at eight in summer.

Art. 18. *Rising*. At the first drum-roll, the prisoners must rise and dress in silence, as the supervisor opens the cell doors. At the second drum-roll, they must be dressed and make their beds. At the third, they must line up and precede to the chapel for morning prayer. There is a five minute-interval between each drum-roll.

Art. 19. The prayers are conducted by the chaplain and followed by a moral or religious reading. This exercise must not last more than half an hour.

Art. 20. *Work*. At a quarter to six in the summer, a quarter to seven in winter, the prisoners go down into the courtyard where they must wash their hands and faces, and receive their first ration of bread. Immediately afterwards, they form into work-teams and go off to work, which must begin at six in summer and seven in winter.

Art. 21. *Meal*. At ten o'clock the prisoners leave their work and go to the refectory; they wash their hands in their courtyards and assemble in divisions. After the dinner, there is recreation until twenty minutes to eleven.

Art. 22. *School*. At twenty minutes to eleven, at the drum-roll, the prisoners form into ranks, and proceed in divisions to the school. The class lasts two hours and consists alternately of reading, writing, drawing and arithmetic.

Art. 23. At twenty minutes to one, the prisoners leave the school, in division, and return to their courtyards for recreation. At five minutes to one, at the drum-roll, they form into work-teams.

Art. 24. At one o'clock they must be back in the workshops: they work until four o'clock.

Art. 25. At four o'clock the prisoners leave their workshops and go into the courtyards where they wash their hands and form into divisions for the refectory.

Art. 26. Supper and the recreation that follows it last until five o'clock: the prisoners then return to the workshops.

Art. 27. At seven o'clock in the summer, at eight in winter, work stops; bread is distributed for the last time in the workshops. For a quarter of an hour one of the prisoners or supervisors reads a passage from some instructive or uplifting work. This is followed by evening prayer.

Art. 28. At half-past seven in summer, half-past eight in winter, the prisoners must be back in their cells after the washing of hands and the inspection of clothes in the courtyard; at the first drum-roll, they must undress, and at the second get into bed. The cell doors are closed and the supervisors go the rounds in the corridors, to ensure order and silence (Faucher, 274-82).

We have, then, a public execution and a time-table. They do not punish the same crimes or the same type of delinquent. But they each define a certain penal style. Less than a century separates them. It was a time when, in Europe and in the United States, the entire economy of punishment was redistributed. It was a time of great "scandals" for traditional justice, a time of innumerable projects for reform. It saw a new theory of law and crime, a new moral or political justification of the right to punish; old laws were abolished, old customs died out. "Modern" codes were planned or drawn up: Russia, 1769; Prussia, 1780; Pennsylvania and Tuscany, 1786; Austria, 1788; France, 1791, Year IV, 1808 and 1810. It was a new age for penal justice.

Among so many changes, I shall consider one: the disappearance of torture as a public spectacle. Today we are rather inclined to ignore it; perhaps, in its time, it gave rise to too much inflated rhetoric; perhaps it has been attributed too readily and too emphatically to a process of "humanization," thus dispensing with the need for further analysis....

Panopticon[1]
MICHEL FOUCAULT

Bentham's *Panopticon* is the architectural figure of this composition. We know the principle on which it was based: at the periphery, an annular building; at the centre, a tower; this tower is pierced with wide windows that open onto the inner side of the ring; the peripheric building is divided into cells, each of which extends the whole width of the building; they have two windows, one on the inside, corresponding to the windows of the tower; the other, on the outside, allows the light to cross the cell from one end to the others. All that is needed, then, is to place a supervisor in a central tower and to shut up in each cell a madman, a patient, a condemned man, a worker or a schoolboy. By the effect of backlighting, one can observe from the tower, standing out precisely against the light, the small captive shadows in the cells of the periphery. They are like so many cages, so many small theatres, in which each actor is alone, perfectly individualized and constantly visible. The panoptic mechanism arranges spatial unities that make it possible to see constantly and to recognize immediately. In short, it reverses the principle of the dungeon; or rather of its three functions— to enclose, to deprive of light and to hide—it preserves only the first and elim- inates the other two. Full lighting and the eye of a supervisor capture better than darkness, which ultimately protected. Visibility is a trap.

To begin with, this made it possible—as a negative effect—to avoid those compact, swarming, howling masses that were to be found in places of con- finement, those painted by Goya or described by Howard. Each individual, in his place, is securely confined to a cell from which he is seen from the front by the supervisor: but the side walls prevent him from coming into contact with his companions. He is seen, but he does not see; he is the object of information, never a subject in communication. The arrangement of his room, opposite the central tower, imposes on him an axial visibility; but the divisions of the ring, those separated cells, imply a lateral invisibility. And this invisibility is a guar- antee of order. If the inmates are convicts, there is no danger of a plot, an attempt at collective escape, the planning of new crimes for the future, bad rec- iprocal influences; if they are patients, there is no danger of contagion; if they are madmen there is no risk of their committing violence upon one another; if they are schoolchildren, there is no copying, no noise, no chatter, no waste of time; if they are workers, there are no disorders, no theft, no coalitions, none of those distractions that slow down the rate of work, make it less perfect or cause accidents. The crowd, a compact mass, a locus of multiple exchanges, individ- ualities merging together, a collective effect, is abolished and replaced by a col- lection of separated individualities. From the point of view of the guardian, it is replaced by a multiplicity that can be numbered and supervised; from the point of view of the inmates, by a sequestered and observed solitude (Bentham, 60-64).

Hence the major effect of the Panopticon: to induce in the inmate a state of conscious and permanent visibility that assures the automatic functioning of power. So to arrange things that the surveillance is permanent in its effects, even if it is discontinuous in its action; that the perfection of power should tend to render its actual exercise unnecessary; that this architectural apparatus should be a machine for creating and sustaining a power relation independent of the person who exercises it; in short, that the inmates should be caught up in a power situation of which they are themselves the bearers. To achieve this, it is at one too much and too little that the prisoner should be constantly observed by an inspector: too little, for what matters is that he knows himself to be observed; too much, because he has no need in fact of being so. In view of this, Bentham laid down the principle that power should be visible and unverifiable.

Visible: the inmate will constantly have before his eyes the tall outline of the central tower from which he is spied upon. Unverifiable: the inmate must never know whether he is being looked at any one moment; but he must be sure that he may always be so. In order to make the presence of absence of the inspector unverifiable, so that the prisoners, in their cells, cannot even see a shadow, Bentham envisaged not only venetian blinds on the windows of the central observation hall, but, on the inside, partitions that intersected the hall at right angles and, in order to pass from one quarter to the other, not doors but zig-zag openings; for the slightest noise, a gleam of light, a brightness in a half-opened door would betray the presence of the guardian.[2] The Panopticon is a machine for dissociating the see/being seen dyad: in the peripheric ring, one is totally seen, without ever seeing; in the central tower, one sees everything without ever being seen.[3]

It is an important mechanism, for it automatizes and disindividualizes power. Power has its principle not so much in a person as in a certain concerted distribution of bodies, surfaces, lights, gazes; in an arrangement whose internal mechanisms produce the relation in which individuals are caught up. The ceremonies, the rituals, the marks by which the sovereign's surplus power was manifested are useless. There is a machinery that assures dissymmetry, disequilibrium, difference. Consequently, it does not matter who exercises power. Any individual, taken almost at random, can operate the machine: in the absence of the director, his family, his friends, his visitors, even his servants (Bentham, 45). Similarly, it does not matter what motive animates him: the curiosity of the indiscreet, the malice of a child, the thirst for knowledge of a philosopher who wishes to visit this museum of human nature, or the perversity of those who take pleasure in spying and punishing. The more numerous those anonymous and temporary observers are, the greater the risk for the inmate of being surprised and the greater his anxious awareness of being observed. The panopticon is a marvellous machine which, whatever use one may wish to put it to, produces homogeneous effects of power.

A real subjection is born mechanically from a fictitious relation. So it is not necessary to use force to constrain the convict to good behaviour, the madman to calm, the worker to work, the schoolboy to application, the patient to the observation of the regulations. Bentham was surprised that panoptic institutions could be so light: there were no more bars, no more chains, no more heavy locks; all that was needed was that the separations should be clear and the openings well arranged. The heaviness of the old "houses of security," with their fortress-like architecture, could be replaced by the simple, economic geometry of a "house of certainty." The efficiency of power, its constraining force have, in a sense, passed over to the other side—to the side of its surface of application. He who is subjected to a field of visibility, and who knows it, assumes responsibility for the constraints of power; he makes them play spontaneously upon himself; he inscribes in himself the power relation in which he simultaneously plays both roles; he becomes the principle of his own subjection. By this very fact, the external power may throw off its physical weight; it tends to the non-corporal; and, the more it approaches this limit, the more constant, profound and permanent are its effects: it is a perpetual victory that avoids any physical confrontation and which is always decided in advance.

Bentham does not say whether he was inspired, in his project, by Le Vaux's menagerie at Versailles: the first menagerie in which the different elements are not, as they traditionally were, distributed in a park (Loisel, 104-7). At the centre was an octagonal pavilion which, on the first floor, consisted of only a single room, the kings's *salon*; on every side large windows looked out onto seven cages (the eighth side was reserved for the entrance), containing different species of animals. By Bentham's time, this menagerie had disappeared. But one finds in the programme of the Panopticon a similar concern with individualizing observation, with characterization and classification, with the analytical arrangement of space. The Panopticon is a royal menagerie; the animal is replaced by man, individual distribution by specific grouping and the king by the machinery of a furtive power. With this exception, the Panopticon also does the work of a naturalist. It makes it possible to draw up differences: among patients, to observe the symptoms of each individual, without the proximity of beds, the circulation of miasmas, the effects of contagion confusing the clinical tables; among schoolchildren, it makes it possible to observe performances (without there being any limitation or copying), to map aptitudes, to assess characters, to draw up rigorous classifications and, in relation to normal development, to distinguish "laziness and stubbornness" from "incurable imbecility"; among workers, it makes it possible to note the aptitudes of each worker, compare the time he takes to perform a task, and if they are paid by the day, to calculate their wages (Bentham, 60-64).

So much for the question of observation. But the Panopticon was also a laboratory; it could be used as a machine to carry out experiments, to alter behaviour, to train or correct individuals. To experiment with medicines and monitor their effects. To try out different punishments on prisoners, according to their crimes and character, and to seek the most effective ones. To teach different techniques simultaneously to the workers, to decide which is the best. To try out pedagogical experiments—and in particular to take up once again the well-debated problem of secluded education, by using orphans. One would see what would happen when, in their sixteenth or eighteenth year, they were presented with other boys or girls; one could verify whether, as Helvetius thought, anyone could learn anything; one would follow "the genealogy of every observable idea"; one could bring up different children according to different systems of thought, making certain children believe that two and two do not make four or that the moon is a cheese, then put them together when they are twenty or twenty-five years old; one would then have discussions that would be worth a great deal more than the sermons or lectures on which so much money is spent; one would have at least an opportunity of making discoveries in the domain of metaphysics. The Panopticon is a privileged place for experiments on men, and for analysing with complete certainty the transformations that may be obtained from them. The Panopticon may even provide an apparatus for supervising its own mechanisms. In this central tower, the director may spy on all the employees that he has under his orders: nurses, doctors, foremen, teachers, warders; he will be able to judge them continuously, alter their behaviour, impose upon them the methods he thinks best; and it will even be possible to observe the director himself. An inspector arriving unexpectedly at the centre of the Panopticon will be able to judge at a glance, without anything being concealed from him, how the entire establishment is functioning. And, in any case, enclosed as he is in the middle of this architectural mechanism, is not the director's own fate entirely bound up with it? The incompetent physician who has allowed contagion to spread, the incompetent prison governor or workshop manager will be the first victims of an epidemic or a revolt. "'By every tie I could devise,' said the master of the Panopticon, 'my own fate had been bound up by me with theirs'" (Bentham, 177). The Panopticon functions as a kind of laboratory of power. Thanks to its mechanisms of observation, it gains in efficiency and in the ability to penetrate into men's behaviour; knowledge follows the advances of power, discovering new objects of knowledge over all the surfaces on which power is exercised.

The plague-stricken town, the panoptic establishment—the differences are important. They mark, at a distance of a century and a half, the transformations of the disciplinary programme. In the first case, there is an exceptional situation: against an extraordinary evil, power is mobilized; it makes itself everywhere present and visible; it invents new mechanisms; it separates, it immobilizes, it partitions; it constructs for a time what is both a counter-city and the perfect society; it imposes an ideal functioning, but one that is reduced, in the final analysis, like the evil that it combats, to a simple dualism of life and death: that which moves brings death, and one kills that which moves. The Panopticon, on the other hand, must be understood as a generalizable model of functioning; a way of defining power relations in terms of the everyday life of men. No doubt Bentham presents it as a particular institution, closed in upon itself. Utopias, perfectly closed in upon themselves, are common enough. As opposed to the ruined prisons, littered with mechanisms of torture, to be seen in Piranese's engravings, the Panopticon presents a cruel, ingenious cage. The fact that it should have given rise, even in our own time, to so many variations, projected or realized, is evidence of the imaginary intensity that it has possessed for almost two hundred years. But the Panopticon must not be understood as a dream building: it is the diagram of a mechanism of power reduced to its ideal form; its functioning, abstracted from any obstacle, resistance or friction, must be represented as a pure architectural and optical system: it is in fact a figure of political technology that may and must be detached from any specific use.

It is polyvalent in its applications; it serves to reform prisoners, but also to treat patients, to instruct schoolchildren, to confine the insane, to supervise workers, to put beggars and idlers to work. It is a type of location of bodies in space, of distribution of individuals in relation to one another, of hierarchical organization, of disposition of centres and channels of power, of definition of the instruments and modes of intervention of power, which can be implemented in hospitals, workshops, schools, prisons. Whenever one is dealing, with a multiplicity of individuals on whom a task or a particular form of behaviour must be imposed, the panoptic schema may be used. It is—necessary modifications apart—applicable "to all establishments whatsoever, in which, within a space not too large be covered or commanded by buildings, a number of persons are meant to be kept under inspection" (Bentham, 40; although Bentham takes the penitentiary house as his prime example, it is because it has many different functions to fulfil—safe custody, confinement, solitude, forced labour and instruction).

In each of its applications, it makes it possible to perfect the exercise of power. It does this in several ways: because it can reduce the number of those who exercise it, while increasing the number of those on whom it is exercised. Because it is possible to intervene at any moment and because the constant pressure acts even before the offences, mistakes or crimes have been committed. Because, in these conditions, its strength is that it never intervenes, it is exercised spontaneously and without noise, it constitutes a mechanism whose effects follow from one another. Because, without any physical instrument other than architecture and geometry, it acts directly on individuals; it gives "power of mind over mind". The panoptic schema makes any apparatus of power more intense: it assures its economy (in material, in personnel, in time); it assures its efficacity by its preventative character, its continuous functioning and its automatic mechanisms. It is a way of obtaining from power "in hitherto unexampled quantity," "a great and new instrument of government...; its great excellence consists in the great strength it is capable of giving to *any* institution it may be thought proper to apply it to" (Bentham, 66).

It's a case of "it's easy once you've thought of it" in the political sphere. It can in fact be integrated into any function (education, medical treatment, production, punishment); it can increase the effect of this function, by being linked closely with it; it can constitute a mixed mechanism in which relations of power (and of knowledge) may be precisely adjusted, in the smallest detail, to the processes that are to be supervised; it can establish a direct proportion between "surplus power" and "surplus production". In short, it arranges things in such a way that the exercise of power is not added on from the outside, like a rigid, heavy constraint, to the functions it invests, but is so subtly present in them as to increase their efficiency by itself increasing its own points of contact. The panoptic mechanism is not simply a hinge, a point of exchange between a mechanism of power and a function; it is a way of making power relations function in a function, and of making a function function through these power relations. Bentham's Preface to *Panopticon* opens with a list of the benefits to be obtained from his "inspection-house": *"Morals reformed—health preserved—industry invigorated—instruction diffused—public burthens lightened—*Economy seated, as it were, upon a rock—the gordian knot of the Poor-Laws not cut, but untied—all by a simple idea in architecture!" (Bentham, 39).

Furthermore, the arrangement of this machine is such that its enclosed nature does not preclude a permanent presence from the outside: we have seen that anyone may come and exercise in the central tower the functions of surveillance, and that, this being the case, he can gain a clear idea of the way in which the surveillance is practised. In fact, any panoptic institution, even if it is as rigorously closed as a penitentiary, may without difficulty be subjected to such irregular and constant inspections: and not only by the appointed inspectors, but also by the public; any member of society will have the right to come and see with his own eyes how the schools, hospitals, factories, prisons function. There is no risk, therefore, that the increase of power created by the panoptic machine may degenerate into tyranny; the disciplinary mechanism will be democratically controlled, since it will be constantly accessible "to the great tribunal committee of the world."[4] This Panopticon, subtly arranged so that an observer may observe, at a glance, so many different individuals, also enables everyone to come and observe any of the observers. The seeing machine was once a sort of dark room into which individuals spied; it has become a transparent building in which the exercise of power may be supervised by society as a whole.

The panoptic schema, without disappearing as such or losing any of its properties, was destined to spread throughout the social body; its vocation was to become a generalized function. The plague stricken town provided an exceptional disciplinary model: perfect, but absolutely violent; to the disease that brought death, power opposed its perpetual threat of death; life inside it was reduced to its simplest expression; it was, against the power of death, the meticulous exercise of the right of the sword. The Panopticon, on the other hand, has a role of amplification; although it arranges power, although it is intended to make it more economic and more effective, it does so not for power itself, nor for the immediate salvation of a threatened society: its aim is to strengthen the social forces—to increase production, to develop the economy, spread education, raise the level of public morality; to increase and multiply.

How is power to be strengthened in such a way that, far from impeding progress, far from weighing upon it with its rules and regulations, it actually facilitates such progress? What intensificator of power will be able at the same time to be a multiplicator of production? How will power, by increasing its forces, be able to increase those of society instead of confiscating them or impeding them? The Panopticon's solution to this problem is that the productive increase of power can be assured only if, on the one hand, it can be exercised continuously in the very foundations of society, in the subtlest possible way, and if, on the other hand, it functions outside these sudden, violent, discontinuous forms that are bound up with the exercise of sovereignty. The body of the king, with its strange material and physical presence, with the force that he himself deploys or transmits to some few others, is at the opposite extreme of this new physics of power represented by panopticism; the domain of panopticism is, on the contrary, that whole lower region, that region of irregular bodies, with their details, their multiple movements, their heterogeneous forces, their spatial relations; what are required are mechanisms that analyse distributions, gaps, series, combinations, and which use instruments that render visible, record, differentiate and compare: a physics of a relational and multiple power, which has its maximum intensity not in the person of the king, but in the bodies that can be individualized by these relations. At the theoretical level, Bentham defines another way of analysing the social body and the power relations that traverse it; in terms of practice, he defines a procedure of subordination of bodies and forces that must increase the utility of power while practising the economy of the prince. Panopticism is the general principle of a new "political anatomy" whose object and end are not the relations of sovereignty but the relations of discipline.

The celebrated, transparent, circular cage, with its high tower, powerful and knowing, may have been for Bentham a project of a perfect disciplinary institution; but he also set out to show how one may "unlock" the disciplines and get them to function in a diffused, multiple, polyvalent way throughout the whole social body. These disciplines, which the classical age had elaborated in specific, relatively enclosed places—barracks, schools, workshops—and whose total implementation had been imagined only at the limited and temporary scale of a plague-stricken town, Bentham dreamt of transforming into a network of mechanisms that would be everywhere and always alert, running through society without interruption in space or in time. The panoptic arrangement provides the formula for this generalization. It programmes, at the level of an elementary and easily transferable mechanism, the basic functioning of a society penetrated through and through with disciplinary mechanisms.

There are two images, then, of discipline. At one extreme, the discipline-blockade, the enclosed institution, established on the edges of society, turned inwards towards negative functions: arresting evil, breaking communications, suspending time. At the other extreme, with panopticism, is the discipline-mechanism: a functional mechanism that must improve the exercise of power by making it lighter, more rapid, more effective, a design of subtle coercion for a society to come. The movement from one project to the other, from a schema of exceptional discipline to one of a generalized surveillance, rests on a historical transformation: the gradual extension of the mechanisms of discipline throughout the seventeenth and eighteenth centuries, their spread throughout the whole social body, the formation of what might be called in general the disciplinary society.

Notes

1. *Editors note*. Before describing the Panopticon, Foucault describes the quarantining of communities struck by the plague. He contrasts this blockade to a new configuration of discipline, a special type of prison.

2. In the *Postscript to the Panopticon*, 1791, Bentham adds dark inspection galleries painted in black around the inspector's lodge, each making it possible to observe two storeys of cells.

3. In his first version of the *Panopticon*, Bentham had also imagined an acoustic surveillance, operated by means of pipes leading from the cells to the central tower. In the *Postscript* he abandoned the idea, perhaps because he could not introduce into it the principle of dis-symmetry and prevent the prisoners from hearing the inspector as well as the inspector hearing them. Julius tried to develop a system of dis-symmetrical listening (Julius, 18).

4. Imagining this continuous flow of visitors entering the central tower by an underground passage and then observing the circular landscape of the Panopticon, was Bentham aware of the Panoramas that Barker was constructing at exactly the same period (the first seems to have dated from 1787) and in which the visitors, occupying the central place, saw unfolding around them a landscape, a city or a battle. The visitors occupied exactly the place of the sovereign gaze.

Bibliography

Bentham, J. *Work*, ed. Bowring, IV, 1843.

Faucher, L. *De la réforme des prisons*, 1938.

Julius, J.H. *Leçons sur les prisons*, I, 1831 (Fr. trans.).

Loisel, G. *Histoires des ménageries*, II, 1912.

Piéces originales et procédures des procès fait à Robert-François Damiens, III, 1757.

Zavaes, A.L. *Damiens le régicide*, 1937.

34

POSTMODERN MARXISM: PAUL WILLIS (1945-)

Paul Willis represents the melting border between Marxists and other types of social theorists; more precisely, his work illustrates how Marxists have adapted symbolic-interactionist theories and the ideas of Foucault. He explores cultural meanings and interactions of everyday life in order to understand how capitalism reproduces itself from generation to generation; he uses an interactionist method to chart patterns of resistance. Like Foucault he sees resistance not primarily in organized movements, but in everyday life and common culture. There is a constant and pervasive play of cultural domination and resistance; this play usually has ambiguous outcomes. The theorist needs a spirit of irony and irreverence and an appreciation of paradox, contradiction and absurdity—attitudes akin to Simmel and Benjamin's way of thinking.

Willis's first major work, *Learning to Labour: How Working Class Kids Get Working Class Jobs*, was a study of the counter-culture of the "lads," white working-class boys in an English secondary school. Willis showed that the lads' rejection of conventional school culture was a form of resistance to capitalism. Their defiance, horseplay, irreverence, pranks, truancy, and collective anti-school spirit reaffirmed the values and solidarity of working-class culture, historically born from workers' resistance to management on the shop floor. This anti-authoritarian "us and them" mentality was learned from their fathers and constantly recreated by young men in small group interactions. But Willis also showed how this resistance was ultimately self-defeating. At an obvious level, the lads' anti-school culture led them to do poorly in school, drop out early, and perpetuate their semi-skilled position in the job market. The anti-school culture is thus a self-condemnation to working class jobs: hence the subtitle of the book.

At a deeper level of Marxist analysis, Willis showed how the very act of resistance to school culture reproduces a central element of capitalism instead of challenging it: The division between mental and manual labour. This division is part of class polarization between the bourgeoisie, associated with mental activity, and the proletariat that performs manual work. In rejecting school culture, the lads throw out the baby of systematic mental activity with the bathwater of school tedium and discipline. They thus condemn themselves not only individually to manual labour jobs, but also collectively to a profound alienation from their intellectual potential. These anti-intellectual patterns of resistance, found among working-class youth throughout capitalist society, add up to the inability of the class to see itself as leading society and developing a hegemonic self-concept. Willis thereby added a crucial dimension of empirical research at the micro level to Gramsci and Lenin's more abstract reflections on how the proletariat has failed to constitute itself as a hegemonic class.

These findings could also be formulated in functional terms; the lads' boisterous anti-school culture has manifest functions for their class by creating working class solidarity, but its latent, unintended function for the capitalist system is to discourage the working class from mental activity and the formation of hegemonic intellectuals. The lads' racism and sexism exacerbate the weaknesses of working-class culture by separating white working-class men from the rest of the class, composed of women and people of colour.

Common Culture is a more mellow and optimistic book, perhaps precisely because working-class jobs disappeared in large numbers during the Thatcher period, forcing young people to develop new forms of oppositional culture. Willis and his research team document these new cultural forms in interviews and observation. Although a traditional Marxist might scoff at the notion that the proletarian vanguard consists of young people mocking the "telly" and shopping in flea markets, Willis suggests that these new forms of symbolic activity can be part of a vital opposition to capitalism. They create new meanings, undermine both consumption and production as central values of capitalism, and preview a post-capitalist culture. We can recognize convergence with Benjamin's optimistic analysis of new media as potential tools for deconstructing capitalist hegemony.

In these selections, Willis defines common culture, discusses its relationship to consumer capitalist culture, and provides examples of symbolic play and cultural expression in the area of style and fashion. In contrast to traditional Marxist analysis, Willis emphasizes language, interaction, the body, and identity. The shaping of common culture is an open-ended process. It will not produce a proletarian revolution in the near future as envisioned by Marxist theory of the old school, but it is part of a long historical process of transformation of consciousness.

Readings

Hebdige, Dick. *Subculture: The Meaning of Style*. London and New York: Routledge, 1993.

MacLeod, Jay. *Ain't No Makin' It*. Boulder, CO: Westview Press, 1995.

Willis, Paul. *Learning to Labor*. New York: Columbia University Press, 1981.

—. *Common Culture: Symbolic Work at Play in the Everyday Cultures of the Young*. Boulder, CO: Westview Press, 1990.

Common Culture
PAUL WILLIS

Symbolic Creativity

The institutions and practices, genres and terms of high art are currently categories of exclusion more than of inclusion. They have no real connection with most young people or their lives. They may encourage some artistic specializations but they certainly discourage much wider and more general symbolic creativity. The official existence of the "arts" in institutions seems to exhaust everything else of its artistic contents. If some things count as "art," the, rest must be "non-art." Because "art" is in the "art gallery," it can't therefore be anywhere else. It is that which is special and heightened, not ordinary and everyday.

The arts establishment, by and large, has done little to dispel these assumptions. It prefers instead to utilize or even promote fears of cultural decline and debasement in order to strengthen its own claims for subsidy, institutional protection and privilege. In general the arts establishment connives to keep alive the myth of the special, creative individual artist holding out against passive mass consumerism, so helping to maintain a self-interested view of élite creativity.

Against this we insist that there is a vibrant symbolic life and symbolic creativity in everyday life, everyday activity and expression—even if it is sometimes invisible, looked down on or spurned. We don't want to invent it or propose it. We want to recognize it—literally re-cognize it. Most young people's lives are not involved with the arts and yet are actually full of expressions, signs and symbols through which individuals and groups seek creatively to establish their presence, identity and meaning. Young people are all the time expressing or attempting to express something about their actual or potential *cultural significance*. This is the realm of living common culture. Vulgar sometimes, perhaps. But also "common" in being everywhere, resistant, hardy. Also "common" in being shared, having things "in common." Where "arts" exclude, "culture" includes. "Art" has been cut short of meanings, where "culture" has not.

As Raymond Williams always insisted, culture is ordinary.[1] It is the extraordinary in the ordinary, which is extraordinary, which makes both into culture, common culture. We are thinking of the extraordinary symbolic creativity of the multitude of ways in which young people use, humanize, decorate and invest with meanings their common and immediate life spaces and social practices—personal styles and choice of clothes; selective and active use of music, TV, magazines; decoration of bedrooms; the rituals of romance and subcultural styles; the style, banter and drama of friendship groups; music-making and dance. Nor are these pursuits and activities trivial or inconsequential. In conditions of late modernization and the widespread crisis of cultural values they can be crucial to the creation and sustenance of individual and group identities, even to cultural survival of identity itself. There is work, even desperate work, in their play....

All arts, dead or living, in or out of their times, can live and do live in our scheme, but they have to earn their keep. We don't wish to be in at the end of "art" but to direct attention back to, if you like, the wellsprings of art. Our project is to establish, or re-establish, some essential, critical, uncluttered and old-fashioned truths. Creative activity, reflection and expression are in all young people's lives all of the time—only they have different names. We aim to spell out some of them.

The basic method we've used to get inside the words and to spell them out has been a loose and general form of ethnography utilizing, in particular, the recorded group discussion. We provide statistical profiles, histories and descriptive contexts where appropriate, but our main aim is to allow young people's words and experiences to come through directly into the written text. Out ethnographic research and presentation have not aspired to a full methodological rigour, and we've ranged widely, sometimes at the cost of depth, for examples of symbolic creativity without really providing accounts of whole ways of life. But we have presented cultural items through the contexts of young people's own practices, meanings and usages of them, as gathered through our direct fieldwork methods. Discussions were taped with a variety of different groups of young people in Wolverhampton.... These provided evidence and data which we've drawn on throughout the book; where not otherwise indicated quoted material comes usually from this source. The book also draws on a range of ethnographic fieldwork materials written up for the original Gulbenkian project (see Preface) and conducted in a variety of places including Sunderland, Leicester, South Birmingham, London and Kidderminster.

We've focused on young people, not because they are "different," locked into some biological stage that enforces its own social condition, but simply because they provide the best and most crucial examples of our argument. The teenage and early adult years are important from a cultural perspective and in special need of a close "qualitative" attention because it is here, at least in the first-world western cultures, where people are formed most self-consciously through their own symbolic and other activities. It is where they form symbolic moulds through which they understand themselves and their possibilities for the rest of their lives. It is also the stage where people begin to construct themselves through nuance and complexity, through difference as well as similarity.

Our main ethnographic materials are drawn form working-class experience. We have not systematically explored class differences. However, we would claim that many of the processes which we discuss hold true as tendencies in middle-class experience too, though in different and more contradictory relation to and producing different effects from school, work, the family and inherited "cultural capital," and are major cross-class cultural levelling forces.

There are, therefore, many commonalities in youth experience and it is these we try to highlight. It is clear, however, that symbolic work and creativity can also differ in form, style and content according to age and "life style" (living with parents or not, whether or not married, with or without children). We have not attempted to delineate this.

We have decided not to try to present a separate cultural picture of ethnic-minority youth. It is beyond our scope to do this in a properly responsible way and our focus is in any case not to provide authoritative accounts of whole cultures but to highlight the symbolic work and creativity of young people, wherever we find them. We draw many such examples from ethnic-minority experience.

Some general points, however, should be made. It is clear from our fieldwork that Caribbean and Asian traditions are very important to young black people. They use their cultural backgrounds as frameworks for living and as repertoires of symbolic resources for interpreting all aspects of their lives. This is a source of much pride to most of them and one of the fundamental means through which they explore what distinguishes them from white youth. This is necessary, not only for the development of their own identities, but also necessary as an affirmation and assertion against an omnipresent racism which tells young blacks that being "English" means being white as well as native born, and that those who are not white can never completely fit into British culture.

But young black people can never look wholly to the prior generation for clues about how to develop their own identities. The experiences of the two generations differ, and some cultural commonalities with white youth must arise from their shared conditions of life—common experiences in the same streets and schools mediated by many of the same cultural media. Often young black people are engaged in a doubly creative task. They are trying to negotiate what it means to be a black person in a white culture at the same time as they are engaged in the same creative activities as their white peers, through which they also explore aspects of their black identities. The balance which young people strike between these things differs from culture to culture and from individual to individual....

Necessary work and symbolic creativity

...But there is another kind of humanly necessary work—often unrecognized but equally necessary—*symbolic work*. This is the application of human capacities to and through, on and with symbolic resources and raw materials (collections of signs and symbols—for instance, the language as we inherit it as well as texts, songs, films, images and artefacts of all kinds) to produce meanings. This is broader than, logically prior to and a condition of material production, but its "necessariness" has been forgotten....

What are some of the basic elements of necessary symbolic work?

First, language as a practice and symbolic resource. Language is the primary instrument that we use to communicate. It is the highest ordering of our sensuous impressions of the world, and the ultimate basis of our hope and capacity to control it. It enables interaction and solidarity with others and allows us to assess our impact on others and theirs on us. It therefore allows us to see ourselves as others.

Second, the active body as a practice and symbolic resource. The body is a site of somatic knowledge as well as a set of signs and symbols. It is the source of productive and communicative activity—signing, symbolizing, feeling.

Third, drama as a practice and symbolic resource. Communicative interaction with others is not automatic. We do not communicate from head to head through wires drilled into our skulls. Communication is achieved through roles, rituals and performances that we produce with others. Dramaturgical components of the symbolic include a variety of non-verbal communications, as well as sensuous cultural practices and communal solidarities. These include dancing, singing, joke-making, story-telling in dynamic settings and through performance.

Fourth and most importantly, symbolic creativity. Language, the body, dramatic forms are, in a way, both raw material and tools. Symbolic creativity is more fully the practice, the making—or their essence, what all practices have in common, what drives them. This is the production of *new* (however small the shift) meanings intrinsically attached to feeling, to energy, to excitement and psychic movement. This is the basis of confidence in dynamic human capacities as realities rather than as potentials—to be made conscious, through some concrete practice or active mediation, of the quality of human consciousness and how it can further be developed through the exercise and application of vital powers. Symbolic creativity can be seen as worthy equivalent to what an all-embracing and inclusive notion of the living arts might include (counterposed, of course, to the current exclusions of "art.") Symbolic creativity may be individual and/or collective. It transforms what is provided and helps to produce specific forms of human identity and capacity. Being Human—human being-ness—means to be creative in the sense of remaking the world for ourselves as we make and find our own place and identity.

What exactly is produced by symbolic work and symbolic creativity?

First, and perhaps most important, they produce and reproduce individual identities—who and what "I am" and could become. These may be diffuse, contradictory or decentred but they are produced through symbolic work including struggles to make meaning. Sensuous human communicative activities are also intersubjective. It is through knowing "the other," including recognizing the self as an other for some others, that a self or selves can be known at all.

Second, symbolic work and creativity place identities in larger wholes. Identities do not stand alone above history, beyond history. They are related in time, place and things. It is symbolic work and creativity which realize the structured collectivity of individuals as well as their differences, which realize the materiality of context as well as the symbolism of self. This reminds us that locations and situations are not only *determinations*—they're also relations and resources to be discovered, explored and experienced. Memberships of race, class, gender, age and region are not only learned, they're lived and experimented with. This is so even if only by pushing up against the oppressive limits of established order and power.

Third and finally, symbolic work and especially creativity develop and affirm our active senses of our own vital capacities, the powers of the self and how they might be applied to the cultural world. This is what makes activity and identity *transitive* and specifically human. It is the dynamic and, therefore, clinching part of identity. It is the expectation of being able to apply power to the world to change it—however minutely. It is how, in the future, there is some human confidence that unities may be formed out of confusion, patterns out of irregularity. This is to be able to make judgements on who's a friend, who's an enemy, when to talk, when to hold silence, when to go, when to stop. But it's also associated with, and helps to form, overall styles of thinking which promise to make most sense of the world for you. It's also a cultural sense of what symbolic forms—languages, images, music, haircuts, styles, clothes—"work" most economically and creatively for the self. A culturally learned sense of the powers of the self is what makes the self in connecting it to others and to the world.

In many ways this is directly a question of cultural survival for many young people. Processes of symbolic work and symbolic creativity are very open, contested and unstable under conditions of late modernization. All young people experience one aspect or another of the contemporary "social condition" of youth: unwilling economic dependence on parents and parental homes; uncertainly regarding future planning; powerlessness and lack of control over immediate circumstances of life; feelings of symbolic as well as material marginality to the main society; imposed institutional and ideological constructions of "youth" which privilege certain readings and definitions of what young people should do, feel or be.[2]

Many of the traditional resources of, and inherited bases for, social meaning, membership, security and psychic certainly have lost their legitimacy for a good proportion of young people. There is no longer a sense of a "whole culture" with allocated places and a shared, universal value system. Organized religion, the monarchy, trade unions, schools, public broadcasting, high culture and its intertwinings with public culture no longer supply ready values and models of duty and meaning to help structure the passage into settled adulthood. This is certainly partly a result of much commented-upon wider processes related to late modernization: secularization; consumerism; individualization; decollectivization; weakening respect for authority, new technologies of production and distribution. But it is also the case that these inherited traditions owe their still continuing and considerable power to the stakes they offer and seem to offer to the individual: some graspable identity within a set of relationships to other identities; some notion of citizenship within a larger whole which offers rights, satisfactions and loyalties as well as duty and submission. However, for many young people, made to feel marginal to this society, and without their own material stake in it, these merely symbolic stakes can seem very remote. These public traditions and meanings cannot make good what they offer, because they are undercut at another more basic level by unfulfilled expectations. These things are for parents and adults, for those who have an interest in and make up the civil body. For the young Black British they're even more remote—they are for other people's parents. No longer can we be blind to the "whiteness" of our major traditional public sources of identity.

Young working-class women may experience this youth condition in a special way. On the one hand they are a target consumption group for many home commodities as well as for feminine-style-and-identity products. On the other hand, and with no money recompense and no real power in the consumer market, they may be making partial, early and exploited "transitions" (often in an imperceptible extension of childhood domestic chores "naturally" expected of girls but not of boys) into domestic roles of care and maintenance. This may seem to be a destination of sorts and a meaningful, useful activity when labour-market opportunities are scarce or difficult, but it can often be a specific unofficial training and subjective preparation for a lifetime's future of domestic drudgery coupled with job "opportunities" only in part-time, low-paid, insecure, usually dead-end "female" service work....

Grounded aesthetics
There are many ways in which the "official arts" are removed from the possibility of a living symbolic *mediation*, even despite their possible symbolic rich-

ness and range. Most of them are out of their time and, even thought this should enforce no veto on current *mediation*, the possibilities of a relevant structuring of symbolic interest are obviously limited. The institutions and practices which support "art," however, seem designed to break any living links or possibilities of inducing a grounded aesthetic appropriation. "Official" art equates aesthetics with artefacts. In literature, for instance, all of our current social sense is read *into* the text as its "close reading"—the legacy of deadness left by I.A. Richards and F.R. Leavis. Art objects are put into the quietness and stillness of separate institutions—which might preserve them, but not their relation to the exigencies of current necessary symbolic work. The past as museum, Art as objects! The reverence and distance encouraged by formality, by institutions, and by the rites of liberal-humanist education as "learning the code," kill dead, for the vast majority, what the internal life of signs might offer through grounded aesthetics to current sensibility and social practice. It is as hard for the "official arts" to offer themselves to grounded aesthetics, as it is for grounded aesthetics to find recognition in the formal canons.

Commercial cultural commodities, conversely, offer no such impediments. At least cultural commodities—for their own bad reasons—are aimed at exchange and therefore at the possibility of use. In responding to, and attempting to exploit, current desires and needs, they are virtually guaranteed to offer some relevance to the tasks of current socially necessary symbolic work. In crucial senses, too, the modern media precisely "mediate" in passing back to audiences, at least in the first instance, symbolic wholes they've taken from the streets, dance-halls and everyday life. Along with this they may also take, however imperfectly and crudely, a field of aesthetic tensions from daily life and from the play of grounded aesthetics there.

Of course, part of the same restless process is that cultural commodities, especially style and fashion "top end down," may become subject overwhelmingly to reification, symbolic rationalization and the drastic reduction of the symbolic resources on offer. But consumers move too. When cultural commodities no longer offer symbolic mediation to grounded aesthetics, they fall "out of fashion." And in the cumulative symbolic landscape of consumer capitalism, dead packaged, reified grounded aesthetics are turned back into primary raw material for other processes of inevitable necessary symbolic work, with only the cultural theorists paranoically labouring back along their "meta-symbolic" routes to "golden age" symbolic homologies. This commercial process may, to say the least, be flawed, but it offers much more to grounded aesthetics than do the dead "official arts."

There may well be a better way, a better way to cultural emancipation than through this continuous instability and trust in the hidden—selfish, blind, grabbing—hand of the market. But "official art" has not shown it yet. Commercial cultural commodities are all most people have. History may be progressing though its bad side. But it progresses. For all its manifest absurdities, the cultural market may open up the way to a better way. We have to make our conditions of life before we can dominate and use them. Cultural pessimism offers us only road-blocks.

Against post-modernist pessimism
The much commented upon incandescence—instability, changeability, luminosity—of cultural commodities ("all that is solid melts into air"[3]) is not some form of spontaneous combustion in commodities or another "wonder" of capitalist production. It is not without or against meaning. This very incandescence passes through *necessary symbolic work,* changes and enables it. The incandescence is not simply a surface market quality. It produces, is driven by, and reproduces further forms and varieties for everyday symbolic work and creativity, some of which remain in the everyday and in common culture far longer than they do on the market....

4. Style, Fashion, and Symbolic Creativity[4]

Like high art and classical music, the world of couture fashion design has its own autonomous, élite tradition which explains itself according to the creative innovations of individual "great men." The exclusive products of the few top designers are comparable in financial terms to the posthumous works of great artists. Reproduction of these exclusive garments filters down selectively to mass-production level, mediated and reinterpreted by the fashion press, in-house department stores and designers, or reproduced cheaply by small fashion manufacturers.

The scenario is one in which fashion ideas initiated in Paris, Milan or New York are in some mediated form felt, seen and bought in department stores throughout the world. In this world a few significant shapes dominate the season and are changed according to the needs and purses of the social élite.

Couture, however, has historically only ever been a small part of the fashion industry, not its apex. Fashion designers have played a much less central role in setting fashion trends than is commonly imagined. Since World War I Britain's textile and garment industry has been progressively diminished parallel to a massive expansion in the popular retail trade in ready-to-wear clothing. The post-war period and the 1960s in particular marked the beginning of a new phase in the mass consumption of clothes, marked by a convergence of innovative design, youth fashion and the invention of synthetic fibres, under the conditions of full employment and increased spending. This convergence of influences helped overturn the previous international trickle-down effect in fashion, allowing a certain democratization of style and fashion that undermined the centrality of the designers.

The expansion in the high-street consumption of clothes has continued apace in the 1980s, the most significant development being the growth of the middle-market fashion industry, making designer-collection clothes accessible to more people through stores like Next, Principles and Burtons. Behind the altered look of the high street, however, lies another set of equally significant changes in popular fashion, clothing and consumption patterns—the impetus of stylistic creativity from below.

Clothes, style and fashion have long been recognized as key elements in young people's expression, exploration and making of their own individual and collective identities. They remain amongst the most visible forms of symbolic cultural creativity and informal artistry in people's lives in our common culture. As in other areas we have looked at, there is here a specific grounded aesthetic dynamic even in apparently passive consumption which stretches into and lies on a continuum with more obviously creative activities. We try to spell out some of this.

In presenting these forms of informal symbolic work this chapter draws from fieldwork in Wolverhampton and Birmingham and, in the case of the hair-style section, London.

Clothes and creative consumption

Clothes shopping has been a central part of post-war youth cultural consumerism. As a cultural practice, however, shopping has tended to be marginalized in much of the writing about youth, style and fashion. Shopping has been considered a private and feminine activity and part of the process of incorporation into the social machinery.

But young people don't just buy passively or uncritically. They always transform the meaning of bought goods, appropriating and recontextualizing mass-market styles. That appropriation entails a form of symbolic work and creativity as young consumers break the ordered categories of clothes, the suggested matches and ideas promoted by shops. They bring their own specific and differentiated grounded aesthetics to bear on consumption, choosing their own colours and matches and personalizing their purchases. Most young people combine elements of clothing to create new meanings. They adopt and adapt clothing items drawn from government surplus stores, for example, or training shoes, track suits, rugby shirts, Fred Perry tops from sportswear shops. They make their own sense of what is commercially available, make their own aesthetic judgments, and sometimes reject the normative definitions and categories of "fashion" promoted by the clothing industry.

While many of the young people we spoke to obtain their ideas about clothes from friends or from simply observing how clothes looked worn on other people, many also use the media to understand and keep up with the latest fashions. They get ideas about clothes from sources such as television programmes, like *The Clothes Show*, fashion and music magazines, or from the personal dress styles of particular pop artists. Aspects of the clothes and outfits worn by pop groups like Bananarama and Amazulu, for example, were taken up *en masse* by young women in the early and mid-1980s, particularly items such as haystack hairstyles, dungarees and children's plimsolls.

Since the early 1980s, media and marketing attention has shifted towards the employee with high salaries such as the 25-40 age group and the "empty-nesters." Changing economic circumstances, particularly the growth in youth unemployment and the start of what will be a long-term decline in the youth population, have made the 16-24-year-old market far less attractive and lucrative. This has meant that there now exists a substantial block of young people for whom the retail boom has provided few benefits. With many working-class youth now denied the sources of income which financed the spectacular subcultures of the 1960s and 1970s, the right to "good clothes" can no longer be automatically assumed.

The young unemployed especially find it difficult to develop their own image and life style through purchased items. For these young people, using clothes to express their identities, stylistically, is something of a luxury. With social identities increasingly defined in terms of the capacity for private, individualized consumption, those who are excluded from that consumption feel frustrated and alienated.

For many working-class young people impotent window shopping is a source of immense frustration. One young woman said that she would not go window shopping for this reason:

> I don't like window shopping very much. Especially if I don't have the money
> ... 'cause if you see something and you want it, you can't afford it. So I don't
> go window shopping unless I have money.

Remarkably, however, even young people with limited spending power still often find ways to dress stylishly and to express their identities through the clothes they wear. Young women and men still manage to dress smartly and make the most out of slender resources, buying secondhand clothes or saving up to buy particular items of clothing. For some the emphasis on presenting a smart or fashionable image is a priority above everything else and results in quite disproportionate amounts being spent on clothes. One young woman said that she bought a clothing item every week, but sacrificed by going "skint" for the rest of the week. Her rationale was that quality was better than quantity:

> I'd rather buy things that'll last me than cheap things what won't, and you
> don't get the quality in them, do you? ... I feel better in myself if I know I've
> got summat on like expensive, instead of cheap.

From subculture to "retro"

The succession of spectacular youth subcultures has shown particular, conspicuous, symbolic creativity in clothes. There is now a long and well-known list of youth subcultural styles, from the teddy boys and the mods, to the skins and punks, which have occupied the attention of sociologists, journalists and fashion commentators alike. The distinct styles of post-war youth subcultures have been interpreted as symbolic solutions to age and class domination, and a means of marking out and winning cultural space for young people. Such styles have been lauded for their symbolic work in borrowing and transforming everyday objects or fashion components, recoding them according to internal subcultural grounded aesthetics. Examples include the teds' appropriation of the Edwardian suit, the skins' appropriation of proletarian work clothes, or the punks' borrowing of safety pins, bin liners and zips.

While only a small minority of young people adopted the complete uniform of youth subcultures, large numbers drew on selective elements of their styles creating their own meanings and uses from them. Many subcultural styles became popularized, finding their way into mainstream working-class and middle-class youth culture. In this way, subcultures became a source of inspiration for the stylistic symbolic work and creativity of all young people. Punk, for example, stimulated a move back to straight-legged trousers, smaller collars and shorter hair amongst young people of all ages. The leggings/thermal underpants first worn by punk girls—which were originally cream and had to be dyed black—were soon being made up new by young market-stall holders. By the summer of 1985 they were being produced in T-shirt cotton and a wide range of colours and had become a definitive fashion item for all women under the age of 40.

But fashion trends arise not only from the street—though always in a dialectic with it. Punk, for example, emanated as much from the art-school avant-garde as it did from the dance halls and housing estates. Many of the stylistic innovators in punk had a firm stake in the commodity market themselves. Indeed, within most post-war youth subcultures, young people have always been directly involved in the production and selling of clothes themselves. A whole economic infrastructure of entrepreneurial activity has accompanied all the major post-war youth style explosions, creating careers for many of those involved.

Punk was perhaps the last major subculture in which there was a convergence of design, subcultural style and small innovative retail businesses. Malcolm McLaren and Vivienne Westwood's shop."Sex" (later renamed "Seditionaries"), set up in the Kings Road in the mid 70s, was one of the few which integrated popular street fashion with the music of the time.

Since punk the stylistic options among an increasingly self-reflexive and stylistically mobile youth have been greatly expanded with revivals of all the major subcultures occurring in the late 1970s and '80s. Punk itself reproduced the entire sartorial history of post-war working-class youth culture in cut-up form, combining elements which had originally belonged to completely different epochs. The wardrobes of past subcultural styles were exhumed, re-adapted and recombined in endlessly different combinations.

Since and including the punk explosion, then, one of the most important trends in youth style has been the rehabilitation and raiding of previous sartorial styles for raw material in young people's own, current symbolic work and creativity, stylistic and cultural expression. Retro style is part of a general trend in contemporary culture which ransacks various historical moments for their key stylistic expressions and then re-inserts and recombines them in current fashion. Clothing items are worn as though in quotation marks, their wearers self-consciously evoking some past, even at the risk of stylistic mismatch and incongruity. These references to past stylistic forms have taken on a kind of iconographic status in pop culture, evoking whole periods of social history, and have been used extensively in popular music and advertising.

Clothes and identity

Clothes, like musical tastes, are an indication of the cultural identities and leisure orientations of different groups of young people. Young people are very adept at the symbolic work of developing their own styles and also at "reading off" and decoding the dress styles of others and relating them to musical, political and social orientations. Thus, as one young woman noted, people who liked "house music," dressed in the "house style"—Dr Martens shoes/ boots, scarves, baggy shirts, old checked jackets with long collars, baggy trousers— "things that don't fit you, but look smart."

But clothes signify more than just musical tastes. No longer are they an automatic reflection of subcultural affiliations or collective social identities. Clothes are also a crucial medium for grounded aesthetics in which young people express and explore their own specific individual identities. Young people learn about their inner selves partly by developing their outer image through clothes. They use style in their symbolic work to express and develop their understanding of themselves as unique persons, to signify who they are, and who they think they are. As one young woman put it, "If I find something I know I like, if I know I like certain clothes, then I know I am that kind of person."

Young people's uses and choices of clothes also involve an active process of conscious, purposeful image-making. Clothes can be used playfully for the sheer pleasure of putting together a costume, or fabricating an identity. As one young woman says:

> To me, what you wear in a morning and what you wear to go out is a fancy dress, that's all I see it as because you enjoy the clothes you wear, right? ... To me, fancy dress is everyday clothes, what you wear to college, go out to work or whatever, or what you wear to go out, it is fancy-dress costume ... I mean, you've got a costume on now, haven't you? I've got a costume on, everybody's got a costume on....

Clothes can make people feel differently in different contexts. For some young people, and especially young women, the clothes they wear on any particular day will influence the way they talk, behave and present themselves. Wearing smart clothes can inspire confidence or may make some young people feel dignified or even snobbish. Wearing trousers, jeans or T-shirts was equated by others with "being yourself," while wearing more feminine, "going out" clothes could be equated with feeling sexy or flirtatious. Clothes can be manipulated to produce the right effect, to induce the right feeling and mood, involving subtle dressing strategies and choices of colours and styles.

Young people make clear distinctions between everyday clothes for college or work, and clothes for going out. They are used symbolically to mark the boundaries between leisure and work. Dressing to go out at night or at the weekend is an important activity which involves symbolic work and specific pleasures all of its own. Clothes are absolutely central in courtship rituals amongst young people. They are used not only to attract the opposite sex, but also to gain friends, win peer-group acceptance, and to appear different or interesting. Young people frequently put on identities when they go out, a process which includes not only dressing-up but also role-playing and putting on different accents. In a grounded aesthetic of the masque, Joan, for example, reports that she wants to look different and to have people think that she is different when she goes out. She wanted to show a different side of her personality to that in college, which involved her talking and dressing differently:

> You don't want to look the same all day, do you, you want to look totally different when you go out at night.... When I go out they don't recognize me, because I am totally dressed up, and they think that isn't Joan, when they look at you good and proper, they think, "God, you look totally different," and that's what you want, you don't want to look the same when you go out.

Dressing appropriately for different social contexts involves its own symbolic work, careful thought and preparation. It is something young people learn by closely scrutinizing how others dress and involves modulating one's dress to fit with different kinds of people in different contexts. As Joan points out:

If I go to a friend's party, I think, "What can I wear?" You know you might take out all your wardrobe just to think, I wanna wear this, I wanna wear that. But really you've got to think of the people there and what they're like. And you've got to think of their dress. You know, some of them might go in trousers, or skirts and blouses.... You can't go in your best suits and, when you go there, people are in trousers, because you'll feel like a right fool. I've done it before and I really felt awful.

Fashion and gender

While all young people use fashion as a means of making and expressing their identities, young women invest more in working on appearance than young men. Appearance is a key means by which women not only express their individual identities and independence, but are simultaneously constituted as objects of, and for, male desire. For young women, making oneself attractive can be a tricky business since appearance can provide the basis of a young woman's reputation. It requires that young women tread the precarious line between discreet and glamourous femininity, that they sexualize their appearance but not too much. One young woman said that her boyfriend liked her to dress in a particular way when with him, but that she liked to dress differently when with her female friends:

> My boyfriend wants me to dress in a skirt all the time, but when I go out with my friends, I usually wear jeans or summat, he don't like me wearing jeans and stuff like that.... He's square ... if I'm going out with my boyfriend, he doesn't like me looking trendy, so when I'm with my friends I like to look trendy, but he doesn't like me looking a tart or anything, he likes me in normal going-out clothes, like jeans and high heels or a long skirt, you know. Not wearing too much make-up.

Since more is at stake for young women than for young men in the realm of fashion, it is not surprising that they embellish it with such rich significance. But young women do not dress for men alone. They also dress for themselves and each other. Particular clothing styles may be used by young women to inspire confidence. Equally for young men style and clothing can be just as much about social esteem as sexual attractiveness. For some it is a considerable investment in a particular kind of masculine narcissistic display: looking "cool." It's a strategy of which young women are only to well aware, as one young woman pointed out:

> They dress to impress us women.... Some of the guys come in [the college] in gold sovereigns, gold necklaces, smart trousers a little way out, jackets and things like that, then they are just waiting for you to say, "Why, you look

nice," you know what I mean? I mean, fair enough, there's times when I've done that, but I knew that was what they were waiting for.

The forms and definitions of femininity and masculinity in style and fashion are continually changing. Subtle pressures are exerted on young people to dress in particular ways by the clothing industry through models, fashion magazines, catalogues and shop layouts. However, this not only involves pressures to dress as masculine men and feminine women, but can also involve adopting styles hitherto seen as confined to the opposite sex. Here, a certain amount of unisex clothing is officially provided by some shops and marketed as such, but young women in particular also do their informal cross-gender buying of men's clothes. Some young women felt that men's clothes were nicer than women's and had more style. One young woman said that she bought men's clothes because, "they're baggy, comfortable" and "have a lot of wear in them." The larger size and baggier look of men's clothes make them suitable for all female sizes and shapes, allowing a more democratic fashion open to all young women. As consumers, young women have consistently broken down some of the gender categories used in shops, despite retailers' attempts rigidly to separate male and female clothes and rule out cross-gender purchasing.

Black hairstyles
The grooming, cutting and styling of hair is an important cultural practice and symbolic activity for all young people. Hair has long been a medium of significant statements about self and society in which symbolic meanings are invested. Hairstyle has also been a central component in a variety of subcultural expressions: from the DA quiff of the teds to the long hair of the hippies to the crop of the skinheads.

Hairstyling practices amongst black British youth, however, are a particularly lively and creative field for particularized grounded aesthetics where young people are able to seize some degree of symbolic control in their everyday lives. Black hairstyles are popular art forms which articulate a variety of aesthetic solutions to some of the problems created by racism, for hair, along with skin colour, is one of the most visible signs of racial difference. Racism, historically, has devalued the material qualities of black people's hair, seeing it only in negative terms. Aesthetic presuppositions have long been closely intertwined with rationalizations of racial domination-aesthetics which stem from Western codes of beauty where whiteness epitomizes all that is good, true and beautiful.

In the 1960s black liberation movements proposed the slogan "Black is beautiful" to contest the hegemony of this white aesthetics with a grounded aesthetics of its own. Fully aware that such hegemony depended on the subjective internalization of these norms and values, the Afro hairstyle was adopted by Afro-Americans as an outward affirmation of an empowering sense of Black Pride. In the Caribbean context, the popularization of Rastafarian beliefs served a similar purpose. Dreadlocks became emblematic of a newly discovered sense of self. After centuries of negation, such styles inverted the binary logic of white bias to celebrate the natural qualities of black hair.

Hair has thus been a key site of semantic struggle over the significance of racial difference, a struggle to negate the very categories of racial oppression itself. In Rastafari, for example, the open signification of dreadness, through the growing of locks, transposes the difference already immanent in the acceptable attribute of dark skin into open symbolic struggle, drawing attention to that least acceptable attribute of "blackness"—woolly hair.

In the 1980s, however, these forms of cultural resistance drawing on a grounded aesthetic of naturalness and authenticity have been joined by another set of cultural strategies in the medium of hair. These turn around a grounded aesthetic of artifice that works in and against the codes of the dominant culture, through hybridity, syncretism and interculturation. Innovation occurs through appropriations of elements from the dominant culture, which are marked off and differentiated by a creolizing logic of symbolic work and stylization that rearticulates and reaccentuates the meaning of those elements.

In accordance with these strategies, the 1980s have seen a whole explosion of diversity and difference in hairstyles amongst black British youth, in tune with constantly evolving and more fluid forms of black British culture. The 1980s have seen a revival of earlier, processed black American hairstyles from the 1940s and '50s (such as the conk and the Do Rag) as well as contemporary styles like curly perms (hair treated by steaming, relaxing and straightening) and "flat tops."

Traditionally read as a sign of self-oppression or aspiring to white ideals, straightening and processed hairstyling techniques are increasingly seen as providing the materials for an open symbolic creativity rather than as inert signs of an inner self-image, or as a sign of alienation or unauthenticity. Straightening is merely one technique among others, and a means to a symbolic end. As one young woman pointed out: "Just because you do your hair in a particular way doesn't alter your attitude as a black person—or it shouldn't anyway."

What constitutes "blackness" is itself subject to historical change and negotiation. As one young black man put it: "The way we conceptualize Africa is based on myth, textual references. You know a lot of Caribbeans have not been to Africa." There is no such thing as total originality. Sources of style are always already culturally formed, already in play. Nothing is totally new. Young black people may choose and shift between many different available hairstyles, drawing on diverse sources for symbolic resources and stylistic inspiration, such as books, magazines or museums, as well as particular black stars in music, fashion, film or sport. Thus people make reference to Grace Jones haircuts (flat top), or Egyptian-style shapes to a haircut. Such references are informed by knowledges which place black hair styles in a historical tradition, a tradition in which young black people consciously position themselves.

The grounded aesthetics of black hairstyling have their own terms and criteria of evaluation. Choosing what kind of style and cut involves important decisions, beginning from that of whether or not to cut one's hair. Dreadlocks, for example, are premised on not cutting and involve long-term cycles of growth and cultivation. Cutting and the decisions which follow on involve choosing from a whole range of techniques and styles, as well as judgements of manageability and convenience, taste and suitability.

Black hairstyling also has its own distinct social relations. Many styles require co-operative and collaborative interaction. They involve skills exchanged between friends and family, and relations of mutuality and intimacy. Hairdressing, as one young black hairdresser comment, is also a site of ritualized communality: "Salons play an important social part as well. People come in, they talk, they meet their friends—it's the atmosphere of the place."

Hairdressing is also supported by its own economic infrastructure, with a substantial hairdressing industry. Large numbers of barber shops and salons now exist in the black community. Hairdressing is a model for ethnic business success stories. The largest Afro-Caribbean owned business in Britain is Dyke and Dyrden, a firm that imports and retails hair-care products to a market that is more or less exclusively black.

Making clothes

Sewing, altering and making clothes are common practices amongst young working-class women. Skills and knowledge are often developed in the home, sometimes handed down from one generation to another, or learnt more formally at school, college or work. June, a young mother of 22, who has been making clothes since she was 14, had originally taken up sewing for practical purposes to make a contribution to the household economy, making dresses for her mother and herself. But this soon expanded into making dresses for, and with, her friends, buying patterns and material from the rag market to experiment with:

> We just used to mess about with bits of material ... and wrap 'em round our heads and sew this on, and sew a hood on things.... And we'd buy patterns and make a skirt.

There are a significant minority of young people who sew and knit their own clothes for reasons that are partly to do with pleasure in their own symbolic work and creativity as well as financial. As one young woman pointed out:

> It saves you money.... 'Cause I mean, there's times when I think, well, I like this, and it cost £50. When I can just go to Birmingham market, buy some material for about a pound a yard ... and look just as good as what was in the shops. And I'm so happy.

There is a symbolic as well as practical pleasure and sense of fulfilment for young people in being able to use their own manual skills and resources to make their own clothes. Joan, for example, says that she specifically enjoys the material process of cutting up patterns: "What I really love about it is getting material on the table and just start cutting. 'Cause I love cutting up the patterns and start stitching it."

Making your own clothes enables you to have some control over what you wear. It means, above all, that you don't have just to follow fashion, you can make clothes that suit you personally and in which you feel more comfortable along the grooves of your own grounded aesthetics. June says that she makes her own clothes because she doesn't like what's on offer in the high-street shops:

> I can walk around the shops, and I'm trying things on, and I can actually give up and think "This is stupid." And the actual price as well, and I look at it ... and how it's put together. I can look at something that's been put together, so ... *badly*!, really, and they're asking such a high price for it. I could make better myself. Like there's certain clothes and certain styles of clothes that I can't easily buy in a shop. For one, they may have gone out of fashion, and it might be a style that I particularly like, that suits me, and I can't go and buy that from a normal shop.

Many young people are both driven and inspired to make their own clothes simply by the high price of clothes in the shops. As one young woman pointed out: "I went to a shop to buy a mohair jumper and it was 60 quid, so I thought I could make that myself. I bought the wool for £11, and made one nearly identical."

Since the late 1970s, the rise in youth unemployment has pushed many young people into self- and semi-employment in the clothes sector of the hidden economy. For some young people, clothes-making is as much a way of negotiating the boredom of the dole as it is a source of income. Bridgette, for example, who knits colourful fashionable jumpers, says that she started knitting because she "couldn't afford to go out, on the dole, so I thought I'd do something constructive, learning to make my own clothes."

Jumble sales and secondhand clothes

Large numbers of young people buy their clothes from secondhand or charity shops, like Oxfam and Barnardo's, or from street and rag markets. Today, more than ever before, young people are having to rely on rag markets and second-hand clothes stores for the creation of style. The 1980s have seen a revitalization of numerous urban street markets with young people forming a major part of their constituency.

Margaret is 19 and unemployed. She goes to jumble sales frequently:

> I thought, why am I going into shops and paying all this money, and saving so hard for a jumper, when I can get it in a secondhand shop. 'Cause if you look around, you can find a jumper that's really nice and you'll pay a couple of quid for it.

For Margaret, as for many young people, there is a specific pleasure in going to jumble sales with friends to rummage through second-hand clothes:

> We always buy things we can experiment with.... All types of coats, jackets that we just cut off to the waist, and things like that. You can actually make something old and quite horrible into something quite nice by just a few nips and slits and turns, you know what I mean. So, it's like, I don't know, it's good fun.... That's what it is more than anything, it's just good fun ... going to jumble sales, like.

Buying secondhand clothes is clearly part of a whole active process of symbolic work and creativity to do with producing appearance. Margaret again:

> You can achieve a certain look, that would be difficult to achieve on such low money, and also difficult to achieve by walking in shops, because they're traditionally made for a size 10 or whatever. And yet, you can find a size-40-chest man's jacket and it gives you the look that you want, but you can't actually go into a shop and buy it ... that certain look. But by turning the sleeves up, or by rolling them over, you can, you know. ... Like, you can get your dad's jacket out the wardrobe, and you know "Oh, this is trendy."

The availability of secondhand men's jackets, trousers, shirts and even shoes has radically transformed the way in which women now dress. Young women buying and adapting secondhand clothes have been at the forefront or some of the major transformations in the female fashion body over the last ten years.

The process began with punk, which helped break down some of the gender restrictions on young women's dress and on female participation in youth subcultures. The androgynous look of punk, particularly its spiky hair style, became part of a general popular feminist style in the late 1970s and early '80s. Since then, substantial numbers of young women have managed to deconstruct feminine styles through novel combinations of masculine and feminine clothing items (such as frilly birthday-party dresses, ribbons and flounces combined with heavyweight boots or Dr Marten shoes). More recently, baggy shirts have proved immensely popular as flexible items of female clothing. Men's raincoats too have been made fashionable amongst young woman, picked up at jumble sales for as little as five pounds. The sleeves would be turned up to fit the length of female arms, simultaneously revealing a high quality striped silk lining.

From secondhand and men's clothes, young women have actively created their own unfixed, fluid and constantly shifting grounded aesthetics of feminine style.

Notes

1. Raymond Williams, "Culture is ordinary" (1958), reprinted in his *Resources of Hope*, Verso, 1988.
2. For a full account of the "new social condition of youth" in relation to youth unemployment, see P. Willis *et al., The Youth* Review, Avebury, 1988.
3. The title of a book by Marshall Berman (Simon and Schuster, New York, 1982) which helped to launch the many faceted and pervasive post-modern debate.
4. [*Editor*: This chapter was written collaboratively by Paul Willis, Simon Jones, Angela McRobbie, and Kokena Mercer.]

CHAPTER SEVEN

HIGHLIGHTING GENDER AND SEXUALITY

INTRODUCTION

One of the most powerful results of the shakeup that transformed theory after 1970 was the emergence of theories of gender. As often the case in the history of theory, such change reflected changes in the real world of everyday life and collective action: in most industrialized nations, women entered the labour force in large numbers and struggled for expanded rights and opportunities. These real-life experiences, struggles, and opportunities affected the work of theorists, leading them to focus on gender issues. Feminist movements and ideologies highlighted gender as a key dimension of inequality and forced social theorists to analyze it with the same attention and seriousness that they brought to the study of class and racial/ethnic stratification.

At least three types of gender theories emerged: macro-level structural analysis, perspectivism, and social construction of gender.

One set of theories focused on the macro-level analysis of gender stratification and gender inequalities. These theories drew on concepts in Marxist, Weberian, and functionalist theories to explain why some societies have (or had) extreme gender inequality, while others have more equality between men and women. Characteristics of the gender system, and more specifically, gender inequality, are related to modes of production, forms of the state and military institutions, class structure, and kinship and inheritance systems. Most of these theories concur in associating the highest level of gender inequality with patrilineal agrarian state-level societies. The rise of women's movements and feminism can also be explained in terms of macro-level analysis that links women's collective action to industrialization and women's entry into the labour force, especially into managerial and professional roles. All of these studies used theories based on macro-level institutional and structural analysis, including functional logic about congruence or articulation of institutions in society as well as concepts derived from Marx and Weber's work. These theories are in an ongoing conversation with Engels's pioneering analysis of gender, class, family structure, private property, and the state.[1] This type of theory is illustrated by the work of Blumberg, Chafetz, Chafetz and Dworkin, Collins, Huber, and Wolf.[2]

A second type of gender theory might be termed "perspectivism" and focuses on using the perspective of women to understand society and institutions. This approach calls for placement of women's experiences and actions—and hence the issue of gender—at the centre of social analysis; shifting the centre leads to new concepts, new research questions, new methods, and a radically different understanding of society. Dorothy Smith's selection outlines the general strategy. A concrete example is provided by James Messerschmidt's work on masculinity and crime. By taking the vastly lower female crime rate as his norm, his research question becomes why men have high crime rates; thus he problematizes what previous theories of criminology had always taken for granted.[3]

A third type of gender theory analyzes social construction of gender, how gender as a category of difference is created in the first place. The category of gender, as a category of thought, discourse, and action, is the puzzle to be solved. Theorists focus on how gender differences are constructed and borders formed in ritual, play, child socialization, interactions of everyday life, and practices of states and organizations.

The real-life experiences of women, including those of large numbers of women entering universities and intellectual life, converged with post-structuralist and deconstructionist theoretical work, especially the writing of Michel Foucault. These new theories focused on how discourse creates social structure and deviance and how power differences are expressed in classification and naming of categories of experience. Discourse differentiates, names, labels, classifies, defines, legitimates, and forms borders. The new theories were radical critiques of these processes, showing us how the basic categories of thought are intimately tied to separation, inequality, and power. The reader may recall that some of these ideas about classification, structure, and the creation of deviance were addressed by Emile Durkheim, and symbolic interactionists had long been interested in labelling as a process that produces deviance; the new theories gave an intense, critical edge to these earlier lines of thought.

The emerging theories fought the status quo on two fronts. First of all, they challenged prevailing notions about gender and sexuality that permeate most societies. They revealed how the line between men and women is established and elaborated in virtually all societies and how a relatively limited physical difference is transformed into a huge social and cultural divide and linked to cruel and pervasive forms of oppression and inequality. They also documented how in many societies, especially those sharing a Judeo-Christian tradition, the difference between heterosexuals and "others" became reified and backed up by viciously punitive practices, from burning at the stake to chemical castration; heterosexism was linked to gender inequalities in so far as it meant the hegemony of narrow norms of masculinity and femininity.

But the emerging theories also opened up a second front, within the sciences and academic disciplines themselves. As Foucault noted, the Enlightenment marked a turning point in discourses of inequality and deviance from religious foundations of discrimination to an ideology of naturalization and normality that made scientific claims in order to legitimate discrimination against women, homosexuals, the insane, and the deviant.

Because discourses of inequality and discrimination became entangled with medicine, the biological sciences, and the social sciences, the new theorists had to challenge and deconstruct existing fields of knowledge. This "second front" had to be within the professions, the academic disciplines, and intellectual life. Sociology and the other human sciences had fallen into the practices of assuming gender differences to be natural, biologically based sex differences. Sociological theory, especially structural-functional theory, perpetuated rather than challenged gender inequality. Therefore much of the writing of the new social theorists was turned against these assumptions and practices of their own field: the naturalization of differences and inequalities between men and women; the language of sex roles which implies a natural division of labour rather than a socially constructed line of difference; the research focus on institutions dominated by men (politics, religious organizations, economic institutions, etc.); the invisibility of women's labour in economics and the sociology of work, especially theoretical neglect of the tasks of social reproduction; the silence of social science on the topic of women's experience; the pervasive assumption that only heterosexual sexuality is normal and natural.

We begin with a short defining piece by Dorothy Smith. It illustrates the idea of the "second front"—the need to begin the deconstruction of gender inequality with a critique of the human sciences, specifically sociology, because it is these disciplines that have legitimated gender inequality. By failing to look at the experience of women, rooted in everyday life, sociologists have not only missed some key elements of human experience, they have legitimated and perpetuated women's marginalization. The first steps toward remedying this situation are to expose it and to become aware that women's experience must be included in the analysis of society. By beginning sociological inquiry with everyday life and embodied experiences of women and other marginalized people, we can end the "bifurcated consciousness" of mainstream sociology, which always acts as though sociologists can be purely external, objective observers who treat other people and relationships as objects that have no effect on the observer. Women sociologists, because of their experiences as women, are in an excellent position to question and overturn this alienated, external, omniscient way of doing sociology. Practices of ruling are tacitly propped up by an objectifying position; to criticize this objectifying way of doing sociology is also to dismantle sociologists' role in legitimating power differences.

Two powerful ethnographic readings embody theories of the social construction of gender and sexualities. Boddy and Herdt force us to reflect on the social construction of men and women in our own society by showing us examples of social construction in two societies that have exceptionally elaborate ideologies and rituals of gender construction: the formation of women in a Sudanese community and that of men among the Sambia of Papua-New Guinea.

Symbolic interactionists had already introduced the concept of borderwork, practices that define distinct categories of people who are identified and labeled as different from each other. (See especially, Barrie Thorne's *Gender Play*.) These practices include labeling, representations, rituals, and sometimes violence. In Part II, we saw how DuBois pioneered the study of how "races" are defined and separated by borderwork in the United States; the ideology of white supremacy rests on this construction of borders and differences. Fields of knowledge like biology, history, and the social sciences were extensively implicated in the construction of "race" and racial hierarchies at the beginning of the century. In our own time, we can observe violent borderwork not only in racist ideology, but also in ethnic conflict in places like the former Yugoslavia. In this chapter we are going to look at similar processes of differentiation, separation, borderwork, and imposition of inequalities in the construction of gender.

Social constructionist theories of gender and sexuality also illustrate the new interest in macro-micro linkages and reaffirm symbolic interactionist claims that society is nothing more than the cumulative product of actions, interactions, and practices. The macro-structures of gender inequality are formed in rituals, play, and borderwork of all kinds, repeated over and over again as part of the routines of everyday life.

Feminist analysis and the central placement of gender in social theory affected many areas of inquiry, for example transforming fields as widely separated and superficially unrelated to gender as criminology and economic development. Highlighting gender has raised a fascinating question that traditional criminology had ignored: why do men outnumber women in criminal behaviour by a 10 to 1 ratio in most industrialized nations? A gender-based analysis could no longer take this disproportion as natural; researchers were forced to ask what it is about the construction of masculinity that generates higher crime rates among men.[4] Gender analysis in theories of economic development contributed to a focus on women in the development process and led a growing number of international agencies, governments, and non-governmental organizations to recognize that development policies must be based on including women in education, credit and loan programs, and technological know-how. Almost all fields of research and knowledge were affected by gender-based theories; the gender perspective provided a new vantage point that led to startling new questions and radical new answers.

Notes

1. Friedrich Engels, *The Origins of the Family, Private Property, and the State* (New York: International Publishers, 1884/1970).
2. See Rae Lesser Blumberg, *Stratification: Socioeconomic and Sexual Inequality* (Dubuque, Ia: William C. Brown, 1978); Janet Saltzman Chafetz, *Sex and Advantage: A Comparative Macro-Structural Theory of Sexual Stratification* (Totowa, NJ: Rowman and Allanheld, 1984); Janet Saltzman Chafetz and A. Gary Dworkin, *Female Revolt: Women's Movements in World and Historical Perspective* (Totowa, NJ: Rowman and Allanheld, 1986); Randall Collins, "A Conflict Theory of Sexual Stratification," *Social Problems* 19 (1971): 3-21; Joan Huber, "A Theory of Family, Economy, and Gender," *Gender, Family and Economy: The Triple Overlap*, ed. Rae Lesser Blumberg (New Delhi: Sage, 1991); and Diane Wolf, "Female Autonomy, the Family, and Industrialization in Java," *Gender, Family and Economy: The Triple Overlap*, ed. Rae Lesser Blumberg (New Delhi: Sage, 1991).
3. James Messerschmidt, *Masculinities and Crime: Critique and Reconceptualization of Theory* (Lanham, MD: Rowman and Littlefield, 1993).
4. Messerschmidt.

Readings

Aslanbegui, Nahid, Steven Pressman, and Gale Summerfield (eds.). *Women in the Age of Economic Transformation*. London and New York: Routledge, 1994.

Chafetz, Janet Saltzman. *Feminist Sociology: An Overview of Contemporary Theories*. Itasca, IL: Peacock, 1988.

Chodorow, Nancy. *Feminism and Psychoanalytic Theory*. New Haven: Yale University Press, 1994.

Collins, Patricia Hill. *Black Feminist Thought: Knowledge, Consciousness, and the Politics of Empowerment*. New York: Unwin Hyman, 1991.

De Beauvoir, Simone. *The Second Sex*. New York: Vintage, 1989.

Lorber, Judith. *Paradoxes of Gender*. New Haven: Yale University Press, 1994.

Messerschmidt, James W. *Masculinities and Crime*. Lanham, MD: Rowman and Littlefield, 1993.

Rogers, Mary. *Contemporary Feminist Theory*. New York: McGraw-Hill, 1998.

Thorne, Barrie. *Gender Play: Girls and Boys in School*. New Brunswick, NJ: Rutgers University Press, 1993.

35

DOROTHY E. SMITH (1926-)

Dorothy Smith focuses on the second front of feminist theory, the exposure of gender-biased assumptions within social science disciplines themselves. In a society in which knowledge, information, and science have leading roles, gender construction in fields of knowledge contributes to legitimation of gender inequality throughout society. Smith's analysis provides an example of Foucault's view that in modern society disciplines (or fields of knowledge) are a key site for creating and circulating discourses that label, classify, and establish power differences. In the case of gender, Smith emphasizes that these power discourses are really silences, an absence of attention to the gender division of labour and the experiences of women. Smith reiterates a point that DuBois made implicitly in the introduction to *The Souls of Black Folk*: the sociological observer is part of the observed society. A challenge to established thought in the discipline is more likely to arise from a sociologist whose own experiences are shaped by marginality in terms of ethnicity, gender, sexual orientation, religion, class, etc.

Du Bois's position as an African American in the United States did not lead him simply to add African American history and culture to the list of interesting sociological topics; he developed an analysis of modern societies as multiethnic fields of unequal power. Similarly, Smith argues that it is not enough for feminists to add "sociology of women" as a good subfield for sociology; the perspective of feminism, based on the experience of women, transforms key assumptions about society and the sociological method itself.

The Conceptual Practices of Power:
A Feminist Sociology of Knowledge
DOROTHY E. SMITH

The opening up of women's experience gives sociologists access to social realities previously unavailable, indeed repressed. But can a feminist sociology be content to describe these realities in the terms of our discipline, merely extending our field of interest to include work on gender roles, the women's movement, women in the labor force, sexuality, the social psychology of women, and so forth? Thinking more boldly or perhaps just thinking the whole thing through further brings us to ask how a sociology might look if it began from women's standpoint and what might happen to a sociology that attempts to deal seriously with that standpoint. Following this line of thought has consequences larger than they seem at first.

It is not enough to supplement an established sociology by addressing ourselves to what has been left out or overlooked, or by making women's issues into sociological issues. That does not change the standpoint built into existing sociological procedures, but merely makes the sociology of women an addendum to the body of objectified knowledge.

The first difficulty is that how sociology is thought—its methods, conceptual schemes, and theories—has been based on and built up within the male social universe, even when women have participated in its doing. This sociology has taken for granted not only an itemized inventory of issues or subject matters (industrial sociology, political sociology, social stratification, and so forth) but the fundamental social and political structures under which these become relevant and are ordered. There is thus a disjunction between how women experience the world and the concepts and theoretical schemes by which society's self-consciousness is inscribed. My early explorations of these issues included a graduate seminar in which we discussed the possibility of a women's sociology. Two students expressed their sense that theories of the emergence of leadership in small groups just did not apply to what had happened in an experimental group situation they had participated in. They could not find the correlates of the theory in their experiences.

A second difficulty is that the worlds opened up by speaking from the standpoint of women have not been and are not on a basis of equality with the objectified bodies of knowledge that have constituted and expressed the standpoint of men. The worlds of men have had, and still have, an authority over the worlds that are traditionally women's and still are predominantly women's— the worlds of household, children, and neighborhood. And though women do not inhabit only these worlds, for the vast majority of women they are the primary ground of our lives, shaping the course of our lives and our participation in other relations. Furthermore, objectified knowledges are part of the world from which our kind of society is governed. The domestic world stands in a dependent relation to that other, and its whole character is subordinate to it.

The two difficulties are related to each other in a special way. The effect of the second interacting with the first is to compel women to think their world in the concepts and terms in which men think theirs. Hence the established social forms of consciousness alienate women from their own experience.

The profession of sociology has been predicated on a universe grounded in men's experience and relationships and still largely appropriated by men as their "territory." Sociology is part of the practice by which we are all governed; that practice establishes its relevances. Thus the institutions that lock sociology into the structures occupied by men are the same institutions that lock women into the situations in which we have found ourselves oppressed. To unlock the latter leads logically to an unlocking of the former. What follows, then, or rather what then becomes possible—for it is of course by no means inevitable—is less a shift in the subject matter than a different conception of how sociology might become a means of understanding our experience and the conditions of our experience (both women's and men's) in contemporary capitalist society....

An important set of procedures that serve to separate the discipline's body of knowledge from its practitioners is known as *objectivity*. The ethic of objectivity and the methods used in its practice are concerned primarily with the separation of knowers from what they know and in particular with the separation of what is known from knowers' interests, "biases," and so forth, that are not authorized by the discipline. In the social sciences the pursuit of objectivity makes it possible for people to be paid to pursue a knowledge to which they are otherwise indifferent. What they feel and think about society can be kept out of what they are professionally or academically interested in. Correlatively, if they are interested in exploring a topic sociologically, they must find ways of converting their private interest into an objectified, unbiased form.

Sociology Participates In the Extralocal Relations of Ruling

Sociologists, when they go to work, enter into the conceptually ordered society they are investigating. They observe, analyze, explain, and examine that world as if there were no problem in how it becomes observable to them. They move among the doings of organizations, governmental processes, and bureaucracies as people who are at home in that medium. The nature of that world itself, how it is know to them, the conditions of its existence, and their relation to it are not called into question. Their methods of observation and inquiry extend into it as procedures that are essentially of the same order as those that bring about the phenomena they are concerned with. Their perspectives and interests may differ, but the substance is the same. They work with facts and information that have been worked up from actualities and appear in the form of documents that are themselves the product of organizational processes, whether their own or those of some other agency. They fit that information back into a framework of entities and organizational processes which they take for granted as known, without asking how it is that they know them or by what social processes the actual events—what people do or utter—are construed as the phenomena known.

Where a traditional gender division of labor prevails, men enter the conceptually organized world of governing without a sense of transition. The male sociologist in these circumstances passes beyond his particular and immediate setting (the office he writes in, the libraries he consults, the streets he travels, the home he returns to) without attending to the shift in consciousness. He works in the very medium he studies.

But, of course, like everyone else, he also exists in the body in the place in which it is. This is also then the place of this sensory organization of immediate experience; the place where his coordinates of here and now, before and after, are organized around himself as center; the place where he confronts people face to face in the physical mode in which he expresses himself to them and they to him as more and other than either can speak. This is the place where things smell, where the irrelevant birds fly away in front of the window, where he has indigestion, where he dies. Into this space must come as actual material events—whether as sounds of speech, scratchings on the surface of paper, which he constitutes as text, or directly—anything he knows of the world. It has to happen here somehow if he is to experience it at all.

Entering the governing mode of our kind of society lifts actors out of the immediate, local, and particular place in which we are in the body. What becomes present to us in the governing mode is a means of passing beyond the local into the conceptual order. This mode of governing creates, at least potentially, a bifurcation of consciousness. It establishes two modes of knowing and experiencing and doing, one located in the body and in the space it occupies and moves in, the other passing beyond it. Sociology is written in and aims at the latter mode of action. Robert Bierstedt writes, "Sociology can liberate the mind from time and space themselves and remove it to a new and transcendental realm where it no longer depends upon these Aristotelian categories."[1] Even observational work aims at description in the categories and hence conceptual forms of the "transcendental realm." Yet the local and particular site of knowing that is the other side of the bifurcated consciousness has not been a site for the development of systematic knowledge.

Women's Exclusion from the Governing Conceptual Mode
The suppression of the local and particular as a site of knowledge has been and remains gender organized. The domestic sites of women's work, traditionally identified with women, are outside and subservient to this structure. Men have functioned as subjects in the mode of governing; women have been anchored in the local and particular phase of the bifurcated world. It has been a condition of a man's being able to enter and become absorbed in the conceptual mode, and to forget the dependence of his being in that mode upon his bodily existence, that he does not have to focus his activities and interests upon his

bodily existence. Full participation in the abstract mode of action requires liberation from attending to needs in the concrete and particular. The organization of work in managerial and professional circles depends upon the alienation of subjects from their bodily and local existence. The structure of work and the structure of career take for granted that these matters have been provided for in such a way that they will not interfere with a man's action and participation in that world. Under the traditional gender regime, providing for a man's liberation from Bierstedt's Aristotelian categories is a woman who keeps house for him, bears and cares for his children, washes his clothes, looks after him when he is sick, and generally provides for the logistics of his bodily existence.

Women's work in and around professional and managerial settings performs analogous functions. Women's work mediates between the abstracted and conceptual and the material form in which it must travel to communicate. Women do the clerical work, the word processing, the interviewing for the survey; they take messages, handle the mail, make appointments, and care for patients. At almost every point women mediate for men at work the relationship between the conceptual mode of action and the actual concrete forms in which it is and must be realized, and the actual material conditions upon which it depends.

Marx's concept of alienation is applicable here in a modified form. The simplest formulation of alienation posits a relation between the work individuals do and an external order oppressing them in which their work contributes to the strength of the order that oppresses them. This is the situation of women in this relation. The more successful women are in mediating the world of concrete particulars so that men do not have to become engaged with (and therefore conscious of) that world as a condition to their abstract activities, the more complete men's absorption in it and the more effective its authority. The dichotomy between the two worlds organized on the basic of gender separates the dual forms of consciousness; the governing consciousness dominates the primary world of a locally situated consciousness but cannot cancel it; the latter is a subordinated, suppressed, absent, but absolutely essential ground of the governing consciousness. The gendered organization of subjectivity dichotomizes the two worlds estranges them, and silences the locally situated consciousness by silencing women....

I am not proposing an immediate and radical transformation of the subject matter and methods of the discipline nor the junking of everything that has gone before. What I am suggesting is more in the nature of a reorganization of the relationship of sociologists to the object of our knowledge and of our problematic. This reorganization involves first placing sociologists where we are actually situated, namely, at the beginning of those acts by which we know or will come to know, and second, making our direct embodied experience of the everyday world the primary ground of our knowledge.

A sociology worked on in this way would not have as its objective a body of knowledge subsisting in and of itself; inquiry would not be justified by its contribution to the heaping up of such a body. We would reject a sociology aimed primarily at itself. We would not be interested in contributing to a body of knowledge whose uses are articulated to relations of ruling in which women participate only marginally, if at all. The professional sociologist is trained to think in the objectified modes of sociological discourse, to think sociology as it has been and is thought; that training and practice has to be discarded. Rather, as sociologists we would be constrained by the actualities of how things come about in people's direct experience, including our own. A sociology for women would offer a knowledge of the social organization and determinations of the properties and events of our directly experienced world.[2] Its analyses would become part of our ordinary interpretations of the experienced world, just as our experience of the sun's sinking below the horizon is transformed by our knowledge that the world turns away from a sun that seems to sink.

The only way of knowing a socially constructed world is knowing it from within. We can never stand outside it. A relation in which sociological phenomena are objectified and presented as external to and independent of the observer is itself a special social practice also known from within. The relation of observer and object of observation, of sociologist to "subject," is a specialized social relationship. Even to be a stranger is to enter a wold constituted from within as strange. The strangeness itself is the mode in which it is experienced.

When Jean Briggs[3] made her ethnographic study of the ways in which an Eskimo people structure and express emotion, what she learned emerged for her in the context of the actual developing relations between her and the family with whom she lived and other members of the group. Her account situates her knowledge in the context of those relationships and in the actual sites in which the world of family subsistence was done. Affections, tensions, and quarrels, in some of which she was implicated, were the living texture in which she learned what she describes. She makes it clear how this context structured her learning and how what she learned and can speak of became observable to her.

Briggs tells us what is normally discarded in the anthropological or sociological telling. Although sociological inquiry is necessarily a social relation, we have learned to dissociate our own part in it. We recover only the object of our knowledge as if it stood all by itself. Sociology does not provide for seeing that there are always two terms to this relation. An alternative sociology must preserve in it the presence, concerns, and experience of the sociologist as knower and discoverer.

To begin from direct experience and to return to it as a constraint or "test" of the adequacy of a systematic knowledge is to begin from where we are located bodily. The actualities of our everyday world are already socially organized. Settings, equipment, environment, schedules, occasions, and so forth, as well as our enterprises and routines, are socially produced and concretely and symbolically organized prior to the moment at which we enter and at which inquiry begins. By taking up a standpoint in our original and immediate knowledge of the world, sociologists can make their discipline's socially organized properties first observable and them problematic.

When I speak of *experience* I do not use the term as a synonym for *perspective*. Nor in proposing a sociology grounded in the sociologist's actual experience am I recommending the self-indulgence of inner exploration or any other enterprise with self as sole focus and object. Such subjectivist interpretations of *experience* are themselves an aspect of that organization of consciousness that suppresses the locally situated side of the bifurcated consciousness and transports us straight into mind country, stashing away the concrete conditions and practices upon which it depends. We can never escape the circles of our own heads if we accept that as our territory. Rather, sociologists' investigation of our directly experienced world as a problem is a mode of discovering or rediscovering the society from within. We begin from our own original but tacit knowledge and from within the acts by which we bring it into our grasp in making it observable and in understanding how it works. We aim not at a reiteration of what we already (tacitly) know, but at an exploration of what passes beyond that knowledge and is deeply implicated in how it is....

The Standpoint of Women as a Place to Start
The standpoint of women situates the inquirer in the site of her bodily existence and in the local actualities of her working world. It is a standpoint that positions inquiry but has no specific content. Those who undertake inquiry from this standpoint begin always from women's experience as it is for women. We are the authoritative speakers of our experience. The standpoint of women situates the sociological subject prior to the entry into the abstracted conceptual mode, vested in texts, that is the order of the relations of ruling. From this standpoint, we know the everyday world through the particularities of our local practices and activities, in the actual places of our work and the actual time it takes. In making the everyday world problematic we also problematize the everyday localized practices of the objectified forms of knowledge organizing our everyday worlds.

A bifurcated consciousness is an effect of the actual social relations in which we participate as part of a daily work life. Entry as subject into the social relations of an objectified consciousness is itself an organization of actual everyday practices. The sociology that objectifies society and social relations and transforms the actualities of people's experience into the synthetic objects of its discourse is an organization of actual practices and activities. We know and use practices of thinking and inquiring sociologically that sever our knowledge of society from the society we know as we live and practice it. The conceptual practices of an alienated knowledge of society are also in and of the everyday world. In and through its conceptual practices and its everyday practices of reading and writing, we enter a mode of consciousness outside the everyday site of our bodily existence and experiencing. The standpoint of women, or at least, *this* standpoint of women at work, in the traditional ways women have worked and continue to work, exposes the alienated knowledge of the relations of ruling as the everyday practices of actual individuals. Thus, though an alienated knowledge also alienates others who are not members of the dominant white male minority, the standpoint of women distinctively opens up for exploration the conceptual practices and activities of the extralocal, objectified relations of ruling as what actual people do.

Notes
1. Robert Bierstedt, "Sociology and general education," in *Sociology and contemporary education*, ed. Charles H. Page (New York: Random House, 1966).
2. Dorothy E. Smith, *The everyday world as problematic: A feminist sociology* (Boston: Northeastern University Press, 1987).
3. Jean Briggs, *Never in anger* (Cambridge: Harvard University Press, 1970).

36

THE SOCIAL CONSTRUCTION OF GENDER

The women's movement and the resurgence of feminism in the 1970s sent shock waves through the community of social theorists. The major lasting impact of feminism on social theory has been the rise of social constructionist theories to a position of dominance in the last decades of the twentieth century. These theories are radical challenges to the notion that there is something natural about society; for social constructionists all aspects of the social order are products of culture.

Social theory had a strong component of social constructionism from the very start. The essence of Comte's thought was that social phenomena are not reducible to or explainable at the level of biological phenomena; social phenomena arise out of the interaction of people and groups in a process that produces culture and society. Durkheim believed that social interaction produces categories of thought. Symbolic interactionists showed how our definitions of reality are created in communication processes. As the most immediate predecessor and strongest influence on social constructionists, Foucault saw historical change as shifts in discursive formations, cultural shifts in the meaning of sexuality, madness, deviance, normality, and the self.

In many respects, social constructionism was not a new line of thought; but feminist social theory gave it a powerful new charge and a field for radical application—the study of gender. In many varieties of structural functional thought, the differences between men and women had appeared to be a natural distinction, based on chromosomal, hormonal, and anatomical differences. Sex roles were seen as social prescriptions that reflected a natural order of maleness and femaleness. Biological differences and sex roles were believed to correspond to one another. Feminist social constructionism challenged this naturalistic view of difference. "Gender" replaced "sex" as the conceptualization of difference. Gender is a process of social and cultural differentiation, of creating boundaries and borders between "men" and "women" whose masculine and feminine identities are thereby established. Gender construction involves both ideas and practices, especially rituals. The reader who would like to explore this line of theory is referred to Judith Lorber's *The Paradox of Gender* and Barrie Thorne's *Gender Play*.

The first example of the social construction of gender comes from the work of Gilbert Herdt, an anthropologist who studied gender ideology and initiation rites among the Sambia of Papua-New Guinea. The second selection, by Janice Boddy, provides a striking example of social constructionist theory in an ethnography of Hofriyat, a village in northern Sudan.

As is often the case, ethnographic writing jars us loose from our taken-for-granted ways of seeing ourselves. By observing and writing about the exotic other, we come to see our own culture more clearly. Ethnography is a mirror; once we see how the Sambia or the Sudanese construct gender, we become sensitive to the construction of gender in western society.

37

GILBERT HERDT (1949-)

In these selections, Herdt describes Sambia ideas about men and women. He observed and reports initiation rites in which these ideas are enacted as adolescents perform fellatio on young men in order to ingest the seminal fluid that is necessary for construction of their manhood. The rites include a painful and dangerous nose-bleeding ceremony as well as instruction about sacred flutes that must be kept secret from women. Herdt concludes his analysis of the formation of Sambia gender identity with the concept of protest masculinity, identity based on a negation of women and women's power. Yet men continue to suspect that women have great powers; one situation in which these powers are revealed is in the accomplishments of women shamans. Herdt's ethnography challenges prevailing western ideas about the nature of gender and sexual orientation.

Readings

Gilmore, David. *Manhood in the Making: Cultural Concepts of Masculinity.* New Haven, CT: Yale University Press, 1990.

Herdt, Gilbert. *Sambia Sexual Culture: Essays from the Field.* Chicago: University of Chicago Press, 1999.

—. (ed.). *Gay Culture in America.* Boston: Beacon Press, 1993.

Schwartz, Pepper, and Virginia Elizabeth Rutter. *The Gender of Sexuality.* Thousand Oaks, CA: Pine Forge Press/Sage, 1998.

The Sambia: Ritual and Gender in New Guinea
GILBERT HERDT

Beliefs About Sexual Differentiation

Sambia see the biological development of the sexes as being strikingly different in most regards. They know that both males and females start life in the womb, and they use anatomical differences at birth to make the sex assignment of the infant. Mothers say boys and girls develop differently soon after birth. Boys fuss more, sleep more poorly than girls, and are more prone to illness, whereas girls nurse more and grow faster. Baby girls babble and toddle before boys, Sambia say. As times goes on, this biological leap continues, girls achieving reproductive competence in adulthood easily, naturally. Boys have it harder. They mature slower and have to be socially aided by rituals to achieve adult fertility. What an ironic view in a warrior culture whose men so much pride themselves on their superiority to women!

New Guinea cultures—like our own in the Middle Ages when we believed in dragons and wizards' alchemy—are animistic, so in their world view they perceive a *structure of essences* that governs all life. We have already seen examples of this biological *essentialist* view in Sambia ideas about nature. Now we need to focus on how the same structure of thought is applied to blood and semen as essences of the body. Remember that Sambia have a simple technology and no science as we know it, so their ideas are a mix of fact and fantasy, unchecked by our sophisticated experimental sciences. The point is that Sambia see blood and semen as the crucial fluids in the working of maleness and femaleness.

Femaleness is vital and fast-growing, whereas maleness is slower in gaining maturation. Maleness is believed to depend on the acquisition of semen— the essence of biological maleness—for precipitating male anatomy *and* masculine behavioural traits. Femaleness rests on the creation and circulation of blood. This essence is held, in turn, to stimulate the production of menstrual blood, menarche, and adult reproductive competence. A girl's menarche is celebrated by women in secret events that socially recognize her "natural" achievements. In girls, who possess a self-activating and functional menstrual blood organ (*tingu*), maturation is viewed as an unbroken process leading from birth and maternal bonding into adulthood and motherhood. In boys, however, two obstacles block male growth. The first is their mother's pollution, food, and overall caretaking, which nurtures them but then stifles their growth. The second is their lack of semen, because the semen organ (*kerekukereku*) can only store, not manufacture, semen—the key to manly reproductive competence. In this model, therefore, femaleness is a natural development leading to feminine adulthood; maleness is not a naturally driven process but rather a personal achievement that men wrest control of through ritual initiations to ensure that they attain adult masculinity. Here we will examine ideas about the essence of blood.... [W]e will see how boys learn the function of semen in promoting masculine gender. Beliefs about both fluids are a basic part of the experience of gender identity in growing up.

Blood is identified by all Sambia with the vitality and longevity of women and their femaleness. Females, unlike males, are thought to be gifted with an innate means of producing blood that hastens the development of growth, menarche, and regular menses. Menstrual blood is also the provider of womb life for the fetus. The male and female parts in reproduction are clearly defined. A man's semen enters the womb and becomes a "pool" that eventually coagulates into fetal skin and bone tissue, which grows inside the female womb. Fetal or womb blood, supplied only by the mother's womb, later becomes part of the circulatory blood needed by all children and adults.

This circulatory blood is thought to be a true stimulator—with certain limits for males—that promotes body functioning and growth and the ability to withstand sickness. The limitations on this idea are centered in concepts through which Sambia define blood itself. First, there is the distinction between circulatory blood and menstrual-womb blood. Both males and females possess circulatory blood (*menjaku*); but only females have menstrual blood (*chenchi*), which is categorized with all other contaminating female fluids. Second, Sambia speak of reproductively competent humans (as well as trees and animals) as being fluid or wet, not dry (that is, either sexually immature or old and used up). In females, fluidity stems from having plentiful circulatory and menstrual blood, vaginal fluids, and that part of her husband's semen a woman "ingests" through sexual intercourse. Males, by contrast, are "drier" because of less fluid; only through their original circulatory blood and later through (artificially ingested) semen are they fluid. Children and old people are most dry; girls are more fluid than boys. Adults—unless sickly or sexually depleted—are generally believed to be fluid. Third, blood is said to be "cold" whereas semen is "hot." Since Sambia see sickness and plagues as active and animated agents (like spirit beings) attracted to heat and repelled by cold, this temperature difference is important in body functioning: the more blood, the less sickness; the more semen, the greater the chance of illness and degeneration. So men are prone to be ill and women healthy. Menstrual periods are compared to a periodic natural defence that rids female bodies of excess menstrual blood and any sickness that manages to penetrate them. Ironically, then, women bounce back from their periods with even greater vitality because of this natural function. The female capacity to create and discharge blood is thus perceived as a sign by the society of the structure and functioning of women's bodies, the fertile powers of birth-giving, procreative sexuality, and health, so men reckon this is why women typically outlive men.

What matters for masculinity is that menstrual-womb blood, though a life-giving female stimulator, also represents after childhood the most dangerous essence for male body functioning. All male circulatory blood originates from the mother's womb, so in later initiation nose-bleedings men attempt to get rid of it. Other female substances—such as skin flakes, saliva, sweat, and especially vaginal fluid—are also classified as polluting and dangerous to men.

Male illness resulting from female sorcery, for example, usually hinges on the fear that a man has been slipped menstrual or vaginal fluids in his food, though menstrual blood is dreaded most. Children cannot help but take in these substances through birth and their mother's feeding and handling. Here are the men's main worries that lead to sexual antagonism. But women have similar concerns. They are careful not to contaminate themselves or others, especially their children, during their periods. Neither women's public statements nor activities, however, reveal anything approaching the intense anxiety aroused in men. Men can be directly harmed since menstrual blood, they believe, can penetrate the urethra during genital-to-genital sex, bringing sickness and thus destroying the manliness that has been so hard won. For this reason, men say, they must also be wary of contact with their own children, who may accidentally transmit and infect men with the traces of their mother's body products.[1] The structure of maleness is relayed through three organs: the semen organ, semen-feeder ducts, and the penis. Together with semen, their essence, they form a physiological system.

All males possess a functional semen organ. Lower mammals, such as dogs and pigs, have the same organ. Females are said to have a semen organ, but its form and function differ from that of males. Here is a remark from Weiyu depicting an image of fetal development:

> Semen makes all the infant: bone, skin, brain [including the spinal column]....
> One thing only—blood—your momma gives to you. Momma gives you blood; [but] everything else, only semen makes. The woman is filled up with blood—the *tingu* makes it and fills it up.

Both semen and blood are involved in sexual differentiation. Semen is the more substantial component, even though blood overwhelms it internally by "filling up" the insides.

The immature male semen organ is "solid and dry" and only changes after the ingestion of semen through homosexual contacts. Boys do not inherit semen from their fathers or mothers. By contrast, the *tingu*, initially holding only a smear of blood, gradually grows, engorged by its own blood, which also fills up the girl's womb. The semen organ in a boy is an empty container. It cannot manufacture the essence; it only accumulates what semen is swallowed. Orally ingested semen modifies the organ's form. A pubescent semen organ is called "soft," because the orally ingested semen, by opening and swelling the organ, softens it from inside.

Women's semen organs are filled by blood or vaginal fluid or both, but not by semen. The male *tingu*, by contrast, is not functional: "Of you and me [men] too—we have a *tingu*. But it is hard and dry.... Women also have a *kereku-*

kereku ... but theirs is filled with vaginal fluid." Tali the ritual expert said this. The prepubescent boy's semen organ is empty, as is his *tingu* organ, Tali has also suggested. No semen or maleness there; so manhood is not possible until homosexual inseminations begin.

How does this bodily change take place? The semen organ is joined by "feeder tubes" to the mouth, navel, and penis. There are two such tubes. One, the esophagus, is shared by all humans. The esophagus transports semen in both women and boys, but to different places. Some (perhaps most) swallowed semen is siphoned off by the "breast ducts" of women and converted into milk before it reaches the stomach or womb. Slight amounts of it may get into a women's womb. None of it goes to her semen organ since she lacks the internal tubes associated with a penis. This is consistent with the men' s view that orally ingested semen goes to "strengthen" a woman or provide milk, while semen "fed" into the vagina goes into the womb for fetal growth. Women, however, generally believe that their own bodies make them strong. Boys lack a vulva, birth canal, and womb; their ingested semen goes first to "strengthen" them by becoming a liquid pool accumulating in the semen organ. Like food and water, semen can be swallowed; but unlike those substances, it is thought to be funnelled undiluted into the semen organ through a feeder tube only males possess. This organ, the "semen tube," directly connects the navel with the penis and testes, and thus with the semen organ. The tubes extend from that organ (in the upper abdominal region) upwards to the navel, and downwards to the stem of the penis. (Another, separate organ, the "urine tube," connects the bladder with the urethra.) Tali has said this: "Both the semen tube and urine tube are joined at the base of the penis, so semen is ejaculated through the urine tube during intercourse." In boys, these semen-related tubes and organs are "closed, hard, and dry" at birth and into childhood, until ritual fellatio matures them.

The prepubescent boy's penis is sexually and reproductively immature, for the boy's body lacks semen. His penis is puny, like a "little leach," men say. It lacks the mature glans penis and foreskin, male biological signs greatly stressed by Sambia. Men and initiates jokingly refer to the adult glans penis as that "ugly nose" and as that "face within the penis [pubic] hair." Such idioms characteristically distinguish the sexually immature from the mature male. Semen has the biological power to change this immaturity. Here is Weiyu on the subject:

> Now when we [males] drink the milk of a man or that of a tree it goes down and paints the *kereku-kereku*. It paints it and it [semen organ] comes up white. And so it makes semen. The penis alone contains nothing... it remains empty. But only the tube—it joins the penis—it shakes it, and it expels semen [at ejaculation].

Later you learn how only adult men drink certain white tree saps to replace their semen. That too is a male secret.

To reach this point of having a potent ejaculation requires years of semen ingestion and appropriate rituals. What matters, to sum up, is that this result is not natural or inevitable; instead, it comes from strict adherence to the male cult's formula.

A harmful effect of women's verbal behaviour during childhood is pinpointed on the boy's nose which is, next to the mouth, the body's main port of entry, and which receives ritual treatment. Here, mother's speech and harangues have a lethal power. A woman's airstream emitted while speaking is thought to emerge from her blood-filled caverns. If it is directed—particularly at close range during anger—toward a boy, the latter is harmed: simply by inhaling her insults and air he is defiled. The nose absorbs and stores her contaminants, thereafter blocking the free movement of circulatory blood and other fluids from the nose throughout his body. Likewise, men say women pollute boys simply by lifting their legs in proximity to them, emitting vaginal smells that boys can breathe in. For this reason, men keep their noses secretly plugged during coitus, avoiding incorporation of the vaginal smell they describe as harmfully foul. Women, incidentally, reject some of these male ideas. Particularly today, younger women say that this is more men's idle talk than reality. We will see ... that ritual nose-bleeding[2] is *the* critical means of expelling these harmful female materials from the male body, since Sambia practice no other form of ceremonial bloodletting.

These sexual development beliefs provide a framework for cultural institutions and for individual behaviour. For boys and girls, these beliefs underlie the normative gender roles they must adapt to and perform as they reach adulthood. The beliefs also provide a structure for experiencing the self as being either male of female. Here, the individual differentiates him- or herself internally in response to such questions as, "Am I male?" "Am I feminine?" "Should I act in such-and-such way to seem more masculine?" These feelings relate to the person's identification with gender roles and social status positions like those of the hunter, the shaman, and the war leader. Beliefs about sexual differentiation provide guidelines for acting masculine or feminine, which merge into gender beliefs, ideas about *being* male or female, in accord with the society's cultural code of evaluative standards. When there is only one world view—one code for appropriate gender behaviour—there may be no great difficulties in learning gender beliefs and in acting upon them in one's life. But what happens when there are two world views, each having different ideas and standards?

The Two Worlds

We have seen that "male" and "female" not only are two sexes but are, for Sambia, two different principles of biological essence, related to two different ways of being social, to the extent that they regard the sexes as different species in many respects. It is only another step—a conceptual leap but an important one—to recognize that this dichotomy creates two distinct symbolic worlds: that of adult men and women. Many New Guinea ethnographers have seen in warfare (the men's aggressive ethos) and the patterning of sexual antagonism the bases for opposition and conflict between the sexes. But how do these factors actually affect child socialization?

Cultures are systems of symbols and behaviours. Sambia men and women clearly have alternative standards in this regard. They do not share all of the same beliefs, they are not guided entirely by the same values, and they disagree on certain fundamentals: Should women have choice in marriage? Are women as polluting to themselves and to men to the extent men believe? Do women experience orgasm? Should men not bear a larger share of garden work, especially now that warfare is over? Should men not be closer to children and do more caretaking of infants? These issues spark conflict between the sexes and suggest basic gender-role differences, fundamental controversies between the worlds of men and women....

The Men's Secret Society

Many warrior societies throughout history have used initiation rites to recruit and train males. This is common in New Guinea, and Sambia are no exception. Indeed, their local warriorhoods exemplify the strong link between war and initiation.

What shall we call the unit that initiates boys? I mean here not the confederacy as described before, because that is the political union of neighbouring hamlets who do collective initiations (called *iku mokeiyu*) together. I mean rather the social and psychological bond that connects men of different villages, their sharing in secret rites—in spite of their warring with one another. We could speak of their being members of a military club, since initiation aimed to producer warriors. The initiation system also created age-graded and ritual-ranked status positions, akin to generals, lieutenants, and soldiers: members of a military order. And we could think of this initiating group as a religious cult, for the clubhouse has the blessings of spirit beings, mystical powers associated with magical formulas, and it conducts fantastic ceremonies—public, private, and secret—which perpetuate the sacred core of Sambia society. Whether we choose to think of it as a military club or cult, initiation is the most colourful and powerful institution in Sambia society. Let us call it a secret society.

This secret club instills the warrior ethos in boys and transmits to them the power called *jerungdu*. Sambia men associate this power with homosexual intercourse and the use of phallic symbols, especially the ritual flutes, that represent the cult and masculinity. The men's club honours the old men and denigrates women, so we may refer to it also as a phallic cult. Much of its power derives from its secrecy; or, to be more precise, from the way the men use secrecy to accomplish military, ritual, and sexual aims. I want to impress upon you that in spite of how exotic and almost archaic this secret society may seem, the account you will read represents not the dead past but the present. The phallic cult of Sambia is alive today.

Initiation for Strength
The main goal of initiation is to make boys big and strong, to make them aggressive warriors. This requires changing them: where they sleep and eat, how they act, whom they interact with, look up to, and obey. This is no easy change. They must be removed, by force if necessary, from the women's domain and placed in the culthouse. This changes them dramatically, for they lose their childhood freedom and must conform to rigid roles. Pre-initiates are seen as boys, not men, for they show feminine traits such as shyness and crying, and they engage in female tasks and routines such as babysitting and weeding. In this sense they belong to the female world, though they are not female. Though they must become participants in the men's secret society, they are too "feminine" in the above ways to be admitted without change—radical change. They must learn new things, but they must also *un*learn old traits and ideas, so that they can truly feel in their gender identity: "I am *not* feminine; I *am* masculine." Such marked change we call *radical resocialization*.

The change from boyhood to manhood is tough and men do not spare boys the ordeals of initiations. To the elders, this is necessary. Warfare was the number-one reality to be reckoned with, and the men still prepare for it. *A war is going on:* this is the old idea that underlies initiation. The whole secret society is oriented toward the constant struggle to survive war.

How are boys to acquire the strength to be warriors? Here the dilemma in Sambia thinking about *jerungdu* is twofold. First, the male body is believed incapable of manufacturing semen, so it must be externally acquired. This means that *jerungdu* itself is not an intrinsic capacity of male functioning but must be artificially created, as we have seen. Second, semen can be "lost" (ejaculated), and, along with it, the *jerungdu* that it sustains. Therefore, ritual measures must be taken to artificially replace what essence is lost in order to prevent weakness and death. No semen, no *jerungdu,* no masculinity. Overcoming these masculine challenges is the long-term goal of Sambia secret initiations. This entire process I call *ritualized masculinization.* Oral ingestion of semen—ritualized fellatio—is critical to the development of *jerungdu* in boys. Only after years of ritualized homosexuality and body treatment do the key sexual signs of strength take physical form. Initiation is thus a means of simulating maleness and masculinity. Be clear about what this means: *jerungdu* is felt to be a real force, not a metaphor or symbol. Fellatio behaviour is a concrete means of attaining it. Men are absolutely convinced of their innate lack of semen and of the need for their rituals, and they transmit their convictions to boys in ritual teaching.

Men likewise stress the cultural values of strength, equivalence, and weakness, which are vague in childhood but made explicit in ritual initiation. *Jerungdu* motivates aggressiveness and assertive protests. Equivalence places initiates in age-mate relationships that require them to match their peers' achievement. The unmanly label *wogaanyu* makes boys conform to masculine standards that despise weakness and passivity in all actions. And females—the softness of femininity—represent a lower and weaker condition. Through initiation boys are radically resocialized to change their cultural orientations, like a sort of brain-washing that traumatically modifies their thought. The effect is to end their attachments to their mothers and to create new aggressive and sexual impulses, thereby directing boys along the lines of culturally standardized male gender role and identity.

Initiation is the true funnel into the warriorhood. It has the pomp and ceremony of a festival and is also sacred, so its secret parts are solemn and dramatic. Initiation occurs at the harvest season, when men recognize the bounty of nature's fertility. Organized by one's fathers, brothers and clan elders, the ritual is done by the most loved and admired people in society. Even one's mother takes pride in the event and in her son's accomplishment. For despite her husband's demands, her workload, the heavy gardening responsibilities expected to ensure the success of the event, her other babies' needs and her own—and notwithstanding her ambivalence in losing a son's companionship and help, or her occasional opposition to the idea of initiation, which sometimes provokes nasty quarrels with her husband—a mother surely recognizes that this is the course a son must take, that the hamlet needs her boy as a defender. Where mother loses a son, father gains a comrade. This is so for all of one's playmates, too, the lads who become age-mates, members of the village warrior class.

The pre-initiated boy, then, is seen as a small person with a penis who is polluted, weak, and not yet manly. He is still polluted from the womb, and has taken in mother's food and saliva. He has been constantly in touch with the contaminated skin of her breasts and body. He is entirely too dependent on her for protection and warmth; her body remains too much of a haven for him. There is more than a hint of femininity about him; he even wears the same type of grass apron as females. He is undisciplined and bawls and throws tantrums when unable to get what he wants. At such times men are openly hostile to boys, taunting them till they cry, saying "Go back to your mother where you belong!" The boy sometimes disobeys his parents and talks back to them. Men cannot forget that their sons are carriers of feminine pollution, so they watch them lest they pollute men, their weapons, or their food. Boys are, of course, kept ignorant of ritual secrets and chased away when these are discussed. Such considerations come to mind when men discuss the need to initiate their maturing sons.

Another urgent thought is that masculinization is literally a matter of life and death. A boy's body has female contaminants inside it that retard masculine development. His body is male: he has male genitals and his *tingu* contains no blood, nor will it activate. Yet for boys to reach puberty requires semen. Milk "nurtures the boy"; sweet potatoes and other "female" foods provide "stomach nourishment" and become only feces, not semen. Women's own bodies internally produce menstruation, the hallmark of reproductive maturity. No comparable mechanism is active in boys to stimulate their biological secondary sex traits. Only semen can do that and only men have semen—boys have none.

What is left to do, then, but initiate boys and thereby masculinize them? Only through initiation can men collectively and immediately put a halt to what they perceive as the stultifying effects of mothering upon their sons. The mother's blood and womb and care, which gave life to and nourished the lad, are finally seen by the secret society as symbols of antilife. To undo these feminizing effects, boys must be drastically detached from women and then ritually treated. Thereafter boys avoid women until marriage, by which time the idealized masculine behaviours of initiation have remade the boy into the image of a warrior....

The Culthouse Scene
Early in the morning, a large group leaves our hamlet for the culthouse and danceground on the other side of the valley. They include Kanteilo, my elder sponsor, Weiyu, Moondi, and younger friends, males at all ages from the village. I am among them. We take up quarters near the culthouse. Other men, some women and children, follow. Soon hundreds of visitors are settling all around us. Tonight the first moonlight rituals and dancing begin. Everyone is beautifully garbed and decorated. Weiyu and Moondi show me around. We see throngs of people from all over, even from other valleys.

A long sequence of nighttime ceremonies is held that first night. The next night these are duplicated, with the third-stage initiates taking prominence. On the third day things calm a bit. That afternoon I went to the culthouse and was amazed to see open homosexual play, which I had not seen before.

How did the men accept me in this scene? This question is basic to all anthropological research. Yet in sensitive settings like this one it is essential to know how and why people accepted an outsider, how he or she influenced their behaviour, and whether they kept secrets. Remember that I had already been in the village eight months. I had lived in the men's house, where homosexual activities were at first hidden from me. I had friends, and several informants had stayed in my house and I ate with them. We had often travelled together. But after four months it was still a scandal when my friend Nilutwo told them he had told me about the secret homosexuality. The men were furious with him. Things were tense for days, What could I do? I waited, and gradually their anger passed. They made me promise I would not tell women and children the secret. As time passed and I was good to my word, they trusted me more. When the initiations rolled around, my friends never doubted I would go to see the secret ceremonies. The men of other hamlets asked about me too. Could I be trusted? A few tried to get me to leave or tried to trick me into missing the ceremonies; but they were exceptional. Most of the people accepted me, for the men with whom I worked always stood up to speak in my behalf. They still do. I was involved in their cult in this sense; I saw the rites and was there when it all happened. Yet I tried to stay off to the sidelines, not wanting to attract undue attention. Some things, like the harsh beatings in initiation, were hard for me to witness. I tried always to describe my own reactions to things too. Thus, I was a participant-observer of the rites, though I did not directly join in or accept as a part of my own personal style all that I saw.

The emotional and sexual tenor of the culthouse scene reveals that Sambia society is temporarily in a state very different from everyday life. Norms and rules are turned on their head. Some anthropologists have referred to this as "ritual time": a time with the license to act out normally forbidden impulses, a sort of free "play" within ritual. Turner (1971) has referred to this as a period of "anti-structure" in society, when relationships are open to reconstitution of ideals and exploration of tabooed feelings. We will see the individual counterpart of anti-structure in the liminal experience of initiates later.

The danceground comes alive at dusk. The weather is cool and clear. Men and initiates are everywhere, though the area is uncrowded. From somewhere, out of sight, flutes can be heard, a part of the male camaraderie celebrating the complete absence of women and children. Homosexual contacts are rampant here. People are open and unabashed, though they do honour certain taboos. Homosexual activity is governed by rules that match incest taboos: all kinsmen and distant relatives are tabooed sexual partners, as are boys' age-mates and ritual guardians. Brothers-in-law may be acceptable homosexual partners, depending on their exact relation to the boy. The mood is festive and light, initiates running around, laughing and clowning, an atmosphere as different from the heavy solemnity characterizing formal rituals as is the night from the day. The following are my very first observations of homosexual play in the dance ground context. Similar things happened in later initiations too.

The culthouse is darkening and noisy, a mass of bodies and movement and laughter. There are two dozen initiates and older bachelors. None of the new *ipmangwi* bachelors are here; they are in ritual seclusion. The elders have absented themselves. Sambia males feel that it is in bad taste for initiates to engage in homoerotic play in the presence of elders. (Homosexual jokes or innuendos, however, alluded to by elders vis-à-vis their peers, are appropriate in front of initiates.) So boys usually refrain from homosexual play when near elders or their fathers. In situations like this one, where elders know what to expect, they conveniently disappear. Several men have built a small fire in the hearth. Some adults who are forbidden to engage in homosexual activities are present. They sit detachedly chatting, incongruously calm in the centre of a storm. All but one of them can sustain this composure—which feels artificial—as seen by his fascination in watching the homoerotic play. The boys are openly initiating foreplay here. Several sitting near the fire are flirting and hanging onto bachelors. Allusions are made to me watching, but no one seems to mind.

Outside on the danceground three boys are hanging on to Sonoko, a bachelor who seems to be in demand. He is talking loudly. A short, strange little Wantuki'u tribesman, who is older but still unmarried, is glued to the second-stage initiate Sollu, a pubescent boy from our hamlet. I am amazed to see Sollu, who is surly, hugging him, their arms locked, faces cheek to cheek. The boy actually nuzzles the man's neck, but there is no kissing. (Sambia do not kiss mouth-to-mouth.) Nearby, several small boys reach underneath the older bachelors' grass aprons to arouse them. A tiny initiate says impatiently to Sonoko: "Come on, shoot me." Occasionally the smiling youths halfheartedly protest that the initiates are pulling on them too hard. In the shadows of the house are several male couples rolling around in the grass. One of them is older, married, and a father—which makes his behaviour immoral by ritual convention, but no one pays attention.

Most of the new third-stage initiates are milling around outside. I walk over to join them. Several feet away in their ritual seclusion hut, filled with elders and off-limits to the younger initiates. Some of these youths flirt with initiates, though the youths are forbidden to inseminate them until they complete their own initiation. Some smaller initiates look nervous in anticipation of the night events. Moondi is among this mob but he appears calm. It is not clear exactly which youths will be initiated; several of them are strangers from outside the Sambia Valley. Two Sambia boys from the village talk with me. Someone hands us baked taro, our first food.

I turn back to the shadowy danceground where sexual exploits and their risque sounds are even more outrageous than those in the culthouse, which seems to excite the crowd. There is still a faint light outside and I am conspicuous. Several times I hear allusions with mild hostility to my presence, but I try to ignore them. A little later, in response to one of these mutterings, I heard my friend Sonoko say: "That's nothing.... He knows." Here—witnessing open homoerotic activities and standing alone, tall, white, Western-clothed—I feel awkward and out of place, more like a voyeur than I ever did, peeping in on a private show, I clutched my pipe nervously and smoked more than usual. There seemed nothing else for me to do if I was to remain and yet ease my tension.

Some two dozen men, bachelors, and initiates are now milling around the danceground, scattered on the great empty space here and there. Some walk in pairs, others in small clusters of bodies, all restlessly flowing clockwise round the circular ground, as if keeping time with some slow, silent hymn (and there was no singing). Initiates are also horsing around among themselves, playing tag, running back and forth, pushing, pulling, and shoving. In the center are several married men who are oddly detached, circling idly among the others. But there are no initiates with them. Nearby are several young and recently married men (without children yet), including my friends Erujundei, Sonoko, Ooterum, and Aatwo (the latter a hard-bitten man in his early twenties whose father is a war leader). Each of them has one or two initiates; Aatwo is with a boy whom he has long favoured. Sonoko has three initiates, who come and go, while I stay on the danceground over the next two hours. The atmosphere remains edgy and exciting. There is rampant sexual foreplay, initiates even competing to hold a man's genitals. From time to time, these couples exit the danceground, into the grass close by, for fellatio; Sambia never permit sex in public. When they reappear minutes later; most walk over and sit inside the culthouse.

There is variation in this sexual behavior but two general patterns emerged. First, most of the couples returned to the culthouse afterward, some—in blatant public "statements"—entering together, while still physically touching, arm in arm. Others, out of embarrassment (as noted by waiting on purpose, then nervously talking to friends), enter separately, moments apart. Second, a few couples would return to the danceground together, but then separate. In some instances the initiate would go to another man, leaving his bachelor on his own or with another boy. Generally, in ordinary life, homosexual partners will split up after sexual intercourse and go in different directions to avoid notice. Several Wantuki'u men joined in, initiates trailing after them. And so did Chemona later on. Like Sonoko, he is very popular with the initiates.

It is the older second-stage initiates, especially the ones recently initiated, who are the most aggressive at this sexual play. Nilangu's own initiates are prominent here: Kambo, Buvuluruton, Sollu, and Dangetnyu. But there were others too. For instance, Merolkopi (Tulutwo's younger blood brother) literally hung on to Nolerutwo, smiling and petting him. Around 7:00 p.m. I heard the youth say matter of factly to the younger Merolkopi (who stood with two other initiates who wanted to be inseminated, all pleading "Me! Me!"): "All right, I mark you to shoot." The initiate lit up in a wide smile. Two other initiates keep teasing and pulling Sonoko's genitals, trying to get him aroused. But twice he said loudly: "Stop it, I've already slept [had sex]!"

Thus it went into the night. On the next night it was the same. And again, at the start of each successive initiation, this free and orgiastic carnival atmosphere was repeated. Never before or since have I seen public erotic behaviour of this sort or on this scale. Homosexual play does occur in other secret situations: at night in the clubhouses, and in the forest or hunting lodges. But it is never this blatant, with open foreplay, and it certainly never occurs on such a wide scale within a large group. The closest situation is that of the rat-hunting lodge, which follows first-stage initiation in the forest. Indeed, the repressive nature of Sambia society makes it seem impossible to casual observers that such frenetic energy could be so easily unleashed in males who, except for these several nights—two or possibly three times in their lives at initiations— are renowned for their reserved, straightlaced behaviour, abhorring public eroticism. Yet, my most singular memory of that night was the *openness* of sexual play—which shocked me—for it meant there were similar past experiences locked inside the adult men I thought I knew before but would never have imagined out in that crowd. Yet, the anthropologist knows that some of the most profound experiences in a society are those that are normally taken for granted or hidden, except on occasions such as this. Participant-observation is thus a valuable "corrective" method in studying people, for in spite of its shortcomings, it can reveal a fuller picture of how they live their lives.

Notes

1. For recent comparative studies on pollution beliefs in Melanesia, see Anna Meigs's (1984) and Fitz John Poole's (1981, 1982) important work, and my own essay on semen as a commodity (Herdt 1984).
2. [*Editor*: Bamboo flutes are jammed into the noses of initiates.]

References

Herdt, Gilbert (ed.) *Ritualized Homosexuality in Melanesia*. Berkeley, CA: Univeristy of California Press, 1984.

Meigs, A.S. *Food, Sex, and Pollution*. Rutgers, NJ: Rutgers University Press, 1984.

Poole, F.J.P. "Transforming 'natural' woman: Female ritual leaders and gender ideology among Bimin-Kuskumin." In S.B. Ortner and H. Whitehead (eds.), *Sexual Meanings* (116-65). Cambridge, England: Cambridge University Press, 1981.

—. "The ritual forging of identity: Aspects of person and self in Bimin-Kuskumin male initiation." In G.H. Herdt (ed.), *Rituals of Manhood: Male Initiation in Papua New Guinea* (100-54). Berkeley, CA: University of California Press, 1982.

38
———

JANICE BODDY (1951-)

The Muslim, Arabic-speaking Sudanese villagers of whom Boddy writes present an extreme situation of the social construction of gender. "Women" (and "men") are literally produced with a pair of scissors. Femininity is inscribed in the human body by a practice of cutting away the clitoris and labia minora and sewing up most of the genital opening, an operation called "infibulation." Men are circumcised. These genital operations exaggerate male/female anatomical differences and transform female anatomy into a sexually anaesthetized and virtually sealed container. An extensive set of prescriptions about behaviour and appearance, such as modest dress for women and the association of women with the enclosed space of the house, further underline gender differences. Preferred partners for first marriages are cousins, which reinforces a sense of closedness and enclosedness. Marriages are, however, quite brittle, and women are easily divorced or set aside in favour of a younger co-wife. Infibulation which ensures women's suitability for marriage also increases the incidence of sterility, a reason for male-initiated divorce.

The enclosure of the Hofriyati women, the literal closedness of their bodies and their social world, is "shown up" in spirit possession, a state of altered consciousness associated with a ritual performance. Gender and enclosure are deconstructed in the ritual performance that expresses possession by a *zār*, a spirit being. In the state of possession, Hofriyati women leave their highly enclosed and interior state (constructed by infibulation, marriage rules, and behavioral norms) to become exterior and other. They are possessed by spirits that are men and/or non-Hofriyati, and in this state, they can become aggressive, lascivious, swaggering, rude, and demanding, or wise and authoritative— all opposites of feminine virtues in Hofriyat. Some are possessed by the spirits of wise, male Muslim elders; others by spirits that are white Christians, Ethiopian or black African prostitutes, nomadic tribesmen, or central African "cannibal sorcerers." These spirits (and other spirits like them) are "other" to the Hofriyati women and radically different from them. In the state of spirit possession, the women dress and act the part of spirit beings who express everything that Hofriyati women are not.

Boddy reports that about 40 per cent of adult women, but only 5 per cent of adult men experience zār possession. It is defined as an illness or affliction, but it is also a ritual performance and an informal local religious cult. Boddy analyzes it not as a psychological phenomenon, but as a cultural one, the creation of a text about gender and culture. The entire complex of infibulation, cousin marriage, appropriate gender behaviour, and zār possession shows us an ongoing process of constructing gender, negotiating it, and playfully deconstructing it. Boddy is implicitly challenging the reader to recognize similar processes of social construction in our own lives.

The selections focus on two rituals—infibulation and spirit possession. They begin with a description and discussion of infibulation and the general interiority and enclosedness of Hofriyati femininity. The selections continue with descriptions of zār possession, especially those instances that create a strong dissociation between the possessed (a Hofriyati woman) and the possessing spirit (which Boddy designates with a capital letter). The dissociation is most complex, striking, and deconstructive when the spirit (a transvestite homosexual or a prostitute) playfully imitates Hofriyati women, so that in the ritual performance the observer sees a real Hofriyati woman playing the part of the spirit "other" (male homosexual, lascivious prostitute) playing the part of a virtuous Hofriyati woman.

Readings
Orsi, Robert. *Thank You, St. Jude: Women's Devotion to the Patron Saint of Hopeless Causes*. New Haven: Yale University Press, 1998.

Wombs and Alien Spirits:
Women, Men, and the Zār Cult in Northern Sudan
JANICE BODDY

Pharaonic Circumcision

My first glimpse of the symbolic matrix informing Hofriyati life came from attempting to understand the practice of female circumcision. During the summer of 1976 I witnessed several of these operations, performed on all girls sometime between the ages of five and ten.[1] Despite my (self-confessed) reluctance, village friends made a point of my attendance, waking me in the dark predawn lest I miss the surgery at daybreak. What follows is a description of one such observation.[2]

June 12, 1976. A band of pink traces the horizon as Zaineb and I thread a maze of walls into the heart of the village. We enter a houseyard washed in shadows. Miriam, the local midwife, has finished circumcising one sister and is preparing to operate on the second. (Sisters close in age are usually circumcised together, otherwise, the operation is an individual affair.) A crowd of women, many of them habōbāt *(grandmothers) have gathered in the yard— not a man in sight. I find myself propelled to the center of the room; it is important, says Zaineb, to see this up close. She bids me record what I see.*

The girl lies docile on an angarīb, *beneath which smoulders incense in a cracked clay pot. Her hands and feet are stained with henna applied the night before. Several kinswomen support her torso; two others hold her legs apart. Miriam thrice injects her genitals with local anesthetic, then, in the silence of the next few moments, takes a small pair of scissors and quickly cuts away her clitoris and labia minora; the rejected tissue is caught in a bowl below the bed. Miriam tells me this is the* lahma juwa, *or inner flesh. I am surprised there is so little blood. She says that haemorrhage is less likely to occur at sunup, before the child has fully risen.* Mushāhara *customs, too, prevent bloodloss, the henna being part of these.[3] Miriam staunches the flow with a white cotton cloth. She removes a surgical needle from her midwife's kit—an elaborate red tin box—and threads it with suture. She sews together the girl's outer labia leaving a small opening at the vulva. After a liberal application of antiseptic the operation is over.*

Women gently lift the sisters as their angarībs *are spread with multicolored* birishs, *"red" bridal mats. The girls seem to be experiencing more shock than pain, and I wonder if the anesthetic has finally taken effect. Amid trills of joyous undulations we adjourn to the courtyard for tea; the girls are also brought outside. There they are invested with the* jirtig: *ritual jewelry, perfumes, and cosmetic pastes worn to protect those whose reproductive ability is vulnerable to attack from malign spirits and the evil eye. The sisters wear bright new dresses, bridal shawls (called* garmosīs, *singular), and their family's gold. Relatives sprinkle guests with cologne, much as they would at a wedding; redolent incense rises on the morning air. Newly circumcised girls are referred to as little brides (arūs); much that is done for a bride is done for them, but in a minor key. Importantly, they have now been rendered marriageable.*

Before Miriam received government training in midwifery, female circumcisions were performed differently in Hofriyat, though their ceremonial aspects were much as I describe. For women circumcised prior to 1969 the operation was more radical, less sterile, and in the absence of anesthetic injections, more painful than it is today. My friends recounted their own experiences. A circular palm-fiber mat with its center removed was fitted over a freshly dug hole in the ground.[4] The girl was seated on the mat at the edge of the hole. As kinswomen held her arms and legs, the midwife, with no apparent concern for sterile procedure, scraped away all of their external genitalia, including the labia majora, using a straight razor. Then she pulled together the skin that remained on either side of the wound and fastened it with thorns inserted at right angles. (Fresh acacia thorns produce a numbness when they pierce the skin and may have helped relieve the pain.) These last were held in place by thread or scraps of cloth wound around their ends. A straw or thin hollow reed was inserted posteriorly so that when the wound healed there would be an opening in the scar for elimination of urine and menstrual blood. The girl's legs were then tied together and she was made to lie on an *angarīb* for up to forty days to promote healing. When the wound was thought to have healed sufficiently the thorns were removed and the girl unbound.

Both operations described are versions of pharaonic circumcision, *tahūr farownīya.*[5] According to villagers the practice is a legacy of the pharaonic past, whence its name. However, analysis of human mummies from that period fails to confirm this assertion so far as premortem vaginal closure is concerned (Ghalioungui 1963: 96; Huelsman 1976: 123; Barclay 1964: 238). From historians' and travelers' accounts we know that the custom has long been practiced in this area. Yet its origins remain obscure. (Abdalla 1982: 63-72; Boddy 1982*a, b*: 685-86; Cloudsley 1983: 101-3; Gruenbaum 1982: 5; Sanderson 1981: 27-29).

Though conventionally termed "circumcision," the procedure is not physically equivalent to the like-named operation performed on boys. In Hofriyati, male circumcision entails removal of the penile prepuce, as it generally does throughout the Middle East, and, indeed, the West. Pharaonic circumcision, however, is more extreme, involving excision of most external genitalia followed by infibulation: intentional occlusion of the vulva and obliteration of the vaginal meatus. It results in the formation of thick, resistant scar tissue, a formidable obstruction to penetration.

A less severe operation, structurally similar to that performed on boys, is currently gaining ground in Khartoum and Omdurman. This is referred to as *masri* (Egyptian) or *sunna* ("orthodox," traditional) circumcision and consists in removing only the propuce or hood of the clitoris. It is not yet practiced in Hofriyat and is a matter of some controversy there. Men working in Saudi Arabia and the Islamic principalities of the Gulf have come under increasing influence from fundamentalist Wahabi Islam; some now perceive infibulations as contrary to Islamic tenets and advocate the less radical operation, considering it to be religiously approved.[6] But women are skeptical of the innovated procedure. While realizing that it is less hazardous to health than pharaonic circumcision, they continue to oppose it on aesthetic and hygienic grounds and in this lies a clue to its deeper significance. Several women I questioned in 1984 made their feelings graphically clear: each depicted *sunna* circumcision by opening her mouth, and pharaonic, by clamping her lips together. "Which is better," they asked, "an ugly opening or a dignified closure?" Women avoid being photographed laughing or smiling for precisely this reason: orifices of the human body, and particularly those of women, are considered most appropriate when closed, or failing that, when minimized....

Creating Female Persons

... When freed from the constraints of naturalistic assumptions, gender is properly seen as a symbolic construct, variable in constitution from one society to the next. The work of scholars such as Gilligan (1982) and Chodorow (1974, 1978) suggests that early gender socialization proceeds in universally similar ways, and establishes certain basic differences in the psychological (interpersonal) orientations of male and female children. Yet, as a growing body of ethnographic literature attests, the specifics of these differences, the contents of and relations between gender categories that inform and reproduce particular gender identities, are socially and culturally relative. Gender socialization is a process whereby humans in the course of interaction are molded and continuously shaped to appropriate images of femaleness and maleness. It is with this contextual aspect of genderization that I am here concerned.

The Hofriyati world is suffused by gender: gender constructs permeate the fabric of meaning and inform the idioms of daily life. Yet to understand women's position in this world, it is not enough to discover its logic; we need also to consider how such meanings are reproduced, continually created and embodied by individual actors. In Hofriyat, I suggest, we need to contemplate the implications of pharaonic circumcision for a female child's developing self-perception. Through this operation and other procedures involving pain or trauma, appropriate feminine dispositions are being inculcated in young girls, dispositions which, following Bourdieu (1977: 15), are inscribed in their bodies not only physically, but also cognitively and emotionally, in the form of mental inclinations, "schemes of perception and thought." But alone the trauma of pharaonic circumcision is insufficient to shape the feminine self, to propel it in culturally prescribed directions: such acts must also be meaningful to those who undergo and reproduce them. Here, as will be seen, meaning is carefully built up through the use of metaphors and associations which combine to establish an identification of circumcised women with morally appropriate fertility, hence to orient them toward their all-important generative and transformative roles in Hofriyat society. Paradoxically, however, to achieve this gender identity, women implicitly repudiate their sexuality.

I noted earlier that in Hofriyat, adult males and females are considered to be different kinds of person, defined by a complementarity attributed only in part to nature. When a child is born it is identified as male or female according to its genitalia. However, to villagers, genitalia are ambiguous and by themselves inadequate determinants of a child's future gender identity. Babies are considered to have the potential to develop into fully female or fully male adults, but this potential cannot be realized without ritual activation and prudent monitoring. A child is formally initiated to its gender between the ages of five and ten, when, as villagers say, he or she has developed a minimal degree of *'agl*, reason, self-awareness, the ability to recognize and follow Allah's laws. It is then that the child is circumcised. Apart from naming, which is sex specific, explicit socialization until this point is similar for male and female children: both are treated fondly and leniently and nursed for as long as two years, though boys, who are considered physically weaker than girls in infancy, may be less precipitately weaned. As babies they are dressed alike,[7] beginning to wear shifts of differently patterned material from about the age of three. Young boys and girls freely play together in the village streets: neither is required to do housework or help with farming. But all this changes dramatically with the child's circumcision, an event long anticipated, for threats of its imminence are often used by adults to scatter play groups too raucous for their ears.

Genital surgery accomplishes the social definition of a child's sex (see Ammar 1954: 121ff.; Assaad 1980: 4ff.; Kennedy 1978*c*: 158); it completes and purifies a child's natural sexual identity by removing physical traits deemed appropriate to his or her opposite: the clitoris and other external genitalia in the case of the females, the prepuce or covering of the penis in the case of males. So doing, the operations implicitly identify neophytes with their gender-appropriate spheres of interaction as adults: the interiors of housed yards enclosed by high mud walls in the case of females; the outside world of farmlands, markets, other villages, and cities in the case of males. Females are associated with enclosure, and enclosure ultimately with fertility; males are associated with the outside, with political and economic engagement of the world beyond the *hōsh*.

But more than this: among Hofriyati, women actively and ongoingly construct other women, in a sense completing Allah's original creation of woman (Hawa, or Eve in the Judeo-Christian tradition) from the body of man. By eliminating any vestiges of maleness, they constitute women as separate entities and distinct social persons, and by so doing, proclaim a triumph for *'agl* over *nafs*.

According to the gender socialization model proposed by Rosaldo (1974) and Chodorow (1974) to account for asymmetrical valuations of the sexes cross culturally, a psychological orientation of females to the domestic sphere and males to the public domain arises and is reproduced largely through the (culturally guided) efforts of male children to differentiate themselves from the feminine world of early socialization. Whereas boys must actively learn to be men, girls can passively "be absorbed into womanhood without effort" (Rosaldo 1974: 25). But this model is incompletely applicable to the Hofriyati context, where a female gender identity is neither wholly ascribed nor automatically assimilated by the female child. Here children of both sexes must actively achieve their gender identities through the directed experience of trauma. Genital operations simultaneously shape a child's body to the culturally appropriate gender image and launch the child on a process of internalizing the inferences of that image, of taking up the dispositions and identifications it suggests are suitable for adult life. The surgery establishes the conditions of adult gender complementarity, and it is in the nature of this complementarity, in its implications of social interaction, that gender asymmetries arise.

Circumcision marks the start of sexual segregation for the child: after their operations, boys should no longer sleep with their mothers and sisters, but accompany their older brothers in the mens's quarters. Similarly, an infibulated girl is increasingly restricted to association with womenfolk and expected to assume greater domestic responsibility. Boys and girls who once played together happily are now unseemly chums. I overheard one mother chastise her eight-year-old daughter for continuing to play with boys: "Get out of the street," she said, "Do you think your cousin will want to marry you if he sees you every day?"

Perhaps the most notable feature of village life is this polarization of the sexes, most marked between men and women of childbearing age. To an outsider it appears as if there are two virtually separate, coexisting societies that only occasionally overlap. Men and women generally do not eat together, they occupy different quarters in the family compound, and they associate with those of their own sex in segregated areas at ceremonies and religious events. Further, while man have ultimate authority over women, this is far less actual than supposed. In everyday affairs, women are more strictly governed by the *habōbāt* than by their male kin, and when it comes to a matter of direct control by her husband, the Hofriyati woman is expert in the art of passive resistance.

The nature of male authority is instructive. A woman is legally under the control and care of her father and, after his death, her brothers for as long as they live. When she marries she also becomes accountable to her husband, but her immediate male kin retain moral responsibility for her welfare. Theoretically, a measure of both economic and moral responsibility passes to her adult sons, especially should she be widowed or divorced. What these men share is the right to allocate and, in the case of her husband, to use the woman's reproductive potential.

Through marriage a man acquires access to his wife's fertility and she, the means to activate it. Children are the capital on which male and female careers are built; yet, since parents have independent claims in their offspring, these careers are distinct. This is important because marriages themselves are fragile and, for men, may be polygamous.

Moreover, men's explicit emphasis on controlling women's sexuality through circumcision, and women's implicit emphasis on thus socializing and controlling their fertility are complementary expressions of the same fundamental paradigm. For the only offspring considered socially and morally viable are those born of circumcised women in arranged and lawful marriages, most appropriately contracted between close kin.[8]

The identification with morally appropriate fertility inculcated in young girls through their circumcisions is reinforced and augmented in everyday life through conversations and interactions informed by a variety of metaphoric associations. As was noted earlier, my closer female friends volunteered that the operation is intended to make women pure (*tahir*), clean (*nazīf*), and smooth (*nā'im*). As I began to learn the various implication of these qualities, gradually piecing together what I was observing with what I was being told, it became increasingly clear that there exists a certain fit between this practice and others. A wide range of activities, concepts, and what villagers refer to as their customs (*'ādāt*) appeared to be guided by a cluster of interrelated idioms and metaphors, sometimes explicitly formulated but more often not. It is this referential substratum that I have described as constituting the informal logic of routine life in Hofriyat. Partly religious and partly secular, it underlies both ritualized and nonritualized behavior, providing a number of overlapping contexts that shape social discourse.

Thus, to determine the fuller significance of female circumcision and glean some insight into the cultural system as a whole, I will trace further applications of its essential qualities: purity, cleanliness, and smoothness. Each interpretation leads to others, the enterprise fanning out from its point of departure until one is faced with a complex of relations in which certain themes, or idioms, predominate. The process is like the weaving of a tapestry: certain threads are left hanging in places, later to be caught up again and worked into the pattern. Symbols interpenetrate, associations ramify, until gradually the images they harbor are revealed.

What follows is based primarily on my observations between 1976 and 1977. To some extent Hofriyati symbolic representations have changed since then: the house ornaments I describe as being made of ostrich egg-shells and dried gourds are no longer to be found. Their disappearance could signify a weakening of the symbolic matrix supporting the central value of fertility[9]— which the suggestion that villagers are moving toward acceptance of the less drastic *"sunna"* circumcision might also sustain. However, I am not convinced this is the case. Villagers are under considerable pressure from external sources (e.g., Egyptian television, Saudi Islam, the national declaration of *sharī'a* law in 1983) to evince a style that is at once more "modern," less "superstitious," and more fundamentally Islamic. Given villagers' history of resilience, locally relevant idioms may have become more implicit or, in assimilating the changes, be assuming other outward forms. It is, perhaps, too soon to tell....

Full Circle: Womb as Oasis
The idiom of (relative) enclosure, premised on the value of the interiority, has gradually emerged in this analysis as one which underwrites a diversity of villagers' practices and ideas. The *hōsh*, the womb, and many more objects of daily life (including, for that matter, women's *tōbs*, which may be thought of as portable enclosures), ideas concerning the human body, reproduction, imperviousness, and the fertility potential of brides, all that was outlined above, appear repeatedly in contexts that play upon this theme. These contexts culminate in another set of associations concerning the hōsh, the womb, and sexual complementarity.

As I noted earlier, the sexes are spatially as well as socially segregated. They occupy opposite sides of the dancing ground at ceremonies, are housed and fed in different households during communal feasts. The *hōsh*, too, is divided into men's and women's quarters, with separate entrances for each. The "front" door (no specified orientation) is known as the men's entrance and is used by official guests and strangers. The men's reception room (*dīwān*) is generally located in the forepart of the courtyard, near this door. The "back" door is know as the women's entrance and is for the use of women, close male kin, and neighbors. Women's quarters are situated in the rear of the compound, as is the kitchen, where *kisra* is baked. When the *hōsh* is considered a politicoeconomic unit, then internal or domestic affairs are overseen by women, while external affairs such as wage labor and marketing are the province of men. Though women are not, strictly speaking, secluded, there is a strong feeling that they ought to remain within the confines of the hōsh unless fetching water or visiting kin. There is thus a fairly firm association of women with internal affairs, enclosedness, and the interior of the *hōsh*, and of men with external affairs, nonenclosedness, and the front of the *hōsh*. The *hōsh*, remember, is symbolic of the womb—here seen as divided into male (outer, vaginal) and female (inner, uterine) domains. These relations provide further images with which Hofriyati think about social reproduction, to which we now return.

The men's entrance to the *hōsh* is known as the *khashm al-bayt*: the "mouth," "opening," or "orifice" of the house. This term also refers to a group of kin. Properly speaking, a *khashm al-bayt* comprises several related lineages, hence a subtribe. But in Hofriyat and elsewhere in Sudan (Barclay 1964: 91) the term is used only in reference to people who live in or originate from a common *hōsh* or *bayt*. It is a lineage section.

Extension of anatomical terms to nonanatomical subjects, as described above, is common in Hofriyat. The supports of an *angarīb* are its "legs" (*kur'ayn*). Importantly, doors and orifices through which things or people pass are "mouth" or "nostrils" (*khashms*), and the insides of houses and other enclosed areas are "bellies" or "stomachs" (*butons*). In the case at hand, the *khashm al-bayt* is associated with males, but the *bayt* itself with females: nonanatomical terms may conversely apply to parts of the anatomy, and the word for "house" is explicitly linked with the womb.

The womb is called the *bayt al-wilāda* the *"house of childbirth,"* and the vaginal opening is its *khashm,* its mouth or door. There thus exists an implicit link between the *khashm al-bayt,* the mens's door to the house yard and, metaphorically, one man's immediate descendants, and the *khash* of the *hayt al wilāda*, a woman's genital opening.[10] The men's door literally opens into an enclosed area occupied by a man's sons and daughters, his "crop." The khashm al bayt al-wilda, the "door" of the womb, also opens into an enclosed area where this crop was sown and nurtured, and which is all the more completely enclosed and purified by a woman's circumcision. Just as the *hōsh* protects a man's descendants, the enclosed, infibulated womb protects a woman's fertility: her potential and, ultimately, that of her husband. Like the *hōsh* poised between the Nile and the desert, the womb of a Hofriyati woman is an oasis, the locus of human fertility, a focal social value for both women and men, hence properly safeguarded and preserved.

Thus pharaonic circumcision is for women in Hofriyat an assertive, symbolic act. Through it they emphasize and embody in their daughters what they hold to be the essence of femininity: uncontaminated, morally appropriate fertility, the right and the physical potential to reproduce the lineage or found a lineage section. In that infibulation purifies, smooths, and makes clean the outer surface of the womb, the enclosure or *hōsh* of the house of childbirth, it socialized or, in fact, culturalizes a woman's fertility. Through occlusion and subsequent enclosures of the vaginal meatus, the womb becomes, and is reestablished as, an ideal social space: enclosed, impervious, virtually impenetrable. Her body becomes a metonym for the resilience of village society in the face of external threat. Much as Sondra Hale (1985) describes for Nubians farther north, women in Hofriyat are truly and concretely "symbols of the homeland."

The infibulated virginal bride, enclosed, pure, ostensibly fertile, is a key symbol in the Hofriyati cultural system (cf. El-Tayib 1987: 64-65). She superbly concentrates its values, figuratively representing interiority, one of its salient organizing precepts. But brides and other women are more than artifacts, symbolic expressions of their culture. They are social actors. And what I have been referring to as the "idiom of enclosure" is not an abstract principle or a set of rules but, following Bourdieu (1977: 15), a disposition "inculcated from the earliest years of life and constantly reinforced by calls to order from the group, that is to say, from the aggregate of individuals endowed with the same dispositions, to whom each is linked by [her] dispositions and interests." This disposition is a permanent one, like that of honor (*nif*) among the Kabyle (Algeria) which supplies Bourdieu's example. It is "embedded in the agents' bodies in the form of mental dispositions, schemes of perception and thought, extremely general in their application" (ibid.). Moreover, the implicit organizing precept of interiority corresponds to Bourdieu's notion of a "generative scheme" that underwrites a wide range of practice: "The 'customary rules' preserved by the group memory are themselves the product of a small batch of schemes enabling agents to generate an infinity of practices adapted to endlessly changing situations, without those schemes ever being constituted as explicit principles" (Bourdieu 1977: 16).

What I consider to be the logic of daily life in Hofriyat is thus an implicit philosophy, an organizing scheme immanent in practice. Interiority is not a reification, an explicitly formulated "rule" whose existence transcends the moment of its evocation. Rather, it is a quality or pattern intrinsic to the background of tacit assumptions in terms of which practice—with all its inevitable uncertainties, ambiguities, and strategies—unfolds. Phrased differently, interiority is the gist of a largely taken for granted world within which the apparently uncomplicated propositions of casual conversation and interaction make sense (cf. Berger and Luckmann 1966: 153). And the polysemic layout of domestic space, the transitive images of femininity and the *hōsh*, the signs embedded in daily activities are as much its techniques as its representations. They are, as Comaroff (1985: 54) puts it, "major media of socialization," "invisibly tuning people's minds and bodies to their inner logic."

Thus the simple, mundane acts of fetching water and baking bread, which girls begin to perform following their circumcisions, or even, perhaps, of eating an orange or opening a tin of fish—all are resonant with implicit meanings. They are metaphors both in thought and practice which, following Fernandez (1974), when predicated upon the inchoate self contribute to its identity. For in appropriating them, in enacting them, a girl becomes an object to herself (p. 122). And as Fernandez suggests, self-objectification must occur—by taking the view of the "other"—before she can become a subject to herself (p. 122). The metaphors predicated on female Hofriyati by themselves and others help to shape their dispositions, their orientations to the world, their selfhood. They are the means by which a woman's subjective reality, closely governed by the cultural construction of womanhood, is—not merely expressed—but realized and maintained. The painful and traumatic experience of circumcision first orients her toward a disposition and self-image compelled by her culture's values. And she is invited to relive that experience at various points in her life: vicariously, through participating in younger women's operations; actually, after each delivery; and metaphorically, with any procedure involving heat or pain, fluids, or other feminine qualities detailed above. Both in ritual and in many small moments throughout her working day, informative values are implicitly restated and her disposition reinforced. Hofriyati men and women, in constituting the latter as embodiments of the moral world, thereby inscribe the apparent political and economic subordination of women within their very selves. As Asad (1986: 153) suggests, it is the very coherence of such cultural concepts constructing womanhood in Hofriyat that renders them so powerful, so compulsive, so politically effective....

Zār

July 20, 1976, 4:00 p.m. The door to my hōsh *bangs open. Asia ducks beneath the lintel, lifts the water container from her head, and pours its contents into my* zīr. *Her face is seamed with sweat. "Allaaah!" she exclaims, the land is hot today! Shufti, ya Janice, I've heard they are drumming in Goz. Do you want to go?"*

Of course!—a zār *is on. But the walk in this heat is a long one, and my leg has been badly swollen for several days.*

"Sadig is borrowing camels from his cousin. You must ride."

Moments later I am teetering sidesaddle, following the equally inexpert Sadig along a trail that hems some withered fields of maize. My camel munches lazily at each low acacia, and I am soon covered in scratches from their thorns. Prodding seems only to anger the beast, and I fear a painful bite, it would have been faster to walk. Still beyond sight of Goz we are reached by the deep bass of drumming, fitful through the sultry air. The camels perk, raise their heads, start trotting toward the sound.

Goz is a newish settlement, an odd assortment of square thatched huts, thorn corrals, and a couple of half-completed mud-brick hōsh*s. The drumming comes from one of these. Ambulatory Hofriyati preceded my arrival; the* zār *has just begun. Ideally, a* zār *should take place in the room of a house, if capacious, but because of the heat, today's has been mounted in the yard.*

*A litany of greetings over, I am seated near the dancing ground, an open area (*mīdān*) bounded on three sides by palm-fiber ground mats. Here sit several dozen chanting women: the spirit possessed. Now and then one rises to her knees and begins to move her upper body in time with the sonorous beat. In the center of the* mīdān *stands the* shaykha—zār *practitioner or "priestess"—a forceful, brawny woman in an electric-pink pullover,* tōb *tied loosely at her*

*waist. She is arguing with a woman just as brash as she, who, between exple-
tives, puffs furiously on a cigarette. I learn that the* shaykha *speaks not to the
woman but to her spirit, in an effort to diagnose the source of the women's
complaint. Observing from the side is a tall, very black, incongruously muscled
figure in a* tb, *large wristwatch, and hairnet—the* shaykha's *reputedly transvestite assistant from south of Shendi. In contrast, the* ayāna—*"sick woman"
and focus of the ceremony—is frail, elderly. She rest quietly on a pillow next
the musicians, facing the front of the* hōsh, *arms and legs curled tight against
her white-tōbed bo*dy.

The shaykha *concludes her discussion, sits down, and starts to drum.
Using only the tips of her fingers, she beats a large earthen* dallūka *stretched
with goat hide, its whitened flanks boldly adorned with mauve geometric
designs. Another* dallūka *responds in shifted accents, joined half a second later
by the* nugarishan, *a tall brass mortar that rings, when struck, like a cowbell,
only deeper. A fourth woman beats a complementary rhythm on an inverted
aluminum washtub or* tisht. *The result is a complicated syncopation, its underlying pattern one long beat, three short. The sound is less soothing than
cacophonous, yet endlessly repeated and accompanied by reiterative chants,
the effect is indeed soporific. The chants, I learn, are called "threads"—*
khuyūt *(a "thread," singular, is* khayt)—*and when sung they are said to be
"pulled."*

The rhythm intensifies; the ayāna *rises to dance. Now visible over her* tōb
*is a red sash attached to a reddish waist cloth in the style of a Sam Browne belt.
She is possessed, my companions say, by* Khawāja *(Westerner) spirits: a doctor, lawyer, and military officer—all of these at once. Yet it is the lattermost she
appears to manifest in dance. Her* tōb *is folded cowl-like over her head,
obscuring her face: she flourishes a cane—hooked, as in vaudevillian bur-
lesque. Her dance is a slow rhythmic walk crisscrossing a chimeric square, feet
first moving side to side, then forward and back. With a leap of the imagination
she is an officer of the desert corps conducting drill. Every so often she bends
rigidly at the hip and, cane pressed to her forehead, bobs her torso up and
down. I am told that her spirits have requested the white* tōb, *cane, cigarettes,
"European" belt, and yet to be purchased, a radio.*

The band takes up the chant of another zār. *The* ayāna *sits; the* shaykha
leaves her drum and starts to dance, tōb *covering her head. Suddenly, the* tōb
is thrown off. She turns on her heel, goose-steps the length of the mīdān, *stops
before me, abruptly pulls herself to attention. She salutes me three or four
times, stiffly, eyes glazed and staring, a grin playing wildly on her face. Her left
hand grips a sword within its sheath; with her right she grasps my own with
unusual strength and pumps it "Western style" in time to the drums. I am shak-
en by this treatment and by thoughts of her sword. The chant sounds like a mil-*

itary march: I recognize the British Pasha spirit, Abu Rīsh, Ya Amīr ad- Daysh *("Owner of Feathers, O commander of the Army"). The drums desist. At once my hand is released. The* shaykha*'s feature assume a more dignified composure and she returns to the center of the* mīdān.

Evening falls. Women rise to dance—or "descend" (nazal), *as the* zār *step is called—throughout the night. Others respond to the spirits' chants from a kneeling position, bobbing up and down from the waist,* tōbs *covering their heads like so many Halloween ghosts. One who stands has mounted a* zār *in the past: she has "slaughtered"* (dabahat, *for* dhabahat) *for the spirits, thus confirming relations with those by which she is possessed. A woman who remains sitting or kneeling has yet to sacrifice; though acknowledged to be possessed, and perhaps even aware of the types of* zayran *that bother her, she remains somewhat uncertain of her spirits and limited to kneeling at their ceremonies until she undertakes a cure. Yet she is no less an adept for this.*

In the waning, eerie light I see a woman—spirit—performing a strange pantomime with a sword, crouching low, sweeping the flat of the weapon back and forth along the ground. She dashes through these postures with skill and grace; I am reminded of a hunter flushing game, or a soldier wary of enemies lying hidden in dense vegetation.

At the start of another chant a tall older woman dressed in red lights a cigarette. She struts down the mdn, *smoking, walking stick held perpendicular to the ground at the end of an outstretched arm, pompous, indifferent, mandarin-like. Some chants later she reappears, transmogrified. Now she and the transvestite stage a sword fight closely resembling the men's dance of a nearby desert people. The combatants leap at each other with apparent abandon, landing within inches of the audience, their sharp unsheathed blades swooping dangerously from aloft. Spectators shrink in terror at their bravado. The two are possessed, I learn by* zāyran *of the* Arab (Nomad) *species.*

Occasionally during the evening's drumming, the shaykha *dances around the* ayna, *encircling her with her arms, coaxing a seemingly reluctant spirit to enter its host and fully reveal itself before the assembly.* But the ayāna *has not risen since her foray into the* mīdān *at the start. She sits, silently watching.*

I notice at the end of each chant that several who have "descended"— standing or kneeling—begin to scratch themselves, and hiccup and burp indiscriminantly. Zaineb tells me these reactions signify the spirit's departure from the body of its host, of a woman's leaving trance....

Zār and Zayran

Smoking, wanton dancing, flailing about, burping and hiccuping, drinking blood and alcohol, wearing male clothing, publicly threatening me with swords, speaking loudly lacking due regard for etiquette, these are hardly the behaviors of Hofriyati women for whom dignity and propriety are leading concerns. But in the context of a $z\bar{a}r$ they are common and expected. The ceremony is rich in complex imagery and movement. Yet it has none of the solemn pageantry of a Mass, nor the predictable, repetitive manipulation of symbols which I, raised as a Catholic, might have found familiar. The tone of a $z\bar{a}r$ resembles neither the subdued formality of Muslim Friday prayer, nor the unorchestrated ceremoniousness of life cycle rites in Hofriyat. It is closer in character to $zikrs$ of the Qadriya and Rhatmiya $s\bar{u}f\bar{\imath}$ orders in Sudan, but lacks their cohesion and transcendent focus. What is singular about a $z\bar{a}r$ is its spontaneity, its imagination whose basis nonetheless is a comprehensive repertoire of symbols and spirit roles—a resource on which participants draw for inspiration. Moves are lightly choreographed—improvisations on well-known themes; "players are interchangeable, costumes readily borrowed and exchanged. But during the performance, neither players' bodies nor their costumes belong to village women—they belong, instead, to $zayran$. $Z\bar{a}r$ rituals are always fraught with tension and surprise, for at any moment a woman might be "seized" by a spirit that Hofriyati did not before know existed, or she did not know she had.

How is all of this to be understood? What is this phenomenon; who or what are these spirits which so dramatically appear in women's bodies?....

...$Z\bar{a}r$ refers to a type of spirit, the illness such spirits can cause by possessing humans, and the rituals necessary to their pacification....

$Maray$ is a beautiful Ethiopian noblewoman whose wantonness is patent; $Sitt\ am\text{-}mand\bar{\imath}l$ (Lady of the Handkerchief) is extremely flirtatious, as is the prostitute $z\bar{a}r\ Lul\bar{\imath}ya$. The case of $Lul\bar{\imath}ya$ is interesting, for villagers' considerable knowledge of Her character extends the covert message about Hofriyati femininity glimpsed with $Hamam\bar{a}\text{-}t\text{-}al\text{-}Bahr$. $Lul\bar{\imath}ya$ demands are for wedding incense, agate beads, a golden nose plug, silver earrings, and a silk $firka\ garmos\bar{\imath}s$, the red and gold ceremonial veil—accoutrements of a Hofriyati bride. When She descends, a red bridal mat is spread, and $Lul\bar{\imath}ya$.in the body of Her host begins to dance in the manner of a bride.

A wedding in the village is a protracted affair. Its climax comes near dawn of the third morning when, after a long night of women's pigeon dancing and bestowing the $shab\bar{a}l$, the bride is led out from seclusion, a $garmoss$ draped over her head, concealing all of her body but her legs. She is positioned on a bridal mat in the center or the courtyard, where she stands, barefoot and immobile, until her husband steps onto the mat and removes the shawl. Now unveiled, she is seen in all her finery and her family's gold, with elaborately hennaed hands covering her face in a gesture of timidity. Gently, the groom releases her arms and she begins the exacting bridal dance: eyes tightly shut, arms extended, back arched, feet moving in tiny mincing steps that barely leave the mat. Toward the end of each song she breaks off her dance and shyly recovers her face, then recommences with the groom's signal, as before, repeating the sequence until she has had enough and her kinswomen lead her away. At no time ought the bride to have seen her husband or the gathering for whom her dance was the focus of rapt attention and long anticipation.

In the *zār mīdān,* when the silken veil is removed, *Lulīya*'s host's hands cover Her face; when these are pulled away She starts to dance, though with less inhibition than the bride and with obvious pretense at shyness. *Lulīya* dramatizes explicitly the *zār*'s implicit, subtle parody of the wedding ... thus reinforcing participants' intuited conclusions in this regard or cultivating an initial awareness of the link. When *Lulīya* presents Herself in the *mīdān,* a *zār* ritual becomes a mock wedding in substance as well as in form.

But what is really happening here? On one level, a wanton, uncircumcised, nominally Christian alien presumes to dance as a chaste, circumcised, Muslim village woman. In the attempt, *Lulīya* tries bravely to suppress Her libertine disposition, but overcompensates, exaggerating the controlled steps of a bride to the point where simulated Hofriyati drama becomes a spirit farce. *Lulīya* is not by nature bashful; Her timidity must be feigned. The spirit's real personality shows through the façade She erects with the aid of her host, illuminating enacted Hofriyati behaviors, behaviors against a background of patently non-Hofriyati traits.

Yet this is not all. For what the audience actually observes is a normally restrained, circumcised Hofriyati matron in the role of a wanton, uncircumcised alien, who in turn "plays" a village maiden who is the epitome of purity and restraint. Here in observing the "other," Hofriyati see the other looking at them; while in looking at the woman entranced, they see themselves looking at the other looking at them. The multiple reflection is dramatically sustained ... then suddenly shatters as *Lulīya* peeks furtively over the hands of Her host, giving Herself away to the uproarious laughter of Her human audience.

The event is an elaborate joke, a forcing together of several normally disparate levels of reality into a few densely packed moments in which so much is stated, so much more implied. It is, in Koestler's (1975: 35-36) terms, a truly creative act, "a double minded, transitory state of unstable equilibrium where the balance of both emotion and thought is disturbed." The episode jolts the commonsense attitudes of those who witness it, calling taken-for-granted values and meanings to conscious attention, raising for consideration the issues of sexuality and fertility; motherhood, licentiousness, virginity, and the dense associative auras that surround these ideas in Hofriyat. No matter how often the joke is told, *Lulīya* always gets a laugh. But it is really Hofriyati womanhood that gets the laugh, at its embodiments' expense.

Still, participants cannot fail to note that however refined the attempt, wanton, uncircumcised aliens cannot ultimately pass for village women: invariably they give themselves away. The integrity of Hofriyati values is preserved in the very moment of their subversion, since only human villagers might genuinely and successfully embody them. Here the implication for expressing village identity through women's bodies is clear....

Another Arab notable for His belligerence is *Bernowi*, a Ta'ishi Bagara *zār* from Kordofan far south of Hofriyat and west of the Nile, who demands that His host carry a spear.[11] *Bernowi* is spirit analogue of the "highest in command in the Khalifa's army." Human Baggara were the principal supporters of Khalifa Abadallahi, the Mahdi's successor after his death in 1885; under him these Arabic speaking cattle herders dominated Sudan. Villagers call "Baggara" the members of an expedition sent by the Khalifa in 1889 officially against Egypt but effectively against the disaffected riverain jaaliyn. And Hofriyati hold the Baggara responsible for the tremendous privations suffered by the village in these troubled times (chapter 1). Thus, when the Baggara warrior *zār* descends, Hofriyati see far more than a woman manifesting traditionally masculine behaviors, or a villager exhibiting the salient traits of an alien ethnic group. What they see is the *zār* counterpart of their historical enemy, who appears, ambivalently summoned, in their midst. The woman "invaded" by *Bernowi* displays physical traits of Hofriyati identity and behavioral traits of Hofriyati's most dreaded adversary at one end and the same time, expressing in the contrast a consciousness of village history, and since *Bernowi* is amenable to negotiation, of how conflict can and should be overcome. The distinction between two sides in a lengthy and uneven quarrel is drawn, only to be temporarily mediated in the ambiguity of possession trance....

Sulayman [Ya Janna] is an adult unwed male homosexual whose name is a complex pun: *Janna* means "one who is veiled or concealed," hence womanlike, and calls up the following supernumerary meanings: one who is possessed (*jinna*), paradise (*al-janna*), harvest or fruit (*janā*)—in colloquial parlance, offspring. The pun and its context evoke the opposed ideas of, on the one hand, femininity, containment, and reproduction, and on the other, male sexual pleasure as will be enjoyed in the afterlife. All of this underscores the essence of *Sulayman's* character in the eyes of Hofriyati women: His misplaced fertility and problematic sexuality.

Sulayman requires His host to chew tobacco, drink *marīsa*—a thick native beer—and wear a man's *jalabīya*, apropos of both Arab and Hofriyati men. But in the *mīdān Sulayman* behaves like a local woman. He fusses constantly with His *jalabīya*, trying with limited success to wear it like a woman's *tōb*, the length of cloth she wraps around her body and pins tenuously in place by holding her left arm close against her chest. *Sulayman* struts simpering around the *mīdān*, impatiently tucking up whatever loose material He can gather from His *jalabīya-tōb* and stuffing it under His host's left arm, all the while holding the hem of His garment lest it drag. The spectacle is ludicrous: here a habitual gesture performed by women dozens of times each day—for *tōbs* are notoriously recalcitrant—is performed by a local woman in masculine clothing, who is, in reality, a male playing the role of a woman.

The structure of this episode reveals the paradox of *Sulayman* and other complex spirit manifestation; here William James's "law of dissociation" is instructive. According to James, if two parts of an object, *a* and *b* regularly occur together, the placement of one of these, *a,* in a novel combination *ax* leads to the discrimination of *a, b, and x* from one another. "What is associated now with one thing and now with another, tends to become disassociated from either and to grow into an object of abstract contemplation by the mind" (James 1918: 506). In the case at hand, when feminine gestures normally associated with feminine dress are portrayed in relation to masculine dress, all three traits are wrenched from their ordinary contexts, thus heightening awareness of the qualities to which they refer. The discipline implicit in the *tōb*: the requirement that a girl begin to wear it when she reaches marriageable age, the fact that it is a portable enclosure which women take care to arrange for maximum coverage before exiting the *hōsh*, now appears in an uncanny light, less as a taken-for granted certainty of the quotidian world. Gender distinctions hegemonically entrenched in villagers' reality are at once emphasized and shown to be problematic, for if femininity is contrasted with masculinity, the foil is sabotaged by the spirts's ambivalent sexuality. The effect is palimpsest of sexual meanings, a double dissociation. It is more than a comic discourse on the ambiguities of gender and sexuality, for in raising these as issues in themselves, it points to the somewhat subversive observation (in Hofriyat) that gender is not a determinable attribute but a cultural construct whose parameters can be modified. Yet at the same time, it demonstrates the necessity of heterosexuality to spirit—human—reproduction, for *sulayman* (an *Arab* who ought to epitomize masculinity, but does not) is childless. A division between female and male is shown to be imperative, while the essence of their contrast, mutable....

There are two female prostitute *zayran* among the Blacks: *Jata*, Lady of the *Rahat*—the thong skirt worn in the past by girls—and *Mūna,* Lady of the *shabāl*—referring to the flick of the hair gesture performed by dancing women at weddings that confers luck on the men who request it. Much like *lulīiya,* the Ethiopian prostitute who tries to pass Herself off as a local bride, when *Jata* and *Mūna* arrive in the *mīdān* They behave like young Hofriyati women. They are, of course, anything but. They are pagan, uncircumcised, and "black," flirtatious and concupiscent, strangers to the moral code that rightly guides village maidens. Once more the effect of their presence in the bodies of their hosts is that of a triple exposure—a palimpsest of signification—here layered with the images of Hofriyati maidenhood, foreign prostitution, Hofriyati matronhood, and complicated by the human/spirit dialectic. The *rahat* was a garment associated with nubile girls and abandoned at marriage: the groom is said to *guta a ar-rahat*, break or cut the *rahat* (now wedding veil) of his bride to indicate her loss of virginity, though intercourse has not yet occurred.[12] The *shahal,* while performed by women of any age, is most appropriately enacted by the "pigeons going to market": unwed women who display themselves to prospective suitors at others' marriage dances. Once against the Hofriyati wedding is educed in the *zār mīdān.*

And again multiple dimensions of contrast expose a number of directions for thought to take. At the most obvious levels, messages could be derived from the antithesis of human host—a married Hofriyati—and spirit—a southern prostitute, the first a circumcised woman who uses her sexuality for the benefit of society in bearing legitimate children, the second an uncircumcised alien existent, a non-Hofriyati pagan who uses Her sexuality inappropriately and immorally, for personal gain. Elements of the one mingle with aspects of the other in the body of the woman entranced, effecting a potential exchange of significance such that concepts like morality, profit, prostitution can be seen in radically altered light. Or one might wish to pursue the relationship between human host and spirit impersonation: between married, sexually active village woman and unmarried, "sexually inactive" village girl. But the comparison cannot be sustained, for things are not what they seem. And this refraction brings the deepest contrast to the fore: between the spirit and Her role; of immoral uncircumcised, concupiscent alien, member of a formerly enslaved ethnic group—whose human analogues now operate in local brothels, pocketing villagers' hard-earned cash—with moral, circumcised, appropriately socialized, yet still virginal village girls. While the spirit is openess demonified, the role She attempts to play is closure or interiority personified. The opposition is mediated by the human host who, in a concrete way, is both of these at once and, no less concretely, is neither. The episode's imaginative convolution forces to consciousness ideas central to Hofriyati identity alongside obverse qualities in an elaborate, three-dimensional puzzle—who is what and to what degree?—that evaporates from the *mīdān* as quickly as it was constituted, when the drumming stops.

Shar: Cannibal Sorcerers

All sorcerer *zayran* are Azande, whose homeland is beyond that of the *Abīd*, in Sudanese Equatoria and northeastern Zaire. They include *Baya-kuba as-Sāhar Juba: Bayakukba* the Sorcerer of Juba (a town in the extreme south), who loves dates; *Nyam Nyam Kubaida, Nyam Nyam* (Zande) the Severe Afflicter, who demands to eat raw liver (*kibda*);[13] and *at-Tumsāh,* The Crocodile, a Zande sorcerer in His animal form.

Crocodiles occasionally travel downstream, from the south, with the annual inundation, and their advent near villagers' farmlands is greatly feared. Every villager has a story about *tumsāh* which terrified some farmer or snatched and devoured a hapless child who strayed too near the river. Its fondness for human flesh makes the crocodile an apt vehicle for Zande sorcerers: all *Sāhar zayran,* like their human counterparts, are reputed to be cannibals. When a sorcerer spirit assumes control of His host during a rite, she suddenly leaps up and starts biting at fellow adepts who scatter in alarm. As a substitute for human flesh, *Sāhar* spirits reluctantly settle for raw meat, of which the possessed might consume half a kilo at a sitting.

Sāhar zayran also demand that their hosts go naked: one seized by a sorcerer attempts to fling off all her clothes, though ultimately she is prevented from doing so by fellow adepts out of trance. *At-Tumsāh,* however, requires that His host don rags and that in addition to nipping at members of the audience, she crawl on her belly as His thread is being drummed. The descent of these spirits is dreaded by those who attend a spirit rite: while *Sāhar* possess few Hofriyati and may not appear in the *mīdāns* for years at a stretch (like crocodiles in the river), there is always a chance that one will manifest Himself unexpectedly, in a participant who had not till then suspected her affliction.

Sāhar represent the darkest side of spirit—indeed human—existence, the power of malevolence and antisocial conduct. In the local idiom of incorporation, they symbolize the violation of others' material and personal integrity: life as villagers most wish it not to be, but as in many ways it really is, its underside a mass of petty jealousies, rivalries, betrayals. Women drum the sorcerers' threads with trepidation. And yet there is a fascination here in tempting fate, in confronting what is most parlous and alarming, most horrific, most alien and antithetical to themselves. Or perhaps it is a need, for the values and ideals of daily life are implicitly revitalized in the apical contrast of village women and *Sāhar zayran.* Participants and possessed emerge from their encounter wiser, perhaps, but usually unscathed....

In its supportive and subversive modes the *zār* reflects women's double consciousness: their commitment to mainstream values and their awareness, however implicit, of their oppression. Possession's power is analogous to that of a satirical allegory in the West, where two lines of thought are joined within a single text and it is entirely up to the reader first to distinguish, then to decide, or not decide, between them. The comparison with allegory is a useful one....

Zār, when viewed as an aesthetic genre, seems designed to open thought, to free it from limitations of prior associations, to pose challenging problems, and encourage reflection on the everyday. Symbolic inversion (cf. Babcock 1978) or negative metaphor (cf. Crapanzano 1977a) is its essence: during possession rites women become men; villagers become Ethiopian, British, Chinese; the powerless and impoverished become powerful and affluent. Essentially irreversible processes—genderization, aging—become reversible; established categories are undermined. Hierarchical orderings are telescoped and undone when Islamic holy men and pagan prostitutes possess the same Hofriyati woman. The external world is internalized, appearing in villagers' homes and through their bodies. The paradox of possession, the merging or juxtapositioning of opposing qualities and mutually exclusive entities, plays with human understanding, directs villagers' attention to the relativity of their categories and the limits of "common sense," is obliquely critical of all that is absolute (cf. Babcock 1978: 16-17; Colie 1966: 7-10; Douglas 1966).

The possession paradox is an immanent signification, it is saturated with potential meaning. Those led to the $z\bar{a}r$ by untoward experience, a challenge to the taken-for-grantedness of daily life are, in its paradox, asked to face that challenge, to explore the taken-for-granted and its alternatives, to examine the dimensions of selfhood from every perceptible angle. Possession provokes those it claims to think about themselves via their inverse spirit counterparts. For paradox, Babcock (1978: 17) notes, "is at once self-critical and creative, 'at once its own subject and its own object, turning endlessly in upon itself,' one inversion leading to the making of another, into the infinite regress of self regard."

Notes

1. Circumcisions are performed on both sexes during school holidays in May and June. In 1984 I saw none because I left the village at the end of April.
2. Portions of the following were previously published in *American Ethnologist* 9 (4): 682-98 and 15 (1): 4-27 (Boddy 1982b, 1988).
3. *Mushāhara* is discussed in chapter 3 [of Boddy's book—Editor].
4. This is also basic to the practice of smoke bathing (later discussed) and was used in rope delivery, an outmoded method of delivery where a woman in labor would support herself by grasping onto ropes suspended from the main ceiling beam of a room. The shallow pit was intended to receive blood and other fluids.
5. The operation post-1969 is referred to as *tahūr wasit*, "intermediate circumcision." In Hofriyati as elsewhere in Sudan, it is often (mistakenly) referred to as *"sunna"* circumcision, discussed in note 6. See also Gruenbaum (1982: 7) and Cloudsley (1983: 109).
6. This is a matter of some debate, though as El Dareer (1982: 71) remarks, to say that circumcision is *"sunna"* makes it unquestionable for Muslims, for whom Islam is not merely a set of religious beliefs, but a way of life. The Hadith stipu-

late that whereas circumcision is required for males *khafd* (reduction) is an embellishment for females. Yet few if any women in Saudi Arabia are circumcised, and even the minor operation has been outlawed in Egypt since 1967 (Cloudsley 1983: 110). Hofriyati are aware that not all Muslim women are circumcised or, more radically, infibulated; they do believe, however, that Bedouin girls in Saudi Arabia undergo a *"sunna"* operation in infancy. In Sudan, *"sunna"* circumcision is often confused with what I have described as the *wasit* or intermediate operation (note 5).

7. However, they wear shirts which leave the genital area exposed, and diapers are not worn.

8. I was told that if a man "only wants children" he should marry a southern Sudanese, for they are prodigiously fertile. If, on the other hand, he wants children who will respect him, support him in his old age, bring honor to the family, behave with grace and tact, exercise good judgment—in short, who are moral beings—his wife must be Hofriyati, a kinswoman, and needless to say, circumcised.

9. On this point, see also Kennedy (1978c: 167).

10. I should point out that the term *khashm* was used only in reference to the men's door, not the women's which was designated merely as wara, "back." They were thus lexically identically differentiated.

11. In Constantinides' (1972: 342) list of spirits, "Barnawi" is a spear-carrying West African Muslim zār from Bornu. If this spirit originated with the urban cult, His ethnic identification appears to have altered in the context of local historical reality. The pattern is not uncommon: spirits' names are borrowed and often encompass more than one zār in the same or another spirit society.

12. The *rahat* is similar in this respect to the beaded girdle of Gisu women (Uganda). La Fontaine (1985a: 138) writes, "to break a woman's beads was considered rape, even if intercourse did not take place."

13. *Kubaida* and *kibda* are derived from the same root.

References

Abdalla, Raqiya Haji Dualeh. *Sisters in Affliction: Circumcision and Infibulation of Women in Africa*. London: Zed Press, 1982.

Ammar, Hamed. *Growing Up in an Egyptian Village*. London: Routledge and Kegan Paul, 1954.

Asad, Talal. "The concept of cultural translation in British social anthropology." In *Writing Culture: The Poetics and Politics of Ethnography*, edited by James Clifford and George E. Marcus, pp. 141-64. Berkeley, CA: University of California Press, 1986.

Assad, Marie Bassili. "Female circumcision in Egypt: Social implications, current research, and prospects for change." *Studies in Family Planning*. 1989, 11 (1): 3-16.

Babcock, Barbara. "Introduction." In *The Reversible World: Symbolic Inversion in Art and Society*, edited by Barbara Babcock, pp. 13-36. Ithaca, NY: Cornell University Press, 1978.

Barclay, Harold. *Buurri al-Lamaab: A Suburban Village in Sudan*. Ithaca, NY: Cornell University Press, 1964.

Berger, Peter, and Thomas Luckmann. *The Social Construction of Reality*. Garden City, NY: Doubleday, 1966.

Boddy, Janice. *Parallel Worlds: Humans, Spirits, and Zār Possession in Rural Northern Sudan*. Ph.D. dissertation, University of British Columbia, 1982a.

—. "Womb as oasis: The symbolic context of pharaonic circumcision in rural northern Sudan." *American Ethnologist*, 1982b, 9 (4),: 682-98.

Bourdieu, Pierre. *Outline of a Theory of Practice*. London: Cambridge University Press, 1977.

Burridge, Kenelm. *Someone, No One: An Essay on Individuality*. Princeton, NJ: Princeton University Press, 1979.

Chodorow, Nancy. "Family structure and feminine personality." In *Woman, Culture and Society*, edited by Michelle Z. Rosaldo and Louise Lamphere, pp. 43-99. Stanford, CA: Stanford University Press, 1974.

—. *The Reproduction of Mothering*. Berkeley, CA: University of California Press, 1978.

Cloudsley, Ann. *Women of Omdurman: Life, Love, and the Cult of Virginity*. London: Ethnographica, 1983.

Comaroff, Jean. *Body of Power, Spirit of Resistance: The Culture and History of a South African People*. Chicago: University of Chicago Press, 1985.

Constantinides, Pamela. "Sickness and the Spirits: A Study of the "Zaar" Spirit Possession Cult in the Northern Sudan." Ph.D. dissertation, University of London, 1972.

Crapanzano, Vincent. "Introduction" to *Case Studies of Spirit Possession*, edited by Vincent Crapanzano and Vivian Garrison, pp. 1-39. New York: John Wiley, 1977.

El Dareer, Asma. *Woman, Why Do You Weep? Circumcision and Its Consequences*. London: Zed Press, 1982.

El-Tayib, D. Griselda. "Women's dress in the northern Sudan." In *The Sudanese Woman*, edited by Susan Kenyon, pp. 40-66. Khartoum: Graduate College Publications, no. 19, University of Khartoum, 1987.

Fernandez, James. "The mission of metaphor in expressive culture." *Current Anthropology* 15: 119-46, 1974.

Geertz, Clifford. *The Interpretation of Cultures*. New York: Basic Books, 1973.

Ghalioungui, Paul. *Magic and Medicinal Science in Ancient Egypt*. London: Hodder and Stoughton, 1963.

Gilligan, Caron. *In a Different Voice: Psychological Theory and Women's Development*. Cambridge, MA: Harvard University Press, 1982.

Gluckman, Max. *Custom and Conflict in Africa*. Glencoe, IL: Free Press, 1965.

Gruenbaum, Ellen. "The movement against clitoridectomy and infibulation in the

Sudan: Public policy and the women's movement." *Medical Anthropology Newsletter*, 13 (2): 4-12, 1982.

Hamnett, Ian. "Ambiguity, classification, and change: The function of riddles." *Man*. N.s. 2: 379-92, 1967.

Huelsman, Ben. R. "An anthropological view of clitoral and other female genital mutilations." In *The Clitoris*, edited by T.P. Lowery and T.S. Lowery, pp. 111-61. St Louis: Warren H. Green, 1976.

James, William. *Principles of Psychology*. Vol I, 1890. Reprint. New York: Henry Holt, 1918.

Kennedy, John G. "Circumcision and excision ceremonies." In *Nubian Ceremonial Life*, edited by John Kennedy, pp. 151-70. Berkeley: University of California Press, 1978.

Koestler, Arthur. *The Act of Creation*. London: Pan, 1964/1975.

La Fontaine, J.S. *Initiation: Ritual Drama and Secret Knowledge around the World*. London: Penguin, 1985.

Langer, Suzanne. *Philosophy in a New Key: A Study in the Symbolism of Reason, Rite, and Art*. New York: Mentor, 1942.

Lewis, Joan. *Ecstatic Religion: An Anthropological Study of Spirit Possession and Shamanism*. Baltimore, MD: Penguin, 1971.

Peckham, Morse. *Man's Rage for Chaos*. New York: Schocken, 1967.

Rosaldo, Michelle A. "Woman, culture, and society: A theoretical overview." In *Woman, Culture, and Society*, edited by M. Rosaldo and L. Lamphere, pp. 17-42. Stanford, CA: Stanford University Press, 1974.

Sutton-Smith, Brian. "Games of order and disorder." Paper presented at the Forms of Symbolic Inversion Symposium, American Anthropological Association, Toronto, 1972.

Todorov, Tzvetan. *Mikhail Bakhtin: The Dialogical Principle*. Minneapolis, MN: University of Minnesota Press, 1984.

Turner, Victor. *From Ritual to Theatre: The Human Seriousness of Play*. New York: Performing Arts Journal Publications, 1982.

Wehr, Hans. *A Dictionary of Modern Written Arabic*. 3rd ed. Edited by J. Milton Cowan. Ithaca, NY: Spoken Language Services, 1976.

CHAPTER EIGHT

GLOBAL VIEWS

INTRODUCTION

It has become commonplace to speak of globalization; everyone now recognizes Marx's insights into the formation of world markets and world cultures. Our last set of readings represent efforts to understand these processes 150 years after Marx and Engels emphasized them in the *Communist Manifesto.*

Several questions shape these theorists' work:

1. What are the linkages between economic processes (global markets) and cultural processes?
2. What are the characteristics of global culture—does it exist at all? Is it postmodern?
3. What is actually "flowing around" during globalization—people, media, capital, artifacts, technology, ideas, and so on? How are these different flows connected? What is the direction of the flows? What is the impact of each type of flow? Are there coherent overall patterns or even a system in these global flows?
4. How are individual and collective identities changing as a result of globalization?
5. What is happening to local cultures as a result of globalization?

The selections begin with a piece by Immanuel Wallerstein that defines the world system. Fredric Jameson grapples with a new, globalized form of culture, postmodern culture. Stuart Hall discusses diaspora (the scattering of peoples) and identity. Arjun Appadurai identifies major types of flows and points to disjunctures between them.

Readings

Harris, Nigel. *The New Untouchables: Immigration and the New World Worker*. London: I.B. Tauris, 1995.

Kwame, Anthony Appiah, and Henry Louis Gates. *Identities*. Chicago: University of Chicago Press, 1995.

Massey, Douglas. *Worlds in Motion: Understanding International Migration at the End of the Millenium*. New York: Oxford University Press, 1998.

Spivak, Gayatri Chakravorty. *A Critique of Postcolonial Reason*. Cambridge, MA: Harvard University Press, 1999.

39

IMMANUEL WALLERSTEIN (1920-)

Marx's enormous unified vision was refracted by later theorists into the analysis of distinct issues: class formation and class struggle; characteristics of capitalist development; technology and the labour process; culture and consciousness. One of the most important themes in Marx's thought was globalization. This was taken up by Lenin at the beginning of the twentieth century, when he analyzed the uneven structure of capitalism as a global system with advanced and backward regions. World systems theory, pioneered by Immanuel Wallerstein, elaborates this perspective and provides a framework for understanding globalization as a central feature of our time. World systems theory was also influenced by a school of French historiography (the Annales school, associated with Ferdinand Braudel) that examined long-term trends in global markets and ways of life linked to the material goods that circulated in these markets.

World systems theory can be summarized as follows.

1. The key unit of analysis for social scientists is the global system as a whole. The perspective of the social sciences should be macro and long-term.
2. The system's subparts are heterogeneous. There are three distinct types of subsystems: states; societies and cultures; and the interlinked markets that form capitalism. These subsystems cut across each other, and the system as a whole derives its dynamism from the disjunctures between states, societies, and markets. The system as a whole is strong and viable precisely because its parts are *not* linked to each other in simple, direct ways.
3. The fundamental or most important element of the system as a whole is the capitalist economy of global markets—a premise that connects Wallerstein to the Marxist theoretical tradition.
4. The system is inherently unevenly developed. It includes three types of regions: an advanced core in which the strongest states, markets, and capitalist firms are located; a semi-periphery; and a periphery that is weak, exploited, and dependent in terms of both states and markets. The core is located in the developed capitalist nations in western Europe, North America, and Japan. The semi-periphery has historically been in eastern Europe and the southern cone of Latin America; perhaps in the last couple of decades one might include the newly industrializing nations of east Asia. The periphery—largely in the global South—pro-

duces raw materials and supplies cheap labour; its states formed recently, after a long period of colonialism, and are relatively weak.

5. Uneven development is not a problem of or for the system; on the contrary, it is an essential, abiding, and sustaining feature of it. This premise has to be understood in a functionalist sense, not as a conspiracy theory about the core and its bourgeoisie. Capital accumulation is made possible by the differences among the regions.

6. The uneven development of the system is reflected in inequalities in conditions of life, with the periphery containing the poorest populations.

7. There are inequalities both within nations and among nations. Both of these forms of inequality are class inequality in the sense that they are the products of global capitalist development. These objectively existing inequalities give rise to various forms of subjective understandings and class struggle. Given the inequalities between the core, semi-periphery, and periphery—inequalities experienced as inequalities among nations—class struggle is sometimes expressed in nationalist or cultural terms. The exploited classes in the periphery believe their struggle must be against the nations of the core, and thereby sometimes fail to see the exploitive character of the dominant classes in their own nation. It is the task of the social scientist to understand the multiple forms of class struggle, including those that are framed in nationalist terms or in terms of cultural and religious revivals.

8. The analysis requires a long, historical time frame, measured in centuries. The world system began to form around 1500 with European voyages of conquest to the western hemisphere, Africa, and southern Asia.

In the following selection from the first volume of his multi-volume history of the world system, Wallerstein points to the emergence of the world system, its uneven structure, and forms of rebellion that appeared in the early centuries of its history.

Readings

Abu-Lughod, Janet. *Before European Hegemony: The World System A.D. 1250-1350.* New York: Oxford University Press, 1991.

Braudel, Fernand. *Civilization and Capitalism.* Berkeley and Los Angeles: University of California Press, 1992.

Wallerstein, Immanuel. *The End of the World as We Know It: Social Science for the Twenty-First Century.* Minneapolis: University of Minnesota Press, 1999.

The Modern World-System
IMMANUEL WALLERSTEIN

In order to describe the origins and initial workings of a world system, I have had to argue a certain conception of a world-system. A world-system is a social system, one that has boundaries, structures, member groups, rules of legitimation, and coherence. Its life is made up of the conflicting forces which hold it together by tension, and tear it apart as each group seeks eternally to remold it to its advantage. It has the characteristics of an organism, in that it has a life-span over which its characteristics change in some respects and remain stable in others. One can define its structures as being at different times strong or weak in terms of the internal logic of its functioning.

What characterizes a social system in my view is the fact that life within it is largely self-contained, and that the dynamics of its development are largely internal. The reader may feel that the use of the term "largely" is a case of academic weaseling. I admit I cannot quantify it. Probably no one ever will be able to do so, as the definition is based on a counterfactual hypothesis: If the system, for any reason, were to be cut off from all external forces (which virtually never happens), the definition implies that the system would continue to function substantially in the same manner. Again, of course, substantially is difficult to convert into hard operational criteria. Nonetheless the point is an important one, and key to many parts of the empirical analyses of this book. Perhaps we should think of self-containment as a theoretical absolute, a sort of social vacuum, rarely visible and even more implausible to create artificially, but still and all a socially-real asymptote, the distance from which is somehow measurable.

Using such a criterion, it is contended here that most entities usually described as social systems—"tribes," communities, nation-states—are not in fact total systems. Indeed, on the contrary, we are arguing that the only real social systems are, on the one hand, those relatively small, highly autonomous subsistence economies not part of some regular tribute-demanding system and, on the other hand, world-systems. These latter are to be sure distinguished from the former because they are relatively large; that is, they are in common parlance "worlds." More precisely, however, they are defined by the fact that their self-containment as an economic-material entity is based on extensive division of labor and that they contain within them a multiplicity of cultures.

It is further argued that thus far there have only existed two varieties of such world-systems: world-empires, in which there is a single political system over most of the area, however attenuated the degree of its effective control; and those systems in which such a single political system does not exist over all or virtually all, of the space. For convenience and for want of a better term, we are using the term "world-economy," to describe the latter.

Finally, we have argued that prior to the modern era, world-economies were highly unstable structures which tended either to be converted into empires or to disintegrate. It is the peculiarity of the modern world-system that a world-economy has survived for 500 years and yet has not come to be transformed into a world-empire—a peculiarity that is the secret of its strength.

This peculiarity is the political side of the form of economic organization called capitalism. Capitalism has been able to flourish precisely because the world-economy has had within its bounds not one but a multiplicity of political systems.

I am not here arguing the classic case of capitalist ideology that capitalism is a system based on the noninterference of the state in economic affairs. Quite the contrary! Capitalism is based on the constant absorption of economic loss by political entities, while economic gain is distributed to "private" hands. What I am arguing rather is that capitalism as an economic mode is based on the fact that the economic factors operate within an arena larger than that which any political entity can totally control. This gives capitalists a freedom of maneuver that is structurally based. It has made possible the constant economic expansion of the world-system, albeit a very skewed distribution of its rewards. The only alternative world-system that could maintain a high level of productivity and change the system of distribution would involve the reintegration of the levels of political and economic decision-making. This would constitute a third possible form of world-system, a socialist world government. This is not a form that presently exists, and it was not even remotely conceivable in the sixteenth century.

The historical reasons why the European world-economy came into existence in the sixteenth century and resisted attempts to transform it into an empire have been expounded at length. We shall not review them here. It should however be noted that the size of a world-economy is a function of the state of technology, and in particular of the possibilities of transport and communication within its bounds. Since this is a constantly changing phenomenon, not always for the better, the boundaries of a world-economy are ever fluid.

We have defined a world-system as one in which there is extensive division of labor. This division is not merely functional—that is, occupational—but geographical. That is to say, the range of economic tasks is not evenly distributed throughout the world-system. In part this is the consequence of ecological considerations, to be sure. But for the most part, it is a function of the social organization of work, one which magnifies and legitimizes the ability of some groups within the system to exploit the labor of others, that is, to receive a larger share of the surplus.

While, in an empire, the political structure tends to link culture with occupation, in a world-economy the political structure tends to link culture with spatial location. The reason is that in a world-economy the first point of political pressure available to groups is the local (national) state structure. Cultural homogenization tends to serve the interests of key groups and the pressures build up to create cultural-national identities.

This is particularly the case in the advantaged areas of the world-economy —what we have called the core-states. In such states, the creation of a strong state machinery coupled with a national culture, a phenomenon often referred to as integration, serves both as a mechanism to protect disparities that have arisen within the world-system, and as an ideological mask and justification for the maintenance of these disparities.

World-economies then are divided into core states and peripheral areas. I do not say peripheral *states* because one characteristic of a peripheral area is that the indigenous state is weak, ranging from its nonexistence (that is, a colonial situation) to one with a low degree of autonomy (that is, a neo-colonial situation).

There are also semiperipheral areas which are in between the core and the periphery on a series of dimensions, such as the complexity of economic activities, strength of the state machinery, cultural integrity, etc. Some of these areas had been core-areas of earlier versions of a given world-economy. Some had been peripheral areas that were later promoted, so to speak, as a result of the changing geopolitics of an expanding world-economy.

The semiperiphery, however, is not an artifice of statistical cutting points, nor is it a residual category. The semiperiphery is a necessary structural element in a world-economy. These areas play a role parallel to that played, *mutatis mutandis,* by middle trading groups in an empire. They are collection points of vital skills that are often politically unpopular. These middle areas (like middle groups in an empire) partially deflect the political pressures which groups primarily located in peripheral areas might otherwise direct against core-states and the groups which operate within and through their state machineries. On the other hand, the interests primarily located in the semiperiphery are located outside the political arena of the core-states, and find it difficult to pursue the ends in political coalitions that might be open to them were they in the same political arena.

The division of a world-economy involves a hierarchy of occupational tasks, in which tasks requiring higher levels of skill and greater capitalization are reserved for higher-ranking areas. Since a capitalist world-economy essentially rewards accumulated capital, including human capital, at a higher rate than "raw" labor power, the geographical maldistribution of these occupational skills involves a strong trend toward self-maintenance. The forces of the marketplace reinforce them rather than undermine them. And the absence of a central political mechanism for the world-economy makes it very difficult to intrude counteracting forces to the maldistribution of rewards.

Hence, the ongoing process of a world-economy tends to expand the economic and social gaps among its varying areas in the very process of its development. One factor that tends to mask this fact is that the process of development of a world-economy brings about technological advances which make it possible to expand the boundaries of a world-economy. In this case, particular regions of the world may change their structural role in the world-economy, to their advantage, even though the disparity of reward between different sectors of the world-economy as a whole may be simultaneously widening. It is in order to observe this crucial phenomenon clearly that we have insisted on the distinction between a peripheral area of a given world-economy and the external arena of the world-economy. The external arena of one century often becomes the periphery of the next—or its semiperiphery. But then too core-states can become semiperipheral and semiperipheral ones peripheral.

While the advantages of the core-states have not ceased to expand throughout the history of the modern world-system, the ability of a particular state to remain in the core sector is not beyond challenge. The hounds are ever to the hares for the position of top dog. Indeed, it may well be that in this kind of system it is not structurally possible to avoid, over a long period of historical time, a circulation of the elites in the sense that the particular country that is dominant at a given time tends to be replaced in this role sooner or later by another country.

We have insisted that the modern world-economy is, and only can be, a capitalist world-economy. It is for this reason that we have rejected the appellation of "feudalism" for the various forms of capitalist agriculture based on coerced labor which grow up in a world-economy....

If world-systems are the only real social systems (other than truly isolated subsistence economies), then it must follow that the emergence, consolidation, and political roles of classes and status groups must be appreciated as elements of this *world*-system. And in turn it follows that one of the key elements in analyzing a class or a status-group is not only the state of its self-consciousness but the geographical scope of its self-definition.

Classes always exist potentially (*an sich*). The issue is under what conditions they become class-conscious (*für sich*), that is, operate as a group in the politico-economic arenas and even to some extent as a cultural entity. Such self-consciousness is a function of conflict situations. But for upper strata open conflict, and hence overt consciousness, is always *faute de mieux*. To the extent that class boundaries are not made explicit, to that extent it is more likely that privileges be maintained.

Since in conflict situations, multiple factions tend to reduce to two by virtue of the forging of alliances, it is by definition not possible to have three or more (conscious) classes. There obviously can be a multitude of occupational interest groups which may organize themselves to operate within the social structure. But such groups are really one variety of status-groups, and indeed often overlap heavily with other kinds of status-groups such as those defined by ethnic, linguistic, or religious criteria.

To say that there cannot be three or more classes is not however to say that there are always two. There may be none, though this is rare and transitional. There may be one, and this is most common. There may be two, and this is most explosive.

We say there may be only one class, although we have also said that classes only actually exist in conflict situations, and conflicts presume two sides. There is no contradiction here. For a conflict may be defined as being between one class which conceives of itself as the universal class, and all the other strata. This has in fact been the usual situation in the modern world-system. The capitalist class (the *bourgeoisie*) has claimed to be the universal class and sought to organize political life to pursue its objectives against two opponents. On the one hand, there were those who spoke for the maintenance of traditional rank distinctions despite the fact that these ranks might have lost their original correlation with economic function. Such elements preferred to define the social structure as a non-class structure. It was to counter this ideology that the bourgeoisie came to operate as a class conscious of itself. But the bourgeoisie had another opponent, the workers....

In the sixteenth century, Europe was like a bucking bronco. The attempt of some groups to establish a world-economy based on a particular division of labor, to create national states in the core areas as politico-economic guarantors of this system, and to get the workers to pay not only the profits but the costs of maintaining the system was not easy. It was to Europe's credit that it was done, since without the thrust of the sixteenth century the modern world would not have been born and, for all its cruelties, it is better that it was born than that it had not been.

It is also Europe's credit that it was not easy, and particularly that it was not easy because the people who paid the short-run costs screamed lustily at the unfairness of it all. The peasants and workers in Poland and England and Brazil and Mexico were all rambunctious in their various ways. As R.H. Tawney says of the agrarian disturbances of sixteenth-century England: "Such movements are a proof of blood and sinew and of high and gallant spirit.... Happy the nation whose people has not forgotten how to rebel."[1]

The mark of the modern world is the imagination of its profiteers and the counter-assertiveness of the oppressed. Exploitation and the refusal to accept exploitation as either inevitable or just constitute the continuing antinomy of the modern era, joined together in a dialectic which has far from reached its climax in the twentieth century.

Notes
1. R.H. Tawney, *The Agrarian Problem in the 16th Century* (New York: Harper & Row), p. 340.

40

FREDRIC JAMESON (1934-)

Fredric Jameson, a professor at Duke University, offers a Marxist-influenced analysis of postmodern culture. While retaining core premises of Marxist theory, he transforms many of its concepts and analytic tools to handle new realities.

Postmodernism is the form of culture associated with late capitalism. Jameson believes that distinct phases of the mode of production have distinct "cultural dominants"—forms of culture. The cultural dominant is not the same as the dominant culture, the culture of economically and politically dominant classes; Jameson gives relatively little attention to classes as coherent purposive social actors. Rather, the cultural dominant is a pattern of representation that appears across different media and art forms. It is an indirect reflection of the underlying mode of production and social conditions, not the product of a class-conscious dominant class. Capitalism itself has distinct phases; currently we are in a phase of extended commodity production ("the consumer society"), "high tech" or electronic technology, multinationalism (or globalization), and media penetration of our unconscious as well as our consciousness. This phase of capitalism shapes postmodern culture.

Since the publication of this essay in 1984, most of these trends have accelerated, with further growth of a politics based on images; the Web, the Net, and the expansion of cyberspace; and postmodern styles in art and architecture.

To help the reader through this erudite and dense essay, I will identify the main points in Jameson's characterization of the postmodern, especially as it contrasts with high modernism, the cultural dominant of the first part of the twentieth century.

1. Jameson begins with aesthetic populism, the blurring or even complete collapse of the boundary between "high culture" ("the arts") and "popular culture."

2. Messages are flattened, with surface intensities emphasized at the expense of "deep meaning." Jameson uses the telling example of the contrast between Vincent Van Gogh's late nineteenth-century modernist painting of peasant shoes and Andy Warhol's *Diamond Dust Shoes*. The former depicts a pair of worn, broken work boots, refers to a life of toil, and implicitly calls for change in the social order; the latter delights in a brilliant, hyperreal representation of party pumps that demands nothing from the viewer except pleasure in viewing the object. In postmod-

ern culture there is only the text (words or images) and no reference to, let alone outrage about, a reality outside the text. This textuality of post-modernism is heightened by cyberspace and virtual reality; attractive Websites do not mean that there is anything, let alone anything attractive, really there.

3. A waning of affect takes place; the search for true feelings disappears. Just as the search for a more just social order is jettisoned, so also is the quest for a truer, unalienated inner self. The belief in the inner self had been expressed in paintings like Edvard Munch's *The Scream* (the expressionistic painting of a distorted man standing on a pier, screaming) and in the Freudian project of recovering repressed, unconscious desires. Postmodernism ends the faith that these true selves exist at all, a theme we already encountered in Foucault.

4. The collective and individual past is lost and replaced by nostalgia, pastiches of cannibalized, de-contextualized fragments of the past, and a playful invention of "retro" styles. So we see 1970s polyester flairs, 1940s platform shoes, and the "look" of movies like *L.A. Confidential* and *The Titanic*. Nostalgia and retro often become a simulacrum, a perfect copy of something for which no original exists. These images are highly marketable commodities. They substitute for a more political, radical, and serious understanding of the past.

5. The psychological expression of postmodernism is a fragmented self. Using the metaphor of mental disorder, Jameson suggests that the postmodern self is schizoid or schizophrenic, while the modern self was neurotic. This metaphor means that the self is now disjointed, multiple, fragmented, and unstable. The rebellion against the Oedipal father, so characteristic of male artists and intellectuals in the phase of modernism, comes to an end, as fewer people have fathers in their families at all.

6. The cityscape and architecture are prime sites for making and seeing postmodern culture. Architecture is the most capitalist of the arts because buildings can only come into being when there is money available for their construction. Postmodern buildings are pastiches of pop culture, for instance, playful references to Las Vegas, 1950s diners, or hot dog stands; others are composed of decontextualized fragments of historical styles in which the past is mocked more than preserved; another popular postmodern building style displays mirrored surfaces like the Bonaventure Hotel in Los Angeles. This transformation of space parallels the destruction of time in postmodernism; both leave us disconnected, disoriented, and emotionally "flattened" to feeling only surface intensities.

7. Postmodern society is evolving toward a social formation that has a dominant form of the economy without a dominant political and cultural class. Postmodern culture is associated with the end of the western bourgeoisie as a dominant cultural and political force. We can now speak of a capitalist class which is increasingly globalized and less and less interested in sustaining a particular form of "high" western culture.

8. The preceding are all symptoms of an underlying transformation of culture that makes radical politics extremely difficult. What is lost or abolished is critical distance, seriousness, the search for authenticity, and faith in the possibility of a radical transcendence of reality. Readers may find that postmodernism echoes Nietzsche's critique of Plato, Socrates, and Christian thought (and by extension, Hegel): the message of postmodern culture is that the search for transcendence is mistaken, we must affirm life as it is. Of course, postmodern culture is Nietzsche in highly commodified form: "Live life with gusto," "just do it," "...as good as it gets" are advertising slogans that express a pop affirmation of life. This playful message is more effectively depoliticizing than coercion and repression.

The author ends by reminding us that these cultural forms are connected to social conditions of late capitalism. He retains a Marxist confidence in the possibility of scientifically analyzing culture, but changing it may prove to be a daunting prospect. Culture is not a free-floating fantasy embodied in texts, media, and artworks. It is part of a new configuration of production, markets, and social relationships. Jameson recognizes that there is no going back to an earlier, serious radical social critique; the new forms of capitalism and capitalist culture must be challenged through new forms of political culture adapted to the postmodern situation, but he does not provide a clear picture of how to create this new oppositional consciousness.

Readings

Berman, Marshall. *All That Is Solid Melts Into Air*. London: Verso, 1982.

Jameson, Fredric. *Postmodernism, or, the Cultural Logic of Late Capitalism*. Durham, NC: Duke University, 1992.

Jameson, Fredric, and Perry Anderson. *Cultural Turn: Selected Writings on the Postmodern*. London: Verso, 1998.

Lyotard, Jean-Francois. *The Postmodern Condition*. Minneapolis: University of Minnesota Press, 1984.

Smart, Barry. *Postmodernity*. London: Routledge, 1993.

Postmodernism, or The Cultural Logic of Late Capitalism
FREDRIC JAMESON

The last few years have been marked by an inverted millenarianism, in which premonitions of the future, catastrophic or redemptive, have been replaced by senses of the end of this or that (the end of ideology, art, or social class; the "crisis" of Leninism, social democracy, or the welfare state, etc., etc.): taken together, all of these perhaps constitute what is increasingly called postmodernism. The case for its existence depends on the hypothesis of some radical break or *coupure,* generally traced back to the end of the 1950s or the early 1960s. As the word itself suggests, this break is most often related to notions of the waning or extinction of the hundred-year-old modern movement (or to its ideological or aesthetic repudiation). Thus, abstract expressionism in painting, existentialism in philosophy, the final forms of representation in the novel, the films of the great *auteurs,* or the modernist school of poetry (as institutionalized and canonized in the works of Wallace Stevens): all these are now seen as the final extraordinary flowering of a high modernist impulse which is spent and exhausted with them. The enumeration of what follows then at once becomes empirical, chaotic, and heterogeneous: Andy Warhol and pop art, but also photorealism, and beyond it, the "new expressionism"; the moment, in music, of John Cage, but also the synthesis of classical and "popular" styles found in composers like Phil Glass and Terry Riley, and also punk and new wave rock (the Beatles and the Stones now standing as the high-modernist moment of that more recent and rapidly evolving tradition); in film, Godard, post-Godard and experimental cinema and video, but also a whole new type of commercial film (about which more below); Burroughs, Pynchon, or Ishmael Reed, on the one hand, and the French *nouveau roman* and its succession on the other, along with alarming new kinds of literary criticism, based on some new aesthetic of textuality or *écriture....* The list might be extended indefinitely; but does it imply any more fundamental change or break than the periodic style-and fashion-changes determined by an older high-modernist imperative of stylistic innovation?[1]

The Rise of Aesthetic Populism

It is in the realm of architecture, however, that modifications in aesthetic production are most dramatically visible, and that their theoretical problems have been most centrally raised and articulated; it was indeed from architectural debates that my own conception of postmodernism—as it will be outlined in the following pages—initially began to emerge. More decisively than in the other arts or media, postmodernist positions in architecture have been inseparable from an implacable critique of architectural high modernism and of the so-called International Style (Frank Lloyd Wright, Le Corbusier, Mies), where formal criticism and analysis (of the high-modernist transformation of the building into a virtual sculpture, or monumental "duck," as Robert Venturi puts it) are at one with reconsiderations on the level of urbanism and of the aesthetic institution. High modernism is thus credited with the destruction of the fabric of the traditional city and of its older neighbourhood culture (by way of the radical disjunction of the new Utopian high-modernist building from its surrounding context); while the prophetic elitism and authoritarianism of the modern movement are remorselessly denounced in the imperious gesture of the charismatic Master.

Postmodernism in architecture will then logically enough stage itself as a kind of aesthetic populism, as the very title of Venturi's influential manifesto, *Learning from Las Vegas*, suggests. However we may ultimately wish to evaluate this populist rhetoric, it has at least the merit of drawing our attention to one fundamental feature of all the postmodernisms enumerated above: namely, the effacement in them of the older (essentially high-modernist) frontier between high culture and so-called mass or commercial culture and the emergence of new kinds of texts infused with the forms, categories and contents of that very Culture Industry so passionately denounced by all the ideologues of the modern, from Leavis and the American New Criticism all the way to Adorno and the Frankfurt School. The postmodernisms have in fact been fascinated precisely by this whole "degraded" landscape of schlock and kitsch, of TV series and Readers' Digest culture, of advertising and motels, of the late show and the grade-B Hollywood film, of so-called paraliterature with its airport paperback categories of the gothic and the romance, the popular biography, the murder mystery and science-fiction or fantasy novel: materials they no longer simply "quote," as a Joyce or a Mahler might have done, but incorporate into their very substance.

Nor should the break in question be thought of as a purely cultural affair: indeed, theories of the postmodern—whether celebratory or couched in the language of moral revulsion and denunciation—bear a strong family resemblance to all those more ambitious sociological generalizations which, at much the same time, bring us the news of the arrival and inauguration of a whole new type of society, most famously baptized "post-industrial society" (Daniel Bell), but often also designated consumer society, media society, information society, electronic society or "high tech," and the like. Such theories have the obvious ideological mission of demonstrating, to their own relief, that the new social formation in question no longer obeys the laws of classical capitalism, namely the primacy of industrial production and the omnipresence of class struggle. The Marxist tradition has therefore resisted them with vehemence, with the signal exception of the economist Ernest Mandel, whose book, *Late Capitalism* sets out not merely to anatomize the historic originality of this new society (which he sees as a third stage or moment in the evolution of capital), but also to demonstrate that it is, if anything, a purer stage of capitalism than any of the moments that preceded it. I will return to this argument later; suffice it for the moment to emphasize a point I have defended in greater detail elsewhere,[2] namely that every position on postmodernism in culture—whether apologia or stigmatization—is also at one and the same time, and *necessarily,* an implicitly or explicitly political stance on the nature of multinational capitalism today.

Postmodernism as Cultural Dominant

A last preliminary word on method: what follows is not to be read as stylistic description, as the account of one cultural style or movement among others. I have rather meant to offer a periodizing hypothesis, and that at a moment in which the very conception of historical periodization has come to seem most problematical indeed. I have argued elsewhere that all isolated or discrete cultural analysis always involves a buried or repressed theory of historical periodization; in any case, the conception of the "genealogy" largely lays to rest traditional theoretical worries about so-called linear history, theories of "stages," and teleological historiography. In the present context, however, lengthier theoretical discussion of such (very real) issues can perhaps be replaced by a few substantive remarks.

One of the concerns frequently aroused by periodizing hypotheses is that these tend to obliterate difference, and to project an idea of the historical period as massive homogeneity (bounded on either side by inexplicable "chronological" metamorphoses and punctuation marks). This is, however, precisely why it seems to me essential to grasp "postmodernism" not as a style, but rather as a cultural dominant: a conception which allows for the presence and coexistence of a range of very different, yet subordinate features.

Consider, for example, the powerful alternative position that postmodernism is itself little more than one more stage of modernism proper (if not, indeed, of the even older romanticism); it may indeed be conceded that all of the features of postmodernism I am about to enumerate can be detected, full-blown, in this or that preceding modernism (including such astonishing genealogical precursors as Gertrude Stein, Raymond Roussel, or Marcel Duchamp, who may be considered outright postmodernists, *avant la lettre*). What has not been taken into account by this view is, however, the social position of the older modernism, or better still, its passionate repudiation by an older Victorian and post-Victorian bourgeoisie, for whom its forms and ethos are received as being variously ugly dissonant, obscure, scandalous, immoral, subversive and generally "anti-social." It will be argued here that a mutation in the sphere of culture has rendered such attitudes archaic. Not only are Picasso and Joyce no longer ugly; they now strike us, on the whole, as rather "realistic"; and this is the result of a canonization and an academic institutionalization of the modern movement generally, which can be traced to the late 1950s. This is indeed surely one of the most plausible explanations for the emergence of postmodernism itself, since the younger generation of the 1960s will now confront the formerly oppositional modern movement as a set of dead classics, which "weigh like a nightmare on the brains of the living," as Marx once said in a different context.

As for the postmodern revolt against all that, however, it must equally be stressed that its own offensive features—from obscurity and sexually explicit material to psychological squalor and overt expressions of social and political defiance, which transcend anything that might have been imagined at the most extreme moments of high modernism—no longer scandalize anyone and are not only received with the greatest complacency but have themselves become institutionalized and are at one with the official culture of Western society.

What has happened is that aesthetic production today has become integrated into commodity production generally: the frantic economic urgency of producing fresh waves of ever more novel-seeming goods (from clothing to airplanes), at ever greater rates of turnover, now assigns an increasingly essential structural function and position to aesthetic innovation and experimentation. Such economic necessities then find recognition in the institutional support of all kinds available for the newer art, from foundations and grants to museums and other forms of patronage. Architecture is, however, of all the arts that closest constitutively to the economic, with which, in the form of commissions and land values, it has a virtually unmediated relationship: it will therefore not be surprising to find the extraordinary flowering of the new postmodern architecture grounded in the patronage of multinational business, whose expansion and development is strictly contemporaneous with it. That these two new phenomena have an even deeper dialectical interrelationship than the simple one-to-one financing of this or that individual project we will try to suggest later on. Yet this is the point at which we must remind the reader of the obvious, namely that this whole global, yet American, postmodern culture is the internal and superstructural expression of a whole new wave of American military and economic domination throughout the world: in this sense, as throughout class history, the underside of culture is blood, torture, death and horror.

The first point to be made about the conception of periodization in dominance, therefore, is that even if all the constitutive features of postmodernism were identical and continuous with those of an older modernism—a position I feel to be demonstrably erroneous but which only an even lengthier analysis of modernism proper could dispel—the two phenomena would still remain utterly distinct in their meaning and social function, owing to the very different positioning of postmodernism in the economic system of late capital, and beyond that, to the transformation of the very sphere of culture in contemporary society.

More on this point at the conclusion of the present essay. I must now briefly address a different kind of objection to periodization, a different kind of concern about its possible obliteration of heterogeneity, which one finds most often on the Left. And it is certain that there is a strange quasi-Sartrean irony— a "winner loses" logic—which tends to surround any effort to describe a "system," a totalizing dynamic, as these are detected in the movement of contemporary society. What happens is that the more powerful the vision of some increasingly total system or logic—the Foucault of the prisons book is the obvious example—the more powerless the reader comes to feel. Insofar as the theorist wins, therefore, by constructing an increasingly closed and terrifying machine, to that very degree he loses, since the critical capacity of his work is thereby paralysed, and the impulses of negation and revolt, not to speak of those of social transformation, are increasingly perceived as vain and trivial in the face of the model itself.

I have felt, however, that it was only in the light of some conception of a dominant cultural logic or hegemonic norm that genuine difference could be measured and assessed. I am very far from feeling that all cultural production today is "postmodern" in the broad sense I will be conferring on this term. The postmodern is however the force field in which very different kinds of cultural impulses—what Raymond Williams has usefully termed "residual" and "emergent" forms of cultural production—must make their way. If we do not achieve some general sense of a cultural dominant, then we fall back into a view of present history as sheer heterogeneity, random difference, a coexistence of a host of distinct forces whose effectivity is undecidable. This has been at any rate the political spirit in which the following analysis was devised: to project some conception of a new systemic cultural norm and its reproduction, in order to reflect more adequately on the most effective forms of any radical cultural politics today.

The exposition will take up in turn the following constitutive features of the postmodern: a new depthlessness, which finds its prolongation both in contemporary "theory" and in a whole new culture of the image or the simulacrum; a consequent weakening of historicity, both in our relationship to public History and in the new forms of our private temporality, whose "schizophrenic" structure (following Lacan) will determine new types of syntax or syntagmatic relationships in the more temporal arts; which can best be grasped by a return to older theories of the sublime; the deep constitutive relationships of all this to a whole new technology, which is itself a figure for a whole new economic world system; and, after a brief account of postmodernist mutations in the lived experience of built space itself, some reflections on the mission of political art in the bewildering new world space of late multinational capital.

1. The Deconstruction of Expression

"Peasant Shoes"

We will begin with one of the canonical works of high modernism in visual art, Van Gogh's well-known painting of the peasant shoes, an example which as you can imagine has not been innocently or randomly chosen. I want to propose two ways of reading this painting, both of which in some fashion reconstruct the reception of the work in a two stage or double-level process.

I first want to suggest that if this copiously reproduced image is not to sink to the level of sheer decoration, it requires us to reconstruct some initial situation out of which the finished work emerges. Unless that situation—which has vanished into the past—is somehow mentally restored, the painting will remain an inert object, a reified end-product, and be unable to be grasped as a symbolic act in its own right, as praxis and as production.

This last term suggests that one way of reconstructing the initial situation to which the work is somehow a response is by stressing the raw materials, the initial content, which it confronts and which it reworks, transforms, and appropriates. In Van Gogh, that content, those initial raw materials, are, I will suggest, to be grasped simply as the whole object world of agricultural misery, of stark rural poverty, and the whole rudimentary human world of backbreaking peasant toil, a world reduced to its most brutal and menaced, primitive and marginalized state.

Fruit trees in this world are ancient and exhausted sticks coming out of poor soil; the people of the village are worn down to their skulls, caricatures of some ultimate grotesque typology of basic human feature types. How is it then that in Van Gogh such things as apple trees explode into a hallucinatory surface of colour, while his village stereotypes are suddenly and garishly overlaid with hues of red and green? I will briefly suggest, in this first interpretative option, that the willed and violent transformation of a drab peasant object world into the most glorious materialization of pure colour in oil paint is to be seen as a Utopian gesture: as an act of compensation which ends up producing a whole new Utopian realm of the senses, or at least of that supreme sense—sight, the visual, the eye—which it now reconstitutes for us as a semi-autonomous space in its own right—part of some new division of labour in the body of capital, some new fragmentation of the emergent sensorium which replicates the specializations and divisions of capitalist life as the same time that it seeks in precisely such fragmentation a desperate Utopian compensation for them.

There is, to be sure, a second reading of Van Gogh which can hardly be ignored when we gaze at this particular painting, and that is Heidegger's central analysis in *Der Ursprung des Kunstwerkes,* which is organized around the idea that the work of art emerges within the gap between Earth and World, or what I would prefer to translate as the meaningless materiality of the body and nature and the meaning-endowment of history and of the social. We will return to that particular gap or rift later on, suffice it here to recall some of the famous phrases, which model the process whereby these henceforth illustrious peasant shoes slowly recreate about themselves the whole missing object-world which was once their lived context. "In them," says Heidegger, "there vibrates the silent call of the earth, its quiet gift of ripening corn and its enigmatic self-refusal in the fallow desolation of the wintry field." "This equipment," he goes on, "belongs to the earth and it is protected in the *world* of the peasant woman ... Van Gogh's painting is the disclosure of what the equipment, the pair of peasant shoes, *is* in truth.... This entity emerges into the unconcealment of its being," by way of the mediation of the work of art, which draws the whole absent world and earth into revelation around itself, along with the heavy tread of the peasant woman, the loneliness of the field path, the hut in the clearing, the worn and broken instruments of labour in the furrows and at the hearth. Heidegger's account needs to be completed by insistence on the renewed materiality of the work, on the transformation of one form of materiality—the earth itself and its paths and physical objects—into that other materiality of oil paint affirmed and foregrounded in its own right and for its own visual pleasures; but has nonetheless a satisfying plausibility.

"Diamond Dust Shoes"
At any rate, both of these readings may be described as *hermeneutical,* in the sense in which the work in its inert, objectal form, is taken as a clue or a symptom for some vaster reality which replaces it as its ultimate truth. Now we need to look at some shoes of a different kind, and it is pleasant to be able to draw for such an image on the recent work of the central figure in contemporary visual art. Any Warhol's *Diamond Dust Shoes* evidently no longer speaks to us with any of the immediacy of Van Gogh's footgear: indeed, I am tempted to say that it does not really speak to us at all. Nothing in this painting organizes even a minimal place for the viewer, who confronts it at the turning of a museum corridor or gallery with all the contingency of some inexplicable natural object. On the level of the content, we have to do with what are now far more clearly fetishes, both in the Freudian and in the Marxian sense (Derrida remarks, somewhere, about the Heideggerian *Paar Bauernschuhe,* that the Van Gogh

footgear are a heterosexual pair, which allows neither for perversion nor for fetishization). Here, however, we have a random collection of dead objects, hanging together on the canvas like so many turnips, as shorn of their earlier life-world as the pile of shoes left over from Auschwitz, or the remainders and tokens of some incomprehensible and tragic fire in the packed dancehall. There is therefore in Warhol no way to complete the hermeneutic gesture, and to restore to these oddments that whole larger lived context of the dance hall or the ball, the world of jetset fashion or of glamour magazines. Yet this is even more paradoxical in the light of biographical information: Warhol began his artistic career as a commercial illustrator for shoe fashions and designer of display windows in which various pumps and slippers figured prominently. Indeed, one is tempted to raise here—far too prematurely—one of the central issues about postmodernism itself and its possible political dimensions: Andy Warhol's work in fact turns centrally around commodification, and the great billboard images of the Coca-Cola bottle or the Campbell's Soup Can, which explicitly foreground the commodity fetishism of a transition to late capital, *ought* to be powerful and critical political statements. If they are not that, then one would surely want to know why, and one would want to begin to wonder a little more seriously about the possibilities of political or critical art in the postmodern period of late capital.

But there are some other significant differences between the high modernist and the postmodernist moment, between the shoes of Van Gogh and the shoes of Andy Warhol, on which we must now very briefly dwell. The first and most evident is the emergence of a new kind of flatness or depthlessness, a new kind of superficiality in the most literal sense—perhaps the supreme formal feature of all the postmodernisms to which we will have occasion to return in a number of other contexts.

Then we must surely come to terms with the role of photography and the photographic/negative in contemporary art of this kind: and it is this indeed which confers its deathly quality on the Warhol image, whose glacéd x-ray elegance mortifies the reified eye of the viewer in a way that would seem to have nothing to do with death or the death obsession or the death anxiety on the level of content. It is indeed as though we had here to do with the inversion of Van Gogh's Utopian gesture: in the earlier work, a stricken world is by some Nietzschean fiat and act of the will transformed into the stridency of Utopian colour. Here, on the contrary, it is as though the external and coloured surface of things—debased and contaminated in advance by their assimilation to glossy advertising images—has been stripped away to reveal the deathly black-and-white substratum of the photographic negative which subtends them. Although this kind of death of the world of appearance becomes thematized in certain of Warhol's pieces—most notably, the traffic accidents or the electric chair series—this is not, I think, a matter of content any longer but of some more fundamental mutation both in the object world itself—now become a set of texts or simulacra—and in the disposition of the subject.

The Waning of Affect

All of which brings me to the third feature I had in mind to develop here briefly, namely what I will call the waning of affect in postmodern culture. Of course, it would be inaccurate to suggest that all affect, all feeling or emotion, all subjectivity, has vanished from the newer image. Indeed, there is a kind of return of the repressed in *Diamond Dust Shoes*, a strange compensatory decorative exhilaration, explicitly designated by the title itself although perhaps more difficult to observe in the reproduction. This is the glitter of gold dust, the spangling of gilt sand, which seals the surface of the painting and yet continues to glint at us. Think, however, of Rimbaud's magical flowers "that look back at you," or of the august premonitory eye- flashes of Rilke's archaic Greek torso which warn the bourgeois subject to change his life: nothing of that sort here, in the gratuitous frivolity of this final decorative overlay.

The waning of affect is, however, perhaps best initially approached by way of the human figure, and it is obvious that what we have said about the commodification of objects holds as strongly for Warhol's human subjects, stars—like Marilyn Monroe—who are themselves commodified and transformed into their own images. And here too a certain brutal return to the older period of high modernism offers a dramatic shorthand parable of the transformation in question. Edward Munch's painting *The Scream* is of course a canonical expression of the great modernist thematics of alienation, anomie, solitude and social fragmentation and isolation, a virtually programmatic emblem of what used to be called the age of anxiety. It will here be read not merely as an embodiment of the expression of that kind of affect, but even more as a virtual deconstruction of the very aesthetic of expression itself, which seems to have dominated much of what we call high modernism, but to have vanished away—for both practical and theoretical reasons—in the world of the postmodern. The very concept of expression presupposes indeed some separation within the subject, and along with that a whole metaphysics of the inside and the outside, of the wordless pain within the monad and the moment in which, often cathartically, that "emotion" is then projected out and externalized, as gesture or cry, as desperate communication and the outward dramatization of inward feeling. And this is perhaps the moment to say something about contemporary theory, which has among other things been committed to the mission of criticizing and discrediting this very hermeneutic model of the inside and the outside and of stigmatizing such models as ideological and metaphysical. But what is today called contemporary theory—or better still, theoretical discourse—is also, I would want to argue, itself very precisely a postmodernist phenomenon. It would therefore be inconsistent to defend the truth of its theoretical insights in a situation in which the very concept of "truth" itself is part of the metaphysical baggage which poststructuralism seeks to abandon. What we can at least suggest is that the poststructuralist critique of the hermeneutic, of what I will shortly call the depth model, is useful for us as a very significant symptom of the very postmodernist culture which is our subject here.

Overhastily, we can say that besides the hermeneutic model of inside and outside which Munch's painting develops, there are at least four other fundamental depth models, which have generally been repudiated in contemporary theory: the dialectical one of essence and appearance (along with a whole range of concepts of ideology or false consciousness which tend to accompany it); the Freudian model of latent and manifest, or of repression (which is of course the target of Michel Foucault's programmatic and symptomatic pamphlet *La Volonté de savoir*); the existential model of authenticity and inauthenticity, whose heroic or tragic thematics are closely related to that other great opposition between alienation and disalienation, itself equally a casualty of the poststructural or postmodern period; and finally, latest in time, the great semiotic opposition between signifier and signified, which was itself rapidly unravelled and deconstructed during its brief heyday in the 1960s and 70s. What replaces these various depth models is for the most part a conception of practices, discourses and textual play, whose new syntagmatic structures we will examine later on: suffice it merely to observe that here too depth is replaced by surface, or by multiple surfaces (what is often called intertextuality is in that sense no longer a matter of depth.)...

Euphoria and Self-Annihilation
Returning now for one last moment to Munch's painting, it seems evident that *The Scream* subtly but elaborately deconstructs its own aesthetic of expression, all the while remaining imprisoned within it. Its gestural content already underscores its own failure, since the realm of the sonorous, the cry, the raw vibrations of the human throat, are incompatible with its medium (something underscored within the work by the homunculus' lack of ears). Yet the absent scream returns more closely towards that even more absent experience of atrocious solitude and anxiety which the scream was itself to "express." Such loops inscribe themselves on the painted surface in the form of those great concentric circles in which sonorous vibration becomes ultimately visible, as on the surface of a sheet of water—in an infinite regress which fans out from the sufferer to become the very geography of a universe in which pain itself now speaks and vibrates through the material sunset and the landscape. The visible world now becomes the wall of the monad on which this "scream running

through nature" (Munch's words) is recorded and transcribed: one thinks of that character of Lautréamont who, growing up inside a sealed and silent membrane, on sight of the monstrousness of the deity, ruptures it with his own scream and thereby rejoins the world of sound and suffering.

All of which suggests some more general historical hypothesis: namely, that concepts such as anxiety and alienation (and the experiences to which they correspond, as in *The Scream)* are no longer appropriate in the world of the postmodern. The great Warhol figures—Marilyn herself, or Edie Sedgewick—the notorious burn-out and self-destruction cases of the ending 1960s, and the great dominant experiences of drugs and schizophrenia—these would seem to have little enough in common anymore, either with the hysterics and neurotics of Freud's own day, or with those canonical experiences of radical isolation and solitude, anomie, private revolt, Van Gogh-type madness, which dominated the period of high modernism. This shift in the dynamics of cultural pathology can be characterized as one in which the alienation of the subject is displaced by the fragmentation of the subject.

Such terms inevitably recall one of the more fashionable themes in contemporary theory—that of the "death" of the subject itself = the end of the autonomous bourgeois monad or ego or individual—and the accompanying stress, whether as some new moral ideal or as empirical description, on the *decentring* of that formerly centred subject or psyche. (Of the two possible formulations of this notion—the historicist one, that a once-existing centred subject, in the period of classical capitalism and the nuclear family, has today in the world of organizational bureaucracy dissolved; and the more radical poststructuralist position for which such a subject never existed in the first place but constituted something like an ideological mirage—I obviously incline towards the former; the latter must in any case take into account something like a "reality of the appearance.")

We must add that the problem of expression is itself closely linked to some conception of the subject as a monad-like container, within which things are felt which are then expressed by projection outwards. What we must now stress, however, is the degree to which the high-modernist conception of a unique *style,* along with the accompanying collective ideals of an artistic or political vanguard or *avant-garde*, themselves stand or fall along with that older notion (or experience) of the so-called centred subject.

Here too Munch's painting stands as a complex reflexion on this complicated situation: it shows us that expression requires the category of the individual monad, but it also shows us the heavy price to be paid for that precondition, dramatizing the unhappy paradox that when you constitute your individual subjectivity as a self-sufficient field and a closed realm in its own right, you thereby also shut yourself off from everything else and condemn yourself to the windless solitude of the monad, buried alive and condemned to a prison-cell without egress.

Postmodernism will presumably signal the end of this dilemma, which it replaces with a new one. The end of the bourgeois ego or monad no doubt brings with it the end of the psychopathologies of that ego as well—what I have generally here been calling the waning of affect. But it means the end of much more—the end for example of style, in the sense of the unique and the personal, the end of the distinctive individual brushstroke (as symbolized by the emergent primacy of mechanical reproduction). As for expression and feelings or emotions, the liberation, in contemporary society, from the older *anomie* of the centred subject may also mean, not merely a liberation from anxiety, but a liberation from every other kind of feeling as well, since there is no longer a self present to do the feeling. This is not to say that the cultural products of the postmodern era are utterly devoid of feeling, but rather that such feelings—which it may be better and more accurate to call "intensities"—are now free-gloating and impersonal, and tend to be dominated by a peculiar kind of euphoria to which I will want to return at the end of this essay.

The waning of affect, however, might also have been characterized, in the narrower context of literary criticism, as the waning of the great high-modernist thematics of time and temporality, the elegiac mysteries of *durée* and of memory (something to be understood fully as a category of literary criticism associated as much with high modernism as with the works themselves). We have often been told, however, that we now inhabit the synchronic rather than the diachronic, and I think it is at least empirically arguable that our daily life, our psychic experience, our cultural languages, are today dominated by categories of space rather than by categories of time, as in the preceding period of high modernism proper.

II. The Postmodern and the Past...

"Historicism" Effaces History

This situation evidently determines what the architecture historians call "historicism," namely the random cannibalization of all the styles of the past, the play of random stylistic allusion, and in general what Henry Lefebvre has called the increasing primacy of the "neo". This omnipresence of pastiche is, however, not incompatible with certain humour (nor is it innocent of all passion) or at least with addiction—with a whole historically original consumers' appetite for a world transformed into sheer images of itself and for pseudo-events and "spectacles" (the term of the Situationists). It is for such objects that we may reserve Plato's conception of the "simulacrum"—the identical copy for which no original has ever existed. Appropriately enough, the culture of the simulacrum comes to *life* in a society where exchange-value has been generalized to the point at which the very memory of use-value is effaced, a society of which Guy Debord has observed, in an extraordinary phrase, that in it "the image has become the final form of commodity reification" (*The Society of the Spectacle*).

The new spatial logic of the simulacrum can now be expected to have a momentous effect on what used to be historical time.

The past is thereby itself modified: what was once, in the historical novel as Lukács defines it, the organic genealogy of the bourgeois collective project—what is still, for the redemptive historiography of an E.P. Thompson or of American "oral history," for the resurrection of the dead of anonymous and silenced generations, the retrospective dimension indispensable to any vital reorientation of our collective future—has meanwhile itself become a vast collection of images, a multitudinous photographic simulacrum. Guy Debord's powerful slogan is now even more apt for the "prehistory" of a society bereft of all historicity, whose own putative past is little more than a set of dusty spectacles. In faithful conformity to poststructuralist linguistic theory, the past as "referent" finds itself gradually bracketed, and then effaced altogether, leaving us with nothing but texts.

The Nostalgia Mode

Yet, it should not be thought that this process is accompanied by indifference: on the contrary, the remarkable current intensification of an addiction to the photographic image is itself a tangible symptom of an omnipresent, omnivorous and well-nigh libidinal historicism. The architects use this (exceedingly polysemous) word for the complacent eclecticism of postmodern architecture, which randomly and without principle but with gusto cannibalizes all the architectural styles of the past and combines them in overstimulating ensembles. Nostalgia does not strike one as an altogether satisfactory word for such fascination (particularly when one thinks of the pain of a properly modernist nostalgia with a past beyond all but aesthetic retrieval), yet it directs our attention to what is a culturally far more generalized manifestation of the process in commercial art and taste, namely the so-called "nostalgia film" (or what the French call "la mode rétro").

These restructure the whole issue of pastiche and project it onto a collective and social level, where the desperate attempt to appropriate a missing past is now refracted through the iron law of fashion change and the emergent ideology of the "generation." *American Graffiti* (1973) set out to recapture as so many films have attempted since, the henceforth mesmerizing lost reality of the Eisenhower era: and one tends to feel that for Americans at least, the 1950s remain the privileged lost object of desire—not merely the stability and prosperity of a pax Americana, but also the first naive innocence of the countercultural impulses of early rock-and-roll and youth gangs (Coppola's *Rumble Fish* will then be the contemporary dirge that laments their passing, itself, however, still contradictorily filmed in genuine "nostalgia film" style). With this initial breakthrough, other generational periods open up for aesthetic colonization: as witness the stylistic recuperation of the American and the Italian 1930s, in Polanski's *Chinatown* and Bertolluci's *Il Conformista* respectively. What is more interesting, and more problematical, are the ultimate attempts, through this new discourse, to lay siege either to our own present and immediate past, or to a more distant history that escapes individual existential memory.

Faced with these ultimate objects—our social, historical and existential present, and the past as "referent"—the incompatibility of a postmodernist "nostalgia" art language with genuine historicity becomes dramatically apparent. The contraction propels this model, however, into complex and interesting new formal inventiveness: it being understood that the nostalgia film was never a matter of some old-fashioned "representation" of historical content, but approached the "past" through stylistic connotation, conveying "pastness" by the glossy qualities of the image, and "1930-ness" or "1950s-ness" by the attributes of fashion (therein following the prescription of the Barthes of *Mythologies,* who saw connotation as the purveying of imaginary and stereotypical idealities, "Sinité," for example, as some Disney-EPCOT "concept" of China.)...

III. The Breakdown of the Signifying Chain

The crisis in historicity now dictates a return, in a new way, to the question of temporal organization in general in the postmodern force field, and indeed, to the problem of the form that time, temporality and the syntagmatic will be able to take in a culture increasingly dominated by space and spatial logic. If, indeed, the subject has lost its capacity actively to extend its pro-tensions and re-tensions across the temporal manifold, and to organize its past and future into coherent experience, it becomes difficult enough to see how the cultural productions of such a subject could result in anything but "heaps of fragments" and in a practice of the randomly heterogeneous and fragmentary and the aleatory. These are, however, very precisely some of the privileged terms in which postmodernist cultural production has been analysed (and even defended, by its own apologists). Yet they are still privative features; the more substantive formulations bear such names as textuality, *écriture,* or schizophrenic writing, and it is to these that we must now briefly turn....

IV. The Hysterical Sublime

Now we need to complete this exploratory account of postmodernist space and time with a final analysis of the euphoria or those intensities which seem so often to characterize the newer cultural experience. Let us stress again the enormity of a transition which leaves behind it the desolation of Hopper's buildings or the stark Midwest syntax of Sheeler's forms, replacing them with the extraordinary surfaces of the photorealist cityscape, where even the automobile wrecks gleam with some new hallucinatory splendour. The exhilaration of these new surfaces is all the more paradoxical in that their essential content—the city itself—has deteriorated or disintegrated to a degree surely still inconceivable in the early years of the 20th century, let alone in the previous era. How urban squalor can be a delight to the eyes, when expressed in commodification, and how an unparalleled quantum leap in the alienation of daily life in the city can now be experienced in the form of a strange new hallucinatory exhilaration—these are some of the questions that confront us in this moment of our inquiry. Nor should the human figure be exempted from investigation, although it seems clear that for the new aesthetic the representation of space itself has come to be felt as incompatible with the representation of the body: a kind of aesthetic division of labour far more pronounced than in any of the earlier generic conceptions of landscape, and a most ominous symptom indeed. The privileged space of the newer art is radically anti-anthropomorphic, as in the empty bathrooms of Doug Bond's work. The ultimate contemporary fetishization of the human body, however, takes a very different direction in the statues of Duane Hanson—what I have already called the simulacrum, whose peculiar function lies in what Sartre would have called the *derealization* of the whole surrounding world of everyday reality. Your moment of doubt and hesitation as to the breath and warmth of these polyester figures, in other words, tends to return upon the real human beings moving about you in the museum, and to transform them also for the briefest instant into so many dead and flesh-coloured simulacra in their own right. The world thereby momentarily loses its depth and threatens to become a glossy skin, a stereoscopic illusion, a rush of filmic images without density. But is this now a terrifying or an exhilarating experience?

It has proved fruitful to think such experience in terms of what Susan Sontag once, in an influential statement, isolated as "camp." I propose a somewhat different cross-light on it, drawing on the equally fashionable current theme of the "sublime," as it has been rediscovered in the works of Edmund Burke and Kant; or perhaps, indeed, one might well want to yoke the two notions together in the form of something like a camp of "hysterical" sublime. The sublime was for Burke, as you will recall, an experience bordering on error, the fitful glimpse, in astonishment, stupor and awe, of what was so enormous as to crush human life altogether: a description then refined by Kant to include the question of representation itself—so that the object of the sublime is now not only a matter of sheer power and of the physical incommensurability of the human organism with nature, but also of the limits of figuration and the incapacity of the human mind to give representation to such enormous forces. Such forces Burke, in his historical moment at the dawn of the modern bourgeois state, was only able to conceptualize in terms of the divine; while even Heidegger continues to entertain a fantastic relationship with some organic precapitalist peasant landscape and village society, which is the final form of the image of nature in our own time.

Today, however, it may be possible to think all this in a different way, at the moment of a radical eclipse of Nature itself: Heidegger's "field path" is after all irredeemably and irrevocably destroyed by late capital, by the green revolutions, by neocolonialism and the megalopopolis, which runs its superhighways over the older fields and vacant lots, and turns Heidegger's "house of being" into condominiums, if not the most miserable unheated rat-infested tenement buildings. The *other* of our society is in that sense no longer Nature at all, as it was in precapitalist societies, but something else which we must now identify.

The Apotheosis of Capitalism

I am anxious that this other thing should not overhastily be grasped as technology per se, since I will want to show that technology is here itself a figure for something else. Yet technology may well serve as adequate shorthand to designate that enormous properly human and anti-natural power of dead human labour soared up in our machinery, an alienated power, which Sartre calls the counterfinality of the practico-inert, which turns back on and against us in unrecognizable forms and seems to constitute the massive dystopian horizon of our collective as well as our individual praxis.

Technology is, however, on the Marxist view the result of the development of capital, rather than some primal cause in its own right. It will therefore be appropriate to distinguish several generations of machine power, several stages of technological revolution within capital itself. I here follow Ernest Mandel who outlines three such fundamental breaks or quantum leaps in the evolution of machinery under capital: "The fundamental revolutions in power technology—the technology of the production of motive machines by machines—thus appears as the determinant moment in revolutions of technology as a whole. Machine production of steam-driven motors since 1848; machine production of electric and combustion motors since the 90s of the 19th century; machine production of electronic and nuclear-powered apparatuses since the 40s of the 20th century—these are the three general revolutions in technology engendered by the capitalist mode of production since the "original" industrial revolution of the later 18th century." (*Late Capitalism*, p. 18).

The periodization underscores the general thesis of Mandel's book *Late Capitalism*, namely that there have been three fundamental moments in capitalism, each one marking a dialectical expansion over the previous stage: these are market capitalism, the monopoly stage or the stage of imperialism, and our own—wrongly called postindustrial, but what might better be termed multinational capital. I have already pointed out that Mandel's intervention in the postindustrial involves the proposition that late or multination or consumer capitalism, far from being inconsistent with Marx's great 19th-century analysis, constitutes on the contrary the purest form of capital yet to have emerged, a prodigious expansion of capital into hitherto uncommodified areas. This purer capitalism of our own time thus eliminates the enclaves of precapitalist organization it had hitherto tolerated and exploited in a tributary way: one is tempted to speak in this connection of a new and historically original penetration and colonization of Nature and the Unconscious: that is, the destruction of precapitalist third world agriculture by the Green Revolution, and the rise of the media and the advertising industry. At any rate, it will also have been clear that my own cultural periodization of the stages of realism, modernism and postmodernism is both inspired and confirmed by Mandel's tripartite scheme....

As I have said, however, I want to avoid the implication that technology is in any way the "ultimately determining instance" either of our present-day social life or of our cultural production: such a thesis is of course ultimately at one with the post-Marxist notion of a "postindustrialist" society. Rather, I want to suggest that our faulty representations of some immense communicational and computer network are themselves but a distorted figuration of something even deeper, namely the whole world system of present-day multinational capitalism. The technology of contemporary society is therefore mesmerizing and fascinating, not so much in its own right, but because it seems to offer some privileged representational shorthand for grasping a network of power and control even more difficult for our minds and imaginations to grasp—namely the whole new decentred global network of the third stage of capital itself. This is a figural process presently best observed in a whole mode of contemporary entertainment literature, which one is tempted to characterize as "high tech paranoia," in which the circuits and networks of some putative global computer hook-up are narratively mobilized by labyrinthine conspiracies of autonomous but deadly interlocking and competing information agencies in a complexity often beyond the capacity of the normal reading mind. Yet conspiracy theory (and its garish narrative manifestations) must be seen as degraded attempt—through the figuration of advanced technology—to think the impossible totality of the contemporary world system. It is therefore in terms of that enormous and threatening, yet only dimly perceivable, other reality of economic and social institutions that in my opinion the postmodern sublime can alone be adequately theorized....

VI. The Abolition of Critical Distance

... What we must now affirm is that it is precisely this whole extraordinarily demoralizing and depressing original new global space which is the "moment of truth" of postmodernism. What has been called the postmodernist "sublime" is only the moment in which this content has become most explicit, has moved the closest to the surface of consciousness, as a coherent new type of space in its own right—even though a certain figural concealment or disguise is still at work here, most notably in the high-technological thematics in which the new spatial content is still dramatized and articulated. Yet the earlier features of the postmodern which were enumerated above can all now be seen as themselves partial (yet constitutive) aspects of the same general spatial object.

The argument for a certain authenticity in these otherwise patently ideological productions depends on the prior proposition that what we have now been calling postmodern (or multinational) space is not merely a cultural ideology or fantasy, but has genuine historical (and socio-economic) reality as a third great original expansion of capitalism around the globe (after the earlier expansions of the national market and the older imperialist system, which each had their own cultural specificity and generated new types of space appropriate to their dynamics). The distorted and unreflexive attempts of new cultural production to explore and to express this new space must then also, in their own fashion, be considered as so many approaches to the representation of (a new) reality (to use a more antiquated language). As paradoxical as the terms may seem, they may thus, following a classic interpretive option, be read as peculiar new forms of realism (or at least of the mimesis of reality), at the same time that they can equally well be analysed as so many attempts to distract and to divert us from that reality or to disguise its contradictions and resolve them in the guise of various formal mystifications.

As for that reality itself, however—the as yet untheorized original space of some new "world system" of multinational or late capitalism (a space whose negative or baleful aspects are only too obvious), the dialectic requires us to hold equally to a positive or "progressive" evaluation of its emergence, as Marx did for the newly unified space of the national markets, or as Lenin did for the older imperialist global network. For neither Marx nor Lenin was socialism a matter of returning to small (and thereby less repressive and comprehensive) systems of social organization: rather, the dimensions attained by capital in their own times were grasped as the promise, the framework, and the precondition for the achievement of some new and more comprehensive socialism. How much the more is this not the case with the even more global and totalizing space of the new world system, which demands the invention and elaboration of an internationalism of a radically new type?...

An aesthetic of cognitive mapping—a pedagogical political culture which seeks to endow the individual subject with some new heightened sense of its place in the global system—will necessarily have to respect this now enormously complex representational dialectic and to invent radically new forms in order to do it justice. This is not, then, clearly a call for a return to some older kind of machinery, some older and more transparent national space, or some more traditional and reassuring perspectival or mimetic enclave: the new political art—if it is indeed possible at all—will have to hold to the truth of postmodernism, that is, to say, to its fundamental object—the world space of multinational capital—at the same time at which it achieves a breakthrough to some as yet unimaginable new mode of representing this last, in which we may again begin to grasp our positioning as individual and collective subjects and regain a capacity to act and struggle which is at present neutralized by our spatial as well as our social confusion. The political form of postmodernism, if there ever is any, will have as its vocation the invention and projection of a global cognitive mapping, on a social as well as a spatial scale.

Notes
1. The present essay draws on lectures and on material previously published in *The Anti-Aesthetic* edited by Hal Foster, (Port Townsend, Washington: Bay Press 1983) and in *Amerika Studien/ American Studies* 29/1 (1984).
2. In the "Politics of Theory," *New German Critique,* 32 Spring/Summer 1984.

41

STUART HALL (1932-)

Stuart Hall's work shows the effects of the melting vision in contemporary social thought. He overcomes many of the postwar oppositions in theory: macro vs. micro; culture vs. social structure; Marxist vs. symbolic interactionist; Marxist analysis vs. analysis of cultural difference. His theoretical work exemplifies the new fluidity of analysis, itself perhaps a product of a greater fluidity in ordinary people's identities and cultural experiences.

Hall identifies himself as a Marxist strongly influenced by Antonio Gramsci's work on hegemony. He devotes his attention to the analysis of culture and the media, especially in Great Britain. In one of his major theoretical projects, he developed the concept "authoritarian populism" to describe the ideological appeal of Thatcherism. The Thatcherite right projected an image of siding with ordinary people against political, social, and economic elites, at the same time that it promised law, order, and social control. A sense of moral panic about crime, racial difference, and moral permissiveness was exploited; working-class and lower middle-class white people who had little to gain from Prime Minister Margaret Thatcher's policies of cutting services and privatizing government functions were nevertheless attracted to anti-elite appeals and "law and order" rhetoric. Authoritarian populism was an attempt—not entirely successful—to broaden the base of Thatcher's support beyond a fairly narrow sector of the business community.

This selection illustrates Hall's continuing interest in cultural analysis. It reflects the real-life conditions of global migration and the formation of multiethnic societies. More and more people live in a *diaspora*, a scattering of an ethnic-cultural group away from its original homeland. *Diaspora* is a Greek word, first applied to the scattering of the Jews throughout the Roman empire and western Asia after the destruction of the temple in Jerusalem. Eventually it was applied to the scattering of tens of millions of Africans into the western hemisphere by the slave trade. Now it describes the condition of people who have migrated transnationally, creating networked extended families and rebuilding communities within increasingly multi-ethnic host societies: West Africans and Maghrebiens (North Africans) in France; Turks in Germany; Chinese throughout southeast Asia and the Americas; Africans, South Asians, and West Indians in Great Britain; Russians stranded in new republics of the former Soviet Union; Mexicans, Cubans, and Central Americans in the United States. These experiences of millions of people have challenged traditional notions of national boundaries and stable national and ethnic identities.

Not only are old prejudices and stereotypes weakening; fixed theoretical notions in the social sciences are also undone. For a long time, social scientists wrote about demographic characteristics as though they were fixed by nature and could be safely taken-for-granted. Social scientists routinely used categories like "race" and "sex" as independent variables, fixed and immutable characteristics of people that could be used to explain their attitudes, collective actions, and behaviours. Religion too was considered a largely unchanging ascribed status.

Hall's essay alerts us to the end of these ideas of immutability, naturalness, ascription, and fixedness, in the social sciences as well as popular thought. We now recognize that people constantly choose and construct their identities. When they move, crossing boundaries and entering new environments, their identity is recontextualized and transformed. They also reconstruct the past, so that it too is continually changing. Both collectively and individually, there are no fixed identities. Social movements do not mobilize support bases according to demographic characteristics; they create support bases by their practices of framing and defining identities.

Readings

Anderson, Benedict. *Imagined Communities*. London: Verso, 1983/1991.

Fanon, Frantz. *The Wretched of the Earth*. New York: Grove Press, 1963.

—. *Black Skin, White Masks*. New York: Grove, 1991.

Hall, Stuart. *Representation: Cultural Representations and Signifying Practices*. Milton Keynes: Open University, 1997.

Hall, Stuart, and Paul Du Gay (eds.). *Questions of Cultural Idenity*. Thousand Oaks, CA, London, and New Delhi: Sage, 1996.

Hall, S., and Tony Jefferson (eds.). *Resistance through Rituals: Youth Subcultures in Postwar Britain*. London: Routledge, 1995.

Cultural Identity and Diaspora
STUART HALL

A new cinema of the Caribbean is emerging, joining the company of the other "Third Cinemas." It is related to, but different from, the vibrant film and other forms of visual representation of the Afro-Caribbean (and Asian) "blacks" of the diasporas of the West—the new post-colonial subjects. All these cultural practices and forms of representation have the black subject at their centre, putting the issue of cultural identity in question. Who is this emergent, new subject of the cinema? From where does he/she speak? Practices of representation always implicate the positions from which we speak or write—the positions of *enunciation*. What recent theories of enunciation suggest is that, though we speak, so to say "in our own name," of ourselves and from our own experience, nevertheless who speaks, and the subject who is spoken of, are never identical, never exactly in the same place. Identity is not as transparent or unproblematic as we think. Perhaps instead of thinking of identity as an already accomplished fact, which the new cultural practices then represent, we should think, instead, of identity as "production" which is never complete, always in process, and always constituted within, not outside representation. This view problematises the very authority and authenticity to which the term "cultural identity" lays claim.

We seek, here, to open a dialogue, and investigation, on the subject of cultural identity and representation. Of course, the "I" who writes here must also be thought of as, itself, "enunciated." We all write and speak from a particular place and time, from a history and a culture which is specific. What we say is always "in context," *positioned*. I was born into and spent my childhood and adolescence in a lower-middle-class family in Jamaica. I have lived all my adult life in England, in the shadow of the black diaspora—"in the belly of the beast." I write against the background of a lifetime's work in cultural studies. If the paper seems preoccupied with the diaspora experience and its narratives of displacement, it is worth remembering that all discourse is "placed," and the heart has its reasons.

There are at least two different ways of thinking about "cultural identity." The first position defines "cultural identity" in terms of one, shared culture, a sort of collective "one true self," hiding inside the many other, more superficial or artificially imposed "selves," which people with a shared history and ancestry hold in common. Within the terms of this definition, our cultural identities reflect the common historical experiences and shared cultural codes which provide us, as "one people," with stable, unchanging and continuous frames of reference and meaning, beneath the shifting divisions and vicissitudes of our actual history. This "oneness," underlying all the other, more superficial differences, is the truth, the essence, of "Caribbeanness," of the black experience. It is this identity which a Caribbean or black diaspora must discover, excavate, bring to light and express through cinematic representation.

Such a conception of cultural identity played a critical role in all post-colonial struggles which have so profoundly reshaped our world. It lay at the centre of the vision of the poets of "Negritude," like Aimé Césaire and Léopold Senghor, and of the Pan-African political project, earlier in the century. It continues to be a very powerful and creative force in emergent forms of representation amongst hitherto marginalised peoples. In post-colonial societies, the rediscovery of this identity is often the object of what Franz Fanon once called a

> passionate research ... directed by the secret hope of discovering beyond the misery of today, beyond self-contempt, resignation and abjuration, some very beautiful and splendid era whose existence rehabilitates us both in regard to ourselves and in regard to others.

New forms of cultural practice in these societies address themselves to this project for the very good reason that, as Fanon puts it, in the recent past,

> Colonisation is not satisfied merely with holding a people in its grip and emptying the native's brain of all form and content. By a kind of perverted logic, it turns to the past of oppressed people, and distorts, disfigures and destroys it.[1]

The question which Fanon's observation poses is, what is the nature of this "profound research" which drives the new forms of visual and cinematic representation? Is it only a matter of unearthing that which the colonial experience buried and overlaid, bringing to light the hidden continuities it suppressed? Or is a quite different practice entailed—not the rediscovery but the *production* of identity. Not an identity grounded in the archaeology, but in the *re-telling* of the past?

We should not, for a moment, underestimate or neglect the importance of the act of imaginative rediscovery which this conception of a rediscovered, essential identity entails. "Hidden histories" have played a critical role in the emergence of many of the most important social movements of our time—feminist, anti-colonial and anti-racist. The photographic work of a generation of Jamaican and Rastafarian artists, or of a visual artist like Armet Francis (a Jamaican-born photographer who has lived in Britain since the age of eight) is a testimony to the continuing creative power of this conception of identity within the emerging practices of representation. Francis's photographs of the peoples of The Black Triangle, taken in Africa, the Caribbean, the USA and the UK, attempt to reconstruct in visual terms "the underlying unity of the black people whom colonisation and slavery distributed across the African diaspora." His text is an act of imaginary reunification.

Crucially, such images offer a way of imposing an imaginary coherence on the experience of dispersal and fragmentation, which is the history of all enforced diasporas. They do this by representing or "figuring" Africa as the mother of these different civilisations. This Triangle is, after all, "centred" in Africa. Africa is the name of the missing term, the great aporia, which lies at the centre of our cultural identity and gives it a meaning which, until recently, it lacked. No one who looks at these textural images now, in the light of the history of transportation, slavery and migration, can fail to understand how the rift of separation, the "loss of identity," which has been integral to the Caribbean experience only begins to be healed when these forgotten connections are once more set in place. Such texts restore an imaginary fullness of plentitude, to set against the broken rubric of our past. They are resources of resistance and identity, with which to confront the fragmented and pathological ways in which that experience has been reconstructed within the dominant regimes of cinematic and visual representation of the West.

There is, however, a second, related but different view of cultural identity. This second position recognises that, as well as the many points of similarity, there are also critical points of deep and significant *difference* which constitute "what we really are"; or rather—since history has intervened—"what we have become." We cannot speak for very long, with any exactness, about "one experience, one identity," without acknowledging its other side—the ruptures and discontinuities which constitute, precisely, the Caribbean's "uniqueness." Cultural identity, in this second sense, is a matter of "becoming" as well as of "being." It belongs to the future as much as to the past. It is not something which already exists, transcending place, time, history and culture. Cultural identities come from somewhere, have histories. But, like everything which is historical, they undergo constant transformation. Far from being eternally fixed in some essentialised past, they are subject to the continuous "play" of history, culture and power. Far from being grounded in mere "recovery" of the past, which is waiting to be found, and which when found, will secure our sense of ourselves into eternity, identities are the names we give to the different ways we are positioned by, and position ourselves within, the narratives of the past.

It is only from this second position that we can properly understand the traumatic character of "the colonial experience." The ways in which black people, black experiences, were positioned and subject-ed in the dominant regimes of representation were the effects of a critical exercise of cultural power and normalisation. Not only, in Said's "Orientalist" sense, were we constructed as different and other within the categories of knowledge of the West by those regimes. They had the power to make us see and experience *ourselves* as "Other." Every regime of representation is a regime of power formed, as Foucault reminds us, by the fatal couplet "power/knowledge." But this kind of knowledge is internal, not external. It is one thing to position a subject or set of peoples as the Other of a dominant discourse. It is quite another thing to subject them to that "knowledge," not only as a matter of imposed will and domination, by the power of inner compulsion and subjective con-formation to the norm. That is the lesson—the sombre majesty—of Fanon's insight into the colonising experience in *Black Skin, White Masks.*

This inner expropriation of cultural identity cripples and deforms. If its silences are not resisted, they produce, in Fanon's vivid phrase, "individuals without an anchor, without horizon, colourless, stateless, rootless—a race of angels."[2] Nevertheless, this idea of otherness as an inner compulsion changes our conception of "cultural identity." In this perspective, cultural identity is not a fixed essence at all, lying unchanged outside history and culture. It is not some universal and transcendental spirit inside us on which history has made no fundamental mark. It is not once-and-for-all. It is not a fixed origin to which we can make some final and absolute Return. Of course, it is not a mere phantasm either. It is *something*—not a mere trick of the imagination. It has its histories—and histories have their real, material and symbolic effects. The past continues to speak to us. But it no longer addresses us as a simple, factual "past," since our relation to it, like the child's relation to the mother, is always-already "after the break." It is always constructed through memory, fantasy, narrative and myth. Cultural identities are the points of identification, the unstable points of identification or suture, which are made, within the discourses of history and culture. Not an essence but a *positioning*. Hence, there is always a politics of identity, a politics of position, which has no absolute guarantee in an unproblematic, transcendental "law of origin."

This second view of cultural identity is much less familiar, and more unsettling. If identity does not proceed, in a straight unbroken line, from some fixed origin, how are we to understand its formation? We might think of black Caribbean identities as "framed" by two axes or vectors, simultaneously operative: the vector of similarity and continuity; and the vector of difference and rupture. Caribbean identities always have to be thought of in terms of the dialogic relationship between these two axes. The one gives us some grounding in, some continuity with, the past. The second reminds us that what we share is precisely the experience of a profound discontinuity: the peoples dragged into slavery, transportation, colonisation, migration, came predominantly from Africa—and when that supply ended, it was temporarily refreshed by indentured labour from the Asian subcontinent. (This neglected fact explains why, when you visit Guyana or Trinidad, you see, symbolically inscribed in the faces of their peoples, the paradoxical "truth" of Christopher Columbus's mistake: you *can* find "Asia" by sailing west, if you know where to look!) In the history of the modern world, there are few more traumatic ruptures to match these enforced separations from Africa—already figured, in the European imaginary, as "the Dark Continent." But the slaves were also from different countries, tribal communities, villages, languages and gods. African religion, which has been so profoundly formative in Caribbean spiritual life, is precisely *different* from Christian monotheism in believing that God is so powerful that he can only be known through a proliferation of spiritual manifestations, present everywhere in the natural and social world. These gods live on, in an underground existence, in the hybridised religious universe of Haitian voodoo, pocomania, Native pentacostalism, Black baptism, Rastafarianism and the black Saints Latin American Catholicism. The paradox is that it was the uprooting of slavery and transportation and the insertion into the plantation economy (as well as the symbolic economy) of the Western world that "unified" these peoples across their differences, in the same moment as it cut them off from direct access to their past.

Difference, therefore, persists—in and alongside continuity. To return to the Caribbean after any long absence is to experience again the shock of the "doubleness" of similarity and difference. Visiting the French Caribbean for the first time, I also saw at once how different Martinique is from, say, Jamaica: and this is no mere difference of topography or climate. It is a profound difference of culture and history. And the difference *matters*. It positions Martiniquains and Jamaicans as *both* the same *and* different. Moreover, the boundaries of difference are continually repositioned in relation to different points of reference. Vis-à-vis the developed West, we are very much "the same." We belong to the marginal, the underdeveloped, the periphery, the "Other." We are at the outer edge, the "rim" of the metropolitan world—always "South" to someone else's *El Notre*.

At the same time, we do not stand in the same relation of the "otherness" to the metropolitan centres. Each has negotiated its economic, political and cultural dependency differently. And this "difference," whether we like it or not, is already inscribed in our cultural identities. In turn, it is this negotiation of identity which makes us, vis-à-vis other Latin American people, with a very similar history, different—Caribbeans, *les Antilliennes* ("islanders" to their mainland). And yet, vis-à-vis one another Jamaican, Haitian, Cuban, Guadeloupean, Barbadian, etc....

How, then, to describe this play of "difference" within identity? The common history—transportation, slavery, colonisation—has been profoundly formative. For all these societies, unifying us across our differences. But it does not constitute a common *origin*, since it was, metaphorically as well as literally, a translation. The inscription of difference is also specific and critical. I use the word "play" because the double meaning of the metaphor is important. It suggests, on the one hand, the instability, the permanent unsettlement, the lack of any final resolution. On the other hand, it reminds us that the place where this "doubleness" is most powerfully to be heard is "playing" within the varieties of Caribbean musics. This cultural "play" could not therefore be represented, cinematically, as a simple, binary opposition—"past/present," "them/us." Its complexity exceeds this binary structure of representation. At different places, times, in relation to different questions, the boundaries are re-sited. They become, not only what they have, at times, certainly been—mutually excluding categories, but also what they sometimes are—differential points along a sliding scale.

One trivial example is the way Martinique both *is* and *is not* "French." It is, of course, a *department* of France, and this is reflected in its standard and style of life: Fort de France is a much richer, more "fashionable" place than Kingston—which is not only visibly poorer, but itself at a point of transition between being "in fashion" in an Anglo-African and Afro-American way—for those who can afford to be in any sort of fashion at all. Yet, what is distinctively "Martiniquais" can only be described in terms of that special and peculiar supplement which the black and mulatto skin adds to the "refinement" and sophistication of a Parisian-derived *haute couture:* that is, a sophistication which, because it is black, is always transgressive.

To capture this sense of difference which is not pure "otherness," we need to deploy the play on words of a theorist like Jacques Derrida. Derrida uses the anomalous "a" in his way of writing "difference"—*differance*—as a marker which sets up a disturbance in our settled understanding or translation of the word/concept. It sets the word in motion to new meanings without erasing the *trace* of its other meanings. His sense of *differance,* as Christopher Norris puts it, thus

> remains suspended between the two French verbs "to differ" and "to defer" (postpone), both of which contribute to its textual force but neither of which can fully capture its meaning. Language depends of difference, as Saussure showed ... the structure of distinctive propositions which make up its basic economy. Where Derrida breaks new ground ... is in the extent to which "differ" shades into "defer" ... the idea that meaning is always deferred, perhaps to this point of an endless supplementarity, by the play of signification.[3]

This second sense of difference challenges the fixed binaries which stabilise meaning and representation and show how meaning is never finished or completed, but keeps on moving to encompass other, additional or supplementary meanings, as Norris puts it elsewhere,[4] "disturb the classical economy of language and representation." Without relations of difference, no representation could occur. But what is then constituted within representation is always open to being deferred, staggered, serialised.

Where, then, does identity come in to this infinite postponement of meaning? Derrida does not help us as much as he might here, though the notion of the "trace" goes some way towards it. This is where it sometimes seems as if Derrida has permitted his profound theoretical insights to be reappropriated by his disciples into a celebration of formal "playfulness," which evacuates them of their political meaning. For if signification depends upon the endless repositioning of its differential terms, meaning, in any specific instance, depends on the contingent and arbitrary stop—the necessary and temporary "break" in the infinite semiosis of language. This does not detract from the original insight. It only threatened to do so if we mistake this "cut" of identity—this *positioning,* which makes meaning possible—as a natural and permanent, rather than an arbitrary and contingent "ending"—whereas I understand every such position as "strategic" and arbitrary, in the sense that there is no permanent equivalence between the particular sentence we close, and its true meaning, as such. Meaning continues to unfold, so to speak, beyond the arbitrary closure which makes it, at any moment, possible. It is always either over- or under-determined, either an excess or a supplement. There is always something "left over."

It is possible, with this conception of "difference," to rethink the positioning and repositioning of Caribbean culture identities in relation to at least three "presences," to borrow Aimé Césaire's and Léopold Senghor's metaphor: *Présence Africaine, Présence Européenne,* and the third, most ambiguous, presence of all—the sliding term, *Présence Americaine.* Of course, I am collapsing, for the moment, the many other cultural "presences" which constitute the complexity of Caribbean identity (Indian, Chinese, Lebanese, etc). I mean America, here, not in its "first-world" sense—the big cousin to the North whose "rim" we occupy, but in the second, broader sense: America, the "New World," *Terra Incognita.*

Présence Africaine is the site of the repressed. Apparently silenced beyond memory by the experience of slavery, Africa was, in fact, present everywhere: in the everyday life and customs of the slave quarters, in the languages and patois of the plantations, in names and words, often disconnected from their taxonomies, in the secret syntactical structures through which other languages were spoken, in the stories and tales told to children, in religious practices and beliefs in the spiritual life, the arts, crafts, musics and rhythms of slave and post-emancipation society. Africa, the signified which could not be represented directly in slavery, remained and remains the unspoken unspeakable "presence" in Caribbean culture. It is "hiding" behind every verbal inflection, every narrative twist of Caribbean cultural life. It is the secret code with which every Western text was "re-read." It is the ground bass of every rhythm and bodily movement. *This* was—is—the "Africa" that "is alive and well in the diaspora."[5]

When I was growing up in the 1940s and 1950s as a child in Kingston, I was surrounded by the signs, music and rhythms of this Africa of the diaspora, which only existed as a result of a long and discontinuous series of transformations. But, although almost everyone around me was some shade of brown or black (Africa "speaks"!), I never once heard a single person refer to themselves or to others as, in some way, or as having been at some time in the past, "African." It was only in the 1970s that this Afro-Caribbean identity became historically available to the great majority of Jamaican people, at home and abroad. In this historic moment, Jamaicans discovered themselves to be "black"—just as, in the same moment, they discovered themselves to be the sons and daughters of "slavery."

This profound cultural discovery, however, was not, and could not be, made directly, without "mediation." It could only be made *through* the impact on popular life of the post-colonial revolution, the civil rights struggles, the culture of Rastafarianism and the music of reggae—the metaphors, the figures or signifiers of a new construction of "Jamaican-ness." These signified a "new" Africa of the New World, grounded in an "old" Africa: a spiritual journey of discovery that led, in the Caribbean, to an indigenous cultural revolution; this is Africa, as we might say, necessarily "deferred"—as a spiritual, cultural and political metaphor.

It is the presence/absence of Africa, in this form, which has made it the privileged signifier of new conceptions of Caribbean identity. Everyone in the Caribbean, of whatever ethnic background, must sooner or later come to terms with this African presence. Black, brown, mulatto, white—all must look *Présence Africaine* in the face, speak its name. But whether it is, in this sense, an *origin* of our identities, unchanged by four hundred years of displacement, dismemberment, transportation, to which we could in any final or literal sense return, is more open to doubt. The original "Africa" is no longer there. It too has been transformed. History is, in that sense, irreversible. We must not collude with the West which, precisely, normalises and appropriates Africa by freezing it into some timeless zone of the primitive, unchanging past. Africa must at last be reckoned with by Caribbean people, but it cannot in any simple sense be merely recovered.

It belongs irrevocably, for us, to what Edward Said once called an "imaginative geography and history,"[6] which helps "the mind to intensify its own sense of itself by dramatising the difference between what is close to it and what is far away." It "has acquired an imaginative or figurative value we can name and feel."[7] Our belongingness to it constitutes what Benedict Anderson calls "an imagined community."[8] To *this* "Africa," which is a necessary part of the Caribbean imaginary, we can't literally go home again.

The character of this displaced "homeward" journey—its length and complexity—comes across vividly, in a variety of texts. Tony Sewell's documentary archival photographs, "Garvey's Children: the Legacy of Marcus Garvey" tell the story of a "return" to an African identity which went, necessarily, by the long route through London and the United States. It "ends," not in Ethiopia but with Garvey's statue in front of the St. Ann Parish Library in Jamaica: not with a traditional tribal chant but with the music of Burning Spear and Bob Marley's "Redemption Song." This is our "long journey" home. Derek Bishton's courageous visual and written text, *Black Heart Man*—the story of the journey of a *white* photographer "on the trail of the promised land"—starts in England, and goes, through Shashemene, the place in Ethiopia to which many Jamaican people have found their way on their search for the Promised Land, and slavery; but it ends in Pinnacle, Jamaica, where the first Rastafarian settlements were established, and "beyond"—among the dispossessed of 20th-century Kingston and the streets of Handsworth, where Bishton's voyage of discovery first began. These symbolic journeys are necessary for us all—and necessarily circular. This is the Africa we must return to—but "by another route": what Africa has *become* in the New World what we have made of "Africa": "Africa"—as we re-tell it through politics, memory and desire.

What of the second, troubling, term in the identity equation—the European presence? For many of us, this is a matter not of too little but of too much. Where Africa was a case of the unspoken, Europe was a case of that which is endlessly speaking—and endlessly speaking *us*. The European presence interrupts the innocence of the whole discourse of "difference" in the Caribbean by introducing the question of power. "Europe" belongs irrevocably to the "play" of power, to the lines of force and consent, to the role of the *dominant,* in Caribbean culture. In terms of colonialism, underdevelopment, poverty and the racism of colour, the European presence is that which, in visual representation, has positioned the black subject within its dominant regimes of representation: the colonial discourse, the literatures of adventure and exploration, the romance of the exotic, the ethnographic and travelling eye, the tropical languages of tourism, travel brochure and Hollywood and the violent, pornographic languages of *ganja* and urban violence.

Because *Présence Européenne* is about exclusion, imposition and expropriation, we are often tempted to locate that power as wholly external to us— an extrinsic force, whose influence can be thrown off like the serpent sheds its skin. What Franz Fanon reminds us, in *Black Skin, White Masks,* is how this power has become a constitutive element in our own identities.

> The movements, the attitudes, the glances of the other fixed me there in the sense in which a chemical solution is fixed by a dye. I was indignant; I demanded an explanation. Nothing happened. I burst apart. Now the fragments have been put together again by another self.[9]

This "look," from—so to speak—the place of the Other, fixes us, not only in its violence, hostility and aggression, but in the ambivalence of its desire. This brings us face to face with the dominating European presence not simply as the site or "scene" of integration where those other presences which it had actively disaggregated were recomposed—re-framed, put together in a new way; but as the site of a profound splitting and doubling—what Homi Bhabha has called "this ambivalent identification of the racist world ... the "Otherness" of the Self inscribed in the perverse palimpsest of colonial identity."[10]

The dialogue of power and resistance, of refusal and recognition, with and against *Présence Européenne* is almost as complex as the "dialogue" with Africa. In terms of popular cultural life, it is nowhere to be found in its pure, pristine state. It is always-already fused, syncretised, with other cultural elements. It is always-already creolised—not lost beyond the Middle Passage, but ever-present: from the harmonics in our musics to the ground-bass of Africa, traversing and intersecting our lives at every point. How can we stage this dialogue so that, finally, we can place it, without terror or violence, rather than being forever placed by it? Can we ever recognise its irreversible influence, whilst resisting its imperialising eye? The enigma is impossible, so far, to resolve. It requires the most complex of cultural strategies. Think, for example, of the dialogue of every Caribbean filmmaker or writer, one way or another, with the dominant cinemas and literature of the West—the complex relationship of young black British filmmakers with the "avant-gardes" of European and American film making. Who could describe this tense and tortured dialogue as a "one way trip"?

The Third, "New World" presence, is not so much power, as ground, place, territory. It is the juncture-point where the many cultural tributaries meet, the "empty" land (the European colonisers emptied it) where strangers from every other part of the globe collided. None of the people who now occupy the islands—black, brown, white, African, European, American, Spanish, French, East Indian, Chinese, Portuguese, Jew, Dutch—originally "belonged" there. It is the space where the creolisations and assimilations and syncretisms were negotiated. The New World is the third term—the primal scene—where the fateful/fatal encounter was staged between Africa and the West. It also has to be understood as the place of many, continuous displacements: of the original pre-Columbian inhabitants, the Arawaks, Caribs and Amerindians, permanently displaced from their homelands and decimated; of other peoples displaced in different ways from Africa, Asia and Europe; the displacements of slavery, colonisation and conquest. It stands for the endless ways in which Caribbean people have been destined to "migrate"; it is the signifier of migration itself— travelling, voyaging and return as fate, as destiny; of the Antillean as the pro- totype of the modern or postmodern New World nomad, continually moving between centre and periphery. This preoccupation with movement and migra- tion Caribbean cinema shares with many other "Third Cinemas," but it is one of our defining themes, and it is destined to cross the narrative of every film script or cinematic image.

Présence Americaine continues to have its silences, its suppressions. Peter Hulme, in his essay on "Islands of enchantment"[11] reminds us that the word "Jamaica" is the Hispanic form of the indigenous Arawak name—"land of wood and water"—which Columbus's renaming ("Santiago") never replaced. The Arawak presence remains today a ghostly one, visible in the islands main- ly in museums and archeological sites, part of the barely knowable or usable "past." Hulme notes that it is not represented in the emblem of the Jamaican National Heritage Trust, for example, which chose instead the figure of Diego Pimienta, "an African who fought for his Spanish masters against the English invasion of the island in 1655"—a deferred, metonymic, sly and sliding repre- sentation of Jamaican identity if ever there was one! He recounts the story of how Prime Minister Edward Seaga tried to alter the Jamaican coat-of-arms, which consists of two Arawak figures holding a shield with five pineapples, surmounted by an alligator. "Can the crushed and extinct Arawaks represent the dauntless character of Jamaicans. Does the low-slung, near extinct crocodile, a cold-blooded reptile, symbolise the warm, soaring spirit of Jamaicans?" Prime Minister Seaga asked rhetorically.[12] There can be few political statements which so eloquently testify to the complexities entailed in the process of trying to represent a diverse people with a diverse history through a single, hegemon- ic "identity." Fortunately, Mr Seaga's invitation to the Jamaican people, who are overwhelmingly of African descent, to start their "remembering" by first "forgetting" something else, got the comeuppance it so richly deserved.

The "New World" presence—America, *Terra Incognita*—is therefore itself the beginning of diaspora, of diversity, of hybridity and difference, what makes Afro-Caribbean people already people of a diaspora. I use this term here metaphorically, not literally: diaspora does not refer us to those scattered tribes whose identity can only be secured in relation to some sacred homeland to which they must at all costs return, even if it means pushing other people into the sea. This is the old, the imperialising, the hegemonising, form of "ethnici- ty." We have seen the fate of the people of Palestine at the hands of this back- ward-looking conception of diaspora—and the complicity of the West with it. The diaspora experience as I intend it here is defined, not by essence or purity, but by the recognition of a necessary heterogeneity and diversity; by a conception of "identity" which lives with and through, not despite, difference; by *hybridity*. Diaspora identities are those which are constantly producing and reproducing themselves anew, through transformation and difference. One can only think here of what is uniquely—"essentially"—Caribbean: precisely the mixes of colour, pigmentation, physiognomic type; the "blends" of tastes that is Caribbean cuisine; the aesthetics of the "cross-overs," of "cut-and-mix," to borrow Dick Hebdige's telling phrase, which is the heart and soul of black music. Young black cultural practitioners and critics in Britain are increasingly coming to acknowledge and explore in their work this "diaspora aesthetic" and its formations in the post-colonial experience:

> Across a whole range of cultural forms there is a "syncretic" dynamic which critically appropriates elements from the master-codes of the dominant culture and "creolises" them, disarticulating given signs and re-articulating their symbolic meaning. The subversive force of this hybridising tendency is most apparent at the level of language itself where Creoles, patois and black English decentre, destabilise and cannibalise the linguistic damnation of "English"—the nation-language of master-discourse—through strategic inflections, re-accentuations and other performative moves in semantic, syntactic and lexical codes.[13]

It is because this New World is constituted for us as place, a narrative of displacement, that it gives rise so profoundly to a certain imaginary plentitude, recreating the endless desire to return to "lost origins," to be one again with the mother, to go back to the beginning. Who can ever forget, when once seen rising up out of that blue-green Caribbean, those islands of enchantment. Who has not known, at this moment, the surge of an overwhelming nostalgia for lost origins, for "times past"? And yet, this "return to the beginning" is like the imaginary in Lacan—it can neither be fulfilled nor requited, and hence is the beginning of the symbolic, of representation, the infinitely renewable source of desire, memory, myth, search, discovery—in short, the reservoir of our cinematic narratives.

We have been trying, in a series of metaphors, to put in play a different sense of our relationship to the past, and thus a different way of thinking about cultural identity, which might constitute new points of recognition in the discourses of the emerging Caribbean cinema and black British cinemas. We have been trying to theorise identity as constituted, not outside but within representation; and hence of cinema, not as a second-order mirror held up to reflect what already exists, but as that form of representation which is able to constitute us as new kinds of subjects, and thereby enable us to discover places from which to speak. Communities, Benedict Anderson argues in *Imagined Communities,* are to be distinguished, not by their falsity/genuineness, but by the style in which they are imagined.[14] This is the vocation of modern black cinemas: by allowing us to see and recognise the different parts and histories of ourselves, to construct those points of identification, those positionalities we call in retrospect our "cultural identities."

We must not therefore be content with delving into the past of a people in order to find coherent elements which will counteract colonialism's attempts to falsify and harm.... A national culture is not a folk-lore, nor an abstract populism that believes it can discover a people's true nature. A national culture is the whole body of efforts made by a people in the sphere of thought to describe, justify and praise the action through which that people has created itself and keeps it self in existence.[15]

Notes

1. Frantz Fanon, "On national culture," in *The Wretched of the Earth,* London, 1963, p. 170.
2. *Ibid.,* p. 176.
3. Christopher Norris, *Deconstruction: Theory and Practice,* London, 1982, p. 32.
4. *Idem, Jacques Derrida,* London, 1987, p. 15.
5. Stuart Hall, *Resistance Through Rituals,* London, 1976.
6. Edward Said, *Orientalism,* London, 1985, p. 55.
7. *Ibid.*
8. Benedict Anderson, *Imagined Communities: Reflections on the origin and rise of nationalism,* London, 1982.
9. Frantz Fanon, *Black Skin, White Masks,* London, 1986, p. 109.
10. Homi Bhabha, "Foreword" to Fanon, *ibid.,* pp. xiv-xv.
11. In *New Formations,* 3, Winter 1987.
12. *Jamaica Hansard,* 9, 1983-4, p. 363. Quoted in Hulme, *ibid.*
13. Kobena Mercer, "Diaspora culture and the dialogic imagination," in M. Cham and C. Watkins (eds), *Blackframes: Critical perspectives on black independent cinema,* 1988, p. 57.
14. Anderson, op. cit., p. 15.
15. Fanon, *Black Skin, White Masks,* p. 188.

42

ARJUN APPADURAI (1949-)

Many people now speak easily and constantly of globalization, but Arjun Appadurai's essay points to the complexities behind this term. He helps us to understand many components of the process and addresses issues raised by social theorists starting with Marx.

Appadurai points out that different spheres of activity are globalized in different ways and at different rates. He indentifies five distinct flows across national boundaries: ethnoscapes (people); mediascapes (media); technoscapes (technologies); finanscapes (capital; investments); and ideoscapes (political ideologies such as human rights, democracy, and nationalism). These flows are not co-ordinated with each other and do not move in the same ways or at the same rate. Many nations make an effort to block out one or another of them; for example, nations may welcome new technologies but attempt to block foreign investment, immigrants, or troublesome ideologies.

Appadurai challenges the notion that globalization is simply a process of cultural imperialism, westernization, or Americanization. The flows are not all from a single westernized or American centre to the periphery, nor are they transmitted in a one-way process of imposition; there are counterflows and regional reinterpretations of culture, as well as regional and local centres. The charting of these counterflows and local eddies is a challenge to world systems theory and its emphasis on centre and periphery; indeed in recent years, Wallerstein has become increasingly interested in local and particularistic opposition to the culture of the centre, the most powerful and developed capitalist nations.

Overall the flows create deterritorialization, a term that is similar to Giddens's "disembedding" of processes from spatial locations. Deterritorialization is one of the processes that weakens the nation-state because people, cultures, and markets cut across state borders.

The essay clarifies and updates Marx's comments on the formation of a world culture. Appadurai also elaborates as well as challenges Wallerstein and the world systems model; on the one hand, he provides further insight into Wallerstein's comments about how resilient capitalism is precisely because states, markets, and cultures/societies and peoples are not rigidly linked. On the other hand, he challenges Wallerstein's view of the dominance of the developed and mostly western centre; in the past, the centre may indeed have been dominant over the periphery and was the source of social change, but the relationship is no longer so one-sided. The reader will also note convergences between Appadurai's conception and McLuhan's notion of the global village and the media's impact on national identities. Appadurai's work fits together with Stuart Hall's essay on identity and diaspora (one type of deterritorialization). These new currents of social theory analyze cultural meanings in the global age and connect them to new media and technologies.

Readings

Appadurai, Arjun. *Modernity at Large: Cultural Dimensions of Globalization.* Minneapolis: University of Minnesota Press, 1996.

Appadurai, Arjun (ed). *The Social Life of Things: Commodities in Cultural Perspective.* New York: Cambridge University Press, 1988.

Sassen, Saskia. *Globalization and Its Discontents: Essays on the New Mobility of People and Money.* New York: New Press, 1998.

Disjuncture and Difference in the Global Cultural Economy
ARJUN APPADURAI

The central problem of today's global interactions is the tension between cultural homogenization and cultural heterogenization. A vast array of empirical facts could be brought to bear on the side of the "homogenization" argument, and much of it has come from the left end of the spectrum of media studies (Hamelink, 1983; Mattelart, 1983; Schiller, 1976), and some from other, less appealing, perspectives (Gans, 1985; Iyer, 1988). Most often, the homogenization argument subspeciates into either an argument about Americanization, or an argument about "commoditization," and very often the two arguments are closely linked. What these arguments fail to consider is that at least as rapidly as forces from various metropolises are brought into new societies they tend to become indigenized on one or other way: this is true of music and housing styles as much as it is true of science and terrorism, spectacles and constitutions. The dynamics of such indigenization have just begun to be explored in a sophisticated manner (Barber, 1987; Feld, 1988; Hannerz, 1987, 1989; Ivy, 1988; Nicoll, 1989; Yoshimoto, 1989), and much more needs to be done. But it is worth noticing that for the people of Irian Jaya, Indonesianization may be more worrisome than Americanization, as Japanization may be for Koreans, Indianization for Sri Lankans, Vietnamization for the Cambodians, Russianization for the people of Soviet Armenia and the Baltic Republics. Such a list of alternative fears to Americanization could be greatly expanded, but it is not a shapeless inventory: for polities of smaller scale, there is always a fear of cultural absorption by polities of larger scale, especially those that are near by. One man's imagined community (Anderson, 1983) is another man's political prison.

This scalar dynamic, which has widespread global manifestations, is also tied to the relationship between nations and states, to which I shall return later in this essay. For the moment let us note that the simplification of these many forces (and fears) of homogenization can also be exploited by nation-states in relation to their own minorities, by posing global commoditization (or capitalism, or some other such external enemy) as more "real" than the threat of its own hegemonic strategies.

The new global cultural economy has to be understood as a complex, overlapping, disjunctive order, which cannot any longer be understood in terms of existing center-periphery models (even those that might account for multiple centers and peripheries). Nor is it susceptible to simple models of push and pull (in terms of migration theory) or of surpluses and deficits (as in traditional models of balance of trade), or of consumers and producers (as in most neo-Marxist theories of development). Even the most complex and flexible theories of global development which have come out of the Marxist tradition (Amin, 1980; Mandel, 1978; Wallerstein, 1974; Wolf, 1982) are inadequately quirky, and they have not come to terms with what Lash and Urry (1987) have recently called "disorganized capitalism." The complexity of the current global economy has to do with certain fundamental disjunctures between economy, culture and politics which we have barely begun to theorize.[1]

I propose that an elementary framework for exploring such disjunctures is to look at the relationship between five dimensions of global cultural flow which can be termed: (a) ethnoscapes; (b) mediascapes; (c) technoscapes; (d) finanscapes; and (e) ideoscapes.[2] I use terms with the common suffix scape to indicate first of all that these are not objectively given relations which look the same from every angle of vision, but rather that they are deeply perspectival constructs, inflected very much by the historical, linguistic and political situatedness of different sorts of actors: nation-states, multinationals, diasporic communities, as well as sub-national groupings and movements (whether religious, political or economic), and even intimate face-to-face groups, such as villages, neighbourhoods and families. Indeed, the individual actor is the last locus of this perspectival set of landscapes, for these landscapes are eventually navigated by agents who both experience and constitute larger formations, in part by their own sense of what these landscapes offer. These landscapes thus, are the building blocks of what, extending Benedict Anderson, I would like to call "imagined worlds," that is, the multiple worlds which are constituted by the historically situated imaginations of persons and groups spread around the globe (Appadurai, 1989). An important fact of the world we live in today is that many persons on the globe live in such imagined "worlds" and not just in imagined communities, and thus are able to contest and sometimes even subvert the "imagined worlds" of the official mind and of the entrepreneurial mentality that surround them. The suffix scape also allows up to point to the fluid, irregular shapes of these landscapes, shapes which characterize international capital as deeply as they do international clothing styles.

By "ethnoscape," I mean the landscape of persons who constitute the shifting world in which we live: tourists, immigrants, refugees, exiles, guestworkers and other moving groups and persons constitute an essential feature of the world, and appear to affect the politics of and between nations to a hitherto unprecedented degree. This is not to say that there are not anywhere relatively stable communities and networks, of kinship, of friendship, of work and of leisure, as well as of birth, residence and other filiative forms. But it is to say that the warp of these stabilities is everywhere shot through with the woof of human motion, as more persons and groups deal with the realities of having to move, or the fantasies of wanting to move. What is more, both these realities as well as these fantasies now function on larger scales, as men and women from villages in India think not just of moving to Poona or Madras, but of moving to Dubai and Houston, and refugees from Sri Lanka find themselves in South India as well as in Canada, just as the Hmong are driven to London as well as to Philadelphia. And as international capital shifts its needs, as production and technology generate different needs, as nation-states shift their policies on refugee populations, these moving groups can never afford to let their imagination rest too long, even if they wished to.

By "technoscape," I mean the global configuration, also ever fluid, of technology, and of the fact that technology, both high and low, both mechanical and informational, now moves at high speeds across various kinds of previously impervious boundaries. Many countries now are the roots of multinational enterprise: a huge steel complex in Libya may involve interests from India, China, Russia and Japan, providing different components of new technological configurations. The odd distribution of technologies, and thus the peculiarities of these technoscapes, are increasingly driven not by any obvious economies of scale, of political control, or of market rationality, but of increasingly complex relationships between money flows, political possibilities and the availability of both low and highly-skilled labor. So, while India exports waiters and chauffers to Dubai and Sharjah, it also exports software engineers to the United

States (indentured briefly to Tata-Burroughs or the World Bank), then laundered through the State Department to become wealthy "resident aliens," who are in turn objects for seductive messages to invest their money and know-how in federal and state projects in India. The global economy can still be described in terms of traditional "indicators" (as the World Bank continues to do) and studied in terms of traditional comparisons (as in Project Link at the University of Pennsylvania), but the complicated technoscapes (and the shifting ethnoscapes), which underlie these "indicators" and "comparisons" are further out of the reach of the "queen of the social sciences" than ever before. How is one to make a meaningful comparison of wages in Japan and the United States, or of real estate costs in New York and Tokyo, without taking sophisticated account of the very complex fiscal and investment flows that link the two economies through a global grid of currency speculation and capital transfer?

Thus it is useful to speak as well of "finanscapes," since the disposition of global capital is now a more mysterious, rapid and difficult landscape to follow than ever before, as currency markets, national stock exchanges, and commodity speculations move megamonies through national turnstiles at blinding speed, with vast absolute implications of small differences in percentage points and time unites. But the critical point is that the global relationship between ethnoscapes, technoscapes and finanscapes is deeply disjunctive and profoundly unpredictable, since each of these landscapes is subject to its own constraints and incentives (some political, some informational and some techno-environmental), at the same time as each acts as a constraint and a parameter for movements in the other. Thus, even an elementary model of global political economy must take into account the shifting relationship between perspectives on human movement, technological flow, and financial transfers, which can accommodate their deeply disjunctive relationships with one another.

Built upon these disjunctures (which hardly form a simple, mechanical global "infrastructure" in any case) are what I have called "mediascapes" and "ideoscapes," though the latter two are closely related landscapes of images. "Mediascapes" refer both to the distribution of the electronic capabilities to produce and disseminate information (newspapers, magazines, television stations, film production studios, etc.), which are now available to a growing number of private and public interests throughout the world; and to the images of the world created by these media. These images of the world involve many complicated inflections, depending on their mode (documentary or entertainment), their hardware (electronic or pre-electronic), their audiences (local, national or transnational) and the interests of those who own and control them. What is most important about these mediascapes is that they provide (especially in their television, film and cassette forms) large and complex repertoires of images, narratives and "ethnoscapes" to viewers throughout the world, in which the world of commodities and the world of "news" and politics are profoundly mixed. What this means is that many audiences throughout the world experience the media themselves as a complicated and interconnected repertoire of print, celluloid, electronic screens and billboards. The lines between the "realistic" and the fictional landscapes they see are blurred, so that the further away these audiences are from the direct experiences of metropolitan life, the more likely they are to construct "imagined worlds" which are chimerical, aesthetic, even fantastic objects, particularly if assessed by the criteria of some other perspective, some other "imagined world."

"Mediascapes," whether produced by private or state interests, tend to be image-centered, narrative-based accounts of strips of reality, and what they offer to those who experience and transform them is a series of elements (such as characters, plots and textual forms) out of which scripts can be formed of imagined lives, their own as well as those of others living in other places. These scripts can and do get disaggregated into complex sets of metaphors by which people live (Lakoff and Johnson, 1980) as they help to constitute narratives of the "other" and proto-narratives of possible lives, fantasies which could become prologemena to the desire for acquisition and movement.

"Ideoscapes" are also concatenations of images, but they are often directly political and frequently have to do with the ideologies of states and the counter-ideologies of movements explicitly oriented to capturing state power or a piece of it. These ideoscapes are composed of elements of the Enlightenment worldview, which consists of a concatenation of ideas, terms and images, including "freedom," "welfare," "rights," "sovereignty," "representation" and the master-term "democracy." The master-narrative of the Enlightenment (and its many variants in England, France and the United States) was constructed with a certain internal logic and presupposed a certain relationship between reading, representation and the public sphere (for the dynamics of this process in the early history of the United States, see Warner, 1990). But their diaspora across the world, especially since the nineteenth century, has loosened the internal coherence which held these terms and images together in a Euro-American master-narrative, and provided instead a loosely structured synopticon of politics, in which different nation-states, as part of their evolution, have organized their political cultures around different "keywords" (Williams, 1976).

As a result of the differential diaspora of these keywords, the political narratives that govern communication between elites and followings in different parts of the world involve problems of both a semantic and a pragmatic nature: semantic to the extent that words (and their lexical equivalents) require careful translation from context to context in their global movements; and pragmatic to the extent that the use of these words by political actors and their audiences may be subject to very different sets of contextual conventions that mediate their translation into public politics. Such conventions are not only matters of the nature of political rhetoric (viz. what does the aging Chinese leadership mean when it refers to the dangers of hooliganism? What does the South Korean leadership mean when it speaks of "discipline" as the key to democratic industrial growth?).

These conventions also involve the far more subtle question of what sets of communicative genres are valued in what way (newspapers versus cinema for example) and what sorts of pragmatic genre conventions govern the collective "readings" of different kinds of text. So, while an Indian audience may be attentive to the resonances of a political speech in terms of some key words and phrases reminiscent of Hindi cinema, a Korean audience may respond to the subtle codings of Buddhist or neo-Confucian rhetorical strategy encoded in a political document. The very relationship of reading to hearing and seeing may vary in important ways that determine the morphology of these different "ideoscapes" as they shape themselves in different national and transnational contexts. This globally variable synaesthesia has hardly even been noted, but it demands urgent analysis. Thus "democracy" has clearly become a master-term, with powerful echoes from Haiti and Poland to the Soviet Union and China, but it sits at the center of a variety of ideoscapes (composed of distinctive pragmatic configurations of rough "translations" of other central terms from the vocabulary of the Enlightenment). This creates ever new terminological kaleidoscopes, as states (and the groups that seek to capture them) seek to pacify populations whose own ethnoscapes are in motion, and whose mediascapes may create severe problems for the ideoscapes with which they are presented. The fluidity of ideoscapes is complicated in particular by the growing diasporas (both voluntary and involuntary) of intellectuals who continuously inject new meaning-streams into the discourse of democracy in different parts of the world.

This extended terminological discussion of the five terms I have coined sets the basis for a tentative formulation about the conditions under which current global flows occur: *they occur in and through the growing disjunctures between ethnoscapes, technoscapes, finanscapes, mediascapes and ideoscapes.* This formulation, the core of my model of global cultural flow, needs some explanation. First, people, machinery, money, images, and ideas now follow increasingly non-isomorphic paths: of course, at all periods in human history, there have been some disjunctures between the flows of these things, but the sheer speed, scale and volume of each of these flows is now so great that the disjunctures have become central to the politics of global culture. The Japanese are notoriously hospitable to ideas and are stereotyped as inclined to export (all) and import (some) goods, but they are also notoriously closed to immigration, like the Swiss, the Swedes and the Saudis. Yet the Swiss and Saudis accept populations of guestworkers, thus creating labor diasporas of Turks, Italians and other circum-mediterranean groups. Some such guestworker groups maintain continuous contact with their home-nations, like the Turks, but others, like high-level South Asian migrants tend to desire lives in their new homes, raising anew the problem of reproduction in a deterritorialized context.

Deterritorialization, in general, is one of the central forces of the modern world, since it brings laboring populations into the lower class sectors and spaces of relatively wealthy societies, while sometimes creating exaggerated and intensified senses of criticism or attachment to politics in the home-state. Deterritorialization, whether of Hindus, Sikhs, Palestinians or Ukranians, is now at the core of a variety of global fundamentalisms, including Islamic and Hindu fundamentalism. In the Hindu case for example (Appadurai and Breckenridge, forthcoming) it is clear that the overseas movement of Indians has been exploited by a variety of interests both within and outside India to create a complicated network of finances and religious identifications, in which the problems of cultural reproduction for Hindus abroad has become tied to the politics of Hindu fundamentalism at home.

At the same time, deterritorialization creates new markets for film companies, art impressarios and travel agencies, who thrive on the need of the deterritorialized population for contact with its homeland. Naturally, these invented homelands, which constitute the mediascapes of deterritorialized groups, can often become sufficiently fantastic and one-sided that they provide the material for new ideoscapes in which ethnic conflicts can begin to erupt. The creation of "Khalistan," an invented homeland of the deterritorialized Sikh population of England, Canada and the United States, is one example of the bloody potential in such mediascapes, as they interact with the "internal colonialism" (Hechter, 1974) of the nation-state. The West Bank, Namibia and Eritrea are other theaters for the enactment of the bloody negotiation between existing nation-states and various deterritorialized groupings.

The idea of deterritorialization may also be applied to money and finance, as money managers seek the best markets for their investments, independent of national boundaries. In turn, these movements of monies are the basis of new kinds of conflict, as Los Angelenos worry about the Japanese buying up their city, and people in Bombay worry about the rich Arabs from the Gulf States who have not only transformed the prices of mangoes in Bombay, but have also substantially altered the profile of hotels, restaurants and other services in the eyes of the local population, just as they continue to do in London. Yet, most residents of Bombay are ambivalent about the Arab presence there, for the flip side of their presence is the absence of friends and kinsmen earning big money in the Middle East and bringing back both money and luxury commodities to Bombay and other cities in India. Such commodities transform consumer taste in these cities, and also often end up smuggled through air and sea ports and peddled in the gray markets of Bombay's streets. In these gray markets, some members of Bombay's middle-classes and of its lumpenproletariat can buy some of these goods, ranging from cartons of Marlboro cigarettes, to Old Spice shaving cream and tapes of Madonna. Similarly gray routes, often subsidized by the moonlighting activities of sailors, diplomats, and airline stewardesses who get to move in and out of the country regularly, keep the gray markets of Bombay, Madras and Calcutta filled with goods not only from the West, but also from the Middle East, Hong Kong and Singapore.

It is this fertile ground of deterritorialization, in which money, commodities and persons are involved in ceaselessly chasing each other around the world, that the mediascapes and ideoscapes of the modern world find their fractured and fragmented counterpart. For the ideas and images produced by mass media often are only partial to the goods and experiences that deterritorialized populations transfer to one another. In Mira Nair's brilliant film, *India Cabaret*, we see the multiple loops of this fractured deterritorialization as young women, barely competent in Bombay's metropolitan glitz, come to seek their fortunes as cabaret dancers and prostitutes in Bombay, entertaining men in clubs with dance formats derived wholly from the prurient dance sequences of Hindi films. These scenes cater in turn to ideas about Western and foreign women and their "looseness", while they provide tawdry career alibis for these women. Some of these women come from Kerala, where cabaret clubs and the pornographic film industry have blossomed, partly in response to the purses and tastes of Keralites returned from the Middle East, where their diasporic lives away from women distort their very sense of what the relations between men and women might be. These tragedies of displacement could certainly be replayed in a more detailed analysis of the relations between the Japanese and German sex tours to Thailand and the tragedies of the sex trade in Bangkok, and in other similar loops which tie together fantasies about the other, the conveniences and seductions of travel, the economics of global trade and the brutal mobility fantasies that dominate gender politics in many parts of Asia and the world at large.

While far more could be said about the cultural politics of deterritorialization and the larger sociology of displacement that it expresses, it is appropriate at this juncture to bring in the role of the nation-state in the disjunctive global economy of culture today. The relationship between states and nations is everywhere an embattled one. It is possible to say that in many societies, the nation and the state have become one another's projects. That is, while nations (or more properly groups with ideas about nationhood) seek to capture or co-opt states and state power, states simultaneously seek to capture and monopolize ideas about nationhood (Baruah, 1986; Chatterjee, 1986; Nandy, 1989). In general separatist, transnational movements, including those which have included terror in their methods, exemplify nations in search of states: Sikhs, Tamil Sri Lankans, Basques, Moros, Quebecois, each of these represent imagined communities which seek to create states of their own or carve pieces out of existing states. States, on the other hand, are everywhere seeking to monopolize the moral resources of community, either by flatly claiming perfect coevality between nation and state, or by systematically museumizing and representing all the groups within them in a variety of heritage politics that seems remarkably uniform throughout the world (Handler, 1988; Herzfeld, 1982; McQueen, 1988). Here, national and international mediascapes are exploited by nation-states to pacify separatists or even the potential fissiparousness of all ideas of difference. Typically, contemporary nation-states do this by exercising taxonomical control over difference; by creating various kinds of international spectacle to domesticate difference; and by seducing small groups with fantasy of self-display on some sort of global or cosmopolitan stage. One important new feature of global cultural politics, tied to the disjunctive relationships between the various landscapes discussed earlier, is that state and nation are at each's throats, and the hyphen that links them is now less an icon of conjuncture than an index of disjuncture. This disjunctive relationship between nation and state has two levels: at the level of any given nation-state, it means that there is a battle of the imagination, with state and nation seeking to cannibalize one another. Here is the seedbed of brutal separatisms, majoritarianisms that seem to have appeared from nowhere, and micro-identities that have become political projects within the nation-state. At another level, this disjunctive relationship is deeply entangled with the global disjunctures discussed throughout this essay: ideas of nationhood appear to be steadily increasing in scale and regularly crossing existing state boundaries: sometimes, as with the Kurds, because previous identities stretched across vast national spaces, or, as with the Tamils in Sri Lanka, the dormant threads of a transnational diaspora have been activated to ignite the micro-politics of a nation-state.

In discussing the cultural politics that have subverted the hyphen that links the nation to the state, it is especially important not to forget its mooring in the irregularities that now characterize "disorganized capital" (Lash and Urry, 1987; Kothari, 1989). It is because labor, finance and technology are now so widely separated that the volatilities that underlie movements for nationhood (as large as transnational Islam on the one hand, or as small as the movement of the Gurkhas for a separate state in the North-East of India) grind against the vulnerabilities which characterize the relationships between state. States find themselves pressed to stay "open" by the forces of media, technology and travel which had fueled consumerism throughout the world and have increased the craving, even in the non-Western world, for new commodities and spectacles.

On the other hand, these very cravings can become caught up in new ethnoscapes, mediascapes, and eventually, ideoscapes, such as "democracy" in China, that the state cannot tolerate as threats to its own control over ideas of nationhood and "peoplehood." States throughout the world are under siege, especially where contests over the ideoscapes of democracy are fierce and fundamental, and where there are radical disjunctures between ideoscapes and technoscapes (as in the case of very small countries that lack contemporary technologies of production and information); or between ideoscapes and finanscapes (as in countries, such as Mexico or Brazil where international lending influences national politics to a very large degree); or between ideoscapes and ethnoscapes (as in Beirut, where diasporic, local and translocal filiations are suicidally at battle); or between ideoscapes and mediascapes (as in many countries in the Middle East and Asia) where the lifestyles represented on both national and international TV and cinema completely overwhelm and undermine the rhetoric of national politics: in the Indian case, the myth of the law-breaking hero has emerged to mediate this naked struggle between the pieties and the realities of Indian politics, which has grown increasingly brutalized and corrupt (Vachani, 1989).

The transnational movement of the martial-arts, particularly through Asia, as mediated by the Hollywood and Hongkong film industries (Zarilli, forthcoming) is a rich illustration of the ways in which long-standing martial arts traditions, reformulated to meet the fantasies of contemporary (sometimes lumpen) youth populations, create new cultures of masculinity and violence, which are in turn the fuel for increased violence in national and international politics. Such violence is in turn the spur to an increasingly rapid and amoral arms trade which penetrates the entire world. The worldwide spread of the AK-47 and the Uzi, in films, in corporate and state security, in terror, and in police and military activity, is a reminder that apparently simple technical uniformities often conceal an increasingly complex set of loops, linking images of violence to aspirations for community in some "imagined world."

Returning then to the "ethnoscapes" with which I began, the central paradox of ethnic politics in today's world is that primordia, (whether of language of skin color of neighborhood or of kinship) have become globalized. That is, sentiments whose greatest force is in their ability to ignite intimacy into a political sentiment and turn locality into a staging ground for identity, have become spread over vast and irregular spaces, as groups move, yet stay linked to one another through sophisticated media capabilities. This is not to deny that such primordia are often the product of invented traditions (Hobsbawm and Ranger, 1983) or retrospective affiliations, but to emphasize that because of the disjunctive and unstable interplay of commerce, media, national policies and consumer fantasies, ethnicity, once a genie contained in the bottle of some sort of locality (however large) has now become a global forces, forever slipping in and through the cracks between states and borders.

But the relationship between the cultural and economic levels of this new set of global disjunctures is not a simple one-way street in which the terms of global cultural politics are set wholly by, or confined wholly within, the vicissitudes of international flows of technology, labor and finance, demanding only a modest modification of existing neo-Marxist models of uneven development and state-formation. There is a deeper change, itself driven by the disjunctures between all the landscapes I have discussed, and constituted by their continuously fluid and uncertain interplay, which concerns the relationship between production and consumption in today's global economy. Here I begin with Marx's famous (and often mined) view of the fetishism of the commodity, and suggest that this fetishism has been replaced in the world at large (now seeing the world as one, large, interactive system, composed of many complex subsystems) by two mutually supportive descendants, the first of which I call production fetishism, and the second of which I call the fetishism of the consumer.

By production fetishism I mean an illusion created by contemporary transnational production loci, which masks translocal capital, transnational earning-flows, global management and often faraway workers (engaged in various kinds of high-tech putting out operations) in the idiom and spectacle of local (sometimes even worker) control, national productivity and territorial sovereignty. To the extent that various kinds of Free Trade Zone have become the models for production at large, especially of high-tech commodities, production has itself become a fetish, masking not social relations as such, but the relations of production, which are increasingly transnational. The locality (both in the sense of the local factory or site or production and in extended sense of the nation-state) becomes a fetish which disguises the globally dispersed forces that actually drive the production process. This generates alienation (in Marx's sense) twice intensified, for its social sense is now compounded by a complicated spatial dynamic which is increasingly global.

As for the fetishism of the consumer, I mean to indicate here that the consumer has been transformed, through commodity flows (and the mediascapes, especially of advertising, that accompany them) into a sign, both in Baudrillard's sense of a simulacrum which only asymptotically approaches the form of a real social agent; and in the sense of a mask for the real seat of agency, which is not the consumer but the producer and the many forces that constitute production. Global advertising is the key technology for the worldwide dissemination of a plethora of creative, and culturally well chosen, ideas of consumer agency. These images of agency are increasingly distortions of a world of merchandising so subtle that the consumer is consistently helped to believe that he or she is an actor, where in fact he or she is at best a chooser.

The globalization of culture is not the same as its homogenization, but globalization involves the use of a variety of instruments of homogenization (armaments, advertising techniques, language hegemonies, clothing styles and the like), which are absorbed into local political and cultural economies, only to be repatriated as heterogeneous dialogues of national sovereignty, free enterprise, fundamentalism, etc. in which the state plays an increasingly delicate role: too much openness to global flows and the nation-state is threatened by revolt—the China syndrome; too little, and the state exits the international stage, as Burma, Albania and North Korea, in various ways have done. In general, the state has become the arbiter of the *repatriation of difference* (in the form of goods, signs, slogans, styles, etc.). But this repatriation or export of the designs and commodities of difference continuously exacerbates the "internal" politics of majoritarianism and homogenization, which is most frequently played out in debates over heritage.

Thus the central feature of global culture today is the politics of the mutual effort of sameness and difference to cannibalize one another and thus to proclaim their successful hijacking of the twin Enlightenment ideas of the triumphantly universal and the resiliently particular. This mutual cannibalization shows its ugly face in riots, in refugee-flows, in state-sponsored torture and in ethnocide (with or without state support). Its brighter side is in the expansion of many individual horizons of hope and fantasy, in the global spread of oral rehydration therapy and other low-tech instruments of well-being, in the susceptibility even of South Africa to the force of global opinion, in the inability of the Polish state to repress its own working-classes, and in the growth of a wide range of progressive, transnational alliances. Examples of both sorts could be multiplied. The critical point is that both sides of the coin of global cultural process today are products of the infinitely varied mutual contest of sameness and difference on a stage characterized by radical disjunctures between different sorts of global flows and the uncertain landscapes created in and through these disjunctures.

[A longer version of this essay appears in *Public Culture* 2 (2), spring 1990. This longer version sets the present formulation in the context of global cultural traffic in earlier historical periods, and draws out some of its implications for the study of cultural forms more generally.]

Notes
1. One major exception if Fredric Jameson, whose (1984) essay on the relationship between postmodernism and late capitalism has in many ways, inspired this essay. However, the debate between Jameson (1986) and Ahmad (1987) in *Social Text*

shows that the creation of a globalizing Marxist narrative, in cultural matters, is difficult territory indeed. My own effort, in this context, is to begin a restructuring of the Marxist narrative (by stressing lags and disjunctures) that many Marxists might find abhorrent. Such a restructuring has to avoid the dangers of obliterating difference within the "third world," of eliding the social referent (as some French postmodernists seem inclined to do) and of retaining the narrative authority of the Marxist tradition, in favor of greater attention to global fragmentation, uncertainty and difference.

2. These ideas are argued more fully in a book I am currently working on, tentatively entitled *Imploding Worlds: Imagination and Disjuncture in the Global Cultural Economy.*

References

Ahmad, A. (1987) "Jameson's Rhetoric of Otherness and the 'National Allegory,'" *Social Text* 17:3-25.

Amin, S. (1980) *Class and Nation: Historically and in the Current Crisis.* New York and London: Monthly Review.

Anderson, B. (1983) *Imagined Communities: Reflections of the Origin and Spread of Nationalism.* London: Verso.

Appadurai, A. (1989) "Global Ethnoscapes: Note and Queries for a Transnational Anthropology," in R. G. Fox (ed.), *Interventions: Anthropology of the Present.*

Appadurai, A. and Breckenridge, C.A. (forthcoming) *A Transnational Culture in the Making: The Asian Indian Diaspora in the United States.* London: Berg.

Barber, K. (1987) "Popular Arts in Africa," *African Studies Review* 30 (3).

Baruah, S. (1986) "Immigration, Ethnic Conflict and Political turmoil, Assam 1979-1985," *Asian Survey* 26 (11).

Chatterjee, P. (1986) *Nationalist Thought and the Colonial World: A Derivative Discourse.* London: Zed Books.

Feld, S. (1988) "Notes on World Beat," *Public Culture* 1 (1): 31-7.

Gans, Eric (1985) *The end of Culture: Toward a Generative Anthropology.* Berkely: University of California.

Hamelink, C. (1983) *Cultural Autonomy in Global* Communications. New York: Longman.

Handler, R. (1988) *Nationalism and the Politics of Culture in Quebec.* Madison: University of Wisconsin.

Hannerz, U. (1987) "The World in Creolization," *Africa* 57 (4): 546-59.

Hannerz, U. (1989) "Notes on the Global Ecumene," *Public Culture* 1 (2): 66-75.

Hechter, M. (1974) Internal Colonialism: *The Celtic Fringe in British National Development, 1536-1966.* Berkeley and Los Angeles: University of California.

Herzfeld, M. (1982) *Ours Once More: Folklore, Ideology and the Making of Modern Greece.* Austin: University of Texas.

Hobsbawm, E. and Ranger, T. (eds) (1983) *The Invention of Tradition.* New York: Columbia University Press.

Ivy, M. (1988) "Tradition and Difference in the Japanese Mass Media," *Public Culture* 1 (1): 21-9.

Iyer, P. (1988) *Video Night in Kathmandu,* New York: Knopf.

Jameson, F. (1984) "Postmodernism, or the Cultural Logic of late Capitalism," *New Left Review* 146 (July-August): 53-92.

Jameson, F. (1986) "Third World Literature in the Era of Multi-National Capitalism," *Social Text* 15 (Fall): 65-88.

Kothari, R. (1989) *State Against Democracy: In Search of Humane Governance.* New York: New Horizons.

Lakoff, G. and Johnson, M. (1980) *Metaphors We live By.* Chicago and London: University of Chicago.

Lash, S. And Urry, J. (1987) *The End of Organized Capitalism.* Madison: University of Wisconsin.

McQueen, H. (1988) "The Australian Stamp: Image, Design and Ideology," *Arena* 84 Spring: 78-96.

Mandel, E. (1978) *Late Capitalism.* London: Verso.

Mattelart, A. (1983) *Transnationals and Third World: The Struggle for Culture.* South Hadley, MA: Bergin and Garvey.

Nandy, A. (1989) "The Political Culture of the Indian State," *Daedalus* 118 (4): 1-26.

Nicoll, F. (1989) "My Trip to Alice," *Criticism, Heresy and Interpretation (CHAI),* 3: 21-32.

Schiller, H. (1976) *Communication and Cultural Domination.* White Plains, NY: International Arts and Sciences.

Vachani, L. (1989) "Narrative, Pleasure and Ideology in the Hindi Film: An Analysis of the Outsider Formula," MA thesis, The Annenberg School of Communication, The University of Pennsylvania.

Wallerstein, I. (1974) *The Modern World-System* (2 volumes). New York and London: Academic Press.

Warner, M. (1990) *The Letters of the Republic: Publication and the Public Sphere.* Cambridge, MA: Harvard.

Williams, R. (1976) *Keywords.* New York: Oxford.

Wolf, E. (1982) *Europe and the People Without History,* Berkeley: University of California.

Yoshimoto, M. (1989) "The Postmodern and Mass Images in Japan," *Public Culture* 1 (2): 8-25.

Zarilli, P. (Forthcoming) "Repositioning the Body: An Indian Martial Art and its Pan-Asian Publics" in C.A. Breckenridge, (ed.), *Producing the Postcolonial: Trajectories to Public Culture in India.*

Sources

Niccolò Machiavelli, selections from *The Prince*, trans. George Bull (Penguin Classics 1961, 3rd rev.ed. 1981), copyright © George Bull, 1961, 1975, 1981. Reprinted with permission of the publisher.

Irving Zeitlin, "The Conservative Reaction," *Ideology and the Development of Sociological Theory*, 6/E by Zeitlin, Irving, © 1993. Reprinted with permission of Prentice-Hall, Inc., Upper Saddle River, NJ.

Edmund Burke, selection from Reflections on the Revolution in France. Doubleday, 1961. Public domain.

Karl Marx and Friedrich Engels, selections from *The German Ideology*, ed. R. Pascal (New York: International Publishers, 1960). Reprinted with permission of the publisher.

Karl Marx, selections from *Capital*, trans. Samuel Moore and Edward Aveling, ed. Friedrich Engels, Vol. 1 (Moscow: Progress Publishers). Reprinted with permission of the publishers.

Stanley Aronowitz and William DiFazio, from *The Jobless Future: Sci-Tech and the Dogma of Work* (University of Minnesota Press, 1994), copyright © 1994 by the Regents of the University of Minnesota. Reprinted with permission of the publisher.

Emile Durkheim, "The Normality of Crime," *Sociological Theory: A Book of Readings*, 8/E, ed. Lewis Coser and Bernard Rosenberg (Free Press of Glencoe, 1969).

Robert Merton, "Social Structure and Anomie," *American Sociological Review* 3: 1 (1938): 672-82. Public domain.

Max Weber, "Class, Status, and Party," *From Max Weber: Essays in Sociology*, ed. and trans. by H.H. Gerth and C. Wright Mills, Translation copyright © 1946, 1958 by H.H. Gerth and C. Wright Mills. Used by permission of Oxford University Press, Inc.

Jeff Goodwin and Theda Skocpol, "Explaining Revolutions in the Contemporary Third World," *Politics & Society* 17:4 (December 1989): 489-509. Reprinted with permission of the authors.

Robert B. Reich, "The New Web of Enterprise," from *The Work of Nations* by Robert Reich. Copyright © 1991 by Robert B. Reich. Reprinted with permission of Alfred A. Knopf Inc.

Georg Simmel, "The Miser and the Spendthrift," from *On Individuality and Social Forms*, ed. Donald N. Levine (University of Chicago Press, 1971, copyright © 1971 by The University of Chicago. Reprinted with permission of the publisher.

Georg Simmel, "The Metropolis and Mental Life." Reprinted with permission of The Free Press, a Division of Simon & Schuster, Inc. from *The Sociology of Georg Simmel*, trans. and ed. by Kurt H. Wolff. Copyright © 1950 by The Free Press; © renewed 1978 by The Free Press.